CHARIOT OF FIRE

RELIGION AND THE BEECHER FAMILY

MARIE CASKEY

NEW HAVEN AND LONDON, YALE UNIVERSITY PRESS, 1978

Published under the direction of the
Department of History of Yale University
with assistance from the income of the
Frederick John Kingsbury Memorial Fund.

Designed by Sally Sullivan Harris
and set in IBM Selectric Baskerville type.
Printed in the United States of America by
The Murray Printing Co., Westford, Mass.

Published in Great Britain, Europe, Africa, and
Asia (except Japan) by Yale University Press,
Ltd., London. Distributed in Latin America by
Kaiman & Polon, Inc., New York City; in
Australia and New Zealand by Book & Film
Services, Artarmon, N.S.W., Australia; and in
Japan by Harper & Row, Publishers, Tokyo
Office.

Library of Congress Cataloging in Publication Data

Caskey, Marie, 1945–
Chariot of fire.

(Yale historical publications : Miscellany ; 117)
Bibliography: p.
Includes index.
1. Religious thought—United States.
2. Beecher family. I. Title. II. Series.
BR525.C38 285',8'0922 [B] 77-5291
ISBN 0-300-02007-4

For
James Burton Carpenter
and
Edmund S. Morgan

CONTENTS

Yale Historical Publications, Miscellany, 117

The Beecher Family in 1859. This group portrait was taken at the Mathew Brady studio on the occasion of the family's last big reunion, which took place at Henry's home in Brooklyn. The only absent member was James Beecher (1828–86), who was then in China serving as a missionary to American sailors. George Beecher had died in 1843.

Note that the daughters are holding Lyman's hands to steady them for the long exposure.

Seated, left to right: Isabella Beecher Hooker (1822–1907), Catharine Esther Beecher (1800–78), Lyman Beecher (1775–1863), Mary Beecher Perkins (1805–1900), and Harriet Beecher Stowe (1811–96).

Standing, left to right: Thomas Kinnicut Beecher (1824–1900), William Henry Beecher (1802–89), Edward Beecher (1803–95), Charles Beecher (1815–1900), and Henry Ward Beecher (1813–87).

ILLUSTRATIONS

The photographs of the Beecher Family in 1859, Edward Beecher, Harriet Beecher Stowe, Henry Ward Beecher, and Thomas Kinnicut Beecher are taken from originals in the Beecher-Scoville Family Papers, Historical Manuscripts, Sterling Memorial Library, Yale University. The photograph of Catharine Esther Beecher is reproduced by permission of the State Historical Society of Wisconsin, Iconographic Collection, and that of Charles Beecher is by courtesy of the Stowe-Day Foundation, Hartford, Connecticut.

PREFACE

This book represents part of a larger study of the Beecher family's religious ideas and activity. Limitations of time and space have forced me to omit the sections dealing with broader institutional change: chapters on the decline of the evangelical ministry (in which the careers of William, George, and James Beecher figure largely); on the evolving character of the church; on the evangelical reform movements in which the Beechers played so important a role; a chapter on the significance of the Tilton trial and ecclesiastical councils; one examining the millenarian ideas of the Beechers; and finally, a chapter on their contributions to the changing life-style of the moralistic middle class.

What I present here is the history of Lyman Beecher and his eleven children, chiefly in terms of their religious experience. I see their formal ideas as dynamically related to life experiences, both those which can be identified as crises or turning points and those which made up the fabric of their everyday life. I have tried to show how the Beechers responded, individually and collectively, to certain demands of their culture. I cannot claim that this family is representative or typical of all evangelical Protestants or all middle-class Yankees. By their very prominence the Beechers were atypical, even apart from the temperamental and intellectual quirks which gave rise to the term "Beecherism." Thus, while willing to treat some of their more singular ideas extensively, I have always tried to show how these ideas reflected the needs and concerns of other eminent Americans and of the voiceless millions for whom they, and the Beecher family, spoke.

In dividing the Beecher children into groupings, my intent is to indicate the divergences among them. Thus, I see Catharine and Isabella Beecher as pursuing much the same goals, even though there may seem to be a world of difference between Catharine's belated Episcopalianism and her sister's Spiritualism. Both sisters came to view religion in almost exclusively moral terms, as the stimulus to right actions undertaken for disinterested (socially useful) reasons. Both argued for moral perfectionism in a way that most clearly repudiated the belief in man's dependency on God which was such an important part of their religious heritage.

Edward and Charles were easily the most serious theologians and scholars in the Beecher family. I call them the prophets of the family because their ideas, however fascinating, were so plainly at variance with the liberalizing, nondoctrinal trends of evangelical theology. The most interesting feature of their beliefs was their congruence with those of their brothers and sisters who proceeded along much more conventional lines.

The Christocentric liberals in the family are most easily identifiable. Their sentimental appeal to the imagery of the home had much in common with Catharine's ideas; but whereas she contemned the affective piety of evangelicalism, Henry and Harriet concentrated upon the "emotive" experience, while paring away the dogmatic growths they saw as obscuring pure faith in Christ. If Harriet retained a deep respect for the theological acuity and psychological insight of New England Theology, it was Thomas who had the deeper sense of man's limitations and frailty. He was, however, as liberal as they in matters of belief and worship.

This is an intellectual biography of a family who were not primarily intellectuals. They were, for better or worse, evangelists first and thinkers second. They believed that they had a crucial role to play in history and wanted to get on with their mission, which was to regenerate society through Christianity. I hope I have communicated this sense of mission and their own sense of what it was to be the children of Lyman Beecher.

It has been no easy task to make a coherent and interesting narrative out of so large and complex a family as the Beechers. My aim has been to depict these lives with both sympathy and detachment. The reader will learn little about how these men and women looked and where they lived. To be continually reminded of their fears and forebodings and confronted with their self-importance and busy optimism is to be plunged into an internal life which may appear too hectic to be truly thoughtful and too self-involved to be truly God-centered. I recall a book review some twenty years ago in which the reviewer, who wished to express lofty disapproval of a biographer, grumbled that the author had committed the tiresome sin of falling in love with his subject. I declare myself guiltless of that charge. And yet there is a great deal to be said for looking closely at a family who tackled life with such vigor and purpose, who lived, as one of them recalled, in an atmosphere charged with "moral oxygen."

It is not the fashion to praise those who go soldiering with Christ and believe that what the country needs is to be remade by a holy band. Even historians of American religious ideas have been prone to contrast the tough-mindedness and clear-eyed realism of the Puritans with the sentimentality and the wide-awake spirit of religious enterprise so characteristic of their Victorian descendants. The "Archimedean money-power" which Herman Melville attributed to the energetic almsgivers of the Evangelical United Front may seem to us, as it did to him, just one more example of self-righteousness masquerading as "disinterested benevolence." We are embarrassed, on the one hand, by the Beechers' veering toward moralistic claptrap and, on the other, by their unabashed adherence to a heroic ideal of discipleship. Without attempting to assay the Beechers' religious commitment for its proportions of sincerity and self-deception, I will only say that theirs was an age of belief; and I have tried to describe and present them as they believed or wanted to believe, because their collective beliefs and collective questionings left a mark on the nation which no historian can ignore.

Of the many historical phenomena I have enjoyed studying, "Beecherism" remains one of the most fascinating. This book started out as a session in David D. Hall's graduate seminar at Yale. He, with Cynthia Eagle Russett, fired my interest in the nineteenth century. Sydney Ahlstrom supervised my dissertation, egged me on in his good-humored way, and kept me at the task until David Brion Davis and C. Duncan Rice went to work on the finished product. Dr. David F. Musto was very helpful in clarifying my ideas on the internal dynamics of families, and of this one in particular. Lawrence E. Dowler and the late Herman Kahn read various chapters with a critical eye. I wish to thank these teachers and colleagues for their discerning criticisms and their generous spirit.

Historical research is inevitably a cooperative venture, and I have been fortunate in having friends like Joseph S. Van Why, Anne Farnam, and Kathryn Kish Sklar, whose own researches on the Beecher family provided a stimulus to mine. Among the countless librarians and archivists who came to my assistance, I wish to thank in particular the staffs of the Stowe-Day Memorial Library, the Schlesinger Library, and Yale's Historical Manuscripts division. Barbara Folsom's excellent editorial work improved the manuscript considerably. Joanne Ainsworth and Edward Tripp of Yale University Press contributed materially to the completion of this book. John M. Espy, a cherished colleague, prepared the index and went over the proofs with great care.

All my family have encouraged me along the way; in particular, my brother, Gary Carpenter, helped with the photographic work, and his wife, Catharine Rolph Carpenter, was a gracious hostess during research visits to Cambridge and Boston. I want also to thank these people, who have been my "stay and shield": Norman Silber, Kenneth W. Keller, Raymond W. Smith, Edward J. Schatzman, Jr., Donald Brosnan, Catherine M. Prelinger, Devon Lee Miller, Jani K. Rachelson, Christopher C. McLeod, and Dr. Julian M. Lieb.

The American Association of University Women provided a fellowship which financed a year of research, and I hope they will be pleased with the outcome.

My greatest debt, however, is to James E. Caskey, Elizabeth Aldrich Davis, and Lawrence N. Powell, who scrutinized the manuscript, showed me how to write plain English, and have kept before me their own high standards of scholarship and teaching.

NOTE ON THE TEXT

I have retained original spelling and punctuation in quoting from manuscript sources, making trivial alterations only where the meaning might be obscure. The abbreviations have been expanded for easier reading, and the paragraphing has been changed in a few cases. The spelling of first names has been regularized in my text but left unaltered in the original sources.

Following is a list of abbreviations for research libraries frequently cited in the notes:

BPL	Boston Public Library
CHS	Cincinnati Historical Society
CSL	Connecticut State Library
HSP	Historical Society of Pennsylvania
LC	Library of Congress
MHCL	Mount Holyoke College Library
MHS	Massachusetts Historical Society
PHS	Presbyterian Historical Society
RBH	Rutherford B. Hayes Library
SDML	Stowe-Day Memorial Library
SLR	Schlesinger Library, Radcliffe
Yale	Historical Manuscripts, Yale

PART 1

BEGINNINGS

1 *AN EVANGELICAL HOUSEHOLD*

When Lyman Beecher moved his family from East Hampton, Long Island[1] to Litchfield, Connecticut in the spring of 1810, he was entering the noontime of his career. Yet he lived nearly fifty-three years more. Moving on to a more prestigious pastorate in Boston, he championed orthodoxy there, left after a drawn battle with Unitarian apostacy, to rise again as president of Lane Seminary in Cincinnati. His fame as a revivalist and controversialist took on luster with each move, but the sixteen years he spent in Litchfield were the most laborious and the most satisfying of his life, the place of memory in his long old age. It was there that most of his eleven children grew up, and the values of that town shaped their adult beliefs. Thus it is fitting to view the Beecher family as it was there.

Lyman Beecher's first few years in Litchfield were especially memorable, "probably a period of more unalloyed happiness than any in his whole life," according to his daughter Catharine. His beloved wife Roxana found new strength and health there, after many trials in East Hampton; and through her skills the drafty, modest parsonage on Litchfield Hill was made as hospitable and as handsomely furnished as artistic contrivance within limited means allowed. One of her sisters, "the fascinating Mary Hubbard," joined in governing an easygoing family.

Mary came into the Beecher family as a refugee from a blighted marriage. While still in her teens, Mary Foote had married a West Indies merchant, the son of the rector of New Haven's Trinity Church. In Havana she discovered that her husband had fathered a mulatto brood whom he kept as slaves. This revelation, and her own abhorrence of slavery, made residence there intolerable. She returned to Connecticut in broken health and eventually moved to East Hampton to serve as Roxana's companion and helper, going with her to Litchfield.

Mary Foote Hubbard died in 1813. Lyman's stepsister Esther Beecher was the third female influence on the burgeoning flock of children. In addition to the East Hampton offspring—Catharine Esther, William Henry, Edward, Mary Foote, and George—Roxana now bore Harriet Elizabeth (an earlier child of that name having died), Henry Ward, and Charles.[2]

Situated on a plateau in the hills of northwestern Connecticut, Litchfield was then, as now, a lovely town whose natural beauty and handsome white frame houses epitomized the prosperous New England community. "Open extensive valleys, hills gracefully arched, rich hollows, and groves formed of lofty trees interspersed everywhere at the most pleasing distances" charmed even so well-traveled a visitor as Timothy Dwight, whose *Travels* also dwelt on "the intelligence of many of its inhabitants of both sexes." The common people of the township, he noted, were "industrious and thrifty, and distinguished for good morals, good order, and decency of deportment."

Litchfield in 1810 was a good place for a man of Lyman's beliefs and talents. A Federalist stronghold in an increasingly democratic climate, it was the home of aristocrats of the old school, some still affecting the powdered wig and small clothes of the Revolutionary era as their badge of gentility. Three-cornered hats, gold-headed canes, knee and shoe buckles were all intended to set them apart from the Democrats whose "infidel" chief wore trousers and leather shoestrings. Litchfield's only rival as cultural center of the state was New Haven; and if the port city had Yale, Litchfield had the nation's first law school and two famous academies—Miss Sarah Pierce's female school and the Morris Academy. Judge Tapping Reeve, founder of the law school, was instrumental in having Beecher called to the town, having been impressed by the minister's temperance, moral reform, and revival activities in Long Island. And from the beginning of his ministry in Litchfield, Beecher had a standing invitation to the town's best homes, for religious exercises, discussions of Federalist strategy, and gossip. Embittered by the niggardly provision in East Hampton, he was gratified by the generosity of his new parishioners and by esteem and affection freely tendered. It was a congenial place for a Yale man, a Federalist, and an evangelical preacher glowing with millennial zeal.[3]

"I was made for action," Lyman observed in his old age. "The Lord drove me, but I was ready." He always took a high view of his calling:

> From the beginning my mind has taken in the Church of God, my country, and the world as given to Christ. It is this that has

> widened the scope of my activities beyond the common sphere of pastoral labor. For I soon found myself harnessed to the Chariot of Christ, whose wheels of fire have rolled onward, high and dreadful to his foes, and glorious to his friends. I could not stop.

Every step he took was a conscious act of discipleship, for he was moved by longings for holiness. His naturally passionate temperament found expression in ceaseless activity, following "the leadings of Providence," in desperate battle and mundane bustle. Beecher was absolutely certain that he and the other soldiers of Christ were fighting the last great battle before the Kingdom of God was established on earth.[4]

He was a many-sided man in whom the emotional element predominated. A pawky sense of humor, astounding physical vigor well into old age, an acute though unprofound intellect, and intense feelings—these were Lyman's chief characteristics. As grand as his aspirations were, a certain butternut rusticity prevented him from appearing awesome. There was also a deep humility in him. He liked to tell stories on himself in which his discomfitures, inelegance, and peculiarities were highlighted. He even enjoyed some of the apocryphal tales inspired by his eccentricity. The first volume of his memoirs, he once joked, would have to be devoted to things he had *not* said.

Humble he might be, but he could make a stinging retort to anyone who tried to employ sarcasm against him. "What is the reason," demanded a tightfisted East Hampton parishioner, that "you ministers are so hungry for money?" "I don't know," his pastor shot back, "unless it is that we see our people growing covetous and going to hell, and want to get it away from them." If old Mr. Fithian had expected a soft answer, he was disabused of the notion and may even have been shocked into restoring the church rate he had threatened to withhold.

Beecher was also so careless in dress and homely in speech that his future ally, the Reverend Nathaniel W. Taylor, mistook him for a common farmer at their first meeting. And Calvin Stowe was not the only friend who thought that a blacksmith's leather apron would have suited Beecher as well as a black gown and Geneva bands. The Southern "chew" sounds that supplanted rural Yankee pronunciation never invaded his speech; he said "creetur" and "nat'ral" to the end of his life. Contemporaries invariably remarked on this quaintness and often portrayed him as the archetypal Yankee—canny, waggish, relentless in logical argument, sinewy, and ungraceful.[5]

The contrast between Lyman Beecher and his first two wives could not have been greater. Both women were from genteel, socially prominent families well above the level of Beecher's foster-father, an unschooled Connecticut farmer. However rustic Beecher may have appeared, with his jerky gait and arm-flailing style of pulpit delivery, he had a very attractive personality. Many of Beecher's critics admitted to a strong personal attachment to him and regretted his heterodoxy the more for it. It is not puzzling that two well-bred ladies found him appealing. Infectious enthusiasm, gameness, and buoyant optimism made him seem perpetually youthful, while a hereditary susceptibility to depression and bad health may have appealed to maternal feelings.[6]

Roxana Foote, whom he married in 1799, lived so vividly in her family's remembrance that it is difficult to separate fact from ideal. Her letters show a calm woman of delicate feelings and deep piety. So timid that she shrank from the public duties expected of a minister's wife, she exhibited a devout submission to hardship and loss rare even in an age when womanhood and piety were nearly synonymous. She bore nine children and managed a huge household with a steady purpose that misfortune could not shake. Although the Footes were not wealthy, Roxana had led a life of ease as the acknowledged "queen" of a cultivated circle in the home of her maternal grandfather, General Andrew Ward, the Revolutionary War hero. When her merchant father Eli died, Ward adopted the ten Foote children, taking them and his widowed daughter to "Castle Ward," his residence in Nutplains, near Guilford, Connecticut. There Roxana and her sisters spent their days spinning, with sentimental novels and French books tied to their distaffs for study. She mastered fine needlework, then an absolute requirement for young ladies. Perhaps, like Nathaniel Taylor's wife, Roxana fell under the spell of Macpherson's Ossianic epics and embroidered "Malvina" on satin, "standing in melancholy attitude by a harp." Horticulture, painting on ivory, and reading history were favorite pastimes. Roxana also liked to play the accompaniment on her guitar when she and her brothers sang Scottish ballads. An émigré from Santo Domingo taught her to speak impeccable French.[7]

Marriage to Lyman Beecher, who was then a newly ordained Presbyterian minister, meant leaving her Episcopalian family (at least one of whom advertised the fact that in remaining outside the true church Beecher was relying on "uncovenanted mercies") and her lighthearted pursuits for a life of struggle and anxiety. As conventional as some of her attainments were, however, Roxana also had a mind that delighted in "scientific and metaphysical" investigations. She "solved mathematical problems" purely "because she enjoyed that kind of mental effort" and found chemistry absorbing.

Marital duties left her few hours for such exercises. Her husband's *Autobiography* gives a pathetic picture of her life as wife and mother. Nine pregnancies in seventeen years, some of which completely prostrated her, keeping school and taking in boarders to eke out her husband's income—such burdens made her life one of ceaseless worry and financial embarrassment. Even with the aid of two capable black womanservants, Roxana's life must have been laborious, especially since her husband was expected to extend hospitality to his clerical brethren. Each cash outlay called for minute calculations, throwing her back on the makeshifts of genteel poverty. It was with understandable resentment that she reflected on "the very low estimation which people appear to have of the blessing of the Gospel ministry" when she figured that East Hampton parishioners squandered more money on tobacco than they were willing to pay for the services of their pastor. This is the only recorded instance when Roxana expressed anything like regret over the difficulties of her position. "I never saw such resignation to God," Lyman marveled, "it was her habitual and only frame of mind." "Even when she suffered most deeply, she showed . . . an entire acquiescence in the Divine Will."[8]

She was endowed with "a habit of regarding all knowledge with reference to its *practical* usefulness and remarkable *perseverance*," which made her an ingenious helpmate to her improvident husband. Armed with an encyclopedia, Roxana invented and experimented in large and small things: a "Russian stove" six times as efficient as the type used in New England ("it annihilates winter," her successor said), a handpainted cotton carpet (the first carpet in East Hampton), and homemade varnish, with which Catharine transformed unfinished furniture into a "chamber set of fine white wood," "ornamented with landscapes, fruits and flowers . . . at that time . . . a great novelty."

Not content with economies of the laundry and kitchen, Roxana adorned the parlor and diningroom of the Litchfield "manse" with watercolors. However amateurish they may have been, they served to stimulate in her children a craving for beauty and for beautiful things, even though Lyman remained indifferent to art throughout his life. Her accomplishments threw a charm over the parsonage which made it seem lovely despite the penurious existence the family often led. In recalling that life, her children made little of its poverty but were effusive in their testimonials to its tranquillity and cultivation. For in fact, Roxana had absorbed many of its shocks and troubles just as she had relieved much of its shabbiness.[9]

After seventeen years of marriage, Roxana died of consumption, leaving eight children. Her death was, in the pious phrase of that time, a triumphant one. Judge Reeve's wife treasured the deathbed vigil as a "great privilege." Roxana "dedicated her sons to God for missionaries" and "made a very feeling and appropriate prayer." Just before she expired, Lyman read to her the passage in Hebrews on the saint's joyous entry to heaven. From this time on the legend of Roxana Beecher flowered and continued to bloom. Lyman preached the funeral sermon, "standing in the little tub pulpit, while her coffin stood below," and though her death stunned him, her happy submission provided "many alleviations" to his grief. He determined to continue in the ministry with unimpaired powers and energy—his letter to Taylor telling of Roxana's death ends with Beecher's laying plans for a tract war against Episcopalians—but he fell into a severe depression which lasted almost a year. Although he took a new wife at the end of that year, Roxana remained his most beloved wife. Indeed, she was made the measure of all women by her husband and children. Her sons had no higher praise for a woman than to compare her to Roxana Beecher: "She is as I should think mother was." Lyman even fell into the habit of referring to his second wife's children as if they were Roxana's.[10]

In death Roxana exerted an even profounder influence on her children than she had done in life. The deathbed dedication of her sons to the ministry prevailed over them with almost tyrannical force, while her example to the three daughters was equally powerful. The memory of her purity and devotion was exalted with the passage of time. No portrait of her survives, although she was described as tall and beautiful. Perhaps this very evanescence contributed to her glorification. Her sons, even as elderly men, spoke feelingly of her moral and spiritual influence, which they believed had shaped their lives. She was their guardian angel, a ministering spirit who awaited them in heaven and lovingly watched over their course on earth. "I never knew my mother," Henry said. "She died when I was three years old that she might be an angel to me all my life." On reading her letters years after her passing, he was struck by their revelation of her religious character. "What these letters were to her life, that are the four Gospels to the life of Christ."

It is impossible to exaggerate the literalness and fervency of this belief. At every crisis, in every family tragedy or jubilee, they testified to the living presence of their mother's spirit. When the Tilton adultery scandal[11] drove Henry to thoughts of suicide, the sight of flowers from Roxana's grave assured him that vindication was certain: "It was a sweet omen. Love never dies. My mother's grave blossomed for me. How much more the Heavens where her spirit dwells!" Roxana's three youngest children, who could barely remember her, seemed most imbued with this attitude of veneration. "Roxana Foote is my madonna!" Charles exclaimed, while Henry publicly avowed that "no devout Catholic ever saw so much in the Virgin Mary as I have seen in my mother."[12]

That there was at least a tinge of superstition to this idea is undeniable, and perhaps there was disingenuousness in appeals to Roxana's memory whenever one of her children came under attack or was caught in a dubious position. But the idealized mother of Litchfield days became a sort of talisman, a touchstone for all action and belief. It is difficult to assign definite causes for this near-idolatry in a rigorously Protestant family. To a large degree, however, the tradition of the sanctified and sanctifying mother was deeply entrenched in the conventional piety of the period. It is also a fact that women predominated in church membership, and often in domestic religious instruction. The vast majority of church members were women and, as such, they had an important role as sponsors of children in baptism. Indeed, they may have sought church membership more actively than men for the sake of their children.

Then there was surely a keen sense of loss in the death of such a remarkable woman. This anguish may have been deepened by guilt. Roxana had died prematurely, and probably, as Lyman stated in his request for dismissal from the Litchfield church, because of "undue exertion" to help clear his debts. Perhaps he grieved, as one daughter later hinted, that he had not been more attentive and solicitous of her health, and realized that he should not have made her undergo so many pregnancies. Roxana also embodied certain powerful religious ideals. Her family and friends believed that she had come as close as was humanly possible to following the self-denying example of Christ. As her children matured and began to depart from Calvinistic conceptions of God, the image of their mother stood before them and mingled with their ideas of the tender-hearted, self-sacrificing Parent, so different from the Sovereign and Judge of their father's conception.[13]

Lyman Beecher's marriage to Harriet Porter must have been affected by this enshrinement of his first wife and was probably marred by it. Had he not been so thoroughly a domestic man, he might have gone on sorrowing, but he sought a new wife rather quickly. He needed someone to govern and nurture his children, and possibly some mothering himself. He went about his selection with characteristic purposefulness, setting out on a ministerial trip with that end in mind, as one of his student charges drily recorded:

> Saturday after the rules were called Miss Pierce went for Mr. Beecher. She said she wished us to pay particular attention . . . as he was going on a long journey again, at which all the girls joined in a laugh. I suppose it was because he was going to Boston to buy him a wife.

This was not, however, the cold-blooded campaign of a harried widower bent on remarriage. Beecher developed a genuine attachment for Harriet Porter, an attachment freely expressed in a torrent of loveletters in which passion, piety, solicitude, and humor were jumbled together.[14]

Jolting homeward in the stagecoach from Boston, where he had secured her promise of marriage on very short acquaintance, Beecher could not wait to send her his thoughts:

> I am now 20 miles from New haven and have not slept since I saw you. But tho my eyelids are heavy I can not resist the propensity of talking with you, for if my voice may not be heard I hope to be able to send back speedily some memorial of the tender recollections which have been the constant attendant of my way. . . . Your image has been constantly with me as distinct as vision could make it—I have not however adopted Van Swedenbourgh's theory of the visibility and actual intercourse of spirits, nor have I on your account been called upon to pay a double passage. Thus you see that instead of a dilatory next-week letter I have not been able to wait even my arrival in New Haven. So much better than my best resolutions!! Is it not ominous of good my Dear? What if I should hold out after this sort to the end?

He asked Harriet to keep a diary "that I may see your thots as they rise and the scenes in which you move and act" and went on to pray that they be made the instruments of his children's conversion.

Although she was startled by such fervent expressions of love from a middle-aged parson, Harriet was nevertheless pleased. "How could you have thought to send back your love from the Stage House," she exclaimed, for "nothing was ever so agreeable. Mr. Dwights remark upon the occasion was 'He is the most thorough man I ever saw.'" Beecher expressed fears of being tempted to love Harriet too well and begged her to strive for weaned affections, to fix her love on God. Yet at the same time he was disappointed that her manner toward him was so subdued and correct. He thought he detected a certain "delicacy of feeling which kept you back from any full and glowing expression of your affection by *language or action* such a man so ardent in his attachments as I am might desire." She must not be alarmed, he added, at the flood of letters from Litchfield, for "I am accustomed they say to do all things verry much in earnest."[15]

A slender beauty with auburn hair, Harriet Porter had been a noted belle. Converted under the doleful preaching of Edward Payson, she turned her back on the fashionable life of Portland and Boston for the way of exemplary devotion. Her family, who were prominent in Maine and Connecticut politics, made no secret of their distaste for her engagement. Apparently because of religious differences—Harriet considered her parents to be lacking in vital piety—but also because of Beecher's circumstances, her family showed little liking for a match between their daughter and an outlandish, threadbare country minister, even if he was important in evangelical circles. Beecher hoped that Harriet's "tender spirit may not be wounded by the opinion of your friends" and implored her not to listen "if the world should meddle and make inauspicious remarks." Supported by her brother-in-law Nathaniel Coffin, a pious Boston merchant, Harriet persisted in the engagement, conceiving of the marriage as entrance into a "wider field of usefulness."[16]

Like his first wife, Beecher's second could not match his ardor. Unlike Roxana, however, Harriet's character had a strong undercurrent of anxiety and self-doubt. She sought the spiritual serenity that Roxana had known, but lived in a state of religious feeling that was troubled, even morbid. As befitted a minister's wife, she enjoyed religious exercises. "She is a holy woman," Lyman wrote after a Thanksgiving family prayer gathering, "and eminently gifted in prayer." In her stepchildren's accounts, however, she emerges as a cold woman whose religiosity bordered on bigotry and whose lack of sympathy left a huge void in her husband's life. Henry and Harriet, particularly, were inclined to set off Roxana's virtues—as they thought they remembered them—by depicting their stepmother unfavorably.

There is no doubt some truth to this unhappy picture. A melancholy woman, Harriet had to struggle for balance, and she spent the last year of her life in a state of extreme mental distress. The sometimes painful facts of her marriage must be taken into account. No woman, no matter how resourceful or appealing, could have competed with the memory of Harriet Porter's predecessor. She wisely accepted the role of foster-mother without trying to exact undivided loyalty and affection from Roxana's children. William probably represented the family's feeling better than the restrospective accounts of Henry and Harriet, when he wrote, "I think father's marriage with our present mother is as blessed an event as ever happened to our family . . . I can but love her, she is so kind and so careful and appears to take as much care of the children as if they were her own." And she had even more children to nurse, clothe, feed, and educate than Roxana, for Lyman fathered four more—Frederick (who died in infancy), Isabella Homes, Thomas Kinnicut, and James Chaplin—even as his oldest sons were reaching college age. Somehow the money for their education had to be wrung from his inadequate salary, or failing that, begged from well-to-do parishioners and relatives. Mistrusting her own regeneration, Harriet now spent many hours on her knees supplicating God to renew Lyman's children as they passed from childhood's comparative innocence to the dangers of adolescence. When Edward left for Yale, she wept with Lyman at the gate, as if he were her own child.[17]

Harriet found valuable support in Lyman's stepsister, who had taken a house next door in Litchfield. Esther Beecher was the original of the energetic Yankee spinsters, gifted in all departments of housewifery, whom her niece Mrs. Stowe portrayed in her novels. Aunt Esther had strenuous conceptions of efficiency, and her futile austerity programs were grist for the family's humor mill. They often teased her about her monomania for frugality, a propensity from which all of them were singularly free.

It was not a bad thing that Esther was so saving. Her brother was so offhand in money matters that he often gave away on impulse rolls of bills accumulated through months of self-denial. Parishioners were dismayed on more than one occasion to see their absentminded pastor hasten to put what he thought was a mite into a missionary collection plate, only to recollect when the cash was on its way to succor the heathen that it was a purse donated by his congregation to meet some pressing family need. One future son-in-law complained, "He forgets this world intirely . . . has no time to look at his pecuniary affairs, hardly knowing whether he has a thousand dollars in his pocket, or owes a thousand which he can never repay." As hard as Beecher sweated in his stony Litchfield acres to raise hogs, hay, fruit, and vegetables in an effort at economic self-sufficiency, he would wipe out that saving—and then some—if a Sabbath-keeping stagecoach line or a missionary appeal moved him.[18]

But it was not in her managerial role that Esther contributed the most to her brother's family. Like the other Beecher women, she was gifted intellectually, well-read, and fluent in repartee. She sympathized entirely with her brother's crusades and projects and was expert enough in theology to serve as chief critic of his writings. So thoroughly did she join in furthering his plans for the children, that one of them described her as the "lens which brought my father's influence to a focus." Witty, with a sense of humor tending toward sarcasm, and a fascinating storyteller, Aunt Esther was the favorite companion of all the young Beechers, who revered her as a spiritual guide and loved her as "a sort of brevet mother."[19]

Acutely conscientious, Esther was always fearful of leaving her duty undone. She once paused when weighed down by cares to reflect on the life she had chosen. "There are many duties to be performed in this world in which the only ground of satisfaction is that they *are duties*," she wrote, "and in the course of my life a *pretty considerable* share of these duties as I think have fallen to my lot. But it is all well." She could have lived comfortably in the home of her niece Mary, who married an affluent Hartford lawyer. But once Lyman's children were grown, she traveled around the country at her own expense, helping to raise a third generation of Beechers. She spent virtually all her small annuity on charity. She lived with George and William in Ohio, with Edward in Illinois, and with Henry and Charles in Indiana, when those states were still on the frontier.

Her letters give interesting pictures of home missionary life in the Old Northwest, as when she stayed with Charles's family at Fort Wayne, Indiana, nursing his wife and children. In bad health herself (she had a heart condition), Esther arrived to find the cholera raging toward Fort Wayne and Charles gone to a college commencement, while his family were suffering for lack of fresh food, being too poor to buy any. The quarterly stipend from the American Home Missionary Society had miscarried, so she had to write to Hartford, asking that her own money be forwarded to pay Charles's grocery bill. It is not surprising that she found herself pining for Connecticut.

Yet Esther seemed incapable of acknowledging needs or wishes apart from her desire for the well-being and success of Lyman and the children. There was a stubborn heroism in her which the children admired. As painful as her heart disease was, she never alluded to the subject, only conceding once that "my heart is still a very uncomfortable companion." In a sense, her heart could only find rest in that utter self-abnegation which was the evangelical ideal. Like her brother, she seems to have inherited a tendency to severe melancholia, yet she did not give way to the groaning, tearful spells of despondency that Lyman experienced. On the whole, her character (excepting the female role of total self-sacrifice) seems to have been more balanced than her brother's.[20]

These four women, Roxana, Mary Hubbard, Harriet Porter, and Esther, instilled in the Beecher children an abiding respect for the moral and intellectual capacities of women. But the person to whom the children were closest was their father. Lyman loved them with the same intensity of feeling expressed toward his wives. His own father, David Beecher (New Haven's version of the learned blacksmith), had shown an indifference to Lyman's welfare that verged on cruelty. David Beecher may have resented the son whose birth caused the death of his "best-beloved" wife. He showed no reluctance in handing the tiny premature infant over to a maternal aunt to be raised. Lyman, who weighed only three-and-one-half pounds at birth, was exhibited by his father as a kind of curiosity, a baby so small that he fit inside an ordinary tankard. Yet Lyman somehow survived the traumas of being wrapped up at birth and laid aside as dead, and of being hand-fed when his nurse's milk made him sick.

He grew up on the Guilford farm of Catherine and Lot Benton, eating plain farm fare and doing heavy chores while his father dined richly in New Haven, enjoying the company of his other children, holding forth to the collegians and state legislators who boarded with him, and dipping into his large library when he was not occupied at the forge. David Beecher could have done much to enrich his son's mind but chose to abandon him to the culturally starved existence of a farmboy. The affection he begrudged his son was freely given by the Bentons, who also paid most of their nephew's academy and college expenses. Even when Lyman attended preparatory school in New Haven, he boarded in the home of an aunt and never spent more than one college term in his father's house.

Lyman's recollections of his father were scanty, and not all of them reflect favorably on the man. A gift of *Goody Two-Shoes* and *Robinson Crusoe* stuck in his memory as an expression of paternal interest, memorable in part because such a rare gesture. David Beecher grumbled so bitterly at having to pay his portion of the boy's Yale expenses that Lyman's stepmother, fearing he would be withdrawn from college, pledged her own property to keep her husband's son in school. The barrenness of their relationship can be gauged from Lyman's

Autobiography. There may be found Lyman's tender affection for Lot Benton. His mourning for his Aunt Catherine and for his mentor, Timothy Dwight, are movingly expressed in his diary and letters. David Beecher's death is not even recorded.[21]

When he became a father himself, Lyman Beecher savored the role. Having "that passionate love of children which makes it a pleasure to nurse and tend them, and which is generally deemed a distinctive element of the woman," he relished fatherhood so much that after twelve children he still delighted in another. Catharine Beecher remembered her mother Roxana as "eminently benevolent, tender, and sympathising," but "I cannot remember that I ever saw her fondle and caress her little ones as my father did." Harriet Porter's daughter gave a similar view, saying that

> towards his children I never knew a man exhibit so much—all the tenderness of a mother and the untiring activity and devotedness of a nurse—father and friend—to me it seems wonderful that with the immense pressure of responsibility so constantly laid upon him—he can find the energy—the heart—to sympathize so entirely with his family and watch over their happiness—in fact I should grow eloquent in praise of my father's domestic character—always excepting his careless habits. . . .

Affection heightened Lyman's fears for the security of their souls. A man who had had many brushes with death in his youth must have had a vivid sense of human vulnerability. His pleas to consider the precariousness of man's mortal foothold were not rhetorical embellishments or merely conventional utterances. Committed as he was to the Edwardsean doctrine of conversion, he felt compelled to put his children through the exquisitely painful exercises necessary to wrest their hearts from Satan and give them to God. In no other thing did he and his children suffer so much.[22]

Catharine, the firstborn, was a witty, resourceful, and it must be conceded, domineering, girl. His inseparable companion in East Hampton, she made her father proud, as she grew into womanhood, both of her domestic skills and her intellectuality. Like her father, she had literary ambitions—and equally limited endowments in this line. Although Horace Mann, a student at Tapping Reeve's school, thought that "she writes very good poetry," perusal of her surviving efforts does not sustain his judgment. Her deathbed hymns and her laments on the plight of the slave and the Cherokee nation show more feeling —and that strictly conventional—than craft or power. Her true superiority lay in metaphysical discussion of a narrow kind and in organizing skill in the field of education, first as a teacher and then as a reformer. Her writings on domestic economy alone entitle her to a place in history.

William, the next oldest child, never attained the eminence usually expected of an eldest son. Frail and sickly, William was undistinguished from the start. A submediocre scholar, he was also, according to Catharine, a weepy boy whose cloudbursts drew a sharp "Look cheerful!" from his father. William did not even go to college. He was the only Beecher son encouraged to learn a trade, that of cabinetmaking. When that ended in failure, he spent years clerking before he could convince his parents that he was suited for the ministry.[23]

Edward, by contrast, showed early promise. He was "loved and idolised" by his brothers and sisters, who regarded him "as a prodigy of learning and wisdom." When Lyman was enfeebled by old age, it was to Edward that the other children turned for counsel and sympathy. Even William deferred to Edward's judgment and opinion. An earnest boy, Edward had the Beecher love of humor and raillery but hid it beneath a sober exterior, earning the nicknames "solemn Ned" and "Edward the silent." Intellectual pride and ambition were prominent in his makeup, and he acknowledged them as his chief character defects. He developed, as did his brother George, an exaggerated sense of his failings and struggled unceasingly to subdue them in his quest for holiness.[24]

A rarity in this family was Mary, the fourth child of Lyman and Roxana. She was a beautiful girl, but except for occasional glints of humor and eloquence in her few surviving letters, she seems to have been a prosy, commonsense person who saw herself as a steadying influence on the brothers and sisters whose passions and eccentricities she did not share. She married well and devoted herself to raising a large family and doing good works in the upper-middle-class circles of Hartford.

Her brother George was more in the Beecher mold. High-strung and painfully sensitive, George had a tormented adolescence and manhood ending in early death, probably by suicide. Like his grandfather and his father, he was a victim of dyspepsia and melancholia. If Edward had vast ambitions and a powerful intellect, George had the first but not the second. Like Edward, he moved entirely in his father's orbit, so much so that one of George's Yale classmates spoke disparagingly of his zeal and family pride.[25]

Harriet, named for her mother's opinionated Tory sister, was an introspective, peculiar child in whom the Beecher tendency to absent-mindedness was strong, as was the family penchant for self-dramatization. She wrote of her Litchfield childhood as vaguely unhappy—though many of her own recollections contradict this picture—because she was made to feel unimportant in a crowded household. Harriet found solace in the companionship of Henry, another bashful, dreamy child. Young Henry was to all appearances a stout, moonfaced dullard. With a mind that seemed "closed almost to the verge of stupidity," he found the Shorter Catechism baffling and did no better at learning his lessons in the district school he briefly attended. He also had a mild speech impediment. His seeming dullness was a great vexation to his father, who had high ambitions for his sons. But Henry did excel in some things—notably fishing, football, and stoicism in the face of repeated canings by his teachers.[26]

Charles was only nine months old when his mother died, and misfortune seemed to cling to him ever after. Entrusted to the care of Roxana's friend Amelia Ogden, he passed his infancy outside his home and was then given over to Aunt Esther. He, like Edward, was athletic and intellectually keen, but during his adolescence he went through a long period of drift and alienation. Ultimately, he became not only Edward's closest friend but also his theological disciple.[27]

Harriet Porter's children differed in some respects from the others. For one thing, they inherited their mother's finely chiseled features and fair, delicate coloring. And from the same source they derived a tendency toward extreme eccentricity, if not insanity. Frederick, the oldest, died of scarlet fever. He was a strikingly handsome child whose loss Lyman felt deeply. Isabella was an intelligent, beautiful daughter whose features and graces captivated her family. She was imperious and self-willed and came to resent the prominence of her siblings, though she remained on good terms with her half-sister Mary, who took the responsibility of rearing Isabella when her mother died. Thomas Beecher, her brother, was a pensive but amiable boy. He resembled Lyman in being prey to unaccountable swings from extreme exuberance to crushing depression. Never a lighthearted youth, he became positively dour in adulthood, though this trait was leavened by a sharp sense of humor and deep humility. James, the youngest and destined to be the unhappiest child, early exhibited traits which indicated emotional imbalance. He was easily the handsomest of the sons and was pampered on that account. His violent temper caused scandals from childhood on, and he eventually suffered a series of nervous breakdowns, culminating in manic-depressive psychosis which ended in suicide.[28]

These eleven children of Lyman Beecher grew up in a home which, though hard pressed financially, was still comfortable and pleasant in a hardworking way. Their mothers strove to ease the father's life, indulging his foibles and taking delight in his successive triumphs. He was the great man in public life, but at home he was often treated more like a precocious little boy or a droll eccentric. That his wives made great sacrifices of their own comfort, inclinations, and health in order to further his career is undeniable. Society at that time expected nothing less. They went further, however, in coping with the emergencies and hardships that his forgetfulness or irresponsibility caused. They were unusually strong women, however mild and self-effacing they might have appeared to be.

Despite Lyman's manifold activities as pastor, revivalist, editor, preacher-theologian, and small farmer, he did not neglect his children. On the contrary, he filled their lives and set his stamp upon them. He was a domineering father because he consciously sought to mold his offspring, to set before them, not merely an amiable paternal model but a saving example. His theology was to be their theology; his crusades, theirs. He led them to share his vision of the Kingdom of God and successfully inculcated the belief that all of them were to have leading roles in the drama which preceded the millennium.

The Beecher children grew up steeped in this sense of mission, both personal and collective. If it was a spur to activity, it was also a burden. If they usually gloried in the mission, they sometimes wearied of it, and in the case of Thomas openly resented it. But on the whole they subscribed enthusiastically to the idea of their own specialness in history. It was an article of faith with them that they, as a family, had a role to play in history—almost, one might say, a role transcending history. Hence the familiar jest that the world was divided into three races: saints, sinners, and Beechers.

Even play hours were dominated by their athletic father, who wrestled and ran races with his boys, the youngest son clinging to his back. There were many times, however, when he fell into spells of depressed apathy and self-absorption. Lyman was, after all, a sufferer from "the hypo," as depression (hypochondria) was then called. At other times his energies were prodigally expended and he seemed to be racing everywhere and undertaking superhuman tasks. Then he could become very forgetful of his children. Nevertheless, he seems to have found many ways to show his concern for them and draw them into his life. Lyman did not wave them away when important visitors were holding forth in the parlor. And he encouraged his children to withdraw to his attic study when they felt out of sorts or had suffered some injury to their pride. While he wrote in his shirt-sleeves, mumbling aloud and swinging his left arm in time to his racing thoughts, they could poke through his tract-barrel, examine the curiosities of the room, inspect the drying bunches of herbs, or simply daydream until their father had finished and was ready for a romp. On occasion he would throw down his work entirely and take his brood on hunting and fishing expeditions. When they went nutting with him in the fall, they were delighted to see how fully he entered into the spirit of the outing, climbing the tallest trees and swinging the tops down to dislodge the nuts. The daughters, who were left out of these masculine excursions, took part in the frequent berrying "forays." Charles recalled how much Harriet enjoyed these occasions, "coming in with a six quart pail full of berries, and her dress wet up to her knees." Even the chores exacted from the children were transformed by Lyman into games or races or uproarious contests, and each contribution was duly lauded so that there was no bad-natured rivalry.[29]

As a disciplinarian Lyman used very effective means, appealing to guilt rather than fear. Catharine recalled that

> Our father was the constant playmate of his children. He rejoiced in all their childish joys, and his ever-ready sympathy consoled their little sorrows. The tones and looks of love were the staple of life to his little ones, while discipline was sometimes administered with tears, more effective even than the rod. Not an hour of life can the writer remember . . . when the full conviction did not exist that, to her father, it was pleasant to gratify and hard to deny any wish of his child.

Henry, who remembered the rod more vividly than his exemplary sister, nonetheless praised his father's methods of government, which rested first on showing how badly misbehavior distressed him, and then on firm application of a quince switch. Tears would always be, for Lyman, the most powerful means of control over his strong-willed children, to whom his tears and sighs were painful. Catharine also remarked on Lyman's wisdom in not laying down a multiplicity of strict rules "whose violation demanded penalties, thus bringing the young under a kind of bondage depressing to the elasticity of childhood." Obedience was exacted according to the capacities of each child, new duties and prohibitions being added as the child matured. Thus, so far as secular duties and responsibilities were concerned,

Lyman's light rein made childhood seem, in a somewhat exaggerated phrase, "a joyous and perpetual play-spell."[30]

Litchfield life was very sociable in its rather countrified way. The Beechers visited in the best homes, so exalted was the minister's status in that day. These rural people preened themselves on their plain-living and high-thinking tradition, the fame of which had spread across the borders of Connecticut. Other places were often compared to Litchfield by its residents—unfavorably if Northampton, Massachusetts—favorably if Boston, Paris, or some other seat of culture. Other New England towns, one inhabitant observed, "cannot pay that attention to polite literature and the belles lettres [and] sciences as Litchfield does where leisure and fashion give scope to that kind of entertainment." Roxana Beecher could shine in conversation "upon literary topics," while her sister Mary Hubbard, in the brief time she graced the town, found many men and women with the same love of poetry and history as she possessed. The stream of clerical visitors to the Beecher home from Boston, Philadelphia, and New York made it a social center for members of the town's higher circles, who craved religious news and sprightly conversation.[31]

That education was highly prized is evident from the acclaim of Litchfield's higher schools. The law school drew students from the entire country, including in its heyday such students as John C. Calhoun and Aaron Burr. Miss Pierce's Academy enrolled girls from wealthy Eastern families. Her pupils were subjected to a regimen of rigorous piety, constant personal surveillance, experimental educational methods, and the usual finishing-school accomplishments. One grace she particularly cultivated was an elegant carriage, which she developed by leading her pupils on promenades through the center of town. There they presented an "interesting and picturesque" sight, moving "to the music of a flute and flageolet." No doubt Lyman had other ends in mind when he secured free tuition for his children in exchange for religious instruction of Miss Pierce's pupils. Like Timothy Dwight before him, he highly valued learning in women. He wanted his daughters to be as well-educated as the standards of that time permitted, and also regarded a thorough grounding in Miss Pierce's methods as a means for them to be self-supporting when the need arose. In all, six of the Beechers (three of them boys) attended the academy for varying periods.[32]

Catharine later made slighting remarks about the place, which she viewed as given over to trivia and "fancywork" despite its unusually high academic standards. According to the "Rules of the Litchfield Academy," the curriculum seems to have been very rigorous by the prevailing standard of female education:

> The course of study prescribed for those who wish to take degrees will consist of the following branches—
>
> Morses Geography, Websters Elements English Grammer, Miss Pierce's History, Arithmetic through Interest, Blair's Lectures, Modern Europe, Ramsey's American Revolution, Natural Philosophy, Chemistry, Paley's Moral Philosophy, Hedge's Logic and Addison [i.e., Allison] on Taste.

But it must be admitted that the results were sometimes indifferent at best. Catharine loafed her way through the program, but took a special chemistry course with the composition teacher, John Pierce Brace, Miss Sarah's nephew. Brace was an amateur student of geology, as so many people were, and took George Beecher on his geologizing rambles. Catharine also shone at the annual exhibition in Miss Pierce's favorite drama, "Jephtha's Daughter." Never inclined to praise others, Catharine probably derived greater benefit from Miss Pierce's instruction and example than she admitted, but she had good reason to be dissatisfied. Many of the educational reforms that Catharine was to undertake in the next five decades reflected her impatience with pioneer educators like Sarah Pierce, whom she considered ineffectual. As Catharine tartly observed, "she carrys a good heart which is a redeeming set-off to the weak spot she carrys in her head."[33]

It was much more difficult for Lyman to secure an education for his sons. After preparatory studies at the Morris Academy, Edward entered his father's alma mater. As little boys he and William had been thrilled by Lyman's enthusiastic forecast when they passed through New Haven: "There boys, look there! That's where you have got to go, one of these days!" During that same visit, Lyman had been naïvely gratified by the attention Edward's large head attracted in a dry-goods store where he bought his son a hat. Even before phrenology, he could interpret this as a sign of incipient genius. Edward had already resolved in secret to become a minister like his father. And what better place to enter on the sacred calling than Yale, where right views and proper influences prevailed? The school was also made dear to the family as the scene of Timothy Dwight's conquest of collegiate infidelity, of Lyman's conversion, and of his preparation for the ministry.

Beecher was intent on having all his sons attend Yale, though he had no means. Fortunately, his late wife's family had prospered, and he borrowed a considerable sum from Roxana's brother George, though not without embarrassment at having to make repeated applications. Even with George Foote's help the family barely scraped along. Edward had to walk to and from Litchfield on his vacations, and to send his laundry home on the stage rather than put his family to the expense of hiring a washerwoman in New Haven. His books he got secondhand, after calculating the cost of each to a nicety. He was not, moreover, terribly straitened by Yale standards. A great many students came from far humbler circumstances than Edward Beecher, and it was not unheard of for students to walk all the way from the Western Reserve in Ohio in order to matriculate. Evidently, the only sacrifice he felt keenly was not being able to afford a watch and chain on which to display his Phi Beta Kappa key. Lyman masked his own disappointment behind a paternal warning against "the foppery" of young men who wore watches. Edward excelled in languages and mathematics, and did well enough in chemistry and geology to be asked by Benjamin Silliman to contribute to Silliman's *Journal*.[34]

By the time George was ready to enter Yale, after preparation under Edward and a stint of schoolteaching to save money, Edward had secured the headmastership of a Hartford school. Catharine had come into a small legacy through the death of her fiancé and was starting her own school. Both were in a position to help Lyman, thus freeing him from dependency on the Footes. He was touched by their readiness to contribute to their younger brothers' education and wrote optimistically of his prospects of solvency:

> I am prepared to do more than I have done in all my life in the way of writing, and . . . it may be as well to take care of me for the church as to give your money to educate a young man or to promote missions. And seeing we are our [own] establishment. It will be best perhaps to keep the old hive in good accommodation for your own sakes as well as mine. I hope when my sermons are in the market and my property at Guilford shall be at my disposal to be able to remunerate you both if you need it, and if you should not need it so much the better, for then there will be the more for George and Henry and Charles. We have now five boarders. . . . It is beside a part of my plan to consume in the family all I can raise . . . and thus to furnish to myself hea[l]th and pleasure and proffit and mental viger.
>
> Henry and Charles have just begun to go to Mrs. Pierce, and Henry

> seems to be taking a new start from which I have considerable hope that he will rouse up and be a scholler which is the best use the Beechers can be put to I believe.

In spite of his projections of Yale careers and honors for his sons, George was the last of them to attend that school. For various reasons, the others attended different colleges. It is plain that Beecher expected them to distinguish themselves academically, but their studies were primarily a preparation for the ministry. Except for William, all the sons were propelled toward that calling from earliest childhood, and their parents and sisters were ready to make any sacrifice to realize this purpose. The older boys entered the ministry as a matter of course. Emulating their father was an ideal they never questioned, though they might have temporary misgivings. For the younger sons, however, having the ministry virtually thrust upon them made life thorny and at times unbearable.[35]

After all, this imperative was just one aspect of a family identity in which religion was the driving force. The symbols by which the family ordered its life were religious ones. They attended services twice on the Sabbath, as well as the weekly prayer meeting and lecture. There was also a monthly concert of prayer for the conversion of the world and the inauguration of the millennium. During awakenings they attended special prayer meetings, inquiry meetings, and revival services. Often the children would wait up on Sunday night for the return of their father, who had driven to a neighboring district to deliver an additional sermon after the completion of his duties in the Litchfield church. Family prayers were a twice-daily observance. Lyman's prayers were brief, but to his children and servants they were impressive and brought his hearers to the verge of tears. Thomas often recalled how he listened with awe as his father daily intoned, "Overturn and overturn till He whose right it is shall come and reign, King of nations and King of saints." When his boys went off to college, he added this supplication, "May they become good ministers of our Lord Jesus Christ," a petition repeated daily for each son in turn. When Thomas left home determined on a scientific career, his father added a plea that God "Remember our son in mercy, and bring him back to be a good minister of Jesus Christ."

Whenever there was special cause for anxiety or hope, the family (even when they were scattered from Vermont to Indiana) observed a concert of prayer. Brothers and sisters also agreed to read the Bible through together, taking a verse a day for study and writing their reflections to each other. They thought their father had a gift for reading the Bible, as though he opened each verse anew, making timely applications of Scripture to daily life. Often after the reading, Lyman would bring out his ancient three-stringed fiddle to accompany the hymns, or the sons would play flute and violin while one of the daughters would join in on the piano. Music was an important feature of family devotions, as it was in Lyman's successive churches. He favored stirring hymns like "Joy to the World," and all the children sang well—some beautifully—making these gatherings pleasurable and moving rather than rigorously formal.[36]

Apart from the religious observances, other things took on a sacred or biblical cast. Among the playthings improvised by the children were Catharine's Old Testament dolls:

> the Queen of Sheba, with a gold crown, and her negro driver . . . seated in a chariot made of half a pumpkin, scooped out, shaped, and furnished with wheels, while four crook-neck squashes were transformed to horses for the chariot. With my brother's knife I whittled out ears and legs . . . and I also made appropriate harness. When all was completed, I was amply rewarded by the surprise and hearty laugh of my father. . . .

Many of their evenings were spent telling humorous stories, gossiping, taking off with good nature on each others' quirks, and listening to Lyman play old-time fiddle-tunes. On rare occasions, if the mood were giddy enough, he would dance in his socks, demonstrating barn-dance steps he had mastered in the lax times before dancing was proscribed as worldly. "There is the strangest and most interesting combination in our family of fun and seriousness," Isabella observed in describing one of these family evenings, for after a boisterous session, "we close with singing a beautiful hymn and with a most tender prayer by our dear father."[37]

The children were also exposed to the more cerebral aspects of the Congregational faith, first as spectators awed by their father's preaching and later as juvenile aspirants to the sanctified life. Two of the boys were overheard one night, discoursing on spiritual topics during a revival. Edward, who was very young, told his brother, "I'm *serious*," and William replied, "Well, I've got a hope!" Far from merely parroting current revival catchwords, however, the children grew up well versed in their father's theology, with its fastidious, sometimes logic-chopping distinctions and definitions.

The utter seriousness with which the common people of Connecticut approached hard points of doctrine was portrayed by another

Litchfield County man, Horace Bushnell. His tribute to the Yankee farmers of his birthplace, "The Age of Homespun," lovingly recounts their grappling with the most sublime questions of eternity, God, free will, and the human soul. How much more exposed to these debates were the children of Lyman Beecher, who enjoyed staging disputations over dinner and during apple-peeling bees, where father and son argued as equals! Like the clergymen of Henry Ward Beecher's novel, they "many a night held glorious wassail of theology, discussing till after midnight, whether sin was born in the nature of a child or began only when developed by action; what was the nature of generous and right actions anterior to a saving change; whether conversion stood in the act of choice on the sinner's part, or was in irresistible and efficacous influence exerted upon him *ab extra.* Over these and kindred savory delights they had dissipated many a night."[38]

These were anything but academic questions to Lyman, and he hoped to impress the truth of his views upon his children. Until he could be sure of their conversion, he believed they were in mortal danger. The world, for the evangelical of Beecher's generation, was full of snares and delusions and none more deadly than irreligion, or as he termed it, "modern infidelity." He inherited the tendency to see infidelity lurking everywhere from Timothy Dwight, who liked to reduce his Yale students to misery with his story of Lorenzo, a fatuous youth seduced by infidel teachings and dragged down the pathway to a criminal death. Beecher tried his hand at the same topic, producing a *Dialogue, Exhibiting Some of the Principles and Practical Consequences of Modern Infidelity*, which attacked not the tenets of deism or free thought but its moral tendencies, all of which were dire.

Infidelity spawned not only sophistry but also debauchery, criminality, and mayhem. Beecher's spokesman, Christianus, rendered this indictment of infidelity and of the moral character of those who (like Thomas Jefferson) embraced its meretricious doctrines:

> My friends, we have passed thro' interesting scenes of joy and woe—full of wonder, and full of instruction. We behold, in living colours, the destructive influence of modern infidelity; and how much good one sinner, inspired with such principles, may destroy. Look at my family—all is order, peace, and love. Look at it again —all is confusion and distress. My son in a dungeon, my daughter torn from my embrace, my nephew dead, my son about to die. Whence this sad reverse? Why Theoret, my nephew, became acquainted with infidel books—he read—he was poisoned. The poison spreads, my son is infected; my prayers are unavailing, my

> counsels are despised, my heart is wrung with anguish, and my grey hairs brought with sorrow to the verge of the grave. . . . Human nature, my friends, is prone, strongly prone to evil. The habits of education, the influence of human laws, the restraints of religion, the ties of blood are all of them needful, and often insufficient to keep back these strong propensities. In spite of them men become vicious; but remove them, and they become monsters.[39]

Because it was a dangerous world for the unwary, and especially for those outside the shelter of Christianity, Beecher's efforts to convert his children were unremitting. They felt the need to become Christians, of course, but their desires for conversion were inevitably bound up in their intense feelings for their father. Thus, Thomas (who never attained a true evangelical conversion) wrote to Isabella that he was striving "to get light soon," so as to spare their father further agony and sorrow. He wanted to offer Lyman evidence of a changed heart, without acquainting him with his doubts, so that his father could learn simultaneously of "my danger and my safety." When Henry made his profession of faith, he suffered internally over his unfitness but dared not reveal to Lyman how far from saved he really felt.[40]

Although Lyman's exhortations and entreaties induced great anxieties in his children, he was not a believer in harrowing conversions, or in terror-filled experiences. He was eager to spare not only his children but all his charges the sort of misery he himself had wallowed in, owing to bad counseling when he was converted.

> They gave me other books to read besides the Bible—a thing I have done practising long since. For cases like mine, [David] Brainerd's Life is a most undesirable thing. It gave me a tinge for years. So Edwards on the Affections—a most overwhelming thing, and to common minds the most entangling. The impressions left by such books were not spiritual, but a state of permanent hypochondria—the horrors of a mind without guidance, motive, or ability to do any thing. They are a bad generation of books, on the whole. . . . I wish I could give you my clinical theology. I have used my evangelical philosophy all my lifetime, and relieved people without number out of the sloughs of high Calvinism.

Beecher's "clinical theology" was a straightforward affair. He wrote two manuals for recent converts and their friends, advising them to aim at a well-adjusted and hopeful religious state. Urging them to get sufficient sleep, exercise, and relaxation, Beecher pointed out the dangers of bad diet and asceticism to people whose religious views were still unsettled. Fasting, excessive devotion to secret prayer, self-isolation, spiritual pride, and morbid self-scrutiny were all to be shunned. Instead of being evidences of holiness in the new convert, they were, rather, inducements to depression or unwholesome mental excitement. To those who berated themselves for not achieving instant holiness, he said, the church is "not heaven, where the spirits of the just are made perfect; but a spiritual hospital."

Beecher was especially severe on notions of a stereotyped pathway to sanctification, for "the commencement of religion is not indicated by any exact order or method of divine manifestation." He directed converts to refrain from anatomizing their souls:

> To demand of the heart feeling, that we may inspect and analyze it at pleasure, is, therefore, the most preposterous demand that could be made; and of course, it is always, and justly refused. And yet, there are multitudes, who thus torture their hearts. . . .

If they must compare themselves to others, presumably farther along the road to holiness, he reminded them that "it would be as vain to seek all the varieties of Christian experience in one person, as to seek all the varieties of human features in one face." Christians must simply maintain a cheerful, healthy outlook on life, show love for Christ in seeking to be like him, obey God in external duties and in their hearts, and urge others "to the *immediate performance* of their religious duty." Above all, Christians must not confuse the symptoms of nervous disease or emotional stress with so-called seriousness and earnestness. This was clinical theology.[41]

While theology and spiritual struggle occupied a prominent place in the family's life, its members also busied themselves with less awesome matters. The Beechers' reading was much the same as that of any educated evangelical family. Milton and Bunyan were, of course, accorded highest praise. They were read countless times, Lyman weeping aloud at Satan's most eloquent speeches and Charles quaking with emotion over the escape of Christian and Hopeful from the Giant Despair's Doubting-Castle. "I trembled all over and could not read," Charles recalled of this passage. "Aunt Esther laughed and gave the book to Henry," who finished the reading with characteristic flourishes. The children were taught to regard themselves as pilgrims and in later life often spoke to each other in the language of Bunyan. Aunt Esther, who "was the equal to any woman in her day in reading, and unequalled in repartee," would have the older children read aloud to her as she did her household chores. They read selections from orthodox religious magazines, such as Jedidiah Morse's *Panoplist* or the New Havenite *Christian Spectator*. Sometimes they would recite from *The Day of Judgment*, and as they read, Esther would comment.[42]

The bulk of their reading consisted of pious and edifying works, such as Cotton Mather's *Magnalia Christi Americana* (in the 1820 Hartford edition by Seth Andrews). Maria Edgeworth, the British educator and moralist, who "was exciting a good deal of attention among the educational circles of Litchfield," provided one of the few juvenile books on this list. *Frank*, a plodding tale of duties well performed, was Roxana's idea of an improving book for young minds. She also made the children aware of the latest developments in the missionary field, a subject of interest to all the family. Hannah More, "then the star of the religious world," held their attention with her plain-speaking tracts on manners and morals. Claudius Buchanan's *Christian Researches in Asia* excited their compassion for the heathen, while John Milner's multivolume *History of the Church of Christ* warmed their hopes for worldwide evangelical unity. Timothy Dwight's *Travels* was read with favor, for obvious reasons. And the family eagerly awaited each number of the magazines that carried Lyman's contributions on the progress of moral reforms and on controverted points of doctrine: besides the *Christian Spectator,* there was the *Connecticut Observer*, and (in Boston) the *Spirit of the Pilgrims.*[43]

The chief modern secular writers in the family library were Sir Walter Scott and Lord Byron. Roxana's brother, Samuel Foote, was a sea captain with literary tastes, who took it upon himself to stock the Beecher shelves with choice and chaste items. He seemed to his nieces and nephews "a sort of brilliant genius of another sphere, bringing gifts and wonders that seemed to wake new faculties in all." Uncle Samuel shared his sisters' love of Scott, Byron, and Moore, and introduced the Beechers to Washington Irving's writings. Although Roxana had formerly loved novels, even taking Richardson's Sir Charles Grandison as her ideal of a gentleman and lover, Lyman forbade such books ("fictions of an injurious tendency") as subversive of morals, intellect, and common sense. He only relented in the case of Scott, whose novels he first read when Catharine inherited a set. The moral tone of the histories (always excepting Scott's unfortunate "sympathy with the war spirit") appealed to Beecher, who pronounced them safe. The family read Scott so avidly that whole poems and entire chapters were committed to memory through simple repetition. They had friendly contests, as they worked piling firewood or making applesauce, to see who knew Scott best.

Local landmarks were named after sites in Scott's poems; a ravine was called "Benvenue" after a Highland gorge and one of the township's lakes was christened "Loch Katrine." Litchfield County must have seemed a little Scotland, with its picturesque scenery and frugal, God-fearing yeomen. With his bristling grey hair and burning eyes, Lyman in the pulpit reminded one observer of a Covenanter, and so he may have seemed to his children, who thought he was a hero. When he stepped briskly out of the house into a tunnel cut through the snowdrifts and set out on his pastoral visits, Beecher disdained the wearing of an overcoat. Wrapping his frayed silk scarf around his neck, he trudged miles in the snow to do his duty by his parishioners. The sense of identification with Scotland's Protestant martyrs was so powerful that twenty-five years later Mrs. Stowe burst into tears at the sight of Hervey's painting of "The Convenanters Celebrating the Lord's Supper."[44]

Lord Byron exerted an equally great fascination for the Beechers who, like many Americans infected with Byronmania, found his genius as marvelous as his depravity was unparalleled. Samuel G. Goodrich ("Peter Parley") could only account for the favorable reception of "the daring if not blasphemous skepticisms of the new poet" by attributing almost hypnotic powers to the profligate's verse:

> He had, in fact—in delineating his own moody and morbid emotions—seemed to open a new mine of poetry in the soul; at least, he was the first to disclose it to the popular mind. By degrees, the public eye—admitted to these gloomy, cavernous regions of thought—became adjusted to their dim and dusky atmosphere, and saw, or seemed to see, a majestic spirit beckoning them deeper and deeper into its labyrinths. Thus, what was at first revolting, came at last to be a fascination.

Byron's preoccupation with his internal state of feeling struck a responsive chord in men and women reared in a tradition of Puritan introspection. It was, possibly, this acute sensitivity to feeling that made Lyman fancy that he and Taylor could have won the poet over to evangelical truth through some earnest conversation. The Byronic hero was to figure prominently in the novels of his daughter Harriet, who was similarly entranced by Byron's vacillation between the sublime and the satanic. Lyman wept bitterly at the news of Byron's death and preached a sermon on his tragic life and demise that stunned its hearers by its eloquence.[45]

As seen in the paternal ban on novels, the family was governed by an unwavering moralism of a legalistic character. Even though Lyman would show off dance steps for his children, he forbade social dancing and made the fiddle screech whenever the boarders, who enjoyed Miss Pierce's balls in Grove Catlin's hotel, took a dancing step. Despite his enjoyment of the school's dramatic exhibitions, Catharine's amateur theatricals in emulation of them were cut short after one performance, and that was tolerated only because her parents wanted to spare her feelings. Lyman's attitudes toward drink were strict and became harder as time passed. He had sold rum, porter, and metheglin at the Yale buttery, and had apparently believed those commodities no more harmful than the cantaloupes he also vended. And in the early years in Litchfield (according to one of his boarders), he treated his clerical guests to "cider and pearlash." He had been a herald of the temperance movement in East Hampton, a reform sparked in part by the victimization of the Montauk Indians, who were kept inebriated by an unscrupulous trader. But temperance gave way in the 1820s to total abstinence, as the diary of Thomas Robbins shows. In fact, Robbins's diary shows a gradual hardening of the moralistic temper over the first half of the nineteenth century. As one of the architects of the temperance movement, Beecher preached lurid sermons decrying the spread of drunkenness and warning the abstemious that drink was the social problem of the century. His temperance rhetoric bore a strong resemblance to his blasts against infidelity. He urged parents to din the horrors of intemperance into their children's ears.

> I do not remember that I ever gave permission to a child to go out on a holiday or gave a pittance of money to be expended for his gratification, unattended by the earnest injunction not to drink ardent spirits or any inebriating liquor; and I cannot but believe that if proper exertions are made in the family to apprize children of the nature and danger of this sin. . . . the whole youthful generation might rise up as a rampart, against which the fiery waves of intemperance would dash in vain. . . .

The first Connecticut temperance organization had been formed in Litchfield in 1789, to curb drunkenness among farmhands and laborers. Limiting its ban to "distilled spirits" and urging the substitution of "wholesome food and common simple drinks of our own production," the declaration pledged its signatories—among them Tapping

Reeve, Colonel Benjamin Tallmadge, and Frederick Wolcott—to temperance for themselves as well as their workers. Thus Beecher's message carried great weight in this town.[46]

Sabbatarianism was likewise enforced. The Beechers did not travel or entertain on the Sabbath but kept within doors, venturing out only to the meetinghouse or on errands of absolute necessity. The children were not permitted to be boisterous or to bring out their toys on Sunday. If their parents were as strict as some evangelicals, they were probably forbidden to laugh as well. Much of the time not taken up with services was devoted to religious instruction and edifying studies. The Sabbath, as was customary in Connecticut, began at sunset on Saturday and lasted until twilight of the next day. Most of the cooking was done ahead of time, and chores such as sewing, laundry, fieldwork, and spinning, were "gotten up" for resumption on Monday. As deadly and drab as so strict a Sabbath now seems, and as monotonous as the children found it, they nevertheless cherished the Puritan observance, both for its tranquillity and its moral influence. Taking to heart Timothy Dwight's injunction, "That chosen, bles'd, accepted day / Oh never never cast away!" they retained this custom long after they had abandoned many of the doctrines of their father's faith. Consistent Sabbath-keeping, of a cheerful and far less legalistic nature, appealed to them as a witness to Christian truth in a materialistic age.[47]

The conception of godly living that guided the Beecher family affronts or amuses us today, according to how we value such qualities as spontaneity, flexibility, consistency, and privacy. But granting a certain bigotry, the moralism of this family was expressive of a genuine ethical commitment, expressive of the old pietistic distinction between the Christian believer and the mere professor. As Henry Smith the Puritan divine defined it: "Now if we be almost Christians, let us see what it is to be almost a Christian. Almost a son is a bastard; almost sweet, is unsavory, almost hot is lukewarm, which God spueth out of his mouth (Rev. 3:16). So almost a Christian is not a Christian."[48]

While religion was at the heart of the Beecher family's identity, there were other elements as well: patriotism, provincialism, and whatever intangibles of time and place molded this family. The Beechers lived in a period when war was a recent reality. The War of 1812, which they vehemently opposed like good Federalists and Christians, was shocking to their most basic beliefs and prejudices. An offensive war, they were certain, was hateful to God. Roxana, who became a pacifist shortly before her death, resolved not to write any more letters, for the postal revenues would help finance the fighting. They, like their neighbors, suffered severely from wartime inflation, but their chief objection was moral. There had been, a generation before, a glorious war. Roxana's grandfather had been a hero of that conflict, as was Harriet Porter's uncle, General King. Lyman's father had participated in the defense of New Haven, though his part was an inglorious one.

Lyman could recall how the Revolution affected life on Lot Benton's farm. New England's willing contributions to the common cause, and especially her farmers' home industries, had given her the advantage, he asserted, over the slaveholding South. Independence did seem to have a peculiarly strong meaning to Yankees. When old Colonel Tallmadge gave his annual reading of the Declaration to hushed crowds on the Fourth of July, he moved them to tearful thankfulness. Perhaps they revived one of the old Revolutionary songs, which were going the way of the old fuguing tunes, such a song as William Billings's "Chester."

Let tyrants shake their iron rod
And slavery drag us all in chains.
We'll fear them not, we trust in God.
New England's God forever reigns.

New England's God and New England ways were the only ones the Beechers knew. To be sure, when the children visited their Anglican relatives, they were awakened to the fact that some segments of New England did not worship as they did, but their loyalty was still to the Puritan tradition of their father. When they read Dwight's *Travels* they would find a declaration of faith in the superior rectitude and wholesomeness of their own small part of America.[49]

If the country was changing, Litchfield was slow to keep pace. Connecticut had ceased to be a land of Puritans and was Yankeedom at its best and worst. The good order, deference, and social harmony of the eighteenth century found its last expression in Dwight's *Greenfield Hill*, which celebrated an organic society with common social purposes. Litchfield had several Democratic newspapers at one time or another, attacking the social and religious verities that Dwight and Beecher believed implicitly. The latter's children saw the quickening flow of emigration from the state. The Litchfield church held special meetings whenever one of its families departed for "New Connecticut" (the Ohio Western Reserve). When an emigrant party passed through town, the children sometimes hid under their beds for fear that the rough, hard pioneers would abduct them to Ohio.[50]

Conditions were changing outside the state, too. Litchfield might boost itself with tributes to the style of its upper class, but it was an upper class whose tastes and enthusiasms were imbued with religious ideals that seemed musty and faintly ridiculous to their social counterparts in Boston and the other capitals to which Litchfieldians habitually compared their little town. Even within town there were prominent men who found the religiosity of its notables excessive. Such a man was Governor Wolcott, a "Toleration man," who ceased inviting the Beechers to his home when they showed unseemly zeal in closing a neighbor's party with prayers and a hymn. (His father, the first Governor Wolcott, had shocked the pious by travelling "on public business" on the Sabbath.) As further proof of the Wolcotts' indifference to the interests of vital piety, the younger Wolcott refused to attend services more than once on Sundays. Harriet Porter may have regarded the orthodox minister as "a messenger from the Court of Heaven," but Democrats and dissenters were working to undermine the established church. Democrats vied with each other at party feasts to lampoon the clergy of the Standing Order. They gave out ribald verses and shouted toasts to "Our brethren in Tripoli and Connecticut—May the former be freed from pirates and the latter from Priest-craft."[51]

Litchfield, Connecticut, was a citadel of religious and political orthodoxy in 1810, when the Beechers arrived, but it was an orthodoxy on the wane. By 1818 the Congregational clergy were cut off from their official ties with the machinery of the state, and if the severance was more symbolic than revolutionary at that late date, it was still a blow to Lyman Beecher. But Beecher rallied almost immediately to become a leading draftsman of the new voluntaryism that was to characterize American denominationalism. Equally important was the shift in evangelical orthodoxy away from the paradoxes of classic Calvinism toward a religion of common sense and the affections. Beecher's "alleviated Calvinism" typified this shift, and his children went on to reject his alleviations. Even so, they retained a vital part of his faith and brought to full fruition his affective piety, just as they clung to their vision of an ideal social order in the sober, diligent, and pious people of Litchfield, the steadiest of towns in the land of steady habits.[52]

2 *LYMAN BEECHER'S THEOLOGY*

In 1846, already in his seventies, Lyman Beecher sat down to write a letter in behalf of his son Thomas, who was leaving Cincinnati and going to the house of Nathaniel Taylor in New Haven. As he addressed his old friend, Beecher was in a retrospective mood and spoke of his recent past as if it were rapidly receding into history:

> You and I are the same as when we projected the Christian Spectator, and battled about the means of grace and episcopacy, and Hartford College, and Nettleton, and Tyler, and Woods, and *Harvey*, if you remember such a one. But now, like Bonaparte's battles and marshals, have all these gone through the little end of Time's telescope into the dim but not uninteresting distance; and how has our generation fallen off, and another and another pushed up behind us, and what things have come to pass which, had we lived in Connecticut, we should have written letters about, and held consultations and talked over so much, but have not talked about at all, and never shall till we have more time in another world.

He would never have admitted it, but his vision of conquering the West lay in ruins along with his dream of an all-embracing evangelical church. Beecher had been a principal character in the strife that had preceded the great Presbyterian schism of 1838, and he had double cause to be sorrowful because so many of his friendships had perished in the conflict that split the church. He never grasped the causes of disunity or comprehended his own unwitting part in promoting it. Although theology was not the single reason for the cleavage, it was the focus of other antagonisms—sectional, political, ecclesiastical, and personal. Even if we do not accord the same attention to questions of theology that Beecher's generation did, we should recognize that his conviction that he was called to define and disseminate new views of God was both his triumph and his undoing.[1]

The relation which theology bears to life is a question of utmost importance in any study of Lyman Beecher's faith and doctrine. In his day and his region, the life of the mind and feelings was very much centered on theology. Timothy Dwight had observed that "among the judicious farmers of this country [New England], particularly among those most addicted to reading, there is a more extensive, and a more accurate, knowledge of the doctrines and precepts of Christianity, than among most men, who have enjoyed the advantages of a superior education." Catherine Sedgwick gave equal weight to the impact of theology upon ordinary life when she recalled her childhood in post-Revolutionary Berkshire County, Massachusetts:

> Both my sisters were very religious. They were educated when the demonstration of religion and its offices made much more a part of life than now—when almost all of women's intellectual life took that tinge. They were both born with tendencies to the elevated and unseen; their religion was their pursuit, their daily responsibility, their aim, and end, and crowning affection. . . . Sister Eliza suffered from the horrors of Calvinism. She was so true, so practical, that she could not evade its realities; she believed its monstrous doctrines, and they made her gloomy. . . .[2]

Although the Sedgwicks found Calvinism monstrous and wound up within the Unitarian fold, many evangelicals who remained nominally Calvinistic wanted to reinterpret its doctrines for the modern age. Lyman Beecher was one of these. It became his chief pursuit to secure, as his contemporary Robert Baird put it, "the union of these two doctrines of *activity* and *dependence*, which are so commonly felt to be subversive of each other; [and] the bringing of both to bear with undiminished force on the minds of the impenitent." It was Beecher's aim to balance these two doctrines. Any argument giving undue weight to man's dependence and submissiveness in the face of God's command that man make himself a new heart seemed absurd to Beecher. He could imagine no folly or cruelty worse than going among inquirers at a revival meeting to tender a vague hope that God's spirit might descend upon them in his own good time.[3]

Lyman Beecher

The theological tradition to which Beecher owed allegiance and which he helped to shape was not the product of closeted scholars, whose definitions "subtile and nice" were so finespun as to shut them up in a world of discourse spheres above that of everyday, intelligent New Englanders. It was a preaching-centered theology, which owed much to the New England Theology but had received a practical, evangelical turn from men who were acute (and, in the case of Nathaniel Taylor, subtle and daring) thinkers, as well as revivalists of great power. This is not the place to consider Sidney Mead's thesis that Beecher's mentor, Timothy Dwight, stood in the Old Calvinist rather than the "Edwardean galaxy." The argument is not a new one and is sufficiently attested by William C. Fowler. More to the point, whatever Dwight's theological antecedents, is the fact that his system was, above all, apologetic and practical. Its purpose was to defend evangelical doctrines and promote active piety. Beecher openly acknowledged his indebtedness to the great New England divines, particularly Edwards and Hopkins, yet he owed his theological temper to Dwight. It was Dwight who composed and presented a system of doctrines as sermons for the Christian life.[4]

Dwight's five-volume *Theology* appealed to human reason and addressed itself to common sense:

> Common Sense, the most valuable faculty, (if I may call it such,) of man, finds all its premises either in revelation, or in facts; adopts arguments, only of the *a posteriori* kind; extends its reasonings through a few steps only; derives its illustrations from familiar sources; discriminates, only where there is a real difference; and admits conclusions, only where it can see their connection with the premises. At theoretical philosophy it laughs. Theoretical divinity it detests. To this faculty the Scriptures are almost universally addressed. The subjects, which they contain, are, to a considerable extent, Metaphysical; and often so abstruse as to defy human investigation. Yet they are almost always treated in the obvious manner of Common Sense.

Thus Dwight characterized not only the direct speeches of Christ but even the Pauline Epistles as eminently suited to the commonsense frame of mind. In keeping with this view, Dwight based all his discussions on revelation and fact. He did not even pause long enough to refute the common objections to the inspiration and authority of Scripture since they were obviously too irrational and pitiable to notice. He treated the Bible as true and binding in every part and supplied abundant illustrations from history and everyday experience to uphold his particular applications.[5]

His system emphasized the practical duties of Christianity almost as much as it delineated correct doctrines:

> Real Religion is ever active; and always inclined to *do*, as well as to *say*. The end, for which man was made, and for which he was redeemed, was, that he might do good, and actively glorify his Creator. . . . Active obedience is the only visible fruit, by which our religious character is discovered to others; and the fruit, by which, in a manner peculiarly happy, it is known to ourselves.

This ethical cast, which Foster calls a "new element" in New England Theology, was perfectly in keeping with Dwight's moralistic, philanthropic, and reformist outlook. He had little but scorn for those who made doctrines obscure or who discouraged the view that religion is active and benevolent.[6]

The signal characteristic of Dwight's theology was his recovery of free agency. Unlike Edwards, whose views of man were swallowed up in the splendor of divine sovereignty, Dwight tried to expound human freedom in such a way as to strike a balance between absolute sovereignty and human agency. In his sermon on the omnipotence and independence of God, Dwight described divine rule in these terms:

> The Kingdom of God is a kingdom of means. With infinite wisdom and benignity he has chosen to adorn his Intelligent creatures with such faculties, as enable them to become subordinate agents in the great system, to coincide voluntarily with him in the furtherance of his perfect designs. . . .

These creatures, he stressed, are "Moral agents," by which "I wish it understood, that I intend *a real agent, a being whose thoughts, affections, and actions, are his own.*" It was necessary to be explicit in defining moral agency because the Edwardseans' discussion of the term had been so perplexed. Dwight admitted that, not only critics of Calvinism (infidels and Arminians), but certain extreme Calvinists as well, had argued that moral agency could not consistently operate in a universe governed by God's immutable decrees. Enemies of Calvinism attacked Calvinists for allegedly "denying the free agency of God himself" by "introducing into the Christian system the Stoical doctrine of Fate, and making an iron-handed Necessity, or blind Destiny, the ultimate and irresistible disposer of all things." Dwight was not so impolite as to name them, but much of his ire was aimed at the so called Consistent Calvinists—Nathanael Emmons, for instance—who had so stated the case for absolute sovereignty that they ran, according to Dwight, into absurdities which affronted reason with arrogant ingenuity. He did not blame their detractors for drawing logical inferences of necessitarianism and fatalism from the premises of the Consistent Calvinists. "It must be acknowledged," Dwight observed, "that this doctrine has been indiscreetly handled" by certain theologians.[7]

The moral government of God, as the first great objective fact of existence, made necessary certain adjustments in New England Theology. God was sovereign but his sovereignty was such as befitted republican conceptions of government.

> In other words, it is a government by motives, addressed to the understanding and affections of rational subjects, and operating on their minds, as inducements to voluntary obedience. No other government is worthy of God: there being, indeed, no other, beside that of mere force and coercion.

Because Dwight wished to vindicate God's government from any imputation of tyranny, he dealt cautiously with the doctrine of decrees—that is, that God has foreordained and predestined all things, including the election of some to sainthood and the relegation of others to endless misery. He objected to the very term "decree," preferring the language of the New Testament, which presented God as acting according to his "counsel," "purpose," "choice," "pleasure," and "will." Dwight suggested that "perhaps it is unnecessary, and would not be useful, to make it a subject of very frequent discussion in the pulpit." Instead of an elaborate argument about decrees and freedom of the will, he offered a general statement: "God's foreknowledge of voluntary actions does in no respect lessen, or affect [man's] freedom; although it renders their future existence absolutely certain."[8]

This and other questions were too difficult for successful human investigation. For dogmatic "disputants" to preach on such topics was not only fruitless but positively dangerous, for many serious-minded men and women "would fail of being instructed; and, if not instructed, would probably be bewildered." Granting that many subjects found in the Scriptures were beyond ordinary understanding, "All such difficulties arise, not from the thing revealed, but from the philosophical curiosity with which it is investigated by ourselves." Again and again in Dwight's sermons rang declarations of human limitation in merely intellectual attempts to understand God's word.

Anyone who was sufficiently clever and enjoyed such diversions could "invent and adopt a philosophical system of religion" and then scour the Bible for supporting proof texts. Enough learned divines in New England were engaged in just such prideful work. But, Dwight challenged them, "Shall a worm of the dust instruct his maker?" He compared "useless metaphysical disquisitions" to spider webs, "invisible, except to an eye fixed in a peculiar position, and possessed of peculiar acuteness." And, like those webs, these discourses were of no practical use. Such squandering of the precious hours of the Sabbath struck Dwight as being impious.[9]

Where inconsistencies remained, they were more apparent than real. There was no real hindrance to intelligent acceptance of both divine sovereignty on the one hand and man's free agency on the other. Both were revealed in the Bible, and human experience, moreover, showed that men were "intuitively conscious of their own free agency." Throughout his sermons and his theology ran the theme of genuine free agency: "all obedience to God is voluntary."[10]

In thus recovering man's free agency, Dwight did not in the least soften his view of man's sinfulness. He reminded his hearers that man's very existence was an act of divine sovereignty. "Man was not only insignificant and unnecessary; but was also rebellious, sinful, and odious to his Maker." Men ought to be humble in remembrance of God's wonderful goodness in providing for their redemption, when "not even a single white spot varies the dark and cheerless turpitude, which is the groundwork of their character." If men doubted this fact, let them examine their own history candidly. Since the death of Christ, "The world has become one vast Calvary; and crucifixion, torture, and death, have been the common work, the rage, the sport, of the race of *Adam*."

As to Adam and his original transgression, Dwight was conspicuously cautious. He formally stated the doctrine of Original Sin in terms that rejected imputation: "in consequence of the Apostacy of Adam, All Men Have Sinned." Selecting his words with great care, he construed Romans 5:20 as stating that "by means of the offence, or transgression of *Adam*, the judgment, or sentence of God, came upon all men unto condemnation; because, and solely because, all men, in that state of things, which was constituted in consequence of the transgression of *Adam*, became sinners." But he was prompt to admit, "I am unable to explain" "*the manner in which the state of things became such*." He was unwilling to add his flawed conjectures to the vast literature on the subject, except to state categorically that the imputation of Adam's sin to his posterity was not a scriptural doctrine. In this, Dwight concurred with his fellow New England Theologians. History adequately witnessed to the result of that first offense, Dwight added, and: "The first great fact in the science of Man is, that he is a depraved being. *This is the first and fundamental fact*, because out of it arise, and by it are characterized, all his volitions, and all his conduct." And, completing the chain of logic, "In consequence of our *Character*, our *Circumstances* have become deplorable." Man's sinfulness was to be attributed, then, to two causes: his subjective character and his objective circumstances.[11]

Yet, Dwight hastened to assert, this sinfulness was not so thoroughgoing as to prevent effectual human effort to avail oneself of God's mercies. Arguing against the Consistent Calvinists, Dwight declared that most men are not as depraved as their faculties would permit. "Those, who make the assertion against which I am contending, will find themselves, if they will examine, rarely believing, that their wives and children, though not Christians, are Fiends." Many characteristics of human nature, "*considered by themselves, are innocent*"—that is to say, morally neutral—such as hunger, thirst, fear of suffering, and desire for happiness. Other characteristics—for example, compassion, generosity, modesty, and the "natural conscientiousness"—"are amiable." No one could claim, Dwight maintained, that these were detestable or vicious qualities in unregenerate man. Man must possess neutral qualities to be able to obey the commands of God, for how could he obey them before conversion if all his volitions and urges were sinful in themselves? Man must be able to give voluntary assent:

> All obedience to God is voluntary. Nothing is, or can be, demanded by him, which is not in its nature voluntary; nor can any thing, but the will of Intelligent beings, be the object of moral law. No man will say, that a brute, a stone, or a stream, can be the object of such law. Faith therefore, being in the most express terms required by a law, or command, of God, must of course be a voluntary exercise of the mind, in such a sense, that it can be rightfully required.[12]

If man is able, as Dwight believed, why then did no one obey God without the aid of divine grace? "Our natural powers are plainly sufficient: our inclination only is defective." This inclination was never changed without the regenerating influence of the Holy Spirit. Once again Dwight refused to speculate about this strange incapacity of man to obey God's commandments. "Those, who *cannot* come" simply "*will* not," because of their "Indisposition to come to Christ." If Dwight had conceded the absolute (physical) inability of man to obey, he would have been forced to admit, as well, the stock excuse of all unrepentant men, that their helplessness excused their rejection of Christ. The Holy Spirit "is the author of the renovation," but it is nonetheless a voluntary choice; "man is as truly active and voluntary in this change, as in any other conduct."

Where Dwight differed sharply from many of his fellow Calvinists was in elevating the role of means in this work of redemption. Although God could easily accomplish man's salvation "without even a remote reference to any means whatever," he had provided many. Family prayer, meditation, self-examination, conversation with godly men and women, reading the Scriptures, and attendance on preaching, were all means of being awakened and converted. God required men to seek and use these helps. In the view of Samuel Hopkins and his followers, the volitions and acts of unregenerate men were wholly sinful; and nothing was more odious to God than the sight of unrenewed men making a show of godliness. Even awakened men who used such means prayerfully were hateful to God, who commanded their immediate submission. Dwight held, on the contrary, that

> The means of grace universally form, when employed in earnest, a preparation of the man, both with respect to the understanding and the affections, for the proper commencement of the agency of the Holy Spirit in renewing his heart. This is not a preparation of *merit* but of *fitness*. It involves no desert of blessing. It infers no obligation on God to communicate it.

But so God had ordained it. The actual renewal involved not man's faculties or physical powers and propensities but his disposition. "Man, in my view, has all the physical power *before*, that he has *at*, or *after*, his regeneration."[13]

This, it may seem, was a bold declaration and not altogether to the liking of those who adhered to the Hopkinsian view. Dwight's view was much more akin to the old Puritan preparationist schemes, although he was no Stoddardean. Many of Dwight's friends and students, Beecher and Taylor among them, said to his face that his views on the means of grace tended to counteract preaching for conversion by undercutting the demand for immediate repentance. The means of grace must not be substituted for immediate, heartfelt submission. Man's own act must not be seen as determining salvation or influencing God's purposes. Beecher was disposed to minimize the difference between himself and Dwight on this point:

> There was a time when a question came up among us about the doings of unregenerate men. Taylor and I pushed for immediate repentance. I didn't go quite so far as Taylor. Instead of *using means of grace*, reading, prayer, etc., we drove them up to instant submission. Dr. Dwight, however, felt as though there might be some use of means. So, though Taylor was his amanuensis, there arose a kind of feeling between them and among the students, and Dr. Dwight felt a grief as though it had produced some coldness.

The impasse was cleared by Beecher who, in his retelling of the story, took advantage of his preceptor's reasonableness to work out their differences through amicable discussion.[14]

Nevertheless, religious education figured much more prominently in Dwight's scheme of salvation than in those of his contemporaries and students. He insisted that "children are by nature prepared to reverence religion." Drawing on his long years of experience as a teacher of young children, Dwight believed that they instinctively revered religion:

> The conscience of man, before it has been warped, and overpowered, by passion, prejudice, and sin, prompts him, of course, to regard this solemn and awful subject, only with emotions of respect. So obvious is this truth, that it has often been acknowledged by Infidels.

This was not Calvinism, as understood by New England Theologians, but Dwight did not insist that he was a Calvinist. He drew, I think, on an older strain of Puritanism less exacting and narrow in its doctrines of conversion and regeneration than that which prevailed in New England. To the pious parent he said, "The salvation of his child is promised to him, and in the most endearing of all methods; viz., as *the consequence of his labour*." "If we *train up* our children *in the way* they *should go*, they will enter it almost of course; follow us to heaven; and be our companions forever." Beecher did not dismiss this conception of Christian nurture but had less confidence in it and in the other means of grace to produce genuine repentance. Many of his children never attained that state which the milder doctrines of his teacher might have induced.[15]

This raises the question, What is the relationship between conversion experience and theology? The evangelical truism was that the most effective preaching was doctrinal preaching. Lyman Beecher certainly thought so. Speaking of his own conversion, he gave it as his considered opinion that "Divine sovereignty does the whole," that evangelical doctrines could be explained in a manner to awaken sinners. His friend Asahel Nettleton, after an emotionally devastating struggle against divine sovereignty and decrees, discovered that "a sweet peace pervaded his soul." God and Christ appeared lovely and precious, while "the doctrines of grace, toward which he had felt such bitter opposition, he contemplated with delight." The ground of his faith in these doctrines, Nettleton testified, was this: "What the Scriptures teach on these points, was confirmed by his experience. He had the witness in himself of the truth of these doctrines."[16]

When he first began preaching, Nettleton preached directly from his own experience, "personating the awakened sinner, and bringing out the feelings of his heart." Later, during the revival of 1821 in Beecher's Litchfield church—a revival which Nettleton sparked and conducted—Nettleton found that the more doctrinally he preached, the hotter the revival waxed. "He brought from his treasure," Bennet Tyler reported, "the doctrines of total depravity, personal election, reprobation, the sovereignty of divine grace, and the universal government of God in working all things after the counsel of his own will [decrees]. And these great doctrines did not *paralyze*, but greatly *promoted* the work."

Judging by his own experience of conversion and his effectiveness as a revivalist, then, Nettleton believed that the surest way to bring rebel hearts to repentance was to present them with uncompromising views of divine sovereignty. "He very much disliked Dr. Dwight's idea of the prayers and doings of the unregenerate, being in certain cases without sin, and of a mere neutral character." Dwight, of course, was a great supporter of revivals, but he also said that the faithful minister must "rear the infant plants, that bud around;/To ope their little minds to truth's pure light." For his students Beecher, Nettleton, and Taylor, however, immediate repentance "did the whole."[17]

If that had, in fact, been the case, Beecher ought to have seen his children ripening one by one into Christians as their understanding matured for the reception of the doctrines of grace. They understood that their father's views were liberal compared to those of his opponents within the Calvinistic fold, and they appreciated his eagerness to render hard doctrines "precious and glorious" by clearing away the obnoxious and obscure phraseology of "hyper-Calvinism." Far from subduing their carnal hearts, however, New Haven Theology repelled and distressed them, as the succeeding chapters will show.

The men who came to be called the New Haven Theologians were bound together by a shared point of view and common convictions concerning the great end of theology. They believed that Timothy Dwight was, in the final analysis, not a follower of John Calvin so much as a Calvinist from conviction, who had worked through the Scriptures prayerfully but with tough-minded realism to arrive at truly evangelical and, because evangelical, unquestionably orthodox views. Beecher and Taylor worked from certain nondoctrinal premises of Dwight's as well. One has only to read Beecher's *Works* or Taylor's *Moral Government* to see how closely they followed Dwight.

Dwight insisted that the Bible was written expressly for plain people, as uncouth and untutored as the Apostles or as naïve and fanciful as children. Hence he placed great emphasis, on the one hand, upon interpreting the Bible according to the *usus loquendi*, the common meaning of words, and on the other, upon using words precisely and perspicuously. He believed that "a multitude of disputes arose from ambiguous phraseology etc. [and] studied with great care the exact meaning of language." Like the Apostles, who proclaimed rules of faith and laws of practice, Dwight held that virtue consisted in acts of benevolence and that religion meant nothing when it had no regard for ethical activity. This was similar to Samuel Hopkins's "disinterested benevolence," but with greater stress on actual practice of humanitarian and charitable works than was found in Hopkins's followers. Another prominent strain in Dwight's thought was his faith in the efficacy and necessity of revivals. He felt that he was witness to the dawn of an era of revivals, which would culminate in one great universal awakening, when the world from "*Nootka* . . . to *Negroland*" would welcome the millennium.[18]

Before proceeding to Lyman Beecher's theological views, it might be useful to consider what is meant by Calvinism and Arminianism. More helpful than any formal definition is Geoffrey Nuttall's observation contrasting the two positions: "The theology of Calvinism arises, naturally and properly, as a theology of the people of God within the household of God. An Arminian theology arises equally naturally and properly, as a theology of mission to the unbeliever." Like all such pronouncements, this must be applied with care and hedged with qualifications. But it is helpful in trying to understand the deviations of the New Haven Theologians from what was conceived by their numerous opponents to be the orthodoxy of the Westminster Confession or of the New England Theology (which are not the same thing).[19]

In the first place, then, Lyman Beecher was not primarily a theologian but a revivalist, polemicist, and ecclesiastical statesman (or politician). And, in the second, he understood theology as an armory and himself as a warrior pledged to win souls and rout infidels and errorists, whether Methodists, Episcopalians, Unitarians, or "nothingarians." He was careful in the controversies that swirled around his friend Taylor never to declare himself a member of the New Haven party, although he was widely assumed, by reason of friendship and public pronouncements, to be one. As for being a Calvinist, he seldom made that claim and, when he did, came to grief because he had no more knowledge of Calvin's *Institutes* than he did of the Hebrew testament. Absolute consistency and system were impossible to the man because he was so imbued with the revival spirit. His doctrinal departures flowed from and reinforced the exigencies of revival preaching. His eagerness to harvest souls moved him, however unconsciously, to bend and whittle some doctrines, suppress others, and clothe still others in novel phraseology.

The dissensions among the orthodox clergy of New England had a long and on the whole unedifying history. It is unnecessary to trace this history in detail, but one fact ought to be borne in mind. Although Hopkinsian theology was the most complete and searching expression of New England Theology, it was by no means the dominant one, either in influence or numbers. In 1804, writing to an English evangelical on "the State of Religion in New England," Jedidiah Morse described the theological complexion of the region in these terms:

> The congregational clergy in New England, generally speaking, may be styled *Calvinistic* in their doctrinal sentiments, with shades of difference from the *severe* views (if I may so speak) of Calvin himself, Edwards, and Hopkins, to the milder schemes of Doddridge, and Baxter. Of this character are, I apprehend, 19/20ths of the clergy. . . . The progress of liberal sentiments in religion in churches, has been slow. I believe if Dr Doddridge were alive, and were to preach his sermons throughout our New England congregational churches, he would in ninety nine instances out of a hundred, be approved.

It is significant that Morse pointed to divisions among the Calvinistic clergy and identified himself with the moderate party. Although he was anxious for all the orthodox to form an alliance against Unitarianism, he complained that "Some *Hopkinsians* so called and who also have become a sect, are inclined to go to the opposite extreme." Morse's paper, the *Panoplist*, occupied a middle ground between the small number of clergy with Arminian (Unitarian) leanings and the stricter party that revolved around Nathanael Emmons, who was generally regarded as Hopkins's heir. One of Morse's confrères, writing of the situation in New Hampshire, noted that the number of ministers "attached to the peculiarities of Hopkinsianism" was small, while the majority of the orthodox still held to "the Calvinistic system of doctrine as maintained by the reformers and the primitive christians of New England"—in other words, the orthodoxy which prevailed before Jonathan Edwards and his school. There were many clergymen and divinity students who regarded Emmons and his friends with horror, who were appalled alike by their grim systematizing and their addiction to following minute propositions to absurd lengths. Elijah Parish, for example, parodied this tendency. "I am reading systematic divinity and metaphysics," he grumbled to Morse, "that I may answer the young gentlemen who are studying *Hopkintonianism* with me. Adieu to tropes and figures, to the smoothly sounding line; now syllogisms, ergos, and corollaries are all my joy: but I must try to hobble on."[20]

When Morse, with Timothy Dwight, led in organizing Andover Seminary as a union seminary rallying the orthodox to fight the Harvard Unitarian influence, he was hard pressed to assure Andover's supporters that the Hopkinsians would be held in check. It was bad enough, as Dwight lamented, that the Hopkinsians had drawn off from the Old Calvinists just when the orthodox needed to present a united front. It would be far worse to have the Hopkinsians gain ascendancy in the new seminary, for their distinctive doctrines were anathema both within and without New England. In 1809, for instance, Abiel Holmes chided his friend Morse for permitting an article to appear in the *Panoplist* discrediting the means of grace. The article was "deemed very exceptionable by some who are well wishers and patrons of that publication. It is pure, unadulterated Hopkinsianism which, it is alleged, was *not* to have place in this work. . . . If the tenets of the Old School are made to give place to those of the New—the disciples of the Old School will desert the standard." The Old School, as Holmes denominated them, represented a strain of Puritanism most akin to Richard Baxter and Philip Doddridge—that is, those clergymen and laymen who called themselves Calvinistic but who were willing in the interests of Christian unity to minimize doctrinal differences and to eschew strict subscription to minutely defined doctrines.[21]

This was the same spirit which animated Dwight's theology and, through him, Beecher's. Early in his career Beecher told John Romeyn that, "abating what I considered the imprudencies of some writers, I was a friend to Hopkinsianism." In 1810, however, he discovered during a preaching engagement in New York City that not only the imprudencies but also the mode of preaching favored by Hopkinsians were in disrepute. "The style of city sermonizing is so different," he wrote his wife, "and so many technical phrases smell of new divinity, that I found myself destitute of good sermons." A survey of his best-known early sermons shows that Beecher, while preaching nothing repugnant to the most conservative within the array of Calvinists, tended to avoid doctrines that to his mind discouraged repentance. Of election and predestination he said very little. In "The Government of God Desirable," Beecher declared:

> If God governs according to his pleasure, he will do no injustice to his impenitent enemies. He will send to misery no harmless animals without souls,—no mere machines,—none who have done, or even attempted to do, as well as they could. He will leave to walk in their own way none who do not deserve to be left; and punish none for walking in it who did not walk therein knowingly, deliberately, and with wilful obstinacy. . . . It seems to be the imagination of some that the kingdom of darkness will be as populous and as vast as the kingdom of light. . . . How could the government of God be celebrated with such raptures in heaven, if it filled with dismay and ruined half the universe? How vast soever, therefore, the kingdom of darkness may be, in itself considered, it is certainly nothing but the prison of the universe, and small, compared to the realms of light and glory.

This sermon, preached before the Synod of New York and New Jersey, was sufficiently well regarded to merit publication at the Synod's direction.

Increasingly Beecher understood his mission as a practical one, and his theology developed in accordance with his pastoral experience. In the words of one of his children, "It was his business, by preaching, to awaken men, answer all their objections, convince them that the doctrines of the Gospel were not at variance with common sense, and lead them to intelligent and honorable repentance." Certain key words and phrases made their appearance in his sermons: "common sense," "honorable" repentance, meeting "all objections." This rationalistic bent was very pronounced, as was his conviction that Gospel truths must be explained in a manner that did not impeach the honorable and just government of God or undermine man's sense of responsibility and obligation. In 1817 he preached a famous sermon at the ordination of Sereno Edwards Dwight, the son of Timothy. "The Bible a Code of Laws" represented God's government in terms that would have pleased the elder Dwight immensely:

> Law, as the medium of moral government, includes precepts and sanctions intelligibly revealed. The precept is directory; it discloses what is to be done. The sanctions are influential; they present the motives to obedience included in the comprehensive terms of reward and punishment. But, to have influence, the precepts and the motives must be presented to the mind. . . . Direct irresistible impulse, moving the mind to action, would not be moral government; and if motives, in the view of which the mind chooses and acts, were coercive of choice, accountability and moral government would be impossible.[22]

Dwight had died that same year, and the leadership of Connecticut orthodoxy fell to Beecher and Taylor. If Beecher had been content to preach variations on Dwight's themes, he might have remained in good odor among the orthodox, but it was soon apparent that he and Taylor had undertaken to improve and clarify certain doctrines. Taylor singled out Edwards's handling of moral agency as the most obscure and vexatious of his doctrines: "For example he thought it to be enough to show that certainty of conduct and moral agency did coexist in fact, without venturing any hypothesis concerning the *quo modo*. Leaving this untouched, he left the loophole for Emmonsism." By Emmonsism, Taylor meant the argument that God "produces" or "creates" all human volitions. Although Emmons insisted that his view did not deny, and in fact upheld, man's free will, why this should be so, given his own premises, was not apparent to his detractors nor demonstrable by his few adherents.

Taylor felt called upon to provide correct views of free agency where Edwards (and Dwight) had defaulted in the obligation to do so. In his *Inquiry into the Freedom of the Will*, Edwards had defined moral agency and free will in terms which Taylor considered an affront to reason:

> Now I can not but think this defect even a gross one. If language has any meaning, a free will is a will which is free, and to say that free will is a power to do as we please or as we will is saying nothing to the purpose. . . . In the second place, he says the will is as the greatest apparent good, and also admits that the appearing

most agreeable to the mind is not distinct from choice or volition. He considers the act subsequent to volition as determined by the volition rather than that the choice itself is, and that the act of volition is determined by what causes an object to appear most agreeable.

Edwards, Taylor observed, skirted the question of what causes the object to appear agreeable in the first place. If that question could be successfully settled, so that genuinely free choosing was demonstrated as a fact, Taylor and Beecher would "give to the world that desideratum which shall show that good sound Calvinism, or, if you please, Beecherism and Taylorism, is but another name for the truth and reality of things as they exist in the nature of God and man, and the relations arising therefrom." The New Haven Theology, or Taylorism, thus arose from the impulse to make free agency even securer than Dwight had.[23]

While Taylor labored over his theological lectures, Beecher was busy conducting the campaign against the Episcopalians, whose proselyting zeal alarmed the orthodox of Connecticut. Almost from the first, Taylor drew fire for his injudicious style of argumentation. He pressed the case for man's free agency, prior to and independent of divine grace, so hard that the Episcopalians, instead of being daunted by his boldness, asked whether the man was really orthodox. It was evident that Taylor's attempts to knock away the allegedly fatalistic props of Calvinism would involve him in deep differences with his own brethren. Beecher was simultaneously preaching the same theme: that, in order to speak of sinning, one had first to admit absolute free agency on the part of man. If man were constrained to do what pleased God, man was not holy. If he were forced by physical necessity to break God's law, he was not guilty.

Since all moral action was voluntary according to Beecher's conception of free agency, he consistently preached moral voluntaryism as the foundation of divine government. When his children received instruction in the Westminster Assembly's Shorter Catechism, they were made to recite a Beecher variant of the text. In place of the declaration that "No mere man since the fall is able perfectly to keep the commandments of God," their father had them say, "No man since the fall is willing to keep the commandments of God." Beecher's readiness to change the very words of the Catechism was in keeping with the New England standard of subscription, which obliged men to subscribe only to the substance of doctrine, not the letter.[24]

Whereas Beecher and Taylor believed they were salvaging Calvinism and confounding its enemies by supplementing the teachings of Edwards, they were viewed by many as importing dangerous novelties into the system. Beecher had made himself famous as a revivalist by his manner of dealing with inquirers.

> I *struck* just according to [their] character and state. It was really almost amusing to see the rapid changes in language and manner I underwent as I passed from one class to another. A large portion, on being questioned, would reveal their state of mind easily, and being plain cases, would need only plain instruction. They believed the Bible, and they believed what I told them as if it was the Bible—as it was; and therefore the truth was made effectual by the Holy Spirit as well as if more conversation was had. . . . Another class would plead inability—can not do any thing. Many of these told me their ministers told them so. Now I rose into the field of metaphysics, and, instead of being simple, I became the philosopher, and began to form my language for purposes of discrimination and power.

And so on he would proceed, according to the emotional and intellectual state of the awakened. "We never knew his equal in difficult cases and solving the doubts which so often amount to chronic infirmities," wrote one of Beecher's students. This same man felt obliged to add, however, that "as a teacher of 'systematic theology,' Dr. Beecher was not very systematic," an opinion shared by many. Beecher may have considered himself adept at playing the philosopher, answering every objection, removing every metaphysical stumbling block, but his friend Ebenezer Porter warned him against indulging this penchant. "I do not think you a metaphysician born to tear up the foundations laid by Edwards," Porter bluntly told Beecher. "You are a rhetorician and a popular reasoner. Your forte is impression by vivid argumentation, and appeal from common sense and boundless stores of illustration."[25]

Beecher ran afoul of the more conservative elements within orthodoxy because of rash pronouncements made in the heat of battle against Unitarianism; Taylor, because of the whole body of his writings. When Beecher went to Boston in 1826, he expected to carry all before him. He had succeeded in wiping out the forces of Unitarianism in his home state of Connecticut and saw no reason why he should not meet with equal success in their citadel, especially when the orthodox of Massachusetts implored his aid and presence. In a typical vein of expansive optimism and hyperbole, Beecher announced, "I rejoice to perceive unequivocal evidence that orthodoxy in Massachusetts is becoming a phalanx terrible as an army with banners, and that our adversaries shall no more be able to frame iniquity by law, and draw sin as with a cart-rope."

By this time, however, the views of Taylor and his colleagues at Yale had diverged enough from those of Andover to attract unfavorable attention within both the Congregational and the Presbyterian communions. Yale had had a separate Theological Department with Taylor at its head since 1822, and it was understood by Taylor's opponents that Yale meant to rival and perhaps supersede Andover, formerly the union seminary but now in the hands of men he considered too conservative. According to the report of a hostile observer, not only were Chauncey Goodrich, Eleazer Fitch, and Edward Beecher aligned with Taylor, but even Josiah Willard Gibbs, the professor of sacred literature. Edward Beecher was only a tutor in 1826, but Joseph Foot found him holding forth on "Dr. Taylor's views" and "our views," while "there seemed to be a general opinion that New Haven had made some advances in theology." Both Lyman and Edward Beecher moved to Boston in 1826, the son taking his place in the pulpit of Park Street Church. The dismay felt by the conservatives may be imagined. If the Beechers claimed to represent the orthodox rebuttal to Unitarianism, what spectacular errors might not be broadcast as authentic Calvinism?[26]

Conservative Presbyterians took note of Lyman's utterances for two reasons. First, there were repeated attempts on the part of liberal (New School) Presbyterians in Philadelphia to induce Beecher to settle amongst them. Second, as a result of the Plan of Union of 1801, New Englanders and Middle States Presbyterians were acting in concert to Christianize the Old Northwest. Isolated evangelists with limited resources found that cooperation forwarded their goals. Despite the talk that was to come at mid-century about Presbyterian opportunists milking Congregationalist cows, such local unions on the frontier appeared at first highly advantageous. But New Englanders, particularly those who espoused or appeared to espouse Hopkinsian views, discovered soon enough that they were regarded with suspicion and jealousy. When Thomas Robbins served a term as a home missionary, he met with antagonism on this account. "The serious people here are generally attached to the literal meaning and terms of the Westminister Confession and Catechisms," he wrote in his diary. "They are particularly alarmed at new terms."

By 1816 hostility toward New Englanders had grown so serious that the Synod of Philadelphia adopted a pastoral letter advising presbyteries to oppose the "introduction of Arian, Socinian, Arminian, and Hopkinsian heresies." The lumping of so-called Hopkinsians with overt enemies to Calvinism was a calculated insult, especially when the Synod declared that they were all "means by which the enemy of the soul would deceive the very elect." What was meant by "Hopkinsianism" among the Presbyterians of the Middle States was any Edwardsean theology that diverged markedly from the letter of the Westminster Confession, as professed according to the stringent standards prevailing in Philadelphia and wherever Scotch-Irish literalist clergymen were to be found. Any theology that took Jonathan Edwards as its starting point was suspect. Edwards, from the Old School Presbyterian point of view, "must be recognized as the spring, whence have flowed many heresies, to plague the Church of God." The chief errors promulgated by these unwelcome allies were the denial of the imputation of Adam's sin, the distinction made between moral and natural inability to obey God, a general (as opposed to limited) atonement, and the insistence upon the governmental theory of the atonement. The latter doctrine undercut any conception of an efficacious atonement.[27]

In Boston, then, while Beecher was still a Congregationalist, he was already being watched by the Old School Presbyterians. They believed that "the divines of New Haven found, in the very heart of the Hopkinsian system, some of the fundamental and most efficient principles of the Pelagian heresy," and no one seemed more pungent and forceful in pressing these views than Lyman Beecher, that "ingenious and eccentric divine." Beecher was aware that people looked to him for the latest practical applications of Taylorite views. Asahel Nettleton, once a close friend of Beecher's, now joined forces with Leonard Woods of Andover and Bennet Tyler to attack Taylor. Taylor soon found himself mired in controversy; each attempt to deal a death blow to one critic produced several rejoinders.

From our vantage point, the differences between Taylor and his brethren seem small, as they did to Leonard Bacon, who was a generation younger. When asked what the difference was between Taylor and Tyler, Bacon quipped, the letter *a*. But that was in 1850. In 1825 the polemics among Calvinists were just beginning, and every deviation in tone and diction was made to seem portentous. Beecher was perplexed by this state of affairs. "The parties on both sides were my special friends," he recalled, "and my labors were unceasing to explain and mitigate, and prevent explosions in the churches of Connecticut and Massachusetts."[28]

In 1825 Asahel Hooker wrote to Beecher, alarmed over Taylor's developing views of Original Sin. Beecher's reflex reaction was to deny that he was a Taylorite as such and to represent Taylor as only slightly, if at all, off the orthodox track. This response was meant to soothe Hooker while not deserting Taylor:

> If any one supposes that I have regarded Brother Taylor as fundamentally erroneous on the subject of original sin, their impression is without foundation. *I have regarded him as adopting one of the half dozen ways in which orthodox men explain and defend that difficult doctrine*, and I have censured him only as changing phraseology needlessly in a few particulars.

At this time Beecher was still in good standing among his colleagues and associates, who hoped to see him break with Taylor. Both Tyler and Nettleton had praised Beecher's 1823 sermon, "The Faith Once Delivered to the Saints," even though it was pilloried by the Unitarian *Christian Examiner* as anti-Calvinistic and a reproach to the orthodox. Nettleton had gone so far as to repel the charge of heterodoxy:

> Probably the writer thinks that you are in sentiment at war with the orthodox at the present day, but he is grandly mistaken so far as Connecticut is concerned. And I do suppose that we do preach moral obligation and dependence different from many of our old divines—that in some things the Calvinism of Connecticut or New England has undergone an important change. Why not take this ground with Unitarians? We feel no concern for Calvinism. Let them dispute it as much as they please; we feel bound to make no defense.[29]

Beecher could not bring himself to break with Taylor. Even if such disloyalty had been possible in him, there was no gainsaying the affinity between their views. He continued, therefore, to murmur soothing sentiments to Taylor's detractors, mostly following the line of denying any novelty to the statements that produced such disquiet, while trying to curb Taylor's combative spirit. Apparently he succeeded in this strategy. In Calvin Stowe's opinion, at any rate, Beecher reined Taylor in at precisely those points where he was readiest and ablest to make a genuine departure from received orthodoxy:

> He checked the theologically more adventurous spirit of Taylor; and by his love prevailed on his friend still to draw as much as possible in the old harness of Edwards. The result was not happy. Though it prevented some temporary evil, it embarrassed and

> embittered the whole strife, and sent Taylor into the ring against the most practiced pugilists with one hand tied behind him. It is true that Taylor and Beecher did agree with Edwards on all the leading topics of Christian theology, but on this [free agency] and its related points they decidedly differed from their master; and though they insisted, and perhaps justly, that Edwards, in order to be consistent with himself and true to the Bible, ought in these respects also to have believed and taught just as they did, yet it was plain that he did not; and it would have been best from the first to have made a clean breast of it and said so. Dr. Taylor, if left to himself, would probably have followed this course.

Taylor finally made a statement in 1828, in his *Concio ad Clerum*, that excited too much opposition for Beecher to claim any longer that there might be many acceptable ways of stating truth. The *Concio ad Clerum* was the manifesto of the New Haven party, and, while its opinions were not strikingly new by this time, they were now advanced uncompromisingly. Taylor concerned himself with providing, as he thought, a modern and reasonable definition of Original Sin. The view that all mankind partook of a racial solidarity with Adam was peculiar to Edwards, and Taylor's rejection of it had no particular significance. He went on, however, to deny the so-called federal view that Adam stood as representative head of the race and to argue against any view of human depravity which made it originate in heredity.

Man's nature, in other words, was not in itself depraved. Man might justly be said to sin *by* nature, but his own nature was not inherently sinful. Man was absolutely a free agent. When he sinned, as he always did until regenerated by the power of the Holy Spirit, he sinned by preference and not through some innate corruption or inherent tendency to sin. To underscore free agency, Taylor introduced the phrase "certainty of sinning, with power to the contrary." Unless man had an actual ability not to sin—a power of contrary choice—his acts could not be called sin. A total predisposition to sin, or prior and outward compulsion to sin, as held by Taylor's adversaries, seemed to relieve man of the responsibility for his own acts. Taylor did not maintain that man did, in fact, make holy rather than sinful choices. Man invariably chose the world instead of God; his sinning was certain. But this certainty of sinning was a fact of life and not a prescription or a physical and mental compulsion.[30]

The *Concio ad Clerum* provoked heated rejoinders, and a protracted pamphlet war began. Taylor, who prided himself on his plain and intelligible writing, discovered that his critics found his new terms baffling or perverse. Ebenezer Porter scoffed at the notion that Taylor's new phraseology was useful and scolded Beecher for employing Taylorite language:

> If you ask me here to specify what I think wrong in your or Dr. Taylor's views, one of the worst faults I find is the indefinite and obscure character of those views. In all the annals of theological discussion, I have seen no match for Dr. Taylor's obscurity. I mean, when a man has good sense as he has, and can preach with perspicuity. And as for you, who certainly can speak and write as clearly as any man on common subjects, I understand that you, as well as Dr. Taylor, are beginning to complain (as system makers have been wont to do) that you are misunderstood.

Ironically, Porter was now berating Dwight's favorite students for the very offense against which Dwight had perennially inveighed. As far as he could grasp Taylorism and the views ascribed to Beecher, Porter thought "these views are not built on the BIBLE, but on philosophical theories as to man's mind and powers of agency," with the result that human agency was vaunted while human dependence on divine grace was lost sight of. The New Havenites, Porter warned Beecher, "are supposed to be thus unwittingly reviving the Arminian notion of gradual regeneration by light, or what has been sometimes termed reliance on *unregenerate doings*."

To be thus misrepresented was maddening to Beecher, who pointedly referred to his widely approved published sermons as containing his "elementary principles" of theology. "They have not, to my knowledge, been misunderstood or created alarm, and in their amplification and application in the pulpit and in the vestry I utter no sentiments at variance with them." He was aggrieved that his friend Porter would take the word of "anonymous brethren," mere "parole testimony, 'the echo' of my sermons," when anyone could read what was in the public domain. He felt he had been injured greatly and hinted that there was a conspiracy to get at him through Taylor, or vice versa:

> You can not, however, be insensible that close upon the confines of honest zeal lie the territories of twilight, and suspicion, and fear, and imagination, and amplification, and whisperings, and rumors, where, through our own imperfections, the enemy [Satan] employs the influential friends of Christ to wound one another, and to propagate distrust, and alienation, and acrimony, almost as injurious to the cause of Christ as heresy itself.

As it turned out, Beecher was correct in divining some sort of conspiracy among clergymen to pin a charge on him, but he was partly to blame for the falling off of old friends. More than once Beecher behaved in a way that seemed to his conservative brethren to prize popular influence over principle. This was the case with Beecher's battle with Charles G. Finney.[31]

His actions with regard to the "New Measures" of the revivalist Finney—first publishing alarms, then threatening to destroy Finney's influence, and finally coming to terms with Finney when his power could no longer be checked—reflected little credit on Beecher. Finney himself never trusted his erstwhile foe and complained, as Porter evidently had, that Beecher tended to be a trimmer and a dodger, who preached far too much in the vein calculated to suit his hearers. Finney's doctrines were sufficiently obnoxious, apart from the supercharged emotionalism and spiritual pride alleged against him, to make association with him dangerous in conservative eyes. To quote his own words, he "preached that the divine agency [in regeneration] was that of teaching and persuasion, that the influence was a moral, and not a physical one." Instead of changing the nature of the sinner, the Holy Spirit changed the "voluntary attitude and preference of the soul."

This was remarkably like the doctrine of Timothy Dwight, but taken with other innovations, it appeared heretical. As in the case of the New Haven party, the consternation produced by these doctrines had more to do with their supposed "practical tendencies" than with their substance. Finneyite and Taylorite views of conversion were labeled Arminian, while Taylor's teachings on Original Sin were denounced as Pelagian. If Beecher was compelled by Finney's popular successes to acknowledge him as a legitimate fellow laborer in revivals, if their cooperation was grounded in similarity of theological views, and if these views appeared to encourage carnal men to assume too much with respect to their own activity and worthiness for salvation, then it followed that the Arminians had won the day. So ran the conservative argument. Men like Beecher were, then, crypto-Arminians, but were too stupid or too self-important to realize how dangerous their innovations were. It was a familiar argument. Beecher himself had considered the "practical tendencies" of Unitarianism the most useful argument against it.[32]

Beecher did not regard himself as heterodox and never conceded that he had used injudicious language in the pulpit or at the anxious bench. Indeed, he argued the wisdom of his course as the only way to win Bostonians back to evangelical truth. Since he himself could not stomach sermons of the "damned if you do/and damned if you don't" school, he could hardly expect other reasonable men to savor them. Instead of being assailed as a mischief-maker in Zion, he ought to be credited with furthering the cause of God in America. His pulpit in Boston would extend evangelical influence, not undermine it. He admitted that he had deliberately preached up human ability and suppressed detailed discussion of human dependence. Boston, after all, was the seat of Unitarianism, and its populace was so accustomed to hearing Calvinism caricatured as fatalistic that they "did not need high-toned Calvinism on the point of dependence; they had been crammed with it, and were dying with excessive aliment." If he had done what Porter and others advised, "it had been infatuation" and would have driven people even further from evangelical truth. "The Antinomianism of perverted Calvinism, and the fatality of philosophical necessity, made it an obvious policy and an imperious duty," he concluded. Beecher's resort to "policy" was unfortunate, and such declarations would be used against him at the worst possible time. Meanwhile, he took his letter to Ebenezer Porter at Andover and spent a day conciliating the men there, leaving them (as he believed) serene in their conviction of his soundness.[33]

Forces were gathering to stop Beecher if he had the effrontery to try to extend his influence. In 1830, when he was weighing an offer from the newly formed Presbyterian seminary in Cincinnati, whose New School supporters wanted Beecher for its president, a party was organizing to keep Beecher away. Its leader was Joshua Lacy Wilson, pastor of the First Presbyterian Church of Cincinnati, and a self-appointed heresy-hunter whose zealotry in behalf of pure Presbyterianism was infamous. Wilson knew enough of Beecher's views to resign from the board of Lane Seminary, and he exerted himself to prevent Beecher's reentry into the Presbyterian Church.

It is difficult to judge how much personal animosities and jealousies figured in the actions of Beecher's enemies. Even Wilson's admirers, however, had to make great allowances for his "pugnacity." In a communion of strict Calvinists there were probably few as literal-minded as he. (Since the Bible prohibited the setting up of graven images, Wilson refused to have a single illustration or portrait in his house.) Yet he was by no means alone in his bellicosity. When Timothy Flint visited Cincinnati, he was scandalized by the incessant verbal bloodletting among the Presbyterian clergy:

> There were hot disputes in the Presbyterian church. I attended the sessions of a Presbytery, assembled professedly to heal these

> divisions. The ministers took the attitude, and made the long speeches of lawyers, in discussing the dispute before this tribunal. They availed themselves of the same vehement action, and pouring out a great deal of rather vapid declamation, proceeded to settle points, that seemed to me of very little importance. The whole scene presented, it may be, a sufficient modicum of talent for the bar, but manifested much want of the appropriate temper, so strongly recommended by St. John the divine.

Beecher left no record that he read Flint's remarks, which had been published in 1826. On the contrary, in the face of vitriolic attacks by Wilson and cries of foul play from Old School Presbyterian partisans, he continued to issue sanguine predictions of fraternal cooperation and churchly amity. Wilson attacked Beecher in the columns of his newspaper, the *Standard*, and implored Beecher to prove himself no hypocrite by staying out of the Presbyterian church.[34]

As it happened, a separate New School presbytery was formed in New York in 1830, and it was to this body that Beecher planned to apply. "This organization," rumbled Samuel J. Baird years later, "became a most active and powerful instrument for corrupting the Church . . . and through it, Dr. Beecher accomplished his extraordinary transit into the Presbyterian Church." A malicious story made the rounds about Beecher's opportunism and cunning. Knowing that he might have to undergo a strict examination, the tale went, he asked an acquaintance from Mississippi to undertake a mock examination. When the Old Schooler asked, "Do you sincerely receive and adopt the Confession of Faith of this Church, as containing the system of doctrine taught in the Holy Scriptures?" Beecher, whether out of principle or bravado, replied, "Yes, but I will not say how much more it contains." He was told that "he was no Presbyterian." After two more attempts to get Beecher to subscribe in due form, the Reverend Mr. Weatherby cut him off with, "no such Yankee answer would do. That it was idle for Dr. Beecher to pretend to be a Presbyterian." Beecher finally confined himself to a simple yes, and on the strength of this experience wrote to the Third Presbytery of New York. He declared himself a conscientious Presbyterian, was received without personal examination, and was immediately dismissed to the Presbytery of Cincinnati, thus qualifying himself with a minimum of effort or scrutiny for the presidency of Lane Seminary.

Whether Beecher acted with such unblushing "policy" cannot now be determined. The Third Presbytery knew that he had been a Presbyterian in East Hampton and could be assumed to understand the platform and usages of the church. In any event, it had long been his lot to be tagged with apocryphal tales. And in the heat of controversy, righteous indignation might fire off shots that were not strictly accurate.[35]

Settled in Cincinnati as president of Lane, Beecher also became pastor of the Second Church. He hoped he was far removed from Eastern strife and wanted to concentrate on winning the West and wresting its inhabitants from the grip of ignorance, atheism, and Catholicism. But the battle in Connecticut followed Beecher to Cincinnati. The Congregationalists of Connecticut and Massachusetts who were most active against Taylor acted in concert with the Old School Presbyterian leaders of Philadelphia, Princeton, and the West. Again the quarrel was about words and moral tendencies, real or alleged. Taylor was not one to see his precious innovations misrepresented or put down. He made a number of unambiguous amplifications of his *Concio ad Clerum* which further inflamed the situation. In replying to Joseph Harvey's *Examination of a Review of Dr. Taylor's Sermon on Human Depravity*, Taylor proposed that Harvey concur with him in restating Calvinist doctrine. "Thus, instead of reading 'out of the heart of man proceed evil thoughts,' we shall read, *out of the ACT* of men, when they know no better, proceed evil thoughts."

Beecher, too, was subjected to a barrage of polemics. In 1833 Asa Rand, an arch conservative, published a *Letter to the Rev. Dr. Beecher on the Influence of His Ministry in Boston*, which maintained that Beecher had misrepresented himself as a champion of orthodoxy against the Unitarians. In the tone of mock deference then favored by Christian controversialists, Rand wondered whether he might not set the reverend gentleman straight and point out to him the unwitting harm he had done. Rand characterized the New Haven Theology as a crypto-Wesleyanism, "a strange mingling of evangelical doctrines with Arminian speculations." By giving undue prominence to human agency in salvation, Beecher encouraged a "lowering down or gliding over the great essential points of scripture doctrine and duty." Rand's opinions did not constitute a particularly astute analysis of Beecher and Taylor's deficiencies, but his language, which was calculated to shock, suited the purposes of Joshua Wilson.[36]

Wilson was also receiving help from other quarters. According to Beecher, the Princeton men "wrote Wilson a flattering letter, explaining the whole campaign, and predicting what the results would be, and attacking us as New England men," before Beecher ever appeared on the scene. Once Wilson could grapple with Beecher face to face, he demanded that the Presbytery of Cincinnati investigate Beecher's doctrinal soundness and appealed to the Synod when the Presbytery declined to take the matter up. These were simply the preliminaries. Wilson took another tack and tried to destroy Beecher through his son George, a student of Taylor's.

George Beecher was seeking licensure as a ministerial candidate befor the Presbytery of Cincinnati. On the second day of his examination, Old School men spoke all day on what they conceived to be his great error, namely, that "he holds that God has no right to require men to do what they are not able to do." Lyman was next to the last speaker. After a concise statement of the congruence between his son's views and the Confession, he ended by warning their opponents that they could not impede the spread of New School sentiments, much less nip them in the bud in Cincinnati. "No, we shall still live; we shall stand on God's earth, and breathe his air, and preach his Gospel as *we* believe it." Wilson rose at last and, in characteristically mean-spirited fashion, informed the Presbytery that "the candidate was not a Christian, and knew nothing experimentally about Christianity, and that he firmly believed that he, and all those who held the same sentiments with him, 'would never see the gates of eternal bliss.'" Thus Wilson attempted to shut George Beecher out of the Presbyterian ministry and heaven in the same breath. Further developments partook of the same spirit.[37]

In Illinois, Edward Beecher was fending off the attacks of William J. Fraser, a counterpart of Wilson, who "assumed the duty of watching us and counteracting our errors." Edward Beecher and Thomas H. Skinner, a New School stalwart, had coauthored *Hints, Designed to Aid Christians in Their Efforts to Convert Men to God* in 1832. Among the directives was one that smacked of New Haven heresy. Ministers and laymen must not let the awakened sinner pray to God for the ability to be saved, for "This would flagrantly misrepresent his case. It is not to be made *able* but *willing*, that he needs." Fraser denounced Beecher and the rest of the faculty of Illinois College as a prelude to stiffer action. Interviewing their students yielded Fraser a budget of compromising testimony; and on March 28, 1833, when the Presbytery of Illinois met at his house, he preferred charges of "unsound teaching" against Beecher, Julian M. Sturtevant, and William Kirby. Edward Beecher, the first to be arraigned, gave a "calm, scholarly, courteous and Christian" defense, to which the rest of the proceedings were anticlimactic.

A month later, after considering the case, the Presbytery voted not to sustain the charges. The litigious Fraser, however, found himself convicted of slander and suspended from the ministry. For some reason he withdrew his appeal of both cases, to the relief of the Illinois College men. Sturtevant later wrote that the synodical decision would have gone against them. In this test of strength the New Englanders came off best, and their victory was widely understood as a vindication of "Presbygationalist" latitude. Thirty-five years later, Samuel J. Baird was still fulminating against the decision which gave "judicial sanction" to "the avowed Pelagianism" of the Illinois College faculty.[38]

Lyman Beecher was gratified by the health and prestige of his seminary, and, as usual, he predicted that the strife would be resolved for the well-being of Christ's church in the West. He wrote to Benjamin Wisner that Wilson was falsely representing him in the *Standard* as arguing that "every man has a right to his own explanation of the Confession of Faith." But he believed that, if "the friends of free agency and moral government stand firm, and act with meekness, patience, and firmness, the present onset will soon be over." He misunderstood the depth of the disaffection.[39]

Back home in Connecticut, conservatives led by Tyler formed a Connecticut Pastoral Union to defend against New Havenite aggression. Its first act, in September 1833, was to found the Theological Institute of Connecticut, at East Windsor, in order to offset the influence of Yale. Prominent in the founding of East Windsor was Asahel Nettleton, who had the temerity to tell friends of the new seminary that Beecher favored the plan, evidently in an attempt to drive a wedge between Beecher and Taylor.[40]

In Cincinnati Joshua Wilson pressed his attack. He preferred formal charges against Beecher in November 1834. In March of the following year, Beecher learned from Albert Barnes that Barnes was about to undergo heresy proceedings in Philadelphia. Beecher now understood the situation to be graver than he had imagined and began talking of an actual schism as a possible outcome. In the month preceding Beecher's trial before the Presbytery, he expended very little time in preparing a defense, counting on his native wit to get him through. To Taylor he wrote, by way of gentle admonition, that, in preaching down the "physical execution of God's decrees and . . . physical regeneration," Taylor must "watch [against] the opposite extreme of a free agency which avails to save by its own actual sufficiency without the Holy Ghost." He expected this to be one of Wilson's key inferences from his and Taylor's teachings. Richard Cary Morse, one of

Jedidiah's sons, sent a stenographer to take a verbatim transcript of the trial for the readers of the *New York Observer* and went in person to observe Beecher's defense. Morse correctly judged that the Presbytery of Cincinnati would give a majority in favor of Beecher. He predicted that the case would ultimately be decided by the General Assembly. Beecher was in fighting trim and had little but contempt for Wilson and his coadjutors:

> He did not know what he undertook. I knew to a hair's breadth every point between Old School and New School, and knew all their difficulties, and how to puzzle with them. In Presbytery he had only inferior men on his side. He knew they were fools. Two of them had been sitting all their lives on goose-eggs till they rotted under them.[41]

Wilson's opening statement was so virulent that his subsequent effort to woo his audience must have sounded hollow. Beecher, he declared, ranked with those whose chief end was "concealing the poison of asps under the pure milk and meat of some salutary truths." Wilson conceded that his own "youthful indiscretions" committed in the heat of judicatory proceedings might lead some to believe him a "litigious, *ultra* partisan in the Presbyterian Church," but this was simply popular "odium." It was only fair to read into the record the opinions of certain well-placed Eastern brethren of Dr. Beecher's—for instance, Asa Rand and the anonymous "Edwardean." By these statements Beecher was convicted of being "a liberal Calvinist." After Wilson had outlined Beecher's views from his published sermons, Beecher gave his defense:

> Dr. Beecher takes the ground of admitting the Sentiments imputed to him and vindicating their agreement with the [Westminster] standards. He aims he says to convince Dr. Wilson himself. Hopeless! the party's course is stereotyped. The Presbytery will acquit, Synod reverse and General Assembly decide. He has been very able today; has vindicated the doctrine of moral ability, appealing to the reason and authority of the church from Justinian to Dr. Wilson himself. One obvious good resulting from the trial is that it brings before the public in a form in which it will be read, the distinguishing doctrines of the Bible.

The case went up to the Synod and ended with an admonition to Beecher to reduce his teachings to more unexceptionable form and publish them.[42]

With Wilson suffering temporary defeat, his allies in the East became active in ferreting out embarrassing letters and soliciting former friends of Beecher's to repudiate him openly. Nettleton and Ithamar Pillsbury worked on Samuel Miller of Princeton, whose letter of 1827 endorsing Beecher's orthodoxy had been read into the trial transcript. Miller discomfited them by replying that Beecher's use of his letter was "fair and legitimate," but he cagily directed their attention to Calvin Stowe's testimony that Beecher was still regarded as sound in 1832. They should try to undermine that statement. Nettleton then set to work to procure a copy of Ebenezer Porter's letter of 1829. This was located and published in the *Hartford Watchman* as Porter's mature view of Beecher and Taylor's errors. Porter was dead, and there was no allusion to the fact that Beecher had consulted with Porter and reached an understanding with him.

Whether Wilson in fact feared to appeal to the General Assembly (if the case went against him he would be censured as a slanderer), or whether he was willing to let the Barnes case decide the issue, he dropped his appeal. Other pressures must be brought to bear on Beecher. Bennet Tyler, who told his son-in-law Stowe that he was glad Beecher had been acquitted, nevertheless wrote a long series of critical letters to John Witherspoon, who took it upon himself to publish them, anonymously, as an assault on Beecher's orthodoxy. Beecher's published defense, *Views in Theology*, was savagely reviewed in Princeton's *Biblical Repertory*, which harped on his "boisterous exaggerations of oratory," his ignorancc of Hebrew and Greek, and his reliance on third-hand accounts of the church fathers. The Princeton reviewer dismissed Beecher's strictures upon Old School Calvinism as the "spectra of his own distempered fancy." "Is it wonderful then, when Dr. Beecher comes forward, lisping the very shibboleth of the New Haven school, teaching that all who do not restrict the nature of sin to spontaneous acts of the mind, believe in physical depravity . . . ?" By now the aim was purely to punish and, if possible, humiliate Beecher, to cordon him off.[43]

The effect of all this upon his family was devastating. Calvin Stowe preached a sermon denouncing the motives and tactics of Beecher's opponents:

> Can it be that the theologians of the present day are so deficient in talent and theological learning, that instead of sustaining their principles and refuting their opponents by reasoning, they must resort to gossip and tattling, weapons hitherto thought appropriate only to the most imbecile of old women? Even

> downright fraud has been practiced . . . the private letters, the confidential conversations, of the dead and the living, have been ransacked, have been obtained under false pretenses, and then with every feature distorted published to the world for the sake of bringing public opinion to bear against some venerable and laborious minister of the gospel—and that too by *brethren in the ministry*!

Stowe was neither Old nor New School in his allegiance, but his words reflected the sentiments of Lyman Beecher's friends and children. They perceived how much confusion had been sown by problems of language. Beecher and Taylor's new terms proved not to be better terms. In the end, as we have seen, the argument boiled down to elusive meanings and to the moral tendencies that could be legitimately or illegitimately inferred from those same fugitive connotations. For some of the Beechers, like Thomas and Henry, the conflict showed that it was ruinous to insist that words, in and of themselves, had sufficient logical power to impress truth upon the mind. They, with Harriet, came to argue that religious sensibility and affective experience were surer guides to truth. Catharine, on the other hand, pressed on with some of the same issues that her father and Taylor had raised, and in her the rationalistic bent of New Haven Theology became even more pronounced.

Edward and Charles did not follow in her track, but neither did they conclude that closely reasoned, frankly speculative theology was dangerous or outmoded. They did, however, take the New England stand on creedal subscription to its logical conclusion. "I cannot believe," Edward wrote his father, "that God will use creeds in the millannium as they are now used. To statements of faith in order that others may know what we teach or believe I have no objection, but I do not think it right to swear to teach according to any human creed, but only according to the Bible." Edward was anxious to see his father's *Views* and added what was hardly a necessary admonition, "I hope you will not deviate from eternal truth in order to conciliate those who love the [Westminster] standards." He was shocked, not so much at the unholy persecution of his revered parent as at the low standard of spirituality prevailing in all the parties to the old Plan of Union. Accused himself of heresy, he rejected judicial sanctions against alleged errorists:

> Many think of whom I am one that no confession of faith which covers so much ground can be a *bond of union* to any body of

> christians for errour or heresy by it, and the decision of such questions by the *votes of a majority*. . . . All the intelligence and piety may be in the minority, and yet the negligence of some one delegate to come in season, or the running of a steamboat on a sand bank may make a man a heretic. This mode of deciding such questions is not in accordance with the laws of the mind, and never will settle a question. . . . Let the operations of the mind be free in fact, and do not compel men to think in chains—fettered by the dread of some odious appellation if green eyed jealousy suspects that they are approximating to the errours of some branded heretic of former days.[44]

Even while his children were experiencing a marked alienation from the Presbyterian way of doing things and concluding to strike out boldly for even more unorthodox ideas, Lyman was taking the offensive in a struggle that could only end in defeat and divison. Gone was the zest for battle, but the zeal for truth, as he perceived it, was as powerful as ever. "I have made up my mind to endure aggression and slander no longer unanswered," he wrote to Thomas Brainerd, a New School man who had left Cincinnati for Philadelphia, "and I expect for a year to come to have my hands full." He took his case to every platform he could find. At the Dartmouth commencement of 1840, he tried "to prove that Edwards was New School." When Henry Tappan's review of Edwards appeared, Beecher seized upon it with avidity and predicted, erroneously as it proved, that this latest critique of Edwards "will produce a revolution in metaphysical theology—which will exclude the appearance of fatalism, and introduce an intelligent and scriptural free agency, such as I have always taught." The East Windsor men must capitulate on this point or show themselves to be the determinists they seemed to be. The great end to be achieved was "a setlement of the long vexed question of Free agency, accountability and moral government and all connected subjects."

Beecher's faith that the truth existed and must emerge from the concussion of logicians was untarnished. Perhaps it was the Yankee in him that made him believe that he could argue any rational mind, even those of Napoleon and Lord Byron, into belief. A man who dropped phrases like "the stated policy of heaven" was bound to believe that he knew the truth and that the one desideratum was rational belief in closely articulated doctrines. Most of his children inclined to believe something else—namely, that faith is after all a gift. And yet their father did not believe that religion consisted exclusively of ratiocination or polemics. He was, in fact, at least as great a thirster after experiential religion and holiness as his children. But, in the bustle and stir of controversy, the New Haven divines and their myriad assailants appeared foremost as bookmen and schoolmen. The next generation would view these contentions with bemused tolerance if not outright bafflement. When Beecher's *Autobiography* appeared, it was, of course, widely noticed. A reviewer for the *New Englander* felt obliged to point out that "Great changes have silently come over the practical beliefs of the Church in respect to the beginning, the nature, the evidences, and the sphere of the Christian life." By 1865 the definitions and syllogisms that had meant so much to Beecher and his contemporaries were passed over in silence, and the best that could be said of Beecher's religion was that it was "a simple, aggressive, and rational Christianity."[45]

PART 2

THE MORALISTS

3 *CATHARINE ESTHER BEECHER*

Lyman sat up with Roxana during her first confinement, and when she gave birth to a girl, he recorded the event in his diary.

> This moment, blessed be God, my dear, dear wife is delivered of a daughter, and my soul, my very soul from agony. Oh, may I never forget the goodness of God who has heard our prayer. Jesus! Thou former of the body and father of the spirit, accept as Thine the immortal soul Thou hast ushered into life. Take, O take it to be Thine before it cling round my heart, and never suffer us to take it back again. May it live to glorify Thee on earth, and to enjoy Thee forever in heaven. Now, Lord, we look to Thee for grace to help us rear it for Thee,–may it be Thine forever, Amen and Amen.

A typically pious, improving sentiment, perhaps. But, by as much as Lyman yearned for and cherished fatherhood, did he fear to make idols of his children, especially the ones who promised well. His eldest child, who would always have special claims on his heart, was named for the aunt who had reared him and for his own mother. With his generous views of women's intellect and character, Lyman expected his daughters to exhibit traits associated with the male sex, such as physical courage, hardiness, and a sense of humor.

Catharine had these in abundance, which was gratifying since William, the secondborn, proved a frail reed, as feckless and maladroit as his sister was plucky and resourceful. Lyman "used to say," Catharine later boasted, "that I was the *best* boy he had." He took her fishing and fixed a special seat for her in his carriage so she could accompany him on his pastoral visits and preaching engagements on Long Island. She easily made the transition from playmate to companion. "Gradually, as I grew older," she remembered with pride, "I began to share with mother in his more elevated trains of thought."

Catharine Esther Beecher *Iconographic Collection, State Historical Society of Wisconsin*

He enjoyed her pranks and escapades and apparently never gave a thought to curbing her high spirits.[1]

Inasmuch as her mother had many onerous duties to discharge, Catharine early mastered the details of feeding and clothing a large family. She exhibited that quality of efficiency and meticulousness celebrated by her sister Harriet as New England "faculty." Despite her household labors, Catharine had more than ample time for study, with leisure for versifying and making visits or playing practical jokes on visiting clergymen. Since she stood high in her class, no one was disposed to rein her in, and she might have gone on being lighthearted and light-minded if her mother had not died. It is plain that Catharine was never quite the giddy goose of her later self-portrait, but Roxana's death forced her without warning into heavy new responsibilities. She undertook to make all the clothing for herself and her seven brothers and sisters, a prodigious task in the days before machine sewing. In this and other efforts, she and Mary, the next oldest daughter, were "cheered and animated" by their father's "happy faculty . . . of discovering and rejoicing over unexpected excellence in character and conduct." Catharine was drawn even closer to her father, whom she pitied in his "solitary, comfortless, and afflicted" state.[2]

The advent of her stepmother Harriet Porter, a "beautiful lady, very fair," more like a "strange princess rather than our own mamma," did not greatly alter Catharine's role. Harriet Porter had been at pains to assure Catharine that she did not wish to supplant Roxana, "Oh no, she must still live, in your memory and affections. . . . To succeed such a woman is indeed a momentous concern." Toward Harriet, Catharine was respectful and civil without being cordial. In many respects she seems to have behaved toward her more like an equal than a submissive daughter. Certainly there was little warmth of affection between them, as compared with Catharine's love for Aunt Esther. Catharine lauded Harriet's skill in domestic matters, her successes in "preserving punctuality, order, and neatness" "without the vulgar practice of scolding."

While she could admire this aspect of her stepmother's character, they had little else in common. Harriet's perfervid piety (which was later to develop into mental illness) may have given Catharine her initial distaste for religious emotionalism. In any case, it did little to commend her to Catharine. Chief among Harriet's reasons for marrying Lyman in the first place was her desire to serve as an instrument of his children's conversion. Lyman had even carried home some of her spiritual meditations in hopes of benefiting Catharine:

> I have just been reading your own account of your *distress* and *joy* to Catherine. She was *moved*, and I availed myself of the opportunity to kneel and pray with her. It was a time of tears to us both. I believe she will lay open her heart to you on the subject. She has I rejoice to percieve great respect and affection also for you and I cannot but hope your coming may be the era of salvation to her soul. She is more sedate and thotful, I believe than common. But how to *love* the invisible god—there is the difficulty.

But neither Harriet's example nor her prayers could convert Catharine.[3]

Catharine's temperament was so optimistic and she was so buoyed up by the affection of her family and the adulation of friends, that it was rare indeed to find her "sedate and thotful" or grieving over her alienation from God. With occasional "serious" turns, she went on in a state of spiritual calm—or as the religious termed it, stupidity—until 1822 when she became engaged to Alexander Metcalf Fisher, the Yale mathematician. Fisher was a child prodigy who had gone from triumph to triumph until he joined the Yale faculty in 1817 as professor of mathematics and natural philosophy. He was the closest thing to a Renaissance man to grace the college since Ezra Stiles. Though Fisher was, like Catharine, unconverted, he was very serious about religion. Edward Beecher hero-worshipped Fisher, and Lyman knew a fine prospect when he saw one, so the family looked for great things from Catharine's union with such a man.

The only one with misgivings, it seemed, was Catharine herself. To her bosom friend, Louisa Wait, she confided her fears about Fisher's demeanor and character:

> The truth is Louisa I feel more and more every day that talents learning and good principals never could make me happy *alone*—I shall need a warm and affectionate heart—and whether I can find it in this case I know not. . . . The more I think of it the more I am sure that I ought to guard my heart from the facination of genius and flattery of attentions till I am sure that my happiness is not risqued.

Writing from New London, where she had gone to teach school, she reiterated her doubts to Lyman: "Were I as secure as you on this point," she wrote, and "if it should be as you wish," "you can not doubt that the sanction and approbation of so dear a parent will be no small part of the happiness of your affectionate child." These and similar expressions betrayed not only the trepidations of an unsophisticated woman (at the age of twenty-one, she had had no previous romances) but also the desire to please Lyman above all.[4]

Observing the proprieties of courtship, Catharine at last consented to a correspondence on matters of mutual interest. "He does write *confounded* pretty letters," she rejoiced. Although none of these letters survive, we have John Hooker's testimony that they were no ordinary love letters. They seem to have been heavily freighted with scholarly exchanges. In due season Fisher smoked Catharine out from her epistolary covert. He arrived in Litchfield, proposed marriage, and was accepted. Catharine was at last satisfied "that I had gained the *whole* heart of one whose equal *I* never saw both as it respects intellect and all that is amiable and desirable in private character." Fisher had planned a tour of Europe to meet "the great scientific characters" and "the great personages at the different courts," and it was thought best to postpone the wedding until his return. Catharine savored her flattering prospects and vowed to practice the piano diligently "for *his* sake who loves to hear me play." Yet in the midst of her triumph, she became disturbed by her continuing failure to give herself to God: "my heart often sinks within me when I think that this may be *my all*, and that Heaven and immortal happiness may be forever lost. . . . Oh when will the day come when like a child returning to a fathers house I can fix my hopes and thoughts above and secure that bright inheritance which can never pass away."[5]

As is well known, Professor Fisher died in the wreck of the *Albion* on April 22, 1822, just off the Irish coast. The news reached New Haven five weeks later, and Lyman hastened to tell his daughter that "the waves of the Atlantic, commissioned by Heaven" had made shipwreck of their common hopes. He expected his letter to shatter Catharine; of himself he wrote that "though my heart in the beginning was set upon this connection, . . . the impression of uncertainty about all things earthly taught me by the lesson of the last six years, have kept my anticipations in check, and prepared me, with less surprise and severity of disappointment, to meet this new scene of sorrow." Thus armored, Lyman proceeded to improve the occasion by asking, "Will you send your thoughts to heaven and find peace, or to the cliffs, and winds, and waves of Ireland, to be afflicted, tossed with tempest, and not comforted?" Not as consolation but almost as a speculative question, he proffered Catharine the slimmest of possibilities that Fisher might have undergone an eleventh-hour repentance and conversion, thus saving his soul from endless perdition.

Lyman's stark, unblinking pronouncements might seem to us cruel. If Fisher had died unregenerate, as he most probably had, then there could be no greater calamity than the eternal ruin of his soul. Perhaps clergymen should not offer their children pulpit utterances in times of crisis, but it was natural for Lyman to pray, "May God preserve you and give me the joy of beholding life spring up from death." Fisher had lost his life, but his death might be the means of Catharine's salvation and, with it, her ultimate victory over death. Edward, the brother closest to Catharine, wrote in a more hopeful vein about Fisher but stopped short of any firm assurances. He, too, sought to impress upon her the fact that the disaster had a larger meaning, that it was God's providential act "to detach you from this earth." Since these and subsequent letters between Lyman, Edward, and Catharine have been regarded as callous, it is only fair to state that such probing emotionalism, brutal as it might seem to modern sensibility, was well nigh universal among the orthodox evangelicals of that time.[6]

Catharine suffered intensely during the next year. She had to go through the process of mourning Fisher, but an important part of that process involved her insistence that her grief must be transmuted to something more noble than merely human sorrow. At first she was too numbed and desolated to think or feel. As she later told Isabella, she felt as though she were trapped in a sort of limbo:

> I remember sister Cate, said once, in regard to Mr. Fisher's loss—that, her feelings, as described to father, at the time—were most singular as well as painful—it seemed as if for months past she had been surrounded by the motion and constant noise of the ever whirling machinery and wheels of a great manufactory and all at once every sound and motion ceased, and all was still as the grave—not a thread, not a circle or circumstance, for the eye or heart to rest upon.

This state of shock gave way to a questing, disputing frame of mind. But let the issue be accurately stated. In the first place, Catharine did not claim (although she may secretly have felt) that God had wrongfully injured her: "I feel that my affliction is what I just deserve." Nor, in the second place, was she maintaining that her father's appraisal of Fisher's spiritual condition was unsound or cruel. Brooding over Fisher's death did force her to turn many of Lyman's preachments and propositions over in her mind, but we have Catharine's own testimony that the crux of her argument with Lyman and Edward was the impossibility, under their system, of reconciling *herself* to God:

> I weep not that my youthful hopes
> All wrecked beneath the billows rest,
> Nor that the heavy hand of Death
> Has stilled the heart that loved me best.
>
> But ah! I mourn the moral night
> That shrouds my eyes in deepest gloom;
> I mourn that, tempest-toss'd on earth,
> I have in heaven no peaceful home.

Her sense of justice was outraged, not because of her father's dogmatic assertion that Fisher's eternal fate must remain uncertain, but because his theology, specifically his doctrine of Original Sin, gave no adequate or persuasive answers to her questions about herself.[7]

The Bible told her that man was wholly selfish and corrupt in his actions, an assertion her own experience confirmed. Writing to Edward, she confessed that her own consciousness convicted her of total depravity. She found evidence in the "painful and humiliating retrospection" of her own life that "I am guilty, but not guilty as if I had received a nature pure and uncontaminated. I can not feel this; I never shall by any mental exertion of my own." New Haven Theology, to be sure, held that man's nature was not corrupt, but that his character and circumstances were such that he unfailingly sinned. But Catharine objected that this did not meet the question. God had, after all, created man with a "perverted inclination" to sin. Why did he not in mercy endow man with "some counteracting aid"?

This seemed a reasonable objection to the doctrine of Original Sin, even in its New Haven phase, yet Catharine's reading of the Scriptures compelled her to admit that her conclusions were "ruinous" and "contrary to the whole tenor of the Gospel." Caught between her own reasonings and the unambiguous declarations of Holy Writ, she experienced a "temptation to skepticism."

> I feel all the time as if there was *something wrong*—something that is unreasonable. Sometimes I think the Bible is misunderstood, and that there must be promises of aid to the exertions of the unrenewed. But then I find as great difficulties on that

> side. There have been moments when I have been so perplexed and darkened as to feel that no one could tell what was truth from the Bible.
>
> But the prevailing feeling is that "these things are so"; that I have been instructed in the truth, and that, if I ever see the consistency and excellency of the truth, it will be through the enlightening operation of the Holy Spirit.
>
> But I am most unhappy in the view which this doctrine presents of my own state and that of my fellow-creatures, except the few who are redeemed from the curse. . . .
>
> I see that my feelings are at open war with the doctrines of grace. I don't know that I ever felt enmity to God, or doubted of his justice and mercy, for I can more easily doubt the truth of these doctrines than the rectitude of God.

This exchange of letters deserves extensive quotation because in them Catharine made the first important critique of Lyman's theology by one of his own children. He upheld his side of the argument so forcefully that some of his letters were "published in their time, and were considered as affording one of the best presentations of New England theology which had then appeared." [8]

Mingled with and perhaps alleviating Catharine's anguish was the realization that she had become an independent thinker, and indeed a judge, of her father's religious system, a fact that was not lost on Lyman. He continued to be proud of Catharine's intellect, even when she exasperated him by what he deemed her sophistry. "The awfully interesting state of her mind" promised good results, Lyman thought, while the discovery that "she is now . . . handling edge-tools with [a] powerful grasp" shed a flattering light on his tutelage. He admitted that "I have at times been at my wit's end to know what to do," she pressed him so hard with her arguments, but "I am not without hope that the crisis approaches in which submission will end the strife." Lyman and Edward offered no novel or even ingenious arguments. Their strategy was to subdue her by appealing to her consciousness of obstinate resistance to God's commands. [9]

A remarkable exchange between Catharine and Lyman revealed the fundamental conflict. Catharine left a note in her father's study, beseeching his help. She was devoid of hope and strength, she wrote, "like a helpless being placed in a frail bark, with only a slender reed to guide its way on the surface of a swift current that no mortal power could ever stem." When she saw herself surging toward the brink of an immense cataract, she turned with desperation to "One standing upon the shore who can relieve my distress, who is all powerful to save; but He regards me not." Lyman answered in kind, endorsing the back of her note with these words:

> Traveling in the greatness of my strength, I have pressed on through tears and blood to her rescue. It is many days, many years, I have stood on the bank unnoticed. . . . At length I sunk the bark in which all her earthly treasure was contained, and . . . again I called, and still I call unheard.

The time of her probation was nearly past, the decision must be made, for all time. Would she persist in her fatal course, spurning divine aid until the current swept her to destruction? [10]

Apart from the inherent drama of the situation, this episode presents interesting features. To take a practical question first, why should father and daughter, living under the same roof and taking meals and walks together, resort to written communications? One obvious answer is that it was the literary fashion of the day. The epistolary novel, not yet out of vogue, depended on just such devices and artifices. Diary keeping and letter writing were far more serious and universal practices than they are today. And more than many of their contemporaries, the Beechers wrote their letters expecting them to be transmitted to posterity. Even if they had had a more modest perception of their place in history, they most probably would have fallen in with the custom of committing delicate matters to paper. There are advantages to writing rather than uttering one's thoughts, the chief of which is the distancing effect of the written word. Not only did letters remove some of the embarrassment or pain of face-to-face contact, they also permitted greater deliberation on the part of the writers, the weighing of words, the deliverance of considered judgments and sentiments, with whatever improvements or clarifications a self-consciously literary mode provided. Furthermore, letters and notes had the additional benefit of permitting (or forcing) the recipient to study the contents with care, to plot out his or her response. Catharine's employment of poetry to express her innermost feelings is of a piece with her letter writing.

An equally striking and related tactic is Catharine's supplication to Lyman in the place of God. It was not fanciful or blasphemous for his daughter to address him as the Almighty, nor for Lyman to speak in the same guise. Nor was this the only time that Lyman assumed the role of God; some of his sermons gained tremendous effectiveness from this assumption. It took no particular egotism to preach in this manner, for revivalists often thundered at their audiences as if the scene were a divine tribunal. And yet there was something more to this particular instance of an earthly father speaking as God. Two parallel cases may help to throw light on the episode.

In the first example we have a curious composition by Richard Cary Morse, also a minister's child:

> Amusing myself with reflecting upon the various scenes of life, I accidentally cast my eyes over the sea, where I beheld multitudes of people sporting in the current, regardless of the danger to which they were every moment exposed of being carried away by it. While thousands of them were perishing in the vast abyss, others forgetful of their ruin and destruction, plunged headlong after them, and were seen no more: but what was still more remarkable, they all seemed to apprehend no danger, but [thought themselves] perfectly safe and secure. Turning round I beheld a venerable old man sitting beneath a craggy rock, intently reading the Bible; upon inquiring of him, why he so busily employed himself in reading and appeared so totally regardless of the scenes which were passing, he replied, "Tired of the busy confusion of the world, I have retired here for the purpose of reading and meditating, and, continued he, let me warn you to be on your guard, lest while you see those numberless crowds sinking into eternity, you likewise perish."

The venerable old man of Richard Morse's religious meditation may or may not have been his father, Jedidiah Morse, a retired clergyman, but it is a fairly safe inference that he was. The note of warning, coupled with a sort of fatalism about the destiny of all but Richard, is reminiscent of Lyman's attitude only in a vague way.[11]

A more conclusive instance occurs in a letter from the Reverend Edward D. Griffin to his teen-aged daughter, Ellen Maria.

> I had, my dear child, a distressing dream about you last night. I dreamed that I was the presiding magistrate in a court which condemned you to die for murder,—and to be executed the next day. You besought for your life; but I told you that I could not help you, and entreated you to prepare to die. And when you appeared disposed to consume the few precious moments in

> prayer to me, I told you that you must not say another word about it. You obeyed, and was silent, and I awoke. And when I awoke, the thought of my poor suppliant child, condemned to death, and pleading with me for her life; and the thought that I might one day see you pleading with me for an eternal life, when I could not afford relief; affected me so much that I could not help praying for you a considerable time, till I fell asleep. Oh my dear child, remember that no modification of the social affections, and of the outward deportment, will answer without a radical change of heart; . . . I beseech you, my darling child, to read over this paragraph morning and evening before you offer your prayers, for the rest of the winter, when something special does not prevent.

Here, in its grossest form, is shown how powerful such tactics were. When the earthly and the heavenly father were identified with each other and seen as handing down a judgment of condemnation unto death, and in the form of a permanent lesson for a child to study, there was no escaping that judgment and its terrors. If, as Theodore Bacon observed, "even the most loyal New Englander may doubt the wholesomeness of the exercises of self-examination and introspection into which devout parents and teachers guided their infant charges," such parents as Beecher, Morse, and the strict Calvinist Griffin more than succeeded in instilling feelings of pessimism and anxiety. God, in their view, was not an indulgent father tender-hearted to a fault. His commandments were plain, his purpose unswerving, and his punishments terrible.[12]

Catharine, then, was to expect nothing in the way of specious paternal consolation. Like any loving parent, Lyman commiserated with his daughter; but as her pastor he could only feel that her spiritual condition was the darker tragedy. Edward, morever, disinterred an old sheet of Catharine's religious resolutions and showed her, point by point, how and why she had broken them all.

> I read your letter with painful interest but indeed I know not what to say to you. What do you expect yourself? You have had unequaled advantages for religious instruction from a child, the spirit has striven with you, mercies have been given you and you idolised them, they have been withdrawn and the world emptied and you wax worse and worse [and] you cannot feel your guilt.
>
> You have preferred the world so long as you though[t] it could make you happy, and now because you do not expect any thing

> more from it you look to God and think it hard that he should not bless these selfish desires with everlasting happiness.
>
> Sit down then and look over your conduct, gather up your virtues and make out your claim and present it to your [master, but] if you dare not to do this why do you feel th[us]? why do your heart and understanding revolt from [the] truth that God would be just should he hide his f[ace] forever from your prayers and tears?

As unsparing as his language was, Edward had said many things of the same import before her bereavement. Fisher's death did not soften his tone; it gave Edward's pleas more poignancy. Neither man, however, presented God to Catharine in purely judicial terms. When it became clear that she could not be made to feel like a contumacious little creature in rebellion against her creator, Edward urged her to dwell on thoughts of Christ. "Think then of the saviour, kind merciful and desirous to save you. . . . He says nothing about feeling your guilt, if you feel your need of him he *will not* cast you away."

Lyman, too, encouraged Catharine to find peace in Jesus as all "merciful, lovely, and compassionate." "I am glad," he told her, "that your vacant eye at last has fixed on these traits of his character." At the same time, however, he warned her that she must never lose sight of the fact that she was a sinner in the eyes of Christ, who helped and pitied her in her fallen state. She must not confuse "the reaction of selfish gratitude" toward Christ "for gracious affection" and entire love to God. Some of this was balm to Catharine's feelings, but Lyman went on to press the necessity of correct views on her:

> His entire character as holy, just, and good, as maintaining the honor and government of God, and saving from sin, is to be taken into view, and, on the ground of our necessity and his sufficiency, we are required with humble boldness to come to him.
>
> But if his purity and justice repel, the softer traits may come in to encourage our approach to Him who will in no wise cast out him that cometh.

In other words, Lyman was pronouncing a caveat against believing that loving the character of Jesus sufficed for salvation. Submitting to the moral government of God was still a sinner's first duty, after which she might lay herself on the bosom of the savior. She must not be swayed by a merely sentimental identification with Jesus or lapse into self-righteousness under the cloak of trusting in Christ.[13]

Lyman seized the opportunity to expound the difference between New England orthodoxy and Timothy Dwight's view of conversion. "I am startled," he burst out, "at the tranquillity produced by reading [John] Newton, and the hope that God will, in his own good time, grant you comfort." Although he conceded that her "tranquillity may not be dangerous," he went on to say why he thought she was imperiling herself:

> I fear only because it is precisely the effect always produced by such directions as Dr. Dwight used to give to awakened sinners, and as the English divines still give. Now who are right, the Old or New English divines? When you consider your own cold, selfish heart, or read the requisitions of the law and the Gospel, and their exposition by the Apostles—if God does not demand immediate spiritual obedience, he does not demand any thing.
>
> Which mode of exhibition is, on the whole, most evangelical and most successful, is as manifest from facts as facts can make manifest. Look at the revivals which are filling our land with salvation; they do not prevail in England. In this country they are confined almost exclusively to the New England manner of exhibiting the truth.

Revivals, he was arguing, were the touchstone of doctrinal truth. If doctrines such as he and Taylor preached every Sabbath, particularly the doctrine of immediate repentance, touched off and sustained revivals, then those doctrines were more acceptable to God than others. Lyman Beecher was hauling "seines full" of the reborn into the church. His teachings succeeded in producing evangelical repentances. Therefore, no matter how obnoxious to the worldly and wicked, they were sound doctrines. And Catharine would do well to believe them.[14]

By now this three-cornered debate had taken on a life of its own, ranging far beyond the providential meaning of Fisher's death. Edward, for his part, sent Catharine this assurance, after reflecting on his late friend's life and character:

> I do not wish to pry into the counsels of God or to decide what is known to him alone, but I still hope and it seems to me on good grounds that what is loss to us is to him gain unspeakable and that he now ranges in fields of knowledge and enjoyment enlarged beyond the highest conceptions of an earthly mind.

He entreated her, moreover, to relent in her quest for absolute certainty in the realm of philosophical theology. Her grief had not abated sufficiently for her mind to sustain such efforts unharmed. While her judgment was still clouded, she ought to suspend her inquiries and wait for light on these difficult questions. "I think," he told her, "you are in danger of speculating too much." He granted her contention that individual guilt was difficult to reconcile with Original Sin and conceded frankly that "I do not expect to throw light on this dark spot, so as to make all things clear; nor ought you to expect to be entirely unembarrassed, where none within the range of my knowledge are free from perplexity."

Following Nathaniel Taylor, Edward declared that sinners were not punished for Original Sin, but for "voluntary moral action" resulting in "actual sin." Self-love, as Taylor maintained, was a neutral quality, and any "selfish exercises beyond this self-love" were entirely voluntary and hence culpable. But arguments which had weighed heavily with Edward would not, he admitted, "satisfy your feelings." The best he could do for her was to recount his own spiritual struggles, which terminated when "I acquired the *practical* feeling" that Christ was "my *only* ground of hope." "This you must have," he insisted, "You ought to think more on his character and less of yourself." He had learned from experience that self-scrutiny and speculative wandering yielded nothing but despondency and emotional fatigue, as they would in her case.[15]

When the initial shock of Fisher's drowning had passed, Catharine set about reordering her life. Five months after the shipwreck she was able to write Louisa Wait, "the bitterness of grief is past. I have done weeping for him I have lost and now I mourn for myself." She described to Louisa how her loss had blasted her religious hopes:

> The first feeling of my heart when I had so recovered from the paralysing shock that I could feel, was, as you have said, that none but God could comfort me--and to him I went for comfort, before him day after day I [laid?] my sorrows and with agonizing supplications, besought him to be my portion and to take the place that had been given to an earthly idol. But week after week and month after month has rolled away and tho' I still seek him sorrowing, he hides his face from me and my prayer is shut out.

She would find a meager portion of earthly happiness, after all, she told Louisa. Not in "the pleasures honours and enjoyments of this world," as would have been the case had she had her wish of marrying an eminent scholar. She must now make good her resolution to "live a few days to speak of the mercy of God and to do some good to my fellow men."[16]

Even though Catharine had been contesting the New Havenite doctrines of her father and brother, or to speak more accurately, their doctrine of Original Sin, she had done so earnestly and soberly, with hopes of having those doctrines vindicated. She had wanted them made reasonable and palatable so that, accepting them, she might find the faith she was seeking. Catharine had as great a stake in "maintaining the honor and government of God" as Edward and Lyman did. It was not surprising, therefore, that she should find a frontal assault on New England Theology disgraceful. In Boston, where she went to visit her stepmother's relatives, she found them all reading Catherine Sedgwick's latest novel, *A New England Tale.* Miss Sedgwick, Catharine learned to her horror, used the novel to make "decided opposition to the great doctrines of religion" and to "shamefully misrepresent their effects upon the character of those that profess them." She could only account for the author's malice by imputing it to Miss Sedgwick's recent desertion of orthodoxy in favor of Unitarianism:

> I think every one who has heretofore known Miss S. will feel both grieved, surprised, and indignant at the course she has pursued. If there ever was one with their eyes open and in the full blaze of truth turned traitor and denied the Lord that bought them it is here, and I can not think of a circumstance to palliate or excuse her [crime].... For the sake of gaining the admiration and applause of a party, she has sacrificed her integrity and she ought to be made to smart for it.

Note Catharine's language. She spoke of Miss Sedgwick as denying the atonement of Christ. There was also the desire to punish or ostracize her for her act of treachery, both against Trinitarian orthodoxy and against Christ.[17]

From the cradle Catharine Beecher had imbibed the teachings her father called "the New England manner of exhibiting the truth." Whatever her private reservations about specific doctrines, she was still (as she thought) stoutly loyal to "evangelical" theology. And perhaps her very outrage at Catherine Sedgwick's apostacy implied uneasiness about her own tendencies in that direction. Beyond the hereditary attachment to the doctrines Sedgwick was trying to explode, Catharine Beecher was not one to deal superficially with things theological, as her brother's attempts to dissuade her from speculation show. A closer look at this novel and its thesis will enable us to understand Catharine Beecher's attitude toward New England Theology and its exponents.

A New England Tale was the first fruit of Catherine Sedgwick's formal connection with the Unitarians. Her father Theodore, the Berkshire County high Federalist, had waited until the last moment to declare himself a Unitarian and had received the sacrament on his deathbed from William Ellery Channing. Theodore Sedgwick had had little use for the Yankee theologizing prevalent in his day:

> My father used to tell with much gusto of Dr. [Joseph] Bellamy that one of his parishioners, who was a notorious scamp, came to him, saying, in the parlance of the [Hopkinsian] divinity that pervaded this part of New England at that period, "I feel that I have obtained a hope!" The doctor looked surprised. "I realize that I am the chief of sinners," continued the hypocritical canter. "Your neighbors have long been of that opinion," rejoined the doctor. The man went on to say out the lesson—"I feel willing to be damned for the glory of God." "Well, my friend, I don't know any one who has the slightest objection!"

If Sedgwick's daughter had been content to satirize "cant and sanctimonious pretence" in the vein of her father's anecdote, the Beechers might have enjoyed it as much as anyone else, the more so since a similar story was told of their father. However, Catherine Sedgwick attacked evangelicalism with more vitriol than suavity. Even apart from its squeaky machinery and absent-minded plot, her novel suffers from her inability to contain her outrage.[18]

Briefly, the story concerns a comely and naturally good orphan farmed out to a hard-handed aunt whose Calvinistic religion is a kind of tough pod in which her dried-up soul rattles around. She abuses young Jane Elton and permits her cousins to treat her like a servant. Because of Aunt Wilson's belief that the elect are exempted from ordinary standards of decency and honesty, her character is repellent, while that of her children is positively odious. Her daughters are vicious and extravagant, and her son is all this plus a liar and a thief. The model of religious character held up to the long-suffering Jane is a Quaker widower and philanthropist, who believes—unlike Mrs. Wilson—that the basic human drives and qualities are good and that there is only one standard of virtue, not two, a carnal and an evangelical. Aunt Wilson's petted son turns road agent, after successfully blaming one of his thefts on Jane and nearly ruining her reputation. When Mrs. Wilson turns to her daughters for consolation, she learns how sharper than a serpent's tooth it is to have pharisaical children.

David Wilson comes to a bad end, and as he broods upon his plight, he turns on his mother. Sedgwick delivers her brief against the antinomian tendencies of Calvinism in a last letter from David to his mother:

> Mother, mother! oh, that I must call you so!—as I do it, I howl a curse with every breath—you have destroyed me. You it was that taught me, when I scarcely knew my right hand from my left, that there was no difference between doing right and doing wrong, in the sight of the God you worship; you taught me, that I could do nothing acceptable to him. If you taught me truly, I have only acted out the nature totally depraved, (your own words), that he gave to me, and I am not to blame for it. I could do nothing to save my own soul; and according to your doctrine, I stand now a better chance than my moral cousin, Jane. If you have taught me falsely, I was not to blame; the peril be on your own soul. My mind was a blank, and you put your own impressions on it; God (if there be a God) reward you according to your deeds!

This, surely, was the argument from moral tendency with a vengeance. Sedgwick's screed on "the old orthodoxy of New-England" which she defended in the preface to the 1852 edition of *A New England Tale*, bears an uncanny resemblance to Lyman Beecher's *Dialogue, Exhibiting Some of the Principles and Practical Consequences of Modern Infidelity* and its predecessors by Timothy Dwight. In all of these, perverted doctrines and philosophies are shown to have shameful or sanguinary consequences destructive to the soul and the social order alike.[19]

It was easy for Catharine Beecher to believe that this was an irresponsible picture of evangelicalism, a caricature. For the time being she was still an evangelical of unimpeachable orthodoxy, and besides that, she was a Beecher and therefore bound to resent Unitarian criticisms of her father's faith. She was questioning that faith herself, but converts are generally questioners, even critics, before they become true believers. Thus neither she nor her father regarded her as an incipient apostate. And so she next traveled to Franklin, Massachusetts, to spend three months in the home of Caleb Fisher, who would have been her father-in-law. Alexander had hoped to see his sisters educated through his money and supervision, but death had cut off this plan. Catharine was hungering for something useful to do and was eager to look after the Fisher girls, saying, "it will be a pleasing mournful employ to supply in some measure their loss."[20]

While Edward Beecher attended to painful details—interviewing a survivor of the *Albion* for last news of Fisher, disposing of Fisher's things, suggesting felicitous phrases for the epitaph Catharine was composing—she was scrutinizing Alexander's private papers, hoping to find evidence on the state of his mind to indicate a regenerate nature. What she learned of his mental state must have been distressing. Beneath his precise, scientific, and rather pedantic demeanor, Fisher had had a tormented religious experience. "Why cannot I employ one week in earnestly seeking religion?" he asked himself. The thought of dying unregenerate obsessed him. "Why cannot I go immediately about preparing for death, while life and health are continued?" A man of great exactitude in evidentiary questions, he assessed data about the afterlife with the same scrupulous care he showed in scientific and mathematical problems. His pastor in Franklin was Nathanael Emmons, whose theological conservatism contrasted sharply with Lyman Beecher's liberalizing tendencies. Fisher became so anxious about his lack of religion that he devoted himself to theological studies under Emmons and then spent a year at Andover. The fruits of his study were a series of theological essays incorporating, with some modifications, the Emmonsite system, which was extremely deterministic. Whether his theological contribution was weighty or slight, Fisher soon realized that ratiocination alone would not renew his heart.[21] He continued to brood over his unregenerate state and came to fear for his sanity. "I am exposed every month to become melancholy and destroy myself," he wrote in a diary. And elsewhere, "Suppose I were a criminal, confined in a dungeon and sentenced to die within a year." Would he yield himself to God under those terms?

Despite the spur of such frightful suppositions, Fisher could not find God in heaven or the Holy Spirit in his heart. Bereft of hope himself, he turned to good works. He began writing a "treatise on Natural Theology" and then projected a grandiose scheme for devising a universal language "on philosophical principles" to be "the medium thro' which heathen nations are to be civilized, enlightened, and taught the gospel." The effects of such an invention would be incalculable; at the least, Fisher's universal language would revolutionize missionary work. The sudden collapse of all language barriers would "conduce to the rapid intellectual improvement of heathen nations." Faith being beyond his grasp, he dreamed of helping to bring it to others. Evidently, his language scheme was a sort of Tower of Babel in reverse, a stupendous undertaking that only a man of genius might dare attempt.

Inevitably, Fisher suffered a severe nervous breakdown. He emerged from this cloud unchanged in his religious condition. The death of Timothy Dwight, whom he had revered, was a further blow. Despair and futility overwhelmed him as he contemplated his eternal future.[22]

Given these glimpses into Fisher's private thoughts, which he had presumably communicated (at least in part) to his pastor, it is surprising to find Emmons declaring that "there is ground to hope that he had experienced a saving change." Emmons was so little inclined to believe in deathbed repentances that when he preached the funeral sermon of one of his sons, he labeled him quite probably unrepentant and therefore lost. Since Emmons could be more encouraging about Alexander Fisher's spiritual condition, it lends weight to the contention that Catharine's despondency arose more from sorrow over the elusiveness of grace in her own life than from a positive dread of hearing Fisher consigned to endless misery and the worm that never dies. She would have been overjoyed, of course, to find evidences of his conversion, but lacking those, she judged his immortal estate in the light of his character.[23]

Lyman and Edward followed her every step with apprehension. Her father, especially, warned her against seeking felicity in earthly occupations. "Guard against those seasons when the clouds clear away," he exhorted her. "I dread such clearings off. Had rather you should walk in darkness and see no light till you trust in the Lord." He felt great tenderness toward his daughter and pressed her to take regular exercise to fend off "nervous excitement" and debility. He was becoming impatient, however, with her harping on the subject of moral inability. "I believe you have speculated enough on that point, perhaps too much. . . . I believe you may as well waive the subject as a matter of speculation, confess your sins, and cry for mercy, remembering that it is indeed your duty to do that which you cry to God to help you to do." She must not plead inability; it was her will that needed changing and she alone could do that, under the influences of the Holy Spirit. Edward seconded Lyman's opinion. "I would not have you read anything of a metaphysical kind," he wrote, and suggested that she frequent Emmons's house and receive his help.[24]

Emmons was a singularly poor choice to comfort a Beecher, notorious as he was for his metaphysical preoccupations and idiosyncratic views. Lyman himself regarded Emmons as a fatalist of the "hyper-Calvinist" species. As for Catharine, she was appalled by his preaching:

> The peculiarities of Dr. Emmons's sentiments, which were exhibited in full almost as soon as I heard him preach, contributed also to bewilder and irritate my wounded heart. To me it seemed as if

> he made us mere machines, and all our wickedness was *put into us*; and then we were required to be *willing* to be forever miserable; and you can imagine how such views, exhibited with no great gentleness, would affect feelings so wrought up as mine were; for I could not perceive, and to this moment I can not perceive, so far as *argument* is concerned, why his reasoning on the first point [that God directly produces all human volitions] is not unanswerable.

Lyman had been prepared for some such argument. He knew that Catharine would seize upon Emmons's determinism as an excuse for her failure to be converted. He met her head on, not with counter-arguments on the nature of volitions, but with preaching to her own consciousness of wickedness and ingratitude:

> My heart bleeds and my eyes are full. But I can not allow my heart to distrust or turn against my God. . . . withold your thots as far as may be from those sorrow moving associations which bring upon you such pressing temptation to murmur and clothe the great and good being in such unlovely characters of Severity, and Secondly, I think an effort of the understanding necessary to detect and dissipate this sophistry of your pained heart, as it respects god and his ways.

> B[e]hold then his eye pondering the mercies bestowed from childhood upward and those which you still hold, and fixed with parental disappointment on the blank which should have borne the record of gratitude and love. . . . if we remember that this is a world of revolt and we are all by nature children of wrath, instead of questioning his goodness on account of the miseries of our own misdoing, or the discipline of his rod. Have we not occasion rather to be filled with grateful amasement at his clemency. . . .[25]

Like a steady rain beating on the soft stone of her obstinacy, came Lyman's injunctions against self-will and self-deception. He warned her not to follow the dictates of her "unsubdued and gainsaying heart," her "affected but rebellious heart." Catharine must acknowledge the "*reality of his requesitions for immediate love and submission*" lest her "heart again . . . take up arms against god." By no means might she expect God to accept her in a spirit of mere seeking for light. It was love entire that he demanded, her complete submission. She must "be aware and think and must tremble at the fearful war which your heart will maintain with a god whose unintermitted and inflexible requisition is the heart, the heart, the heart."[26]

Catharine would not retreat from her position that the Bible yielded gracious promises of aid to the ordinary, devout seeker. When Dr. Emmons preached that awakened sinners were more hateful to God than inveterate sinners, she felt an impulse to kneel in his meetinghouse and thank Jesus that "he was not so hard a master [as Emmons], but that he had left behind him so many gracious words of kindness and encouragement to all the wretched and guilty who would come to him for strength to do his will." Theologians might blind themselves to the plain meaning of the Gospels, but her own judgment confirmed her conviction that "the certain knowledge which the mind has of its own faculties and operations" was the surest basis for interpreting the Bible. As he had promised, so (Catharine claimed) Christ would act, in pity and in mercy. As for New England Theology, she reiterated her earlier declaration that she could "more easily doubt the truth of these doctrines than the rectitude of God." If, therefore, she and Lyman understood God's word differently—"which is easiest to abandon, confidence in my own consciousness or in your interpretation of the Bible?"—Lyman could only reply that "it is your *feeling* that makes you think so and not the analogy of the faith [once] delivered to the saints."[27]

The debate remained locked at this point. Catharine professed to be puzzled and mystified by her father's arguments, but in this she was rather disingenuous. By setting up Nathanael Emmons as the more consistent (and extreme) spokesman for New England Theology, she could more easily expose and flay his doctrines and make them take the brunt of her attack. To Lyman's contention that her consciousness, which she had set up as the supreme authority in understanding revelation, was itself the creature of selfishness, she had no answer except the simple assertion that her father was wrong. Within eight years she would take this argument and elevate it into a system of mental and moral philosophy, going beyond the appeal to individual consiousness to say that the mind is perfectly constituted and needs only early training and precept to attain right views, and with them salvation.

The experiences of those eight key years, which coalesced into her *Elements of Mental and Moral Philosophy*, are easily enumerated. With Lyman's encouragement, Catharine established a select girls' school in Hartford, taking Mary and Harriet into her household as unpaid teachers. With her brightest pupils (among them Harriet) she gradually worked through the vast questions which she and Lyman had debated inconclusively. Before she achieved her synthesis of common-sense realism, educational theory, and sentimental idealization of home influences, Catharine had made her mark as an innovative and extraordinarily gifted teacher. Her pupils almost idolized her:

> By her extreme mildness and gentle firmness, she has acquired such an ascendancy over her pupils, that her wish is their law. She is invariably cheerful, and merry with the merry, and though superior to all around her, she places all quite at their ease. The truth and humility of her character are beautiful and endearing. . . . She seems to be a blessing to the world. The mind and character of her pupils are so admirably trained, that they must dispense good wherever they are.

Catharine Beecher's mature religious views, which were very far from those of her father and brothers, derived as much from her educational successes as from her speculative writings or from settled views of Christian doctrine. In the beginning of this educational career, however, she seemed bent on proving how truly evangelical she was, even while she set about to undermine New England orthodoxy.[28]

The clearest instance of her desire to assert her orthodoxy was the revival of 1826, which began in her school. "Our house," she wrote Edward, "is literally a house of prayer." She directed the revival within her walls much as she had seen Edward and Lyman directing theirs. Calling the young women together, she exhorted them to stand fast in the faith, commend themselves to unbelievers by their loving demeanor, avoid artificial excitement and religious enthusiasm, and labor with the unregenerate in a spirit of meekness and hope. If Lyman was going to argue that Gospel doctrines were revival-producing doctrines, how could he reconcile the fact of her revival with what he supposed to be her doctrinal vagaries? For he did not doubt that it was a genuine awakening.

He was never forced to answer the question, however, because there was no recurrence of the revival spirit in Catharine's domains. Lyman rejoiced in her success and gave her equal commendation with her brother: "It is my hope that God has raised you [Edward] up to promote revivals in colleges and Catharine to promote them in female schools." Without ever forbidding her to continue this work, nevertheless, he may have managed to communicate to Catharine a sense of uneasiness over her assumption of a traditionally male role. Revivals led by persons not connected with the ordained clergy were, at this date, irregular and sometimes suspect. Whatever the case, Lyman did not discourage Catharine's leaning toward a religious vocation.[29]

The revival which began in the Hartford Female Seminary and spread to the churches of that city affected Catharine's life profoundly. An immediate result of the revival was her decision to present herself for membership in the First Church. So long as she retained scruples about her fitness for membership, she had refrained from declaring herself a Christian. Now, although her views had not changed and were, in fact, moving further from orthodoxy, she felt she could in good conscience agree to abide by the church covenant and walk in the Congregational way.

Whatever Lyman's secret thoughts on the subject of her conversion, he was prepared to believe her fully awakened to evangelical truth as a result of the recent revival. She, with her sisters Mary and Harriet, became members of the First Church. The more important and lasting result of the revival was the heightening of her conviction that she was called by God to be a religious teacher, in a sphere different from but in no way inferior to that of her father and brothers. Catharine's conversion and calling must be considered together to understand how these events shaped her life. In the first place, she did not experience what the orthodox called a "saving change." She described her motives and the discovery of her religious vocation in terms that linked the two with her fascination for moral philosophy:

> Soon I became deeply interested in this study; for I had been led to my profession [of faith] by most profound and agitating fears of dangers in the life to come, not only for myself, but for a dear friend who, according to the views in which I had been trained, had died unprepared. "What must we do to be saved?" became the agonizing inquiry for myself and all I loved most.[30]

She continued to rely on Edward, but no longer for spiritual guidance. Rather, he was to serve as critic of her nascent mental and moral philosophy, as this letter of 1828 shows:

> My school is not yet what I intend to make a school before I stop. . . . I have many plans and some very good ones, which I must defer laying open till I can have time and opportunity to talk with you face to face. Mean time my plan for a Sunday School book is waiting to hear what you have to say on the various points presented for your consideration. Do you know how sadly we need some text book on Moral Philosophy for our Academies and Schools? It is a shame with all our talk about *moral*

> influence, *moral* nature and every other moral thing, that every other philosophy, can find some duodecimo to shine in, except *moral philosophy*.

Paley's classic treatise she dismissed as "an *im*moral philosophy" and "worse than none," and in the absence of a satisfactory substitute for Paley, she had concluded to write her own.[31]

Indeed, Catharine Beecher produced three books within ten years. In addition to the *Elements*, which she published anonymously, there were her *Letters on Difficulties in Religion* and *The Moral Instructor*. Taken together, these books presented both a departure from Lyman's theology and a confirmation of many of its premises. Catharine's system was as truly "clinical" as her father's. Like him, she claimed to take Gospel teachings in their bearings on the life experiences of inquirers and new converts. But whereas Lyman hammered out his views in the heat of revivals, Catharine took hers from the lessons of the classroom. Religious instruction was of paramount importance in her school. Even if she had not been convinced that the Scriptures construed according to common sense were the best source of religion, the presence in her school of girls from different denominations and sections of the country would probably have necessitated a nonsectarian approach to the subject. Not content to cull tidbits from available textbooks, and not disposed to echo Nathaniel Taylor or Joel Hawes's sermons, she "sought and read Locke, Reid, Stewart, Brown and other works in English, and also went to those who read Greek and German for the views of Aristotle and Kant." From these formidable researches Catharine distilled two principles: "that our Heavenly Parent is chiefly glorious as the Great Happiness Maker" and that man is endowed by this same Father with a perfect mental constitution which requires only proper cultivation to bring it to correct views of God and a desire to be his child.[32]

Certain features of her system, as taught to her pupils as the basis for their Bible readings, excited great alarm among the clergy and lay religious leaders of Hartford. In particular, her appeal to the final authority of human consciousness, while superficially similar to Nathaniel Taylor's appeal to reason and common sense, went beyond current rationalism to make the consciousness of unregenerate man a perfect umpire in spiritual matters. Her insistence on depicting God as sharing human feelings (a heresy known as patripassianism) and her conviction that neither divine leadings nor the indwelling of the Holy Spirit were necessary for regeneration, were also attacked as unsound. When Catharine realized the full extent of her heterodoxy, and the horror it excited, she suppressed the *Elements*. In most respects, her later views were but an elaboration of these ideas. At first she attempted to reconcile them with New Haven or New School doctrines, but she later recognized the futility of her efforts and frankly avowed herself a Pelagian.[33]

Although she spoke of Pelagianism—characteristically hoping to turn a stigma into a badge of honor—her religious beliefs were little different from the moralism of her generation. In the well-worn channels of doctrinal controversy, Catharine's views could still annoy and alarm, but it is difficult to see them as anything but congruent with middle-class piety. By 1840 her religious system had dropped the doctrine of Original Sin as contrary to reason and pernicious in its effects. She went on to teach that such sin as man possessed was shallowly rooted. Her religious teachings did not acknowledge the existence of what the poet George Herbert had called "cunning bosome-sinne." Man's wrongdoing resulted from faulty instruction or lack of nurture, an assertion which should not be confused with the views of Catharine's contemporary, Horace Bushnell.

In calling Catharine's views moralistic and middle-class, I do not mean to say that they were thereby shabby or tiresome. Intellectual historians have been apt to complain of the sentimentalism and intellectual flabbiness of the post-Edwardean era in theology, and it was, for the most part, lacking in "tough-mindedness" and unblinking realism. But we are not called upon to believe as the Victorians did, nor even to applaud them.

Whatever her family thought of her religious views, they were more concerned over Catharine's behavior. She seemed determined to vindicate her ideas and convert church leaders to her way of thinking. In 1831 we find her writing to Archibald Alexander of Princeton, inviting herself to his home for a protracted discussion of her *Elements*, a copy of which was to precede her. She grandly announced that she had just communed with Benjamin Wisner on these topics. Her brothers, inevitably, were subjected to the same treatment. Whenever she had worked out a variation on her key ideas, she would visit them each in turn, arriving out of the blue. She remained for days, or even weeks, monopolizing their evenings and making herself tiresome by her pertinacity and self-importance. Nathaniel Taylor grew to dread her visits but could hardly turn away the daughter of his oldest friend. She importuned Edwards A. Park and his wife to read the manuscript of her *Common Sense*, charging them to be prepared to debate its propositions when she reached their home.

The publication of Catharine's *Appeal to the People* was accompanied by another flurry of consultations and confrontations with unwilling disputants. To Nathaniel Wright, an elder in Lyman's Second Church of Cincinnati, she proposed a visit of several days. Although she was hampered by poor health and the elderly Wright by deafness, Catharine saw no reason why she should not descend on his home, provided he took care not to upset her in her state of "nervous excitability." At the same time she was challenging Wright to debate her, she sent articles to the *New York Observer* and the *New York Evening Post* and a letter to Henry showing just why her views alone were consistent with Scripture while her brother's were halfway measures and false steps.

These actions were painful to the whole family, but particularly to the male members. When she assumed a hectoring tone with John Hooker, in a letter full of unsolicited advice about his career, Hooker, the mildest of men, complained to Isabella, "I have no wish to get into an argument [with Catharine], for in a few weeks we should be in the *Biblical Repository*."[34]

John Hooker was referring to Catharine's famous dispute with Leonard Woods on the subject of fatalism and free will. In her essay, Catharine had argued for a generic principle of contingency and buttressed it with appeals to the New Havenite doctrine of "power of contrary choice" and motives as occasional (rather than producing) causes. Not content with publishing her remarks, she engaged Charles and Edward in a three-way controversy. They maintained that she was an acute thinker but prone to get out of difficulties by semantic dodges, which landed her in straits such as the most elementary lessons in logic ought to have prevented. Charles wrote a long-winded account of his disputes with Catharine to their father, concluding on a note of exasperation and dismissal:

> I have simply to say in respect to these controversies that 1. with Edward I consider them as barren of wholesome fruit as the scholastic jargon of the middle ages. 2. As to Catharine's mind it is the last that should flatter itself with the hope of *disentangling* the subject. 3. That as to Edward—she neither does nor can comprehend him—by reason that his region of truth and thought is too far above her. 4. That the only source of truth is *slow*, patient —comprehensive induction and generalisation.

When Catharine made a visit to George Beecher shortly afterward, Lyman wrote George in advance, "I have charged her and charge you not to break her back and foot—by over much metaphysical discussion in which when provoked she has no great knack of holding her tongue."[35]

Her keen frustration at not being able to win important men over to her views and her resentment over not being taken seriously by male clerics led Catharine to publish increasingly anticlerical pieces, culminating in the bizarre *Truth Stranger Than Fiction*. Without going into all the details of this New Haven scandal of 1848-50, it is still necessary to discuss it in order to show why her ostensible purpose in publishing the book conflicted with her real purposes. Catharine had been the teacher of Delia Bacon, Leonard Bacon's sister. Delia was a bluestocking who made a living conducting classes in history and literature for older women who could afford to pay for private instruction. In the late 1840s Delia became enamoured of a Yale divinity student, Alexander MacWhorter, who was a close friend of Nathaniel Taylor.

After a prolonged and rather irregular courtship, MacWhorter broke off the relationship, giving as his reason his disgust with Delia's unwomanly aggressiveness. His friends, animated by an unholy glee, spread the tale around the College and the Divinity School, depicting Delia as a love-starved spinster with no self-respect or modesty. Leonard Bacon felt obliged to bring MacWhorter to account for ruining Delia's reputation (and with it her prospects of earning a living), but the New Haven West Ministerial Association—dominated by Taylor—returned a statement clearing MacWhorter.

At this point Catharine Beecher intervened. According to her, Delia actually got down on her knees and begged her not to write the book, but Catharine's disinterestedness would brook no refusal, even when Leonard added his pleas to Delia's tearful entreaties to let the matter drop. *Truth Stranger Than Fiction* was designed as an exposé of hypocrisy in high places. Catharine used code names for the principals, but there was no disguising their identities. She even tried to enlist Horace Greeley's aid in marketing the book. It was a peculiar production. In her treatment of Delia, Catharine was more damning than exculpatory, dwelling at length on Delia's character defects and excessive pride, and reproducing gossip that tended to make her look foolish, if not downright stupid. Actually, the book's aim was a larger one. Catharine intended her readers to interpret this seamy episode as an indictment of the clergy, who used unmerited social power to destroy a defenseless woman and to uphold their own spiritual authority.[36]

Nathaniel Taylor realized that he was the target and implored his old friend Beecher to repudiate the book, at least privately. Catharine's family was appalled at this latest outbreak of Catharine's tendency to bear grudges and ventilate her resentments publicly. After several more such incidents, albeit on a smaller scale, she became persona non grata at most of the Beecher hearths. The tender-hearted Charles (who had not suffered public indignities at Catharine's hands) lamented his sister's exclusion from the family:

> Now I know she has peculiarities that repel some from her. And yet it seems sad to me to see her cast out as it were from the family circle by Mary, and Hatty and you[Henry]—Not that she is really cast out—but—something virtually pretty near it. Yet she is sincere, and kind, and benevolent. That is she seems to have been so, both by natural impulse and on principle. Cannot she be made to feel more of the warm sympathy of fraternal affection in her loneliness?[37]

Given her animosity toward the clergy, it was natural that Catharine should look with increasing favor on lay religious instruction of the type she had pioneered in Hartford. She believed that women, by nature and education, were best suited to guide infant minds to religious truth. This was her alternative to the vast evangelical united front, with its missions empire and tract and bible societies. She argued that every home was a temple of religious instruction, with the mother as a sort of priestess. The end of this instruction was not, however, the same as that sought by her father Lyman. In the last analysis, Catharine Beecher's idea of religion made it a kind of rational ethical almanac in which the highest virtue was not "disinterested benevolence" or love to being-in-general, but womanly self-sacrifice—self-sacrifice of the kind which instills guilt and therefore obedience in its beneficiaries.

After 1840 her religious ideas changed hardly at all. She simply became bolder and more truculent in publishing them. When her brother George died in 1843, she took it upon herself to publish his letters and diaries under the title *Biographical Remains.* She presented his life as proof of the efficacy of self-culture in overcoming severe constitutional handicaps:

> It is the history of a mind which, embarrassed with infirmities of temperament, with the impediments of habit, with the weakness and discouragements of disease, found motives and influences that imparted unwonted strength and vigor, and secured remarkable

success, and these are so presented as to awaken hope and encouragement in all, who amid similar embarrassments, are pressing forward to the mark for the prize of their high calling.

But she also showed how evangelical religion induced the morbidity of temperament so marked in George's diaries. In reaction against this, Catharine looked with great favor on Unitarianism and Episcopalianism. On "strictly *theological dogma*," she aligned herself with the Unitarians. In matters of faith and order, however, she inclined very strongly toward Episcopalianism. In 1846 she told Bishop Alonzo Potter that she identified with the religion of her mother, Roxana. "I rejoice in the prosperity and lament the trials of your church the same as if it were my own." She went on to criticize the principles of her father's communion in these terms: "the *grand mistake* in the religious world is, in bringing children up—first to be *poisoned* and then arranging all measures for their *cure* instead of turning the main effort to preventive training."[38]

When Charles Beecher came to prepare materials for his father's *Autobiography*, he recognized the importance of Catharine's spiritual crisis in drawing the lines of dissent from Lyman's theology. Like her brothers and sisters after her, Catharine Beecher came to understand religion as a way of life, and the religious experience as a growth in grace. Whereas they, however, continued to assert a heroic ideal of Christian discipleship, she, more than the rest, equated high spirituality with the possession of domestic virtues. Until 1862 she argued as one remaining within the evangelical tradition, but in that year, at the age of sixty-one, she finally made her belated departure when she was confirmed as an Episcopalian.

Whereas Catharine had once assailed Catherine Sedgwick for her opposition to Calvinistic doctrines and evangelical church order, she herself had long since crossed over to rationalistic ground. Her repudiation of the views she had once believed absolutely necessary to piety and morals was, if anything, more forcible and heated than Sedgwick's complaints about "the cruel doctrines of Geneva." If Catharine was drawn closer, by identification with the Foote family and by the logic of her arguments, to the Episcopal Church, it was not the Episcopalianism of the Thirty-Nine Articles. Her ultimate position amounted to a unitarianism of the deity, with Jesus Christ reduced to the supreme moral instructor. Eternal punishment remained a vital part of her beliefs, as a rational necessity to insure unswerving obedience to God's commandments. Above all, for Catharine Beecher, true religion was to be found only among those who extended "their arms towards the children, enfolding them and protecting them like tender lambs."[39]

4 *ISABELLA BEECHER HOOKER*

Harriet Porter died in the midst of her husband's heresy trial, leaving her books and dresses to her thirteen-year-old daughter Isabella. Isabella had been separated from her mother, remaining in Hartford to receive her schooling. Mary Beecher Perkins, seventeen years Isabella's senior, supervised her half-sister's upbringing. Growing up in the Perkins's affluent circle, Isabella lived up to her pet name of "Belle" and became a stylish young lady like her mother before her. Sensitivity about class lines and an aggressive belief in modishness and refinement characterized her well into middle age. She early developed, as well, a yearning for recognition and a disarmingly flagrant vanity. Writing to her serious-minded, unassuming fiancé, Isabella reminded him that

> the opinions and tastes of Miss Belle have been consulted by her parents and *sisters* (old enough to claim that dignity) until she has learned to feel pretty extensively her own importance—and now that she has come to years of discretion—her old and almost idolised father comes to her almost as an equal—and tho' kindly influencing and modifying, always leaves her to choose and *act* for herself.

It was a fact that her family was apt to treat Isabella like a rare and fragile creature. Henry boasted of her "youthful feats" as a musician and scholar, while Charles ungallantly contrasted his sisters to his half-sister:

> I presume Mary and Kate and Hatty will all dawn upon our darkness; a perfect constellation of every thing but—beauty—Nature could not afford much more than was necessary to complete one such specimen as yourself Bell . . . and that is why the rest are so "expressive"—but "plain."[1]

Isabella Beecher Hooker

It was not until she was seventeen that Isabella was reunited with her father, as Lyman ruefully admitted:

> With my elder children I formed and kept up an acquaintance from the cradle. But after the vortex of public cares and labours took me, I have been obliged to be introduced to [the younger] by circumstances. I knew that you loved me from early childhood, but did not know how much of it might survive the needed crosses and self denials of education. . . . If it is a pleasure to children to be beloved by their parents there is to them no greater joy on earth than its full hearted return.

In the months preceding her return visit to Cincinnati, Isabella underwent the conversion experience. Remembering her own sufferings, Mary shrank from importuning or interrogating Isabella, as Catharine might have done. Instead, she resorted to the familiar device of leaving a note on her sister's writing table. In it Mary assured Isabella that the time was ripe for her reception into the community of believers: "the remembrance of your mother's prayers may come up before God–His spirit is evidently decending and his ear is ready to hear and his arm to save." God was gracious and desired her salvation. Almost timidly, Mary added that "Whatever aid I can give I will give most joyfully–I will go with you to any meetings you may chuse and tho' I do not feel competent to guide I shall be ever ready to converse with you if you feel inclined."

Thomas Beecher, with his precocious Puritan sombreness, exhorted his sister, "Do read *Persuasives to early piety by J. G. Pike* . . . and with it the *bible* together with prayer, and I shall always pray for you." He warned her not to fall by the wayside, for "I fear your heart has grown callous." Mary, Aunt Esther, and the Reverend Joel Hawes apparently did not require the aid of James Pike's gloomy tract. Under their guidance Isabella's conversion was relatively serene and unmarked by significant episodes of despair or terror. Hawes did not even question the reality of her conversion, as he had done with her sister Harriet.[2]

Lyman greeted his daughter's entrance into the church of Christ with unreserved joy:

> My longing for your salvation and desire of your prayer and example and influence on your younger brothers–as well as a state of mind some what sorrowful–at the dark aspect of Lane events, rendered the goodness of God like the bursting out from darkness of an effulgent sun, and made me weep for my past distrust, and present gratitude and joy—

Although he had some misgivings about her understanding of sanctification ("you seem inclined to legal views"), he spared her any close examination of the genuineness of her regeneration. He encouraged her solicitude for the spiritual travails of others but warned against indiscriminate zeal, cautioning, "Your desire to benefit others should be wakeful—but this does not imply . . . that you should every day slam-bang at somebody as a matter of duty with out rule or reason." He recommended that she let Edward be her guide in such matters. Nevertheless, Isabella's conviction that she was uniquely destined to be a spiritual leader became the theme of her life.[3]

Piety was the keynote of her correspondence with John Hooker, the Farmington, Connecticut, lawyer she was to marry. Hooker, a direct descendant of Hartford's founder, the Reverend Thomas Hooker, was an amiable man whose adventures as a foremast hand in the China and India trade would seem incongruous in one whose character was so mild and self-effacing had not so many other college youths done the same. Hooker had interrupted his studies at Yale to sail on the bark *Marblehead* in the first of his many quests after good health. He found the experience a "school of manliness and self-reliance and courage," despite the "serious moral peril" which environed sailors. His bravery was most severely tested in an encounter with pirates, which, though harrowing at the time, he later recalled as a wonderful adventure.

Manliness, which Hooker valued above everything else, did not consist in physical courage, however. Manliness was moral courage, absolute probity, and a chivalrous regard for the weak and disinherited. Even his religious beliefs came to be weighed against this moral standard, though at the time he was courting Isabella, he retained a large measure of orthodox evangelical fervor. He insisted that Isabella read and take to heart the example of one *Martha*, a pious lady whose self-crucifying life her brother the Reverend Andrew Reed had commemorated in a fashion almost necrophiliac. Isabella replied tartly that she had already studied the life and good works of Martha Reed "with no christian delight." She went on to admit that she had previously disliked "those whom I had known to be pointed out as the most self-denying, holy characters." Such people, to her mind, appeared "unrefined—comparatively uneducated—who seem to care nothing for the works of taste and the comforts of a cultivated state of society—whose chief merit in my estimation, was, a sort of go ahead zeal—that made them I suppose useful ministers—now I could not feel that with my present tastes and education, such characters were pleasing—and therefore did not wish to become a devoted christian—these were mistaken ideas I think—and now I can say with truth that such *is* my desire and will I trust be my constant effort." Isabella was probably sincere in her wish to conform to such once-despised examples, and the knowledge that her future husband wanted her to emulate sterling female Christians must have kindled in her the desire to be seen as pious.[4]

It proved to be a temporary state of mind. She had never liked the rigorously observant Sabbath of the Beechers and Hookers, which even the Perkinses (for a time) upheld. Isabella did not pretend to see the good of it. Whether she acted upon John, who pledged, "the probability is that I shall never contradict a wish of yours which I have the power to gratify," or whether he was insensibly falling away from his family faith already, they gradually developed a more genial and relaxed religious attitude without, however, losing any moral earnestness. John expressed fears lest Isabella think she had "fallen into the iron hands of a rigid bigot," when she complained of his urgings that she perfect her Christian character through self-examination. But there was never any danger that she would think him excessively religious. In fact, she resented the fact that he demurred at Lyman's demand that he enter the ministry.[5]

John was sufficiently devout and impressionable to consider throwing over his promising legal career to take up the cross of a home missionary, but he wondered whether his delicate wife could stand up to the privations and labors of such a life. Lyman, who would not be denied in such matters, pressed him to make the decision. "We shall not be able I suppose to enroll your name in the great Family Bible," he wrote John when he gave his consent to the engagement, "but you may consider yourself as already enrolled with Isabella and all the rest on the tablet of our hearts and so entirely in mine." Though Hooker was not "a son by birth," Lyman saw no reason why his prospective son-in-law should not do as his own male children and prepare for the ministry. He began pressuring him to do his duty and help save the great West from irreligion and ignorance, but the Hookers and Perkinses objected strenuously. They felt Lyman had no right to urge John into the ministry when it was plainly not his calling. Isabella herself, once the glamor of the idea had worn off, discovered that she was disinclined to become a migratory poor relation of the Perkinses, and John abandoned the project.

Catharine had sided with Mary and Harriet, who knew their sister too well to share Lyman's illusions about her happiness as a home missionary's helpmate. With her usual plain speaking, Catharine described to Hooker the most prominent strains in Isabella's character. She noted that, on the one hand, Isabella seemed to enjoy being "feeble and sickly." John should not abet her, or dream of a cottage idyll in Farmington "with your father and mother to pet her, and you with nothing to do half the day but coo over her." On the other hand, and coexisting with Isabella's languishing nature, was a powerful need to dominate. "Bell is formed by nature to *take the lead*—She will learn every year more and more of her power *to influence others*." Voluntary poverty and social obscurity could never content a woman like Isabella. If she were a minister's wife, she would thrive only in a metropolitan setting, with plenty of money and leisure.[6]

The analysis proved accurate. John Hooker's devotion did include a large element of commiseration, as when he declared ten years later: "I can not tell you how your misfortunes make me love you. If I were a man of wealth and leisure how I should love to go around with you to every Bethesda where a cripple could be healed." In the absence of wealth he still managed to send his wife to a number of sanitaria and spas. As for her need to rule, which was to take a decidedly pathological turn later in life, Isabella frankly expected to dominate her husband in many matters. For his part he confessed, "I believe I am rather wanting in decision." He defined marriage as having "a dear—loving confiding—noble companion . . . who will read and study with me—think with me—become daily more and more one with me." "I do admire intellect in woman—indeed I almost adore it," he exclaimed, stressing his expectation that he would serve as Isabella's intellectual mentor.[7]

Isabella made it plain that she would not settle into a round of complaisant mediocrity and household drudgery. While visiting her brother William, whose wife was an accomplished, resourceful, but unhappily married woman, Isabella reflected on Beecher marriages:

> I have—for some moments in looking at the families of some even of my brothers and sisters—felt misgivings—many and great—but then, I feel that there is a radical defect in their plan—one which can be avoided—they did not start rightly . . . resolve upon self-denial, self-sacrifice, and consideration of the others feelings as much as their own. . . . If I tho't my married life would be such as I have seen exhibited in my own family—I never could bring myself to fulfill an engagement, other wise delightful.

Beyond her pessimistic, albeit partly just, assessment of her family's matrimonial record, Isabella expressed philosophical objections to current views of the institution. She engaged George and Sarah Beecher in a "most labored discussion of the relative position of a wife—to her husband—her duty of submission etc." with reference to scriptural doctrines. She concluded that "while ministers and others insist most strenuously, on the duties of the lady, the husband's fulfilment of his obligations is taken for granted—and 'husbands *love* your wives even as Christ loved the church' seems an entirely superfluous command." This moral myopia she attributed to the fact that "I do believe the love of power is inate, in all minds . . . [and] there seems no good to result." Considering her youth (she was seventeen) and the date of these opinions, which seem to have arisen from private ruminations rather than any crystallized political awareness, Isabella's incipient feminism is all the more remarkable.[8]

John and Isabella were married on August 5, 1841; Isabella was nineteen, John, six years her senior. Despite some very painful passages, it was a relatively harmonious marriage. If sometimes strained, their affection was constant, and the mutual dependency tremendous. And this in spite of the fact that John was the more openly loving and forgiving of the two. Hooker, who was accustomed to call Isabella his "covenant angel," could write twenty-eight years later, "It is wonder enough such a woman should be—but greater wonder that God should have given her to me."

For her part, Isabella did not reciprocate this rapturous devotion. She often complained of John's faults: his precipitancy in some matters and excessive caution in others, his childlike bond to her, and his seeming inability to grasp the concrete advantages of becoming a shrewd man of the world. In one crucial instance, however, he proved the dominant partner, and his determination to convert his wife to abolitionism was a momentous fact, not only for her but for her whole family.[9]

At first Mrs. Hooker seemed content to be a homebody and a dutiful companion to the elder Hookers, who doted on her. But John and the Perkinses liked to see her moving in fashionable society. Her assets were many—chiefly her delicate beauty, sportive conversation, and rather bold charm. John Pitkin Norton, their neighbor and one of John's abolitionist allies, admired Isabella, who often entertained him. In one account of the Hookers' party games, Norton wrote, "Mrs. Hooker, indeed, acted like a perfect witch, she was entirely carried away, by excitement and fun." At a boating party for her sisters, Isabella practiced more witchery and enchanted the guests by singing duets on the water with Norton "with pretty good success."

Ice cream feasts, picnics, and family readings and rides made for an easeful, gracious life, though Isabella was piqued by criticism from friends and family of her worldly literary tastes. One book "of the novel cast . . . full of wit as well as romance" seemed innocuous to Isabella, but her in-laws gravely informed her that it "would probably shock some of Father's moral reform tendencies."[10]

After the death of their first child Thomas, they had three more children. Isabella's relationship with them was troubled. Once, while sitting by her daughter Alice's sickbed, Isabella told her, in what must have been a painful admission, "I wish you would hang onto me a little. I should so like to have you." Alice, who was fourteen, soberly replied: "I cant. I'm just like you. Mary and Eddie must do the hanging—that's enough I'm sure." Of Mary, however, Isabella complained, "There is a fretfulness and irritability, leading to much whining and hanging round 'mama' that I would fain overcome." However much she may have disliked Mary's clinging dependency, she also reacted sharply against her excessive self-will. Incensed at one of Mary's "obstinate fit[s]," Isabella gave her a thrashing so severe that she injured her own back, while Mary remained defiant. "How the little creature could bear such blows and yet hold out I cannot imagine—my own hand smarted fairly with them and the whalebone must have stung well." The trials of motherhood and housewifery brought Isabella very low, as she confessed to Harriet Stowe. She excused herself for not inviting her impoverished sister for a long stay, because "my poor head I fear which is none of the strongest at best, would utterly fail me in such a crisis—confusion, noise of children and extra care completely upset me. . . . I can hardly account for my brain weakness, and my incapacity for the daily duties which many perform so easily."[11]

Her afflictions, both physical and emotional, increased in variety and intensity. She had long been a sufferer from back pains; *prolapsus uteri* was another serious complaint of long standing; she suffered also from chronic digestive and bowel upsets; her rheumatic "twinges" worsened. Nasal polyps destroyed her sense of smell, and the resulting loss of appetite aggravated her general feelings of debility and decline. Physical prostration, "neurasthenia," and ennui threatened to make her a lifelong invalid, as she often warned John, himself a frequenter of health spas, and in the language of the time, a valetudinarian.[12]

To assess the causes of Isabella's discontent and ill health is difficult. There was, undeniably, a maternal history of mental illness. Some of Isabella's complaints were remarkably similar to her brother

James's, particularly the continual references to weakness or confusion in the brain and the sensations of panic over routine domestic and personal responsibilities. In the absence of clearer indications, however, it is best not to venture diagnostic remarks. Her own perceptions of the situation indicate a bitter chafing over the stupidity of woman's work and her own unfitness to lumber along in the domestic routine. She saw her siblings engaged in work of a more attractive and significant nature, her brothers as clergymen and reformers, her sisters as authors. (What she thought of Mary Perkins's conventionality is not known.) Isabella was developing a serious interest in social and political reforms, particularly in their legal and constitutional aspects. True to his word, John encouraged his wife to read law with him and discuss the public issues of the day.

She developed an even keener and more personal sense of the wrongs inflicted on women by law, custom, and culture. But as was true of so many women of her generation, she came to feminism through antislavery. Hooker's brother-in-law Francis Gillette, later a United States senator, was one of the earliest abolitionists in Farmington, and may have been instrumental in Hooker's conversion to the cause in 1840. In order to bring Isabella around to his way of thinking, John pressed his arguments for emancipation with a force and energy he never dared to exhibit in other discussions. His frequent absences on business and as reporter for the state supreme court made it necessary for him to commit his arguments to letters, which Isabella was bound to mull over.

His abolitionist sentiments initially met with scornful outrage, but at length Isabella began to entertain doubts about her father's wisdom in supporting colonization and struggling to suppress ecclesiastical cleavages over slavery. Her earlier cooling toward evangelical theology may have contributed to her willingness to criticize Lyman's political views as well. Hooker had, however, to neutralize powerful influences from Isabella's sisters, especially Mary, whose hostility to "the raging waves of Ultraism, which threaten to engulph all the common sense of the country" was animated by Thomas Perkins's obdurate conservatism. "We at the north," Perkins told Isabella, had "nothing to do with slavery—absolutely nothing—any more than we have with Hindoo idolatry . . . Dr. Hawes, might as well have confessed the latter, in his fast-day prayer, as a *national* sin, as the former."

The moral obtuseness of such declarations could not have impressed Isabella favorably; for whatever their feelings about abolitionism, the Beechers were all agreed that slavery was a barbaric institution in a free republic and that its eventual eradication was necessary to transform America into a righteous nation. Catharine, nevertheless, hewed to Perkins's line on the subversive character of slavery's more radical opponents: Weld and Birney did more harm than good with their intemperate attacks on the institution and its defenders. When Catharine wrote that the self-righteous apostles of abolitionism had subjected slaveholders to verbal abuse that "would form a large page in the vocabulary of Billingsgate," Isabella could agree wholeheartedly, although Catharine's other propositions were embarrassing to the Beechers. They could not help wincing at her plumping for expediency over ethics. Isabella disliked breaches of decorum as much as Mary and Catharine did. She continually threw into John's teeth the charge that abolitionists were bigots whose favorite weapons were sarcasm and character assassination. Southerners and their native institutions ought to be treated with civility, no matter how much gentlewomen and clergymen might deplore specific features of slavery. Reason and moderation were to be praised in antislavery men like her brothers George, William, and Edward. As for John's attitude, "I do believe," she wrote him, "that you and I shall never fully harmonise until you cease to think and speak so contemptuously of those who differ from you."[13]

Though the fashionable town of Farmington was seemingly remote from slavery, as compared to Cincinnati where Lyman Beecher and the Stowes lived, the Hookers could not escape personal involvement with the institution or knowledge of its evils. John Hooker's uncle and namesake had settled in South Carolina and undoubtedly reported back on conditions there. Hooker himself braved social ostracism to take a black man to his church. He also negotiated the freedom of a fugitive slave, the Reverend James W. C. Pennington. Though Pennington had become an eminent preacher in Hartford, he was still (under the name James Pembroke) the property of his former master and lived in fear of being reenslaved. To insure that Pennington could not be returned South on some legal pretext, Hooker purchased Pennington and manumitted him in Connecticut. Before this, he had interested himself in the welfare of the *Amistad* mutineers. His parents' hired man was a runaway slave whose wife and children were still in bondage. The Hookers were appalled by this discovery and felt it keenly when "he cried so in telling his story that he could hardly speak." Reflecting on the man's tragedy, John wrote Isabella, "It really does seem as if a justice-loving God could not much longer withold his avenging thunders."[14]

Knowing her eagerness for disputation, and appealing to her sense of fair play and pride in being consulted as an equal, John challenged her to uphold her family's side of the debate openly. As it was, several of her half-brothers had already allied themselves with Weld and Birney, while she continued to speak for the conservatives in her family. "Your censures," John commented, "are too severe for one to inflict, who refuses to give the object of his censure, a fair hearing." It was an "immense and sublime question," and he was ashamed that she followed the lead of Mary Perkins in refusing to canvass the topic. He could hardly credit "the position that you have taken that you will not *read* upon the subject." He himself disavowed the extremism of some of the abolitionists, "the ultraism—the garrisonism, Abby Kellyism, nonresistanceism etc.—and above all the anti clerical spirit, which has been so much mingled up with AntiSlavery." As for her accusation that abolitionist discourse was characterized by "coarseness" and "meanness," he dared her to compare that rhetoric to Lyman Beecher's:

> Are you willing to read over carefully your dear Fathers sermon on duelling—and see why almost every argument against the severe language used by the abolitionists (and which I condemn as heartily as you) will not apply to that sermon. I never knew a slaveholder more severely attacked and *abused*—than the Southern Duellists are by your Father.

Other people had remarked on Lyman's inconsistency in violently assailing duelling—a comparatively restricted vice—while urging moderation and compromise on slavery.[15]

Within a year of their marriage, Isabella had begun to come around to John's position. She was soon won over completely, writing of a discussion with the Perkinses, "I suppose they talk here very much as I used to—but it does not strike me either pleasantly or as becoming intelligent, reading, christian people." Yet she opposed John's plan of accepting the Liberty Party nomination for Congress when Mary convinced her that it was a quixotic gesture, a needless sacrifice of reputation and opportunities for preferment. By 1844, however, she was actively forwarding his Liberty Party work. He counted on her assistance in planning and running antislavery meetings, although she could not, of course, address the gatherings for fear of compromising her reputation. His lecture tours of the state began to win small numbers over to abolitionism, but he was disappointed at the limited gains. "How strange," he puzzled, "that in *this country*—and among the sons of the Pilgrims, *such* a cause should be unpopular." He served one term in the Connecticut House of Representatives as Farmington's abolitionist spokesman.

John believed that Isabella's conversion to the cause had capped their union. "How I thank God that you are a whole souled abolitionist. I do not know how much this consideration has contributed to our perfect happiness in one another." Their mutual dedication to a highly unpopular reform did, in fact, consolidate certain elements of their relationship, not the least of which was their increasing tendency to strive for social and political regeneration without regard to the fundamentally religious vision of Lyman Beecher.[16]

By 1850, Isabella was delighted to observe, Henry had finally arrived at sufficiently militant views on slavery. And within two years she announced that "Hatty [Stowe] is coming strait onto our Anti-slavery platform—she has been you know a father and Mr. Stowe abolitionist heretofore." In belatedly declaring herself a John and Isabella Hooker abolitionist, Harriet did not acknowledge the Hookers' lead. Isabella remarked that "she was so absorbed in the dawn of her own ideas she did not once remember that in common with others of our family she *had* doubted the wisdom of such practice."

Isabella felt vindicated, and there can be no doubt that she and John had helped urge the more conservative members of the family along toward abolition. But she was only too aware that it was Harriet, and not she, who had written *Uncle Tom's Cabin*. Long plagued by doubts whether "I have powers of attraction yet," Isabella coveted a like distinction. John's adoration of her was pleasant enough, but she wanted lasting fame, not ephemeral, tame tributes to her good looks and intelligence. John seemed hardly to grasp the extent of her feelings of uselessness and insignificance, as when she brooded over lacking "individuality," or wrote him from a health resort, "oh my *soul*, if you would only teach me how to earn money—but there's no use hoping. I cant write a book—nor draw pictures—nor do any other productive work. I have always told you, that you overestimated your wife."[17]

Protracted stays at hydropathic and other cures in the 1850s did not alleviate Isabella's malaise, but in 1860 she began to catch glimpses of future greatness. She made a visit to the Gleason Water Cure in Elmira, New York, where Thomas Beecher had his pastorate. On renewing her friendship with this nettlesome brother, she came to envy his usefulness in the ministry, which contrasted so painfully with her own bitterness and sense of stultification. At one point she fancied herself as a hydropathic gynecologist and wrote home of her novel ideas for relieving female suffering, but she soon dropped the idea. In the light-hearted, convivial atmosphere of the Gleason Cure, she had leisure for stock-taking and warm support for various schemes of reordering her life to secure health, energy, and mental repose. "Tell papa," she triumphantly wrote Alice Hooker, that "Mrs. Gleason says—that my sleeping so late in the morning, is the one thing, that has saved him from having a *nervous, fidgetty,* perhaps even *crazy* wife. She highly approves my past practice in this and most other respects." Isabella hinted that she "might easily become" a permanent martyr to ill health unless the entire domestic regime was altered to accommodate her needs for leisure and quiet. She fended off her family's pleas for a speedy return with threats of imminent collapse, and took up a number of projects.

In keeping with the dietary and dress reforms associated with hydropathy and rival therapies, Isabella adopted the Bloomer costume for outdoor wear. Between wet packs, sitz baths, and uterine injections, she busied herself in drafting a treatise on political economy. Her husband, whose collegiate humor often came to his aid in coping with her notions, chaffed her about her latest preoccupation: "dont speculate I beg upon political economy and go into a brain fever in trying to save the world from bankruptcy. Domestic economy almost killed you before you left home." Microscopy then caught her interest, and she demanded that John scrape up the money for a suitable instrument so she could show her children the circulation of the blood, "one of the most exciting sights I ever beheld . . . it is wonderful!" These, however, were passing fancies compared to the idea that was assuming paramount importance in her life. She came more and more to think of herself as an inspired religious teacher.[18]

John had openly ridiculed the claim that God was the author of *Uncle Tom's Cabin*, a statement which in his eyes made Mrs. Stowe appear foolish and enthusiastical, no matter how much it might appeal to certain segments of her readership. Now he found his own wife speaking increasingly of divine leadings, unfoldings, and "dispensations" revealing the direction of her personal fulfillment. Musing aloud about past and future, she indicated the channel in which her thoughts ran:

> It is funny, how, every where I go—I have to run on the credit of my relations—no where, but at home can I lay claim to a particle of individuality—to any distinction of goodness, smartness or anything else whatever. . . . It becomes more and more evident to

> me—that I have great power of personal influence—family name goes a great way no doubt—but there is a magnetism of heart and eye and voice, that is quite individual. Oh how I wish I might exert this on a broad scale, to sweep people along in the right path. Approbativeness—real love of admiration is as strong perhaps as in the days of childhood and youth—but benevolence is uppermost, I am quite sure of that—and thank God for the assurance.

Her phrenological character, as she read it, did admit of selfish motives, but she praised God for enabling her to rise to disinterestedness as well. With gathering realization of divine superintendance, came the belief that her marriage, which she had been tempted to think unsatisfactory, was peculiarly blessed. "I do rejoice and wonder every day and increasingly," she confided to John, "that our union combines all the main elements of a high and noble character . . . an almost perfect whole." Isabella confessed that she had verged on contempt for John's sickliness and meekness. God had now led her to understand that "nothing very exquisite can be very strong—that, that word implies a physical, material quality which in inconsistent with this species of mental beauty." In other words, John's excellence lay in his likeness to feminine ideality.[19]

As Isabella groped her way toward a plan of sanctified activity, many dimly remembered fragments of her early life, especially of her mother's affection and anxiety for her children, came back to her clothed in light and power. She believed that Harriet Porter's spirit hovered overhead, while the "nearness and love of Christ" was daily more apparent, in seemingly trivial "signs" that might have escaped a less exalted person than Isabella. She felt absolute assurance that her mother and Jesus Christ sponsored her career of conspicuous benevolence. They had helped her discover new qualities in her husband, whose sweet good nature could be shaped into something more positive, without losing any of its gentleness. By 1864, moreover, John's financial affairs had prospered to the point where he could think of exchanging a life of toil for one of "gentlemanly liesure [*sic*] and independence." Isabella's enthusiasm for doing good on a grand scale must have been catching, for John now envisioned a lofty new calling:

> I have often thought myself a miserable failure, but I am clear now what my vocation is and what I was made for—It is to go about and see to God's natural world and see that it is all in order—I feel now the force of the command . . . "to go into all the world and preach, etc."

By this time, however, John's conception of religion included a far larger element of practical good works and a far smaller element of evangelical theology and spirituality. He saw himself superintending "God's natural world"; and as for going out to preach, he wanted to preach man's moral perfectibility, not God's transcendence and man's dependence. Neither was there much concern for the gospel of Christ, although John continued to invoke his name. Isabella shared these ideas, but what her husband failed to grasp was the strength of her conviction that she had a superhuman, anointed role to play in bringing their religious ideals and aspirations to fruition.[20]

When the Civil War broke out, Isabella entered a new phase of life. She was caught up in unquestionably important activities and she relished them. There was heroism to be found in nursing, and if she did not, as John urged, "come down to homespun and hock and beans" for the Union's sake, she vicariously shared in her brother Jim's military triumphs and sufferings. It was also during the war that she and John became woman suffragists. Many of their favorite watering holes combined therapeutic baths or vegetarian regimens with feminist and spiritualistic proselytizing. What seemed divagations or crotchets to many of the Beechers appealed to the Hookers, who liked to unite the search for health with new directions in reform. "I am in love with the idea of habitually spending our winters in New York and right here at Dr. [George H.] Taylors," John wrote in 1869, "taking movements [physical therapy] if we wish."

As Dr. Taylor was attuned to many of the current reform fads, including some on the fringes of respectability, the Hookers had no lack of opportunities to canvass the field of uplift and benevolence. Isabella participated in the founding of the New England Woman Suffrage Association and became an intimate friend of Paulina Wright Davis, Elizabeth Cady Stanton, and Susan B. Anthony. Over the next decade she rose to become a second-echelon leader in the radical suffragist wing, helping to organize lobbies and writing for the *Revolution*, called by Parker Pillsbury and Mrs. Stanton "the Great Organ of the Age." Isabella made a tour of Illinois, Iowa, and Kansas in 1870, addressing suffrage groups, forming "parlor associations," and distributing tracts. There was no longer any scorn for Abbey Kelleyism, and Isabella developed into a distinguished public speaker. Putting her knowledge of the law to good use, she drafted with her husband the first Connecticut law giving distinct equal property rights to married women, a law finally enacted by the General Assembly in 1877, seven years after its first introduction. Meanwhile, she organized a national woman's suffrage convention in Washington, D.C., to publicize her contention that women were entitled to the vote under the citizenship provision of the Fourteenth Amendment. She memorialized Congress to that effect, arguing that no new constitutional amendment was required. Representative George W. Julian and Samuel Bowles, editor of the *Springfield Republican*, became allies of the Hookers.[21]

It was during her first suffrage convention in Washington that Isabella met Victoria Claflin Woodhull and was swept into her train. Isabella was slowly learning that reform activism could require association with flamboyant, even disreputable, personalities. Much of her social snobbery had already fallen away, and she found in the militancy of the radical feminists something like real disregard for social niceties and fastidious friendships. From being a starchy upholder of manners and morals, Isabella changed into a dogged defender of people like Mrs. Woodhull, whose sexual irregularities and general naughtiness offended the rest of the Beechers. It was a part, undoubtedly, of Isabella's feminist ideology.

But it was also an element of her messianic identity which required her, as she confided to her secret notebooks, to be "all things to all men." In 1873 she published *Womanhood: Its Sanctities and Fidelities*, which made a frank argument for sex education, especially of boys, and supported Josephine Butler's campaign to repeal England's Contagious Diseases Act. By providing for the regulation and inspection of prostitution, the act, in the view of feminists, upheld the sexual double standard. Isabella's tract, while ostensibly a liberated view of sexuality, actually argued for the repression of sex through voluntary self-limitation by husbands who could not expect their delicate and far less amatory wives to submit to their excessive demands.[22]

Victoria Woodhull figured very largely and catastrophically in the lives of all the Beechers, particularly Isabella and Henry. Space does not permit discussion of the Beecher-Tilton adultery scandal, but Mrs. Woodhull's role in it must be mentioned in connection with Isabella Hooker. *Woodhull & Claflin's Weekly*, Victoria's newspaper, published the first accusations of adultery against Henry Ward Beecher. The decision to publish involved not only Victoria's commitment to free love (a doctrine she later renounced) but also revenge against Harriet Beecher Stowe, who had caricatured Victoria in her novel, *My Wife and I*. The repercussions of Victoria's act were terrific, and the scandal, complete with court battles and ecclesiastical councils, dragged on for almost a decade. Isabella, on the basis of corroborative evidence from Stanton and Anthony, chose to side with Victoria.

The rest of the Beechers were horrified, not simply at Isabella's disloyalty to Henry, but also at her repeated attempts to invade Henry's church in order to issue a confession from the pulpit in his name. Her addiction, as they saw it, to strange friendships and even stranger ideas, could no longer be tolerated. Victoria Woodhull was responsible, it is said, for convincing Isabella that she was a powerful spiritualistic medium and a messiah. "No one could understand," Mrs. Stowe bitterly told a friend, "the secret of her influence over my poor sister—an incredible infatuation continuing even now. I trust God will in some way deliver her for she was and is a lovely woman and before this witch took [control] of her we were all so happy."[23]

Despite Isabella's frequent descriptions of herself as eminently sympathizing and tactful, she sometimes exhibited a curious insensitivity to the feelings of others. She projected a kind of theatrical self-awareness and had a tendency to manipulate people and events to produce dramatic effects. When, for example, her brother James wrote her a confidential letter about his wife's alcoholism, she immediately despatched it to John, with directions to their daughter to "read the first page aloud to you—in a low pathetic voice—and see if the style does not remind you of Dickens." This incapacity to enter fully into her brothers' and sisters' feelings was to harm her standing in the family. Even less than they could she distinguish between private and public matters. And so, while she viewed her public statements in the Tilton affair as the debt owed to honesty and the sexual single standard, her family concluded that Isabella's attacks on Henry were instigated by Victoria Woodhull for her own dark purposes. And, moreover, the peculiar character of Isabella's speeches and acts was put down to mental disease. To Eliza Stowe, Harriet wrote, "Your aunt is like many monomaniacs, all right if the wrong string is not jarred."[24]

There was undoubtedly a degree of self-protection in the Beechers' attribution of craziness and gullibility to their sister, but it cannot be denied that her behavior was extremely provocative. Her siblings ostracized her, when they were not imploring her to come to her senses and repudiate Victoria Woodhull. There were even accusations by Henry's wife that Isabella was trying to blackmail him. John Hooker was overwhelmed by the scandal and his wife's part in it. Though he was a sincere feminist, he was essentially a private, prudish man. He would have preferred to continue with his gardening, versifying, and secret giving, rather than to become the subject of gossip and the object of contempt. When their neighbors forbade Isabella to enter their homes, John felt he had no choice but to share in her punishment. In 1874 he took Isabella to Europe for an extended stay, hoping to wait out the scandal. Though skeptical of her claims, he investigated psychic phenomena and was gradually converted to Spiritualism. When they returned to Hartford in 1876, the situation had brightened somewhat. The cabin-fever atmosphere began dissipating and the neighbors slowly let down the bars to hospitality. Even while they were reacquiring social acceptablility, however, John found himself domiciled with a wife whose delusions seemed almost monstrous to a man of his equable, conventional nature.[25]

Whenever he would try to argue Isabella out of her messianic fantasies, she would harangue him by the hour about the sinfulness of his attempts to thwart the Grand Design and choke off her "individuality." She had long since stopped attending Congregational churches and cleaved to Trinity, Episcopal, all the while compiling and laboriously annotating a series of notebooks which recorded spiritual visitations, divine illuminations, and prophecies of millennial grandeur (see chapter 10). Out of loyalty to Isabella, John also left the Congregational church and seemed stalled in a half-blown Christian spiritualism that was tepid by his wife's standards. She continually upbraided him for his lack of faith. Their moderate wealth had been consumed by financial reverses, sponsorship of reform causes, and their flight to Europe. While John grimly set himself to retrench and recoup, Isabella dozed catlike on their tin roof, receiving spirit rappings through her parasol.[26]

The years from 1877 to her death at the age of eighty-four were to outward appearances sedate in all respects but those connected with feminism and Spiritualism. Besides converting her husband and their son Ned, Isabella found a warily receptive audience for her spiritualistic teachings in her sisters. They seem to have been largely ignorant of her private visions, but the Beechers still concurred in regarding her as slightly aberrant. In 1896 Isabella served as an official at the World's Congress of Religions, where she read a universal creed of her own devising, with statements taken from the world's major faiths. The Hookers gave lectures on Spiritualism in various Connecticut towns and sent communications to the *Banner of Light.* Isabella briefly corresponded with William James and Alfred Russel Wallace on psychic phenomena.

The death in 1886 of their daughter Mary was a terrible loss to the

Hookers, who devoted many evenings to conversing with her departed spirit. Isabella begged for assurances that Mary had not resented her mother's shrinking from physical embraces during the last stages of her consumption. The height of their experience came one day when Mary's spirit materialized before them on a mountainside. The sheer number of their acquaintances who dabbled in seances and automatic writing is amazing, although these sorts of diversions and investigations were taken for granted.

In 1888, for instance, Isabella wrote Alice that she was on her way to "a social gathering of spiritualists this evening in connection with a missionary sewing society." Whether her messianic dream had withered completely is difficult to judge. Isabella continued to repeat that "there is so much work for me to do in the spiritual realm." Her final resting place of faith seems to have been a withdrawal to a more modest perception of her lifework. "As yet we are on the threshold of these great palaces of truth wherein dwelleth righteousness. Let us all contribute our mite to the building and furnishing and great shall be our reward."[27]

PART 3

THE PROPHETS

5 *EDWARD BEECHER*

> The change which he meditated in the theology of the church, he sometimes compared to that from the Ptolemaic to the Copernican, from the Geocentric to the heliocentric system of astronomy. To be a moral Copernicus, he confessed was his ambition, his idol.

As characterized by his admiring younger brother Charles, Edward Beecher believed he had been appointed to a very special role in the destiny of nations. He thought he was a prophet and a general of the Lord's hosts, identifying himself with Moses, Joshua, and Caleb. This assurance of being entrusted with a holy mission was not in itself strange for a Beecher, but in Edward the idea was peculiarly strong and explicit, and peculiarly doomed to disappointment.[2]

He was much like his brothers and sisters in having a large fund of energy, tremendous drive, and a nervous disposition. His capacity for work and his tolerance for discomfort were remarkable. Edward was also like them in having "quite a nonchalantic air" in his dress and bearing, and in having, though he was eminently respectable, enough idiosyncrasies to be considered eccentric by his contemporaries. Growing up in East Hampton, "he was always so in the sphere of his father's mind" that he was in deeper sympathy with Lyman's teaching, and formed a closer filial bond than perhaps any of the children, Catharine excepted.[3]

In 1818 he entered Yale, where he more than fulfilled Lyman's expectations. "Edward has just returned to College in good health and with every prospect of making a first rate scholler," ran a typical paternal report. Edward went on to win the Berkleian Prize in classics and graduated as valedictorian. Under the drilling of Chauncey A. Goodrich, professor of rhetoric and oratory, Edward became a gifted speaker. His father boasted of one exercise, "he poured it out Lyman Beecher like and made the class stare." It was also to Goodrich, rather than the college chaplain, that Edward turned for spiritual counseling.

Edward Beecher

He was converted in his senior year, after experiencing "a sort of unnerving despondency." Unlike George, he did not undergo a protracted harrowing. Although Edward's conversion experience was painful in some respects, in the end, Charles said, it was like a planet slipping back into orbit. Yet despite the fact that he had aspired to the ministry since early boyhood, Edward made no immediate plans to attend divinity school. About this time he received the first in a series of spiritual influxes which he believed came directly from God. He began to have faint but precious glimmerings of some specially consecrated role, and at graduation time he wrote Catharine:

> I feel very little anxiety for my future life; whether I live or die, am prosperous or unfortunate, am distinguished or unknown matters little to me. I feel willing to trust all to providence. I feel assured that I have something to do before I die and when that is done, I should rejoice to leave this for a better world. I habitually think of death with pleasure and when I am dejected and depressed I can more easily elevate my spirits by thinking on death and heaven than in any other way. How sweet will be the heavenly rest. . . .[4]

Edward had courted a New Haven girl, unconverted and in other ways unacceptable to his family, and he dutifully decided against marrying her. The next two years he spent in Hartford, where he was headmaster of the Hartford Grammar School. Though he managed the school ably, he disliked the business of having "to beat knowledge into thick sculls." Evidently feeling a more certain call to the ministry, he entered Andover, but studied there less than a year before accepting a coveted tutorship at Yale College in May of 1825. "New Haven is the best place for you, both as it concerns Papa, George and yourself," Catharine observed, adding complacently, "I cannot say that I ever feared much that you would be much altered by Andover . . . but still I should prefer you should have models more to my taste."

She meant, of course, that Andover's theological conservatism was anathema to the Beechers. These two eldest children were strongly attached to each other, intimately involved in each other's plans and projects, and given to sage pronouncements of approbation or rebuke of their younger siblings' behavior. Where Catharine was exigent and officious, however, Edward was mild and diplomatic. As his brothers and sisters passed into adolescence, Edward became a kind of second father to them. If Mary was perplexed by her studies and found the learned commentaries in Lyman's library dry and discouraging, she would write to her brother:

> [I] wish I could study it with you, how often have I tho't so, when I have met with any beautiful passage or any part that needed explanation. I do not forget that none teacheth like God . . . but still I suppose he works by means and tho' I may not chuse I should rejoice if you were the instrument.[5]

He adopted a similar role in his relations with the undergraduates at Yale, although Charles exaggerated when he later wrote that Edward had virtually wrought a revival in the College. A student of that time, later a colleague of Edward's, stated that "there was no general religious awakening in college during my student life." Edward undoubtedly encountered cases of "infidelity" among his collegians, and perhaps set a boy or two back on the path to piety, but the perennial undergraduate flouting of traditional religious observances was often cried up as rampant irreligion. Serving as unofficial chaplain to such a flock was good preparation for greater labors. Lyman was grooming Edward to be his chief successor, and was seeking an outstanding pastorate for his brightest son. "I hope," Catharine urged him, that "Providence may make you[r] way plain so that you may at last be led as a fellow labourer with Papa to that peculiarly interesting and desolated field" of Unitarian Boston. Lyman announced to Edward the possibility of a professorship at Dartmouth, but pressed him in the same breath to turn it down. If he must be a professor, let him wait for an opening at Yale; but in the final analysis, "if your feelings and judgment coincide with mine, I think you will prefer [real?] pastoral life."[6]

When Dartmouth formally asked Edward to accept the professorship, he was very taken with the idea of teaching moral philosophy and leading a retired, studious life. "I need more intellectual growth," "I like the country best for my health," he wrote his father. Most of all he wanted the leisure, and a small but assured income, to pursue a topic which was to become one of his major interests, "Experimental religion as connected with the culture of all the human faculties." Lyman brought great pressure to bear on Edward to incline him, instead, to an active parish ministry. His influence secured Edward a call from the prestigious Park Street Church in Boston. Edward had, to be sure, distinguished himself in his studies and when he assisted his father during revivals. He was a preacher and evangelist of promise, even if he was a neophyte. Nevertheless, it is difficult to know exactly what prompted such a call to a man as young and untried as Edward Beecher, who was barely twenty-three. Apart from Lyman's activity on Edward's behalf, the church must have had great expectations. He was ordained on December 26, 1826, and installed the following day, his father preaching the installation sermon.[7]

Edward faced special problems at Park Street Church. Evangelicals considered it "the Gibraltar of orthodoxy," but Unitarians scoffed at it as "Brimstone Corner." In his very first pastorate Edward Beecher was expected not only to acquit himself well but also to stand forth as a slayer of Unitarianism in its home territory. Despite his father's backing and proximity, or perhaps because of it, he had a difficult time. It started auspiciously enough. The church committee had taken the special step, probably in deference to Lyman's views, of prohibiting liquor at the installation ceremonies. On this the church and society and their new pastor were agreed. Edward threw himself into the work with characteristic abandon and rigorously applied the discipline of the church to errant members, particularly in cases of fornication and drunkenness. Although the chastening was tempered with mercy, a number of cases eventually ended in excommunication, but only after the most careful investigations and negotiations with the offenders.

Far from making the new minister unpopular, his strictness commended him to the militantly puritan flock. He drove himself so hard that he was obliged to request a vacation only eighteen months after his settlement, in order to rest his nerves. He went off to Maine, where his stepmother had relatives, including a cousin whom Edward began courting. Although he was supposed to be recuperating, he preached a revival instead, and returned to Park Street crowned with the laurels of a distant victory. In 1830 the church and society asked him to offer an evening lecture series and he refused. Dissatisfaction with his ministry began spreading. Unimpressive preaching, which seems an unlikely reason, was the complaint of one parishioner, who assailed Beecher in a letter so insulting that the church officially discountenanced it. Ebenezer Parker berated Beecher for his shortcomings, complaining of the small return on "the great sacrafices" entailed in supporting him, and comparing him unfavorably with the "men of the most brilliant talents" who had preceded him.[8]

Beecher had been married only a few months when Parker's missive arrived, bearing the news that there was widespread dissaffection and disillusionment among the congregation. If, as Parker charged, Lyman had been warned, he had kept it from Edward. Just when Edward was settling comfortably into domestic life with Isabella[9] and congratulating himself on his blessed labors in Maine, he received this startling disclosure. Though he could claim plenty of support among the membership, he realized it was a serious matter. He had been preoccupied with outside tasks, though in all fairness he had been brought to Boston with the idea of serving as his father's lieutenant. He had assisted Lyman in a revival and had been set to work as a controversialist for the *Spirit of the Pilgrims* as well. But even more engrossing than these tasks were his private thoughts, speculations "on the profoundest questions" of sin, accountability, and regeneration.[10]

There had been a serious doctrinal stumbling block to his acceptance of the Park Street call—namely, the proper mode of administering baptism. Lyman had responded to Edward's doubts by dismissing them out of hand. Simple reliance on Scripture was his unalterable rule, or so he claimed, and he recommended it to Edward, for

> What you do know from the bible on these subjects is enough without ecclesiastical history and combats with Windmills in the fog of distant ages. . . . And tho your extreme conscientiousness would be appreciated by heaven it would not be I think by man certainly not by some who might lay hold of it as the occasion of mischief. . . .

Though he might take pride in his son's intellecutal curiosity and encyclopedic learning, Lyman felt he ought to put a curb on Edward's restless habit of inquiry. Notwithstanding Beecherism and Taylorism, which was only doctrine "accommodated to use," after all, Lyman mistrusted the speculative frame of mind. He was fated, within a few years, to be accused of neology himself, but in the meantime he considered his own orthodoxy unimpeachable and wanted Edward's to stay within bounds. With Edward it was always the case that "my mind refuses to rest, and my conscience is unsatisfied until I can survey the field so as to convince myself." But with his canny father urging him to keep silent, Edward finally suppressed his doubts and agreed to be ordained with the issue of baptism unresolved.[11]

If he had been against ventilating scruples about baptismal modes, Lyman was all the more anxious to discourage Edward from airing his convictions on the all-encompassing themes of Original Sin and the character of God. Edward would later publish a book on baptism, heavily philological and patristic, whose tone was so judicious and irenic that Baptists alone found it offensive. But his new views on the history of redemption were such as to shock and dismay evangelicals when finally published some twenty-five years after their inception. The fact that Edward had been, as he confided to Lyman, vouchsafed a series of divine illuminations corroborating his novel views, did not allay his father's fears.[12]

Edward Beecher believed (as did his brother Charles) that God himself had put the seal on his theological innovations, but there may be a more naturalistic explanation overlooked by the two brothers in their desire to give Edward absolute precedence. In the first place, he was carefully and laboriously studying the Church Fathers at the time his revelations occurred. The special subject of inquiry was baptism, but in the course of his readings he was bound to come across a broad range of cosmological and soteriological thought, as, for example, the *Peri Archon* of Origen, whose ideas on baptism Beecher appears to have consulted.

Although Beecher never acknowledged the influence of Origen on his own theology, and may in fact have arrived at his idea of preexistence entirely independently of him, it nevertheless seems likely that the Greek theologian molded, if he did not directly inspire, Edward Beecher's Copernican revolution in theology. Like Origen, Beecher resorted to the theory of the preexistence of souls in order to account for the diversity of human fates in a universe where freedom of the will was central to God's redemptive purposes. And it is possible to see Origen's universalism influencing Beecher's later views of future retribution. Beecher's ideas were not, however, merely repristinated Origenic heresies. He specifically took issue with Origen on several important points and, while not a wholehearted critic of the Alexandrian Father, Beecher was nevertheless severe in his judgments against his errors. In seeking other explanations for Edward Beecher's peculiar doctrines than the one he himself gave, we may conjecture that the exposure to Origen was crucial.[13]

The credit, or blame, for Edward's abrupt recoil from New England orthodoxy could just as well have fallen on William Ellery Channing, whose influence Beecher did acknowledge, with gratitude. He was an unlikely candidate to become an ardent admirer of Channing's. He had applauded his father's decision to take the battle against Unitarianism into its home ground, which he regarded, with proper evangelical horror, as a city of snares. When Catharine, then in the turmoil of religious doubt, ventured there in 1822, Edward pleaded with her not to risk it. "I fear to have you go [to Boston] in your present state of mind." As late as 1826, of course, he was identified with the New Haven party and was, to all appearances, a thoroughgoing Taylorite.

But disillusionment with Taylor had set in when Edward was grappling with the baptismal question. "I have not been in circumstances favourable to the candid discussion of the subject," he had complained to Lyman. "I have said little on the subject to Dr. Taylor, for in many respects I do not believe that he has examined it as attentively as I have, although his mind is decided."

Edward told himself that he could not shirk the duty of intellectual honesty, not even though older men like Taylor and Lyman Beecher bypassed "candid discussion" to settle on the false bottom of received opinion. They might regard his scrupulousness as a symptom of arrested adolescence or intellectual arrogance, but he was certain that God required men to seek the whole truth. Therefore, when he was faced with Channing's views of God and man, which were clearly at variance with those of his teachers, Beecher did not permit hereditary prejudices to interfere with his reading of Channing. He found, in Channing's emphasis on the paternal character of God and the honorableness of his dealings with man, a vision of the created world which stimulated and exalted him. However much he might incline toward Channing's theology, Beecher retained deep conceptions of man's sinfulness. His developing theology sought to reconcile the two positions within a cosmological framework of grand proportions.[14]

These ideas were not presented publicly until 1853. For the present Edward yielded to his father's importunings. Lyman was not alone in wanting his son to muffle his heresies. The Footes had long ago feared that Calvinistic doctrines were driving Roxana crazy. Conversely, Edward's current views were attributed to mental strain. "Many who once loved and respected me," he mourned, wondered "whether I had not lost the balance of my mind, and become unconsciously the slave of that visionary certainty which is caused by nervous excitement." At best, then, his family and friends regarded him as an enthusiast, although it is uncertain whether they were more upset by his claim to divine illuminations or by his heretical ideas. In the meantime, there were present problems of a critical nature. He had faced down the opposition within Park Street Church and might have remained there, although ministers in such situations often found their lot miserable. But Lyman had more plans for Edward. The West, not Boston, was the new theater of Christian warfare, and Edward must be on hand for the great battle.[15]

Providence, in the persons of the earnest Yale graduates known as the Illinois Band, drew Edward's attention to "the great western Valley," where a college was established under Yale Band sponsorship.

It needed his leadership badly. His work as a tutor had not been in vain. Since, as Lyman delicately phrased it, there were "many and great things in favor of his going, and nothing very inviting in his remaining where he is," the offer of a college presidency was opportune. Edward had wanted to instruct and spiritualize the young men of Dartmouth, and how much more pressing was the cause of Illinois College! For the next thirteen years he was president, often in absentia, of this small but hopeful Western school. It was a period of activity even more intense and unremitting than the Boston pastorate. Besides fulfilling the conventional duties of a college president, the chief of which were instruction and fund-raising, he reared a large family, devoted thousands of hours to secret prayer and meditation on his theology, researched and wrote his book on baptism, and supported the antislavery movement in Illinois.[16]

As a Beecher who was still associated with Taylor in the public mind, Edward was suspected of unsound doctrines from the moment he arrived in Jacksonville. Both his theology, or rather the New Haven views still imputed to him, and his ideas of reform brought odium on Illinois College. And as often as the Yale Band might profess freedom from strict New England notions of church polity, they were as often accused of hauling the Trojan horse of independency before the walls of presbyterianism. Beecher was astute enough to recognize how sore an issue it was, and when William Carter and Julian Sturtevant decided to organize a Congregationalist church in Jacksonville, he carefully dissociated himself and the college from their act. Equally hazardous was the course the New Englanders were taking with regard to home missions. A number of the Yale Band were agents of the American Home Missionary Society, which the Ohioan Joshua Wilson declared aimed at nothing less than to "overthrow Presbyterianism as it now exists." Conciliating such men as Wilson was impossible, for part and parcel of his distrust of the AHMS was his dread of Yankee theologies and their purveyors, as shown in the Old School effort to convict Beecher and his colleagues of heresy described earlier.[17]

As if it were not enough that Beecher and his faculty had taught their young charges the doctrine of "voluntary depravity" (as the Old School sneered) and gotten off scot free, he adopted the still more obnoxious heresy of immediate emancipation for slaves. His close friendship with the martyred Elijah Lovejoy, and his own publications and activities in behalf of the Illinois Antislavery Society, caused the college to be stigmatized as a propagator of "ultra" reforms. "Many individuals of wealth and social standing and even of religious reputation," who were in a position to aid the school either hung back or openly castigated its president and faculty.[18]

With the panic of 1837 Beecher, like his father at Lane Seminary, had to sacrifice inordinate amounts of time, energy, and pride to the task of imploring pious Eastern benefactors to sustain the college, which had rafts of equally impecunious and worthy competitors. Beecher's devotion to the ideal of educating the West had not diminished, but he was discouraged and frustrated. His patient, timid wife had suffered many privations on his account. When she first arrived in Illinois, she had had to live "sucker style" in a rude log dwelling. Malaria was endemic; a Morgan County jest had it that "everybody is shaking so hard with the durn ague, they can't find time to die." The Beechers' first son was mentally defective, the aftermath of a childhood disease. Mrs. Beecher bore six more children during their stay in Jacksonville. Cholera nearly killed her, and her resulting weakness and invalidism must have grieved her husband.[19]

There were happier times, of course, as when Beecher was chosen to make a welcoming address for Daniel Webster and shared the platform with him. But on balance, Beecher felt called to the more impelling pursuit of spreading correct views of God. By way of apology for his scholarly *Baptism*, he wrote:

> Almost exhausted by efforts to sustain the college over which I preside[d], in a time of unparalleled pecuniary embarrassment, without an adequate library at the college, compelled to visit distant libraries, some more than a thousand miles distant, and to make researches at long intervals, loaded with pecuniary cares and anxieties, compelled often to write on journeys, in steamboats and canal-boats, and taverns, no one can be more deeply sensible than I am of the necessary imperfections of my performance.

Mingled with the humility of such a statement was frustration and, perhaps, resentment over thwarted ambitions. Beecher was ambitious not merely to do good but to revolutionize man's ways of thinking about God and about his own soul. He displayed a confidence in the persuasive force of reasonable argument so characteristic of his age, but what gave his faith in free inquiry and rational discourse its poignancy was his conviction that he had been called by God to discharge a holy duty.

And so, like his brothers and sisters, Edward Beecher turned his prodigious energies to the work of making the nation see the truth.

The Beechers, their critics said, were not only arrogant, but they also had a penchant for championing outlandish ideas. The road to popularity seldom lies in the direction of zealotry. And it is equally true that those who seek to elevate private visions into universal systems of belief are doomed to dismissal as intellectual or spiritual cranks. Knowing that his own family treated his grand idea as a baroque curiosity, he aspired nevertheless to convert the entire Christian world to his theological vision. The energy and passion with which he undertook this work are nothing short of amazing, and one hardly knows whether to attribute his single-mindedness to perversity or to intellectual integrity.

Although Beecher was quick to heap scorn on other men's craving for eminence and deprecated such tendencies in himself, the appetite was still there. Thus, when he repeatedly belittled a Baptist polemicist's reputation as a latter-day Jonathan Edwards, Beecher was poking fun at a distinction he himself privately desired. His pride and his yearning for worldly acclaim were strong, and he often prayed to God to deliver him from them. Returning East, where he could carry on his writing with fewer distractions and make the most of his opportunities for research, would enable him to bring his redemptive scheme to fruition. He therefore resigned the presidency of Illinois College, although he continued to raise money for the school. His father and he were instrumental in the founding of the Society for the Promotion of Collegiate and Theological Education at the West (SPCTEW).[20]

Salem Street Church in Boston's North End, one of the hivings-out of Lyman Beecher's old Hanover Street Church, called Edward to be their pastor. He was installed there on March 13, 1844. "The present call," he wrote the church, "has also brought to a crisis my deliberations on other plans, long since formed . . . the execution of which, I have seen for a few years past, might require a residence in the East." This oblique reference to his gestating theology was amplified in his diary, where he recorded, "It is proposed to extirpate from the Christian System the common doctrine of the fall in Adam." He aimed at nothing less than the overthrow of Augustinian theology. Beecher's aim was to elucidate his own Christian System in a treatise learned and exhaustive yet persuasive to the popular mind. Considering the task he had set himself of renovating theology, and through it the Kingdom of God, and given the conditions under which he worked, his achievement was remarkable. He closely supervised the work of his church, preached regularly to large congregations, and continued speaking and writing on political and moral issues, all the while laboring secretly over his huge book.[21]

In 1845 came a controversy with Amos Anson Phelps in the *Boston Recorder*, a religious newspaper, over the policy of the American Board of Commissioners for Foreign Missions toward slavery. No mere paper war, it marked Beecher's alienation from the Garrisonians, who attacked his doctrine of "organic sin" as a "jingle of words without meaning." Beecher allied with Calvin Stowe and Leonard Bacon in supporting the ABCFM's policy of noninterference with slavery. He contended that the sin of slavery involved the whole of society (hence its "organic" quality), but in such a way that the simple fact of owning slaves did not make a given individual a sinner, provided he was otherwise religious and humane. To proscribe such a man was beyond the necessities of Christian duty. Bacon, who was spokesman for the American Colonization Society, and Stowe, who was also a colonizationist, were sufficiently conservative to be regarded as hostile to all Abolitionism. Beecher, though a conservative abolitionist himself, came under fire as a fence-sitter. One of Phelps's friends thus described Edward Beecher's dilemma:

> [I saw] Dr. Bacon and E. Beecher at New Haven, and sounded them [out]. They both wish, and honestly so, I believe, that the Board should take different ground from that on which they [the ABCFM] now stand. But they are both afraid of being among the "abolitionists"—and will be sure to avoid any course which will compel them to seem to act in unison with such men as you: indeed they almost so said in express terms.

Beecher's middle ground on abolitionism is of interest here as representative of his family's stance in the late 1840s and early 1850s. With the death of his brother George in 1843, the family had lost its most militant abolitionist.[22]

Other causes engaged Edward's attention during this period. He helped forward his sister Catharine's education plan for the West, which dove-tailed with the efforts of the SPCTEW. A holy war must be prosecuted by female teachers and young theologues against "our crafty antagonists" from Rome, who were plotting to sap the foundations of the Republic from beachheads in the "mission-field of the Great Valley." Edward was terribly alarmed over the incursions of Roman Catholics everywhere. He saw them as diabolically clever, amoral schemers whose end was to subvert republican freedom and substitute popish idolatry and authoritarianism. These views, which represented no advance in liberality over Lyman's notorious *Plea for the West*, received detailed documentation in Edward's *Papal Conspiracy Exposed*, a scholarly diatribe—but a diatribe nonetheless.[23]

Temperance also enlisted his energies, as Isabella Hooker noted, in a revealing description of her brother:

> He goes to the bottom of everything he touches mentally—his play is harder study than the labor of most men. Chess for instance is his diversion now—and he sits like a marble statue by the hour together—studying games from one of the five great volumes which adorn his library. I wouldn't be the wife of such a man for a great deal—but I like to observe such minds. I find that he and many other competent men are intent on enforcing Maine law in the city—and they seem to have little apprehension of any failure.

Beecher was so much in earnest about temperance that he studied the subject exhaustively. His church called upon him to provide a learned opinion on the question of whether wine might be used in communion. (Fired with zeal, they even went so far as to investigate Jewish methods of extracting the juice of raisins for nonintoxicating communion "wine" in accord with ancient practice.) Another sketch of Beecher from this same period stressed, in addition to his intellectuality and reforming zeal, Edward's ability to mingle with diverse groups of men:

> Unlike many of his cloth, he does not deem it a duty to shut himself up in his study continually, for fear of rendering himself "too common" to excite the wonder of the people on the Sabbath. . . . You will see him in the streets, and at the exchange, in the reading-rooms, in the police court, at the public meetings in Faneuil Hall and Tremont Temple. He is a sociable, accessible, generous man, and capital company. . . . It is because he mingles with the people that he is in advance of many of his clerical brethren.[24]

Although he easily established himself as one of Boston's leading clergymen, Edward soon thought of moving on. Even before 1848, when he began pressing inquiries about a New York City pulpit, he found his Salem Street salary inadequate. In addition to high board bills for his retarded son, Edward had to pay heavy medical fees for several other children—he had a sickly brood—while paying for the private schooling of his older sons. Henry C. Bowen, an extremely influential member of Henry Ward Beecher's Plymouth Church, was happy to look after Edward's interests in New York. When it appeared that he was ready to leave Boston, however, he suddenly received an offer to edit a new religious journal. Leading Boston Congregationalists entreated Edward to accept the post. It was widely believed,

Edward told Henry, that "none of the papers represent the congregationalism of New England worthily," and it was his own opinion that "New England is in perishing need of a paper, worthy of her position and principles." Though his friends thought that "my nervous system was too sensitive for the wear and tear of editorial life," Edward finally refused a call to New York. He became editor-in-chief of the *Congregationalist*, whose first issue appeared on May 26, 1849, declaring its platform to be Congregational and Calvinist unity and the non-extension of slavery in the territories.[25]

The supplementary income was welcome, but the editorial tasks came on top of a grueling self-imposed schedule. Only a man accustomed to writing at length every day could have survived such a program. In 1853, at last, he published the matured system first conceived in 1826. *The Conflict of Ages,* long since forgotten, was Edward Beecher's major contribution, as he deemed it, to theology. By pushing back the Fall to a previous state of existence, and treating present life as a remedial stage wherein a long and truly suffering God acts to save the incarnated souls he loves so tenderly, Beecher sought to provide a vitalizing restatement of Calvinism. He wanted to retain profound views of human depravity in conjunction with a new moral understanding of how and why God's eternal decrees operated to save the deserving.

Whatever hopes Beecher may have entertained of unifying Christians behind his views, he met with tremendous hostility from all the nominally Calvinistic camps, while other evangelicals were equally baffled or offended by the *Conflict of Ages.* However much evangelicals praised him for his erudition and judicious style of criticism, they treated his major propositions as mystical arcana. Preexistence was equated with Brahminism and Gnosticism (even though Beecher explicitly repudiated Gnostic thought), while his patripassianism was dismissed as an ancient heresy in no need of reviving.

Beecher received a far more appreciative, if dissenting, hearing from Universalists and Unitarians (Moses Ballou, Thomas Starr King) and others even farther from the pale (Henry James, Sr.). One Universalist, long an attendant at Plymouth Church, gloatingly demanded of Henry, "Has not your brother, Dr. Edward Beecher, written a book which is giving (with many of your own Church and communion) the death blow to 'Orthodoxy?'" Beecher had expected opposition and misunderstanding but was unprepared for the storm of criticism and the intimations that the labor of a lifetime was just another outburst of Beecher eccentricity. In the face of the "undeserved popular odium [raised] against me" by conservative Congregationalists, he resigned his post. He had never used the *Congregationalist* to spread his private views but felt that his resignation was necessary to protect the paper's reputation for orthodoxy and saneness.[26]

Edward remained with Salem Street Church for another two years, during which time he helped organize the Boston ministers against the Nebraska Act. It was also his particular influence on Harriet Stowe which prompted her to write her novel against the Fugitive Slave Law. Then, once again, he felt the urge to move to a new "sphere of great importance and extended influence." A Congregationalist church was being formed in Galesburg, Illinois, near Knox College. A concurrent appointment as Lecturer on Church Institutions at the new Chicago Theological Seminary made the call to Galesburg especially attractive, even though the lectureship was uncompensated and would require a weekly trip of 300 miles. Edward turned to Henry for financial help, since the Galesburg church could not pay full salary, but it was Calvin Stowe who finally undertook to raise the money, and Henry helped out later, when a tornado destroyed the church steeple.[27]

"All the ties are now cut, that hold me to New England," he exulted, "and I begin to realize that I am a Western man once more." His congregation parted with him tearfully. The council which declared in his favor took care to state that his "peculiar views" were not at issue, affirming their confidence that he was still "devoutly attached to the great principles of godliness." The people of Salem Street Church pleaded with him to stay, but he would not be swayed. Neither they, nor he, saw his departure as a flight, but he was bitterly disappointed in the reception of his book and wanted time to prepare a sequel which, he prayed, would move men to acceptance where the first volume had failed.

Once in Galesburg, he became a popular man right away, as well as a local character. His absentmindedness and other foibles endeared him to a people who also liked his playful humor and refusal to stand on ceremony. Four of his sons attended Knox College, and his brother Charles served briefly as professor of rhetoric (elocution). Edward made the weekly trip to Chicago by train. Though stung almost to despair over the fate of the *Conflict*, he took comfort from thoughts of God's work in the West: "He will redeem this continent, he will redeem this great West. Visions of his glory were around me when I came on the cars from Chicago. As I looked over the prairie, I saw the glory of God."[28]

An old feud between Jonathan Blanchard, president of Knox, and

George Washington Gale, Galesburg's founder, eventually involved Beecher. When Gale tried to pack the college board to insure Presbyterian domination and Blanchard opposed him, Beecher sided with the Congregational faction. His support of the Blanchard party was so vocal that the pro-Gale, Presbyterian forces accused Beecher of exhibiting a "fiendlike malignity." Like so many other ecclesiastical struggles of an equally unedifying character, this one had a double origin in a bitter division over church polity and the slavery question. Increasingly, New England church polity was associated with free inquiry and abolitionism. It may be doubted whether Edward Beecher was in fact a conductor on the Underground Railway, but his support of antislavery remained strong. He was present when Lincoln debated Douglas at Galesburg and lived out the Civil War in Illinois. *The Concord of Ages*, published in 1860, was his response to critics of the *Conflict*, but the second book went largely unnoticed. Its publication preceded by three years Charles Beecher's trial for heresy, for having preached Edward's theology as well as liberal doctrines of his own. Edward, a widely acknowledged expert on Congregational councils, pleaded his brother's case before the Georgetown, Massachusetts, church and then successfully appealed it.[29]

In 1871, when Beecher was approaching his sixty-eighth year, a small group in his church tried to maneuver him out. The great majority of members came to his defense, but fearing disunity, he resigned and moved back East. He settled in Brooklyn, where he did editorial work for the *Christian Union*, Henry's paper, and worshipped at Plymouth Church. He continued his scholarly researches and published a *History of Opinions on the Scriptural Doctrine of Retribution*, in which he approximated to Charles's view that the punishment of sinners was not endless but rather reformatory. The Brooklyn church councils of 1874, called to try Henry for his alleged misconduct in the case of Elizabeth and Theodore Tilton, again found Edward in the role of advocate for an accused brother. If he had any doubts about Henry's character, he kept them strictly to himself and "stood like a rock before Henry when Slander assailed him."[30]

In 1885 Edward became stated supply at the small Parkville Congregational Church, near Brooklyn. A railroad accident in 1889 cost him a leg and put an end to his trips to the Parkville Church. Thereafter he had to content himself with occasional services to Henry's flock. He had taken such pride in his athletic abilities that his family expected him to be more than normally depressed over the amputation. Instead, while recuperating, he philosophically discussed the

Andover controversy with Charles, "and the Biblical doctrine of the resurrection–also whether the loss of hearing which Charles has suffered or the loss of a leg is greatest." He was later fitted with an artificial leg. The death of most of his children left Edward bereft of support, but "owing to the kindness of friends," he had "an ample income . . . and so the strain of poverty and the poor house is forever removed."

In 1891 Edward and Isabella adopted a daughter, Voice Adams, who helped care for them in their old age. His mental decline was rapid after this, but like his father at the same stage in life, he still craved useful activity, and Isabella wrote, "He thinks every day is Sunday. He wonders why we do not go to church." When he died in 1895, he received an Episcopal service, but his brother Thomas agreed to speak as well. "An avalanche does not stop for a tiny gravestone," Thomas Beecher intoned, underlining his conviction that the Beecher family's prodigious labors were only small steps and missteps in the inevitable march of godliness. He went on to stress his brother's faithfulness and holiness. The man who had aimed at becoming a second Jonathan Edwards, and even a Copernicus, in theology was remembered after all chiefly for his glowing piety. Of all the tributes to Edward Beecher, he himself would have chosen for his epitaph the simplest, that from a colleague at Chicago Theological Seminary who said, "Like the old Connecticut divine Dr. Bellamy, 'he made God great.'"[31]

6 *CHARLES BEECHER*

None of Lyman Beecher's children settled comfortably into the household of their father's faith. He did not encourage an unthinking submission to his theological views and, as has been seen, prodded his children into a precocious awareness of the complexities and difficulties of theology. But for all his fostering of their dialectical skills, Lyman was chiefly concerned with his children's religious experience. Conversion was for him, above all, a subduing of the proud and treacherous heart so that the loyalties and affections would come to center on God alone. This was his message to Catharine, who in the end did not heed it.

Himself a passionate man, Lyman did not mistrust passion or ardor in themselves. His success as a revivalist owed much to his ability to excite and channel the feelings in settings supercharged with emotionalism. Neither did he look upon the cultivated intellect with suspicion, as did the Methodists and many Baptists. That, too, could be enlisted in the service of God. What he did fear was the surrender of both emotion and intellect to an imperious self, which sought fulfillment in unsanctified strivings after sensual pleasure or worldly preeminence. Such a self was the subject of Lord Byron's poetry, and while Lyman deprecated the poet's self-absorption, he could comprehend it. Conversion, in Edwardsean terms, meant the loss of selfhood in love to being-in-general. The opposite development, exaltation of self, meant eternal ruin. It was precisely this craving to exalt self which seized Charles Beecher and made of him a romantic rebel against evangelical piety.

Charles Beecher's spiritual crisis received conventional treatment in his father's *Autobiography*, with many of its details suppressed or shaded to produce the effect of a supremely happy ending, complete with answers to Lyman's prayers. This chapter will aim at developing the story more fully and disclosing some of the conflicts that lay beneath the surface of family solidarity and loyalty. Because Charles's story is so well documented, it is possible to present details that are lacking for other members of the family. Thus the focus here will be on the period of crisis, with an epilogue relating the rather unexpected outcome.

As editor of his father's memoirs, Charles Beecher looked back on his own spiritual wanderings of 1834–45 as the crowning tragedy of Lyman's years at Lane Seminary:

> In addition to the suffering attendant upon the anti-slavery imbroglio, the assault upon his orthodoxy, the death of his [second] wife, and the sudden failure of his [financial] support, he was obliged to witness the descent of one of his sons and pupils into the midnight of fatalism, and to find his favorite author, President [Jonathan] Edwards, the occasion of the disastrous change.

As Charles thought, this episode was a key event in the Beecher family's history. But he mistook its significance when he characterized it as an ultimate triumph for Lyman, as the chapter heading, "The Lost Found," might suggest. The outcome actually pointed the way for the children's movement away from their father's orthodoxy, rather than vindicating it. At the same time, it marked Charles's acceptance of a species of evangelical theology, albeit of a highly individual character.[1]

When Charles matriculated at Bowdoin College he was only sixteen, but he became engaged in his freshman year to a cousin, Sarah Leland Coffin. He seems to have been a popular student. He was good-looking, frank, and affable, and was also a natural athlete. His considerable talents as a musician and linguist commended him to the faculty, who were delighted to have a son of Lyman Beecher among them. Always a serious-minded boy, he began a "protracted and ever unsuccessful struggle to bring myself to an ideal standard of perfection in the religious life." The same quest for perfection preceded George Beecher's suicide, but it began ordinarily enough for his younger brother. Charles asked his family for data for a spiritual autobiography, to discern "how the Lord has led me, to gather warning, instruction and energy." Scanning his short and uneventful life, he warmed with the conviction that God had only to "*perfect* in me the good work he has begun–I love to study myself."[2]

Not surprisingly, he found a program of seclusion and prayer unsettling to his health. He became dyspeptic; vigorous exercise and change of habits did not restore his sense of well-being. Meanwhile,

Charles Beecher

following Henry's lead, he developed a strong curiosity about phrenology and formed a phrenological study group at Bowdoin much like Henry's Amherst club. Charles's reflections on the implications of phrenology took a different direction from Henry's, however. Whereas Henry adduced phrenological doctrines as a welcome ally of Christianity, his brother argued that the new science, in common with Edwards's theology properly understood, destroyed any possibility of freedom of the will. Without free will, there could be no such thing as religious faith or hope. Both systems, to his mind, involved an iron determinism which could not be explained away.

New Haven Theology had developed in large part precisely to convince men that free agency was not only a reality but the keystone of God's system. Lyman's arguments about divine government and free agency did not convince Charles. Even Henry could not dissuade his brother from this stand. Charles found metaphysical speculation as "intensely exciting as it was new," and enjoyed vanquishing his earnest but inept classmates in philosophical debates. Although he nowhere recorded his arguments, we may assume that he attacked Edwards for not venturing an explanation of the state anterior to choice and that he interpreted phrenology as physical determinism along the lines of anatomy-as-destiny. Either position was destructive of freedom of the will and both taken together were lethal, since Charles apparently rejected any broader conceptions of contingency in the universe. Charles soon progressed from speculation to skepticism, finally lapsing into "entire disbelief" of revealed religion.[3]

In the staidly orthodox circles of Bowdoin, his "infidelity," which he flaunted undergraduate-fashion, was bound to create a sensation. He was not content to brood in his closet over these terrible themes; he wanted to dazzle the Maine farmboys and ministerial candidates with his superior knowledge. Charles went around drooping and glowering Byronically and trying to engage his friends in disputation. To his father and aunt he wrote:

> My *poem* that I spoke to you of, went off very well; but because the hero of it was an infidel, and killed himself, besides being a parricide and murderer, with the presum[p]tion to talk of happiness after death, it met with considerable criticism. Prof. [Egbert C.] Smyth said, "'twas a heathenish thing"—and somebody else said, "'twas hardly orthodox enough for Dr. Beecher's son!"

As provoking as this disclosure was meant to be, it was as much an appeal for help as a challenge. Charles sought a confrontation, hoping his father could overwhelm him in fair debate and bring him back to safety. At no time did he claim that his philosophical discoveries were liberating or gratifying, however much he may have enjoyed scandalizing the college. He had become "an infidel" precisely because he had once desired to perfect his Christian character.[4]

"I love to study myself" summed up his attitude and activities. He reveled in introspection, and by his own account, savored only "romance–poetry." The mood into which Charles had fallen was familiar to his family. They despised it as effete and narcissistic. Henry, for one, satirized "the *inwardism* of Germany and of the fluttery, callow imitators" in America, men like the "New England transcendentalists" who "only make a mock of their German brethren–They are like courteor[s] who imitate all the Kings defects–and lisp and stutter and limp because he does–whe[n] he does it by desease." The family concurred in viewing Charles's difficulties as the product of adolescence. His theological doubts were the cavilings of an argumentative boy, arrogant with newly discovered intellectual powers. Many young men, so the conventional wisdom ran, were made better Christians for having passed through trials of faith. Their attitude was one of guarded, prayerful optimism: once directly under Lyman's tutelage, Charles would weary of philosophizing and acknowledge that he was in error.[5]

Charles graduated from Bowdoin and, with Henry, rejoined the family at Walnut Hills, the little village where Lane Seminary was located. Lyman was hopeful that Charles would come around to sound beliefs and recruited an even more disputatious child, Catharine, to argue Charles out of his fallacies. Whether her weightiest arguments were simply unconvincing or whether her brothers tended to discount her opinions because of her sex, Catharine proved unsuccessful in reclaiming Charles for orthodoxy. As she herself was none too orthodox, her arguments about mental philosophy may have aggravated rather than alleviated Charles's disbelief. Lyman was well aware of the "immemorial tendencies to heresy and error" of mental philosophy and was anxious to turn Charles's thoughts toward more practical questions. Henry despaired of reasoning with him. They quarreled and for several years were almost strangers, where before they had been the closest companions. While Charles was experiencing "the prostration of all hope," his energetic brother attended classes, took copious notes, and approvingly epitomized Lyman's lectures and sermons ("Father preached to day on divine sovreignty–It was very clear.") Henry echoed Lyman's denunciations of balls, drink, nudity in art, and "sensual gratification" in general, exposed the sophistries of Universalism from a public platform, and threw himself into the task of becoming the model preacher, pastor, and evangelist.[6]

Henry, who was not without his own theological doubts, nevertheless chose to labor cheerfully. His very successes as an aspiring minister served to underscore Charles's rejection of that calling. No small part of the latter's unhappiness and resentment stemmed from the family's inflexible determination to make a minister of him. Lyman was adamant in his belief that all educated men of piety were morally obligated to become clergymen or missionaries. Where his sons were concerned, he invoked Roxana's deathbed covenant with God, dedicating her sons to him. In his deepening distress, Charles protested against both his father's exigency and his mother's deathbed decree. He felt himself both spiritually unfit for the role and temperamentally unsuited to it. He demanded the right to choose a different profession and told his family he was going to be a musician. The Beechers dismissed the idea. He would undoubtedly recover his faith, whereupon he would recognize where his duty and his talents lay. Instead of talking incessantly about "Romance" and setting up music as his idol, he ought to become sober-minded and open himself to religious influences.[7]

Charles insisted on exploring all his doubts, though he was repeatedly being told that they were baseless. Henry alone expressed open anger toward him. Whatever his sufferings, however, Charles knew that he was the object of affectionate concern, even when it took bullying forms. Esther and Lyman were especially skillful in reminding him of the gravity of his sin against his sainted mother, and while he debated Lyman with seeming insouciance, he felt he was sinning against him as well. Equally serious was the problem his irreligion created with regard to Sarah Coffin who, he decided, should not have to marry "a confirmed infidel." His love for Sarah had in any case cooled to a cousinly attachment. Whether to avoid disappointing family expectations, or whether he lacked the will to break off the engagement, his irresolution added another painful element to the process of alienation. He desperately wanted to be rescued from his spiritual, professional, and personal dilemma, but without hurting Lyman or Sarah.

In this keyed-up state of mixed anguish and expectation, Charles fell in love. Mary Wright, six years his junior and the daughter of one of Lyman's wealthiest parishioners, caught his eye in the winter of 1836. He concluded that his feeling for Sarah was simply a relic of "the usual impetuosity of boyhood," while his love for Mary was incandescent. Just as he had earlier thrown himself into a fever of speculation and sensibility, he now gave himself over to this new passion, "every nerve quivering with poetry and enthusiasm." He had to keep his quiverings well concealed, however, because Mary's family protected her jealously. Though she was barely in her teens when Charles fell in love with her, he thought of her as a full-blown woman, perfect in beauty and possessing a powerful intellect. Henry, who was also attracted to her, described her as "so fresh of face—so intelligent and pure, " and compared his own fiancée unfavorably to Mary.

At first Charles's delicacy over Sarah checked his amorous impulses. He still loved Sarah "as a sister" and pitied her for her "paralytic turns." But he soon experienced a veritable "delirium of love" for Mary Wright. Casting about for an honorable excuse to break his engagement, Charles revived the argument about his infidelity which made him "unfit for union with a religious person." He implored Edward Beecher, in whose home Sarah was living, to pave the way for a quiet break. Charles's actions were muddled at this point. He may have had genuine scruples about yoking Sarah to an unbeliever, but if it had been true that he was irretrievably lost in atheism, he could hardly have expected Nathaniel Wright, a Presbyterian elder, to look with favor on his suit.[8]

Surrounded, as he had always been, with family counselors at home and in school, Charles continued in defiance of their wishes. Henry accused him of following childish inclinations in place of duty and reminded him that he was wounding their father terribly. The entire family derided the notion that Charles was suited for the life of a professional musician. He then evolved the plan of becoming a professor of ancient and modern languages. With characteristic immodesty, he calculated that a mere year of preparation would be necessary if he resolved to "become at once a severe student and reserve only three or four hours a day to music." While struggling to find the right professional niche, he had also to deal with the problem of Sarah. He interrupted his studies to make a visit to Jacksonville, Illinois, but returned to Cincinnati without breaking the engagement. The matter remained unresolved for an entire year until March of 1838, when Charles wrote Isabella simply, "P.S. Connexion with Sarah terminated. Her character and conduct admirable. I remain at home a year at least—study languages with Stowe."[9]

At one point during this year, Charles moved out of his father's Walnut Hills home to take a cheap room in Cincinnati where he passed a wretched period trying to support himself by giving music lessons. Home had been an oppressive place from which, he told himself, he could only find relief by living as "an exile." He wanted to prove that he was not just a visionary adolescent, but he ended up in debt and "suffered to the verge of insanity" from loneliness and brooding. He was relieved when Lyman appeared and insisted on taking him home. This effort to free himself from dependency on his domineering family ended shabbily, but the embarassing dénouement to his first real assertion of independence actually stiffened his resolve to become free of both family and "respectable" conventional society.[10]

Since Lyman and the rest of the household seemed uncomprehending and insensitive, Charles turned to his half-sister Isabella for a confidante. Isabella was by far the prettiest of his sisters and regarded herself as a woman of boundless empathy. Since she was undergoing the stress of conversion, Charles became, rather incongruously, her spiritual counselor. He may be forgiven the rather superior tone of his letters to her, for he was perfectly sincere when he warned Isabella against allowing pride of intellect, his own besetting sin, to thwart "that religion which consists in humility and entire dependence [upon God]." He still hoped that some one would successfully contest his gloomy views and invited the help of Aunt Esther and his sister Mary, while seeming to shrink from them. "You will percieve," he wrote Isabella, "that this is not a matter to be talked about to Mary or to Aunt E. or any one–tho' you may use your own discretion." In other words, he did not guard his privacy as jealously as he claimed to. For that matter, his family did not scrupulously respect it. There was a season of continual correspondence. Thus Henry: "Read Charles letter in answer to George, poor fellow–he has suffered." They trained their thoughts on Charles's condition and cast about for remedies. George found a shocking parallel in his own parish:

> One young man, who had studied for the ministry, having studied Phrenology, drank in infidel principles, from some who have written on this subject, and rejected revealed religion as a vain thing. This shows how important it is for a minister to be acquainted with Phrenology, that he may point out the fallacies of infidels, who pervert it to their own ends.[11]

None of the Beechers blamed phrenology or philosophical inquiry, as such, for Charles's spiritual dilemma. Lyman's attitude is best seen in Henry's reflections on the case:

Some tho'ts suggested by Chas state

> It seems to me that nothing is more deplorable than a strong intellect, *acting the wrong way*, i.e., *a priori* instead of inductively. It seems to me that in metaphysics as in everything else we are to begin on facts, on the *underhill* side, and ascend so long as principles can be maintained consistently.
>
> A strong mind gets hold of principles far above his perfect controll, although he may in some measure grasp them. But *exact* reasoning on them is and must be eminently fallacious because, the least *variation*, the least over or understatement, the smallest change of revelation will destroy the truth of the thing started upon.
>
> Can I construct an irrefutable argument vs Fatality from facts upward? If I had no vexation to earn money—I would certainly *try*.

Underlying Henry's analysis was Lyman's belief in the superiority of common-sense reasoning, as well as his exasperation with youthful addiction to speculative modes of thought. Without common sense, Lyman had warned in 1835:

> No wonder that theology should be regarded as the region of chaos and old night—starless and dreamy—fanciful and feverish—where the atoms of truth and error hold everlasting conflict of attraction, and repulsion, and fermentation, and revolution—without the possibility of system, or knowledge, or obligation to know the truth, or accountability for error.

And was there not, on Henry's part, the suggestion that metaphysical inquiries were well enough for people like his brother, who had no "vexation to earn money," but unjustified for men of affairs like himself?[12]

Just as Charles's prideful intellect had alarmed his family, so his waxing self-confessed "enthusiasm" was seen as a bar to spirituality. They could partially excuse him on grounds of "Beecher temperament." Everyone knew that the Beechers were high-strung, moody, and vulnerable to emotional storms. But they found the prolongation of Charles's turbulent state abnormal and unconducive to right thinking and feeling. Surrounded by sage advisers (who perhaps mistook their importunity for tact), he had little excuse for continuing his rebellion against God. Although they correctly diagnosed his malady as an excess of feeling, they did not perceive that his yearnings had an earthly object.[13]

Charles was very much the lovestruck sufferer. He may have feared to reveal his devotion openly, for there is no evidence that Mary reciprocated his feeling. Or he may have enjoyed worshipping an unattainable goddess. In either case, he seems to have relished the role. He carried a pencil "purloined" from her as a love-token and spent hours gazing at it. Spying in at her window at night, he came close to being detected in his secret passion. He began to write love poems, taking the nom de plume of "Vivian." Vivian coexisted with another character—namely, "Anthony Awful," a tragicomic poetaster invented to amuse Isabella. While Vivian composed lyrics whose theme was Mary Wright, Anthony turned out a chatty "Walnut Hills News Letter," retailing family news and local gossip for the Connecticut Beechers. Although the tone of the newsletter was generally sunny or mock-heroic, Anthony occasionally struck a bitter note, as in this soliloquy:

> Why is creation so empty? Why hath my soul no voice to respond to it in its ceaseless going forth thro' all created beauty, in search of some *being* of kindred yearnings—of kindred loneliness. . . . Why find I none on whom to pour forth all that is within me? Where is the *God* of creation?

This revelation of Charles's spiritual condition suddenly gave way to crude reality when Anthony's reverie was punctured by the appearance of Jim Beecher, loafing along inattentive to his duties, and Charles had to step out of Anthony's character to shout, "Hello Jim, go drive those pigs into their pen."[14]

In this abrupt shift of tone, Charles was acknowledging that his threnodic flights were vulnerable to deflation. The ridiculous Anthony Awful yearned for "the ideal," just as if he were a Vivian, and longed for perfect communion. Charles's aside to his brother brought his dramatic outpouring down to the level of the commonplace and earthy. The crudely comic element jostled the would-be sublime. The point is not that Charles was merely posturing, or even that he was sporadically brought up short by his own recognition of striking attitudes and making extravagant gestures. This capacity to turn humor against himself was not simply a saving grace amidst his overheated emotional display. His amusement at himself was part of his self-consciousness, which allowed the play of irony. It is this, rather than his self-dramatization, which marks him as the romantic he thought he was. Even as he experienced anguish, disappointment, confusion, and humiliation, he was capable of inducing other emotions, which he then analyzed and exploited as a means of clarifying and mastering his desires, fleshly and spiritual. He loved, as he said, to study himself.

He explained away his abandonment of Sarah by insisting that "I am and ever must be an enthusiast and an idealist. She is practical—real—common-sense." To Charles's poetic imagination, Mary represented the opposite pole, that of ideality. There is no evidence that Mary Wright, who was simply one of several pretty family friends, was so different from prosy, capable Sarah. They were, in fact, both semi-invalids.

Charles's infatuation was by now becoming a public one. Although his family only slowly divined that he was in love with Mary, his best friend easily discovered the secret, and Charles cut him off. Vivian's poetic effusions then found their way into a Cincinnati newspaper, and their author and his beloved were soon known. "Ma'am Scandal," as Henry called the church grapevine, had already linked his own name to Mary's (and not without reason), but Vivian's verses established Charles as her suitor. He later claimed that the publication pained him, but his professed desire for secrecy is questionable.

To compound the offense of the Vivian publication, Charles went through an elaborate series of steps to plant a ring, his love-token for Mary, where she could find it. Far from mystifying the girl and her parents, the ploy enraged the Wrights, who were beginning to view Charles as a strange bird. They were naturally reluctant to have their daughter's name become common fame. While insisting that his love was a melancholy, terrible secret, Charles was advertising his devotion in the hackneyed modes of the day. Vivian was more than a nòm de plume; he was the persona in whom religious and romantic rebellion became identified.[15]

Much as his brothers and sisters were finding their theological bearings in public controversy, sometimes with each other, Charles was acting out his inner turmoil in a highly public manner. The Beechers were accustomed to exposing their private agonies to public gaze. Charles loudly regretted that his flamboyant actions had been bruited about, yet he took the additional step of detailing them at great length to his bewildered idol's father. In a letter combining the style of spiritual autobiography with gift-book sensibility, he related the history of his religious difficulties, broken engagement, alienation from father and friends, ill-considered publication, and the pathetic outcome. After emptying his bitter cup, he apologized to Wright for his "unfinished style" and volunteered to provide "further information on any point." Concluding that he had gravely offended the Wrights and injured his long-suffering family, he announced his departure for the deep South, where "I may possibly begin to live for others." He swore that his love for Mary was hallowed and undying and begged her father's forgiveness which, however, Wright withheld.[16]

Charles left for New Orleans in late December of 1838, taking passage on a boat headed down "La Belle Rivière" to the Mississippi. He was to teach in a private school operated by Henry's brother-in-law, Talbut Bullard, an older man of known piety. Though the Beechers hoped the change of scene would cure Charles, they viewed the move anxiously. "Poor Charles," Henry wrote Isabella, "has walked a dark and thorny path. . . . He is unhappy except when he violently overcomes his feelings and then his mood is extravagant—and never as I could find was he quiet except the quiet of *moodiness*." Once more, Charles was operating in a situation controlled by his family who had, in effect, deputized the kindly Bullard to monitor Charles's spiritual condition. When he made his farewells at the dock, he knew that "Sunday morning has been set aside as a time of family concert to pray for him." He would never forget the moment when Lyman, with "quivering lip" implored him, "My son, eternity is long!"[17]

Though he may be faulted for his erratic performance as a father, Lyman had, after his fashion, a clear perception of the problems that beset his son. He explicitly singled out adolescent storm-and-stress and the burden of choosing a vocation, without, however, admitting how heavily the family bore down on Charles with their demands that he uphold the Beecher tradition. Writing to Isabella, a newly converted Christian, Lyman gave an astute, if skewed, analysis of Charles's frustrations:

> He has been in the hand of god who has successively kept him from going over the precipice as he rushed up to it and as often warned him off, from the project he set his heart upon, and turned him to one thing after another at which his mind had revolted—1st. his Idol music, because he could not reach the "beau ideal" of excellence in execution with out an independent support—and could not support himself by it if obtained and loathed the druggery of common teaching. From that therefore at my suggestion he turned. To the study of greek, to be a professor in some College—and drove it as hard as he had the violin till his nerves cracked—and he loathed it as he did the fiddle. Then came a time without object and employment and intolerable "ennue" [ennui]. To escape which he drove up to the cave

> and rowed the boat upstream. But during all this time he complains of solitude, and speaks of his pride as disqualifying him for friendship with any mind he can find. The meaning of which is. The constitutional craving of an immortal mind—for a kind of society and satisfaction which no finite mind can afford. . . . He has not as you will see come straight in his phrenological philosophy—but since God has kept him back from so many perils—and has checked and brought round his fiery course to so many points of relative improvement, we ought to be patient.

Charles would have conceded the justice of some of Lyman's points, but felt that it was his family and friends who had baffled his plans, not a superintending Providence. They had especially harped on his obligation to shoulder the "labour and self support at which he had so violently revolted," the "druggery" of routine tasks. They criticized his unmanly reliance on his father's small resources. With the decline of Lane Seminary, Lyman, who was oblivious to personal comfort and equipage so long as churchly affairs prospered, had reached a new low in shabbiness. His letters home playfully referred to travel detours to "beg a little by the way" for the seminary, but secondhand clothing stores and a mendicant ministry were galling to a son who shrank from whatever was "coarse, vulgar and unetherial."[18]

Arrived in New Orleans, Charles tried to resign himself to "the hurry of human toil for contemptible gold," but he was still preoccupied with scrutinizing his soul. He wrote home of his "consciousness of [mental] disease" and spoke increasingly of his dread of madness. He found the perfect Platonic metaphor for his state. His soul was a harp "beaten by many a storm till its strings, some relaxed—others stretched to unnatural tension, refuse to his soliciting hand the expected harmony—but startle him by unmeasured discord." Existence had become a nightmare of discord, and the consciousness of having betrayed his father's hopes weighed heavily on him. In his deepening depression he wanted only to "dream thro this contemptible existence as swiftly as possible—undeluded by the notion that happiness—or tranquil repose is [not] unattainable." Nevertheless, he promised, "You shall hear frequently." For the next two years, the Beechers listened for "eolian murmurs" from the strings of Charles's "disordered soul."[19]

Instead of teaching under Bullard, Charles first worked as a bill collector, traveling the Louisiana coast on horseback. When in town, he gave music lessons and played the organ at a Protestant church. Though befriended by the Bullards, he felt his isolation keenly and sent back long accounts portraying the sufferings of a *déraciné*. Far from seducing him by its elegance and openness, Southern society disgusted him. He found it diseased with "the accursed malaria of business life—and the pestilential effluvia of Slavery. . . . They talk about liking it—getting used to the South—prejudices—habits and all that." But even among the wealthy planters, who were "generous people," he could not escape the presence of "abhorred slavery." Neither did he shrug off tales of priestly debauchery among the region's Roman clergy. His experiences in New Orleans would later give color and power to *Uncle Tom's Cabin*.

To relieve, or perhaps to enhance, his sadness, Charles learned Beethoven's waltz, "La Doleur," and read Rousseau, whose "sensibility and intense emotion" touched him deeply. Rousseau's character reminded Charles of a close friend, whose inability "to do what is required of a man in society at the present day places him above rather than below the ordinary level of humanity." He and Charles agreed in celebrating the sublime and denigrating getting-and-spending. Charles longed to "rescue" Stillman "from the ordeal of *realization*." His own occupations, meanwhile, were sordid enough, though the exotic scenery of the interior and the physical hazards met there mitigated the daily grind. His letters to Isabella pictured "poor Vivian" as a grubby itinerant, jogging through swamps beset by snakes and alligators, to collect a few dollars at each stop. He soon began looking for a way out of this latest ordeal of realization.[20]

In August of 1839 Charles suffered an attack of yellow fever. It was even reported in Cincinnati that he had died. This event seems to have been critical in his recovery from spiritual prostration, but since it is passed over in the letters, save for the usual thanks for providential escape, its importance can only be inferred, taken with the facts of Charles's felt isolation, continuing dependence on his family, and recoil from Southern culture. During his recuperation he began to assess his situation soberly. His schemes of becoming a West African planter or a Texas colonist—strange choices for an antislavery man—evaporated along with his dream of a European tour. He began working out his plans and prospects with care. To his father he wrote at first only of his continuing despair and isolation:

> The idea of cerebral disease is now ever present and continued reflection [brings] only conviction, that there is and always has been some constitutional disqualification, something as tho' one mind were a magnet and all other magnets of the same pole, thus repelling it, till it should find itself driven from among men.

> It was so at Groton—Bowdoin, Walnut Hills [and] is so here. Among men, all day, there is no intercourse and cannot be.

Charles entreated Isabella to help him, and he secured assurances from Sarah that she fully forgave him for his actions. This knowledge, which he owed to his sister, "bestowed a sense of *freedom*," and Charles felt he could now divulge to Lyman the cause of his continuing despair. He had decided to stake everything on winning Mary Wright.[21]

Though he still scorned business as an "infernal monomania," he prefaced his statement with a detailed résumé of his financial prospects. He felt certain he could earn "Enough for a life, at once literary—social—and above mediocrity in respect to style." Despite the national depression, he could count on an income of $1,500 from commercial life or teaching, with additional money from teaching music. His current job as a "sub-Levee-agent in the Tow-boat-business" would develop him physically, "annihilating for the time, idealism, and substituting practical readiness." He was willing to deny his true nature in order to win Mary on her parents' terms and expected his father to help him. These terms included, however, that her suitor be a man of decent religious opinions. Charles was now able, he believed, to fulfill even this requirement, because he had the most powerful of motives for regaining his faith:

> I expect [he wrote Lyman] not ever to arrive in the same realm of doctrine over which you so well preside. But I do expect—unless the light of my hope be extinguished—to own a god—a savior —a Bible as the sovereign—the friend—the rule of my life.

Repudiating the New Haven Theology, Charles turned instead to "the character of Christ and to the precept and example of *practical value*. While at the same time I shall seek to elaborate a system of truth praying for enlightenment." This statement is almost identical to Catharine's resolution of her spiritual difficulties.[22]

As his brothers and sisters were to do, Charles found a new center of faith in Christ rather than the sovereign judge and ruler his father held up for adoration, but with this difference—that it was Charles's love for Mary which, he argued, would effect the needed change of heart necessary to make him a Christian. He seemed aware that Lyman could not accept the idea that Mary Wright should supercede Christ as the hope of his salvation. "You may call this idolatry—" Charles protested, anticipating his father's objections, "But I tell you, it is *Nature*." He had yearned since boyhood, he reminded Lyman, for union with an all-sufficient being. He now pleaded with his father to weigh his case and decide it for him, either granting his son a life of "peace, usefulness [and] piety," or watching impassively as he descended toward "vagabondism—or I know not what indescribable subversion of my present characteristics, and apathetic assumption of hitherto impossible relations." If Lyman would not help him to become pious, then he must become dissolute.[23]

Like Catharine before him, Charles placed himself entirely in Lyman's hands. And there was the same identification of Lyman with God. The confusion of persons was plain, when Charles wrote, "Oh my father—can he deny me. . . . I leave it with you. And with him—and with God." Lyman must decide, for eternity. To Isabella, Charles wrote that he expected to break down completely if his hopes were allowed to die:

> You have never stood by the dark cave of Insanity—and looked with horror in at the dark door—and down the frightful chasms—nor heard beneath—the hurrying waters—the hideous noises—the shrieks and the laughter—feeling meanwhile your own brain boil—and every nerve thrill with a dreadful joy mingled with horror.

Laying the burden on his father was, he swore, "the final effort" of a terrified mind seeking repose. Surely Lyman would not spurn his tearful petition.[24]

Lyman's promises of aid gave Charles new energy founded on hope:

> The first words which I wrote in my diary were "There must be a God, and he must have been leading me." So quick did the awakening of a hope in my heart of hearts enable me to trample unbelief under foot. . . . Thus is the love I bear for Mary henceforth an holy one, and identified with the religion of my heart.

The religion of his heart had an erotic basis, which he only now was ready to acknowledge. In a "Ballad" written on his sickbed, Charles began to work up to the point by equating unrequited passion with physical death. The fair one's beauty and melancholy enraptured the "Exile," who gazed at her from concealment, taking in "Her vesture unrestrain'd transgressing," which "Betray'd her bosom round," while "That half revealed bosom swelling/Heav'd many a bitter sigh." Just as his letters had breathed forth Wertherian weltschmerz, so his verses were marked by the same extravagance of expression, as when the Exile declaimed, "The grave! the grave! I'm hastening thither." To remark on his poetic excesses is not to accuse Charles of mere posturing. He was trying to give expression to deeply felt anguish in a romantic idiom of which he was not a master. The straining for dramatic effect was a common failing—though in view of Henry's later success as an orator, perhaps a strength—of Charles's family.[25]

It is difficult to believe that Lyman expected to win his son's suit. Everything in his theology and his understanding of faith would have rejected Charles's too ready identification of his kind of "religion of the heart" with genuine holy affections and submission, even though the sentimentalism of the day came near to endorsing such a transference of feeling and loyalty. Charles did not claim, as orthodox evangelicals would, that Mary was to be the humble instrument of his conversion. She, though of a devout nature, was herself unconverted and was, rather, the immediate object of Charles's yearnings. Lyman could only hope that his son's willingness to cease searching for philosophical certitude, to begin trusting entirely in God (or Lyman), was the germ of genuine faith. It is otherwise difficult to understand his subsequent actions. Just as Lyman had almost badgered Catharine into her fateful betrothal to Alexander Fisher, he now took steps, however unconscious, that would result in dashing Charles's plans.

The entire episode had greatly embarrassed the Wrights and mortified the Beechers. None of them had supported Charles, and Henry had openly obstructed him, when he dogged Mary's steps and inflicted unsought attentions on her. Now Lyman clashed with her father, seemingly over an unrelated issue, and at the risk of offending one of the financial mainstays of the Second Church. With Catharine as amanuensis, he drafted a long-winded letter attacking Wright for introducing dancing parties into his home. Even Isabella, the most fashionable Beecher, complained while visiting Cincinnati that "now it is carried so far—that none of us can attend." Lyman accused Wright of allowing worldliness and frivolity to insinuate themselves among the young, thus destroying the influence of "the visible church," and with it the religious character of the young.

Hedonism was bound to undermine Lyman's revival efforts. Wright mulled over the charges before replying in a letter full of heat and sarcasm. He characterized his venerable pastor as the type of Christian who wanted to legislate morals on nonscriptural grounds and impose social tyranny in the name of a spurious godliness. Teetotalism, abolitionism, and kindred fanaticisms were the inevitable result, as Lyman had learned to his sorrow when Lane Seminary was all but wrecked by abolitionism. Lyman neither gained his point about the dancing nor advanced his son's cause.[26]

Unaware of the further breach between the two families, Charles gloried in a heavy schedule of work. Still clouding his future, however, was the matter of his heretical views, which far from remaining a private torment, now became a public issue. Charles had remained a member of the Bowdoin Street Church in Boston (formerly Hanover Church), which he had joined when his father was pastor. To satisfy his tender conscience, he had formally requested excommunication, and the church now acted upon his request. Julius A. Palmer, a deacon of that church and a friend of Lyman, charged his son as follows:

> 1. He disbelieves in the existence of a God. 2d. He disbelieves that the Scriptures were given by inspiration of God and are a perfect rule of faith and practice. 3d. He disbelieves that the wicked will finally go into punishment which shall be without end.

Charles had not foreseen how seriously the church would take his application, and it came to a head when he least wanted it, just when he had renounced "the sublime misery of a Byron—or the ill-greatness of a Voltaire." The Byronic poem of college days and his recourse to a New Orleans newspaper to air his religious doubts were now embarrassments. It was he himself who had repeatedly taken the labels "infidel" and "atheist," and there was truth to the third of Palmer's charges, though Charles was by no means the only Beecher who had misgivings about eternal punishment. By injudicious publicity and inadvertence in church legalities, Charles had further damaged his reputation. Many things were combining to defeat his hopes: his father's meddling, Mary's indifference, his own recklessness.[27]

Lyman, with testimonials from Talbut Bullard to Charles's newfound religious character, was able to avert discipline by Bowdoin Street Church. He advised Charles no longer to press his suit with the Wrights. Charles acquiesced in this decision, because by March of 1840 Mary's health was so affected by all the excitement that she was believed to be in mortal danger. Her ailment ("preternatural irritation" of the heart) required large doses of digitalis and complete quiet. Events pushed Charles toward finally admitting that Mary was lost to him. Despite Isabella's warnings, an officious female cousin interfered in the affair.

Meanwhile, the failure of his company cast him out of employment, and "out of the contaminated atmosphere of business life." As though he dimly recognized the fate of his futile passion, he spent the nights of late March and April writing "Eoline." "The excitement is so painful," he wrote his sisters, but "the pleasure of writing is intense—

greater than the stimulus of opium—or coffee—I tremble—and often weep . . . from the extacy of my emotions." The theme of this slight tale was the fatal results of enthusiasm and excessive idealism.[28]

Renunciation of "the Ideal" was also a renunciation of the woman who embodied ideality. "Eoline; or the Wind Spirit" was published in *Godey's Lady's Book* and was in good company, since the magazine catered to a readership fascinated by religious and quasi-religious themes. In his Rhineland allegory, Charles compressed his entire history of youthful enthusiasm and family conflict. Karl, a young dreamer, has drudging, unsympathetic parents, who scoff at his ambition of achieving greatness as a violinist. The father subjects Karl to "daily tirades," "vainly trying to make him a blacksmith." (Charles's shrinking from his father's profession is seen in his making the man revert to the Beechers' ancestral trade.) Reduced from eminent churchman to village smithy, Lyman is portrayed as narrow-minded and neglectful. Having called Karl a drone and prated in fairy-tale English, he drops out of sight, soon to appear in a new guise.

Karl proves himself a violinist of extraordinary talent, but when he cannot attain the zenith of excellence, he turns his back on his patron and admirers and retires to a simple cottage on an isolated knoll. There he constructs "a large Eolian" (the wind harp so much in vogue in romantic literature). He becomes a hermit, pining for a kindred spirit. Eoline, "daughter of the king of the winds," comes to him in a dream and promises to materialize from the harp's strings if Karl will swear to be faithful to her. Before she can become embodied, however, Karl is visited by his patron, whose daughter Bertha secretly loves Karl, and a grave, fatherly monk. The monk is horrified to hear Karl's story and begs him "not to peril his soul by seeking prohibited communion." While awaiting Eoline's appearance, he pleads with Karl for his soul, echoing Lyman's words: "'Remember my son,' said he in a tremulous accent, 'Eternity is long!'"

Though his forebodings only increase when he sees Eoline, the monk agrees to marry Karl and the incarnated wind-spirit. When Karl takes Eoline, she tells him that "she may confer possession of any power his soul most covets," but he will pay a dreadful price. Karl asks for superhuman powers of musicianship and exults in permanently securing not only genius but "extasy." He does not realize that his powers derive from the very substance of his etherial wife, who is drained of vitality during his performances. Once he wins unparalleled renown, Karl unaccountably tires of Eoline, who commits suicide. Karl and Bertha consummate their illicit love during a wild storm, and the next day the troubled monk seals their union. Karl's next performance terrifies his audience. His violin gives forth "the screams of torment of the damned," while Karl himself wears the visage of a madman. Whirled aloft by vengeful wind-spirits, he is hurled to the floor of the concert hall. His heart-broken friends convey him to his cottage, where he hears the last chords of the eolian harp and dies.[29]

A basic ambivalence underlies this tale. Eoline/Mary is depicted as a creature of God, beautiful, sympathetic, and pure, yet she confers "calamity" along with her gift of genius. An immortal spirit, she chooses mortality, hence physical death, for love of Karl, who betrays her. Thus their union is doubly doomed. A similar doubleness affects Charles's portrayal of his father. The blacksmith/monk is either stolidly uncomprehending or perspicacious, according to his role. The one cannot appreciate cravings for genius; the other does understand this appetite and warns that fulfillment of Karl's "unnatural longings" will destroy his soul. And just as Charles was poles apart from Sarah ("She is real—I am ideal"), so Eoline is a transcendent, fragile creature next to the scheming, seductive Bertha. The monk seals both marriages with his priestly authority, and both are fatal. It is as though he is both accomplice and judge.

If Charles sought to show in "Eoline" that sublimity and transcendence are terrible to their possessors, he succeeded, at some cost to clarity. The woman he could not have in any event, he now renounced, without, however, abandoning completely his search for a soaring ideal. What he did jettison were the obsessive introspection and solipsism of his Byronic phase. He tried to find new emotional and intellectual poise in a personal and religious outlook, after discovering in 1840 that peace and fulfillment were not to be found in Mary Wright. "Eoline" was a partial statement, however flawed, of Charles's resolve to seek new foundations. The tale itself was confused and confusing, and cannot be compared to his sister Harriet's literary explorations of the meaning of faith. Yet the intent was the same: to come to terms with disturbing and arresting religious ideas and to communicate these conflicts to other Christians and would-be Christians.

In May, less than two months after completing his story, Charles sought a reconciliation with Sarah and began to talk hesitantly of entering the ministry. It was three more years before he began to feel certain of his faith, but barring the usual doubts of converts, he never looked back. "I have begun," he rejoiced, "to restore peace to father's heart." Yet he also spoke of his continuing terror in the face of life and occasionally fell prey to crippling apathy. More than ever he counted on his family to sustain and comfort him. Though his "judgment" confirmed his decision to give Mary up, his "heart" was still "agonised." "Nevertheless," he concluded, "I believe it would be safe for me to marry Sarah."[30]

From the retrospect of Lyman's *Autobiography*, Mary Wright might never have existed. The entire treatment of Charles's long spiritual orphanage omits any reference to his love for Mary, and the woman who emerges as the saving force is his mother Roxana, whose prayers are said to have rescued her son. As far as Lyman was concerned, Charles was another Augustine, and the child of so many prayers could not be lost. Oddly enough, neither are Charles's theological difficulties presented. The chapter is almost a sentimental set piece. It was not Lyman's logic or authority, or Charles's maturation, that brought him back to Christianity, but rather the tie to Charles's heart which reached down from heaven where his mother dwelled.

Charles's spiritual problems did not vanish overnight, but he felt that he had quenched his "thirst for the mysterious, the speculative, the daring—the recondite." The authority to whom he now turned was the English lay theologian, Isaac Taylor, whose *Natural History of Enthusiasm* maintained that "Christianity has in some short periods of its history been entirely dissociated from philosophical modes of thought and expression: and assuredly it has prospered in such periods." Taylor denounced "moping sentimentalism" on the one hand and "dogmas, awfully clothed in the clouds of metaphysical phraseology" on the other. "The religion of the heart," he warned, "may be supplanted by a religion of the imagination, just in the same way that the social affections are often dislodged or corrupted by factitious sensibilities."

As a diagnosis of Charles's tendencies Taylor's words were very apt. Most important of his statements, from the point of view of Charles's speculative difficulties, was Taylor's insistence on inductive reasoning. Perhaps more useful to Charles Beecher than this unsparing dissection of the enthusiastic frame of mind was Taylor's criticism of Jonathan Edwards, whose *Inquiry into the Freedom of the Will* had first unsettled Charles's faith. Instead of attempting to overturn Edwards's logic, Taylor applauded him for confuting the Arminians, while yet urging that "*pious* Calvinists should at length meet *pious* Arminians on common ground; and that the difference between the two parties should for ever be merged in a Biblical doctrine." It was not "metaphysical theology" as practiced by men like Edwards which would enable

Christians to find truth, but "a better understanding of the special nature and unique constitution of the Document of Faith, which, unlike any other writing, is at once simply the work of human minds; and not less absolutely the work of the Divine mind."[31]

It may be asked why Isaac Taylor's statements were more authoritative than Lyman's "clinical theology," Nathaniel Taylor's Scottish realism, or even Timothy Dwight's common-sense theology. Henry, no theologian at all, had already arrived at the conclusion that inductive reasoning was the only sound reasoning and a good corrective to his brother's arid system-building. For one thing, Isaac Taylor denied the claim that systematic divinity was a worthwhile endeavor, so long as men reposed too great a trust in their own abstractions, confusing them with biblical theology. For another, his tone was much more irenic and catholic than the men under whom Charles had studied. Another clue to Taylor's appeal for Charles Beecher lies in the former's preoccupation with the physiology of the human mind, a subject which, in the form of phrenology, continued to hold sway over Charles and Henry and had great attractions for their sisters as well. One major theme of their collective theological explorations was a desire to know how the mind operated during and after life, and whether "constitutional" flaws did not account for human depravity and self-will.

Taylor was not the only source for Charles's new beliefs. Like so many young men of his time, Beecher discovered Thomas Carlyle and the German evangelical theologians. Ultimately, the most important discovery he made was one shared by his brothers and sisters, who rediscovered the Bible and Christ. Charles's pastoral theology was both Christocentric and noncreedal. His earliest publications were *The Bible a Sufficient Creed* and *Pen Pictures of the Bible*, an imaginative re-creation of life in biblical times. It was Harriet and Henry whose Christocentric theology developed into Liberal Orthodoxy, however; while Charles, following the lead of Edward Beecher, became absorbed in abstruse cosmological and prophetic investigations which led the two brothers into a theological backwater in the 1850s and 1860s. It would make a nice symmetry to leave Charles securely in possession of a simplified, biblical, and liberal theology after his decade of philosophical entanglement. The truth is, however, that far from escaping the craving for the recondite and mysterious, Charles Beecher became a disciple of his brother Edward, whose theology was nothing if not speculative.[32]

After a brief stay in New Orleans with his bride Sarah, Charles moved to Indianapolis to be with Henry, whose influence, it was thought, would be both soothing and tonic. Henry kept Charles under close scrutiny and by March of 1843 was able to report that "on the whole *I feel Charles is safe.*" Although he was worried that Charles had not yet discovered "*fulness* of intense personal love to Christ," he was pleased that Charles was thoroughly in earnest about doing his duty to Christ. Henry recommended time and study for his brother but wished he would let certain questions alone. In Fort Wayne, Indiana, for instance, Charles's first pastorate, he got the reputation of leaning toward Unitarianism from talking so much about the life of Christ and so little about Presbyterian doctrines or Christian duty. "I do not believe that he is *tainted*," Henry wrote Lyman when he got wind of the controversy, but "what he needs much to do" was some "*practical preaching.*" The Beechers must rally to Charles's support and stop the mouths of his critics.

Charles found Presbyterianism a straitjacket in many ways, not the least of which was its strict confessionalism. The most distasteful feature of the Presbyterian church was its enormous appetite for polemics. He described his feelings in a letter to Amelia Ogden, who was a sort of godmother to him, according to Roxana's dying wish. When he arrived in Fort Wayne to assume office in a church organized by his brother Henry, he had found that "the whole subject of experimental religion, the ministry, the church, had become profoundly disreputable, and the daughter of Zion was surrendered to the sneers and unresisted ridicule of the profane." Having just emerged himself from "many dark mountains of sin, and rugged roads of unbelief," Charles felt a great sympathy for these benighted souls. To his consternation, his boorish charges, however ignorant they were of "experimental religion," were well versed in "debates on rival parties in the Church." They came to him, not seeking the path of salvation but "to wrangle in Law" and "to listen to political harangues."

> "Beecher," I have heard myself addressed *of a Sunday morning.* "Beecher, you must put in your best licks to day!" "You must *knock the socks* off those Old School folks!" And so they stood by to see me fight. Fight? for what? for Christ? They never dreamed of that, they wanted to hear what I had to say for *New School.* Now I had nothing particular to say for new School. I always supposed my father knew all about that. I *didn't* and told them so. "Well," said they, "What did you come up here for?"

Henry, confronted with the same situation, would have deplored it as much, but he also would have seen the humor in it.[33]

Charles was a different sort of man. He was determined to find his own truth, to be absolutely thorough in his investigations, and once having found the truth, to defend it at all costs against all comers. It was probably this temperamental affinity which drew him, in the end, to Edward rather than to Henry or Harriet. Charles later claimed that he had believed in preexistence since his early teens. Perhaps he did, in a Wordsworthian sense, as a sort of moral intuition. He did not, however, accept his brother Edward's doctrines. In 1846, when they engaged in a correspondence about Edward's "system of God," Charles expressed complete disapproval:

> There is nothing that so completely tends to destroy my confidence in you and in all your results as such language as this. I do not believe that "the system of God," has been revealed except in some partial details and relations. Nor that it is possible for your mind, however daring and however powerful, nor any other mind (created mind)—to grasp that system—and measure all the hight and depth and length and breadth of the great theme [of] the origin of evil. And the very fact that any mind proposes to do such a thing—much more supposes that it has done it, is enough to stamp discredit upon the whole of its proceedings.

His own attitude, which he recommended to Edward, was one of patient, prayerful inquiry. If facts and theories were at odds, it was far better to "leave their connections for eternity to disclose" than to engage, as Catharine was doing, in a futile effort to harmonize all knowledge in a single volume. It is strange that Charles became so loyal a follower of his older brother, not only adopting the entire theory but elaborating upon it in a massive book of his own, *Redeemer and Redeemed*, a new theory of the Atonement.[34]

In the absence of fuller documentation, this major shift in Charles Beecher's theology cannot be explained adequately. Relatively little is known of this period of his life, particularly of his private thoughts, but a pattern emerges from such evidence as there is. He left Fort Wayne in great discouragement, for reasons which are unclear. They were unclear at the time to his congregation. Hugh McCulloch alluded to "the necessity, real or supposed, that led you to brake off your connexion with our little Society." Charles talked of returning to Fort Wayne, but the recurrence of malarial symptoms in his wife made him reluctant to return to the Middle West. Once in the East, he asked his family to find him employment. He briefly supplied Plymouth Church during Henry's absence, but was churchless until the Free Presbyterian Church of Newark, New Jersey, asked him to be stated supply. After a trial period, he was called to be their pastor but served less than three years. While pastor of the church, he persuaded the members to affiliate with the Congregational churches of New York and Brooklyn.

He took several long leaves of absence, once to help his sister with the final stages of *Uncle Tom's Cabin*, and again, to accompany Mrs. Stowe to England and Europe as her secretary and escort. Ill health also required vacations away from the church. His antislavery scruples had cost him a call to the District of Columbia and also caused him trouble in Newark. His fellow ministers kept him out of their pulpits, and when the church published his sermon calling for violation of the Fugitive Slave Law, the child who distributed it was threatened with violence. It was a time of illness, depression, political strife, and professional insecurity. He could barely support his family and had to rely on the Hookers and Stowes for gifts of money, books, and hand-me-down clothing.[35]

Charles adopted an increasingly catastrophic view of national events and sacred history. To his friend Hugh McCulloch he wrote, "the prophesyings of my former ministry are being fulfilled. That great crisis of world-convulsion is coming. This sin-sick delirious world will never know peace, nor sanity, until the foot of the Crucified once more hallows the soil." Harriet and Lyman received this prediction:

> Tell Father that the great Tribulation is begun. This guilty land will not escape. The church instead of premature peans, had better weep in sackcloth and ashes. The crowns are taken from the [horns?]. The name of blasphemy is written no more henceforth on [the] imperial Head, or regal coronet, but all over the *democratic body politic*. The Woman will first ride the Democratic beast and become drunk with blood. Then she herself will be destroyed. Democracy became Anarchy, and universal confederacy against God. Antichrist will rise to the surface, and ride on the foam-wave, and then will come the End. Whom the *Lord* will destroy with the brightness of his coming. Father may not live to see it. But I for one expect either to die by violence or to live in the fastnesses and retreats of the forest. The plot is laid. The explosion will come soon.

Charles now saw himself no longer as a wanderer in spiritual byways but as a prophet. His profound sense of alienation from modern political society and his jubilation at the coming disaster made him more akin to the title character of Mrs. Stowe's *Dred* than to Henry

Ward or Lyman Beecher, whose visions of a regenerated America were optimistic and melioristic by comparison.[36]

Evidently, Charles's eschatological views were connected with his conversion to Edward's theology. In 1848, for example, Charles told Lyman that their prophetic ideas differed because Lyman clung to the wrong view of the origin of evil: "Your prophetical system, is obliged to make Original Sin, or the doctrine of the Fall in Adam, one of its starting points. . . . while I regard that as the corner stone of the Antichristian system, as now manifoldly spread over the Romish, Greek, and Protestant communities." He had, that is to say, come around to Edward's view that the Augustinian dogma regarding Original Sin was fallacious and unholy. He now had to reconcile this rejection of Augustine with his own conceptions of sin, which were deep and far-reaching.

In 1852 we find McCulloch treating Charles as a fully convinced spokesman for Edward's ideas: "you get rid of the ugly points of Calvinism by reference to a pre-existent state." And when Beecher went abroad with his sister, he made a discovery at the Louvre that confirmed his belief. He visited and revisited the gallery where the winged bulls of Nineveh were displayed and meditated aloud on their meaning:

> What I have never seen noticed [is] the magnificent phrenological development of the heads. The brow is absolutely prodigious—broad, high, projecting, massive. It is the brow of a divinity indeed, or of a cherub, which I am persuaded is the true designation of these creatures. They are to me but the earliest known attempts to preserve the cherubim that formed the fiery portals of the Eden temple until quenched in the surges of the deluge. Out of those eyes of serene, benign, profound reflection, therefore, not thirty, but sixty centuries look down upon me. I seem to be standing at those mysterious Eden gates, where Adam and Eve first guided the worship of a world, amid the sad, yet sublime symbols of a previous existence in heavenly realms.

This is as far as the evidence will take us. Charles's desertion of a position identified with the sentimental liberalism of Henry and Harriet must remain, to some extent, an enigma. Perhaps it involved the recrudescence of his youthful relish for speculative thought, or perhaps the personal attraction to Edward prevailed. William Beecher was also a convert to Edward's views, and there the case may be more clearly made for a worshipful attitude toward Edward's independent intellect. Alternatively, Charles may have extracted something special from his long experience of spiritual drift which made a holistic "system of God" necessary, even if it was a bizarre, idiosyncratic system. Whatever the answer, he turned his back on the lessons of Isaac Taylor and of his brother Henry to become an isolated figure in American theology. Nevertheless, with Edward he succeeded in identifying some of the critical questions of evangelical theology, and in so doing played an active part in his family's collective religious pilgrimage.[37]

PART 4

CHRISTOCENTRIC LIBERALS

7 HARRIET BEECHER STOWE

Harriet Elizabeth Beecher was a child when Professor Fisher's death disrupted the precarious spiritual peace of her family, but she silently stored away impressions and ideas which she made the theme of one of her best novels. She was a plain girl, intelligent but given to spells of listlessness and dreamy abstraction. Her self-confidence was not bolstered by her father's saying that a girl with her mental endowments ought to have been a male. But she, at least, was credited with brains. Her brother Henry, it was feared, was positively stupid. Henry was out getting into scrapes and neglecting his lessons, while Harriet spent hours poring over Mather's *Magnalia*. For all this, the two children were devoted to each other and remained closely attached as adults.

Harriet's early years were uneventful, though she did win local acclaim for her schoolgirl essay on a set topic, "Can the Immortality of the Soul be Proved by the Light of Nature?," whose precocious argumentative skill and stodgy polish gratified Lyman. The most memorable, because painful, events were her mother's death and her sister's bereavement. When Harriet was thirteen she became a student at the Hartford Female Seminary. Within two years she was one of Catharine's assistants, and it was at that juncture that Catharine began a class in mental and moral philosophy, raising questions that would inspire and haunt Harriet throughout her life.[1]

In the summer of 1825 Harriet was converted upon hearing her father preach "Jesus as a soul friend offered to every human being." Lyman's joyous acceptance of her testimony was in marked contrast to the searching scrutiny to which it was subjected by the Reverend Joel Hawes, pastor of the First Church of Hartford. Even Catharine demanded to know how Harriet could attain assurance so easily. Harriet fell into a melancholy soul struggle. Her best friend, Georgiana May, was also beset with religious doubts. "Georgiana's difficulties

Harriet Beecher Stowe

are different from Harriet's: she is speculating about doctrines, etc.," Catharine reported, and prescribed a vacation for them. The girls sought elevation of spirits in a visit to Nutplains, where the Foote homestead was. The comforting rituals and stately forms of the Episcopal Church must have afforded relief from the doctrinal and psychological perplexities of Calvinism.[2]

Harriet next turned to her brother Edward, whose sympathy alleviated her condition. "You," she recalled sixty years later, "were my earliest religious teacher; your letters to me while a school-girl in Hartford gave me a high Christian aim and standard which I hope I have never lost." But at the time she protested that "your speaking so much philosophically has a tendency to repress confidence." She objected to Edward's understanding of God's nature in terms which exactly reproduced their father's theology of divine moral government. Finally, in 1830, she came to accept Catharine and Edward's view of Christ as divinely suffering, not merely in his human aspect but as God manifest.[3]

Because it was a family concern, the Hartford Seminary did not yield an independent income for Harriet, who accepted her heavy teaching load without question, since it helped pay for her brothers' college expenses. She was a good-natured woman and, when the mood struck her, a lively conversationalist, but too backward or frumpy to attract suitors. When she was not with Catharine or George, she lived in Lyman's Boston home. And, when he left Boston to assume the presidency of Lane Seminary, she accompanied the family there, to help operate Catharine's new school, the Western Female Institute. Catharine was nothing if not imperious and, as a sister-in-law reported, "very clever to deal with" in money matters—so Harriet soon learned to her grief. The Beechers moved among the literary and professional elite of Cincinnati, virtually all transplanted Yankees, who comprised the Semi-Colon Club, dedicated to literary entertainments and refined good cheer. Some of Harriet's offhand sketches of New England life were very favorably received by the club, and she also uncovered a suitor among its members.[4]

Calvin Ellis Stowe, professor of biblical literature at Lane, was a widower, his first wife, Eliza Tyler, having been a close friend of Harriet's. Harriet and Calvin were married on January 6, 1836. The exodus of the "Lane Rebels" and the consequent withdrawal of Lewis Tappan's money reduced Stowe's salary to a pittance. Just when Harriet needed her sister's help, Catharine refused to recognize Harriet's claim to part of the assets of the Western Female Institute.

Harriet began married life with a pathetically small outfit of household goods, and was soon mired in domestic problems. She bore six children and had the burden of another "child" in her neurasthenic husband. Besides being a melancholiac, Calvin was a glutton, and the digestive upsets which plagued him were the precursors of kidney and liver disease. He was so preoccupied with the state of his health that he vied with his father-in-law for the distinction of being the worst sufferer from depression and dyspepsia. Mrs. Stowe learned very early how to handle her husband during his blue spells, and developed a playful attitude toward him. To supplement his uncertain income, Harriet produced sketches and tales for annual giftbooks like *The Token* and *Friendship's Garland*, turning out such items as "a fanciful conciet of the *twelve months* meeting as embodied beings in a fairy cave," all the while toiling at tasks devoid of such fairy charm. This woman, "all honey and flowers" to a later generation, was so ground down by domestic worries that she began to suffer from depression. Calvin's handwringing style of dire prognostication probably aggravated her inherited susceptibility to melancholia.[5]

Events piled up in such a way as to make her aim of Christian resignation difficult: her father's desperate and ultimately futile efforts to restore the seminary to prosperity; squabbling with Catharine over the demise of their school; vicarious suffering over the bad marriage Henry had made (he who was "more angel than brother"); and the explosive political and racial situation in Cincinnati. Yet her greatest anxieties centered on her spiritual condition. It was useless to turn to Calvin for support. He was in constant religious turmoil himself and expected his wife to sustain him, to brighten his pathway with the light of her own piety. When he was not imploring her to help him find Christ, he was scolding her for her shortcomings as a housekeeper. Once, after drawing up a bill of particulars, he stopped short with, "I cannot presume to catalogue any further, for it makes me too sick." Harriet admitted that she had little gift for household management even in the best of times, and she was distressed to discover that she had "no life, no energy, no appetite." As she passed her thirty-fourth birthday, she asked, "When the brain gives out, as mine often does, then what is to be done?" In late July of the same year she nearly died of cholera. Her father and her sister Mary fully expected her to succumb, and it was only their heroic exertions that took "the stamp of death" from her face. Mary nursed her through the night "in the dining room hot as an oven and thronged with muscetoes" until the crisis was past.[6]

A trip East with Mary improved Harriet's health, but she was still feeble and gave every indication of impending collapse. Money was often bestowed on the Beechers by secret donors. A timely cash donation now paid Harriet's expenses at Dr. Robert Wesselhoeft's water cure in Brattleboro, Vermont, where she was accompanied by her sisters. Life at Brattleboro had a tonic effect on Harriet, who experienced both the rigors of hydropathy and the novelty of a completely carefree existence. From May of 1846 to March of the next year she benefited from the wholesome diet, vigorous exercise, and easygoing social life of the Wesselhoeft regimen. By letter the Stowes again exchanged criticisms and pledged to seek a higher spiritual and conjugal felicity.[7]

Harriet finally returned to Walnut Hills. Physically renewed, she was inwardly mournful and rebellious. Domestic trials were as onerous as ever, resignation as elusive a boon. Despite their poverty, it was now Calvin's turn to go to Brattleboro to recruit. During his absence the Stowes lost a son. The cholera epidemic of 1849 killed their baby, Samuel Charles. For a woman as ardently maternal as Harriet, the shock of Charley's death was shattering. Two years earlier she had ministered to Henry and Eunice when their son George died. She had assured them then that God's chastening rod was held by a loving hand, moved by compassion to effect that "entire submission" for which true Christians longed.

> What we can calmly endure and soon recover from is not the medicine strong enough for our case, it must be that which shakes the soul to the centre and takes with it our very life blood—it must be something for which we get no relief from any earthly source and that casts us of necessity on Him alone. . . . There is a tendency in the weariness of sorrow to despise and undervalue this affliction as of no use to us and only a gratuitous torture—to be weary of it as a yoke we would gladly cast away and escape from—The very keenness of it confuses our sense of the benefit it is to us and we do not perceive that it is of any use. . . . But *afterward* as the Bible tells us it shall yield peaceable fruits and then may come a time even in this life when you shall bless your Heavenly Friend even for this bitter sorrow.

The deaths of infants signified, she had reminded them, not the cruelty of God but rather his tender mercy. For "the task of piloting a soul thro the breakers of this life appears so hazardous and fearful" that she as a mother "should breathe a long sigh of relief that one at least had so easily won the victory." Such sentiments, so true to conventional piety, were not easy to live up to. They fell unctuously from the tongue and were the staple of religious writings of the time, but they were sorely tested in each crisis of life, especially family crises.[8]

At the same time that Harriet was supplicating the Lord for deeper faith, her family believed her to be more nearly sanctified than they. Her letter to her surviving brothers after George Beecher's violent death had exalted their spirits. Calvin had shown her letters to his clerical brethren as examples of wonderful piety. And Isabella, ignorant of Charley Stowe's death, begged Harriet to shed her luminous spirituality on her sister's dead heart:

> The Lord has been very kind to you my dear sister in lifting you above the world in spirit, tho' pressed down and sorrowful oft through the flesh, and no gift from a Father's hand can equal this—the most satisfying, consoling, delightful token of adoption.

Even cholera, Isabella thought, could hold no terrors for a woman so full of faith. If Harriet could be blessed with surpassing peace "in the midst of sorrow and death," then "how rich must be your experience" in ordinary times, "unless, indeed affliction and apprehension call out the sentiments of piety and submission, as they always do with me, in a peculiar manner." Several years later Isabella again spoke of Harriet as having high spiritual authority:

> I am hoping for much good from free conversation with sister Harriet. She is certainly a christian of the highest order and has no temptation to form or adhere to theories merely—and she has the largest charity. If she does not pierce some of my clouds, I shall live in their shadow many years I fear.

What struck others about Harriet's religious experience was its warmth and simplicity. No mere theorizer, as the Beechers believed Catharine to be, Harriet seemed to her brothers and sisters to live as nearly like Christ as anyone could, finding "peaceable fruits" in the shocks and blows of life.[9]

What passed after Charley's death confirmed the Beechers' belief in Harriet's spiritual maturity. She strove to apply the lessons of her letter to Henry and Eunice to her own loss. Charley's death brought spiritual consolations greater than personal resignation. In a real sense, his dying evoked the emotional responses which ultimately produced *Uncle Tom's Cabin*. "It was at his dying bed and at his grave," Harriet later wrote, "that I learned what a poor slave mother may feel when her child is torn away from her." Cholera was as cruel a tyrant as any slaveholder, and in the political climate of the late 1840s, when Harriet was groping for a meaning for Charley's death, she settled upon slavery as a metaphor for her own troubled existence. This identity of suffering cut across racial lines, she told Henry, and was the more poignant when one recognized the peculiar susceptibilities of the African race:

> I have known a great many slaves—had them in my family, known their history and feelings and seen how alike their heart beats to any other throbbing heart and above all what woman deepest feels I have seen the strength of their instinctive and domestic attachments in which *as a race* they excel the anglo saxon. The poor slave on whom the burden of domestic bereavement falls heaviest is precisely the creature of all Gods creatures that feels it deepest.

From this position, Mrs. Stowe developed an even more explicit argument, which linked her own tragedy with that of the slave. By reason of their extraordinary sufferings, slaves were the very type of Christ:

> The African race appear as yet to have been companions only of the sufferings of Christ. In the melancholy scene of his death—while Europe in the person of the Roman delivered him unto death, and Asia in the person of the Jew clamored for his execution—Africa was represented in the person of Simon the Cyrenean, who came patiently bearing after him the load of the cross; and ever since then poor Africa has been toiling on, bearing the weary cross of contempt and oppression after Jesus. But they who suffer with him shall also reign; and when the unwritten annals of slavery shall appear in the judgment, many Simons who have gone meekly bearing their cross after Jesus to unknown graves, shall rise to thrones and crowns! [10]

As Isabella had said, affliction and apprehension, which were the lot of women (and even more so of slaves), induced a higher piety. This was a truism which reflected human reality, according to Timothy Dwight:

> This interesting fact is probably owing, chiefly, if not wholly, to the anger, sorrow, and death, to which the sex are especially exposed; and which, always before their eyes, operate as solemn, and effectual monitions of their speedy departure to the eternal world. In this way they are usually more sober-minded, more

> attentive to spiritual and eternal things, and more disposed to give them their due influence, than men; and, thus far oftener to become the subjects of piety, and the heirs of endless life.

Harriet and her sisters were encouraged by such pronouncements to believe that it was a distinctive part of God's government to make intense suffering yield fruits of piety. Reactions to bereavement varied, but it was a reflex of piety to try to transmute human grief to something nobler. Lydia Sigourney, Hartford's honeyed poetess, specialized in couplets which few lacrimal glands could resist. A tenacious convention was the "mourning piece," which Catharine Beecher (herself addicted to elegiac versifying) dismissed as "an embroidered tombstone under an apparition by courtesy called a weeping willow, with a row of darkly-clad weeping females approaching it." Harriet's way of coming to terms with the death of her child, while partaking of such sentimentalism, derived its special power to impress others from her psychological discernment.[11]

In virtually all her fiction, just as in *Uncle Tom's Cabin*, Mrs. Stowe attempted to discover to her readers the mutuality of thought and feeling, and their impress upon national and racial character. Her earliest expression of this theme is to be found in her reflections on Madame de Staël's *Corinne*:

> In America feelings vehement and absorbing like hers become still more deep, morbid, and impassioned by the constant habits of self-government which the rigid forms of our society demand. They are repressed, and they burn inward till they burn the very soul, leaving only dust and ashes. . . . All that is enthusiastic, all that is impassioned in admiration of nature, of writing, of character, in devotional thought and emotion, or in the emotions of affection, I have felt with vehement and absorbing intensity,—felt till my mind is exhausted, and seems to be sinking into deadness.

It was in part her astuteness in interpreting religious affections that made her family look upon her as eminently qualified to give spiritual guidance. She tried her best with Charles, who appreciated her efforts. But he decried her tendency to anatomize and analyze as the psychological counterpart of Catharine's penchant for philosophizing:

> But she [Harriet] is a little too wise withall—and because she has experienced about all the mental phenomena possible to a woman, is irresistibly inclined to assist others in their passage thro' the

> same path (as she thinks) by telling them how she felt, and how she came to stop feeling so—and what they will find out by and bye. It is true that this is not her characteristic but her occasional failing. Probably she considers it the exclusive prerogative of Cate, and is thus more cautious. . . . She is not in her letter[s] pouring forth feeling merely *because she feels it* but planning by the combination of such and such feelings or thoughts to produce a given effect.

Even her private communications, it would seem, were emphatically didactic—to a degree remarkable even among the Beechers. What could have been more natural than Harriet's seeking to minister to an enslaved race, arouse the national conscience, and deliver herself of a novel, all in the act of assuaging a private grief?[12]

After the initial success of *Uncle Tom*, Harriet made a tour of England and the Continent in 1853, publishing her impressions in *Sunny Memories of Foreign Lands,* a collection of her travel letters, with extracts from Charles Beecher's travel diary. Almost the first experience she recorded was passing the Kinsale lighthouse, the place where Professor Fisher had met his death. She made a sketch of the scene, a memorial to Catharine's anguish, now vividly recalled. "Surely, without the revelation of God in Jesus," Harriet reflected, "who could believe in the divine goodness?" Everywhere in Britain she was confronted with the history of the Puritans from whom she was descended. Their present disrepute disturbed her, but her defense of their iconoclasm and severe doctrines displayed both loyalty and chagrin. When she heard the celebrated Dissenter, the Reverend Baptist Noel, she characterized his preaching in these terms:

> It was a sermon in the style of Tholuck and other German sermonizers, who seem to hold that the purpose of preaching is not to rouse the soul by an antagonistic struggle with sin through the reason, but to soothe the passions, quiet the will, and bring the mind into a frame of mind in which it shall incline to follow its own convictions of duty. . . . To me, brought up on the very battle field of controversial theology, accustomed to hear every religious idea guarded by definitions, and thoroughly hammered on a logical anvil before the preacher thought of making any use of it for heart or conscience, though I enjoyed the discourse extremely, I could not help wondering what an American theological professor would make of such a sermon.

She concluded that, while American evangelicals could profit from

Noel's example, "If I could have but one of the two manners, I should prefer our own, because I think that this habit of preaching is one of the strongest educational forces that forms the mind of our country."

Thus Harriet gave her assent to both the manner and the matter of preaching by her father's generation at the very time when Catharine Beecher was attempting to discredit their ideas and authority. From Geneva, Mrs. Stowe wrote home, "Calvinism, in its essential features, never will cease from the earth, and men with strong minds and wills always discover it. The predestination of a sovereign will is written over all things." By this she meant that God's purposes were plainly declared in the face of nature and in natural laws, a doctrine that could be called predestinarian only by courtesy. That she chose to call it Calvinism was a measure of her personal loyalty to inherited tradition.[13]

It is necessary to establish the complexity of Harriet's attitude toward her theological heritage in order to comprehend the genesis of *The Minister's Wooing*. This novel, like *Uncle Tom*, originated in Harriet's reaction to the death of a son, this time the Stowe's eldest. If Harriet was passionately devoted to her children, Calvin was equally as fond a parent. He was, she said, in the language of phrenology, "a man gifted with an uncommon development of philoprogenitiveness." Henry Stowe, named for Harriet's favorite brother, had accompanied her on her second European tour and was the recipient of her confidences. When he went away to school, his mother insisted that he write exactly how his room was arranged and furnished, how he spent each day, the names and characters of his friends. To the extent that Calvin Stowe was undependable in practical matters, Henry replaced his father as Harriet's manly support.

She monitored his religious growth very carefully. In 1855 she wrote to him with tenderness and urgency of Aunt Esther's death: "Henry death is *a great experience*—we cant tell what we are ourselves till a friend dies and then we see a great deal—it is just as if the gate opening when they went in gave us a glimpse of the glory and made this world *dark* in comparison." Harriet did not dwell on Esther's terrible physical sufferings but reminded Henry of the moral struggle which had occupied his great-aunt's entire life:

> Henry, she was a great sufferer. She had high feelings a proud nature—great intensity of feeling—and all these had to be made subject to Christ. No nun in a convent ever lived a more self denying life—and it has been a long one. But at last every thing within was conquered and before she died Christ gave her the

victory, and she was made perfect in love. My dear boy the light of her example makes me feel my deficiencies—I am afraid when I am gone you cannot remember so much of me, but I am going to try and be more faithful. *I do love you* Henry, and I know you do love me—but oh my darling, I want you to choose my Redeemer—your Father's and mother's God for your own.

The Stowes had doted on this son, who was the most intelligent as well as the most attractive and self-reliant of their offspring. They also believed that he was the most advanced spiritually. "Henry was the only one of our children," Harriet told Isabella Hooker, "that we had begun not to feel anxious for and to hope to rely on him ourselves."[14]

Henry Stowe drowned on July 9, 1857, shortly after returning to Dartmouth from a vacation. He was nineteen and unconverted. Mrs. Stowe exhibited touching calm when she learned the news. "Dear soul! she bowed her head, and said nothing for some moments—then asked with clasped hands—And now how can I best keep up till I get there?" Calvin, she feared, would feel the immediate shock more than she. She sent words of comfort to their son Fred and to her father, "who she knew would feel it very much especially as he would think his [Henry's] case a hopeless one. She on the contrary has seen light from the first." Harriet consoled her family and friends by recounting her talks with Henry and bringing out his letters. They seemed to show that he was on the brink of saving faith when he was cut off, a point she urged in his favor in a letter to Lyman:

My dearest Father

Lest your kind heart be too much distressed for me I write one word. This affliction comes from One nearer and dearer than all earthly friends who loves us better than we love ourselves—this may suffice.

In regard to Henry's eternal estate I have good hope—the *lamb* of my flock he was. I *rested* on him as on no other and He who has taken [him] will care for him. He who spared not his *own son*—how shall he not with him freely give us all things?

Pray for my *other children.*[15]

Her feelings of assurance soon faded, however, not because of any unkind words from Lyman but because her own trust in Christ was not absolute. Far from shrinking from Lyman or engaging him in open and wounding debate, Harriet leaned on him and imagined that she drew sustenance from his presence. "Papa and Mamma are here and we have been reading the memoir," she wrote of long sessions in her Andover home working over the manuscript of Lyman's *Autobiography*. The book in her view was "Glorious–beautiful." Yet we must believe that experiencing again that entire life, from her father's impassioned attempts to convert Roxana to his retirement from the flagging seminary, stirred many memories and set trains of thought into motion, however unconscious. There were the chapters devoted to Catharine's spiritual agonies, to George's death, to Charles's loss of faith, to the crumbling of Lyman's friendships, to the persecutions and prosecutions that had saddened the last fifteen years of his active life.

If Lyman's understanding of God's plan of salvation and of man's redemptive activity was correct, then why were both volumes of his memoirs replete with evidences of how little his views had prevailed with his children? As Harriet sought to sanctify her most recent loss, to emerge victorious from this latest trial, she often gave way to doubt. Her sisters tried to comfort her by pleading gentler views of God's dealings with the unconverted. She replied to Catharine and Mary that she had been assailed by "the Devil trying to seperate me from the love of Christ," but that faith had prevailed:

> The most . . . agonising doubts of Henrys state were thrown into my mind–as if it had been said to me, You trusted in God did you? You believed that he loved you--you had perfect confidence that he would never take your child till the work of grace was mature–and now he has turned him out without warning without a moments preparation–and where is he? I saw at last, that these thoughts were irrational that they contradicted the stated belief of my calmer moments that they were dishonorable to God and that it was my duty to resist them and to assume and sturdily maintain that Jesus had taken my dearest one in love to his bosom and since then the Enemy has left me in peace.

To a cousin wrestling with similar doubts, Harriet sent this message: "Say to her that I believe that if she commends her child with earnest devotion to her Savior and herself to its christian nurture that he stands pledged and promised to ensure its eternal salvation."[16]

Now, as at other times, Harriet drew great strength from her husband, whose profound influence on her has been ignored or belittled by her biographers, even including their son Charles E. Stowe. All of them have depicted Calvin Stowe as a kind of humorous caricature, abetted in this view by Harriet's own indulgent attitude toward him. But, while acknowledging that Stowe was a noted biblical scholar, no historian has ever examined either his scholarship or the effects of that scholarship on the changing religious ideas of his more famous wife. Not only his biblical studies but also his pulpit views were, as Harriet herself indicated time and again, the single most important influence on her theological development, particularly since they reinforced the liberal preachments of her brother Henry, who himself owed a considerable debt to Stowe.[17]

Calvin's influence was threefold. In the first place, he was temperamentally disinclined to doctrinal controversy, as both intellectually barren and tending to distress and divide the family of Christ. During his years at Lane, he learned to hate party divisions "when he was raced through muddy lanes, and rattled over corduroy roads, under the vigorous generalship of Dr. Beecher, all that he might give his vote for or against some point of doctrine, which, in his opinion, common sense had decided ages ago." A most painful example of discord over small points of doctrine affected Stowe doubly, because his first wife's father, the Reverend Dr. Bennet Tyler, had changed from friend to rancorous foe of Lyman Beecher. Stowe even took it upon himself, in vain as it proved, to effect a reconciliation between his two fathers-in-law. Tyler's intransigence appalled him, just as instances of clerical enmity against her father outraged Harriet and left her with a jaundiced view of ecclesiastical politics.[18]

The second and most direct contribution of Stowe to his wife's theological education lay in his knowledge of and affinity for, the mediating theology of the German pietistic theologians, especially Frederick Tholuck ("your great Apollo," Harriet called him). In the German's view, philosophy was neither to be despised as inimical to traditional faith nor enthroned as an all-sufficient science. There need be no antagonism between Christianity, as affirmed in the great historical confessions, and the modern spirit of free inquiry. Both would harmonize in an enlightened and trusting supernaturalism. The German theology was biblical, historical, and Christocentric. Stowe, who had translated both Jahn's *History of the Hebrew Commonwealth* and Lowth's *Lectures on the Sacred Poetry of the Hebrews* in the 1820s, maintained that the critical insights of such scholars gave precious aids to Christians. By showing how God had acted in history, preacher-theologians recovered both the spiritual authority and the consolations of the Old Testament. They thus refuted those who denied that the Hebrews had been in direct communion with God and had transmitted his word to the rest of the human race.

Although historians, translators, and exegetes contributed greatly to man's understanding of the word of God, metaphysicians, in Stowe's view, did not:

> For universal obligatory belief, for the salvation of the soul and the conversion of the world, the simple, direct, aphoristic, matter of fact teachings of the Bible are enough without the jointings and tinkerings and inharmonious harmonizings of speculative philosophy. It is the *sincere milk of the word* which men need in order that *they may grow thereby*; and not the hard, biting, indigestible cheese which theologians so often make of it. Not that theologians are blameworthy for speculating, it is the nature of the mind to investigate and to systematise.

Religion, as he defined it in his sermons, was "the union of the soul to God," and must ever be held essential, whereas theology and "ecclesiastics" were decidedly secondary in importance. "They are, if I may so express it, the shed under which religion shelters herself among sinful men." Furthermore, throughout recorded time believers had always agreed upon the vitals of faith. "It is manifest that there is, and ever has been, very little difference of opinion among experimental christians as to what constitutes true religion." Where there were fundamental paradoxes, genuine Christians never sought to resolve them through study and theorizing:

> The Bible takes marvellously little pains to make one truth *appear to be consistent* with another; it is enough that common sense teaches that real truths must always be consistent. The Bible asserts the power of sovereignty of God in terms as strong and absolute as it possibly could have done if man had no free-agency at all—and it affirms the free agency of man as fully as it could have done, if God exerted over him no control whatever. God has manifested no anxiety on this matter, and has left men to settle it among themselves.

The point must not be lost, Stowe told his congregations, that men could never settle such questions and ought humbly to admit it. As soon maintain that unregenerate men could find true happiness as that they could reason their way through "speculative difficulties." Did not Ecclesiastes preach the folly of both endeavors?[19]

Stowe's quarrel with the Edwardseans was precisely on this issue. Justifying the ways of God to men was a profitless task, even in the hands of a Jonathan Edwards, whose intellectual capacities Stowe eulogized in the most glowing language. The greatness of Edwards, who was "both the Calvin and the Fenelon of his class," lay instead in his unexampled piety and in his ministry to the spiritually dead, both white and Indian. His evangelistic preaching and his teachings on the nature of religion were more valuable, in Stowe's eyes, than his philosophy. Harriet Stowe was herself an astute lay theologian and well versed in the intricacies of the variant Edwardsean theologies, but for critical insights into the thought of Edwards and his heirs, we must grant Calvin Stowe due recognition.[20]

The third area in which Stowe's expertise provided his wife with ammunition for her attacks on orthodox theology (orthodox, that is, by her father's lights) was that of eschatology and prophecy. In the instance under consideration—Harriet's reaction to their son's untimely death—she relied upon her husband's interpretation of the Scriptures as the bedrock of her affective, maternal response, which affirmed Henry's continued and blissful existence. When she searched the Old and New Testaments for supporting texts, Calvin supervised her studies, directed her to learned commentaries, and made translations of pertinent passages for her. In the letter to her sisters before quoted, Harriet triumphantly announced his decision:

> Mr. Stowe says that the text "By which he (Christ) went and preached unto the spirits in prison" [1 Peter 3:19] can by no means be interpreted without great violence to the text to mean any thing more or less than that Christ's soul while his body lay in the grave went and declared the news of salvation to those spirits who were disobedient in the time of Noah—This you see at once opens a wide field of thought.

Stowe had formerly helped Isabella with her studies of Revelations ("he is not satisfied with any English commentary on the book") and encouraged her to pursue New Testament studies with her brother James. Harriet herself aided Calvin materially in his major work, the *Origin and History of the Books of the Bible*, while her own nonfictional books, the *Key to Uncle Tom's Cabin* (1853), *Woman in Sacred History* (1873), and *Footsteps of the Master* (1877), resulted from collaboration with Stowe and, to a lesser extent, with Edward Beecher. Calvin read and criticized her drafts, suggested lines of investigation, and brought many sources, including apocryphal and traditionary ones, to her attention.[21]

Having seen how much Calvin led and supported Harriet with his intellect and his conception of faith, we shall return to her writing of *The Minister's Wooing*. Harriet was striving to find language expressive of both grief and hope. To her twins Eliza and Hatty she wrote, "Had he lived, we had hoped to see all wrong gradually fall from his soul as the worn-out calyx drops from the perfected flower." She had been the gardener and Henry's soul the seed. As for Jesus, he was not (as the Devil seemed to say in her inner ear) so cruel as to cut that soul off unrepentant and unfulfilled. "I know that he has taken it to his own garden," she said. Calvin could only add, "I am submissive, but not reconciled." To Georgiana, the youngest daughter, Harriet spoke of weariness unto death when thoughts of what Henry might have become made her "feel again all the bitterness of the eternal 'No' which says I must never, never, in this life, see that face, lean on that arm, hear that voice." It was during this period of mourning, feeling a "deep wound in my heart" but also "golden hours of calm," that Harriet dictated her novel.[22]

Harriet clearly intended to handle New England Theology sympathetically yet expose its terrible effects on the human spirit, expose, as Catherine Sedgwick had said, "the cruel doctrines of Geneva." Mrs. Stowe singled out one of the extremest and subtlest forms, the theology of Samuel Hopkins. Let it be noted that she did not assail New Haven Theology, which by its liberalizing nature presented too small a target. It was not, I think, that she felt any great reluctance to criticize or discredit her father's doctrines openly, for the children's collaboration on the *Autobiography of Lyman Beecher* had already produced that effect, even though it was undertaken as a gesture of filial piety. She felt, instead, the need to take on an opponent who was both more extreme in his elaborations of Reformed doctrine and far less sympathetic than her father.

Just such a figure was Hopkins, the metaphysician par excellence, a byword for prolixity and aridity in the pulpit, a minister who had lost his congregation because of the coldly severe tenor of his preaching. It was to his credit, of course, that he had conducted a humanitarian crusade against slavery in slave-trading Newport, Rhode Island. What Harriet stressed, however, was the psychological result of his chilling doctrines, voicing at the same time a sincere protest against those descendants of the Puritans who had forgotten, or simply dismissed as tiresome, the invigorating intellectuality of the theological mind of New England. It was not because Hopkins was hardhearted, but because he was "at once reverential and logical" that "his religious teachings were characterized by an ideality so high as quite to discourage ordinary virtue." Hopkinsian theology, in Harriet's view, demanded instant perfection of the believer, for "Short of that absolute self-abnegation, that unconditional surrender to the Infinite, there was nothing meritorious." Esther Beecher, Harriet believed, had attained "absolute self-abnegation," but only after a struggle of decades.[23]

Harriet pictured the redemptive power of God as a ladder planted in the best affections of the ordinary human heart. It is from this earthy, and even base, human heart that the soul ascends, "refining as she goes, till she outgrows the human, and changes, as she rises, into the image of the divine." Like Jacob's ladder, this redemptive vision was the highest hope of the human spirit, a dream of the heart that gazed heavenward until the hope was lost to sight. And, like Jacob's ladder, it was not only a hope but a gracious promise.

> At the very top of this ladder, at the threshold of Paradise, blazes dazzling and crystalline that celestial grade where the soul knows self no more, having learned, through a long experience of devotion, how blest it is to lose herself in that eternal Love and Beauty of which all earthly fairness and grandeur are but the dim type, the distant shadow. This highest step, this saintly elevation, which but few selectest spirits ever on earth attain, to raise the soul to which the Eternal Father organized every relation of human existence and strung every cord of human love; for which this world is one long discipline, for which the soul's education is constantly varied, for which all its multiplied powers tend with upward hands of dumb and ignorant aspiration, this Ultima Thule of virtue had been seized upon by our sage as the all of religion. He knocked out every round of the ladder but the highest, and then, pointing to its hopeless splendor, said to the world, "Go up thither and be saved!"

What the wisdom of Moses had seen in writing of the Lord's promises, that salvation was to be brought about through "every relation of human existence," this was destroyed by the "subtile mental analysis" and uncompromising severity of Samuel Hopkins. Mrs. Stowe's metaphor of the ladder to heaven was simply the most lyrical expression of anti-Calvinistic theology, and her major criticism was strikingly similar to those of Horace Bushnell, on the one hand, and his opponent Edward Beecher, on the other. By insisting that every sinner, no matter how God had endowed or hobbled him, must vault straightway to the height of entire holiness, Hopkins had defeated his very purpose as a servant of God. How, Harriet was asking, could he be said to *minister* to his people when his sermons induced only "deep inward sadness" in "the most earnest and devoted, whose whole life had been a constant travail of endeavor, a tissue of almost unearthly disinterestedness"?

The victims of such a theology were many, but those who felt its terrors most were women like Mrs. Marvyn, the unconverted mother of an unconverted son lost at sea. She had labored and prayed to be won to Christ. Taking Dr. Hopkins's teachings with utmost seriousness, she had become despondent and now saw herself and her son as irretrievably lost and hateful to the God she longed to worship with her whole heart. In the New England of Jonathan Edwards and Samuel Hopkins, "the problems of the Augustinian faith" were presented in the most fearful form to the most intellectually earnest of people, with no countervailing forces to lessen their impact:

> No rite, no form, no paternal relation, no faith or prayer of the church, earthly or heavenly, interposed the slightest shield between the trembling spirit and Eternal Justice. The individual entered eternity alone, as if he had no interceding relation in the universe.
>
> This, then, was the awful dread which was constantly underlying life. This it was which caused the tolling bell in green hollows and lonely dells to be a sound which shook the soul and searched the heart with fearful questions. And this it was that was lying with mountain weight on the soul of the mother, too keenly agonized to feel that doubt in such a case was any less a torture than the most dreadful certainty.

Harriet was representing Hopkinsian theology, and the theologies it stood for, as stranding souls alone, stripping them of every prop or support, and thus abandoning them to a lonely battle against overwhelming forces. It was, to use an overworked term, an existential struggle of the cruelest and most awesome kind.

Of all Harriet's novels *The Minister's Wooing* is the most explicitly autobiographical. Later works would present a milder, sunnier picture of New England religion and its spokesmen (Lyman Beecher made less relentlessly logical), but in this book she worked out so many of the complexities of her family's relationships to their father that virtually every member of the family speaks, most often through the female characters. Mary Scudder, the spiritualized heroine, confutes Dr. Hopkins's doctrine of disinterested love to God (the much execrated test of the "willingness to be damned"—actually a Puritan legacy and not a Hopkinsian innovation). Mary addresses Hopkins in the words of Roxana Foote, as she had written them to Lyman

Beecher in 1798. Lyman had acçepted Roxana's teaching—"Do not God's children love Him because He first loved them?"—and had marveled at his wife as the very embodiment of disinterestedness. When Mrs. Marvyn confides in Mary, she speaks just as Catharine had written in debating her father: "I am quite sure there must be dreadful mistakes somewhere." Edward Beecher's aim, to uphold the honor of God in his dealings with men, is present throughout. And Harriet voices Henry Ward's teaching that "much of our misery in life is only Gods *drugging* us while we resist" through Candace, the black servant, who speaks words of simple consolation just as her namesake in Litchfield had done.

Harriet had stated the entire argument of *The Minister's Wooing* when she had maintained that "Christ would not have been for years the daily confidant of all my cares for Henry, walking with me as [an] intimate companion and working in his childhood" and "at last when his mind was in the most hopeful and progressive state hurrying him away unprepared." This was not only unthinkable, but as she had said, "dishonorable to God." The conception, so important to all the Beechers, that rightminded men and women must ever view God's character and teachings in a light wholly tending to his honor, is pointed up by exchanges such as these between Harriet and her sisters. In the relatively short time which had elapsed since Timothy Dwight had warned man, "a worm of the dust," against trying to "instruct his Maker," it was no longer a mark of active piety to accept bereavement, and its eternal consequences, as a providential occurrence not to be questioned. The piety which could accept even the forlorn hope and the needless sacrifice as the requisition of a benevolent ruler—that piety was increasingly seen as impious in its implications about the character of God. For Harriet Stowe, the suggestion that God had given her a son only that he might be lost forever and in the power of Satan was a lie. No, she had told Catharine and Mary, "No such slander as this shall the Devil ever fix on my Lord and my God."

Just as Harriet had pictured the aspiring soul as feminine, rising upward toward union with God, so she identified herself with Christ. Christ alone could feel what a mother felt. Her own heart was like his. It bore the pattern of Christ's heart and thus revealed the power of his saving love:

> He who made me capable of such an absorbing unselfish devotion as I feel for my children so that I could willingly sacrifice my eternal salvation for theirs—He certainly did not make me capable of more love more disinterestedness than he has himself. He

> invented mothers hearts—and he certainly has the pattern in his own and my poor weak rush light of love is enough to show me that some things cannot be—Mr. Stowe said Sunday that the mysteries of Gods government must be swallowed up by the greater mystery of the love of Christ even as Arons rod swallowed up the rods of the magicians.[24]

Her readers welcomed Harriet's argument that theology served the cause of religion only when it illuminated the passageways of the human heart and showed the heart's likeness to God's. Yet there was a tendency, understandable enough, for the popular press to dilute her message. A reviewer for the *Times*, for example, predicted, "It will be widely read, and will produce a very marked effect upon the popular theology of the day." Mrs. Stowe's "theological inculcations," he wryly observed, had brought denunciations from "those who devote a large portion of their time and thought to hunting heresies in . . . the Beecher family." But her chief purpose had been twofold, he said: first, to "prejudice the public mind against" predestination and election and, second, to prove that Christianity's "effects upon life, upon personal character, upon social relations, and upon the mind and heart of individuals, is certainly an essential element of its validity."

Such an assessment said both too little and too much. The complexity and ambivalence of Harriet's attitude toward "Calvinistic Puritanism" was not apparent to the reviewer, though it was important to her more thoughtful readers, such as James Russell Lowell. On the other hand, her conviction that Christianity is a richly realized and vividly spiritualized life was reduced almost to the equation that Christianity is moral character. Both the ruggedness and the mental acuteness of eighteenth-century Puritanism were slighted by superficial readers, while the muscularity and the sweetness were enhanced. The divine condescension and the mystery of grace were shuffled offstage.[25]

In her private life, meanwhile, Harriet continued to strive with her children, to urge a very high spirituality upon them. The twins were receiving a very costly European finishing, which fitted them, in the end, to be housekeepers for their mother. When Harriet received word that Hatty had been unfortunate in love, she wrote words of comfort, but also preached strenuous self-abnegation:

> My child you are like a bird in a storm which if it abide near the earth is tossed and baffled about and cannot fly—it has no resource but to soar *very* high above the region of storms and

> there find a clearer sky and calmer heavens. It is only by becoming very pure—*very* unselfish by living in the highest faculties that God has given you that you can find rest. A pure tender unselfish love kept deep within the heart may be a teacher and ministering angel to the soul, if it deepens our sympathy with humanity and makes us comprehend more vividly the sacredness of the heart which God gives to every human being. But if it becomes a selfish and solitary brooding [love]—if it draws *in* our sympathies from common human beings to fasten them on an ideal image then it becomes a morbid spot in the heart. God made you for a large hearted brave, noble woman—but you must come out of self—and live in others.

Harriet was marking key passages in the Bible for Hatty to study and reflect on, but: "As to the theology you have been hearing throw it out of your thoughts. It is if true at all truth which produces on you all the impression of falsehood." Let Hatty examine her own short history and she would see how gently she had been dealt with and how far above childish self-love she had already risen. It was God's plan and will that she should grow in grace, almost imperceptibly:

> My desires for you are unutterable that you may not fall short of that beauty and loveliness and perfection for which you were made—Oh *believe* my child that you are in loving hands—loving as they are resistless and that the current so strong which we feel bearing us along in spite of our struggles is not the current of a cruel fate but of a *loving care*—we are held in a very gentle but very firm hand—and creatures who are to outlast the stars—and live when all this earth is a forgotten dream must not expect to understand the discipline by which their Father prepares them for immortality.

In a curious way, Mrs. Stowe was presenting a predestinarian view to her daughter. Thirty-five years before this, Lyman had told Catharine that the current which was bearing her along in spite of her struggles was the torrent of her own wicked self-love, her hatred of God, her worship of earthly good. She despised and turned off his mercies. And if God chose, as in justice he was bound to choose, to drown her in the fast-running river, to sink her bark of depravity, rebellion, and self-will, how should she complain? But for Harriet, writing to a young girl whose trials were merely unrequited love and a fondness for finery, éclat, and good times, the soul's bark ran before a fair breeze, moved by a God who never hid his face.[26]

The maternal yearnings that had softened young Henry's heart toward Christ produced just the opposite effect in his sister Hatty. Catharine diagnosed Hatty's spiritual ailment in a letter to Henry Ward and challenged him, with bristling antagonism, to produce aliment for the hungry young soul of his niece:

> I write now to say that I want you to preach one sermon *for me*, as the representative and advocate of a large class of suffering minds, who as yet can find no one whose public teachings gives them a chance to get to Heaven. . . . Where a person is *self-reliant* and can pick out what suits and cast off what does not it comes out all right. But there is a class of the weak—the discouraged—the lambs of the fold, who are torn and wounded by the thorns of Calvinism—and it is for them I plead. Among these—you will find sister Harriets oldest daughter Hattie and I could find you many more.

Intellect, will, responsiveness to generosity and nobility of character: all these, according to Catharine, were prominent in Hatty. But she was, phrenologically speaking, "lacking in hope," while her "approbativeness" was "large."[27]

The depressing theology which Harriet had bade Hatty to put out of her mind had wounded her deeply, Catharine agreed. "Andover Calvinism administered in four [decisive?] phases by the four professors" had confused Hatty. Her intellect could not assent to such doctrines, but neither could she easily dismiss them. Further confusion had been sown by having "all its hideousness shown up by her uncles Edward and Charles, her mother and her Aunt." Moreover, what her closest relatives had taught her to abhor was not balanced by any constructive, consistent theology suitable to one of her age and intellect. The critical factor, in Catharine's view, was not mind but temperament. Hatty was, like her aunt, "fastidiously averse" to displays of ripe emotion, "a real Footism." Since the "*Footish*" temperament was all "*undemonstrative*," "That *emotive* experience toward Christ, which her mother exhibits does not suit her taste or nature any more than it did Uncle Samuels and mine. She *cant* feel so and *dont wish* to." Thus, it would seem that Hatty shrank, with increasing aversion, from the model of religious experience which her mother pressed upon her with importunate affection. Catharine might have said of Hatty, as she did of another relative, "All that is impassioned in religion goes against his taste."[28]

Harriet worked on Hatty's mind and spirit for three more years, but by 1862 she had concluded that her daughter had to "cast down an anchor somewhere," and not "in our [Andover] chapel nor in our denomination." Congregational orthodoxy was "unsuited to your nature and instead of doing you good I think does you harm." To ease Hatty's change of allegiance, her mother applied for a pew in the local Episcopal church and urged her to be confirmed with her Aunt Catharine. In preparation for the momentous step, she also wanted Hatty to "talk with Dr. [Frederic Dan] Huntington on the subject. He is the very ideal of le Bon Pasteur and having struggled thro many difficulties himself has a large and charitable judgement for all who struggle and are doubtful."

Huntington, it must be noted, had entered the Episcopal fold from the opposite side, from the rationalistic and, as he thought, dreary piety of Unitarianism. He had found within his new church a warmer, richer affective religion, just at the time when Catharine Beecher came to dislike and mistrust the "*emotive* experience" of evangelicalism and to seek a more decorous, rational religion. Episcopalianism was a shelter for both people, as Harriet hoped it would be for her daughters. Harriet herself preferred the Episcopal form of administering the sacrament. "To have my children with me in the fold of Christ, to unite with them in the sacrament has been the thing of all others I have longed for," she wrote shortly before Hatty, Eliza, Georgiana, and Catharine entered the Episcopal church.[29]

The young women's newfound safety brought no surcease from their mother's ministrations. "I think," she confided to them, that "I have never burned with such fervent aspirations for you—my soul has seemed to be nothing but a prayer that God will accept of you for *a work*—and make you do something *worth* all the prayers of years." Their religious life must vindicate their mother's Christian nurture. They could not settle down as ordinary churchgoers. They were Beechers, after all. Their lives must be consecrated and heroic, even if their "sphere" were more restricted than their mother's.

> I want you not to be drones and idlers in christs army—I want you to win *laurels*—such laurels as christ gives to those who have overcome *self* and borne and suffered in his behalf. If Christ should say to me of any one of you—you may choose for her wealth, position ease and with it the final salvation of her soul—but with low attainments in goodness—or—she shall have trouble and misfortune, but her soul shall rise with every trial—she shall be crowned with fortitude and become glorious in enduring love—I would not hesitate—which to choose—*would* you!

The better to help the girls "*purpose to lead a new life*," Harriet wrote down her thoughts on Christian discipleship. This was not to be The Little Women playing at making the Pilgrim's Progress, but rather "a sort of working chart--embodying all the results of my years of study and prayer—I want to give it to you to keep by you as a memorial of me—for you may live many years when I am gone and what I say to you now will bear remembering years hence—you will know and love me better and understand me better years hence than now." The list of their common blind spots and character defects was devastating, including superciliousness, a preference for fashion and luxury over industry and simplicity, light-mindedness, and a cruel sense of humor that got easy laughs by mimicking the physically afflicted and by fastening nicknames on unfashionable people. These were hardly the high-minded young gentlewomen of their Aunt Catharine's portrait. Such deplorable traits would have been disgusting had it not been for the fact that they were merely the relics of childhood. Harriet encouraged her girls to believe that the rough spots in their Christian character would be smoothed away by the kind discipline of the Anglican church. She entered into her daughters' new religious life with enthusiasm, as Henry slyly observed:

> Stopped at Andover half a day. All were well. . . . *The girls* spend much time with the prayer book,—play cards as a natural relief from devotion. Aunt Hattie is encouraging them by studying all the Magnalia of Episcopacy, with great zeal. The old Dr. set them back a little by disclosing the fact, that part of the collects, etc. are taken from the Apocrypha. No matter. All right now. The Prayer Book makes up any little lack of canonicity.

Henry could not help being amused at the Episcopal zeal of his favorite sister, but his Protestantism was offended, as was his evangelical prejudice against card playing.[30]

Lyman Beecher's death in the new year of 1863 was a relief to his family, who had grieved over his senility and his manifest eagerness to depart. As Lent approached, Harriet worked simultaneously on the proofs of his *Autobiography* and penned her reflections on the season. She reminded her daughters that Lent was "a venerable touching monument of the life and death of our best Friend," as celebrated by "the great majority of nominal christians." Only "that portion of the christian church which sprung from the influence of the Puritans," she told them, forswore those celebrations. The Puritanic element, "tho strong in piety and intelligence," was "greatly a minority in numbers." She waxed lyrical about Lent for the edification of the girls (one of whom, Georgiana, married a ritualistic Episcopal priest), sermonizing at the same time about her father's death. "Ever since my fathers death there has been a deep earnest feeling which has constantly been saying to me–*Be in earnest* in religion. It seemed to me the lesson of his whole life." This earnestness, which in Harriet and Calvin was still evangelical, did not strike root in their daughters. When the family had to unite in facing a crisis, Harriet found her girls deficient in piety.[31]

Their younger brother Fred had been wounded severely at Gettysburg, discharged from the army, and sent home. Harriet, who had secured him his place in a combat unit, believed that his sacrifice was not too great to save the Union but she was also horrified by the after effects of his injury. Fred Stowe had become an alcoholic while in the service, and his enslavement to liquor rapidly worsened after he left the army. Despite intensive medical treatment and a long ocean voyage with his father, Fred could not shake his craving for drink, which he used, he said, to still his head pains. Harriet, who was building a gorgeous Italianate mansion in Hartford, kept Fred in that city, hoping the physicians could afford him relief from his pain and wean him from drinking.

Fred, too, sought comfort and forgiveness in the Episcopal church, which he approached with "no great exstatic joy" but in the hope that God "is taking care of me" and would quench his thirst for alcohol. He had only to recall the recent death of his Uncle James Beecher's wife, who died in the throes of delirium tremens after a disgraceful career as the shameless woman of the Beecher family, to realize how keenly his own habit was wounding his family. In April of 1864, Harriet bought a pew in Hartford's St. John's Church, but her happiness over this new connection–she was never actually confirmed–was dimmed by the recognition that Fred was "hopelessly bound to this habit" and would always be disappearing on "sprees."[32]

The Stowes tried various courses of action to save their son. Harriet made him manager of her newly acquired plantation in Florida; but he was not equal to the assignment and was not, as she had hoped, isolated from supplies of liquor. Medical consultants were called in with regularity, but their measures had no effect. Harriet, unlike Fred's sisters, never gave him up entirely, and even managed to improve the occasion:

I read Gods providence to us as a family, in taking away him that

> would have been our pride and reliance, and leaving him for whom we fear, for whom we suffer, as meant to teach us the great lesson of pitifulness to all who sin—and sinning, suffer. . . . If we receive this trial aright it will make us tenderer gentler more Christ like,—and therefore is sent on us.

But they could not see beyond the immediate social disgrace to the providential purposes of God, as their mother hoped they would. Fred, in one of his attempts to rise above "the sin that easily besets him," now formally joined the Episcopal church. As his condition worsened, his mother urged a concert of prayer upon her other children. She told them to be "strong to endure—strong to fight the Devil in Gods name and to dispute every inch of Ground for this soul. . . . Fred will not fall away so as finally to perish."[33]

Fred Stowe voluntarily entered an asylum for alcoholics, but his sisters exhibited no greater forbearance, to his sorrow:

> Do not let the feeling of shame bear too heav[i]ly on you at the thought of my being here it is better far that I should be here than out in the world disgraceing the name you bear it is fare more honorable to have it said that he is here then to have it said that he has gone to the bad. I will raise out of the [slough?] and stand a free man an honor to the name I bear. . . . We proberly shall neaver be togeather for any length of time but I hope you will endevor to forgive, what you can neaver so long as I live forget, and with the memories of the past let the thought of their having been repented of with a deep and sincear repentence remove thier sting.

To his father, whose love persevered, Fred wrote of his dreadful shame and, again, of his resting upon religion: "I can not write much to night but at some other time I will give you an account of the way I came at last to seek Gods healp in this matter." His mother implored Hatty and Eliza to console Fred, but with trepidation. "It is a subject on which I feel too deeply ever to speak to you," she wrote, betraying the breach that had opened between them.

Fred was sent South again, to manage his mother's orange groves. In the end, for a second time, he went to sea in hopes of avoiding temptation. With the intercession of his aunt Isabella Hooker, he secured permission from his parents to join the merchant marine. He was already thirty-one, but still very much the sweet-tempered, feckless little boy of the family. On going ashore at San Francisco, he disappeared and no word ever came of his case, although the Stowes pressed inquiries for years. He was eventually presumed dead or shanghaied, unless he was living on in self-imposed exile under an assumed name. His mother's faith in his ultimate restoration was cruelly unrewarded.[34]

During the last thirty years of her life, Harriet underwent no thoroughgoing religious or theological changes, but there were significant developments in her mature ideas of faith and worship. Of these the chief were her belief in maintaining and refining an evangelical theology as a necessary constituent of faith; her attempts to mediate between the beliefs and practices of her childhood religion and that of the Episcopal church; and her insistence that religion was best taught by women, whose claim to authority lay in their hearts.

Despite fame and wealth, Harriet was buffeted by so many private griefs that her emotional and spiritual resources were often strained. Her daughter Georgiana, like many other genteel invalids of the time, became addicted to opiates. Harriet suffered for and with her as Georgiana went through various crises of mental illness. The spinster twins, who were extremely competent household managers, relieved Harriet of most of her routine domestic worries and also handled a great deal of her correspondence. Her remaining son, Charles, caused her unending anxiety. After many educational and disciplinary trials with the pampered Charley—who stretched but never snapped his fond parents' patience—the Stowes consented, with many misgivings, to send him to Bonn to study languages and theology. Harriet kept up her practice of weekly letters and, as with Eliza and Hatty, she wrote almost exclusively of the need to attain saving faith.

On one occasion, having just come from Georgiana's sickbed, Harriet wrote Charley her thoughts on "entire consecration":

> After all that is said about the higher life I think it can be resumed in two things. First *really* to do what we profess to do. Second *really* to *believe* what we profess to believe. All christians when they join the church profess to devote themselves wholly to the service of God—They profess to do this every time they take the communion. Why then are they not wholly the Lords? . . . Second all christians profess to believe that they have an Almighty Friend perfect in wisdom and goodness and armed with Almighty Power. . . . Why then are they not cheerful, exultant—Why are they restless uneasy worried, worn with care. Either because of a divided heart—of something kept back from God—or for want of full *faith*

that the things he says are so—and that the blessings he gives are real and are ours.

Her belief, unlike Catharine's, was that the human heart remains very much divided and that full faith is difficult to achieve. In all her family letters there was this brooding sense of the doubleness of religious experience. True Christians were supposed, according to the promises of the Bible, to be led to faith as easily as if they were children, and yet they had to take such pains about it. When her close friend, the very pious Susan Howard, lost a brother, Harriet sent her words of consolation but also of challenge: "A kind note from Hattie Stowe says—'Your brother is not dead but promoted. Can you *believe*?'" This was the lesson Harriet wanted to impress on her son.[35]

Her letters to Charles Stowe shed light on the major religious themes of her later years. When Charles returned from Europe, he took a church in Saco, Maine, and almost immediately experienced hostility to his doctrines. In part the criticisms may have been aimed at him rather than his theology. Although, as his aunt Eunice Beecher wrote, "he *is smart* as far as scholarly attainments go," he was also "self conceited and arrogant" and at best "a strang[e] compound." He also had to contend, so his mother claimed, against the common belief that blood was thicker than orthodoxy. As a "pestilent young sprig of Beecherdom," Charles Stowe could expect conservative Maine Congregationalists to eye him suspiciously. "I trust . . . you will be careful," she counseled her son, "and not give needless cause of controversy and division that souls be turned from seeking their personal salvation into a doctrinal mangle." It was not New England Theology or any school of distinctively Reformed dogma that she wanted Charles to preach. Neither did she want him to purvey a sentimentalized rationalism:

I advise you to preach a positive doctrine of *retribution* in the future stated in the line of Whatsoever a man soweth that also shall he reap. The fault of Unitarian and Universalist preaching is that they lack energy. Gods law becomes a piece of good advice in their hands and God a good father. . . . God *is* a loving father but his laws are not to be trifled with and that he does allow aweful retribution to follow breach of natural and moral law can be made clear by every mans own experience of life. The inflexibility of natural law its terrible certainty and unpitying hold on the sinner can be made quite clear—Moral laws have a hold no less certain and distinct—the natural laws are only visible symbols of the moral laws.

Future punishment, she told Charles, was not a theoretical proposition or an antiquated dogma. It was provable by "acts in nature and experience confirming scripture declaration," proofs which "will carry every mans conscience." As she wrote in *Oldtown Folks,* quoting herself from *Sunny Memories*, Calvinism is engraved all over nature and into man's consciousness, regardless of dogma. But modern preachers shied away from unpopular subjects, hence the vagueness of their pronouncements on future punishment:

> Now the fault of our pulpit generally is that *they do not preach retribution at all.* Now the good fathers in Maine have, and every human being has, a sort of practical sense that this so[r]t of thing will not do. . . . I hope you will never say or do any thing to express a young mans self esteem and that might look like want of reverence for the hardy old christian soldiers who have been bearing the burden of the day in Maine.[36]

On these grounds she based her unyielding hostility to the Unitarians. They stripped away unpopular and awkward doctrines in order to present a genial religion to their followers, but in the process they destroyed some precious saving truths. Harriet recalled Moses Stuart's advice: "Never preach *against* old formulas—quietly substitute truth for error or as Proff. Stuart used to say to his scholars, be thetic—not *anti* thetic." The trouble with the Unitarians was that they had declared war on the entire evangelical system of truths without any thought of appropriating the sound elements or of providing constructive ideas in their place:

> [Theodore] Parker was only a destructive [force]—a great pity it was. His teaching began in Theism but his sheep are wandering among the tombs of atheism. . . . God is love—salvation free—the Spirit and the bride [groom] say Come—But *Come* you must or be lost—such as I read it is Gods message.

It was the message of Harriet's friend John Greenleaf Whittier as well, and she commended his religious poetry to Charles. Quaker illuminism had always appealed to Harriet, though Quaker piety in the 1870s was an attenuated and moralized one. Her generosity toward Quakerism and her inveterate opposition to Unitarianism were of a piece with her emotional stance toward religion in general. When Charles, and some of his congregation, began leaning toward Unitarian views, his mother prescribed a course of studies on the life of Christ as a specific against atheism.[37]

In 1881, as Charles's tendencies toward Unitarianism were becoming more pronounced, his mother wrote impassioned protests. He seemed to be attacking her spiritual authority as well as the doctrines she believed in. "I have hitherto found you disposed to listen appreciatively and sympathetically to what I say," she wrote, "and I am surprised and grieved now to see in your letters no reference to it." The Unitarian denomination she dismissed as nothing but "a little body dissociated from the great body of Christs church—Latin Greek Anglican and American." His affinity for the views of conservative Unitarians only showed that they themselves were converging on "more orthodox" positions, and "in many cases coming out and joining them as Dr. Huntingdon and others." The group which Charles imagined to be united was actually wracked with division. "Thus the *name* [Unitarian] covers every form of dissent and unbelief down to that of men like [Minot J.] Savage who believes no more in Christ than a Jewish rabbi. I have heard most atrocious radicalism in E[dward] Hale's pulpit—not from him but from br[other] ministers."

She also reminded Charles, in case he should overlook it, of "the imputation of changeableness" that had clung to him:

> I have always regretted that you did not finish your course at New Haven—your sudden change there however had the Bishops order for its justification but it was a pity—and made necessary the finishing of your course in Germany and it is doubtful to me whether the scholarly advantages you gained there balance the lack of faith—the filling of your head with rationalistic doubtings, whose bats wings every once and a while flap and flit about you when you are trying the simple old paths of childlike trust. For you to go into a denomination of skeptics and rationalisers of whom scarce any two believe alike, would I think be *peculiarly* bad for you—who are altogether too much given to rationalistic dangers—and too little faith.

The recent history of Unitarianism was depressing, a history of honest men dividing into camps. Men like Cyrus A. Bartol, whose sermons she had once praised as "models of undenominational Christian preaching," were now "going down into the baldest naturalism." On the other hand, Bartol's coreligionist George Merriam had become "too orthodox for unitarian pulpits and too Unitarian for orthodoxy and is thrown out of the ministry," while the Stowes' "earnest" friend, Annie Fields, had stopped going to Unitarian services for lack of spiritual sustenance.[38]

Let Charles compare the disarray of Unitarianism with the successes of his Beecher uncles:

> Uncle Henry and Uncle Tom . . . differ[ed] in many points with

> the received orthodoxy of their day—but they made no noise about it—they preached what they *sincerely did believe* and left what they were in doubt about to the further teachings of Gods Holy Spirit. Clinging to Christ making definite efforts to bring souls into union with him they found work enough for man or angel to do without chasing after or fighting over disputed theological subtleties and noble christian churches have grown up under their labors.

Charles had formerly said of Henry Ward Beecher that his sermons were "food for him—they *stimulate* and open *new thoughts!* The only man's sermons that do!" Now, Harriet was pained to hear, "You 'despise Liberal Orthodoxy for its slovenly inconsistency and its dishonesty.'" This was an unjust and ignorant judgment:

> What I, and your uncle Henry believe and teach is not either slovenly, or inconsistent and we are neither of us dishonest. Your uncle is precicely the model I would hold up to you, of how a manly and honest man should guide himself in the ministry in an age when God is shedding new light on religion thro the development of his own natural laws in Science—what he could not conscientiously preach he let alone. . . . He never said any thing about Adam's fall one way or the other—but preached simply that all had sinned and needed to repent. He preached Christ as the Savior from Sin—as the Friend—Comforter and Guide. He preached the certain punishment of sin here and hereafter. The need of Gods Holy Spirit—Gods willingness to give it. Prayer—and its answer. The Bible—and its inspiration and how to use it. . . . Now if he had yielded to disgust—gone over to Unitarianism—there would have been lots of scandal a bitter controversy—but no Plymouth Church.

Liberal Orthodoxy also taught the Atonement as God's greatest act of love. And that "there is a Hell a fearful one," for "*Sin* is *Hell* and much of the suffering of this life is the burning of the fire of Hell in our own bosoms—temper, pride self will—these are Hell fire and if we do not flee to Christ and accept his healing power his Holy spirit they will burn worse after death than here." Harriet begged her son to recognize his danger. She warned that "the great Enemy of whom Christ warns" was watching for the chance to trip him into "some hasty step that may be a fatal one in your future life."

If not for his own soul, Charles ought to be fearful for the souls in his care. "I cannot describe," she told him, "the ardor with which I desire and pray that you may be made a minister after Christ's own heart." If Mrs. Stowe was aware how much like her father she sounded in importuning her son, she never acknowledged it. In one letter she felt called upon to defend herself from Charles's expressed fear that she was becoming too excitable:

> You say my letters appear to be written under nervous excitement—perhaps they were—but your letters did seem to give ground for alarm. . . . Your declaration that you mean to leave these speculative matters and go about *work* for Christ meets my wishes and has been unspeakable relief to me. . . . You are *so* outspoken that you are in great danger with your speculative habits of deranging the faith of simple souls.[39]

Her own faith—she would have accounted herself a simple soul—was a triumphant one in the end, but in part because she managed to block off distressing signs of dissent from Catharine and Henry, and because she was a very evangelical Episcopalian and could have a religion very much of her choosing. Catharine's views were almost as rationalistic as those of the men Harriet denounced, for instance, O. B. Frothingham. Save for Catharine's retention of future punishment, her ideas on the nature of man's redemption were extremely rationalistic. As for Henry, whose "music and motion" and generalship she begged for in Charles Stowes's behalf, he was so far gone down the road of liberalism that he had abandoned the tenets of liberal Congregationalism, including the modified doctrine of future retribution which Harriet believed was the shibboleth separating orthodoxy from naturalism. What she made of Henry's apostacy she never said.[40]

The Stowes' Episcopalianism also contained incongruous elements. Their son-in-law Henry F. Allen was an Anglo-Catholic, who proselyted even among Henry Ward Beecher's children, and Harriet loved many of the trappings of high-church worship, particularly the profusion of floral decorations and Gothic ornaments. In the Stowes' own little mission church in Mandarin, Florida, Calvin preached from a "Gothic desk" of his wife's construction, which she had cobbled out of other pieces of furniture. But Stowe, who had reentered the Presbyterian ministry (without any Anglican interlude), preached in his own fashion. Since he believed that the Anglican Thirty-Nine Articles were the best extant summation of Calvinistic doctrine, his sermons were probably not standard Episcopalian fare. After Eunice Beecher worshipped at their flower-decked church in the woods, she reported sourly to Henry:

> I for one can't find rest in the Episcopal Church, certainly not in such a mongrel 'alf and 'alf as to humor the [Stowe] girls,

To: Lewis

Date: July 7 Time: 11:30

WHILE YOU WERE OUT

Ms. Elizabeth Yetter

of

Phone

Area Code Number Extension

TELEPHONED	X	PLEASE CALL	X
CALLED TO SEE YOU		WILL CALL AGAIN	
WANTS TO SEE YOU		URGENT	

RETURNED YOUR CALL

Message: Please call at:
([illegible]) [illegible]-5388 or
([illegible]) 741-[illegible]

SCD
Operator

AMPAD EFFICIENCY®
23-000 40 SHT. PAD
23-001 250 SHT. DISPENSER BOX

To Lewis

Date July 7 Time 11:30

WHILE YOU WERE OUT

Ms. Elizabeth Yetter

of

Phone

Area Code Number Extension

TELEPHONED	X	PLEASE CALL	X
CALLED TO SEE YOU		WILL CALL AGAIN	
WANTS TO SEE YOU		URGENT	
RETURNED YOUR CALL			

Message Please call at:
(201) 968-5388 or
(201) 741-8166

sgp
Operator

> they manage to make of this church here. Have just returned from Communion Service, and it has made me home sick, for dear old Plymouth [Church] and *the one* who makes that service something more than a mere form—or ceremony. I can't see how Hattie Stowe with her "higher life" tendencies can be content with such poor fare.[41]

Harriet did, in fact, feel yearnings toward Catholicism, but not the Catholicism of contemporary Rome. She dreamed of a half-historical, half-legendary epoch before primitive Christianity had become altogether imperial and papistical. In 1874, when Charles Stowe was in Rome, she had relived some of her first favorable impressions of Catholic worship, but she sadly concluded:

> St. Peters is a lovely building in conception—yet in many of the architectural ornaments how tawdry and how unlike is the Pope borne on the shoulders of the pye bald followers with fans of peacocks feathers to Jesus meek and lowly entering Jerusalem upon an ass! About as much like as the giggered and fussed up and party colored feather dusters which are distributed as palm leaves! as much like palm leaves in their beauty as the Pope and Cardinals are like Christ and his Apostles—just about.

She wanted to share all Charles's feelings, which, she was certain, were fundamentally Protestant:

> I know *all* your feelings have felt them all—I have that half to my mind which exquisitely feels all the devout attraction of the Romish Church—but I have as you have the half also that sees the *impossibility* of the hierarchy representing either in spirit or in results on society what Christ is—or wills us to be—May he keep you under the shadow of his wings.

Yet the pope and his retainers were not so much worse than the mass of nominal Christians. Even the disciples, after all, had doubted that the dead Christ would arise. Harriet followed her son through Rome in her mind:

> I thought all day of you in St. Peters of the silver trumpets that sound down from the dome when the great moment of the elevation of the host comes—It is a most sublime scenic effect—but how different from the little quiet upper room where Jesus broke the bread and gave the wine to twelve simple fishermen.

The voices of the *castrati* symbolized the tragedy of the Roman Church. "The miserere sung by emasculated beings is indeed a wild wierd wonderful wail—but to me it speaks the anguish of souls crushed under that immature system and crying in vain for an absent Lord." And finally, she rested as much as ever on revivalistic religion:

> [Dwight L.] Moody's Easter sermon which consisted of a simple homely earnest recital of the story of the resurrection from the four gospels had more of Christ than all I saw in Holy Week put together. It seems now that the revival under Moody will shake Boston and all the state.[42]

Her reservations about Catholicism were unchanged from the views expressed in *Agnes of Sorrento* (1862), published fifteen years earlier. In that novel Harriet had depicted Girolamo Savonarola as "an Italian Luther," striving to "disentangle Christianity from Ecclesiasticism" but ultimately "obstructed by the full energy of the whole aroused serpent brood which hissed and knotted in the holy places of Rome." She characterized his famous hymns as minglings of "the Moravian quaintness and energy with the Wesleyan purity and tenderness." The heroine, Agnes, was another Mary Scudder. Her serenity was like that of "the veriest Puritan maiden that ever worshipped in a New-England meeting-house." Mrs. Stowe's attitude toward the reliquaries, which had so amused her and Charles Beecher in 1853 was somewhat ambivalent. She was unwilling to denounce Roman superstition in the usual Protestant vein, because she admired the Catholic attitude of veneration. Yet, on the whole, we see in *Agnes of Sorrento* Harriet's determination to claim as Protestant whatever features of late medieval Catholicism were most praiseworthy.[43]

Also present in *Agnes* was Harriet's conviction that women had a peculiarly sacred and powerful role in Christianity. This was present from the beginning but had been obscured or slighted, particularly by Protestants. This belief, which she voiced in a number of books, must not be confused with the sentimental cult of feminine saintliness, although it derived in part from that source, nor was it merely a transplanted, hybridized Mariolatry. Mrs. Stowe's thesis was twofold: first, that women were intended by God to minister, equally with men, to fellow seekers; second, that this was proven by the Scriptures themselves, in their revelation of a female prophetic tradition. It must be clear by now that when Harriet wrote or spoke to her brothers and sons, it was—in her own mind at least—as their intellectual equal and, by common agreement, as their spiritual preceptor.

This religious authority, based on acute theological learning and biblical studies under her husband's guiding hand, imbues all her letters, particularly those to Charles Stowe.

It is not surprising, then, to find that she regarded herself as qualified to fill certain sacerdotal functions. When she described a Mandarin communion service, she announced, as by right, "I am sole servitor. . . . We all know and love each other so much in our little neighborhood that the feast is more domestic and intimate than in larger places." She was, in fact, a self-appointed home missionary to Mandarin and its vicinity, and she savored the role with its ecumenical possibilities. "All unite," she wrote, "Congregationalists, baptist[s] methodists Episcopalians and it seems good." There she led a married women's bible class. When they studied the raising of Lazarus, their womanly hearts were touched because "there was not hardly one among us that had not had a great loss—a sorrow—a grave to weep over." In virtually all her letters to Charles, Harriet directed him to read certain books, not just Christian classics that any mother might recommend, but critical studies, commentaries, and the like, which she herself had already assimilated and knowledgeably criticized. "In Andover," a typical sentence ran, "I always warned our young men not to study *theories* and arguments but to follow Christ in the sacred narrative."[44]

She found her second argument, the existence of an ancient tradition of female prophecy, in the Old Testament, which she had undertaken to explicate because she wished to see it rehabilitated as a source of revelation equal with the New Testament:

> It was with some fear, for myself that I began these OT studies —but by keeping a prayerful attitude—by suspending first judgments and laying every difficulty in a filial spirit at the feet of my Father, I found a sweetness, light and comfort in those studies not inferior to what I find in the New Testament.

In *My Wife and I* (1872), a "society" novel, Mrs. Stowe editorialized about the folly of modern minds in neglecting the Scriptures:

> A throughly educated graduate of most of our colleges is unprepared to read intelligently many parts of Isaiah or Ezekiel or Paul's epistles. The scripture lessons of the church service often strike his ear as a strange quaint babble of peculiar sounds, without rhyme or reason [and] . . . he is only preserved by a sort of educational awe from regarding them as the jargon of barbarians. Meanwhile, this literature of the Bible, strange, weird, sibylline,

> and full of unfulfilled needs and requirements of study, is being assailed in detail through all the courses of a boy's college life.[45]

Woman in Sacred History was the result of Mrs. Stowe's studies, her attempt to redress the balance through character sketches of the prominent women of the Bible. Where the sources were fugitive or the stories apocryphal, she pieced them out with legendary materials from early Catholic sources or contented herself with substituting her own highly colored emotional messages, procedures her husband presumably endorsed. The "sacerdotal nations," as she called Christendom, had much to learn from "That pure ideal of a sacred woman springing from the bosom of the family, at once wife, mother, poetess, leader, inspirer, prophetess," an ideal "peculiar to sacred history" of Judeo-Christian lands and peoples. Deborah the prophetess, Delilah the destroyer, Jezebel, Esther, Judith, and even the Witch of Endor took their places alongside New Testament women like the widow of Nain, Lydia, Mary Magdalene, Martha, and above all, Mary the mother of Jesus. Mrs. Stowe was not interested in presenting lovely heroines only, as the inclusion of Bible villainesses shows. She wanted to show how powerful such women had been, whether for good or ill.

From modern times she selected a curious but revealing example, an elderly black woman of Brunswick, Maine, whose childlike piety was a great blessing on the town whose almoner she was. In this unnamed Christian worthy were embodied all the virtues Mrs. Stowe had come to associate with entire holiness: a member of a despised race (a race which, nevertheless, was supposed to be more feeling and more trusting than others), a pauper, a woman who had known many kinds of suffering. This one woman was, from the worldly point of view, a victim, a dependent, and a negligible factor. But her faith had enabled her not only to rise above the world but to serve as a light to others. So Mrs. Stowe felt, drawing upon the very old tradition that the saints of the eternal kingdom are often found among the disinherited and despised of this world.[46]

Even so, Mrs. Stowe's Bible figures were mostly women of power and authority. The lavish, garishly colored lithographs accompanying the tales heightened the mystery, power, and sensuous womanliness of her subjects. But, above all, the prophetesses—vessels of divine revelation—were shown excelling in their domestic attachments and finding exaltation in the cycle of conception, parturition, nursing and nurture, and vicarious living through adult children still bound by the maternal tie. Mary, the mother of Christ, was not the goddess of beauty or mere earthly power and wisdom. She was the goddess of poverty, sorrow, pity, and mercy:

> In Mary, womanhood, in its highest and tenderest development of the MOTHER, had been the object of worship. Motherhood with large capacities of sorrow, with the memory of bitter sufferings, with sympathies large enough to embrace every anguish of humanity!—such an object of veneration has inconceivable power.

Women, then, had not been mere auxiliaries, supernumeraries in the drama of redemption. They had been anointed by God to speak for him.[47]

A third idea, which first emerged in this book, was certainly heterodox, but it was not an idea peculiar to Harriet. She believed not only that Christ partook of human nature through his incarnation, but that his humanity was distinctively feminine. The feminine element in Christ's nature was Mary's contribution to her son's greatness. It was her physical and psychological endowment as a woman that Mary, representing mankind, had given, sealing the human nature to the divine. This theme was repeated, with greater insistence, in *Footsteps of the Master*, a devotional manual of the Christian year. "The blessedness of Mary," Harriet wrote, "was that she was the one human being who had the right of ownership and intimate oneness with the Beloved." From a single line of a single gospel concerning the childhood of Christ, Mrs. Stowe concluded that

> He was entirely her own. She had a security in possessing him such as is accorded to other mothers. . . . Neither was she called to separate from him. . . . To love, to adore, to possess the beloved object in perfect security, guarded by a divine promise—this blessedness was given to but one woman of all the human race.

The fruits of this blessedness were not for Mary alone, for her son Jesus ("we should call him LOVE, itself"), who embodied "the feminine element exalted and taken in union with divinity," transcended time and history. His greatness was Mary's greatness, and the Catholic veneration of the Virgin, from which Protestants shrank with such aversion, was an instinctive recognition of this fact.[48]

Woman in Sacred History and *Footsteps of the Master* are not among Harriet Beecher Stowe's better-known works. Even now it would be hard to say how widely accepted her ideas were. They were genuine attempts to popularize biblical studies at a time when the old Protestant bibliolatry was giving way to naturalism. More than that, these books were Mrs. Stowe's attempts to come to terms with her own role in her family and in history. If anyone typified a heroine of sacred history, Harriet did. She had always seen herself acting within a providential scheme, as an instrument of God. By writing *Uncle Tom's Cabin* and *Dred* she was not merely his instrument, but a hammer of God. There are few Americans whose impact upon their generation was greater than hers. Yet she had persisted in viewing herself as an ordinary womanly woman, badly dressed, extremely vague at times, saddled with an eccentric but endearing old professor of a husband. She turned out potboiling pieces often enough and was always worried about money. Her children were neither handsome nor exceptionally intelligent and they were not remarkable for resourcefulness or initiative. Most painful of all, they evidenced none of the ardent piety she herself felt.

All the same, she was not the scatty little woman of her public remarks. When the Emancipation Proclamation was brought to the Senate, the entire floor and gallery rose to acknowledge Mrs. Stowe's presence and roared its acclamation. Perhaps she would have felt differently if Henry Stowe had lived to be the great man she and Calvin had imagined he would be. As she had written, Christ provided the pattern of woman's heart. In Mrs. Marvyn and James Marvyn, Harriet embodied not only herself and Henry Stowe idealized, but Mary the mother of Christ:

> None of the peculiar developments of the female nature have a more exquisite vitality than the sentiment of a frail, delicate, repressed, timid woman for a strong, manly, generous son. There is her ideal expressed; there is the out-speaking and out-acting of all she trembles to think, yet burns to say or do; here is the hero that shall speak for her, the heart into which she has poured hers, and that shall give to her tremulous and hidden aspirations a strong and vigorous expression.

Mrs. Stowe must have known that she was a prophet, and a prophet honored in her own country. A Beecher could be no less. But her power and influence, she said, came from the love and tenderness of a woman's heart, the heart of a suffering mother.[49]

Harriet continued to work out her theological perplexities. One, for instance, was the true interpretation of the Atonement, to which she devoted a series of letters to her son. When Catharine Beecher died in

1878, Harriet envied the rest her sister had found in "the Everlasting Arms" and wrote to their sister Mary: "God takes care of love and shelters it for he is Love. The world was a cold place to Him when he lived here—from cradle to grave and it is not here that his children have their rest ever." Calvin took a very long time to die of Bright's disease, and she consoled him by telling him that "when patience has had her perfect work he will be sent for."

Harriet herself looked forward to dying and did not even regret Henry's passing. After senility claimed her in 1890, she continued to give out autographs to admirers. "Trust in the Lord and Do good" was the only thought to which her old mind remained riveted. Just before her mind failed her, however, Harriet had written to a close friend about her heavenly desires:

> The inconceivable loveliness of Christ! It seems that about Him there is a sphere where the enthusiasm of love is the calm habit of the soul, that without words, without the necessity of demonstrations of affection, heart beats to heart, soul answers soul, we respond to the Infinite Love, and we feel his answer in us, and there is no need of words.

If there is one phrase that captures the religion of Harriet Beecher Stowe, it is her own, "the enthusiasm of love." It was not the "disinterested benevolence" of Samuel Hopkins, or even the millennial ardor of her father, but a domesticized, highly personal vision of a love between a gentle Jesus and his children, his brothers, and his sisters. Mrs. Stowe's theology was liberal and Christ-centered, but compared to her brother Henry's, it was also more akin to the evangelicalism of Lyman Beecher's generation.[50]

8 *HENRY WARD BEECHER*

When Henry Ward Beecher died at the age of seventy-three, such was his fame that hundreds of other famous men and women vied for the distinction of doing him honor. John Rogers, whose work Beecher had admired, cast a limited-edition statue of the preacher, and Edward Bok compiled a commemorative volume containing tributes by Louis Pasteur, William Gladstone, Elizabeth Blackwell, William Tecumseh Sherman, and Dion Boucicault, among others. The most quoted of these appreciations is that of Robert Ingersoll, the militant atheist, who declared, "Henry Ward Beecher was born in a Puritan penitentiary, of which his father was one of the wardens."

Ingersoll's anti-Calvinist screed was more than simple rant enlisted against cant because of his obvious sympathy with Beecher and his insightful, if bloated, description of the sources of Beecher's rebellion against Puritanical religion:

> Through the grated windows of his cell, this child, this boy, this man caught glimpses of the outer world, of fields and skies. New thoughts were in his brain, new hopes within his heart. Another heaven bent above his life. There came a revelation of the beautiful and real. Theology grew mean and small.
>
> Nature wooed, and won, and saved this mighty soul.
>
> Her countless hands were sowing seeds within his tropic brain. All sights and sounds—all colors, forms, and fragments were stores within the treasury of his mind. . . .

Except for Ingersoll's animus against "utterly heartless and inhuman" New England Congregationalism, the passage quoted could well have been taken from Beecher's own romantic theological statement, his unsuccessful novel *Norwood.*[1]

But the Puritan penitentiary of Ingersoll's depiction proves upon closer examination to have been much less confining to Henry than to his brothers and sisters. Like them, he was accustomed to portray his early life with a mixture of warm nostalgia and righteous indignation. On the whole, his memories were fond ones:

> Before I was ten years old I had learned to sew, to knit, to scour knives—and to dirty them. I had learned to wash dishes—and to prepare them for washing. I could set and clear the table . . . cut and split and bring in wood. I could make fires—and it was no small art to build a fire with green oak on a roaring winter morning. I had learned how to feed cattle, and curry horses, and go to school—and not to study.

These small-town virtues of industry and energetic goodwill, combined with a certain playfulness, remained with Beecher in later years, even when he was able to celebrate the humble life from within a richly appointed townhouse.[2]

He could not get accustomed as a child to thinking of his father as a great public figure: "My predominant feeling was that he was a man of great moral excellence." Although Lyman boxed his sons' ears on occasion and even thrashed the boys, his chief appeal was to their affection for him. In the same spirit was the freedom with which he showed his feelings, particularly his tenderness. In a sermon of 1883 Henry told his congregation how Lyman had comforted him when he had a painful toothache:

> I went into my father's room, and he put his hand upon my head, and with tones of great kindness and love said, "You have got the toothache, my dear boy! Come get in with me and cuddle down by my side,"—how that filled me with affection, and such gladness that I forgot the toothache! It was quite lost and gone. I slept.

The sermon topic which this vignette illustrated was "The Rest of God."[3]

While he was exceptionally close to his father, Henry perhaps felt a more inveterate antipathy for his stepmother, Harriet Porter, than did the rest of Roxana's children:

> Now, my nature was enthusiastic and outgushing; I was like the convovulvus—I wanted to be running on somebody all the time. But my [step] mother was stately and not easy to approach. She was a beautiful person, serene and ladylike. She never lacked self-possession in speech, gesture, or posture. She was polished; but to my young thoughts she was cold. As I look back I do not

Henry Ward Beecher

> recollect ever to have had from her one breath of summer. . . . I revered her, but I was not attracted to her. I felt that she was ready to die, and that I was not. I knew that at about twilight she prayed; and I had a great shrinking from going past her door at that time.

In this characteristic self-revelation, it was he, and not his stepmother, whom Henry likened to the wild morning glory. Her cool, deathly presence threw a pall over his thoughts and feelings. By contrast, when he was eighteen Henry came across some of his parents' old letters and was deeply impressed with Roxana's:

> Her letter to father in which she treats of "love to *God*, whether we should love him because he has done us good or not," etc., I was very much pleased with. And I could not help observing that her letters were superior, more refined and conclusive, than the corresponding ones of father's. . . . Her piety was doubted by herself, although no one who reads her description of her feelings can doubt for a moment that Christ was found within her heart.

In after years Henry was wont to declare that Roxana Beecher was to him as the Virgin Mary was to Roman Catholics.[4]

The mothering that Harriet Porter seemed incapable of providing was bestowed on Henry by three persons: Esther Beecher, Aunt Chandler (another family connection), and his sister Harriet. Aunt Chandler remains a shadowy figure, one of the numerous female relatives who attached themselves to the Beecher household at various times. Of Esther Beecher, Henry said that her "great soul" glorified religion in his young eyes. His bond to Hatty was intense and enduring, and it was to her that he confided his grievances and ambitions. She seldom failed to take his part, a tendency that became more pronounced when he reached adulthood. Hatty sensed instinctively that Henry would become the great man of the family and lamented the misunderstandings and indifference he encountered on every hand:

> He is too good for me—I sit and think over all his sorrows, all the injustice that was at one time done him and all his gentle child-like tenderness of heart, till I think it cannot be that Heaven will not claim its own, and take him to the world where alone he will find those like him.[5]

Henry was a fair-haired, pink-faced child tending toward fatness, who ran around Litchfield in hand-me-downs, his locks carefully soaped into forehead curls by his doting sisters. Although he may not have been the tongue-tied blockhead he was later reputed to have been (a description his brother Charles indignantly denied), Henry was a poor student in a bright family. Nevertheless, his spirits were resilient and he impressed everyone by his unfailing good humor and boisterous, mischievous ordinariness. He was, seemingly, a thoroughly uncomplicated child among high-strung siblings. Henry was, furthermore, a remarkable mimic. He liked to stand chest-deep in hay, wearing huge "blue goggles" scavenged from some trashpile, to deliver a juvenile sermon:

> Then he would mount his airy perch, and begin his sermon to his school-mates; he used no articulate words, but a jargon of word-sounds, with rising and falling inflections, wonderfully mimicking those of his father. The rotund phrasing, the sudden fall to solemnity, the sweeping paternal gesture, the upbrushing of the hair, were all imitated perfectly by the son.

Henry always ended these performances by tumbling down the hay, a departure from decorum not unlike those which scandalized his clerical brethren in later life. Like his sisters, and especially his brothers, Henry was to find ridicule, whether gentle or witheringly sarcastic, a potent weapon against the sterner features of orthodoxy.[6]

He did not distinguish himself at Miss Pierce's school, at Catharine's school, at the Boston Latin School, or at the Mount Pleasant Classical Institute, where he was sent to prepare for Yale. At one point, he became so unhappy over his enslavement to the classroom that he made up his mind to run away to sea. Lyman, who did not fancy the idea of Henry's sailing before the mast, took him aside and made a bargain with him, assuring him that he could go to sea when he had thoroughly mastered the mathematics necessary for a ship's officer to know. Ciphering was not Henry's forte, and the romantic dream went glimmering away.

Amherst College, rather than Yale, became the family's choice for Henry. At Mount Pleasant he had profited immensely from the elocutionary drill of an Englishman, John E. Lovell, who did more than anyone else to instill self-confidence and feelings of mastery in the boy. At Amherst Henry continued to practice debate and oratory but scanted his other studies, except for classes in natural history and geology under Edward Hitchcock, the geologist-theologian. The "science" which attracted him most, however, was phrenology. He began to organize his thoughts regarding the relationship between men's organic endowments and their spiritual and intellectual ones. Character, as Henry called it, became his chief study. He kept a notebook on "outlines of the lives who have made themselves or have attained any great end by decision of character" and also observed the acts and thoughts of ordinary men around him. At the same time, Henry decided to buff up his social manner and become a man of the polite world. He did not desire mere social standing, however, for he identified his career with his father's. But he became convinced that evangelicals took too grim and coarse a view of life, shunning refinements and graces which enhanced the Christian life.

Henry asked Harriet to help him find a young lady suited to wed a Western home missionary, and when Lyman finally decided to go to Lane Seminary, his son exulted in the move. "It will make the people of the west think that Jacob and his family are again going down to Egypt." Reflecting on the fact that they would not be universally welcome, he also pictured the Hoosiers and Suckers complaining, "Surely the Locusts of Egypt are come upon us in the form of the Beecher family." Henry knew all too well that his father's theology and social aims were anathema to large segments of those Lyman liked to call the perishing millions of the West.[7]

Before he graduated from Amherst, Henry became engaged to Eunice White Bullard, the daughter of a Sutton, Massachusetts, physician and farmer. They resigned themselves to a long engagement because Henry had to undergo a five-year training as a minister and home missionary. He was eager to take his place among the Beechers in Ohio and made glowing predictions to his prospective wife. But from the first he was caught up in the maelstrom of Presbyterian schism. When his father was haled before the presbytery in the first round of heresy proceedings, Henry was assigned clerk to take stenographic notes of the trial and followed Lyman through the entire routine of prosecution and appeal. That their father was vindicated only heightened his children's indignation, and none had as little use for church law and church lawyers as Henry. After one ordinary synodical meeting he recorded Lyman's opinion of the whole business:

> Father remarked that "nothing laid such a tax on a man's patience, whether personally interested or not, as ecclesiastical judicial proceedings–It is a burlesque on law–" He remarked also that these contentions in the church, was [*sic*] preparing the way for the subversion of the Presbyterian government and [the] universal triumph of *congregationalism*.

The heresy trial, which scandalized the Beechers, drew them protectively around their father. However, their own questionings of Lyman's doctrines did not abate on that account. Their misgivings derived heightened significance from being debated against the backdrop of the conservative prosecution.[8]

It is an interesting feature of Henry's letters and journals of this period that he was, for the most part, mute on these topics. Everything else, whether it reflected favorably on him or not, was duly recorded: illnesses, literary opinions, lapses from faith, ambitions, romantic scrapes (although he was engaged, he remained an incurable flirt). He seemed to sail effortlessly through the turbulent waters of theological controversy at the very time when Charles was nearly shipwrecked in atheism, George was veering dangerously close to Oberlin perfectionism, and Edward was marooned on a reef of ancient heresy. Thomas Beecher was favorably impressed by his brother Henry's comparative freedom from metaphysical wrangling.[9]

Yet, if Henry's later reflections on this period are to be believed, he too was caught up in a tormented revolt against Calvinistic orthodoxy. As he explained for the benefit of his Brooklyn congregation and his biographers after he had become famous, his sojourn at Lane Seminary was a time of trouble for his soul. While at Amherst, he asserted, he had come under the influence of an (unnamed) Old School preacher and, assuming the truth of Old School doctrines, he had speculated upon their implications until "they came near wrecking me; for I became sceptical, not malignantly but honestly, and it was to me a matter of great distress and anguish. It continued for years, and no logic ever relieved me." He told Lyman Abbott, his colleague and biographer, that "The salvation of humanity by Divine agency, through the salvation of individuals was to him the great end to be obtained, but the means to this end was a problem, the complexity of which rendered him, as he neared the close of his theological course, the victim of deep depression." This account seems to point toward quite a different source of religious doubt than the first. Here we see Henry stalled, or overcome, by the practical question of how to bring individuals to God. If he experienced uneasiness over specific doctrines, for example Original Sin, he did not so state to Abbott.

In another recollection, he emphasized his loneliness and feelings of alienation from God: "till after I was twenty-one years old, I groped without the knowledge of God in Christ Jesus." (His father believed him to be converted, since Henry had made a profession of faith in his teens and joined the church.) A fourth statement stressed still other aspects of his experience of spiritual unrest and hunger:

> I went from my college life immediately to the West and there I fell into another fuliginous Christian atmosphere when the old school and the new school Presbyterians were wrangling, and my father was tried for believing that a man could obey the commandments of God, and Dr. Wilson was contending against him . . . and the line of division ran all through the State, and there was that tremendous whirl of old school theology, old Calvinism and new Calvinism, and by the time I got away from the theological seminary I was so sick—no tongue can tell how sick I was of the whole medley. How I despised and hated this abyss of whirling controversies that seemed to me to be filled with all manner of evil things, with everything indeed but Christ.

The elements of his disaffection, as he remembered them here, were these: hatred of theological controversy and of church division on doctrinal questions, a pietistic tendency to set religion over against doctrine, and, besides these, a rebellious longing to undertake, like Charles, a secular career.[10]

The resolution of his difficulties came with unexpected ease and suddenness. Henry experienced a brief moment of illumination on a "blessed morning of May," when "it pleased God to reveal to my wandering soul the idea that it was His nature to love man in his sins for the sake of helping him out of them." God, it seemed to Henry, was speaking in accents of maternal love. He revealed "that He felt toward me as my mother felt toward me." The very grass and the creatures of the forest seemed transformed as Henry wandered under the trees of Walnut Hills praising God. Several years later he received a second, no less dramatic, illumination, "the disclosure of Christ ever present with me—a Christ that never was far from me, but was always near me, as a Companion and Friend, to uphold and sustain me. This was the last and the best revelation of God's Spirit to my soul." In another version, with a different emphasis, Beecher said:

> I had a conception of the depths of the nature of the Divine Being that made metaphysical doctrines and philosophical formulas more repugnant to me than they had ever been before, and I entered into a vow and covenant that if I were permitted to preach, I would know nothing but Christ and him crucified among his people.[11]

Close examination of Henry's journal does not sustain his later public declarations about his radical change of heart. On the contrary, he readily studied his father's sermons and only rarely dissented (on technical points) from Lyman's opinions. In March of 1836, in fact, he made an entry that indicated how short of dwelling with God he was:

> I have for some time past—but especialy to day been in a very singular state of mind. I cannot think of the Love of God without great emotion—a stirring up within my bosom—a glow of feeling tenderness and tears—yet it does not command the will. I do not find that it produces in me such entire strong determinations to give up all for him—to live entirely for him—I fear that it is but the natural action of a Great theme upon my emotive constitution, having in it nothing of that character which constitutes pious *emotion*.

Six months later, after recovering from a "Brain and intermittent fever," Henry meditated on the question, "What is the spirit of Christ Jesus, without which we are none of his?" Unlike his sister Harriet, who believed in perfect conformity to the spirit of Christ, Henry concluded that "so much as [he] was *above* us, is not incumbent on us." As for his distaste for theological jargon and hair-splitting, it is also a fact that his journal contains detailed outlines of arguments and theories scarcely less technical than those of his father or Dr. Wilson.

In another respect Henry's recollections were at fault. Far from wanting to follow Charles out of the ministry, he kept up a regular volley of arguments on Lyman's behalf. The question is not whether Henry unconsciously rebelled against Lyman and identified with Charles, but whether his autobiographical statements were at fault. In this particular case, Henry dismissed Charles's self-justification:

> Chas sent (3d) letter to father on leaving the ministry and becoming a musician—Father grieved some what indignant—Charles has fo[u]nded his determination on *feeling*, his plans on *hopes*, and his arguments upon obstinacy. He reasons that as his *feelings* or constitution are more congenial with music than divinity—therefore he can do more good as a musician than as a divine. This does not at all reach the bottom of the question.

Implicit in his scorn for Charles's arguments was his own distrust of unchecked emotionalism, as appeared in his commentary on Lord Byron:

> Read Byron's Journal—he had just the *feelings* all will, who have large *capacities* and *not object* of feeling. It was *feeling*, feeling, feeling—but not gratified within limits of *right*, it sickened and

> wasted him. It always *will*. Feeling gives *pleasure*, not *content*. *Contentment* is the exclusive boon of a good conscience. This he had not. The guilt of reckless atheism is superficial and *stupid*.

But Henry did not believe, as Charles did, that the ministry precluded esthetic enjoyment and fulfillment.[12]

The remarkable thing about Henry, which virtually sets him off from his brothers, was his uncomplicated, unflagging assurance in his calling. He would be not only a successful minister in the eyes of the world but one richly endowed with sensibility, whose very appreciation of the arts would enhance his character and contribute to his effectiveness. "There are in fact," he wrote to one of his female admirers, "three classes of divines--the ascetic, the neuter, and the sunshiny." The ebullient young preacher put himself in the third category:

> the glorious sunshiny ones—I envy them—I emulate. These are they who, think there is a time for relaxation and elegant enjoyment. . . . Litterature is not to them frivolous, the glorious poets —the orators, the heart stirring dramatist, serious or comic, beginning from remote antiquity and thronging thicker and thicker untill now, these they love,—whatever elevates, dignifies and enobles—whatever softens our native coarseness and purifies—whatever draws away from sensual gratifications and assimilates us to a higher order of enjoyment, that they deem the part of religion to encourage and cultivate. . . .[13]

The effulgent beams of Henry's sunshine first brightened Lawrenceburgh, Indiana, "a destitute place indeed," whose feeble Presbyterian church installed him in October of 1838. "For about two years," wrote the historian of Henry's first charge, "a meteor blazed in the firmament of Lawrenceburgh." The meteor, if it blazed at all, blazed fitfully. In fact, his ministry was decidedly unsuccessful for a variety of reasons, none of them having to do with his orthodoxy. James Barr Walker, himself a Presbyterian minister of heterodox views, was present by chance when Beecher preached his first sermon as pastor, "an extempore sermon against the doctrine of Universalism." Walker and his wife were impressed by "the manner of his preaching and his easy social manner" and predicted that "popularity rather than power would characterize his ministry."[14]

He had, first, to maneuver through Old School obstacles even to get installed as pastor. As a reflex of anti-Beecher feeling, Oxford Presbytery did its best to keep Henry out of the ministry. In a satirical account of the examination written for his brother George, Henry took off on the Old School party, which dominated Oxford Presbytery:

> Father Craigh was appointed to *squeak* the questions. They examined me to their hearts' content. I was a model to behold, and so were they! Elders opened their mouths, gave their noses a fresh blowing, fixed their spectacles, and hitched forward on their seats. The ministers clinched their confessions of faith with desperate fervor and looked unutterably orthodox. . . . There he sat, the young candidate begotten of a heretic, nursed at Lane; but, with such a name and parentage and education, what remarkable modesty, extraordinary meekness, and how deferential to the *eminently acute* questioners who sat gazing upon the prodigy!

With their quaint Scottish burr and their cast-iron Confession, they were the very essence of old-fogeyism, and Beecher was prepared to see them hoist on their own petard. He was animated, in part, by a genuine feeling of indignation over their treatment of his father, but also, it must be confessed, by a mischievous spirit. The Old School examiners subjected Henry to the most rigorous examination possible and were astounded to find him not only apprised of the most current distinctions between their doctrines and those promulgated at Lane, but suspiciously prompt in trotting out irreproachable replies. Not content with grilling him for one day, they protracted the examination. Finally, he reported to his family, they began to wonder whether he was not, by Scotch-Irish standards "a leetle too orthodox." Stumped by Beecher's apparent soundness, the presbytery sustained him, and he duly accepted the call to Lawrenceburgh.

But the matter did not end there. On the following day a majority of the presbytery voted that all licentiates and candidates must declare their adherence to the Old School. Beecher had no choice but to withdraw from Oxford Presbytery. He and his church then declared themselves independent. The patent injustice of the Old School majority's action was not lost on those parties within the whole church who, like Calvin Stowe, still hoped to keep a middle ground between Old and New School. Robert Hamilton Bishop, himself a Scotch Presbyterian, publicly denounced the maneuver and urged Beecher to stand fast in hope the act would be repealed:

> It is no inconsiderable matter in these days that Dr. Beecher has at least one son, who, after a full and free examination before the Oxford Presbytery, has been pronounced to be orthodox and

> sound in the faith; and that, in order to exclude the son of the *archheretic*, *a new term* of ministerial communion had to be introduced.

Thus Henry's very entrance upon ministerial life was marred by months of ecclesiastical strife.[15]

That in itself would have had a dampening effect on his spirits even had there not been domestic problems. He and Eunice lived wretchedly on his church's meager offerings—how wretchedly Eunice told the world in her autobiographical novel, *From Dawn to Daylight*—and his various "little plans and devises for *pastoral labor*" met with sullen indifference, if not outright hostility, from church members and unregenerates alike. Eunice from the first looked down on the uncouth dress and accents of Henry's flock, and although she earned some praise for her unflagging industry and her skill as a nurse, she was decidedly unpopular. A woman who always anticipated snubs and meanness and took offense when none was meant, she went through her long married life with Henry, despising his sisters and quarreling with his brothers. She regarded herself as a martyr to his growing fame, and bombarded him with letters beseeching him to love her passionately in spite of her insignificance and ignorance. "The dark clouds are growing still more sombre," she moaned after her engagement was announced. Phrases like "the wild pulsations of this aching heart" filled her letters, which more or less routinely announced that she expected momentarily to "lay this suffering body among the clods of the valley." Most of Henry's family exhibited nothing but goodwill and generosity toward his wife, but this did not mitigate her dislike and jealousy of them, a hatred she tried to pass on to her children. Henry, characteristically, pretended neither to comprehend nor to hear Eunice's recriminations and outpourings of bitterness.[16]

His parishioners were also unhappy with him. One with whom he was on good terms finally took him aside and "opened to me much dissatisfaction among my people—Chiefly on two points 1. my pecuniary circumstances or *credit* too freely exercised 2. infrequency of visitation during the summer. It depressed me exceedingly." Henry despatched Eunice to her uncle's home to beg a loan of $200 and resolved upon a reformed course of life so as not to damage "our cause at [the] west." He was very much aware that he was under public scrutiny, even though the post he occupied was an obscure one compared to Lyman's or Edward's. Misconduct or incompetence "would be eminently disasterous and all those things in Presbytery matters which *now*, bid fair to turn to great advantage would become very prejudicial."

As the case turned out, Oxford Presbytery refused to reverse itself, and Beecher was ultimately installed over his church by the New School Presbytery of Cincinnati. By this time, however, he had tired of his dreary situation and was casting about for a new, more prosperous church. The faults for which his Lawrenceburgh parishioners criticized him he fairly acknowledged to be grave ones. "Self-estimation" led his own list, followed by lack of application to preaching, carelessness about debt, and "my desire for *fine* living." His repeated resolutions to overcome his bad habits produced little change in his behavior, but his removal to less straitened circumstances made these faults less apparent.[17]

As a Presbyterian he had to contend not only with the fault-finding spirit of his congregation but also with the gibes of his chief competitors, the Methodists. They delighted in attacking the Calvinistic errors of the "Presbygationalists" and their college and seminary training. Beecher was disgusted by their ignorance, even more by their pride in that ignorance, and by their uncharitable attitude toward ministers outside their communion, whom they publicly insulted and lampooned. They did not have a learned ministry, but the Methodists were clearly in the ascendancy around Lawrenceburgh. Beecher studied their methods and laid out a campaign to recapture Methodist territory:

> Let it be remembered that I am surrounded by malignant, prosolyting, spiritualy proud professors—not half of whom even pretend to have experienced a saving change and that I am opposing a church which lets into full communion *any who choose*, without any change of heart or preparation whatsoever except seriousness and desire to be better.

If he contemned his Methodist counterparts, he was determined not to imitate their pugnacious tactics. When he launched his counterattack he wanted to "let it be *done*, without sounding a trumpet befor me—*do it*—and call no names—etc."[18]

At the same time he was readying for combat with the Methodists, Beecher was dismayed by the widening disunity within his own church. When the New School-Old School schism finally came, with Lyman, George, and Edward prominent in the formal organization of the New School as a separate church, Henry deplored the division. He preached a sermon which, even in its surviving outline, suggests the power he could attain when speaking on a subject that deeply moved him. "God has a controversy with us—for *our sins*," he proclaimed.

Worldliness and other personal sins like Sabbath-breaking were rife among professed Christians. "What triffling with God, what gross neglect of known duty," he lamented. Far worse was the "deep insensibility to human woe" and the "fraud violence and cruelty" inflicted upon the Indians in their forced removal from Georgia. Sectarianism had also infected the church, with terrible consequences for the peace and usefulness of its leaders and members.

In a letter to one of his brethren in the ministry, Henry analyzed the sources of faction and schism, while stating his own positive standard of Presbyterian communion:

> I ask no questions about old or new school in giving my confidence. I am unwilling to be hemmed in by the narrow lines of Schools and parties—but, standing a free man in God's church, I look about to see who is *most loved of God*; and the holiest, humblest and most useful man, is dearest to me, whether *in* or *out* of my particular church. Where there is a *heart right before God* there cannot be grounds for refusing fellowship and communion. Alas! if our ministers had been holier men—if prayer had kept pace with fear, if heresy hunters had searched for excellencies as keenly as they did for faults, we should never have been a divided church till the day of Zion's redemption—and bonds of steel could not have bound us so strongly, as would the sympathy and union of holy hearts—bent on the glorious work of bringing to God again, this lost, and suffering world![19]

Beecher laid the blame for the catastrophe upon the Scottish and Scotch-Irish element in the church. He contrasted Scottish with American Presbyterianism in political terms. "Scotch Presbyterianism is a church and state matter and wields therby signal powers—American Presbyterianism is simply republicanism, of few and simple powers. Scotch is *akin* to absolutism—the other is democratic. Can these two thrive well together?" Those most determined to make their will prevail against the good of the church as a whole, were also those most versed in the arbitrary uses of power. "*Edicts, ordinances* —summary excision, execution, and *then* trials—these are natural to the *kirk*, why not to its latest offspring?" Here Henry reflected his family's New England republican ideology and loyalty to Congregational independence.[20]

His hereditary allegiance to independent church polity and his own conviction that the vastness of America precluded effective national church organization upon independent principles led Beecher to doubt that the New School would long remain intact. He made a prediction about the fate of the New School, one he lived to see fulfilled:

> But, what is more to the point to my mind—every indication of Providence seems tending to break up large ecclesiastical establishments. I believe there will be a *Southern* and two *northern* churches formed out of ours—a hundred men can live together better than *two*. They form a *public sentiment*: two cannot—so a hundred denominations would be more peaceable than two overgrown ones. The more—the more will it become absolutely necessary to *tolerate*; and toleration is a step brother of Charity. So that God may design great good, by what seems to us evil.

Within sixteen years of this prophecy the Albany Conference, with the Beechers present, organized a national Congregational church, a denomination apart from the New School Presbyterians, though differing very little in doctrine. And Beecher himself went through further transformations in the direction of ecumenism.[21]

But his immediate concern was the unsuccess of his ministry in Lawrenceburgh. He did try to moderate his spending and to become more conscientious and industrious. The church, which was very poor, felt it had much to complain of, but the true causes of disaffection between Henry and his church were lost in the dust stirred up by Eunice's accusations, published decades later. Although Beecher was not held in great favor in Lawrenceburgh, the Second Presbyterian Church of Indianapolis was eager to call him. On the strength of an endorsement by Samuel Merrill, a leading Indianapolis Presbyterian, the Second Church made strong overtures. The call came on May 13, 1839, and Beecher shortly left Lawrenceburgh, embittered by the hardships he and his family had undergone and saddened by the loss of an infant son. Within months he was making his influence felt in the capital and wrote optimistically to Lyman, who saw a great future for him as a Western preacher. He sent glowing reports to Henry's brothers and sisters. Isabella was especially pleased by his sudden success. "I think he is going somewhat in father's track," she wrote, and, greatest accolade of all, she predicted that Henry "will perhaps one day—come somewhere near him in eminence."[22]

As 1839 drew to a close, Henry entered a solemn resolution in his journal, a statement which reflects his mature views of religion and the ministry as well as anything else he wrote or said:

> If God will give me grace I will preach faithful[ly] all parts of the Gospel necessary for conversion of men and perfecting them

> in holiness. But in his strength, I am resolved, never to become a *disputant* or *champion* on any of those points which *divide truly evangelical christians.*
>
> [1.] If I feel it a duty ever to speak of such topics I will strive to do it so as to soften and win the feeling and promote charity rather than bitter sectarianism.
> 2. Resolve that I will strive to cherish *secret feelings* of love to all other churches beside my own;–to say nothing evil of them nor to desire their members;–nor their decline.
> 3. Resolved, that in public and private, I will give my life to bringing all christians to [the] work of spreading the *true* power of [the] Gospel–the love of Christ.

If there ever was, in fact, a unique event, a divine disclosure that seized Henry and sent him traveling down a different path from the one he had chosen in college, it must have occurred shortly after he settled in Indianapolis. What is recorded in his journal, however, is a resolution which seems to have been drawn from a growing consciousness of the desirability of church harmony. The conception of the true power of the Gospel, which he now expressed, derived from several sources, the most important being his success as a revivalist and the increasing influence on his thought of Calvin Stowe. He preached regularly in his own church and ministered to as many outlying congregations and churches as he could reach on horseback. Critics who later attacked him for his indolence and love of comfort and display were often unaware of the extreme hardships and sacrifices of this period.[23]

But he had already begun to take himself seriously as an apostle not only of the Gospel but of culture. If he was shabbily dressed in cast-off clothing, he still spoke mellifluously on subjects like nudity in art, recent experiments in agricultural chemistry, phrenology, and Macaulay's histories. He was editor, in 1845, of the *Indiana Farmer and Gardener*, which disseminated useful knowledge together with the young preacher's exhortations to his readers to leave off their shiftless practices and low manners. Always the prodigal spender, Henry moved into a new house in 1840. "The house is finished in a very much more expensive way than fathers," he told his sister, and gloried in the "beautiful mantel pieces–doors and windows costly mouldings and in [the] front room panel work below the windows. The fire places are *iron back* and *iron sides*." He enunciated an esthetic theory to justify these expenditures. Ministers should avail themselves of those and other such luxuries (they were luxuries by Western standards) in order to set an example for the community. Loveliness and comfort had beneficial effects upon character, and the good minister was obliged to consider this fact when offering himself as a model. His work for the *Indiana Farmer* was an unpaid public service, an effort to let light into dim but eager minds bent upon self-improvement. If people said Beecher lived beyond his means and kept too rich a table for himself and his boarders, that too was service, not self-indulgence.

Gardening was one of his passions, especially the cultivation of flowers and ornamental shrubs, of which he amassed a remarkable collection before leaving Indianapolis. Not content with the mere raising and showing of flowers, he must employ them as moral instructors. Often, if his wife's account is to be believed, he would pluck rare blossoms and buds from his garden and stroll about the streets (hog wallows, actually) looking for a suitably benighted passerby in need of floral edification. He would present the flower or nosegay to the stranger, say a few appropriate words, and wander away to meditate on the moral influence of flowers. Considering what a grim, raw, malaria-infested spot Indianapolis was in the 1840s, it is easy to believe that its inhabitants found Beecher's behavior whimsical. If he delighted strangers with his affable demeanor, he was also famous as a man of tremendous stamina and physical courage. Bullies gave him a wide berth when they learned that he was quick and fearless.[24]

Already, then, Beecher had developed those characteristics for which he would be world-famous in the 1860s. On the one hand, he could say, without blushing, that "a hollyhock is a moral and accountable being," while declaring, on the other hand, that Sharps rifles sent to Bloody Kansas were a salutary gospel for border ruffians and slavemasters. Beecher could be by turns sentimental, skittish, bellicose, pompous, or jaunty. He loved making money and spending it with a free hand, and airily referred to large sums as mere bagatelles. At the same time, he dressed simply, ate sparingly, and paid great attention to his physical fitness so that he would be true to manly values. The combination of a mild, yielding nature with the truculent, masculine image belonged to him in far greater measure than to any of his brothers, who found both his hobbies and his public antics hard to take. He was successful in establishing himself in the mind of the public as a distinct personality.

But it was not on the strength of his personality alone that Henry won a following. He was, from 1842 onward, an extremely successful revivalist. Before leaving Lawrenceburgh he had assisted Lyman in the revival at Miami College in Ohio, and his labors there won tributes from all the Beechers, even Catharine. Once he had established a network of ministerial connections in Indiana, Beecher was able to awaken large parts of the state. Called to Terre Haute to aid in a revival there, he helped bring conditions to a crisis and then proceeded to preach revival sermons on his homeward journey. His "heart was on fire; and it rained a stream of prayer all the way home from Terre Haute to Indianapolis. It was like an Aurora Borealis, I have no doubt, ray upon ray, for that whole distance, if angels could have seen it." In his own church, however, three nights of preaching failed to spark an awakening. Beecher was despondent, even mortified and angry at his people's apathy. But on the third night a solitary inquirer remained behind, a serving girl who "smelt of the kitchen and looked kitchen all over." Beecher felt a momentary burst of wounded pride:

> I said to myself that after so much work it was too bad. It was just a glance, an arrow which the Devil shot at me, but which went past. The next minutes I had an overwhelming revulsion in my soul; and I said to myself, "If God pleases, I will work for the poorest of his creatures. I will work for the heart of a vagabond, if I am permitted to do it, and bring him to Christ Jesus." I felt it; and I thanked God that night for that girl's staying.

The revival which ensued spilled over into other churches in the area, and, with Beecher as the leading spirit, the Baptists and Methodists also reaped notable harvests.[25]

The feeling of brotherly amity was briefly imperiled by the Campbellites, who raised the divisive issue of the proper mode of baptism for the new converts. Beecher had no use for the Campbellite mentality, as was shown by his remarks in an 1840 journal entry:

> *Campbellism* . . . Only ground on which it could be placed is imitation of *primitive order*—If this is to be imitated so litterally why then, do we not see consistency—Why use a *printed book*, why not use a MSS for [the] Apostles did! If no liberty in mode of preaching to vary, but bound to their example, how comes it that necessity extends only halfway round?

It would have been easy for Beecher to take to platform or press to deride the Campbellite position. Only a year before he had preached a series of sermons on baptism examining the controversy in the light of biblical history, patristic scholarship, and philogy. Edward Beecher was an authority on the subject and undoubtedly provided Henry with arguments and references. Instead of attacking the Campbellites, Henry's strategy was to disarm their prejudices. He cordially agreed to a grand union baptism with his fellow ministers, and personally baptized his Presbyterian converts by sprinkling, affusion, or immersion in the White River, whichever they felt to be the scriptural mode. It was his principle, from this point on, never to be a stickler on points of church order but rather to welcome converts into his church by whatever means he felt most appropriate and congenial.[26]

By such acts and by a general course of magnanimity and friendliness, Beecher won the loyalty and cooperation of numerous Indiana clergymen. They looked upon him as an evangelist of extraordinary gifts and dedication and accepted his help gratefully. The success of the revivals gratified him. In 1842 alone he led three revivals, and in after years several more. His credentials as a revivalist were firmly established, and his fame reached the East.

But it was less the techniques of the revival which fascinated Henry than the psychology of revivalism. He was developing what he later called the "social law" of revivals. His oratorical talents, which were not inconsiderable to begin with, brought great results. He took careful note of everything connected with his own revival preaching and that of others and concluded that revivalism, far from being a relic of his father's generation or an outcropping of fanaticism and nervous excitement, was a natural expression of the mutual attraction and loyalty that could be generated in a mass grouping of people looking for a new focus of feeling, allegiance, and purpose. It was the duty of the minister to channel this collective yearning into religious awakening or renewal.

Beecher became increasingly a preacher and exhorter and less of a pastor. Pastoral visiting and counseling, for which he had shown so little inclination in Lawrenceburgh, now seemed even less important. As his pastoral work fell off, his skills as a preacher grew. His object, as he stated it, was to show his hearers that "Religion [is] not an *essence to be received*," but consisted of "Reconciliation, Exercise of love, Action thro' life—flowing from it." Although he continued to consider such recondite topics as the argument that God is the author of sin or the development of the human faculties in Heaven, he became disenchanted with heavy doctrinal sermons. The usual orthodox argument was, of course, that the most effectual revival preaching was doctrinal preaching. Yet it was doctrinal sermons which had brought the most odium and suspicion upon Henry's father.

Henry reckoned that it was three or four years before he became a truly effective preacher, and he attributed his success to a new style of preaching. A "careful examination of the Apostles' preaching" led him to draw up certain rules. First, the Apostles had "a foundation of historical truth, common to them and their auditors." Second, they distilled this truth and pressed it upon their congregations "in the form of an intense personal application and appeal." Third, they spoke only in "the language of common life." In a sermon preached before his father's Cincinnati church in 1843, Henry made precisely these points. Taking the learned ministry as his subject, he demanded a new standard of preaching for the Presbyterian clergy. The original disciples of Christ, he said, were like businessmen, not scholars pursuing pet theories but pragmatists with facts to demonstrate to a skeptical public. Comparing their character and methods with those of the present day, Beecher found a glaring discrepancy between the standard of his church and the apostolic church:

> And the complaint I utter against learned preaching is not that it is studious—not that it is accurate—but that it has become too dainty to *walk among facts* and chooses to *fly among principles*. . . . He who would *work up* the gospel to give it a dignity—is a man who would tie ribbons on an oak to make it pretty—would criticise Niagara Falls to give it grace—and suggest amendments to a storm or the thunder of a raging Ocean.

Furthermore, Presbyterians were too apt to stress "the accompaniments of the gospel instead of the thing itself." By "accompaniments" Beecher meant church ordinances and government as well as moral precepts. In his own case, he was more comfortable with homely imagery, although, as the above passage indicates, he was given to oratorical flights. In his 1841 sermons on baptism, for instance, he used images from gardening and building, two tasks at which he was skilled and with which he could count on his audience to be familiar. When he reread the sermons of Jonathan Edwards, he found confirmation of his idea. Edwards, whatever his fascination with metaphysics, preached directly from Scripture. Even though the result had been "a kind of moral inquisition," the fact remained that Edwards's success lay in concentrating scriptural truths until they became "a fire upon the life, the hearts, the character, the conduct of living men, just as they lived in Edwards's days."[27]

Unlike Lyman Beecher, who preached of eternal damnation, Henry veered away from such topics and eventually abandoned them altogether. Of Edwards's "Sinners in the Hands of an Angry God," Henry said, "I think a person of moral sensibility alone at midnight, reading that awful discourse, would wellnigh go crazy." Only a few years earlier he himself had been prepared to tell of the judgment to come. "As I was writing my sermon, this eve," he had recorded in 1837, "it struck me forcibly and affectingly, that Christ who *died for men*, and strove so unweariedly to save them and is interceding for them above, is at last to be *their judge* and condemn [them]–strange!" As he pondered this paradox, he had laid out a neat frame for a sermon:

> Savior and condemner–one prerogative
> 1. Who will know so well as Christ, the guilt of *rejecting* him–how much suffering is despised what atonement for sin–what endurance–
> 2. Who knows so well as Christ–how much and how obstinately men have sinned against him.
>
> Consider: How terrible [it] will be to have Jesus Christ for a Jud[g]e. (1) because that must be a dreadful and stern and hopeless necessity which transforms such love to *wrath* (2) because all our hope is in Christ–all chance, and he being lost to us, all is lost. So that being a judge, is to us the shutting up [of] all further mercy.
>
> Terrible again, because he is the very one so deeply injured and we are to *confront him.*

Christ the judge was, after all, a Scripture teaching that no one who believed in the divinity of Christ could gainsay. Yet Henry began suppressing such ideas and images in his sermons. By 1843 he was preaching the "salient points of the gospel" in this fashion:

> *God became incarnate* (this is the gospel message) *for your sins–man–he died–Now he offers you full release. He is in Heaven and remembers For you Christ–Christ–Christ.* His personall love–love–love–His free pardon–pardon–pardon. *Purity of life flowing from love to him.*

Whereas Beecher had been accustomed as a boy to think that Jesus was an "official personage," he now came to understand and to preach that Christ was "just what a mother is to a child."[28]

What was the source of this new understanding of Christ and the Christian life? It may have been, as Beecher later told his congregations, the fruit of a divine illumination, a revelation that would be made known to every convert, for "no man is a Christian until he has experienced it." There are, however, identifiable sources of a more historical nature. Henry's theological development, despite his depiction of it as highly individualized and original, followed the lines along which American liberal theology was developing. Among the characteristics of liberalizing theology which fit the Henry Ward Beecher mold were a confidence that religious truth could be perceived intuitively, an appeal to experience, a great stress upon the human consciousness and therefore upon religious education, and a highly Christocentric vision. These were ideas encountered first by Edward Beecher, who became an admirer of William Ellery Channing, and by Calvin Stowe, who was a student of the German evangelicals.[29]

Like Edward Beecher, Henry was strongly attracted to Channing's theology. He later acknowledged Channing's pervasive influence upon American religion in terms which implicitly rejected his father's manner of upholding truth. When the Beechers were in Boston, Henry recalled, he had been plunged into "the very centre and heat of that great controversy which was raging, in which my father was an eloquent thunderer on one side, and in which Dr. Channing was an eloquent silent man on the other side." Yet, though Channing was a great man, Beecher maintained, "mankind behind him was greater, the time was greater, and the all-informing spirit of God was greater yet." Thus, with a twist to his father's argument that the truth of doctrines was to be tested by their efficacy in producing revivals of religion, Henry came to argue that the touchstone of religious truth was the moral sense of mankind, quickened by the Holy Spirit to be sure, but nonetheless an independent judge.[30]

Toward the Germans, however, he maintained a critical posture. Speaking of leading figures among the Germans, he said:

> There they are shut up from all outward action and enterprise, they are *driven* inward. I regard this *inwardism* and idealism in which they all indulge Jacobi, Goethe, Lessing, Tholuck, etc. as the desease of that state—When men have, according to their own notions of *Wholeness* (see notes to Goethes songs) a free development of exterior life and full stimulus of inward—then the nearest are they to a constitutional and designed state. . . . We doubtless tend to the other extreme. There is a development of the exterior a call for labor and enterprise which draws us to the physical too much—but as this subsides and it will or wealth enables more to study I think the American mind will hit the just medium.

Henry found within himself the requisite balance between inner consciousness and outward energy and drive.[31]

A telling example of such morbid inwardness was to be found in George Beecher, who died a possible suicide in 1843, although his family never acknowledged his death to be anything but accidental.[32] However they tried to come to terms with George's violent death, the loss to Henry was a bitter one. "George's translation to heaven" drew consolations to his widow from Henry. He rejoiced that "the *tyrant Death*" had been vanquished by George's faith, which bore him aloft "when he *broke through* this worlds crust." George had been extremely generous to Henry and Eunice when they first started out in Lawrenceburgh and had extended many invitations to Henry to preach in his church at Chillicothe, Ohio. A typical letter from Henry to George expressed feelings both of brotherly kinship and of deference: "I wish, George, you could be here a while and help me. . . . We have grown almost strangers to each other since you groped off to Rochester, and I would fain have some of our long talks again." He had urged George not to publish his views on perfectionism and warned him not to let "perplexities" of doctrine assume too large a part in his thought. It was well known how melancholy and introspective George had become, the opposite, in fact, of his hearty, jolly brother Henry.[33]

Despite his reflexive rejection of German subjectivism as an emotional and intellectual illness, Henry could not have avoided serious consideration of the views of the German theologians when he maintained such close ties to his brother-in-law, Calvin Stowe. In addition to Stowe, there was a cousin by marriage, Henry Boynton Smith, a New School Presbyterian who came back from Germany fired with admiration for the safer aspects of German critical scholarship. He had a long talk with Isabella Beecher, who was eager for firsthand impressions of Tholuck, whom she called "my paragon of all excellence." Henry surely must have been aware that such men as Tholuck found warm allies among liberals in America.

Stowe, however, was the main external influence on Beecher, as far as theological questions could be said to have engaged his interest. Before Henry left Indianapolis, refusing a call to Park Street Church, Boston, in favor of the pulpit of Plymouth Church, Henry was revising his views of the Atonement. In 1847, when he preached at various Brooklyn churches, he presented this view of the life and work of Christ:

> Reasons why Christ should leave the earth—old [sermon] body, new section at close which developes better than ever before the

> fact that all Gods dealings are with reference, by *education*, to making us *independent, industrious, active*—That he works not *for* us, but to make us work. . . .
>
> Presented a view of Preparation of Christ for work of sympathising with man—most desirable aspect—and attacking demon by effection. Yet it was but an outline—If more thoroughly explored, and its body filled up—would be an important pillar in a row to illustrate Christ—and atonement.

A few months later he visited Stowe at the water cure in Brattleboro and sounded him out on some difficult questions:

> I was greatly comforted to find that Stowe held my identical views on the *Atonement*, and gave me some information where materials were to be found—so that I begin to feel that there is excellent *company* for my heresy.[34]

The best statement of Beecher's and Stowe's doctrine of the Atonement is found in a book published by James Barr Walker. His *Philosophy of the Plan of Salvation*, first published anonymously in 1845, was prefaced with an essay by Calvin Stowe endorsing Walker's theory. The manuscript had been submitted to the Beechers for criticism, and Catharine, "then regarded as the literary Cynosure of the family," gave Walker "honest and true" advice as to its merits. Briefly stated, it was Walker's thesis that the Atonement is best understood as the necessary and sole sufficient demonstration to sinful men of the "spirituality and holiness of the divine law" in such terms as to "prepare man to love a spiritual deliverer." A need must first be created. When the need was supplied, the once needful would love the one who gave them plenitude. Walker was careful to distinguish between his theory and the so-called spectacular theory of the Atonement. "Truth, whether sanctioned by conscience or not, has no power, as has been shown, to *produce love in the heart.*" Affection, like gravity in the physical realm, had once held the soul to God. That principle of attraction broken, the moral world needed a restoration of "harmonious and happy motion," which could only be provided by Christ's exhibition of supreme love in and through his humanly and divinely suffering sacrifice.[35]

If, as Henry joked, his ideas were heretical, it was not owing to their glaring novelty. He could always seek refuge in the standard defense of the heterodox—namely, that they are only engaged, honestly and prayerfully, in recovering the essence of Christianity as voiced in the Gospels and preached by the early church. If others scented danger in such an undertaking, that merely showed how far they had apostatized from the primitive faith. And, in fact, at no time prior to 1875 would Beecher's numerous critics be able to muster organized attacks on his theology, and then only in relation to its alleged moral tendencies. As far as he was concerned in the 1840s, however, the only moral tendencies of his preachments were wholesome ones.

Beecher never distinguished between proclaiming and interpreting Holy Writ and the social activist sphere. James Walker's judgment that he would be popular but not powerful proved completely wrong. He became very powerful, both in terms of influence and ability to make things happen. His very popularity served as armor against his critics. In 1844, when his *Seven Lectures to Young Men* appeared, Henry was established in the public eye as a trenchant critic of social evils. Leonard Bacon declared that he could hear a new Lyman Beecher in those lectures, "the old Boanerges thundering with a youthful voice." Sloth, reckless spending, card-playing, drinking, and consorting with prostitutes were the subjects of his combined exposé and monition, which became the best-selling of all his books and enjoyed large sales well into the present century. The alternative to sodden sinfulness, as he said in his brotherly chats with the young men of the city, was a forthright, active, and manly religion.[36]

This view found much favor in the cities of the East. When he removed to Brooklyn in 1848, Beecher was prepared to find a congenial circle and a large public audience. He had discovered, while preaching trial sermons in New York, that it was "possible with a sermon extremely faulty in respect to its absolute rhetorical formation to produce nevertheless strong effects." His pulpit style, which had met with much favor in the West, now took on a new individuality. The peculiarities, if anything, increased—not such uncouth Western traits as the holy whine that Henry and Thomas Beecher loved to mimic, but sparkles and flourishes of Henry's own.[37]

Situated in Brooklyn, which still had a lingering small-town flavor, Plymouth Church had a middle-class congregation of heavily Yankee origins. Henry expected his church to grow rapidly and received assurances from its leaders that it would be an influential pulpit. He reflected on the recent past in a letter to his sister Harriet:

> Here I have several days of *absolute rest*. And they are among the very few—perhaps the only ones I have had for ten years—except at Walnut Hills. So, when I came away from home, I sought out

> from my letters the notes which I used to receive from you, and which I have always preciously kept. . . . I have sat me down, and read them over again, one by one, with long pauses between, filled with all the thoughts and fancies and feelings which such an uncontrollable head as mine backed up by such a rebellious heart, might be supposed to have. So I have lived over again the years we lived together before the plunge into matrimony first gave you, and next me, to [the] sea of life and all its innumerable waves. I seem almost like a wrecked sailor, escaped upon a little island and looking back on the waters—and imagining the harbor and the home beyond from which he sailed—So these notes have brought up the past: I have thought over and loved them over. I see myself again as I was then: and *you* as you were then and how we felt; and thought of how the world had served us, and wondered what, if observation were taken anew would be the latitude and longitude of our hearts now etc. etc.

The sense of nostalgia mingled with unease suggests a certain trepidation for the future, with regrets about past decisions, but such feelings quickly vanished.[38]

Henry was almost immediately enthroned as a prince of the New York and Brooklyn pulpit, and, through his frequent visits to colleges to deliver uplifting lectures to the young men, he became very well known in college and seminary circles. He was soon talked of as the peer of Horace Bushnell, among others. A letter from one of Beecher's newfound admirers will serve to illustrate how he was regarded and how appealing his theology was:

> I truly believe that B.[ushnell] is a greatly abused man—but by no one worse than himself. His vanity and love of notoriety will be the ruin of him. He certainly has got hold of two or three—perhaps more—fine thoughts, and probably twice as many fine cro[t]chets. . . . And the good Dr. might remember that he is set to march for souls, and find some bigger business than to turn himself into a theological kaleidoscope, turning over and over and shaking his pretty parti-colored novelties into diverse startling shapes, to the delight of shallow-pated admirers and the horror of bald-pated heresy-hunters. . . .
>
> There are two things that make me laugh. One is, to hear *you* likened to *Bushnell*! to whom I venture to intimate a suspicion that you are just the moral (and of course the intellectual)

> *antipodes*—As thus: he is a man who thinks head-foremost—you are a man who think[s] heart-foremost.

One of the "shallow-pated admirerers" of Bushnell was Thomas Beecher, who at this time believed himself to be very akin to his brother Henry in religious ideas.[39]

The apparent confusion concerning the implications of Bushnell's theology was to some extent real. But to say that Henry Ward Beecher was poles apart from Horace Bushnell was just as inaccurate as to say that they were consciously allied. Beecher was a renowned revivalist; Bushnell eschewed revivals and crisis-centered religion in favor of Christian nurture. Beecher was quietly heterodox and irenic in spirit (though he became snarled from time to time in doctrinal squabbles); Bushnell by contrast, though privately a sweet-natured man, managed to antagonize many of his clerical brethren, who thought he was deliberately adopting strange or dangerous terms. Beecher's new views were more often flowery or muscular in tone and never speculative. He had neither the inclination nor, it would seem, the intellect, to engage in detailed or difficult theological study.

Not that Bushnell himself was a very learned man. He was certainly far less so than Calvin Stowe, for instance, or Edward Beecher, but his intellect was keener, capable of fresher insights. Bushnell's ties to the Beecher family were not intimate, even though Mary and Thomas Perkins were members of his Hartford church. The Perkinses often took Isabella's children to services with their own, but the Hookers were not regular attendants. The rest of the Beechers, Thomas being an important exception, were highly critical of Bushnell. On one occasion, Bushnell was the direct target of a Beecher sermon:

> Edward Beecher preached at me *sub rosa* before the Pastoral Association [of Boston] yesterday, on pantheism. A new paper, called the *Congregationalist*, edited by Edward Beecher, [Gilbert] Havens, and [Increase] Tarbox, is out with the first number, having a communication from Baker full sail against me.

Within three months, however, Bushnell was gratified to find Lyman Beecher interceding on his behalf with the Fairfield West Association, which was debating whether to eject Bushnell for heterodoxy:

> Dr. Beecher came to me in a most fatherly way, the other day; and after a full talk the old man was perfectly satisfied of my soundness (apart from speculative theory), rejoiced with tears at the discovery, went directly over to Farmington and saw Dr.

> [Noah] Porter; and the substance of the report of the committee, *i.e.*, of the majority, was arranged, giving me a hearty clearance.

Although the Hartford preacher had few contacts with Henry Ward Beecher, he was brought to a grudging admiration of Beecher's sermon style:

> Beecher preached the most dramatic and, in one sense, most effective sermon I ever heard from him, but in all the philosophy of it unspeakably crude and naturalistic; and yet I was greatly moved notwithstanding, and, I trust, profited. The close was eloquent enough to be a sermon by itself.[40]

In the final analysis, it may be said that the difference between Bushnell and Beecher centered on two points: their conception of the place of theology in religion and their ideal of the ministry. The likenesses between the two men are striking but more difficult to measure. To take their differences first, it is plain that Bushnell believed that theology was not only possible but that it should be refined and subtle, without losing its power to influence men toward Christ. Hence his strictures on the crudeness of Beecher's philosophy. On the other hand, Beecher insisted that the ministry should be active in all the great reforms of the day. If he was not on the cutting edge of reform, he knew well enough when to join the ranks of antislavery and how to mobilize the most effective mass support for it. Staging mock slave auctions at Plymouth Church was one such stroke of genius (or bad taste, according to Beecher's detractors). It would have been hard for a son of Lyman Beecher to be anything but a reformer, although Thomas managed to stand apart from most movements and to carp at their self-righteous excesses.

In a commemorative sermon before his church in 1853, Bushnell made a strong public declaration in favor of quietism. Although the Old School had been foremost in denouncing him as a liberal heresiarch, he sympathized with some of their views:

> Indeed, I had a certain peculiar sympathy with the style of piety in the Old-School brethren, especially in all the points where it was contrasted with the flashiness of a super-active, all-to-do manner, such as then distinguished the movement party of the times.

The "movement party" was, of course, the side on which the Beechers were aligned.[41]

Beecher and Bushnell did share common ground, and it is surprising to find Beecher disavowing this community of understanding. Perhaps he liked to call no man master, or perhaps he really believed that his own religious experience was not to be likened to another's and could not be grounded in formal philosophical statements. In any case, there was a common experience that both men believed had altered their lives: the revelation of a personal Christ. Bushnell's experience occurred relatively late in life, after he had already published some of his important theological works. Beecher's happened near the outset of his career. Whereas Bushnell was loathe to talk about his experience, saying only, "I was set on by the personal discovery of Christ, and of God as represented in him," Beecher did not consider the subject too sacred for public discourse. What happened to Bushnell in 1848 inspired and animated his subsequent theological productions. Beecher's appeal to the authority of a profound personal experience of Christ was just that: a nontheological source of authority for his declarations of new truths, declarations very similar to Bushnell's but dissimilar in that Beecher claimed to have found his truths in holy Nature, not in Reason and the Understanding.[42]

Beecher's reputation grew rapidly. One account of his preaching, written in 1848, praised him as a master sermonizer: "He could make them laugh or weep by turns, he was very pathetic and solemn, then again very animated and full of humorous remarks." Another, seventeen years later, stressed the same characteristics, which recalled the style of Lyman Beecher, greatly loosened up:

> I cannot think of any other occasion in my life when I felt so charmed with the preacher as on this occasion. His illustrations (in which he abounds) were most happily chosen, making his argument clear and convincing. A stroke of humor was occasionally thrown in, hitting so palpably that one could not refrain from smiling, some passages were most sublime. . . . There is a great difference between the oratory of Mr. Beecher and that of Wendell Philips. Beecher is animated, vivacious, exerting himself to make a vivid impression on his hearers; and is a vast ways in advance of Philips as a public speaker. Now I think of it, I was more charmed, more carried away by [John] Gough (or Goff) than by Beecher. The two are much alike in their style of oratory, but Beecher is but moderately what Gough is extremely. The two are unquestionably the first popular speakers of the present day.

By 1865, then, Beecher was established in the public mind as one of the great orators of the day. He was more flamboyant than Wendell Phillips and leavened his discourses and speeches with copious amounts of comedy. Yet compared to Gough, a reformed drunk and former actor who had made his stage debut in a play burlesquing Lyman Beecher and other temperance advocates, Beecher was only moderately theatrical. Many of the thousands who were drawn to Plymouth Church came prepared to see a performance as dramatic as any on the New York stage, which Beecher denounced for its corrupting influence. One of Beecher's biographers and intimate friends remembered how affectingly his pastor could impersonate men from all walks of life, getting down not only their carriage, but their tricks of speech, facial movements, and mannerisms. A Thanksgiving Day sermon, for example, might feature Beecher conducting "an imaginary interview between a shipowner of kindly Christian feeling and an old sailor," complete with the tobacco-chewing sailor removing his cud and wiping his hands on his trousers before grasping the shipowner's hand. Beecher's followers had heard his orthodoxy questioned, but few went away from Plymouth Church without concluding that there was "nothing, that is in the slightest degree unsound or heterodox."[43]

Where Beecher might have come to grief, but did not, was in his public pronouncements outside the pulpit. Numerous books poured from him, seemingly without effort. In fact, his utterances were so prized by his congregation that they hired a crack stenographer to record his every word, whether in the pulpit or out. He was once again an editor, this time for the *Independent*, which was among the leading religious papers of the day. His little pieces in the *Independent*—sermonettes, essays, reveries, and offhand reflections—appeared in a prominent place, signed with an asterisk, hence their collective title of *Star Papers*. One such essay, written in 1852, evoked bitter criticism from coreligionists who feared he was giving away too much ground to the Universalists. Writing from Oneida County, New York, an aggrieved minister claimed that

> errorists take advantage of your admissions to fortify themselves in their positions—So I am told is it with Unitarians and Universalists in this region. We are surrounded with them. . . . It seems to me while we should avoid the *mode* of bitter *denunciation*, we should likewise be very careful not to make *allowances* which may be seized [upon] as virtually sacrificing the proud fundamentals of that Christianity which teaches *salvation* by the *blood* of *Christ* in connection with *representation* by the *Holy Ghost*—and which points as the alternative to an endless damnation.

Henry, who was decidedly not a controversialist (as his father most emphatically was), developed techniques for defusing potentially furious debates. It was his custom, as befitted a great public figure, to write what were in effect open letters to minor clergymen and anxious parents in remote parts of the country.[44]

In this case, he flattered the Reverend Charles Jones of the Holland Patent by replying at length. Of course, he affirmed, he believed the wicked would be punished in the future life, and it was a salutary doctrine. Would not the Reverend Jones agree that, "to the mass, the force of these views does not lie in *the love of God,* but in the *exemption from* punishment consequent on that love"? The "impress from superior motives" might produce as genuine a conversion as fear. On the whole, taking the Universalists as a body, "I have to say frankly that I see nothing in them which should prevent a true regenerative and spiritual union with Christ." The Unitarians were a much tougher case. "The absence of Christ from preaching, a living, loving, divine Christ—very God—must be to me a capital deficiency." His own theology was still evangelical and Trinitarian in its outlines:

> In my judgment the thorough sinfulness of man, the regeneration of the heart, the effusion of Divine influence, the Truth of God manifest in the flesh, the love and power of a crucified Savior, are the elements of all the *religious* power that there is in preaching. And it is my impression that all preaching which has substantially left out these will be found either to have been perfectly useless, or to have reared up churches without moral stamina.
>
> Nay more—
>
> 1. If a man really understand whereof he affirms, and sharply and intelligently rejects the need of regeneration, arising from heartsinfulness, the divinity and atonement of Christ and the Holy Spirit, I do not conceive it possible for him to be a *Christian*. He may be a worshipper—a just man—a man that *fears God*. But he will not be, he cannot be a disciple of Christ in any such sense as I suppose the Bible to require.
>
> 2. But when we reflect how many persons hold with a kind of *outward* grasp their theological views, how many have no efficacious opinions, how many are led through their affections, their social sympathies, their practical reason. . . . multitudes who are in Unitarian churches . . . are really humble penitent and spiritual Christians. Their faith in Christ is real and vital; and the heart takes him—as all sufficient and divine in spite of all the dry technics of their head.

Beecher concluded by urging Jones to circulate the letter among clergymen of the latter's acquaintance, but asked that it not be published, as Beecher's enemies, headed by Iraneus Prime of the *New York Observer*, were seeking means to harass and embarrass him:

> For those in error—for infidels—for the outcast—I have always had an especial yearning and my ministry is much more a ministry to the *world* than to the *Church*. . . . My life has been but a long labor for them and this is not the first time that my Zeal has seemed to Christians in the camp to carry me too near the lines of the enemy.[45]

Beecher counted on disarming his critics by utter candor and did succeed in great measure. He also, however, wrote in lazy, if affecting language, so that phrases like "the divinity and atonement of Christ and the Holy Spirit" littered his pronouncements. His understanding of Christ, the key to his theology, underwent remarkable changes, but with no gains in clarity of expression. In 1844 he was accustomed to speak of Christ as "the captain of our salvation made *perfect thro suffering*," a view completely congruent with that of Calvin Stowe and James Barr Walker. By 1875, after long experience as a minister, he was telling his people that "Christ is in Himself the Atonement," a declaration Edward Beecher thought both inaccurate and irresponsible. Edward, who was then attempting to defend his brother from accusations of false teaching made in connection with the Tilton trial, pointed out that Henry's vagueness had left him open to such charges.

Charles Hodge of Princeton, for one, wondered why Henry's views of the Atonement were so illogical and contradictory. Sometimes Henry preached that the death of Christ prepared the way for God's forgiveness toward man. But at other times, as Hodge complained, he held that no such preparation for divine mercy was necessary, because God loved man unreservedly. In this case, the sufferings of Christ were demonstrations of that love, not a necessary reconciliation or expiation. When Edward urged him to make his meaning plainer, Henry dismissed theology as "that machinery of false philosophy," a view completely at odds with his older brother's. The most that Edward was able to extract from Henry was a statement that he still taught "the general relation of the death of Christ to the universe."[46]

Henry respected and deferred to Edward. But there was a puckish, impatient quality in Henry's attitude toward theological discourse, an attitude which grieved Edward. On one occasion, when he gently reproved Henry for taking two diametrically opposed stands within a few minutes and challenged him to choose between them, Henry replied that he believed both, to the delight of his audience and the consternation of Edward. Then there was the time when a fellow minister asked Edward what was wrong with one of Henry's articles. Edward replied, "I said, 'Henry, you have put into that article all your doubts and kept out of it all you believe.'" By the time this exchange took place in 1876, Edward Beecher and his kind were so far behind the middle-class conception of religion that he invariably suffered when compared to his younger brother. The sermons which had been criticized as insufficiently weighty at Park Street in 1829 and which had met with warm approval at Salem Street in the 1850s now seemed, as one minister said, "kiln-dried with metaphysical philosophy and top-heavy with encyclopedic erudition." The very possibility of theology, as Edward understood the enterprise, was rapidly waning.[47]

Meanwhile, Henry's auditors were waxing enthusiastic over his teachings. The historian of Plymouth Church quoted an encomium from the *Brooklyn Eagle* that swelled the chorus of praise from the secular press for Beecher's syncretistic theology:

> It is easy to refer Mr. Beecher's composite creed to its sources. His allegorical picturesque views come from the Swedish seer [Swedenborg]. His assent only to the knowable was the doctrine of Compte and Locke, albeit the latter would have shrunk from the full acceptance of his own premise. His exaltation of love and of the fatherhood at the expense of the royalty of God is Channingism in expression. In his espousal of restorational punishment, Mr. Beecher and Dr. [Edwin Hubbell] Chapin and the Pope cross hands across the sulphurous chasm of Calvinism. The Plymouth preacher has insensibly assorted his creed from many denominations.

The appearance of such an endorsement, with its conception of the Beecher creed as a sort of ecumenical burgoo, in an official history of his church, shows how far the man had strayed from the orthodox evangelical fold.[48]

Long before this assessment of 1872, moreover, Beecher had enunciated views which justly alarmed the conservatives of his denomination. In 1859, ostensibly taking issue with Theodore Parker's theology, Beecher made a statement that was suspiciously antitrinitarian. He exalted Christ above the "dim and shadowy effluence" of the Father and the "invisible film of thought" that was the Holy Spirit. The appreciative flutter in Unitarian quarters may well be imagined. Some of their spokesmen naturally taunted Beecher, daring him to declare himself among their number publicly. He issued highly unsatisfactory affirmations of the Trinity at intervals, as in 1882, when he told a friend that

> In my own case, the Father is the *formless* God. He fills the Universe—he must be,—if the conditions of human life, and the history of the Race, are in any way to be accounted for, a Being, out of reach of our ways of thinking—and this very immensity—richness of attribute, and way of creating and governing carries his Being up into nebulous indistinctness.

Such statements, with their echo of Herbert Spencer's Unknowable, distressed Congregationalists, Baptists, and Methodists alike. Edward Beecher repeatedly urged Henry to reconsider his views of Spencer who, in Edward's view, was the rankest sort of atheistic materialist. But Henry's Christology remained unchanged.

> When therefore Christ appears I rush to him, as suited to my greater need—I do not trouble myself to prove his Divinity—Equality with God, in a strict theologic sense—He is *mine*—His limitation is my richness.

By this date the climate of religious opinion had so changed that such statements made no great noise, save among thoroughgoing conservatives, who used the religious press to try to curb Beecher's influence on laymen.[49]

Mention of changing climate of opinion inevitably leads one to ask, in what way changed and by whom? Beecher himself had an answer, already quoted, that the Holy Spirit moved with might according to God's will in disclosing new religious truths. When he stood before a huge throng in 1880 to praise Channing, Beecher concluded that the passage of time since the Beechers were in Boston showed that "those two men, my father and Dr. Channing, that stood over against each other,—to my young seeming,—as wide apart as the east from the west, I see standing together, and travelling in precisely the same lines, and toward precisely the same results."

Those results were the theology known as Liberal Orthodoxy, for which Henry Ward Beecher and Harriet Beecher Stowe were spokesmen, if somewhat singular ones. The middle ground was that of the Liberal Orthodox and the conservative Unitarians, who, Harriet maintained, were approximating evangelical views. One such conservative Unitarian, Catherine Sedgwick, paid tribute to

Beecher in these words, contrasting him to her former orthodox pastor:

> Dr. [Stephen] West belonged to other times than ours. His three-cornered beaver, and Henry Ward Beecher's Cavalier hat, fitly denote past and present clerical dynasties; the first formal, elaborate, fixed; the last easy, comfortable, flexible, and assuming nothing superior to the mass.

Some of Beecher's fellow ministers objected that this was exactly the difficulty with Beecher, that he vulgarized his message for mass consumption, preferring the plaudits of the curiosity-seekers who crammed Plymouth Church to the approval of sober-minded, orthodox Congregationalists.[50]

Beecher himself dwelled on the time past as a kind of distant heroic age, when ministers and common people alike pursued Miltonic themes:

> New England, because of her conscience, because of her devout faith, became a thinker,—a thinker as diverse, as various, as fruitful as any in the world, the Greek not excepted; not perhaps so perfect, so crystalline, yet in variety, in scope, in penetration, not second even to the Athenian. Because New England believed in moral sentiment, her children became not only fruitful in thought, but fruitful also in art, not in the external forms of art . . . but, if art be that which is framed by the imagination, working with reason and feeling, you shall find throughout New England most unmistakeable traces of the art-feeling and the art-life; and perhaps if the Puritans carved fewer statues, they made more men.

Beecher's eulogy of the New England Puritans was similar to Macaulay's tribute to the Roundheads in his essay on Milton. There was the same admiration for the Puritan tendency to dwell in eternity and to look God full in the face. Such men, to Macaulay's mind, were heroic, as they were to Beecher's, however much he might deplore their shortcomings. Such men were Lyman Beecher and Nathaniel W. Taylor, as Henry Beecher characterized them in a speech in 1870:

> O, it was charming to see men who believed in what they taught with such an abandonment of faith that not the visible world, nor human life, nor household love was so real and so transcendent to them as abstract truth! Nor is it without a certain beauty, that, the farther away from fact the thread was spun, the more

> attenuated the philosophy became, the more important it seemed. The globe and the universe, to their thinking, hung upon distinctions finer than a spider's finest film.

He prized such an attitude in somewhat the same way he gazed upon the costly treasures in his Brooklyn house, his Oriental rugs, Chinese porcelains, and ancient folios. Beecher said more than he knew when, speaking in 1880, he told his audience that religion-as-veneration, the religion of his father, was no longer possible in "our scrambling, active land."[51]

He, as much as any single figure, as Catherine Sedgwick implied, was responsible for reshaping religious ideas and ideals to keep pace with the new spirit. Strolling across his Berkshire farmland in 1854, Beecher meditated on the meaning to be found in the myriad forms of animal life surrounding him. He drew a lesson from animal creation:

> The line that divides between the animal and the divine is the line of suffering. The animal, for its own pleasure, inflicts suffering. The divine endures suffering for another's pleasure. Not when he went up to the proportions of original glory was Christ the greatest; but when he descended, and wore our form, and bore our sins and sorrows, that by his stripes we might be healed!

This may seem an orthodox enough thought, but taken in the context of the Beechers' patripassianism, their view of Christ as suffering in his divine nature, it was unorthodox. Yet, even in that sense, was it really heretical? James Barr Walker's *Philosophy of the Plan of Salvation* had met with great acceptance by that date, perhaps because Walker had the wisdom not to advance an explicitly patripassian argument. His book, in fact, became the most widely distributed and translated book of its kind in the world.

In any event, Beecher did not have to flinch before clerical critics when he found such great support among his parishioners, who were to be found wherever his books were read. A bereaved mother writing in 1874 blessed Beecher for his Yale lecture, which "so brought down, and at the same time lifted my conception of the Savior" that he appeared "so tender, near and human that I felt I could lay my boy's hand in his with a sweet cheerfulness, and even see him draw the veil and shut me out, for a time, in the dark. . . . Be assured you have helped to pour sweetness into the wounded heart of a mother whom you never saw."[52]

The number and character of the things which Beecher felt ought to be expressed in a creed were reduced over the years. To say "I confess" such things was, in his belief, momentous still. Yet he could say that "the Athanasian Creed is gigantic spider web weaving. I leave it to those who want to get stuck on it." Although spider-web weaving had been one of Lyman Beecher's preoccupations, and although such power and subtlety of mind still commanded his respect, Henry decided in the 1880s to relegate those ideas to the category of relics of spiritual barbarism. "They are infantine conceptions." He had living examples of such tendencies in Edward and Charles Beecher. Their scholarly attainments, particularly in philology, were considerable, and Henry was happy to acknowledge their aid.

But a far more congenial scholar was Calvin Stowe, who hated metaphysical speculation as he hated the Devil. Henry himself, according to a close friend, had such a deficient memory that it was "impossible down to the end of his life for him to quote anything except the briefest and most familiar passages of the Bible (and hardly those with accuracy)." Perhaps it was a case of prudent retreat from a battlefield in which he was poorly armed. But this is not to say that he was an ignorant man. He knew the "technics" of New England Theology well enough to produce wry parodies of it. If he was not so acute a critic of that theology as Harriet or Edward, he was able to come to terms with it without the heart-wrenching doubts of the one or the sense of isolation and futility of the other.[53]

Henry's success lay in proffering a brand of religious intuitionism and naturalism. Christians, he believed, could "never come to a sense of *a living and present God*, until we also include in our methods the old Hebrew way of beholding God in living activity, moving in the heavens and along the earth." Books like the *Star Papers, Eyes and Ears,* and *A Summer Parish* expressed this idea through metaphors and vignettes of nature. Beecher owed something, no doubt, to Edward Hitchcock's vision of God acting on nature, but his reveries had a taste and odor all their own. One of his better-known essays, "Nature a Minister of Happiness," portrayed him sauntering forth on a hot summer day:

> Every sense is calmly alive, and every faculty that lies back of sense is quietly exultant. My soul is like a hive, and it swarms with thoughts and feelings going nimbly out, and returning with golden thighs to the growing comb. Each hour is a perfect hour, clear, full, and unsated. It is the joy of being alive. It is the experience of that living joy which God meant to exhale from each faculty, just as odors do from flowers. Such days are let down

> from heaven. On such days the gate that looks toward the earth has surely been set wide open, and hours are but the spaces which lie between the angels that God sends to bear to us immortal joys.

Paeans to Nature and Nature's God flooded the pages of Beecher's novel *Norwood*, which teems with overripe similes and metaphors. The sensuousness of his prose captivated his audiences, who even bought a volume made up entirely of his similes. The very dandelions taught theology, for "their passing away is more spiritual than their bloom. Nothing can be more airy and beautiful than the transparent seed-globe—a fairy dome of splendid architecture." Writing to a woman friend, Beecher described his sensations after a ride across the prairies of Illinois in 1859:

> This was my first sight of the Mississippi, although I had often been not far from it. The banks were full and the river presented a most noble appearance. I had the advantage of seeing a seven miles stretch of it. It affected me as the Ocean always does and made me gasp. Deep feeling always makes me draw long breaths and sigh. . . . There is something enchanting to me in the free out door singing of birds. That God made such things indicates what thoughts pass through his mind and what his disposition is. . . . I think that the Bible is God's spelling-book. And after we have learned our letters there, and how to read, *then* the material world and human life reveal more of God than we can learn any where else. At any rate the most near and touching views of Divine Nature.

This conviction of revelation through natural and human means, particularly through intimate intercourse with Nature, did not completely supercede the Scriptures, but there was a definite tendency on Beecher's part to restrict the necessary lessons to lovely, harmonious, and joyful ones. In *Norwood* he depicted himself as the physician-philosopher Dr. Wentworth, who catechized his beautiful daughter Rose in this vein, playing on the phrasing of the Westminster Shorter Catechism:

> "Rose, what do the apple-trees principally teach?"
> "They make me think how beautiful God is!"[54]

The theology of Henry Ward Beecher was so genial, diffuse, and unencumbered by doctrine that his aged father grew alarmed. A sermon, "For God so loved the world," "annoyed him exceedingly," and Lyman complained that his son "had no business to tell sinners of the love of God without telling them of the wrath of God." He speculated aloud as to why Henry would stray so far from the faith once delivered to the saints: "I cannot tell how much the motive of helping men that would not listen to any thing but such like preaching has to do with Henry." For Henry's part, he saw no reason to vex his hearers with horrifying images and tormenting ideas. Too many people continued to think that religion was supposed to have a frightening aspect:

> One of our great troubles, as ministers, is to keep people from wishing to be awfully converted. There are those who will not come into God's kingdom unless they can come as Dante went into paradise—by going through hell. They wish to walk over the burning marl, and to snuff the sulphureous air.

Beecher wanted to coax and charm such gloomy people away from their religion of fear. God's retributive justice was not important; it was his fatherly affection that really mattered, and even more important than God's love was the love and patience of Christ.[55]

A warm, joyous naturalism like Henry's was easily assimilated into progressive evolutionism, and it is no surprise to find him hailing Darwin and Spencer as geniuses. At the same time, however, he was anxious lest an atheistic naturalism gain too much sway. He followed the English scene closely, and in 1862 asked President Woolsey of Yale to write a critical series on the *Essays and Reviews* for the benefit of *Independent* readers:

> It is not so much a discussion of the questions, on their merits [that is required], as a *view* of the discussion, an analysis and history of the great topics, each, that are under search. The Puseyite *tendency,* away from reason and *to* authority, generates a reactionary tendency away from old grounds to naturalism, to reason and science. The questions of *Inspiration*, of the *Death of Christ*, etc. are going through a remarkable history. The philosophy and results of what is going on are most important. Can you spare time to prepare such articles?

Several years later, Beecher decided that he must undertake a defense of Christianity, not a polemical or obscurantist defense but a *Life of Christ*:

> At a time when a chill mist of doubt is rising over all the Sacred Records, from an excessive addiction to material science, it would seem that good service might be rendered to religion by reasserting,

in language and by methods congenial to the wants of modern thought, the Divinity of our Lord and Saviour, Jesus Christ.

While he was carrying out his researches, Beecher could derive inspiration from a recent gift by a wealthy member of his congregation, who had brought back olivewood from the Mount of Olives and had it made into pulpit furniture for the Plymouth pastor.[56]

After 1868, when he began the *Life of Christ*, Beecher added no new elements to his theology. In 1876, after weathering the worst shocks of the Tilton scandal, he started a new religious newspaper named the *Christian Union*, whose aims he outlined to David O. Mears, a liberal ally. "It shall be a gentleman!" he insisted, in contrast to the narrowly denominational, partisan character of other religious papers. And "Its spirit shall be sweet, and breathe cheerfully." Most importantly, "I am determined that it shall steadily work toward a higher type of personal religion. Without entertaining the crude notion prevalent about 'Higher Life,' I mean that the *Christian Union* shall steadfastly have its face set as if it would go up to New Jerusalem." This "personal religion" was preached in the paper not only by Henry but also by Harriet and Thomas, with occasional contributions by Edward and Charles, who, however, continued to hold themselves apart from Liberal Orthodoxy.

Henry, meanwhile, continued to pour out books, chiefly sermon collections. In 1880 he preached a Fourth of July sermon declaring his independence from orthodox interpretations of the Fall and the Atonement. Defending himself against charges of apostacy and ultrarationalism, Beecher claimed, quite rightly, that he was only giving public statement to the private views of his more timid brethren. "There has been a great change in the temper and views, of the Evangelical Churches, within the past 30 years," he wrote, and "in the direction of putting emphasis on *Christian disposition* and not on *theology*."

Nevertheless, he subscribed to a fund to enable Andover theologian Edwards A. Park to write his "Body of Divinity which is to give Princeton a black eye." He told Park, probably in jest, that he might one day publish his own systematic theology. The closest he came to it was *Evolution and Religion*, a collection of sermons on the love of God and the march of humanity "to etherial light by and by." The book was sufficiently thoughtful and fresh to merit high praise from Frank Hugh Foster, the historian of New England Theology. In it Beecher openly declared his freedom from scriptural revelation, upheld arguments for moral and spiritual perfectionism, and presented a God who was immanent and active in the world of Nature. As a postscript to the story, or rather as an indication of Beecher's ascendancy, it is worth noting that Park labored long over his system of theology only to discover that it was too outmoded to publish.

As for Beecher, he occasionally expressed a wistful desire to have leisure for revising his sermons, but he recognized that even in their raw, unburnished state, taken directly from his lips as he paced the platform, they had exerted as much influence as any man's, not excepting those of his father, with whom he continued to identify, even while speaking to a different age:

> My sympathy toward abstract truth was strong in early life. But as my affectional nature developed in greater power, my mind, from a strong *practical* sense hereditary, betook to *clinical* theology. I have been a worker upon men rather than upon *thought*. Now all this time I have never had ambition but *sympathy—inspiration*. Intensely active in an intensely active period, I have gone in a chariot of fire.[57]

9 THOMAS KINNICUT BEECHER

Thomas Beecher, like his brothers and sisters, was seldom at a loss for words, especially words of remonstrance and rebuke; and since he was a Beecher, his sayings became famous. One incident in particular may serve as a window into his life. Once, at Henry's behest, Thomas came down from Elmira to preach in his brother's absence from Brooklyn. But when Thomas rose to greet the congregation and the standing-room-only crowd of spectators, there was a mass exodus of those who were disappointed to see that someone other than Henry Ward Beecher was filling the Plymouth pulpit. The younger Beecher raised his arm and proclaimed: "Those who came here to worship Henry Ward Beecher are excused. Those who wish to worship God will remain."[1]

By this declaration Thomas meant no ill will toward Henry, whom he loved with something approaching hero-worship, but he did feel, and often told others, that his great misfortune—in a life filled with misfortunes—was to be born a Beecher. As much as that birthright gave him in terms of family pride, friendships, and connections, it was also a stumbling block and even a bar, Thomas believed, to personal happiness and professional usefulness. He felt this from the first and continued to wrestle with the problem of family identity to the end of his long life.

It is often the lot of the last children of a large brood to feel comparatively insignificant, lost in admiration of their older siblings' achievements, and Thomas felt both awe and envy. "I always had a feeling of pride and confidence in the ability of my brothers to do anything," he confided to his sister Isabella. In addition to such feelings, and mingling with them, was a pronounced strain of melancholy. As a boy of fifteen Thomas wrote Isabella in a typically desponding vein:

The fact is, that I have just made a discovery that I wonder I

Thomas Kinnicut Beecher

> never made before (viz) that I am not one of those who are to be happy in this world for if anything in the world can give me a conception of the *lower regions*—it is—to sit down and think of my lot.

Despondency and consciousness of alienation from the workaday world were hardly the exclusive affliction of Thomas, for we have read similar expressions of gloom and loneliness from Charles's pen. Melancholia frequently visited various of the Beechers, as well as John Hooker and Calvin Stowe. But in Thomas an awareness of the sadness of things was so marked that Henry once complained, "I always get the blues when I go toward Elmira." Thomas early made up his mind that life was a vale of tears. Happiness was an illusion for which children might strive in their innocence of the true state of man, but the wise man was one who perceived the reality of life—its limited possibilities for felicity and infinite possibilities for suffering and sin—and combatted evil in the hope of transcending it. Any attempt to understand Thomas's religious experience must take his dark view of life as the starting point.[2]

When Lyman shifted his center of operations to Cincinnati, Thomas was only six, and his mother was an ailing woman whose last years—she died five years later at the age of forty-five—were harried and dark. Perhaps some of her pessimism and anxiety were communicated to her son. Thomas remembered his mother as "that willowy fair-faced being whom I called mother, and who fasted on my birthdays and prayed to God to give me a new heart." His longings to attain religion were inseparable from love for his "sainted mother, who found in it her sure support thro' trial and death, and by it ascended to heaven to the bosom of our lord." Although Harriet's three children grew accustomed to hearing their father talk as if Roxana Foote had been their mother, one cannot help suspecting that Lyman's habit rankled. In any case, Isabella, Thomas, and James drew together in an intense but often quarrelsome alliance ("the second Beecher brood," Max Eastman called them), mourning their mother's death when no one else did.[3]

Thomas was raised as much by his brothers as by his father. Lyman's preoccupation with churchmanship and theological controversy often kept him away from home, and his older sons, particularly Edward, automatically assumed many parental burdens for him. Henry and Charles were more like companions than fathers to Thomas, but they still exercised a degree of paternal oversight and authority. Thomas attached himself first to one and then to another of his brothers in rapid succession. Charles helped him prepare for college, and he was enrolled at Illinois, where Edward was president.

Still unconverted, Thomas labored mightily for spiritual rebirth, but with no success:

> But yet I hope [he wrote Isabella] soon to become one of the visible church on earth that I may with the more assurance go on in persuading others to choose the right way. I know of nothing I deplore more than my yielding to temtation so easily especially of some particular kind. It seems as if my nature never could be subdued and yet I think that each offence shall be the last one of that kind; when I make resolutions it seems as if they never would be broken over and yet each day shows the breaking of one or more resolutions. Dear sister pray for me and while our prayers are mutually ascending may it please the Lord to lift the cloud from our eyes and show us the way in which we should act.

There is a fine line separating the language of real spiritual struggle from mere religious catchphrases and evangelical jargon, and it must be observed that Thomas's youthful letters smell more of the tract and the copybook than was usual in his family. He himself sensed a certain artificiality pervading his attempts to disclose his feelings to his sister, who, he feared, must "be amused at the untalented and homely effusion[s] of my pen." He apologized for the tone and contents of his letters:

> But you are weary I know of my weak attempt at philosophizing. . . . In theory I eschew all abstractions or metaphysical reasonings—taking as my theme and profession—*things* not principles—matter and not mind. Nevertheless such has been the thorough steeping I have undergone, in the successive conversations of Henry, Charles, Cate, George and Father, that despite my better resolutions tis as natural as breathing for me to descant by the hour, upon abstract questions which do gender strife yielding no profit.

He had got the glossary and grammar by heart, and even knew the "technics," but he could not make himself feel as he was supposed to.[4]

Nevertheless, Thomas was persuaded to declare himself ready to become a church member, in part because of his attachment to Aunt Esther, whose hopes for his conversion he hated to disappoint.

Privately he felt more than the usual misgivings about the step. He wondered whether he would not set a bad example for James and their stepbrother Joseph Jackson. "My great fear," he told Isabella, "is in regard to the boys—I am afraid that I shall not live well enough to show them that the standard of the church is not lowered by my uniting with it." But his real anxiety was over his confusion of belief and his family's urgency in pressing him to declare his intention to enter the ministry. "The fact is," he protested, "that Father never understood my inclinations or talents, disposition or capabilities." He loathed his studies and had no liking for professional life. To become a minister, he believed, "would cost my reason if not my life. I have once in devotion and prayer and in sincerity devoted myself to the Lord but to become his ambassador to men is more than I can do." He told Isabella that he was only marking time, remaining in college to please their father while secretly searching for avenues of escape.[5]

Living in Edward's household, Thomas was initially delighted with his brother's personality and ideas and looked upon him as a model:

> You cannot conceive what advantages and privileges I do have here in the line of sermons, advice, explanation[s] etc.; tho Bro E. has many doctrines of which I am not as yet capable of judging—yet if I were seeking any person now living after whom I might safely pattern [myself] it would be Bro E. He is the most consistent, most faithful—(i.e.) full of faith, and the strongest practical believer in the providence of God of any persons that I ever saw.

As to Edward's theory of the preexistence of souls, Thomas had no means of deciding, but he was drawn to Edward's view of God, which represented the deity as a compassionate and truly suffering God. Yet, when Thomas asked Edward for help in understanding the doctrine of election, he was disappointed by what he considered "sophistical reasoning" on Edward's part.

Thomas's disaffection from Edward grew apace. He came to resent his authority and called his doctrines into question. Whether he lost confidence in Edward as a result of picking holes in the latter's system, or (just as likely) rejected Edward's theology in the process of establishing his independence, Thomas was quickly disenchanted with him. He remained on good terms, however, with Charles and sought his concurrence in his decision to give up college and their father's dream of seeing all the sons in the ministry.[6]

Shortly after the new year opened in 1842, Thomas wrote Lyman pleading for release from "the profession which you practice with such happiness and peace of mind to yourself and acceptance to all your hearers." "I fear this announcement gives you pain, perhaps causes much sorrow while reading it," he anticipated, and proceeded to lay out in great detail the objections he had already rehearsed with Isabella two years before. He even quoted at length from a letter of Edward's, addressed to Lyman almost twenty years before, arguing the impossibility of entering the ministry when major philosophical doubts remained unresolved. The will of God, Thomas insisted, indicated a different calling for him, one that would take account of his special intellectual endowments and physical needs. Not for him the "quiet, monotonous, retired life of a minister." He wanted to be an engineer. Evidently he conceived of the ministry in different terms from the other men in his family, who could hardly be said to lead secluded lives. Thomas proposed that his father use his "extensive acquaintance and influence" to secure his admission to West Point. Failing that, Thomas would try to get his scientific training locally, perhaps with the astronomer O. M. Mitchell.[7]

Charles wrote Lyman by the same mail, expressing surprise at the suddenness of his brother's decision but partially supporting it. Charles also feared the effect of the blow on Lyman and expressed contrition over his own former willfulness and folly:

> I well remember [the] scenes through which I myself passed. I believe however that you will be less pained now than then, because the difficulty is not in the present case of so radical and inexorable a cast. And because I must own that I think Thomas has shown more consideration for your feelings than I did.

He thought Thomas's case was less desperate than his own for several reasons. Thomas, for one thing, was not prone to entanglement in the ropes and chains of theological controversy. For another, he had always tried to be a good son in every sense of the word: obedient, deferential, honest, forthright, and virtuous. Perhaps he tried even harder to please Lyman because of the flagrant misbehavior of his brother James.

James Beecher had given his family many bad moments, but the worst was to come. His irascibility, extravagance, and arrogance had involved him in numerous quarrels and scrapes. He talked a lot about his high sense of honor, which would brook no insult, real or imagined. Lyman, who was horrified to see his son acting like a Southern Hotspur instead of a fledgling parson, had to withdraw him from one school where the students carried sidearms and bowie knives to settle their disputes. Despite their strong resemblance, Thomas and James were unlike. Whereas James alternated between winsome charm and downright surliness, Thomas was grave, mild, and self-effacing. Whatever Thomas's faults, he was basically serious-minded and gave the appearance of precocious maturity, so that his family counted on his eventually becoming religious.

Charles liked James, but he positively loved Thomas and worried about him constantly. He dismissed Thomas's argument that he was intellectually unfit for the ministry and judged that his real disqualification was spiritual. Speaking as he did on this subject, Charles was reflecting not only on Thomas's low spirituality but on his as well. Charles had his own doubts about entering the ministry and admitted as much to Lyman. "I must own that while I have seen in Thomas all honorable, estimable, and it may be christian traits—I have not seen that love of Christ—which you feel, which Henry feels—and which I understand, and *would* feel." He recommended that Lyman permit Thomas to have his way, for the present, but to make sure that he would remain under Edward's eye or be sent to Yale, where he would be surrounded by proper influences. Charles felt as if he were reliving his decade of spiritual wandering: "Good bye—my dear father—and believe me—that to perceive as I do how you now feel gives me even more pain than I felt when I inflicted the blow. I feel at last, as I ought to have felt then."[8]

To Isabella, Charles disclosed similar views but with greater emphasis on their brother's unformed religious character. "I think it quite certain that he can't be a minister with his present notions of godliness. For to say [the] truth he has been on short allowance of spiritual grog for some time." That being the case, the family could hardly expect Thomas to man "a life boat wherein he can cruise for shipwrecked sinners—he will have to bail hard—caulk cracks—and skull hard with a cracked oar, to escape Davy Jones's locker himself. How powerful all this may be, to keep him out of the pulpit awhile you will admit." This, Charles felt, was only a phase through which their brother was passing. In his present state of mind Thomas might respond positively to the military discipline of West Point, but if he were turned loose without strict guidance, he would undergo a lengthy harrowing by the sorrows of the world, "picking up here and there with many tears scraps of knowledge—and volumes of experience—untill finally perchance he have conned one great lesson—God is great—and life is a lesson he sets us to learn."[9]

While Charles identified with Thomas in his adolescent rebelliousness and predicted that he would ultimately emerge with a deeper knowledge of God, Lyman had concluded that Thomas "has been injured in his speculations by Charles." Thomas was not, in fact, indulging in any speculations. He was rapidly advancing toward complete skepticism, in reaction, he told Isabella, against Edward's example. Given his disinclination to criticize Edward openly, it was not surprising that his other brother received the blame for his religious condition, for Charles, "tho convalescent, is not wholly restored." Ironically, Lyman did not grasp what was so plain to Thomas: that it was Edward's speculative system which was fascinating Charles and would lead him into strange byways of theology. Bent on becoming independent and making his mark outside the ministry, Thomas spurned Edward and drew away from Charles as well, choosing Henry as his model:

> I think I like Henry the best. He is the most like father of all his sons, and as a speaker and writer far surpasses any divine I have ever heard, i.e., in my opinion. Then for versatility of talent—one moment a farmer—next a nursery man—then a horticulturist—lawyer—doctor—minister—etc. he is certainly without equal among my friends. And then for warmth of affection, and adaptation for domestic usefulness—and happiness—he is hardly second to our dear father who on these points I feel by daily experience that he is peerless.

Again Thomas confided to his sister what he did not dare hint to the rest of the family:

> My dear sister I will not disguise from you—that I feel terribly unsettled in my religious constitution. Tis what I have long feared—and I know not, nor can any one predict save the Omniscient, where my resting place will be. I am in darkness on the philosophy of religion—the reality of it and the practice of it.

His twin doubts were the authenticity of the Scriptures and the existence of God. Yet, fatal as such doubts must be, an even graver obstacle to belief, in his mind, was the character of his own family. It is not unusual to find a young man making the discovery that his family is not utterly consistent in practicing what they preach, but Thomas's dissatisfaction ran deeper than that. "Again supposing both these points proved, I see so much in the church, and among our own family even to give me a disrespect to religion, that I feel doubts arising as it regards embracing a system whose lights and glory appear to me so slim and faulty."[10]

None of the Beechers, he was saying, were whole-hearted Christians. Since they could not exhibit perfect Christian character, who could? Or, more bluntly, what was the virtue of a system that produced such flawed results? Even those members of his family whom he conceded to be fervent in their piety seemed pitiably confused in their intellect. It was Thomas's opinion that the faith which Charles had recovered with such pains was rooted in "*self deception*" of the same stripe as Edward's. As for Edward, on whom Charles obviously leaned, Thomas was thoroughly disillusioned:

> I once almost worshipped Edward—as some of my letters to you indicate—but I am undeceived now. Either Edward is insane on some points—or else he is not a christian, of the same kind as our father or brother Henry. And I say without fear or hesitation that if religion were to make *me* another *Edward*—I say God deliver me from being pious. But if I could be a second *Father*, or Henry, untold wealth would not swerve my choice. . . . Edward loves me I know sincerely, and I love him dearly as I love any of my brothers, but I pity more than I respect him.

Affection and lingering admiration kept him from exposing Edward, Thomas added. "'Tis not prudent for me to make known—so long as I am in college, where he is President, the grounds of my opinion as respects him—but they shall be known to the faculty—to father and to all our family so soon as I leave here," he declared darkly.

The vehemence of Thomas's language indicated not only contempt for Edward's strange theological ideas but for his character as well. Perhaps he considered Edward a hypocrite for secretly holding views at variance with New School orthodoxy. Perhaps he thought Edward was unnecessarily exposing the college to ruin by pressing his antislavery cause—with which Thomas disagreed—too zealously. If he did not quarrel openly with Edward, Thomas expressed his hostility in other ways. In one instance, he asked the faculty to allow him to skip Saturday evening prayers. When they demanded the reason for his unusual request, he coolly announced that he preferred hunting to praying. A more serious show of disrespect caused his suspension from Illinois College for "repeated disorders tending to disturb the worship of God in chapel."[11]

Thomas's religious problems, like Charles's, were compounded by an unhappy love-life, which was due in turn to his indecision in finding a vocation that would enable him to marry and raise a family. Suppressing the name of his young lady, Thomas confessed to Isabella that "for the first time in my life," he felt "an emotion of true and ardent love—in my heart—but owing to the unsettled state of my future prospects, I made no one my confidant and my penchant is as yet unknown and unsuspected." He turned over the possibilities of becoming a trapper or hunter in the Rockies or sailing to the Indies as an ordinary seaman. The West Point plan evaporated (for reasons unknown). He then canvassed law and medicine as possibilities. Teaching and clerking offered themselves but did not appeal to Thomas, who disliked sedentary occupations. Then he wondered whether one of his mother's wealthy cousins would like to take him on a commercial voyage. There was also the Naval College, if he still wanted an engineering or military career.

He was casting about for an occupation without any expectation that one would turn up. He had presentiments of leading a life of poverty and obscurity and dreaded the day when he might be reduced to teaching at a district school in the West, in "a log School house" with only "dirty, semi brutes for my pupils." Thomas lacked Edward's enthusiasm for education and James's empathy for the rough, reckless ways of Western men. What he needed, he told his sister, was exacting work for his hands, something like surgery. Perhaps he ought to be trained as a "philosophical [scientific] instrument maker—or a clock and watch maker," the kind of work that would exploit his mechanical aptitude while fulfilling his need for money and respectability.[12]

Never as gregarious as his brothers and sisters, Thomas now chose to lead a solitary life, confiding only in Isabella and becoming more and more "melancholy and dumpish." He got his hands on a German book which suited his mood precisely. Immersing himself in Wilhelm DeWette's *Theodore*, a long theological novel recently translated by James Freeman Clarke, Thomas found "much that is agreeable true and beautiful in it—and sometimes I fancy myself somewhat in 'Theodores' situation both in *religion* and *love*."

It may be doubted whether Thomas grasped the intricate, labored delineation of rival schools of German theology and biblical criticism, with DeWette's strictures on them. But the bare outlines of the novel did speak to Thomas's condition. The titular hero, a well-bred skeptic with a scientific turn of mind, is consecrated to the ministry by his saintly mother, undergoes numerous tests and a few heartbreaks before winning a wife, recovering his faith, and settling down as an enlightened village pastor in his hereditary domains. In the absence of further testimony from Thomas, it would be pointless—not to say naïve—to take too literally his statement about the congruency between his life and that of DeWette's fictional mouthpiece. One of Theodore's speeches deserves quotation, however:

> "In me the understanding, for a long time, exalted itself too highly; and how much pains did it cost me to force it back again into its proper limits! And how can I be sure that it will not again rebel. . . . Our faith is not completely satisfactory till we have renounced all attempts to understand precisely what we believe. What a mistake is committed by those who think they have contributed to the religious benefit of mankind when they scatter among the community acute explanations of truth!"[13]

Several other statements by DeWette are striking, in view of Thomas Beecher's subsequent theological development. First, there is DeWette's examination of the shortcomings of nineteenth-century Protestantism: its excessive tendency toward intellectuality; its low views of church communion; and its nearly inhuman standard of spirituality which few men could meet. Second, DeWette's scathing criticism of bibliolatry and religious enthusiasm is a recurrent theme. One of the characters, the spiritually proud Walter, may have reminded Thomas of his brother Edward. What did Thomas mean when he called Edward Beecher insane? Edward's scheme of preexistence was outlandish in his brother's eyes, but the intensity of Thomas's feeling may have been an expression of alarm over Edward's claim to have received his doctrines through immediate revelation. Theodore's narrow-minded friend Walter believes himself to be in union with Christ, but

> Theodore could not but consider his friend's state of mind as a diseased one. . . . In the fancied communion with the Redeemer, lay the most extraordinary self-conceit and presumption. . . . This pretended intercourse with Christ, is it any thing else than a dialogue with ourselves, in which it is a happy accident if the better part of our nature assumes the part of the Savior?

And lastly, there is DeWette's definition of Christianity as a unique way of life, as discipleship in the whole of one's being, yet without extravagance or asceticism:

> "a Christian is one who has faith in Christ, the Redeemer, and who communes with his church, not one who receives the

Scriptures and its verbal contents. . . . For those who regard Christianity as a *life*, there is nothing disagreeable in this view; it is only when we make the essence of it consist in words and letters, that we are terrified by it. The regeneration of Protestantism depends on bringing Christianity back again into life."[14]

Thomas finally revealed to Isabella the identity of the girl he loved. She was Catherine Mussey, daughter of Dr. Reuben Dimond Mussey, a Cincinnati physician and dietary reformer who was one of Lyman's parishioners. There were many obstacles in the way of such a match, not the least of which was Thomas's consciousness of cutting a poor figure in society. In the spring of 1843 his father suggested that he make a visit to Henry in Indianapolis. Whereas Lyman hoped that Henry's influence would steady Thomas's religious opinions, Thomas seized upon the occasion as an opportunity to "attain a little of that polish—and those accomplishments of life—of which I am conscious that I am entirely destitute." He vowed not to return to Walnut Hills until he had made himself worthy of Catherine Mussey by acquiring "those requisites for a scholar and gentleman, as well as a christian which shall render the disparity less between her and myself." He needed no urging to become an inmate of Henry's house. Thomas regarded Henry as the great man of the family, the one after whom he must pattern himself. Whatever his expectations about this stay in Indianapolis, Thomas went home a changed man, probably having gained little by way of manners and modishness but very much in earnest about religion.[15]

Years later, Thomas recalled his brother as a heroic figure carrying revival fires across the prairies and swamps of Indiana on "his long-boned, fast-walking sorrel, with well-worn and ill-fitted saddlebags . . . as courageous as Paul, as gentle as John." In March of 1845, when a revival was brewing in Henry's church, Thomas surprised his family by announcing laconically, "Well, I think I had better go and help Henry." Lyman, his sense of justice and his pride in Thomas's scientific abilities swaying him for once, had felt compelled to free him from the obligation to the enter the ministry. Since "my heart had let go of its favorite purpose that he should preach," Lyman wrote Henry, it would be boon enough if the older brother should convert the younger. In Thomas's later retelling of the story, it was all a family conspiracy. "Hearing of the great revival in Henry's church, he asked leave to go and see Henry and try conclusions with him;—which the old father was prompt to grant," he recalled. In this version Thomas intended to dispute with Henry, not serve as his lay assistant. He portrayed his father as the physician of his soul, passing the patient on to another skilled practitioner.[16]

Harriet did her part by writing Thomas a long, very characteristic letter detailing her own struggles and the exultant resolution of them. He must not despond over the tyranny of his powerful intellect or be ashamed of his unfulfilled yearnings for ideal spirituality:

> That repressed and crushed longing, useless, unreasonable, without end or purpose, is all that remains to the captive of a noble lineage and high inheritance; and even though it become mania or moroseness, or though it unfit him for the office of a patient drudge without fitting him for any thing else, 'tis all one, there it is, a mournful fragment of something divine.

Soul union with Christ, Harriet preached, was the chief end of man, who must bow to the "inflexible WILL" and through that submission find conciliation with God. It was source of torment, wondering how mortal man with his inchoate yet burning longings for holiness was to escape the dead weight of earthly cares. Thomas must learn the lesson that Harriet believed herself to have read in God's word:

> I often saw, as by a dart of sunlight, that an entire IDENTITY of my will with God's would remove all disquiet, and give joy even to suffering. . . . When self-despair was final, and I merely undertook at the word of Christ, then *came* the long-expected and wished help. *All* changed. Whereas my heart ran with a strong current to the world, now it runs with a current the other way. What it once cost an effort to remember, now it costs an effort to forget. The will of Christ seems to me the steady pulse of my being, and I go because I can not help [it]. Skeptical doubt can not exist. I seem to see the full blaze of the Shekinah every where.

If Harriet offered the lesson of her experience of Christ, Henry's treatment was also tailored to Thomas's state of mind:

> There were no arguments. Nothing was proved. Can you tell how the bones of the unborn babe grow in the womb? So Christ was formed in *Consciousness*. Like some white bird high-flying, that drops down through the smoke into a walled city fortified against all comers, carrying under wing a message from afar, so came to me the vision of Christ, as with matchless words brother Henry told the story, without theology or dialectic. . . .

What Henry and Harriet gave their brother was not a revival-induced change of heart, not a fully articulated system of beliefs, but the germ of faith. Even this germ was hidden far from sight, so that it appeared that Thomas, while inclined to be pious, was still far from Christian. "The Christ formed in me," he said, "was shut in doubly by the hull of frolic and frivolity; and by the hard shell of intellectual pride and scientific attainment."[17]

In the fall of 1844 Thomas decided upon a medical career. His father was anxious to keep him nearby as long as he was still unconverted and assented to this latest plan. Thomas had had some success in making scientific instruments, which brought him to the notice of the founders of the Ohio Medical College in Cincinnati. Nothing came of this project, however, and Thomas was soon adrift, though he continued to study chemistry and mechanics. Filial obedience was deeply ingrained in him and, lacking any definite plans, he acceded to Lyman's renewed requests to make his home at Walnut Hills, serving his father as factotum and amanuensis. With no one else was Thomas so companionable. A family friend described their relationship perfectly when he wrote, "He and the old gentleman are forever poking fun at each other, to their own great delight and the entertainment of others."

When they weren't joking together, Lyman and Thomas found pleasure in long walks and talks. Furthermore, Thomas was virtually alone in getting along with Lydia Beecher, his stepmother, and her son Joseph Jackson, both of whom the other Beecher children despised as interlopers. When Charles and Henry asked Thomas to help them with a projected biography of their father—a scheme kept secret from Lyman—Thomas fell in with the idea enthusiastically. He began making a "Diary of his [Lyman's] 'talk talk' reminiscences, anecdotes, etc." Inevitably, it became awkward for Thomas to remain at home, when neighbors and friends began to hint that he was an idler and a sponger. "I was impatient to be gone, and many a passionate discussion came up between us about the matter," he recalled. As much as he longed for independence, he could not make the break. He knew of Lyman's unceasing worries for him and he admitted to himself that he worried about his aged father too much. In the end he could not resist his father's plea: "Tom, I love you; you mustn't go 'way and leave me. They're all gone—Jim's at college. I want one chicken under my wing."[18]

Lyman knew his son too well to waste breath in arguing doctrines with him. But he believed that the leaven was working in him. All his son required, he thought, were the proper influences. He wrote to his old friend Chauncey Goodrich, suggesting that Yale College might find the funds to support Thomas in postgraduate studies (in the paternal orbit of Goodrich and Taylor). Beecher gave his son high marks for intelligence but deplored his arrogance:

> But he is a child of a vigorous mind. Keen and powerful and dextrous in argument, to make the worse appear the better reason if he pleases, and unhappily is apprised of his comparative mental ascendancy, and being where there were but few competitors [Illinois College] has probably augmented his self estimation.

Lyman craftily refrained from engaging Thomas in debate. If he could not be at Yale, to learn truth from the New Haven divines, Thomas must learn practical lessons in piety at home, without benefit of the theological wrangling he relished.

When Henry wrote Lyman that Charles was at last convinced of his worthiness for the ministry, the old man made an epic journey on horseback to Fort Wayne, Indiana, to deliver the ordination sermon. Lyman emerged a genuine hero in Henry's account, where filial pride, amazement, and envy of the feat were mingled:

> Father got here the Saturday night before I did. He is you know 70 years old. When he got to St. Mary's on Friday night, (the termination of the Canal) he had *69* miles to ride, the road terrible—It was impossible to do it on Saturday—so waiting for the moon to rise he started at *ten o'clock* on Friday *night* and rode all night and all day Saturday—and Sunday preached twice and is hearty as a buck! I should like these Sunday-travelling young men members of churches to compare their excuses for travelling on Sunday with his—and their conduct with his.

Hugh McCulloch recalled how old Beecher arrived at the McCulloch home, leaped off his steaming horse, and after a short rubdown ventured out with his rifle to bag game for the McCulloch table, to repay them for their hospitality. Though "covered from foot to head with mud," he made light of the feat, which staggered the congregation in Fort Wayne. His joy in Charles's calling had buoyed him up during the long ride.

Thomas found himself rejoicing in the event too, despite his misgivings about Charles's metaphysical bent. He interpreted Charles's recovery as a triumph for the entire family. Charles, he was pleased to see, "has got at last to be as desirous to read and study as he ever was to fiddle and sing, etc., and if his health only holds out he will yet prove the smartest Beecher that father has educated and ordained." Lyman's remarkable physical vigor, his devotion to his sons, and his conscientious Sabbath-keeping could only have impressed Thomas, who was accustomed to judge men's beliefs by the light of their conduct. He received, from this and other acts of Lyman's, profound impressions of what his father meant by the sacrificial life. But still Thomas was unconverted.[19]

After his hopes of sending Thomas to Yale collapsed, Lyman feared that his son would drift into an unsuitable career. In addition to his secretarial duties, Thomas made and sold common tinwares and worked in a machine shop "making philosophical instruments, working glass and building lathes, etc., until now I can command $5.00 pr week for my services as a journeyman mechanic." Even the lure of such wages seemed small recompense to Lyman, who insisted that Thomas must not waste his education. Thomas continued at home and was restive without being openly rebellious. Drawn as he was to his father, he regretted that the other children saw so little of Lyman. Thomas scolded Edward in particular for his cavalier attitude:

> Although father appreciates the extent of your duties and their engrossing nature, yet he feels now and then as though you might send him at least a word or two of love and remembrance—and not leave the newspapers to be the only medium through which he can hear of you.

The only other child remaining with Lyman was Catharine. She, Thomas groaned, was full of crotchets and "writes and rides her education scheme as assiduously as ever, and once in a while wishes I would devote myself thereto." Catharine prevailed upon her brother to accompany her on one of her Western educational tours, as no gentlewoman could travel without a masculine escort. While she sat on the platforms, Thomas stood before strange audiences and read his sister's speeches and observations to them. This prolonged association did nothing to cement their relationship.[20]

Perhaps some of Catharine's educational zeal rubbed off on Thomas, nevertheless, for he next concluded to try teaching. He found a place in Philadelphia, undoubtedly through family connections, taking charge of the old Northeast Grammar School. The school had once been a thriving enterprise but had fallen on hard times, and dwindled in enrollment as its reputation sank. With his family's encouragement and a loan backed by John Hooker, Thomas entered on his new duties in July of 1846. He was then twenty-two and acutely conscious, as he wrote to Isabella, of "the depth of disquiet and discontent springing from the ambitious insignificance that has ground my life for years."

He saw no future in teaching and continued to dream of mastering "chemistry—Natural Philosophy and science in general." If he could make his mark as a scientist, he thought, he might still have a chance of winning Catherine Mussey.[21]

His experiences at the school made teaching even more distasteful than he had anticipated. "You see my boys—i.e., nine out of ten of them are of the very worst sort—of no family or with no home feeling. They glory in cheating me—and take more pleasure in seeing me whip a fellow than they would in seeing me laboring with constant success for their welfare." Beecher did not try to disguise his contempt for his students, his shrinking from their filthiness. "Then, too, they are dirty, ragged, lousy and obscene—i.e., a great number of them—my first idea was to turn all such right out of the school. But as Edward says, 'It is for the good of just such as these that public schools are established.'" Only constant self-exhortations and the dream of winning out over Catherine Mussey's other suitors kept Thomas going.[22]

Besides the problems of the school, over which he shed many tears, Thomas was also forced to take his brother James in hand. The two brothers had been separated for years, attending different schools. After James was suspended from Dartmouth for assaulting a student, disrupting chapel, and other offenses, he joined Thomas in Philadelphia. He formed a strong attachment to his older brother, a dependency that continued for the rest of James's life. If "ambitious insignificance" marked Thomas's life, it was even truer of the youngest Beecher. James attributed all his troubles to the machinations of malign forces and spoke darkly of combinations raised against him. It was useless for Lyman, Henry, or Thomas to remind him that his own incivility and recklessness were the real sources of difficulty and not collegiate cabals or faculty vendettas.

Although he was unpleasantly surprised by James's cynicism and bad manners, Thomas took the attitude that there was a noble man underneath the adolescent and treated him as an equal. James repaid this kindness by genuine devotion and loyalty, but he also created new problems for Thomas. He borrowed freely from Thomas and, when Thomas's money ran out, applied to their destitute father to make good the loans. His seeming callousness and his very evident lack of foresight worried his older brother, who wanted very much to "prepare him for the social pecuniary and personal trials he will encounter when he makes his debut for himself." He assured the rest of the family that James needed only silent examples of manliness to counter the hedonism and selfishness of his "singularly decieved and disproportioned" character. Ultimately James left Philadelphia unchanged and, if anything, even wilder than before. His failure to kindle a sense of responsibility and independence in James haunted Thomas for many years, and made their relationship as bitter as it was tender.[23]

Thomas's correspondence with Catherine Mussey came to an end when she revealed her engagement to a wealthy Cincinnati lawyer, who was also (unlike Thomas) pious. Beecher was crushed by her decision but wrote Isabella that "by as much as I love Catie, just so much do I rejoice, that she has found so worthy a mate." He resigned himself to remaining single the rest of his life. His disappointment in Catherine was countered by the success of his school. He could report that it was "conquered–it begins to grow . . . [and] now I have some sunshine gleams of created intelligence, *my work*, such as gives me almost a painful pleasure."

His pedagogical successes prompted him to govern by precept alone, and he stopped whipping the pupils, at that time an accepted practice. The boys he had initially shunned as delinquents became his firm friends, and they grew to hero-worship Beecher. Yet he still regarded teaching as a temporary occupation and planned to use his savings to finance two years of advanced scientific study in England and Europe. He hoped his father would give the plan his blessings now that Lyman had apparently withdrawn all objections to a secular career. Science, not education or divinity, was to be his calling.[24]

Having settled his career to his own satisfaction, Thomas was now faced with an important choice in joining a church. He was still feeling his way slowly in matters of religion and received, he claimed, no help from the ministers he consulted and heard. He bypassed the New School Presbyterian churches of his father's friends, Albert Barnes and Thomas Brainerd, in favor of Christ Church, Episcopal, a choice dictated as much by his love of sacred music as by conviction.

Nonetheless, he had positive complaints about the evangelical churches in the city, informing his father that "vital religion can be hardly said to exist any longer in Philadelphia." If Lyman was surprised by this announcement, he let it pass unchallenged, knowing that Thomas was apt to be fault-finding and superior. Thomas explained to Lyman exactly what was wrong with his clerical brethren:

> The lamp is gone out, and where with shall it be lighted. Even the appointed lights gleam but according to the light of private christians around them. Where Mr. Barnes represents the learning,

Dr. Bethune the eloquence, Dr. Chambers the popular address, and Mr. Brainerd the sympathy of the pastoral office, alas for the church. Learning without emotion, eloquence without aptness, popular reform without physical executive energy—these may be each parts but never a whole for a successful ministry—leaders of a progressive christian church.

Beecher's disparagement of his father's allies showed the extent of his alienation from the ministry and his lack of enthusiasm for the evangelical alliance which Lyman had struggled so hard to erect. Thomas never permitted himself to acknowledge, much less voice, any feelings of contempt for Lyman himself. In the future Thomas Beecher's colleagues would have occasion to murmur against his captious spirit, a tendency toward censoriousness mitigated only by his equally severe self-criticism.

His disapprobation of the Presbyterian church led him to consider deserting it for the Episcopalian, and he sounded his father out on the question of his confirmation. Lyman, who was visiting Philadelphia, discussed the decision in these terms, as Thomas recounted the story to Charles:

"Tom," said he, "your mother loved the Episcopal Church (he often counted me a son of your mother, Charley). She was a good woman. The Episcopal Church is as good as any. Go there, if you can do any good by going; I have no objection at all; only, whatever Church you go to, be a Christian and work.

The less exacting terms of communion which the Episcopal church offered made it a logical choice as shelter for a man like Thomas Beecher, who could not or would not conform to the evangelical standard of church membership. Lyman was anxious to see him safely within the embrace of religion and had genuine respect for the Episcopalians, notwithstanding his former battles with their leaders in Connecticut. His reasonableness and sympathy touched Thomas and drew the men even closer to one another.[25]

In spite of his father's recommendation, or perhaps because of it, Thomas returned to the Presbyterian fold and presented himself before the session of the Pine Street Church with a remarkable confession of faith: "I don't believe the Bible, but I believe on Jesus Christ —Bible or no Bible." Privately he told Lyman, "What I shall hold to all my life I know not . . . [but] I know that I shall always love Christ—love my parents and friends—and shall always wish to love and make a friend of every one I meet and associate with." He believed that all churches without exception had apostatized from the primitive faith, which he seems to have conceived of as a unitarianism; yet he had no positive religious affirmations of his own, "for how shall I learn save from the Bible—a sealed book to me." He believed intuitively "in the most *absolute fatality*--yet not so as to unnerve my arm from labor, nor my feet from walking aright."

Thomas's beliefs amounted to a kind of theistic stoicism and love of Christ without faith in his gospel. Such views, for whose consistency he did not argue, were "anathema" to the orthodox mind, but "a consciousness of honest seeking after truth must be my present support." Baring his heart to his family would leave them in possession of "the solving key to my life and principles," he told Harriet Stowe, who sympathized with his protracted struggle. But there remained the dilemma of his public professions. "How to manage the matter with acquaintances in prayer, meetings and families, I am at a loss." He could not worship in good conscience, even while considering himself in some sense part of the Christian fellowship, because there was nothing and no one to worship. Yet he was fearful of casting discredit upon his family by the appearance of irreligion and of damaging "religion and its interests." His departure from Philadelphia in 1848 relieved him of this burden. He moved to Hartford, where he became principal of the recently organized Hartford High School.[26]

A much more momentous change, which altered the course of Thomas Beecher's life, was his coming under the influence of Horace Bushnell. Before encountering Bushnell, Thomas had found no one outside his own family capable of being a religious teacher. Excepting Beecher sermons, "I *never* hear any preaching that gives me any pleasure or suggists any new thoughts." In Bushnell's preaching he suddenly discovered a personal revelation of the meaning of religion and of the religious affections. Compare his grudging but deeply felt concession to Lyman in 1846, "For the world as it is, Religion is God's best gift," with his joyful declaration to Harriet two years later that "science—piety—and peace—and call it what you will has to my mind now a glorious element of *experimentality*, round whom it centres." This change of mind and heart Thomas credited to the one man capable of leading him, "Mr. Bushnell [who] has got hold of the life of religion." He predicted that

> unless a certain intellectuality that pervades his whole being, overgrow the young germ of experimental religion in his heart, overgrow it by reason of strong polemic opposition, he will develop most richly the scheme of love—and the christian philosophy

of the Bible as based upon the heart, in distinction from that human philosophy that springs from detached but strong perceptions of detached parts of a great fact that must be considered as *one* to be seen at all.[27]

What was this but a reaffirmation, in Beecher's groping terms, of DeWette's "Christianity as a *life*"? To be sure, Bushnell's apprehension of German idealism was mediated through Coleridge, and it is unlikely that Thomas knew very precisely the sources of Bushnell's theology, or cared to know. He saw Bushnell as a man who had traveled the same arduous, sorrowful pathways to arrive at the same truth for which Thomas had been seeking. Bushnell's understanding of religious truth, which Beecher well knew to be both heretical and philosophically unsound by his father's lights, confirmed his own rejection of "abstract questions which do gender strife yielding no profit." He only feared that Bushnell would become entangled in theological controversy and be deflected from his real mission. He coincided with Bushnell in his view of "the absolute *experimentality* that characterises the gospel religion as I now hold it." Beecher defined its meaning for Harriet as "aiming to identify, or rather to be identified with its author and centre." Experimentality had revolutionized Thomas's religious beliefs:

[It] is the element which to my mind gives most light and disperses the most fog. By this long word which I have coined, I want to express an idea that I know you have, but which one word will not express. . . . So true have I found [it] that "the light hath shined into the darkness and the darkness comprehendeth it not"; or, as Dr. Bushnell would delight to express it, truth in religion exists as truth, not by itself subjectively—but by its believers state of mind and age of experience. For (and here his bold sentence would scan orthodox) religious truth exists not! (as does a material world—liable to make itself apparent by collision destructive with other worlds unless harmony reign) nor can we know it in any manner such as we use to learn other facts.

Well! words are contrivances to conceal ideas. So truly do I believe them so, that I shall not open my eyes very wondrously wide if perchance a man were to understand me to describe a funereal cell with sable hangings, when all the while I was thinking and talking of a golden sunset, such as seems to realise all the figures by which the Bible reveals to us heaven.[28]

Another of Bushnell's doctrines reinforced Thomas's conviction that what was called Christian character, the highest social affections united and developed through divine grace, was the one thing needful. These "generous emotions," the "susceptibilities that are the germ of the religious element in man," were fostered by the family and the community as "the natural course of things according to the laws that regulate moral appetites." This process ended unfailingly in "gospel regeneration and Christian union. This is in brief what I believe Dr. Bushnell means when he writes and talks about: Christian Nurture."[29]

These were the ideas Beecher distilled from reading and hearing Horace Bushnell, whom he revered as a teacher without wanting to follow him through the mazes of theological controversy. He feared that Bushnell would succumb to the polemical spirit and blunt the force of his doctrines by defending them too often or being compelled to strive for the absolute consistency which Beecher thought fatal to theology. The elusiveness or, as Beecher held, the nonexistence of religious truth, was a liberating discovery only insofar as its discoverers had the courage to sustain it:

> And yet how much do I fear that many may, in ardor for the propagation of a happiness [they] themselves enjoy, talk so much of it, that finally they will be on the outside themselves, standing in the rain to admire and praise their noble house. . . . I could *preach* all my religion away in a week. And therefore do I fear much for the future usefulness of Dr. Bushnells ministrations. I hope, in this I am to find myself wrong in my prognostics.[30]

Eager to impart these new ideas to his family, Thomas wrote to Henry, who hailed him as a brother not only in the flesh but also in the spirit. The fraternal bond between the two was being intensified by a new crisis in James Beecher's life, which Henry and Thomas had to master together, Lyman being too aged and too far distant to protect James any longer. In a typically expansive vein, Henry welcomed Thomas as an initiate. "I glory and rejoice to know that you are high enough up on the sides of Mt Zion to begin to see the wide circuit of life—and that you are advanced so far as to know how much deeper *feeling* is, than *thinking*." He wept with joy to know that Thomas had finally learned the first lessons in religion, of which one of the most important was, as Harriet would write in *Oldtown Folks*, that in any serious theological debate, moral earnestness stripped mere logical arguments of their force. Henry understood, of course, that Thomas would find few men with any pretensions to orthodoxy who would admit to like views. But orthodoxy mattered little when "You can claim relationship to many of the most intense portions of [the] Bible which is, of all books on Earth, the Book of the Heart."[31]

To Thomas's sweeping admiration for Bushnell, however, Henry gave a corrective. "Oh how I could weep when I think of such a soul as Isaiah, who had no mode of embodying in action, and so realizing the intense emotions of his *heart*! and how glorious a period is that in which we live in which . . . [there is] the most *unbounded* opportunity for individual exertion." Bushnell fell short of the gospel standard of spirituality. He lacked "this outward sympathy . . . that tremendous sweep, which the Pauline, because Christlike, mind takes, when from these crystal mountains it descends for the poor multitudes."

One wonders what Thomas thought when he read his brother's near dismissal of the man who had affected him so profoundly and given him confidence in the views it had cost him so much to reach. Henry wrote, in a rather snubbing way clearly meant to point the contrast between his own religion and that of the Hartford theologian's: "The moment one feels the *working zeal*—all mysticism and obscurity become impossible. [Men] rescuing people from fire or flood use the shortest and most direct methods." Henry's disagreement with Bushnell, he seemed to be saying, was too basic to admit of spiritual kinship, no matter how much Thomas wanted to see it. Comparisons to Bushnell did not flatter Henry, who felt a rough and ready impatience with theologizing and an urgent need to champion social and political reforms, and on the same grand scale as his father. As he observed to a close friend:

> Although I cannot agree with Bushnell, I can as little with his respondents; nor do I see any benefit in a controversy. . . . It seems to me the only thing on earth truth is good for is to convert men from evil to holiness.[32]

If, as Thomas had come to believe, Christianity was to be found in the integrity of living as a disciple of Christ, then perhaps Henry's "working zeal" was the best fruit of such a life. Henry seemed to distrust intellection as much as his brother. But whereas Thomas was reluctant to preach his religion for fear of diluting and dissipating it, Henry claimed to find value only in preaching and doing. And the deeds for which the Beechers were praised and damned were the grand reform campaigns which Lyman had believed would quicken the coming of the Kingdom.

Already it was becoming plain that Thomas would part company with his brothers and sisters. Never had he evinced the slightest sympathy for the family's reform designs, nor had he shown the least symptom of being infected with reforming zeal. Even such an apolitical scheme as Catharine's female education project seemed overblown and meddlesome to him. From the retrospect of 1889, a nostalgic but bitter Thomas Beecher described the "worthy confessors" whose example had inspired him as a young man:

> Then comes a drift period 1836–43, and never a saint was in all that time added to my company. Sister Harriet floated in at or about this time telling me a manner of Christian experience. And took her unchanging place. Henry Ward—not as you have known him, but as I knew him 1844-5 preaching Christ 17 weeks, every evening and Sunday too. Yes—*my* Henry is a saint—and all his after and stormy tribulations to the contrary notwithstanding. The foundation cannot move.

Still later he desired Isabella to invite him to Hartford for one last look at their mentally decayed sister, for he wished to "look upon the wreck of Hattie; to tranquilly summon from the far past the memories of the loved . . . to adjust once more the visions of love and fidelity—as it was before the tornado struck us scattering the Beecher fleet along lines of notoriety toward will o' wisps of reform, over restless waters of 'agitation'—such a sympozium would command me." It was a phase of their lives that he could never comprehend, much less enter into. This may account for his growing coolness toward Isabella, once his confidante. Her abolitionist husband had convinced her to take a stand with the Liberty Party. And at the same time there began appearing in Thomas's letters complaints of his family's unwillingness to fathom the deeps of his nature, complaints voiced before the 1850s but now expressed more passionately and hopelessly. The confiding, exultant tone of his letters to Harriet and Henry in 1848 gave way to increasingly morose and tetchy communications, sometimes sparring, sometimes entreating.[33]

The process of estrangement from his family, in such marked contrast to his former intimacy and dependency, was accelerated by events. In Hartford he met and courted Olivia Day, the daughter of Jeremiah Day, president of Yale. Livy Day found her suitor's outlandish ways endearing, as she wrote to a friend:

> I wish Tom wouldn't talk in his tempestuous, dreadfully entertaining way. I have been entreating him to go out and walk, and

> he has actually disappeared now, and left me to a moment's quiet, but I fear it is only a reprieve.

Livy combined good looks with intelligence and fluent speech, as a male friend of the Days noted, but with a telling qualification: "I missed that desire to please which adds so much to the attractiveness of a woman." Thomas Beecher did not require to be pleased and flattered, but rather to be stimulated and comforted. John Hooker, who often piqued his wife by overpraising other women's minds, positively gloated over Livy's intellect, "the most peaceful, classick, vivacious and richly furnished mind that I ever fell in with." Thomas savored her letters so exceedingly, Hooker reported, that

> He rather desires to prolong his courtship than to abridge it—and says to Livy that she must stop writing if she ever wants to get married. He seems perfectly contented with his bird in the bush—and seems far more disposed to hear her warble and chatter from the spray—than to hear her simply sing from her cage.[34]

At a date which cannot be determined precisely, but after he had met Livy, Thomas began preaching and decided to enter the ministry after all, when Lyman had given him up as lost to a secular career. The change was as sudden as it was unexpected. A last-minute appeal to supply a Hartford pulpit for one day seemed to him a providential call to the ministry. One would give a great deal to know what precipitated this decision but, as there are no details of the incident, it can only be conjectured that his changed circumstances, particularly his falling in love with Livy Day and the new state of certainty over his beliefs, worked on a mind that had never quite escaped the sense of family mission. Without any further preparation than that afforded by growing up in a family of clergymen, Thomas commenced preaching in various Connecticut towns, concentrating, apparently, on disseminating Bushnell's views along with doctrines of his own, advocating probationary views of the future life. One auditor came away impressed equally by his homiletic talents and his personal singularity:

> His voice is very fine clear as a trumpet and his articulation uncommon. The sermon was a very strange and eccentric one full of strange and sometimes undignified passages but it was full of feeling and genius and eloquence, not well balanced exactly but real. . . . Mr. Beecher is full of sensibility and enthusiasm and if he does not run wild entirely will make a noble preacher.

As for his eccentricity, Professor James Hadley of Yale had a long talk with Thomas and noted with relief, "Saw less of Beecherism than I had looked for."[35]

As it happened, Catharine Beecher was roiling the usually tranquil waters of New Haven with her most recent, and most inflammatory, appeal to the public, *Truth Stranger Than Fiction*. Her enemies, who were in the majority at Yale, regarded the tract as an excuse to pillory Nathaniel Taylor and hold the rest of the Yale faculty up to derision. Thomas's marriage to Jeremiah Day's daughter, in a ceremony performed by Henry, took place at the height of the uproar, and Thomas could not have been indifferent to the gossip and scornful amusement aimed at his family. Catharine's officiousness in the affairs of the Bacon family probably helped to sour Thomas's attitude toward crusading zealotry, especially his family's brand of it.[36]

They, meanwhile, watched his first essays at preaching closely and not without anxiety. Henry felt that his and Thomas's fortunes were linked and predicted victory for their principles:

> The New England forms of religious development have always been stern—and impenetrable solemnity—i.e., the exercise of the organ of veneration in religion is yet the habit of some of the best men and christians. Now it is not possible to divulge a [new] principle without producing horror by it. . . . I shall be pummeled some—but in ten years there will not be a reputable thinker who is not on the same ground.

Harriet surveyed their brother's development with less confidence in the outcome. She, no less than Henry, endorsed the view that feeling was superior to mere thinking, but she retained a respect for New England Theology and its defenders that was alien to Henry's more buoyant, brash spirit. Unlike him, she came to her views painfully, even fearfully, and not as an audacious prince of the pulpit sure of his audience and even surer of his power to persuade and enthrall. Thomas could leap over the barriers set by New England Theology, this "skilful engine of torture," as Harriet called it, and land straight in the Bushnell camp, but Harriet wondered whether he was mature enough to grasp the dangers inherent in Bushnellism. "What do you think of Tom's preaching?" she asked Isabella, who had more opportunities to hear it. "Where do you go to church," she pressed her sister further, "at Bushnels or Hawes?" Bushnell's doctrine of Christian nurture appealed to Isabella and Mary, but the rest of the family were highly critical of him, particularly Catharine, who accused him of preaching a disguised doctrine of baptismal regeneration and who thought he was clinging to evangelical dogmas that ought to have no place in his theology.[37]

While Henry could joke with Thomas about religion-as-veneration, a phrenological code-word for tendencies toward intolerance and bigotry, Harriet was unwilling to see evangelical doctrines smashed up wholesale. She wanted her brothers to exonerate the best features of the older orthodoxy while moving ahead toward a new one. She was afraid that Bushnell would encourage Thomas's low views of Scripture:

> For my part I begin to be a little afraid that the Bushnell movement may go too far—and [fail?] to hold on to the old ground—that is to say they are apt to push their freedom too far and too fast. We must try to keep a Bible to live and die by and to hold to strict and accurate ideas of inspiration and if Tom is sound then I should be willing to [let him] go ahead in preaching and preach himself clear just as beer works clear.

As the wife of a biblical scholar, Harriet was far better apprised of new developments in biblical interpretation and criticism than most ministers. Thomas had earlier come to believe that the Scriptures were at best an imperfect revelation of Christ. He was proud to stand openly with Bushnell and, when Henry defaulted in his promise to preach Thomas's ordination sermon, he turned to Bushnell. Eventually he dedicated a book to Bushnell, *Our Seven Churches*, a small volume of ecumenical discourses inspired by Bushnell's *Christian Comprehensiveness.* If Thomas Beecher concerned himself with Bushnell's studies of the Atonement, he left no record of it; his debt was far more general.[38]

Thomas's first call was to the New England Congregational Church of Williamsburgh, New York (now a part of Brooklyn). Like Charles, he owed his first church to Henry. The New England Church was formed under Henry's auspices by men desiring to build a church "which should illustrate an anti-slavery and reformatory spirit." Thomas was surrounded by such men in Williamsburgh. Even his neighbors, John Hooker approvingly noted, were "the strongest sort of abolitionists." Hooker took Thomas and Livy to a great anti-slavery convocation to hear Henry speak, but Thomas remained aloof from the movement. He was neither warm for emancipation nor hot against the slave-power. Years later it was said that he quit the New England Church because of the peculations of its leading laymen, who were stalwarts for reform and high-minded politics. If true, the story sheds additional light on his sardonic observations about reformers.[39]

Although he was deeply in love with Livy, his happiness in marriage was not unalloyed. His salary was small and Livy was unable to economize. Though she may have seemed serene to Hooker, she shared with Thomas a pessimism about the present life that made them want to escape the world, and her few surviving letters have a gloomy tinge. Writing to a bereaved friend, Livy, who was pregnant, wondered when she herself would "enter into the secrets of the suffering." "You no doubt feel," she said, "that all your friends should be praying for you —but oh Lizzie—in the high and holy seclusion where sorrow shuts you up with God, pray rather for us, who, in the daily joys of life, are *able* to keep away from Him, and so to cheat ourselves of all real joy." Livy's desire to know suffering did not go long unfulfilled. Her pregnancy made her so ill that Henry, fearing she would die, tried to persuade Thomas to move into his house where Eunice could nurse her around the clock. Livy died before the plan could be tried.[40]

Thomas's reaction to Livy's death and the death of their infant was so entirely controlled that his sisters were scandalized by his "excentric" behavior. Mary was shocked by his almost casual demeanor. "I feel myself repulsed and displeased continually by his outward manner and style of language," she huffed. "Though I dislike and eschew as he does the *heathenish* manner in which a christian death and burial is generally regarded. . . . I cannot concieve of any one, be he a christian or not—losing what has become dear and necessary as their own hearts blood, without suffering." They were not content to accept his explanations and demanded further justification for his outward coolness and indifference to sorrow.

His answers were frank but equally incomprehensible. Livy's death was "a cause of thanksgiving," a merciful providence:

> I cannot make you see as I do without any effort—that for Livy to have lived and become a mother would have been as foul an incongruity as it would have been for *Undine* to have been transformed into a steady dutch vrow, nursing her children through the measles.
>
> I cannot make you see that God's Providence culminated so appropriately and symmetrically in her death—I mean in preparing her *to go*—and me to stay, that now I keep wondering why I did not prophesy it—and expect it as the only answer possible to all our prayers.

> Every day since our betrothal we have talked of death—as near to us. She supposed of *me*. I supposed of her. From no prayer was it ever absent. Our love, knew only separation and trial here. My heart was torn for her. Hers was always anxious for me, and we walked hand in hand in heaven—more hours than on earth.

Thomas repelled as unsisterly Isabella's suggestion that he had borne himself badly. After all the "solemn sighing," "trite and pathetic talk," and "awful sober look[s]" he had endured for the sake of convention, he had hoped to find Isabella willing to sit with him and "give thanks with assured hope, that Christ has harvested a soul—and a soul has ceased from tribulation." He denounced her grief over Livy's youth and beauty lost in decay as "*unchristian,*" but he did concede that most men and women would be as graceless as Isabella in the same circumstances:

> I am not anxious to compel men to feel as I do. I will not pronounce it exemplary or pious or even sane. It is simply my *fact*—that after twenty six years of despair, Christ gave me *Livy*—and some mysterious elixir of *something*—so that when He took her, I rejoiced and did not weep, and cannot.[41]

Over the next year he tried in vain to make this point intelligible to his family, to communicate the truth of his gospel of "the Christian's rest." He expressed first surprise and then sorrow over their inability to seize the truth that was so precious to him. "One of my mistakes most often repeated," he lamented, "is the one of supposing that because a person is kindread to me, therefore they are like me." His sense of dwelling apart from them, both emotionally and spiritually, increased:

> I feel more and more the dreamlike perceptions of gross events. . . . All fervors and all passions which burn or boil seem to me so many facts, powerless to move me—they troop along in herds, like the living beasts when Adam named them. All events—national, municipal, ecclesiastical and domestic, seem to me no longer exciting—they are only interesting. My opinions take place, undisturbed by fear or any passion. That sublime aphorism which Senator Seward quoted in the peroration of his great speech—"Man proposes but God disposes"—is wrought into the very web and substance of my thoughts. . . . I cannot tell you what a rest this is to my spirit.[42]

These are curious letters and reveal a great deal about Thomas. His relationship to Livy, like his bonds to his brothers and sisters, was as painful as it was intense. There seems to have been on his part a constant expectation of being disappointed. Hence his alternations between hero-worship and sudden, total disillusionment. Only Lyman seems to have remained unblemished in Thomas's mind. The attachment to Catherine Mussey never met the test of actuality. Livy Day, on the other hand, was elevated to sainthood after her untimely death. A marriage which found its happiest moments in mutual longings for death and separation must have been a very complicated one. No matter how turbulent other Beecher marriages might have been, they were active partnerships.

Perhaps visualizing Livy as a saint in heaven was somehow bound up with Thomas's feelings for his mother. His yielding Livy up without a murmur, and his gratitude that she had escaped the "foul incongruity" of motherhood, cannot be explained as a reflex of conventional piety. Perhaps it was his disgust at the thought of Livy's fulfilling her biological function which startled his sisters into condemning his attitude. It is even stranger to find Thomas still preaching about the primacy of the "social affections" and the family state just when he was exulting in the flight of his wife from earthly thrall. He maintained, in fact, that the highest field of Christian endeavor was the family:

> Had you but known how often with longing, tearful pathos I have sketched a quiet faithful mother, as my highest conception of a christian hero, and have sighed with a perpetual sorrow that for *me* there is no such plain path of unmistakable duty and usefulness. . . . Belle—all that I have of vital lasting piety as a well spring in my soul, I seem to owe to the experience of love which bound me to Livy. Christ is the bridegroom—and the redeemed are the bride. . . . Tho' I cannot solve the mystery of life, yet I know *some* things—and none more surely than the divine authority and gracious effects of *true* marriages between "believers."

The theme of escape and transcendence, not merely from the world but from the flesh, emerges even more clearly in a letter Thomas wrote to Henry's son-in-law:

> My theory of the universe and of this world is one that no amount of pounding or bruising can ever make your buoyant and loving heart accept. To me the death of your little boy chimes in with a unison of evil. I say it was bad. It was wrong. It was of the

> devil, who has the power of death. I hate him, and I hate his works, and I hate this world. It is a world where Jesus could not live, my Livy couldn't nor your boy. They all died too soon. 99 in every 100 die too soon. Death has passed upon all. This is a gloomy world. I give it up. I have no part in it. I wont plan—I wont hope—I wont fear. I will only endeavor to keep from its evil, bind up its gashes, shine into its darkness, prophesy heaven and wait—wait—singing songs in the night.[43]

His letters and sermons from the time of Livy's death are steeped in this sombreness, which he called triumph. Even his remarriage in 1857 to Julia Jones, Livy's "nearest and dearest friend and lifelong companion," did not temper the sternness of his piety. Saying that his heart was heavy and craved peace, he next accepted a call to the Park Church in Elmira, New York. He was careful to spell out the terms of his acceptance in detail, one of the major stipulations being his refusal to be installed as settled pastor. He made this reservation for personal and ecclesiastical reasons:

> Thomas was sensitive, liable to depression—original in his modes of thought and unable to coincide with established formulas. He went to Elmira an ordained Evangelist, took the church first for three months, and has continued to work there as Pastor ever since—never having been installed there—and so not having to come under the scrutiny of any counsel of minister[s] who might raise controversy on his doctrines. Christ was his all—his teacher his God and his guide and has led him, notwithstanding many weaknesses and faults into a fruitful ministry.

Once in Elmira he undertook a heroic effort at church building. At first his people were few and many of them impoverished. The meetinghouse was unheated; he preached under much the same conditions as Connecticut preachers of the previous century, his tumbler of water freezing on the lectern. His congregation multiplied and he won immense popularity among the townspeople, as well as great disfavor with fellow clergymen.[44]

Thomas became one of the leading citizens of Elmira, a liberal dispenser of charity and personal services, and a frequent candidate for office on such tickets as the Greenback Party's. His backers continued to draft him as a candidate, in spite of his habit of casting aspersions on the wisdom of all politicians. "The reputation of the entire Beecher family for eccentricity was rank, but it was declared in Elmira that 'Tom Beecher' was the worst of the lot." He rode an adult-sized tricycle, drank beer, and chided fellow ministers as teetotaling fanatics, kept an office in a seedy downtown building rather than maintaining an official parish house, and placed repentant streetwalkers in the homes of church members in an effort to rescue the fallen women of the town.

Epithets bounced off Beecher's head, gibes like "the Opera House preacher," aimed at him by ministers who disapproved of his holding services in a theater while the new church was being erected. When the ministerial association tried to blackball Beecher, he sweetly appeared for each meeting and, though snubbed and ignored, took his part in the proceedings, getting off sage and sly observations, to the discomfiture of those members who were trying to represent him as a buffoon. Julia Beecher magnified the couple's reputation for being impervious to public opinion by bobbing her hair, pulling on Congress boots in place of feminine footgear, and contradicting her husband at prayer meetings and church socials. She was a gifted sculptor and made a bust from memory of Livy Day, which she and Thomas enshrined in the woods. Whereas her husband was either jubilant or maudlin, Julia was relentlessly cheerful. Toward him she took the attitude of a resourceful governess coping with a loveable, clever, but extremely difficult child.[45]

Even this security and his much-acclaimed successes threw Thomas into despair. In 1863, during the war he thought so useless, a conflict provoked by Yankee bigotry and meddling, he groaned:

> I am consumed with desire to be at some absorbing work, such as the age calls for. But no gate or door opens. I'm sick of ministerial nonsense—mine, [Nathaniel J.] Burtons—Henrys and all, and yet am a minister more and better than ever!

Eleven years later he summed up his ministry in equally crabbed terms. "Left to our own choice," he informed the readers of the *Elmira Weekly Gazette*, "we should never act again as a public teacher of morals and religion. But having had the duty laid upon us, we continue to testify as often as opportunity serves, and as strongly as our ability permits." When Isabella wrote from Hartford praising her minister, Thomas replied:

> Good. I'm glad you love your pastor. Enthusiasm is a good thing to 'em as has any. I hope he is more than I am or can be in this 'ere disappointing delusive world. I am getting ready to go adrift ere long from here. As for Julie, poor girl, she is worthy of anyone. . . . She is pastor, I am log.

Although he did not desert his post in 1857, as this letter threatened, but remained in Elmira the rest of his life, Beecher suffered from frequent protracted illnesses and nervous crises. Julia described his state of mind during one such low spell. "His heart is sore for the weak ones, in the Church, and in [the] society," she confided to their benefactor, Mrs. Langdon. "He cried as he told me some things that had been said to him of their trials. And for him it *is* impossible to know of such things without sharing all with the sufferers." His generosity toward his parishioners and the poor outside his church was prompted by two things: his genuine compassion for the afflicted, and his suspicion of easeful living. He had vowed that avarice would never stand in the way of godliness. And so, although Park Church gave him a very large salary, most of it went to charity. Typically, he shunned prosperity and practiced asceticism, wearing the same severe tunic and cloth cap every day.[46]

In 1867 his health gave way completely from combined fatigue and anxiety. He made a long voyage around the Horn to San Francisco and back, working with his hands at carpentry and road building to pay his expenses. Again, in 1871, he made a trip to England, with letters of introduction from Henry. But as soon as he was back in harness the old worries weighed him down. While his brothers took the view that their ministry was the widest possible, embracing the regeneration of society, Thomas was overwhelmed by the problems of his church alone. He maintained from the beginning a pessimistic view of the possibilities and ends of church organization, while at the same time encouraging progressive ideas of church building. He became famous for developing one of the first so-called institutional churches, one with a broad range of social, recreational, educational, and charitable services and facilities. But at bottom he regarded the church as a company of "ill-balanced, passionate and partly sanctified ones. The church is a family, and needs the steadying influence of uniform and well digested teaching." Such teaching was not to be secured by heeding the "frothy scum of thought, which rises from the fermentations of restless and depraved minds," minds of the sort that too greatly influenced his brother Henry. Thomas's own lesson to his people was a simple one: "The gospel is an adventure of grace and condescension."[47]

To his own family he still preached the gospel of purification through suffering. When his nephew Frederick Beecher lost an infant son, Thomas wrote, "Now you are not a *boy* any longer. We make room for you . . . in full citizenship of a world that groaneth in pain—

waiting for the manifestation of Gods son." Yet his experience had not led him to relish death and dying. There was no necromania about his beliefs. Dying was simply a fact, which Christians ought to bear in their hearts the better to recognize what a gracious gift it was to overcome death in Christ and the Resurrection. "The evidence of true piety is to be gathered," he insisted, "from the Godly conversation of a man during the days of his health and vigor." The only kind of death he believed to be edifying was suicide, when undertaken for "chivalrous" reasons—a declaration which affronted clergy, lay believers, politicians, and law enforcement officers alike.[48]

Thomas Beecher could not make himself understand why Harriet, Edward, and Charles experienced such difficulties about doctrines and theories. Nor could he comprehend why Catharine proclaimed a secular regeneration or why Isabella was so determined to spread her very peculiar ectoplasmic gospel. Least of all could he sympathize with Henry's radiant, hopeful views of man's nature and destiny. His brother James, who alone of all the family was in complete sympathy with Thomas, had begun his ministry in 1855. Thomas welcomed James into the brotherhood with a letter that represented the crystallization of his experience:

> I have boldly shaken the stoutest arguments upon which men build their conceit of truth, and they all rattle with weakness. I have listened to men's pleas on every hand, and find universally that the destructive arguments of men are valid, the constructive contemptible.
>
> I agree that slavery exhibits monstrous iniquity, but so does liberty; I agree that popery is an awful delusion, but so is Protestantism. I agree that Theodore Parker curdles my blood with his blasphemy, but so does Edward Beecher. I agree that marriage is a blessed estate, yet it is also a cursed condition for nine out of every ten. Were I a one-eyed reformer, I should be a great, red-hot zealous man. But I have looked and loved and longed and suffered. I see more things at a time than most men do. I give it up.

It might appear that Thomas Beecher, in his vision of radical weakness and evil, was the only remaining Calvinist in his family. Yet there was no emphasis in his beliefs on the free sovereignty of God. He gave first place to the love of Christ. One important element of Calvinism—namely, its activism—animated the other Beechers, who continued to believe that the world was the theater of redemption, with man playing an important role. This is missing from Thomas

Beecher's religion. In his belligerent tone of negation, his deliberate resort to paradox and misanthropic irony, he might almost be taken for another Thomas Carlyle, stalking down the Chemung Valley. But in the end, Beecher's religion was one of confession and affirmation. "We as a race, are lost children in a mazy wilderness of life. Let us be gentle, humble, good, forgiving, patient, kind. By and by our elder brother will come to lead us to our home."[49]

PART 5

CHANGING VIEWS OF MAN AND GOD

10 SPIRITUALISM

"Would it be like Him to suffer two souls to grow together here, so that the separation of a day is pain, and then wrench them apart for all eternity? It would be what Madame de Gasparin calls, 'fearful irony on the part of God.'"

The bat-like fallacies of our godless metaphysics vanish before the unfolding of our present theme.

"Egeria, we stand upon the threshold of the temple; its penetralia lie open before us; we have defeated death!"[1]

The problem of Spiritualism[2] and the Beecher family's interest in it could be discussed in a number of ways. It would be easy to accept Thomas Huxley's contention that, while gossip of any sort is tiresome, disembodied gossip is especially inconsequential. William James, by contrast, never ceased investigating psychic phenomena. Enough has been said already to indicate that the excursions of at least one of the Beechers into the unseen world were voyages into a delusionary universe or, to put it more bluntly, symptoms of mental disorder. Rather than dwelling on Isabella Hooker's delusions, however, it is the aim of this chapter to show how pervasive and compelling the subject of Spiritualism was in the lives of the Beechers.[3]

Some of the sources are fugitive and tantalizing, and some of the Beechers were not very forthcoming about their explorations into the occult. In the main, however, it can readily be shown that their curiosity about spiritualistic phenomena arose from deep personal needs. Furthermore, as the epigraphs to this chapter are intended to suggest, Spiritualism may also have informed their eschatological thought in ways that a superficial survey of spirit-rappings and table-tippings could not convey. Sydney Ahlstrom has spoken of a "New England subculture" of mesmeric healing and "harmonial religion" from which arose the heroic figure of Mary Baker Eddy. If we add to this the tediously orphic Andrew Jackson Davis ("the Poughkeepsie seer"), Kate and Margaretta Fox, and the sibyls and svengalis in the novels of Hawthorne, Henry James, and Orestes Brownson, there begins to emerge a picture of hectic, yeasty passion for intercourse with the world beyond death.[4]

There may seem to be a vast gulf separating Lyman Beecher's belief in Heaven and the ministrations of departed spirits from his daughter's invisible realm opened to the eyes of an anointed prophet. Yet a careful examination of the case leads to the conclusion that the family shared many of Isabella's ideas. Put another way, the Beechers' beliefs about the afterlife and their attempts to pierce the veil separating earthly and heavenly existence provided the context in which Isabella worked out her own peculiar vision.

We must recur to a theme by now familiar, namely, the glorification of Roxana Beecher. Roxana's children had an abiding conviction that their dead mother's persevering love inspired their growth in grace, sponsored their entry into the church of Christ, warded off temptations, and secured them against repining and fatal doubt. Lyman repeatedly attested to her continuing presence. He was still so tied to her that shortly after her death he "wrote to her a letter, in which he poured out all his soul." Some time later, grieving over troubles in his parish, he dreamed that Roxana and her sister had returned to console him. "I awoke joyful, and I was lighthearted for weeks after." Years later, when Charles was passing through his crisis of faith, he published a poem in a New Orleans newspaper expressing his grief. One of the stanzas horrified his father:

> My mother! whither art thou fled?
> Seest thou these tears that for thee flow?
> Or in the realms of shadowy dead,
> Knowest thou no more of mortal woe?

When Lyman read these lines, he implored his son not to desecrate Roxana's memory:

> Your address to your mother is overwhelming to me. That you should address her *in doubt* whether she now adores as an angel amid the resplendent joys and glories of heaven, or is bereft of consciousness amid the shadowy dead by annihilation. . . . Oh my dear Charles, would to God that this blessed mother could look upon you as in life, and in my dreams since her death, she has looked and smiled on me.

Charles's recovery from infidelity evoked from Lyman renewed expressions of faith in Roxana's undying influence. "His mother has been long in heaven," he told a friend, "but she bound chords about her child's heart before she left which have drawn him back. He has never been able to break them."[5]

The passages just quoted open up three areas for discussion. First, Protestants believed in the glorification of the dying elect. This may seem a commonplace, but as the nineteenth century progressed, there was far less certainty about the soul's ultimate destiny. Second, there was a yearning to know mediately and immediately what this state was like. Charles's poem shows that there could be very different notions of the condition of the departed soul. Although Timothy Dwight's *Theology* devoted almost 150 pages to an orthodox description of this condition, the question of "the change at death" was hotly disputed by Universalist factions. A third observation has to do with what may be called the spiritual continuum. There was a widespread inquiring after, and belief in, paranormal confirmation of the teachings of theology and devotional works concerning the last things. Hence the validity that was accorded dreams such as Lyman's, and the attention paid to deathbed testimonies, ghostly visitations, and psychic phenomena in general. Mrs. Stowe gave voice to these preoccupations in another context when, quoting Philip Doddridge, she said of her native region, "In no other country were the soul and the spiritual life ever such intense realities, and everything contemplated so much (to use a current New England phrase) 'in reference to eternity.'"[6]

Lyman knew exactly what Heaven was like, so much so that he seldom expounded the theme. There are, however, two statements about his Heaven worth quoting. In a funeral sermon of 1806 he depicted this realm in conventional language. "This world above, the local residence of the redeemed, is a place of most exquisite natural beauty and glory. . . . Heaven, moreover, while exempt from the calamities of earth, will abound with sublime, perfect, and unutterable joy." Interestingly, he chose to portray Hell less as a place of physical torment than as a sink of hatred and selfishness. Forty years later, Beecher enlarged his prospect of Heaven in a very characteristic statement, but one which reflected speculations on the future state that were gaining currency. Speaking to a class of Lane seminarians, he said:

Next to exemption from sin would be the blessedness of intense

> mental activity without weariness. I could hardly consent to go to heaven only to sit by purling streams or beds of roses, fanned by fragrant breezes and lulled to repose by heavenly music. The nature and laws of mind must be reversed before mental inaction, mere rest can constitute the blessedness ascribed to the heavenly state. It is the rest of high and untiring and productive benevolence centred in the worship and service of God.

Clearly, Lyman's expectations were a projection of his own unflagging zeal to do good. The scene he painted was thronged with figures much like himself: David, Paul, Richard Baxter, Isaac Watts, George Whitefield, David Brainerd, and Timothy Dwight. Beecher's heroes had not "gone above to spend an eternity in Psalm singing! No—benevolent action is the life of their souls."[7]

This belief in the persistence of individual characteristics undoubtedly colored his children's hopes as well. They spoke often of Roxana's deathbed, when their father had read from Hebrews the vision of the city of God and the innumerable company of angels their mother had gone to join. In spite of their conviction that earthly affections should be weaned affections, they did not try to disguise their keen, impetuous family attachments. They were clear as to the duty of restraining themselves from too fond a love of family and friends, but found the burden grievous. Isabella once told her husband of her difficulties in this regard:

> At least I can truly say that I think that I love the Lord, less for what He has bestowed, than for what He *is*—and in that view I sometimes love to think of our happiness as a sort of causeless miracle—a divine effluence into which we floated as motes in a sunbeam—no hand guiding and no envious or sorrow stricken ones beholding. . . . My chief spiritual trouble of a religious nature—has been of late—that these family ties are too exquisite, too worthy, to be dropped with the body—they are institutions, good enough for Hades certainly, in the Paradisaical portion—and decidedly *heavenly* to my mind.

Though James Beecher knew that his idea of Heaven was not a correct one, he confessed to his wife the hope that Heaven was not so much the general assembly of the firstborn as a place of family reunion:

> As you know to me Heaven is where Father and Mother and Aunt Esther are, rather than or I should say, more than where God is. For God is here, they are not. And I count it the will of God that

we keep fast hold of our broken loves, not to mourn over them, but to be drawn by them. That where the treasure is the heart may go.[8]

These highly personalized ideas of the blessed estate of just men and women made perfect were matched by equally vivid ideas of the future abode of the unregenerate. Although Lyman Beecher was not a hellfire preacher, he did not spare his hearers terrible images of future suffering. Horace Mann, whose Unitarian sensibilities were usually offended by the preaching of "rigid hide-bound Calvinist[s]," represented Beecher as a relatively liberal exponent of the "rigorous principles of his creed." Thus, when Mann reported one of Beecher's sermons, we can be sure that it was less horrific than many of its kind:

> The design of the first sermon, which I heard him preach was to arouse and inspirit the languid; and scatter dread and dismay in the paths of the [scum?]. . . . He divided sinners into several distinct classes, laid open the motives which deterred each respective class from attending to their highest interests, carried one by one through the dark valley of the shadow of death, to the throne of God, and then personating the Almighty, he pronounced their terrible doom. He showed the hillock of undried clay that rose over their bodies, reared their sable monuments and read to us the inscriptions, which *truth* would dictate, and which they, if they had possessed the power would have indicted, amidst groans of unutterable torture. But, this was not sufficient. He took a single sinner, young and vigorous . . . he carried him through the successive gradations of honor, put the sceptre of power in his hand. . . . But age advanced and the strong hand forgot its grasp, and the wreath withered from his brow. Disease now stretches him upon the death bed. One after another, the cords of life are broken; the extremities grow cold; the dews of death gush from his temples. Death gives the blow and he sinks to remediless perdition. After all, said he, what can I say or do. I feel like a single solitery individual attempting to oppose an army . . . struggling to oppose your swift career while you are rushing by me on all sides to leap into the pit of hell.

If this seems like so much chromolithographed luridness, it did not so strike its hearers. Even Mann, while deploring pulpit appeals to fear, conceded admiringly that "I never heard such a sermon in my life."[9]

Dread and anxiety were, of course, operating in such an environment. We can hardly credit assertions by Lyman's children that the religion of their childhood was never "gloomy" or "repulsive," when their father was so skilled at "personating" the terrible Judge. More painful than pictures of a crackling torment was the awful uncertainty that confronted souls as they loosed their hold on earthly life. Even Lyman could not be sure of joining Dwight and Payson and Taylor. The year before Beecher's death, one of his children tried to rally him by reminding him that he would soon be with his beloved brother Taylor. He had been trapped in a hale body while his mind decayed; but far from welcoming the release of death, as his children expected, Lyman despondently told them, "There is that to go through first that I can not contemplate." It was not death he dreaded, but dying.[10]

The "triumphant" deathbed scenes of nineteenth-century fiction were reflections, however exaggerated or stereotyped, of real experiences and feelings. (The Uncle Tom plays, pirated from Mrs. Stowe's novel, with their glory robes and apparatus for hoisting Little Eva off the mundane sphere, gave exuberant, if vulgar, expression to conventional feelings.) To take an ordinary example from an ordinary memoir, Martha Reed's dying agonies were minutely recorded by her clergyman brother for the purposes of edification. She assured him that although she was "in *exquisite pain*," she was "free *from care and alarm*" and continually looked heavenward. In his recounting of the final crisis, Reed told of the family encircling the bed, their eyes trained on Martha's heaving chest. Their own breathing became labored, as in a dying rhythm. With her final exhalation, "we recovered our inspiration by an hysterical effort; trembling seized us; we fell back into our seats, and burst into a flood of tears." Rare were accounts of doughty types like Frederick Porcher's uncle, an amateur scientist, who passed away making observations on his dying faculties, "philosophizing and experimenting" to the last.[11]

Truer to the pious pattern were two other deathbed accounts, the one intended to be inspirational, the other expressive of morbidity. Timothy Dwight's deathbed was described by his sons as a saving example to other Christians:

> Though frequently bewildered through excess of pain, yet no distressing fear assailed him. He saw the presence of the grim Destroyer with tranquility and hope; yielded up his soul without a struggle, and, as we trust with undoubting confidence, found a glorious welcome into the "House not made with hands; eternal in the heavens."

We have, however, a very different description from the diary of

Alexander M. Fisher, an intimate of the Dwights, who was distressed over the manner of President Dwight's passing. Because of Dwight's protracted illness, which had induced lethargy and a "partial derangement," Fisher recorded, "little passed, from which we can draw any inference respecting the degree in which he enjoyed the consolations of religion in the last period of his life."

Before attempting to reconcile these disparate reports, it might be instructive to compare them to another deathwatch. Frances Willard bitterly recalled her parents' importunate interrogation of her dying sister:

> "Do you see the Christ?" they asked. "Is He close to you?" "Is He coming closer?" "My darling, you will meet us, won't you, at the Beautiful Gate?" Such were their eager questions while she was trying to make them understand that she wished them to be careful not to bury her alive!

The preoccupation with holy dying displayed in both cases is too plain to require further comment. What is interesting is the tremendous weight such scenes carried. Even if President Dwight's expiration was unattended by blissful or hortatory utterances, his sons seem to have felt obliged to fill in the picture to produce a properly edifying effect. On the other hand, Fisher's melancholy report may have reflected his own fearful obsessions. As for the Willards' inappropriate, even callous, inquisitiveness about what lay beyond the Beautiful Gate, it reflected what was surely a widespread eagerness to catch glimpses of the future world. When a soul was on the verge of disenthrallment, just before the last corporeal thread was snapped, deathbed watchers might be vouchsafed some glimpse of the world into which that soul was passing.[12]

At the heart of the matter, prompting this concentration of attention, was a need for reassurance. Although Frances Willard despised her parents' crude approach, she did not scorn the need to know, and she herself became a Spiritualist. Although Porcher intended to ridicule conventional piety by adducing the example of his irreligious uncle, he did not treat death and its mysteries lightly. One of his aunts, he explained, exhibited mediumistic powers which baffled him.[13]

Reassurance was not to be found, for many Christians, in the plain declarations of the Bible. Gospel teachings on the subject had never been sufficient to quell doubts or suppress inquiries. To speak only of the Beechers' lifetime, there were, from Joseph Butler's *Analogy* to Mark Twain's irreverent *Captain Stormfield*, countless treatises, poems, and novels touching on or wholly devoted to authoritative declarations about the location, inhabitants, hierarchies, and modes of existence of the hereafter. It will be useful to examine some of these statements and show how they provided a background to the Beechers' speculations about the last things: death, resurrection, judgment, and immortality.[14]

Isaac Taylor of Stanford Rivers (1787-1865) is a convenient starting point. Now little known, he was acclaimed during his lifetime for a learned and mystical piety. That he came of Dissenting stock but early entered the Church of England probably enhanced his appeal to a large American audience who themselves were often alienated from their Reformed origins. "For one reader in England," he wrote to his sister, also an author, "we have ten or twenty in America." It has already been shown how Taylor's strictures on enthusiasm enlightened Charles Beecher and how his essay on Edwards helped Beecher recover from fatalism. Taylor's other influential book, the *Physical Theory of Another Life*, was equally important to the Beechers and to many others of their day.[15]

Taylor's appropriation of Baconian inductive philosophy provided an underpinning of natural law and scientific logic to the speculations of the *Physical Theory*. Taylor combined induction from known laws of mind and matter with a far-reaching extrapolation by analogy. He posited a duality of animal and spiritual *body* and asked, "what are likely to be the prerogatives of the latter, as compared with the former; or in what manner the actual powers of the present structure of human nature may be conceived of as expanded or advantaged, consistently with those great principles of analogy which we find to characterize the Divine operations in all their departments. " Analogy led Taylor to suggest that in the future life the intellect would be freed from the "trammels of calculation and the subtilties of logic" so that "we shall be freed from the operose methods of calculation and reasoning, and be endowed with the power of intuitively perceiving all the properties and conditions, as well of mathematical as of metaphysical entities:—the mind, not made indolent by this advantage, would start forward, as from an advanced position, and move on with rapidity toward new and higher ground." Other developments would include a "PLENARY MEMORY . . . needed for penetrating the mind with a sense of its own condition, and for rendering it its own equitable censor"; communication by means of thought transference or mental telepathy; and, in consequence of all these, "the gradual accumulation and consolidation of an ABSOLUTE PHILOSOPHY—metaphysical, theological, and moral."[16]

The key concept of Isaac Taylor's system, which he claimed to derive from Paul, was that of "spiritual corporeity"—that is, the transition by strictly natural processes from the present physical condition to one of inconceivably greater refinement, "an imperishable corporeity." In other words, the change would not be from carnality to a disembodied spirituality, but from one mode of physical existence to a higher one. The passions, the intellect, and the moral sentiments, while remaining the same in character, would be greatly intensified and put to active uses in what the Beechers would surely have called a wider sphere of usefulness:

> During this, our planetary stage of existence, we have our lodging in the murky suburbs of creation; but yet a distant view of royal palaces and gardens of delight is afforded to us, nor are we left without significant indications of what is there to be found. There may be those perhaps, who would resent it as a trivial and unworthy supposition that heaven can be anything except a grave convocation of rational worshippers, convened in perpetuity upon ethereal clouds, and occupied for ever in one and the same ecstatic manner.

Far from endorsing this static model of the future life, Taylor conjectured that within the galaxy was another, invisible, universe "elaborate in structure and replete with life;—life agitated by momentous interests, and perhaps by frivolous interests." Thus he envisioned "two collocated systems," one material, the other metamaterial. In the second, as in the first, activity was the mainspring of the system.[17]

In Taylor's parallel galaxy, however, benevolence did not automatically triumph, nor would it necessarily be universal. He could easily imagine a liberated soul, such as that of a "ruffian slave dealer," "proudly careering through mid-heaven," only to be vanquished when he encountered more powerful beings who would chain him in "an abyss." There he would "chafe, and taste the retributive miseries of captivity, and the fruitless strivings and writhings of a power sufficient, if it were not bound, to bear him from star to star." While Taylor posited an abyss corresponding to the orthodox Hell, the torments were not those of fire and torture, but the nullification of infinitely increased capacities and faculties. This punishment Taylor apparently conceived to be endless.

As for mundane, planetary evil, he reaffirmed the ancient belief in "malign influences." The author of evil was, of course, Satan, but he operated by purely moral and spiritual means. There was also a race of demons (pre-Adamite in origin, Taylor suggested) who manifested themselves visibly and palpably but, again, according to natural laws. To dismiss the existence of such beings and agencies was, Taylor argued, a large step in the direction of atheism. The present world was, in fact, a "haunted planet." All these reasonings, it must be emphasized, were said by Taylor to accord strictly with revelation and natural law.[18]

It might be supposed that Lyman Beecher, who likewise affirmed the value of analogical reasoning as a means of shedding light on inspired truths, derived his later views of Heaven from Isaac Taylor, and indeed he did cite Taylor's *Physical Theory* in his theological lectures. But it was not from Taylor alone that Beecher drew his ideas. In 1831, five years before the appearance of Taylor's book, Catharine Beecher had printed her *Elements of Mental and Moral Philosophy*, which anticipated some of his arguments. Chapter 28, on the "Consequences in a Future State of the Disordered Operation of Mind," was a description of the development after death of human minds, the benevolent becoming purely beneficent and holy; the selfish, irremediably base. Her conclusions, she announced, were based on reason, while alternative theories were "mere suppositions." Selfish minds thrown together and endowed with bodily form would make a terrible postmundane prison for each other. Grown weary of tormenting their fellows, they would be wracked by remorse and despair, but not by physical sufferings. Catharine did not attempt a theodicy. To the question why God, foreseeing all, had chosen to form the human mind with capacities for selfishness and hatred, Catharine replied, "Revelation gives no answer."[19]

Not only did Isaac Taylor influence the Beechers with his views of the life to come and his method of reasoning, he also spawned a host of American books with a similar purpose. Of these, three works are of special interest, both because of their great popularity and because they knitted together hundreds of scientific, mystical, and eschatological sources. Two of these were, by the standard of that time, scholarly books: Edmund H. Sears's *Athanasia*, and Robert Dale Owen's *Footfalls on the Boundary of Another World*. Sears was a Unitarian clergyman and popular author of pronouncedly mystical tendencies, whose devotional writings had a vogue outside his own denomination. *Athanasia*, retitled *Foregleams and Foreshadows of Immortality*, went through at least twelve editions. Owen was the leading American Spiritualist of his generation, a convert from free thought. His *Footfalls* did not deal with Spiritualism as such, but confined itself to the spiritual continuum, as evidenced in spontaneous phenomena. He was convinced that the gathering, classification, and presentation of data on apparitions, prescience, prophetic dreams, acts of supernatural retribution, poltergeists, and mysterious noises, would provide the "solid, reliable building-stones" with which "some future architect" could erect a theory of supramundane existence. As it happened, Owen himself took on the latter task, in his *Debateable Land.*[20]

Harriet Stowe read both *Footfalls* and *Foregleams* and professed herself highly edified. Though reluctant to publicize her views, she privately assured Owen that she had profited from his studies. His inferences, she told him, "are certainly in agreement with the whole analogy of nature as well as our instinctive convictions of justice and right and I know not that they are contravened by Scripture." She was delighted that his researches seemed to confirm her own views of future punishment, based on intensive study of the Bible and animated by grief over the death of Henry Stowe:

> I have yet to see the passage that asserts that probation ends with *this* life—for tho many passages assert a final separation of the good and the evil at a period called the day of judgment I know no passage which warrants saying that probation ends *until* then.

The story of Lazarus and Dives posed no great difficulty, she asserted, because "Nobody of course in these days interprets that literally. All we can make [of it] is that a life of selfish self indulgence ends in great misery in the future state--That the misery is disciplinary and not penal may be inferred from the parental tone in which the Father exhorts to patience." She had studied commentaries from Calvin onward, and these concurred, she told Owen, in construing 1 Peter 3:18–20 as showing that Christ had preached in Hell. The Apostles' Creed fully confirmed the belief of primitive Christians that Jesus had a mission to departed souls. Mrs. Stowe had almost nothing to say about the evidential value of Owen's data, but seemed rather to stress the general congruence between his views and hers.[21]

In discussing the change at death, Owen maintained that the ministration of spirits to the living showed that

> Death destroys not, in any sense, either the life or the identity of man. Nor does it permit the spirit, an angel suddenly become immaculate, to aspire at once to heaven. Far less does it condemn that spirit, a demon instantly debased, to sink incontinently to hell.

Modern-day Protestantism might declare his doctrine heretical but modern teachings on this subject were wrong according to Owen. In fact, post-Reformation doctrine involved an apostacy from "the faith, universally confessed, of primitive Christianity." By denying the existence of Hades and purgatorial discipline, Luther had done great injury to Christian belief. The alternatives after Luther were immediate translation to Heaven or Hell, or eons of joyless residence in a "dreary gulf" between earthly life and the Last Judgment. Restore Hades to the Protestant conception of the afterlife, and theology would recover the truly Christian hope, "Hope to encourage, Mercy to plead, and Love—the earth-clog shaken off that dimmed her purity—still selecting her chosen ones, but to be separated from them no more." Rather than "a heaven too immaculate for progress, too holy for human avocation or human endeavor," there would be first Hades, "an abode of emancipated spirits, but of *human* spirits." "Transplanted from earth to a more genial land," spirits willing, working, and persevering to the end would ultimately be prepared for an even lovelier existence beyond Hades. What the final stage would be, Owen did not pretend to know, nor did he invoke the Scriptures. He could only say that "We know not whither ultramundane progress may lead."

It is difficult to believe that Harriet accepted Owen's doctrine entirely, unless she was prepared to abandon her assurance that her mother had experienced immediate translation to blessedness. But the idea of a probationary state was necessary to her theology, and arguments affirming "ultramundane progress" greatly relieved her mind with regard to her dearest son. When *The Debateable Land* appeared in 1871, she thanked Owen on behalf of her brother Henry, who commended his "calm and philosophic spirit." They even compared Owen's achievement to that of Darwin. Harriet also pressed his findings on a skeptical George Eliot. Mrs. Stowe read Owen selectively, just as Owen had appropriated arguments from Edmund Sears without taking account of the radical divergence between his doctrines and Sears's.[22]

Whereas Owen was preoccupied with phenomena and considered theology primarily (if not exclusively) in its moral aspects, Sears's view was completely spiritualized. The tone of *Foregleams* was totally hostile to materialism, even in its subtler manifestations. The intense spirituality of Sears undoubtedly appealed to Mrs. Stowe's "higher life tendencies" (as Eunice Beecher sneeringly called them). Sears's conceptions of creation and of God's works were altogether different from Owen's. While Owen constantly recurred to the natural laws which governed life after death, Sears dismissed such ideas. When learned men of piety—the Reverend Joseph Tracy and his coreligionist Edward Hitchcock—filled religious journals with disquisitions on the processes of bodily resurrection in the light of modern psychology and chemistry, Sears rebuked them. The lamps of modern science shed feeble light compared to divine revelation and the truths about man's immortal estate implanted by God himself in his creatures' consciousness. These truths were so universal that all the world's religions shadowed them forth, however imperfectly.

Sears's antimaterialism rested on his proposition that the "inmost principle of matter is the Divine Life itself,—not the Divine Essence as the Pantheist would say, but an effluence from it." His statements on this subject are so like those of Jonathan Edwards that, even in the absence of explicit acknowledgement, we must suspect Sears's indebtedness to the last great Calvinist. Sears argued that creation was continuous:

> And is it not therefore true,—not that he created it [matter] once out of nothing,—but that he creates it every moment out of himself? And does not the great truth begin to dawn upon us that the relation of creator and created subsists all the while, and if suspended for a single instant, the universe vanishes like a bubble that breaks in air?

Traditional religion, Sears believed, had portrayed God's workings in excessively mechanistic terms. Creation in this view, while marvelous, was still only something of an engineering feat. The rhapsodies of the Cambridge Platonists on the divine ingenuity were at bottom celebrations of a mechanistic worldview.[23]

And this worldview had gained ground with ever accelerating force. The soberest traditionalists would not dream of overturning the watchmaker idea of God, though they imagined that their ideas of God were more pious than those of the deists. Sears averred that "The subjects of Creation, Providence, Divine Government, Eschatology, all are affected with our naturalism, and God becomes an almighty mechanic, and not a Creator and Governor." The Tracy-Hitchcock school, who congratulated themselves on reconciling science and Scripture, presented no advance over older eschatology. As far as Sears was concerned, theologians still encouraged the view of God as a sort of divine bricklayer or potter who would set up shop at the last trump and commence constructing or patching up the dead from whatever materials lay at hand. The God-as-potter notion vitiated eschatology by its fundamental materialism and, in this view, any ideas of immortality must partake of a gross, cloddish quality. Sears rejected Isaac Taylor's theories on the same grounds and gave a penetrating analysis of the leading principle of Spiritualism, when he wrote that the spiritual world was "Not as the author of the Physical Theory conjectures, nor as the current 'Spiritualism' teaches,—that the spiritual world is a subtilized natural one on the plane of materialism."[24]

Taylor and Owen alike strenuously upheld the doctrine that natural laws governed the realm beyond death. Taylor was, in fact, one of the authorities most often cited by Owen. What struck Sears as the fatal flaw in their reasonings was to them the most impressive and persuasive element of their systems. Catharine Beecher's views on the afterlife were clearly allied to the Taylor and Owen schools of thought rather than to Sears's. This was in keeping with her naturalistic outlook.

Instead of interpreting spiritual growth after the soul's departure from its fleshly tenement as a natural, quasi-physical process, Sears interpreted Paul to mean that during life there was a "continuous putting off the natural body and putting on the Divine," an "excarnation of man which abolishes his relations to material things, and makes him eternally the denizen of a spiritual wor[l]d." Again echoing Edwards, Sears defined regeneration as the unfolding of "the angelic affections . . . until all necessity for self-denial has ceased, and the Divine Love has a spontaneous flow into our whole external life. So long as there is self-denial, there is conflict between the Holy Spirit working in us and our own unextinguished selfishness." Although Sears envisioned regeneration as a gradual process, this was no centuries-long postmundane probation where the self was chastened and tempered by schooling in self-sacrifice. Though not instantaneous in Sears's conception, regeneration was much closer to the Pauline and Edwardsean disinterested love.[25]

But there is a danger of misrepresenting Sears as a neo-Edwardsean, which he certainly was not. Beyond his probable debt to Edwards, he also drew heavily on the doctrines of Emmanuel Swedenborg, particularly the idea of "degrees" of spiritual ascent and amplitude. He expressed regret that Swedenborg's influence on theology had not been greater. Another well from which Sears drew was that of the Alexandrian Fathers. In any case, Sears's theory did present a subtle, truly spiritualized theory of the condition of immortal souls, jettisoning his contemporaries' naturalistic cargo. Mrs. Stowe, however, seemed to experience no difficulty in approving the views of both Owen and Sears.[26]

No greater contrast to *Foregleams* could be found than that Victorian celestial guidebook, Mrs. Ward's *The Gates Ajar.* The immense popularity of this novel makes it plain that the decline of Calvinistic religion, with its cruel paradoxes and hard sayings, did not diminish anxiety about death and immortality. The novel concerns bereavement and consolation in a post-Civil War setting redolent of suppressed incestuous sexuality. Mary, the heroine, has lost her only brother in the war. Unable to accept the loss with Christian resignation, she withdraws into a feverish state of lamentation, brooding over the injustice of Royal's fate, "snatched away in an instant by a dreadful God" and brought home in his uniform to sleep under the snow. The male protagonists, Deacon Quirk, a typical canting Yankee, and the Reverend Dr. Bland, offer the young spinster nothing but stale homilies. When her recently widowed Aunt Winifred comes to stay, Mary senses that Winifred's wisdom far exceeds that of Dr. Bland. Aunt Winifred resolves to put an end to Bland's unwitting persecution of her tender lamb: "She put her arm around me with a quick movement, as if she would shield me from Deacon Quirk and Dr. Bland." And indeed Winifred Forceythe proceeds to expose their Calvinism in all its cruelty. Hundreds of pages of girlish confidences and maternal chats expound the author's theme: Heaven is simply earth made jollier, fancier, and busier.[27]

Theology, biblical exegesis, archaeology, hermeneutics, and psychology are of use only insofar as they substantiate Aunt Winifred's housewifely vision. Like the author, whose grandfather was Moses Stuart,—or like the Beecher women for that matter—Mrs. Forceythe is a competent lay theologian. Yet she confesses that all her learned studies had only baffled her. She could not reconcile the dogma of savants with her own reading of the Bible, "this book of gracious promises," or with the ultimate authority, "common sense." The text is studded with citations to scholarly books; it is a veritable thesaurus of eschatological theories and controversies. But these are only cloves in the hefty ham of Aunt Winifred's own theology. Her doctrines are a potpourri of supposition, invention, and reverie. *The Gates Ajar* is virtually a parody of Isaac Taylor. Did Taylor conjecture that Heaven might be located in the incandescent realms of the sun? Aunt Winifred thinks that Paradise is just like Kansas. She promises Quirk's bumpkin son that he will trade his homely features for those of an Adonis and that his Yankee itch for tinkering will be satisfied in the creation of unheard-of mechanical marvels. In the many mansions of her Father's house are best parlors with tinkling pianos.

Apart from such homey details, there was a serious argumentative purpose to the book. Among other things, the novel urges rejection of the authority of male ecclesiastics and closeted scholars and celebrates an extremely individualistic, extra-ecclesiastical faith. Not only must men and women learn to view Heaven as a brisker, nicer earth, they must dare to be their own guides to this higher knowledge. Heaven is nothing more or less than a projection of whatever the individual feels is most valuable, touching, or lovely in his or her present life. James Beecher told his wife that Heaven is made precious chiefly by the presence of loved ones. Elizabeth Ward gave a baldly heretical version of this same sentiment when she made Mrs. Forceythe speak of the yearning for lost friends and relatives:

> ". . . if we could speak to them, or they to us, there would be no death, for there would be no separation. The last, the surest, in some cases the only test of loyalty to God, would thus be taken away. Roman Catholic nature is human nature, when it comes on its knees before a saint. Many lives—all such lives as yours and mine —would become—"
>
> "Would become what?" [Mary asks.]
>
> "One long defiance to the First Commandment."

Mary is properly aghast at such a conclusion, but she finally recognizes her aunt's moral and intellectual courage, for Winifred has said aloud what Mary has kept suppressed, in admitting that love of family may supercede love of a remote deity. When Winifred converts Dr. Bland to her doctrine, the women's victory is complete. Mrs. Forceythe's painful death from cancer only heightens the triumph, because she is traveling to regions where she will not be a stranger.[28]

The purpose of this extended discussion of Owen, Sears, and Ward is to point out an unremitting endeavor by many authors to describe, or even map out, the future world in terms acceptable, on the one hand, to an increasingly scientific temper and, on the other, to the spirituality of Protestants whose lineage was Puritan. There was a tension between "naturalism" and a generalized fear of materialistic, mechanistic philosophy. As evangelical Protestants like the Beechers shed many of the constraints of Reformed dogma, particularly the belief in double predestination and endless retribution, they grew more uneasy about the immortality of their souls. For the Beechers this uneasiness took the form of fearing that their theological innovations might bleed away the saving power of the Gospels. Thomas

Beecher, whose theology was entirely a pastoral one, was bold enough to declare publicly his belief in the soul's probation after death. As early as 1850 he was proclaiming it to his congregations, as Isabella reported to Henry:

> It *was* a capital sermon—and the first I have ever heard on the state of the soul between death and judgment. He announced Hades explicitly and the gospel preached there to those who have never really heard it in this life—the argument was clear and logical—illustrations admirable—application so serious and discriminating, as to make all abuse of the new doctrine improbable if not impossible. It was one of a series of sermons—he has been long concocting—and the way has been admirably prepared by previous discourses—on physiology—law of *physical* death, etc., etc.[29]

His brothers and sisters proceeded with greater caution but gave equal attention to these questions. In 1857 Charles, who was working up materials for his father's autobiography, wrote his reflections to Henry:

> I have extracted all that reveals Fathers agency in reference to the great problems of the conversion of his children. It is deeply affecting. It is really one of the most solemn things I have attended to for a long time. It fills me with concern for my own children, and my own great Stupidity in regard to them, and above all, my unbelief in regard to their danger. Is *eternal* punishment a reality? Father thought so. He never doubted [it]. Strike that idea out of his mind, and his whole career would be changed, his whole influence on us modified. . . . Yet Isabella and Mary I fear reject father's belief in it. Do you really believe that the wicked will exist forever, and continue forever in sin? The only point on which my mind recoils, is, on the question of their endless *existence.* If they exist, I can conceive that they might be unchangeably wicked, and of course miserable. But do you believe this? How can we affect *our* children as Father did us, if we have not the same concern for them, the same sense of their awful danger?

There was still, as the preceding pages and these letters show, a reluctance to give up the idea of sanctions in the afterlife against those who had been malign forces while living. There was also a growing fondness for the idea that the tenor of the infinitesimally short span of earthly life did not constitute the soul's only chance for eternal happiness.[30]

Whatever the solutions proposed, whether Isaac Taylor's or Catharine Beecher's, there was a significant retreat from belief in immutable divine decrees. If not wholeheartedly universalist, many of these authors professed universalistic beliefs, particularly probationary ones. Millennialism, perfectionism, and illuminism also figured prominently in many such theories, as we will see in the discussion of Spiritualism.

The Beechers' profound interest in paranormal phenomena, which certainly antedated the Hydesville rappings, opens up another aspect of the problem. Long before Kate and Margaretta Fox burst onto the American scene in 1847 with their spirit-rappings in a western New York farmhouse, the Beechers had occult dealings of their own, though these took far more genteel forms. Unlike the Foxes, Lyman's children certainly never graced P. T. Barnum's Lyceum and seldom publicized their strange powers. One Beecher, Henry Ward, exhibited a rather grand indifference to the whole excitement, although Harriet tried to make him out an inquirer.

The most dramatic story was that of Calvin Stowe. From early boyhood he had been afflicted by striking visual and auditory hallucinations, mostly the former. "Constitutionally feeble," and with a "nervous system easily excitable," young Stowe saw "a multitude of animated and active objects" so real that he "knew no difference between them and any other of the objects which met my eye." Though he could not touch and could only seldom hear these creatures, he "kept up a lively conversation with them . . . by a peculiar sort of spiritual intercommunion." These spectral beings were of two classes, beneficent and maleficent, manifesting themselves according to Calvin's mood. When happy, he saw fairies and musicians who played airs and disported themselves in his bedroom. When melancholy (as he often was), he was visited by mischievous or terrible things. Sometimes when his mood shifted abruptly, sinister beings would appear and frighten away the pleasant ones. It was only when his mother reacted with alarm to his queries that he realized the companionable creatures were imaginary.[31]

In his account of these visions, which Stowe detailed to the Semi-Colon Club of Cincinnati many years later, he was careful to state that they were a "delusion of the imagination," to associate them with his rapidly fluctuating emotional states, and implicitly to connect them with the morbidity of his temperament, which craved solitude and dusk and delighted in ghost stories. On one occasion he was terrified to awaken and find a spectral skeleton in his bed. On another he looked down on a panorama of Hell, whose inhabitants lacked the standard goatlike appendages and red skin but were instead "in all respects stoutly built and well-dressed gentlemen" of ash-blue coloring. Ascending clouds, like tornadoes with a kind of brute intelligence, served these modish devils as instruments of torture. As the boy looked on, he saw a crew of devils and their furious clouds ambush an obnoxious neighbor of the Stowes.[32]

However delusionary Stowe believed these childhood visions to be, he later saw hallucinations of real objects and people. Some, particularly images of his wife, were so vivid that they made him doubt whether he was seeing Harriet or only a visual imprint of her as she puttered about their house. Still stranger, if a secondhand account can be believed, were his interviews with the Devil. Stowe was alleged to have told a ministerial friend that he had personally battled with Satan and vanquished him with telling passages from Ephesians. He also claimed to have chatted with Goethe in the shady groves of Nook Farm near the Stowe cottage and to have received great enlightenment as to the poet's intent in *Faust*, Part Two. In any case, Stowe and his family seem to have made a perfect adjustment to his hallucinations, and he had no qualms about letting Harriet incorporate his Semi-Colon Club report, almost verbatim, into *Oldtown Folks*, just as she did his Yankee saws, ghost stories, and nuggets of local color.[33]

A far different, and to Stowe very credible, account of a vision was given to him by an elderly native of his hometown, an unschooled pauper of famous piety. He had told Stowe his story many times, and during a visit in 1844 Stowe took the trouble to record it as the "Religious Experience of John Ross of Natick Mass. as written down from his lips by Calvin E. Stowe of Cincinnati June 14, 1844."[34] In his prefatory remarks, Stowe described Ross as formerly a hopeless drunkard, a "vulgar, noisy disagreeable fellow, of a very weak mind and profane beyond description. . . . To all appearances he was a brutal slavering idiot." His only redeeming trait was his kindliness toward his family. One morning he got out of bed miraculously transformed. He was sober, mild, and religious, though mute as to the cause of the sudden change. He shrank from declaring himself converted but ministered to "the poor sick, afflicted, and forsaken within 10 or 12 miles." Ross carried himself so straitly and meekly that, after two rebuffs by a frankly incredulous Congregational church, he was accepted as a member and walked orderly the rest of his life. Even the Natick Unitarians were forced by his case to revise their stand against supernatural instantaneous regeneration, a doctrine they had spurned as a relic of Calvinism.

Ross told Stowe that he received two visions of the Christ child in August of 1824 while lying in bed. He was not spiritually aroused or in any way predisposed to receive religious impressions—they simply came to him. His spirit was carried to a stream in a nearby meadow, where he first saw Christ as a newborn infant in Mary's arms. The baby was wrapped in a linen cloth or napkin. "*He was all love and beauty*." When Ross asked Mary to let him hold the baby, she "said No he will go to no one but his Father." Mary relented as far as giving Ross the child's swaddling cloth, and in that moment Ross felt himself to be "a vile miserable wicked wretch filthier than a dung heap—and Christ so loving and beautiful." As soon as it was light, Ross opened his long unused Bible to read about Christ's childhood, and "For 2 days I walked about in a maze." Christ, grown older but still a small child, appeared to Ross a second time in Coolidge's meadow. His mother placed the child in Ross's arms. "I was too afraid to be happy and too happy to be afraid." The child gave him unspoken assurance of salvation, and Ross's regeneration was accomplished "on the 2nd day of the next April at a quarter past two in the morning," when he suddenly "felt him in my spirit—my sins were forgiven—my distress was all gone." Christ had cleansed him as he had the lepers and had made him see when before he was blind. This was John Ross's simple and sufficient understanding of the experience.

Stowe was apparently eager to believe Ross. He posed a series of questions designed to show that the visitations were not normal occurrences, such as dreams. When he asked Ross whether he was actually present at the stream where Christ appeared, Ross answered, "My spirit was there[;] my body, that, was in bed." And again, "I know what it is to be asleep and dreaming and I know I was not." When Stowe asked about Mary's features, Ross replied, "Why Christ is all in all . . . she is more like other folks." There was a circumstantiality about the account that lent it veracity. There were homely touches, such as Ross's use of the rustic "creek" in place of the correct "brook," and the language of his witness to his radical change of heart: "I am very poor—all alone old, and poor—but it makes no odds—Christ is with me." This simplicity tended to counterbalance some of the stock religious expressions he also used, as when describing his "unspeakable wickedness." And the whole relation had a muted Bunyanesque quality that must have deeply touched a man like Stowe, anxious to distinguish true visions from neurological anomalies, and who had slept as a child with *The Pilgrim's Progress* next to his heart.[35]

Ross's relation was very important to Stowe. Not only did he make several copies of it, but he also used it in his sermons. What better way to preach for conversion than to give such a persuasive account of Christ's personal ministry? This story, with others, formed a stock of private experiences which the Stowes believed to be indisputable evidence of supernaturalism.[36]

At the same time Stowe was visiting his old haunts and transcribing Ross's experience, Harriet was vacationing at Henry's home in Indianapolis, where she and her brother experimented with mesmerism. Harriet reported to Calvin that Henry almost threw her into convulsions during the first session: "spasms and shocks of heat and prickly sensation[s] ran all over me, my lungs were violently constricted and my head in dreadful commotion." After some practice, Henry was able to produce a "semi somnolent state" in which his sister's hands wandered as if moved by a will of their own, while "amid all the bodily effects my mind and powers of observation seemed uncommonly bright and active." Another session induced near torpor, and "thus you see I have come to the verge of the spirit land." She instructed Calvin to query her brother Edward whether "he does not think there is an animal magnetic fluid." Eunice evidently expressed strong misgivings about the proceedings, because Harriet later teased her, "dont you remember you almost thought you had some hobgoblin magician for a husband last summer! How you did scud out of the room!"[37]

Months later Harriet was still fascinated by the topic and consulted a pair of professional mesmerists whose itinerations had brought them to Cincinnati. A chance acquaintance with Mrs. Bonneville turned into a fast friendship. Harriet invited her to live as a guest in the Stowe home, and she in turn initiated Harriet into further mesmeric mysteries. Harriet explained Mrs. Bonneville's theories to Henry:

> Her view of the subject is that the mesmeric fluid is a powerful remedial agent in the cure of nervous diseases particularly—such as all forms of convulsions hysteria epilepsy paralysis neuralgia in general and it is to the dissemination of light and knowledge on the subject that she considers herself devoted. They had patients in the city by the hundreds . . . and the pretty little graceful creature spent time and strength enough to wear her health out in mesmeric manipulations to this intent.

The curative powers of mesmerism must have attracted a woman whose family was overstocked with nervous diseases, but Harriet felt ambivalent about mesmerism as such. She told Henry that their experiments had been dangerous but still urged him to pursue his investigations, for "I think you have an immense power in this way and the time may come when you can relieve pain by trying it." She herself proved adept at helping a suffering friend fall asleep by making "soothing passes."[38]

Mesmeric powers were not confined to Henry and Harriet. Their brother William, who was so incompetent at other things, was by his own admission the family's most skillful magnetizer. In October of 1842, on his way to attend the Synod of Genesee, he stopped over with a family whose son was cataleptic. As William explained in *Fowler's Phrenological Journal*, he discovered that he could magnetize the child, who then exhibited singular powers. While in a separate room the child could taste and smell substances in Beecher's mouth. As Beecher serially touched various of the boy's phrenological "organs"—Benevolence, Reverence, Combativeness, and so forth—his behavior corresponded. He also showed remarkable clairvoyant powers, minutely describing Beecher's study in Batavia, New York, many miles away. Upon being subjected to further mesmerizing, the child was cured of his fits and his spinal injury. Experimentation on other subjects convinced Beecher that he could cure toothaches and headaches, tic doloureux, and assorted pains and swellings. Delving into the sources of mesmeric power was beyond him, he confessed. Possibly it was diabolical in origin, but "as a remedial agent mesmerism is to accomplish much good." Of the more occult manifestations he was more skeptical, saying, "I am not, however, a full believer in all which is affirmed of clairvoyants—what I see and know, I believe."[39]

Beecher's disclaimers and his suggestion that mesmeric powers could be abused provoked one Henry Jones to publish *Animal Magnetism Repudiated as Sorcery*. As the title indicates, the reality of mesmeric phenomena was not at issue. The Bible, with Jones's own experiences, proved that they were authentic. They were the evil wonders foretold by the Scriptures as signs of the opening of the last days. The works of mesmerists were "too perfectly in the Image of Satan himself, to be considered as having a better origin." Robbery, seduction, paralysis, and maiming could just as well form the repertoire of the skilled mesmerist as healing or other meritorious works. This obscure pamphlet is only worth mentioning because it reflected a common view, and its arguments were to be repeated throughout the century by opposers of Spiritualism—Charles Beecher among them.[40]

Neither Henry nor William (after his initial experiments) is known to have practiced magnetic healing outside the family circle. But other members of the family did not hesitate to consult psychic healers of varying schools and pretensions. As she was something of an authority on hygiene and human physiology, Catharine's account of her hauling and mauling at the hands of successive "celebrated physicians" is instructive, especially since she could not suppress the humor of the whole sad story. Her "delicate and scrofulous constitution" made her health precarious, and the death of Professor Fisher was so severe a blow that she spent decades trying to salvage health and peace of mind. Her overwrought state had induced a "semi-paralysis of the nerves of motion, attended by an extreme sensitiveness of the whole nervous system." After orthodox medicine (allopathy) had failed her, she resorted to homeopathy and "galvanism." "Dr. Buchanan and his theory of Neurology," the details of which are vague, "produced a strong impression in reference to future probable discoveries of the remedial agency of *animal magnetism.*" Said magnetism was then essayed in experiments featuring a bright silver sixpence and a long-suffering brother who spent "day after day" making mesmeric passes over his afflicted sister. Neither this nor consultation with a highly touted clairvoyant availed to restore the power to Catharine's "nervous fountain." Sherwood's Electro-Magnetic Machine had no better effect, and after an entire year of hydropathy, with never a "water cure crisis" to repay her for her sufferings and cash outlay, Catharine repaired to a man who detected disease "by a peculiar magnetic power in the ends of his fingers." Weeks of this treatment failed to produce the requisite "mucus crisis," and Catharine was understandably disappointed.[41]

She explained to her confidante, Mrs. Bannister, that this Dr. Ruggles combined magnetic diagnosis "in detecting the *seat of diseased action*" with conventional hydropathy. As evidence of the serious failure of orthodox medicine, Catharine observed that "He has turned away multitudes this summer and yet has been thronged," and, where accepted therapies had proved worthless, "His cures have many of them been *remarkable*." Though Catharine ultimately had doubts about the efficacy of mesmeric healing and reservations about its use, she remained alert to evidences of magnetic forces. One facet of her medical history deserves further comment. Although she received no physical benefits from the clairvoyant whom she consulted, the woman did display unaccountable powers that deeply impressed her. She continued to sit with clairvoyants and attempted to develop a purely natural explanation for their seemingly occult knowledge.[42]

The rise of Spiritualism as a religious movement did not sweep the Beechers along with it. Even Isabella and John Hooker were late converts to Spiritualism. The Beechers' public comments on the novelty were wary or sarcastic. With their omnivorous reading habits, they must have been well apprised of Spiritualistic developments. It is interesting that one of the earliest so-called harmonial communities in the United States was the Cincinnati Brotherhood, led by a former steamboat hand who located his brethren on the Ohio River, where they hoped to work out his system of scientific and moral revelations. Surely the Beechers would have been interested observers of this community, which lasted from 1845 to 1848.

One of Mrs. Stowe's early references to Spiritualism as such was a flip aside in one of her letters to the *National Era*, where she joked about "The spiritual rapping fraternity, who are *au fait* in all that relates to man's capabilities, and who are now speaking *ex cathedra* of all things celestial, and terrestrial, past, present, and to come." By the time she made her triumphal tour of England and the Continent, she found that the contagion of Spiritualism had spread there. Charles recorded in his travel diary that in Paris they "attended the *salon* of Lady Elgin," where they were introduced to "the Marquis de M., whose book on the spiritual rappings comes out next week. We conversed on the rappings *ad nauseum*." On her second visit to Europe, Harriet attended seances at the residence of Robert Dale Owen, then American consul at Naples. She remained unconverted but unwilling to denounce the movement.[43]

Henry had no such scruples. He called himself a "stout unbeliever in the spiritual origins of these phenomena" and warned that "A belief in modern spiritualism seems to weaken the hold of the Bible upon conscience, the affections, and to substitute diluted sentimentalism and tedious platitudes instead of inspired truth." Henry's rejection of Spiritualism was in marked contrast to the curiosity and awe of his brothers and sisters.[44]

Catharine's interest was a serious one. Her *Letters on Health and Happiness* included a long "Note" on animal magnetism and spirit-rapping, which hypothesized that animal magnetism worked by a transfer of invisible nervous fluid "very much as electricity accumulates in a Leyden jar." She dismissed Spiritualism as a lower-class excitement akin to Mormonism, with identical tendencies to corrupt morals and stultify the mind. Applying the tests of empiricism and common sense to the phenomena, she concluded:

I have as yet never seen any thing claimed to be "spiritual

> manifestations" that could not be easily accounted for as is here suggested. And the progress of time is more and more exhibiting the folly and inconsistency of the popular delusion that brings back the spirits of departed friends to perform fantastic tricks, and to make known inane and contradictory revelations.

Catharine's experiences with Kate Fox did nothing to alter her judgment. Sometime in the late 1860s, she lived in the same boardinghouse with Kate Fox and her companion Laura Edmonds, daughter of Judge John Worth Edmonds, one of Spiritualism's most prominent converts. Catharine's attitude toward them may be judged from the wry tone of her recollections. She remembered that the women "cut up all sorts of capers," trying to mystify her. When they assured her that they had seen a vision of Lyman, "kneeling before her offering her a rose as the emblem of her purity," she knew them for frauds—if well-meaning frauds. Fanaticism was vulgar, or symptomatic of "disordered mind," and their secret wisdom had therefore no appeal. While Catharine tended to shrug off supernatural explanations of such phenomena, she remained an active investigator.[45]

Charles, meanwhile, had undergone a reversal of opinion. Spirit-rappings were not salon foolery after all, but demonic displays. In April of 1853 he made a report to the Congregational Association of New York and Brooklyn giving his preliminary conclusions. His *Review of the "Spiritual Manifestations"* created a stir, as would any major pronouncement on the subject from a Beecher. No less than three, and presumably more, pamphlets were published as rejoinders to Beecher's report. Samuel B. Brittan, publisher of the *Spiritual Telegraph* and sometime colleague of Andrew Jackson Davis, praised Beecher for demanding a dispassionate investigation of the phenomena but complained of his Procrustean standards:

> Instead of subjecting the facts of the Bible to the principles of science for trial, he reverses the order, and proceeds to try *Science by Scripture*, or by the more questionable standard set up at Westminster. . . . We may as well quote from the "Pilgrim's Progress" to illustrate the art of steam navigation. . . . We are by no means prepared to admit that the law which is to determine our faith in modern Spiritual phenomena is written in any six lines of the Westminister Confession; or, indeed, that it is written in that Confession at all.

As for Beecher's ascription of the phenomena to diabolic agents, Brittan demanded, "if the purest instructions emanate, in these days, from the Devil, how can we know that he has not been the world's spiritual teacher in all past ages." Another critic scored Beecher for claiming that saving faith was never accompanied by spiritual manifestations. How, on that basis, would he account for Paul's conversion or that of Paul's jailor? If such manifestations were invariably suspect, were Christ's miracles diabolic, or alternatively, simply electrical?[46]

Edward C. Rogers, a self-styled medical electrician, attacked Beecher from the opposite side. He explained the manifestations as purely automatic cerebral activity "analogous to that of a mesmerized patient,—that of a mere automatic machine; the same, also, as the brain of the clairvoyant, the dreamer, the somnambule, the insane." Beecher had singled Rogers out for abuse as an utter materialist, but he countered that Beecher's demonic theory was far worse. By removing the subject from the sphere of science, he "thrusts it into the hopper of a vulgar credulity, into which has run a constant stream of filthy superstition since the birth of man." Furthermore, his unbecoming eagerness to invoke devilish agents as the cause of cerebral automatisms would help spread the contagion of "nervous mania." Rogers warned that the recrudescence of belief in demonic possession would hamper the advance of psychiatric therapy.[47]

Charles Beecher was not unaware of the undercurrents that fed the stream of Spiritualism, apart from what he conceived to be Satanic agency. As Sears had done, Beecher indicted Spiritualism as tending toward a "polytheistic pantheism, disguising under the name of spirit a subtle but genuine materialism." Even a casual perusal of Spiritualistic literature would have confirmed Beecher's worst fears. Brittan, in fact, boasted that Spiritualism had succeeded in scuttling Calvinism. Spiritualism in its many forms taught gradualism and progressivism in moral growth. This perfectionism and related doctrines of Swedenborgian provenance undercut the historic doctrines of both Protestantism and Catholicism. What Henry Ward Beecher dismissed as "diluted sentimentalism" thoroughly alarmed his more excitable brother.[48]

Henry and Charles probably had in mind Andrew Jackson Davis (1826–1910), the renowned medical clairvoyant and trance-speaker, through whom Swedenborg, Galen, and other master spirits communicated moral, scientific, and political revelations corroborative of an anticlerical, anti-Calvinistic theology and a peaceably radical social ethic. Davis's "arcana" were hamstrung by what even a sympathetic historian of Spiritualism called an "anaemic optimism."

Nevertheless, Davis hobbled on and on through volume after volume of diffuse philosophy. These claimed to have "*penetrated* the hidden and sequestered parts of numerous questions," bringing forth moral and philosophical treasures from "the *penetralia* of the imperishable Univercoelum." Besides affirming the "post-mundane perpetuity of acquired characteristics," Davis undertook to make "psychometric examinations" by feeling locks of hair. All his books crudely caricatured Luther and Calvin and offered in their stead a broadly optimistic and genial "harmonial" philosophy. Davis's religion, if it were to offend present-day readers at all, would offend chiefly by its milky cheerfulness. But to Charles Beecher and other clergymen, such views were very threatening.[49]

Protestants were not alone in recoiling from Spiritualism. Orestes Brownson, American Catholicism's militant apologist, devoted a long novel to dissecting Spiritualism, exposing its Yankee and Calvinistic origins, and showing that its teachings were dangerously radical. *The Spirit-Rapper* purported to be the confessions of a lapsed Spiritualist, snatched at the last minute from the jaws of atheistic materialism. Although the novel now seems almost preposterous in its reactionary harangues, it was a serious study of Spiritualism as a social movement. Brownson dwells on the illicit sexuality associated with enthusiastic religion and wittily takes off on the omnibus reforms of Yankee, Quaker, and renegade Catholic sectarians. (His Transcendentalist spokesmen, incidentally, spout some of the cleverest parodies of the Concord sages ever written.) Though far less successful novelistically than Howells's *The Undiscovered Country*, *The Spirit-Rapper* is a brilliant blast at the nineteenth-century reform mentality. For this discussion, the important features are Brownson's warning against allying with infernal powers and his expression of Catholic hostility to a movement which sometimes represented itself as a rapprochement with Roman doctrines of supernaturalism and miracles.[50]

Charles Beecher was, then, far from alone in his dread of the diabolical element in Spiritualism. Despite his warnings, however, his sister Harriet continued to dabble in Spiritualism. Her sly remarks and idle curiosity gave way to serious inquiry in 1859, when Henry Stowe died. The Stowes' yearning to establish that he was in the realms of the blissful led them into investigative sittings with various mediums, and as the years passed they pressed on with their quest. They read ponderous treatises on mysticism and spirit-writing and explored the workings of Planchette (the ouija board), all the while hoping for some striking confirmation of their feeling that Henry was near and trying to communicate. As in her other religious studies, Harriet relied on Calvin Stowe's scholarly knowledge, and they studied French and German theses together. On another level, Harriet made a point of collecting ghost stories from her acquaintances and trying to authenticate them. Her letter to Robert Dale Owen, already quoted, shows her train of thought in 1860.[51]

In assessing Harriet's views of Spiritualism, it is necessary to distinguish between her actual experiences, as nearly as they can be reconstructed, and her public statements, which were sometimes more wishful than accurate. How, for instance, is her statement regarding her brother Henry's adult conversion experience to be interpreted? She claimed, in a biographical sketch published in 1868, that after his terrible travail of soul, Henry passed through "a period of spiritual clairvoyance" from which he emerged with "the talisman of his ministry," a Christocentric theology. Given her absorption in Spiritualism, her choice of the term *clairvoyance* was probably not accidental. While it is true that Beecher's understanding of his experience involved a kind of divine illuminism, he held nothing like his sister's mature views on mysticism.[52]

Although that event was highly colored by Harriet and Henry in retrospect, it is nevertheless true that she herself underwent a sort of clairvoyant experience, which she identified as such immediately. In 1863 occurred a strange episode that Harriet uncharacteristically chose not to divulge to the world. One sleepless night, while in a state of anxiety over her son Fred, who was fighting with the Union Army, Harriet had a distinct, overpowering impression that "some soul was to depart that night." She and her daughter Georgiana rose to read the Anglican prayers for the dying. Harriet suddenly knew that the death throes were those of Annie Beecher, James's alcoholic wife:

> I said to Georgie "Why have we given up praying for poor Annie! Did not Christ cast seven devils out of Mary Magdalene? Is not Christ able to save those souls whose bodies have become defiled." . . . By an irresistible impulse I seemed to raise her up in my arms [and] commend her to Jesus. I seemed to stand with her before the cross and give her up to him. . . . Christ [h]as said to the Evil Spirit "I charge [you] to come out of her and vex her no more" and I see her sitting at his feet clothed and in her right mind.

The impression was so vivid that Harriet had Georgie note the date and hour. The following day a telegram bore the news of Annie Beecher's sudden death, and Harriet was certain that they had "prayed beside Annies dying bed last night" and their prayers had prevailed to help heal her soul.[53]

Another of Harriet's reticences concerned her sitting with Kate Fox of doubtful repute. In her public statements Harriet always protested her ignorance of paid mediums and, even when describing sittings with nonprofessionals, she suppressed their names. It is little wonder, then, that she did not care to be publicly associated with one of the Hydesville rappers. Yet she did take part in four, and possibly more, seances at which Kate Fox Jencken presided. Dr. George Taylor, proprietor of the Swedish Movement Cure in New York City, a favorite Beecher health estabishment, was a Spiritualist. Over the years Kate Fox Jencken gave the Taylors over one hundred sittings. It was probably the Hookers who conveyed the Stowes to the Taylor home, where Catharine Beecher joined them. Calvin Stowe was also present at one of the seances, but neither of the Stowes ever divulged the nature of the messages they received.[54]

In 1870 Harriet, who had been spending a lot of time with Planchette, published a series of articles on Spiritualism in Henry's mass circulation religious paper, the *Christian Union*. She begged her readers not to judge the movement by "what is published in the *Banner of Light*, and other papers of that class," papers which carried contributions by the Hookers. Harriet accounted for the charlatanry encountered within the movement by the "trembling agony of eagerness" and "willingness to be deceived" of those who had been bereaved in the recent war. Another force making self-deception so common was the "wild craving of the human soul for the region of future immortality." She dealt very little with mediumistic communications as such, but presented a long historical survey of early Christian beliefs and rites centering on the communion of saints. There was, she explained, a genuine Christian spiritualism which must be distinguished from spurious varieties which depended on sensational feats or dispensed immoral advice. It was no coincidence that Calvin Stowe's articles on mysticism appeared simultaneously in the *Christian Union.* Taken together, these showed why people like the Stowes could be attracted to Spiritualism, even while deploring its excesses.[55]

In defining mysticism, Calvin Stowe said only that "the sanctified soul has communion with God, it knows God's heart," a doctrine identical to that of Edward Beecher. To the objection that mysticism was irrational or dangerous, he answered, "the Bible is mysticism, and the whole Christian system is a mystical system." He did not include raving fanatics or initiates of esoteric cults in the category of Christian mystics. Neither did his wife define Christian spiritualism in terms of bogus prophets and pythonesses who imposed their "juggleries" on the gullible. She claimed to have nothing but contempt for the breathless but trivial messages imparted by supposed mediums. There was a pure body of scriptural spiritualism (or mysticism). The rest was an inevitable excrescence. The great need of the age was the deepening of Christian experience for all who professed belief in Christ. In Harriet's view, "The pastures of the Church have been suffered to become bare and barren of one species of food which the sheep crave and sicken for the want of."[56]

A subsequent article, "A Look Beyond the Veil," presented Harriet's resolution of the torturing enigma of her son's immortal estate. Transition to any new state of being presupposed gradual development, she observed, and therefore the "sphere of the new born immortal will be mercifully regulated according to his spiritual progress." A tender Father "may lead us from regions not unlike our earth, and as it were, shading off into our mortal life—upward and onward—as we can bear it." Here may be seen her adoption of Swedenborgian ideas, which she acknowledged explicitly some years later. "Vague ideas of blessedness and glory" were meaningless to the grief-stricken. Who would wish to think of their loved one as a "solemn angel, rapt away from earth in a distant divine latitude"? Just as Owen and Mrs. Ward insisted, there was continuity between this life and the next. Angelic spirits retained all their solicitude for their earthly friends and lovers. Harriet was speaking not only for herself and Calvin but also for her father when she wrote:

> We sincerely believe that it has sometimes been God's will to vouchsafe to faithful souls some glimpses of the spiritual world, and by the loved voice or presence of the departed, seen in night visions or by vivid impressions of them, to relieve some crisis of agony—to give lightness, peace and joy.

This was no exhortation to weaned affections but rather a declaration that earthly ties need not be broken at all.[57]

Calvin Stowe followed this up with an essay on "The Wicked Spirits in the Skies," which argued that there was an ontological reality corresponding to what secularists vaguely referred to as the power of evil. Weakening of belief in Satan and in "the existence and agency of fallen spirits" was an ominous development. In *Spiritual Manifestations* (1879), Charles Beecher echoed his brother-in-law's dismay at the increasing disbelief in diabolism. Beecher declared himself a

Christian spiritualist in contradistinction to the Spiritualist movement. Like the Stowes, he believed absolutely in the reality and activity of invisible spirits. The first four chapters of his book were devoted to what he believed were veridical accounts of spirit agency, a number of them volunteered by friends and family.

One of the more significant of these experiences was revealed in a fleeting reference to Calvin Stowe's belief in his dead son's presence. When Charles asked, "Have you ever seen and touched departed friends?" he answered, "Yes. I have seen H.[enry], and felt his hand in my own." Given Stowe's dread of Satanic delusion, it must have been a very striking demonstration to convince him that the apparition was indeed Henry's spirit, not merely one of his usual hallucinations or a devilish imposture.[58]

The reality of such occurrences was so central to Charles Beecher's eschatology that he subjected the accounts to less than rigorous scrutiny. In the famous Stratford poltergeist haunting, certified as authentic by no less an authority than Andrew Jackson Davis, Beecher was so ready to ascribe the phenomena to spirit agencies that he ignored evidences of trickery and self-deception which were obvious to more skeptical investigators. Davis himself hinted that Dr. Phelps's stepson produced some of the mysterious effects himself; but, by a strained casuistry satirized by Howells, Spiritualists were accustomed to excuse fraudulent manipulations as necessary incitements to genuine spirits. The picture of Connecticut divines gravely endeavoring to decipher hieroglyphics incised on a turnip is worthy of Mark Twain, but the ludicrousness of the scene escaped Charles Beecher.[59]

Beecher's book had two purposes. The first was to welcome the purer phases and leaders of Spiritualism for reviving biblical belief in spirits; the second was to bolster his own millenarian theory. He treated Spiritualism as a deeply rooted popular movement unfettered by ecclesiastical structure or confessional requirements. The movement was characterized by a solid body of shared beliefs tending, as he believed, to lend great weight to evangelical Christianity. Opponents of Spiritualism were powerless to check its growth, at any rate, because it was a "household religion, which is rapidly extending throughout Christendom." Regardless of the crude or disgusting things perpetrated by the movement's bad elements, it would flourish because it was engaged with the great question of the age. "Vague rumors have gone abroad that God is dead," Beecher declared, but "can the soul coldly discuss the possibilities of such spiritual orphanage?"[60]

What he hoped to see happen was the dissemination of correct views of the great end of spiritualistic activity. According to Beecher's redemptive scheme, human history was only one of the theaters of combat in a celestial political struggle. Over the eons the Satanic (or "cosmocratic") party had wrestled for primacy with the forces of God. The Satanic and angelic parties were now locked in deadly combat over "the principles of good [moral] government." Beecher asserted that the end of the present dispensation would be signalized by the opening of the sixth seal, which would bring on a "very great and grand crisis of catastrophism." The "cosmocratic empire" would stage its last desperate assault on the citadel of God. Dreadful wonders would be seen and heard as fallen angels sought to enlist men under the Satanic banner. Hence the recent deluge of vicious, depraved spirit communications. "Millions of low and deceptive spirits," Beecher warned, were engaged in putting about the damnable lie that the millennium had already begun under Spiritualistic auspices:

> Hence, when the claim is put forth that the millennium is begun, —that the resurrection is now actually taking place in the materializations of the day,—spiritualists ought to be on their guard; and since they admit Christ and the apostles to be the strongest, purest, and most reliable mediums that have existed, they should carefully study their predictions respecting this great crisis.

Let the credulous masses be swayed by the good news of Christ, not by grandiloquent cosmocratic slogans and works of the Devil. Men should not allow themselves to be courted by necromancers who promised to initiate them into forbidden mysteries. Illicit spiritual communion might be an intoxicating prospect, but it was abhorred by God. The only spiritual manifestation permitted to men in the present dispensation was the communion which Christ had promised to believers, the indwelling of his Holy Spirit.[61]

Charles's own history of youthful enthusiasm, which he shuddered to think of, would have been enough to make him leery of any teachings which tended to undermine Scripture or depreciate Christ's unique role and authority. His extreme fear of perverted philosophy and spiritual pride was not allayed by his association with his half-sister Isabella. When Charles warned against human accomplices of the cosmocratic party, he might well have had in mind three persons: Isabella Beecher Hooker, Theodore Tilton, and Victoria Claflin Woodhull.

When Thomas Nast caricatured Mrs. Woodhull with bat's wings and cloven hooves, it was no mere whim. "The Woodhull," as her enemies called her, denying her the dignity of her married title, was supposed to fascinate adherents by sinister means. The Beechers could only account for Isabella's devotion to Victoria by supposing a mysterious enthrallment. Isabella was seemingly besotted with the woman, whom the rest of the Beechers regarded as a vulgar adventuress, who advertised the benefits of free love in a manner suggesting that she herself was a sexual opportunist. And she was the kind of medium who might use her powers for vile ends. Theodore Tilton, formerly a close friend and editorial colleague of Henry Ward Beecher, and also Mrs. Woodhull's sometime paramour, wrote a strange little biographical sketch extolling her psychic powers.

He portrayed the Claflin sisters, Victoria and Tennessee (otherwise Tennie C.) as gorgeous fauna in a Jukes-like brood of hellcats and subnormal yokels. The sordidness of Victoria's surroundings had been made bearable to her by heavenly visitants. "She has entertained angels, and not unawares," Tilton prated. At the age of three Victoria had been transported to the spirit world. The stately Demosthenes made many calls on the Claflin shack to tutor Victoria and detail prophecies of future greatness for his little charge. When she was only ten, two angels had assisted her as she restored an ailing infant to roseate health. Even her marriage, four years later, to the dissolute Dr. Canning Woodhull had not dimmed her hopes. In spite of ill usage at his drunken hands, she had grown more eloquent and bewitching, and her miraculous healing powers reached their height. When the Woodhulls' imbecile son Byron died, she had pressed the cold corpse to her bosom and warmed it back to life. Jesus Christ, she explained to Tilton, had "re-wrought the miracle of Lazarus for a sorrowing woman's sake."[62]

In 1870, after she had been won over by Mrs. Woodhull, Isabella Hooker began hinting at a role even more elevated than the one she had revealed to her husband and children a decade before. Writing to Alice, she counseled her about how to cope with life's disappointments:

> We are not only becoming purified ourselves but lo we are already ministering spirits to others—entering by a subtle power of sympathy into their heart of hearts and giving them comfort, guidance even, almost without a word. I remember when the reality, the delicious sense of all this came to me, as a verification of old

> time teachings. . . . You are too young yet to *realise* what I mean and I should be sorry if you could—but some day you will enter into it all and call to mind what I have written and said so many times. . . .

It has often been said that Victoria Woodhull was chiefly responsible for giving Isabella delusions of grandeur, and she did tell her that 1876 would be a momentous year for her. But whatever Victoria told Isabella about her cosmic destiny and powers, it is clear that she was already prepared to believe great things about herself.[63]

The Hookers' passionate involvement in diverse but allied reforms has already been mentioned. Feminism naturally succeeded antislavery as their favorite crusade, and it is logical to look for clues to Isabella's mental state in that sphere. First, however, her grand illusion must be described. Isabella came to believe that she had been appointed as the savior of the world, a messiah whose mission was to inaugurate a world government with herself as vicegerent of Christ. The establishment of this world government, which she called the maternal (or matriarchal) government, would usher in the millennium, that hope of all the centuries since Christ. The maternal government would be visibly instituted and universally acknowledged. Isabella would rule personally, with the aid of a cabinet of relatives and neighbors. Her private Notebooks (now mostly lost or sequestered) described the general workings of this government down to provisional lists of cabinet officers. In addition to this cabinet, Isabella would have a number of women apostles who were being secretly prepared and tested by God until they could be exalted to his daughter's right hand. Signs and wonders would accompany their coming.

A curious characteristic of Isabella's jottings is the way in which the empyrean and everyday realms interpenetrated. One moment she would be noting down instructions for the servants, and the next communing with the late Horace Bushnell. Yet there was no violent shifting of gears. Instead, the Notebooks[64] reveal a confiding, dogged optimism. Throughout this mass of fussy, sometimes self-doubting, rumination are scattered touchingly honest glimpses into Isabella's character. She was conscientious enough to wonder if making John a cabinet officer was not nepotistical. Self-flattery was prominent, which might be expected of a messiah, a messiah who hoped to hang on to her good looks and who was very proud of her cleverness in household management. There was also self-pity, for she was married to a nearly bankrupt and very demoralized man, who felt obliged to tell her she was crazy. The Hookers' finances were in a sorry condition, and the cloud of the Tilton scandal was still lowering over their Nook Farm mansion when Isabella began the Notebooks in 1876.

Isabella's continuing misery over the loss of her mother was evidently a catalyst to her delusions. In the past she had often alluded to Harriet and felt a great burden of responsibility for her brothers. She felt she had a sacred trust with regard to their welfare and happiness and tried to look after them, a task made difficult by their odd personalities and their suspicion that Isabella was even odder than they. Considering how prominent and self-consciously apostolic the Beechers were, the idea that she had been entrusted with sacred obligations was hardly strange, nor was her belief that she would become a significant public figure. Some features of her private experience were, however, definitely pathological. It does no disservice to Mrs. Hooker to say this flatly, even while attempting to make historical sense of her congeries of doctrines and superstitions.

Her Notebooks allude to a brief vision she had at the age of thirteen, presumably some glimpse of her dead mother. It is not certain that she saw anything very distinct or that she understood it to be a vision at the time. It may have been an evanescent but powerful feeling or dream that was only promoted to the rank of a "vision" in retrospect. Her conversion to Spiritualism provided a language, a tradition, and a phenomenology by which she could give such experiences a temporal perspective and teleology.

The second of Isabella's visions occurred in Paris, where she had fled with John to escape the repercussions of the Tilton scandal. Her mother's spirit came to her there and abided with her as her own Angel of the Annunciation. Isabella typically applied Scriptural titles to persons who played important roles in her private world, and typically the implied parallels were skewed or inaccurate. When the Hookers returned to Hartford, Isabella made a "sanctum" of one of the upper rooms of their home and consecrated it to her mother. Greenery, ornamental grasses, and scarves were arranged to good effect under the guidance of the Hookers' son Thomas, who had died in infancy but had developed into an artist in the spirit world. Isabella had no portrait of her mother, so she substituted a copy of a Madonna given to her in happier days by her now estranged sister Harriet Stowe.

Many were the notables who graced that small Victorian retiring room. Josef Haydn usually accompanied Thomas Hooker, bearing greetings (in his quaint German accent) from other spirits who wanted to become Isabella's mentors. Joan of Arc was among them but, try as she might, Isabella had a terrible struggle to learn French, despite wearing silk stockings to retain the magnetic effluences requisite to brainwork. Judge John Edmonds was a frequent visitor, and he (with the late Samuel Bowles) scolded John Hooker, through Isabella's mouth, for his want of faith. Harriet Martineau volunteered her services as an instructor in political economy. All these great men and women thronged the sanctum in order to encourage Isabella and to instruct her in the many branches of knowledge she must master in order to govern the world wisely. Deceased theologians also entered these sacred precincts. Lyman Beecher renounced his Calvinism. Bushnell likewise recanted his theological errors and also begged Isabella's forgiveness for vilifying the women's rights movement. Lyman put his seal on Isabella's messianic appointment by materializing in her sanctum. Even Roxana Beecher, the wife who had overshadowed Isabella's own mother, came to support Isabella and pay her honor.

Catharine Beecher was a prominent figure in the Notebooks. Although Isabella tried to sway her to an open avowal of Spiritualism, Catharine maintained a scientific reserve on the subject, while conceding that she had witnessed many things she could not explain. Immediately after her death in 1878, Catharine began manifesting herself in the sanctum, not materially but through Isabella. Just as in life, she was peremptory and pushy, trying to seize control of Isabella when another spirit was talking through her. Isabella gave Catharine a tongue-lashing for attempting to encroach upon her "individuality" —an old complaint—and Catharine was humbled. She professed herself eager to be schooled in the higher knowledge of the realm she had just entered and repented of her former skepticism, begging Isabella for guidance.

Isabella's spirit friends did everything they could to sustain her, but just how far Isabella's husband and children believed her claims is hard to tell. At first John and Ned Hooker humored her in small matters. John dutifully recorded lawyerlike attestations in her Notebooks, declaring that he and Ned stood ready to test her prophecies. Her prediction of a murderous assault on their despised son-in-law, Eugene Burton, produced a major fiasco. John, having called in the Hartford plainclothes police in anticipation of the attack, was mortified. He was furious with Isabella, but when he accused her of monomania, she countered with a reminder of his own family history of insanity. Ned Hooker, meanwhile, proved more credulous. He had practiced tourniquet-tying and marksmanship the better to aid his brother-in-law when the ruffians broke in, and the utter failure of his mother's prophecy left him equable and optimistic.

While John Hooker fumed and licked his wounds—explaining the episode to the police must have required some ingenuity—Isabella took Ned aside. Encouraged by his filial attitude, she had decided to impart a great secret to him. Ned had been immaculately conceived and was consecrated as a divine healer and thaumaturge. His success in rallying a dying patient with mesmeric passes when homeopathic treatment had failed, seemed to him a confirmation of his mother's disclosure of his supernatural powers. This may have incited in him a desire to believe the rest of her revelations, but there are no documents from his own hand. In any case, he came very close to *folie à deux* in believing he was a divine physician, and perhaps his father was eventually added to the circle of believers in Isabella's superhuman powers, an instance of *folie à trois, quatre. . . .*

The immaculate conception of her son was a logical extension of Isabella's beliefs about her own identity. The Angel of the Annunciation had revealed a wondrous truth to her daughter, one almost too awesome to be borne. Isabella was the twin sister of Jesus Christ, the Comforter promised to his disciples (John 14:16–26). At first she resisted the idea, fearing it might be a Satanic ploy, but she convinced herself that God would not permit the spirit of her sainted mother to deceive and thereby destroy her. Isabella began calling herself the Comforter. She apparently differentiated between herself as the incarnate sister of Christ, and the Holy Spirit. Whether she believed herself, like Christ, to have preexisted since before the world, she did not say. The important fact to her was the government of the world by no mere woman but by the sister-Comforter, coequal with Christ. That Christ himself presided over his sister's elevation was verified by his materialization in her sanctum.

It must be plain by now that Mrs. Hooker believed herself to be in almost constant contact with another world and its inhabitants, and further, that she herself was divine. It may be asked whether she was hallucinating or behaving in a crazy manner. Hundreds of thousands—perhaps millions—of her contemporaries also thought they were in touch with disembodied spirits, but one would hesitate to say that every man or woman who chatted with Benjamin Franklin in a darkened parlor or who believed that a dead relative was thumping messages on a table, was insane. Receiving religious instruction from the spirits of Persian sages and noble savages, or even witnessing ectoplasmic manifestations were, and are, common enough experiences. Credulity is not insanity. As DeWette had observed in *Theodore*, dialogues with oneself are all too common.

The phenomena that surrounded Isabella Hooker took several forms. One of these was spirit-rappings. They generally occurred as gentle popping or snapping sounds in her parasol. It was her custom on hot days to clamber onto the tin roof below her dressing-room window. While she mused and dozed, she would feel slight raps, the usual mode of communication with her mother. Another means of communication with the spirit world was automatic writing. Isabella would inscribe messages from a control or succession of controls (as the communicating spirits were called). On rare occasions, Isabella's handwriting would give way to a strange hand, such as Samuel Bowles's, inditing messages of special import.

A third type of manifestation particularly congenial to Isabella was inspired utterance (also known as trance-speaking). Russel Wallace named her in his autobiography as a well-known trance-speaker, and she was evidently quite noted for her abilities in that line. A histrionic flair undoubtedly enhanced her "personations" of dead acquaintances. She considered herself especially proficient in representing female relatives, such as Kate Edes, William Beecher's wife. While they spoke through Isabella, she would make characteristic gestures and facial expressions to lend verisimilitude to the spirits' projections of themselves. Thomas Beecher was not, however, impressed with Isabella's rendition of his first wife and he received Livy's purported messages with coolness. But others of Isabella's bereaved friends derived consolation from these performances.[65]

Her ability to revive flagging hopes of immortality, her privity to the secrets of death and resurrection, and her genuine (if self-aggrandizing) solicitude for mourners, gave Isabella power and authority. After due allowance is made for her skills as an actress and speaker, the fact remains that her authority, however warped or pitiable it may seem, rested on a community of beliefs and hopes. Many of her supposed revelations and disclosures were simply ancient superstitions woven into current forms; others were more recent cults, such as Pyramidology (which lives on today).[66] All these occult ideas took on personal symbolic meaning in the closely woven fabric of Isabella's life and thoughts. Any dabbler in the occult—and Nook Farm apparently abounded with them—might look to Pyramidology for arcane knowledge. But the "secrets" of the pyramids took on special significance when Isabella decided to make over one of her mother's cloaks. An heirloom of doubtful value was then transformed by a local seamstress into a "coat of many colors," emblematic of Joseph, the biblical type of whom Isabella was the antitype. But this is a rather outré example.

Of greater importance, ultimately, were the kinds of questions which absorbed every earnest Christian or lapsed Christian. Many of these subjects have been touched upon already: the nature of the change at death, the condition of the blessed and their communion with the living, the existence and activity of beneficent and evil spirits, the works of Satan and the fallen angels, future retribution versus future probation, paranormal experiences, and the expansion of extra-ecclesiastical religious life.

Another belief, shared by Catharine and Harriet, may be added to these: the superiority of women as religious teachers. Further, and here Harriet went beyond Catharine, there was the revival of a female prophetic tradition. Isabella stated her belief in the general superiority of women in her 1869 correspondence with John Stuart Mill on the "comparative endowment of the sexes":

> Of late I have been impressed more and more with the closer likeness to the divine nature which woman seems to bear, in that she is more sensibly, if not more truly, a creator than man is. . . . What father can say, "Thou art *my* child," as a mother can?—and through what channels does he count the life-beat of his child as his own? And to my mind there is more sense of power in this sense of motherhood than in all things else; that power we all reach after by virtue of our divine ancestry. To create is to live; to express our own beings through another and another is everlasting youth; and to mould, guide, and control this offshoot of our being, itself an independent power,—this is the glory of existence, its very most supreme delight. To my conception a mother is the only being in this world who thus approximates the divine nature. So feeble in comparison is the father's relation to her child, so lost in her higher and diviner relation, that it is within the experience of many a mother, whether recognized by herself or not, that from the moment of blessed annunciation to heavenly birth, she, like the Virgin of old, has known no father to her child save the Holy Ghost.

Anticipating Mill's rejection of such a doctrine, Mrs. Hooker protested that she wrote not out of spiritual pride but from "an inordinate love of justice." She went on to announce that women had a glorious future: "cleaving the future, I see such honor and power coming to woman as makes me tremble."[67]

In this letter of 1869 are plainly forecast the outlines of Isabella's messianic vision and her conviction of Ned's immaculate conception (a doctrine she did not understand in the Catholic sense). But there is little there to distinguish her conceptions of divine motherhood from Harriet's published opinion. What made the difference was, as James Beecher declared, an inherited predisposition to insanity:

> I think sister Belle would have done far better to come here this winter than to be browsing around Brooklyn and Elmira where she will only make a nuisance of herself. She might have my pulpit every Sunday and I am very sure would attract quite an audience. She could explain her spiritual mysteries to Mr. Dibbles and her higher life and womans rights to Mr. Nelson Kelly.

James was sure that his wife would be equally amused at the mental image of the elegant Mrs. Hooker propounding her doctrines to the farouche woodsmen of Ulster County, New York. But he went on to attribute her strangeness and perversity to a tainted heredity:

> I am sure that there runs a streak of insanity in our mothers three children—or rather a monomania, assuming diverse forms. I recognise it in Tom and myself. The only advantage I have is in being absolutely conscious of the fact. Tom is partially so. Belle is absolutely unconscious and is therefore the craziest of the three. However she is almost sixty. If she got well, she couldnt do much good, and if she grows worse, she cannot do much harm—and a very few years will clear us all out, and in a dozen years or so if any body should ask who were those Beechers any how, there will be nobody able to answer the question.

In this outbreak of bitterness from one who was to succumb to madness himself, there are clear indications of what made Isabella's delusion so Beecherish. There was the urgent sense of mission, a task of global dimensions; the feeling that, as with Wesley, the world was one's parish; the frequent want of proportion between ends perceived and means employed; and the insistence on mounting a pulpit to proclaim the good news. There were, after all, only a few steps between the beliefs espoused by the community of faith in which Isabella was reared and her own peculiar doctrines. What was indisputably bizarre about her was her self-deification, but that which was idiosyncratic or fanatical in her, found less alarming but persistent expression in her brothers and sisters, with the possible exception of Henry and Thomas.[68]

Charles had many entreating talks with Isabella. She described one such discussion to her daughter Mary, indicating why Charles's advice carried no weight with her:

> Uncle Charles who left here Friday after a few days visit at the Stowes with his dear sweet wife, told me he was looking daily for the coming of Christ—and though cautioning me kindly against spiritualism as of the devil probably, I found in all our conversation that our views were very similar as to the interpretations of the Bible and life generally. And when he told me he was sure there was a conspiracy against Henry—he being utterly innocent, *which was of the devil surely*, my confidence in his judgment of Spiritualism was weakened—especially as he acknowledged the phenomena to be largely true.

If Charles had glanced over his sister's Notebooks and discovered her references to Christ's materialization, he would have been shocked beyond expression. He could readily believe that his brother Edward had received divine illuminations or that his sister Harriet had written *Uncle Tom* under divine inspiration. Isabella's experiences were quite another matter. Even without divulging the secret of her messiahship, she managed to convey to Charles enough of her private beliefs to convince him she was putting her soul into mortal danger. In fact, his conversations with her in 1877 probably contributed to the urgent warnings of *Spiritual Manifestations*.[69]

When Charles's book appeared, Thomas gave it a favorable review in the *Independent*. As early as 1872, and possibly before, Thomas endorsed a view of Spiritualism similar to Charles's, though less favorable and credulous. In a sermon at the Elmira Opera House, Thomas told his congregation that he had studied the phenomena for twenty years

> until the whole habit of my mind has been changed in this regard. Instead of being surprised to hear that there are spiritual manifestations abounding throughout the land, I am daily more and more surprised and grateful that as yet I have been able to keep them out of my own house and out of my own body. . . . There is very little doubt in my mind that the clamor and confusion and strife of opinion of these days are to be attributed largely to spiritual influences.

Like Charles and Harriet, he insisted that Spiritualism had no revelations worthy of superceding the Bible. The value of Spiritualism lay in converting atheists back to supernaturalism, by appealing to their empirical side. Such teachings as purported to come down from the Summerland were nothing but "pious truisms—goody slush!" The virtue of his brother's book, "repulsive title" notwithstanding, was its elevation of the subject above the "flavorous froth of popular thought."[70]

These views, needless to say, did not deflect Isabella from her course. She and John remained Spiritualists to the end. What is more interesting and, moreover, of historical significance, is her family's perseverance in the same quest. Harriet, for all her public cautions against Spiritualistic impostures, continued to seek out mediums and to construct new proofs of immortality and divine forgiveness. In 1884 she publicly endorsed Swedenborgianism in these words:

> The thinking religious mind of New England has in many directions received precious helps from the mind of Swedenborg, and whoever has learned to see this spiritual teaching in the events of this present life has gained a key that unlocks many a mystery and opens many a treasure of consolation and hope.

As for Isabella's mediumship, Harriet took comfort from the possibility that her sister was in touch with Fred Stowe, whose fate his parents could never learn:

> I wish dear sister you would do me one other favor. Copy and send to me the supposed communication from my poor Fred—also poor Annie. Mr. Stowe wants to see them and I want to see them again. I committed Fred to my Savior, who knows all—who lives to save and goeth after that which is lost until *he find it*.

Frances Beecher also sought help from Isabella and her medium friends when James's insanity appeared hopeless. Despite Isabella's exertions and assurances of divine healing influences, Frankie Beecher went away convinced that there was nothing in Spiritualism for her and her suffering husband.[71]

Even Edward Beecher, who had once named Spiritualism as one of the ancient errors revived by the enemy of man in the last days, turned to spirit communications in his old age. He and his wife sat with a number of mediums, usually in company with Isabella and John Hooker. There is preserved an artifact of the Spiritualistic investigations of Edward's wife: a letter purporting to come from Anna Jones, her sister and lifelong companion. When Mrs. Beecher was discovered to have inoperable cancer and her physicians had pronounced her case fatal, Edward engaged the services of "an educated clairvoyant who has brought wonderful results in desperate cases."

The identity of this healer is uncertain, but if a surmise may be permitted, she was probably Voice Adams, the young woman they later adopted. If so, while she brought Mrs. Beecher relief from pain, she also disrupted family ties. Edward's relatives were convinced that Voice had insinuated herself into an afflicted circle and imposed upon two elderly people who grew more confused and insecure as their faculties waned. Charles's wife, recalling the time before Voice had come into their midst, protested to Edward's son:

> Well I wrote down what I saw and felt and sent it yesterday to your mother—no allusion was made to any *shadow* between us—and Voice, "Oh no we never mention her." Mary Blood and I have grieved ourselves ill over the strange change in your parents, but 'tis a temporary hallucination. When the soul lets down the bars of the spirit world with out placing the Holy Spirit to keep watch and ward—lying spirits in the body or out can forge the names of loved ones, cousin Ann [Anna Jones] for instance Uncle Henry (who sends wonderful letters which your dear mother accepts as genuine). . . .[72]

After Thomas Beecher died, his wife Julia was certain he still lingered in his old home. She kept his favorite chair empty, in case his spirit should seek out its familiar places. When attending church, she felt that "of all the places Tom would be likely to visit—there—with them with all his people he must be, and I almost but not quite see him." Julia joined the Society for Psychical Research, begged her friends for true ghost stories, and craved but never received a communication from her husband.[73]

Isabella's messianic fervor seems to have glimmered away. The evidence is inconclusive, but she did write to her surviving daughter in terms suggesting that her elevation was to be postponed until she departed earth. Isabella still expected to have "young apostles" and, "whatever my part in this revelation," she believed that "the bald statements of ultra Calvinism and modified Calvinism in all their hideousness" would give way to a "conception of the true heart of God." The spectacle of the Fox sisters recanting and then unrecanting their Spiritualism moved her very little, for "it is not worth while to write about disagreeable things." She welcomed the rise of Christian Science as a long-overdue development: "nearly all the women I meet are more or less interested in some form of spiritual healing." Nevertheless, she deplored Mrs. Eddy's disloyalty to her Spiritualist preceptors and expressed outrage at her claims to be a messiah.[74]

The Hookers celebrated the twenty-seventh day of each month as a worldwide communion day of the saints, inviting any spirit to speak through them. They remained in touch with Russel Wallace and other prominent Spiritualists who had kept the faith despite ridicule and exposures of fraudulent mediums. They contributed liberally to churches of all denominations, including the Roman Catholic. John compiled a directory of "Spirit Friends" numbering over 450, with whom the Hookers had communicated—guides like Lincoln, Swedenborg, Isabella of Spain, Frederick Douglass, Thomas Arnold, Theodore and Angelina Grimké Weld—in short, all the figures of recent and remote history who had dedicated themselves to religious liberty and human betterment.[75]

Hoxie Fairchild has spoken in a related context of "Protestant Christianity in a more or less delightfully phosphorescent state of decay." Perhaps Isabella Hooker's belief that the millennium would begin in Hartford, Connecticut, is an illustration of Fairchild's hostile commentary on the degradation of Protestant dogma and religious sensibility in the nineteenth century. Even when she moderated her talk of making all things new by a single stroke and contented herself with reconnoitering the undiscovered country, her ideas and activities are bound to appear outlandish. They had always appeared so to Henry. Of what use was a labored, intricate anthropology or eschatology to a preacher who pronounced himself "a cordial Christian evolutionist"? He could not be expected to agonize over God's decrees when he believed, and preached, that "Christ is only God made easy."

To those who believe that theology is an important human enterprise, Henry Ward Beecher's cheerful way of resolving difficult questions might seem evasive, but it was, after all, his Liberal Orthodoxy which prevailed. It is not accurate—nor would it be just, however—to set his experience over against that of his brothers and sisters and to conclude that their involvement with Spiritualism evidences the moribund state of evangelical Protestantism.[76]

That Spiritualism was a cul de sac is undeniable. The movement survives today, of course, but under decidedly sectarian auspices.

Occultism has burgeoned again, but without accessions from the mainstream churches. What is important about the Spiritualism of the Beechers' day is the way it reached down to tap so many cultural roots, and the seriousness with which the Beechers and like-minded people approached the subject. Painful bereavement, on the one hand, and a desperate hunger for empirical verification of immortality, on the other, animated their inquiries and undoubtedly colored their conclusions. They wanted to be certain that their loved ones lived on in spirit but, even more, that they were still a family with unsevered ties and persevering love. It was all this, and something more. After all, Henry had suffered bereavements as crushing as his brothers and sisters had, but he did not become a Spiritualist or even explore the subject. Neither did Thomas require Spiritualism to assure him that Livy had conquered death and lived in the presence of Christ.

Healing, both physical and emotional, as Catharine and Isabella's experiences show, was another attraction of the occult sciences. Suffering was not something to be borne stoically as long as new aids were available in mesmerism and mental cures. When extraordinary healers were found among the Spiritualists, they and their patients could point to the very great healing emphasis of the Gospels. It is, however, significant, that none of the Beecher men tried to incorporate healing arts into their ministry. Another facet of Spiritualism which appealed to the Hookers but seemed inane to the rest of the Beechers was its social and political optimism and perfectionism.

Ultimately, the Beechers were drawn to Spiritualism for religious reasons. They saw it as a much-needed force prevailing against scientific materialism and religious indifference. It gave added force to supernaturalism in general and, specifically, to the belief in angels and demons. Spiritualism, in its own way, bolstered the Beechers' inherited belief in the soul's activity in behalf of its salvation, and also seemed to reassert God's miraculous intervention in the orderly and wonderful world of his creation, a creation he loved and labored for. The Beechers were searching for new theological bearings, and whatever their individual differences, they were certain of one thing: that evangelical Protestantism needed new views of the character of God and of the endowments and possibilities of his creatures.

11 THE FAMILY OF GOD

Despite striking divergences in the Beechers' religious thought, which fall into the three rather distinct patterns that emerged from their individual religious experience, there is also a strong family resemblance in their theology. Charles Beecher once employed a simile in speaking of Jonathan Edwards which applies equally well to the Beechers:

> A man's theological system is like an old hereditary mansion;—taken as a whole it may be gloomy, ruinous, forbidding. Yet there may be a room or two of Southern aspect, in which the man lives. Into the ghostly walks, and corridors and haunted chambers, and appalling dungeons, he may never, or seldom enter. . . . As a man does not build the Ancestral Castle which he inhabits, so Edwards did not make the ecclesiastical and theological scheme in which he sojourned. On the contrary he was a progressive. He was intent on fitting up a new wing;—or a new Conservatory.

This was his reflection upon Calvinistic theology when he discussed it in 1881 with Oliver Wendell Holmes, who was even less at home in the tradition than Charles.

If the religion of Lyman Beecher was an old and commodious house, its Calvinistic framework had been obscured by the time his children set to work altering and refitting it for their habitation. New Haven Theology, despite its claims to restating Calvinism in modern terms, was anti-Calvinistic in its implications. Edward and Charles Beecher, like their father, devoted their lives to trying to conserve vital elements of evangelical theology and assumed that because their intent was conservative, their results were too. They never felt comfortable in the presence of Calvinism. Charles even tried to represent Edwards as a sojourner in Calvinism rather than its defender.[1]

In this final chapter I shall examine the Beechers' doctrines of God and human nature, always bearing in mind that the religious experiences earlier described were forces for change as powerful as any explicit doctrinal considerations. Their ideas, while not as systematic or as searching as those of Hopkins and Edwards, gained coherence and dignity from being rooted in a long cultural and intellectual heritage, and they gained authority by appealing to and interpreting the hopes and desires of millions of men and women. These desires and hopes, as well as the fearful legacy of Reformed belief, found expression in popular art, fiction, poetry, and hymnody, and in the multiplication of sects. Spiritualism was but one expression of changing religious beliefs. As I have tried to show, the impulses that led intelligent people to enter the Spiritualist ranks were mixed. Acute spiritual unrest was sometimes combined with scientific curiosity; mere inquisitiveness prompted some, while fanaticism urged others on; maternal anxieties moved still others, who might also be morbid or superstitious; the avowed skeptic was often a sentimentalist; the materialist was often afraid to jettison supernaturalism completely.

The phrase "religious difficulties" has recurred throughout this study with such variants as "theological problems" and "doctrinal difficulties." Although religion and theology are not the same thing, the problems the Beechers wrestled with throughout their lives are perennial problems of belief to the skeptical, the pietistic, or the formally theological mind, and their problems of faith often found theological expression. It will be well to state the most important of these problems at the outset, without attempting to show that one flows from or generates another in any precise, logical order. They all have to do with vindicating God's ways to man, with explaining the paradoxes of Christian revelation in rational terms.

(1) Theodicy attempts to account for the existence of moral evil, specifically man's sinfulness, in a benevolent divine economy. (2) The question of just desert takes the form of asking why men's lots differ, why the wicked often seem to flourish while the good and the holy suffer. Doctrinally speaking, it involves examination of election and reprobation. (3) Another issue is the general one of the ethical content and character of divine law. (4) There is also the problem of anthropomorphism, the extent to which man is justified in interpreting God in human terms. (5) The last of these questions concerns the way of salvation. What are the respective roles of God and man, and how far may man be said to be active in his own behalf?

The Beechers did not give these five problems equal attention, nor were they equally troubled or stimulated by all of them. For Edward Beecher, as we have seen, the first question assumed prominence in his major writings, while the others were clustered around it. His father, on the other hand, concerned himself almost exclusively with the last, a pattern his daughter Catharine followed. Those members of the family most attracted by Spiritualism were beset by deep doubts about the second of these questions.

With these five points in mind, we can begin examining Lyman Beecher's views of God and man. Beecher was not a powerful systematic thinker, although Frank Hugh Foster, after he had lost faith in New England Theology himself, credited him with being "one of the most incisive and clear thinkers" of that school, and another historian devoted a study to systematizing his thought, with more success than Beecher himself had enjoyed. Beecher's mind gave out before he could collect and revise his sermons and lectures, and in any event, few if any Congregationalists were producing bodies of divinity by that time, no matter how assiduous their Presbyterian counterparts were in that line of endeavor. Nevertheless, his *Views in Theology*, though published under duress and with a view to propitiating his opponents, provides ample material when examined in conjunction with his published *Works* and his manuscript "Theological Lectures." His letters to his children also set out his theology and anthropology in vivid language.[2]

His ideas about God were much like Timothy Dwight's and Nathaniel Taylor's. One theme was set before the Christian and the sinner alike: the moral government of God. Dwight held the nature of God to be an abstruse question beyond profitable discussion, although he was willing enough to tell Arians, Sabellians, and Socinians that their anti-Trinitarian views were unscriptural. As for the character of God, Dwight showed as little inclination to dwell on that subject. The one fact for men to understand and celebrate was that God ruled creation. "This Glorious and Perfect Being, as the Creator, Preserver, and Benefactor, of the Universe, is, of the most absoute right, the Ruler of the Work which He has made, and the Lawgiver of all his moral creatures." The titles Dwight gave to God were primarily political or judicial; even when he called God Father, Dwight as often as not was thinking of God's family as a miniature constitutional monarchy. God was not an Oriental despot but a deity fit for republicans, and neither was he blind necessity. Even so, Dwight's depiction of God in heaven stressed his transcendence and impassibility: "Independent of all possible beings and events, he sits at the head of this Universe, unchanged, and incapable of change, amid all the successions, tossings, and tumults, by which it is agitated. When empires are overthrown, or Angels fall; when Suns are extinguished, and Systems return to their original nothing; he is equally impassive and unmoved as when sparrows expire, or the hairs fall from our heads. . . . Nothing can frustrate his designs, and nothing disappoint, or vary, his purposes." Such a God, far from being unamiable to his subjects, was admirable in his fixity of purpose and unalterable justice. While to believers he appeared as benevolence itself, to sinners, however, this was "a character of God inconceivably awful."

Dwight had no answer to the problem of moral evil. If God was the epitome of benevolence, and if he ruled with unswerving justice and boundless mercy, why did he permit evil to exist? "The truth is," Dwight confessed, "the subject of Moral Evil is too extensive, and too mysterious, to be comprehended by our Understanding. . . . Where knowledge is unattainable, it is both our duty and interest to trust humbly and submissively to the instructions of Him, who is THE ONLY WISE." The nearest Dwight could come to explaining why man, who had been created virtuous, had fallen from grace and become wicked, was to offer his own version of the fortunate Fall. The felicity of Adam was as nothing compared to that to be enjoyed by his descendants "after the Mediatorial Kingdom is finished." For all their God-given powers of reasoning, men were still limited in their views of his ends and purposes. "With respect to the subject in hand," Dwight said of moral evil, "*we* are emmets; and take our surveys from the top of a mole-hill."[3]

Lyman Beecher, like his teacher, wanted to convince men that their Ruler was a beneficent deity. "Ever since the Fall," he told an audience of Cincinnati workingmen, "the fear of God has usurped the place of filial confidence, and has been excessive. . . . In all false religions, fear has ever been the dominant principle of worship, and rage and cruelty the principles to be appeased." This was not so in Christianity, evangelical Christianity in particular. God was not a hideous idol demanding sacrifices. He was a moral governor who had published his gospel "*to reassure his ruined guilty creatures of his unextinguished kindness FOR THEM, and to bring them back, reconciled and forgiven, to his fellowship and favor.*" Such was Beecher's answer to the "infidel" argument that the Christian God was no better than a heathen fiend.

Yet he also warned that it was wrong to "stop the mighty thunderings and the voice of the trumpet, and array with smiles the face of Heaven alike upon the righteous and the wicked." Too genial a view of God was fatal. His friend Nathaniel Taylor agreed that such a view was dishonorable to God. Only a God who abhors sin can be truly benevolent. When, "instead of viewing him in the character of a just and righteous Sovereign, we are to render him in no other relation than that of a benignant, tender parent," God emerged as a being "who so delights in the happiness of his family, that to promote it he will sacrifice all that can be called law, justice, and equity." Who would desire a God who loved not wisely, but too well?

Moreover, erroneous ideas of God would lull sinners into false security. Beecher's second wife understood this and wept bitterly over her parents' blindness:

> My Father thinks there is no difficulty at all in understanding the scriptures and he reduces every passage to suit his moderate views. He has no doubt he shall be saved because he always has and intends to do the best he can and "Christ will do the rest"—And truly if a man might build upon morality [alone], none could with a better pretext than he, for I have often thot in his temperate, amiable, self denying habits he is a reproach to those who profess to be actuated by better principles. By great desease, bodily suffering and discouragement my Mother is brought to an indifferency of feeling to everything in this world or the next. She has little or no concern for her salvation "because God is good" and "she has suffered exceedingly in this world for sin but has not merited eternal displeasure." She has been apparently many times on the verge of eternity and felt calm and undismayed and therefore she thinks she always shall—Oh, who shall bring them from their error or rescue them from remediless ruin?

A correct view, unlike that of Dr. and Mrs. Porter, would have balanced the wrathful and the tender aspects of God. Sinners who would not heed his gracious invitations must be driven to his shelter. Beecher's efforts to magnify God's amiability without compromising his just anger amused Unitarian Boston. Shops offered for sale a two-headed caricature of Beecher, with one aspect beaming and paternal while the other glowered ferociously amidst lightning bolts. A fairer representation of his image of God was his sermon on Niagara Falls. Niagara's thunderings called to mind the omnipotence of God, and its cataracts were an emblem of "his indignation which shall beat upon the wicked in the gulf below the eternal pit." The thick mist represented "the smoke of their torments," while "nothing but the warbling of unearthly voices seems necessary to make one feel that hell and destruction is uncovered before him." But in the midst of these images of horror and destruction God caused a rainbow to shine, the "brilliant type of mercy."[4]

This same omnipotent God whose hatred of sin was absolute had created the universe with evil in it. Nettleton's explanation of this puzzling fact was deceptively simple: "If the soul be innocent, it can be redeemed from nothing." This is a different response from Dwight's sturdy assertion of the fortunate Fall, different in bluntly affirming a paradox: belief in redemption requires the recognition that the God who saves from sin has permitted that very sin to exist and may indeed be its actual author. As Frances M. Young has said, atonement "proclaims the conquest of evil" and "asserts the power of God over evil," while theodicy, on the other hand, "seeks to explain its existence" and "regards evil as a threat either to God's goodness or his sovereignty."

Lyman Beecher never doubted God's goodness, and he tended to see the existence of moral evil from a purely governmental viewpoint. So he explained it to his theological students, in a moving vindication of God's government. He painted a picture of the intelligent universe arrayed to decide the question. Should God create man and the angels with free will and thus bring into being the conditions that would produce sinfulness? As the students sat spellbound, their teacher, "as if standing in the place of the Creator himself, and putting the question to vote, shall I create or not create?" "made the shout go up as the voice of ten thousand times ten thousand, *create! create!*" As Beecher's colleague recalled the scene, "no man who heard that lecture could help thanking God that He had decided it for him by making him a free agent, and a fit subject of just that government of law and grace which God is administering over our world." When pressed by objections to his teachings on human depravity, Beecher brushed aside protests against God's justice and rectitude as the reflex of obstinate ingratitude. "Some cry out 'mysterious! mysterious!' because God has not so created us that we can not make mistakes. There is no mystery about it. As well ask why God has not created tallow candles to light up the universe."[5]

The substance of this particular solution to the problem of moral evil was not novel in its thesis that genuine free agency made man liable to sin. It was not even the exclusive hallmark of New Haven Theology. But New Haven Theology carried two further implications.

In the first place, it made sin exclusively the product of man's moral activity. This, as Edward Beecher charged, could have highly pessimistic implications about the possession of free will. In the second place, while removing any trace of belief that God is the author of sin, it infringed upon his omnipotence by suggesting that he was powerless to prevent it. Taylor was less cautious than Lyman Beecher in admitting as much:

> In the assertion that *it may be* impossible that God should prevent all sin in a moral system, I refer merely to an impossibility which may exist in the nature of things, and of course not to the want of any conceivable power in God; to an impossibility to which power bears no relation, and with which it has no concern.

The distinction Taylor drew was unconvincing to his critics, who held that nothing was impossible for God, but his more general proposition about moral agency was the keynote of Beecher's theology. Both men reiterated their belief that God saw fit to rule according to morality and reason. The exertion of sheer physical power, or resort to physical coercion, was unthinkable in a moral governor:

> Every subject of such a kingdom must be a free agent; i.e., he must possess the power to sin, and to continue to sin, in defiance of all influence from truth and motives—from the spirit and power of God, and go on in sin. . . . God knows, as does every wise human legislator, that by securing the loyalty of one, or of a few, he may occasion the hopeless and eternal rebellion of many.

Taylor and Beecher saw no alternative to New Haven doctrine, for if they were to concede that God decreed sin as the means to achieve the greatest good, they must admit that God prefers some of his creatures to hate him. Under Taylor's system, by contrast, God knows that some of his creatures will rebel and that many will misuse their freedom. Even though he is grieved by that knowledge, he knows that freedom is the best gift for his creatures. Nettleton's argument that God makes men sinful in order that he may rescue some and thus uphold his own free sovereignty, seemed folly to Taylor:

> It is true indeed that God could never have redeemed from sin if there had been no sin. But what kind of mercy is that which produces evil merely for the sake of putting an end to it? Does a kind father push his children into a pit, or down a precipice, for the sake of showing how merciful he can be in bringing deliverance and in healing their bones? Does a benevolent God design,

> and so order his providence, that our whole race shall fall into the gulf of sin and ruin, for the sake of showing his mercy in their rescue. . . ? Or does it better accord with God's character to suppose, that when men have freely plunged themselves into this ruin, against his law and against his will, God *then* comes in the glory of his mercy to redeem and save?[6]

In revising the doctrine of depravity, the New Haven divines were forced to grapple with the doctrine of decrees, that is, predestination (foreordination) and election. Dwight advised ministers not to preach decrees often, for "in the ardour of investigation, disputants will, of course, be in danger of asserting many things, which are neither satisfactorily evinced, maturely considered, nor well understood, by themselves." No single subject had provoked more futile controversy. The carnal heart was, of course, averse to the doctrine, but Dwight affirmed that the rational mind likewise rejected its pagan connotations. He stated the doctrine as best he could: "God's foreknowledge of voluntary actions does in no respect lessen, or affect, their freedom; although it renders their future existence absolutely certain."

If this appears a rather obvious phraseology, it must be remembered against whom he was contending. Taylor followed Dwight's lead in ascribing "heathen origin" and "heathen import" to the words *decree* and *predestination.* To illustrate the dangers of misapplying the word *predestinate*, he construed Romans 8:29 to mean a "moral conformity to Christ, a conception inconsistent with the heathen notion of *destiny*." Because of the semantic and philosophical drawbacks to *decrees*, Taylor replaced the term with his own, "the providential purposes of God," a phrase stressing a moral government of free agents. The import of New Haven Theology was, of course, averse to the Emmonsite doctrine of direct divine efficiency. No better expression of the New Haven position on decrees can be found than this of Beecher's:

> *THE DECREES OF GOD are His determination to create a universe of free agents, to exist forever under the perfect laws of his moral government, perfectly administered; for the gratification and manifestation of his benevolence, for the perfect enjoyment of all his obedient subjects; with all that is implied therein, and all the consequences foreseen.*[7]

One looks in vain in either Beecher's or Taylor's works for a fully developed Christology, for their exclusive interest was the moral government of God. New England Theology, by contrast, had not neglected the offices, miracles, and gospel of Christ. Christ as mediator received due worship and supplication because he had made a covenant with God whereby he became priest and prophet. Soteriology was an important aspect of New England Theology, as it had been of the earlier Covenant theology. According to New England Theology, his Atonement served a "governmental" purpose: that is, its primary effect was not to satisfy justice by sacrificing an innocent Christ in place of guilty man, but rather to demonstrate God's hatred of sin and his love for his creatures. New Haven Theology bypassed this characteristic New England doctrine and contented itself with saying of Christ, as Taylor did, that he was "A JUST GOD, AND YET A SAVIOUR." Although Beecher, while a student, had composed a brief life of Christ, he did not make such themes prominent in his preaching. In the following pages I shall explore the ways in which the Beechers adjusted their ideas of God, which often resulted in elevating the role of Christ.[8]

It is important to distinguish between two developments that are often confused under the heading of "Christocentric liberalism." On the one hand, there is the tendency, given expression in Channing's sermons, to celebrate the parental character of God. Although this was (and is) commonly called the "fatherhood of God," it was not unusual to ascribe maternity to God as well. On the other hand, there was the tendency toward christomonism, that is, making Jesus Christ the sole object of devotion and prayer. Frequently associated with these two developments was an increasing readiness to treat man's filial relation to the deity as in itself divine. This last trend may be illustrated by the once popular distinction between Unitarianism and Universalism: the one held that man is too good to be condemned by God, while the other argued that God is too good to condemn man.[9]

The relationship between the Beechers' understanding of God and man, and their broader theological departures, was dynamic. In some instances a changed conception of God's character or man's capacities necessitated adjustment of other doctrines; and, in other cases, the reverse was true. The previous chapter has shown the movement among Spiritualists toward a meliorist view of human nature, and with it a powerful upsurge in the popularity of probationary doctrines of the future life. Human character, as it developed on earth, was far from wicked. And though it was, as most Spiritualists agreed, limited and flawed, the soul would pass on to higher stages, cheered and speeded by loving spirits whose chief end was to guide it on its journey home. God was similarly clothed in endearing associations; but he was, on the whole, a rather vague benignity, made more remote at the same time that he was less menacing. Spiritualism was nothing if not humanitarian and optimistic, but it failed to make a special place for Christ and can by no means be called Christocentric. Thus, while the Beechers were attracted by Spiritualistic beliefs and practices, they did not find there compelling images of the God they continued to worship.

Abandonment of their father's idea of God included rejection of his way of talking about God. The style of theologizing favored by New England Theologians, and their father's school in particular, was parodied by Henry in the person of a Southern commentator:

> The fact is, there is too much brain here in New England. Every body is racing and chasing after causes. I believe your people think they have the responsibility of the universe on their shoulders. When the Bible said, "Canst thou find out the Almighty to perfection?" there were no Yankees about. Since then, about five hundred ministers in this very New England think they have done it. . . . Did you hear that young sprout preach, last Sunday afternoon, fresh from New Haven? He was amazingly precocious. He went on glibly unfolding moral government. "God *must* do this," and "God, from the nature of things, *cannot* do that." There was not a thing about the Infinite and Eternal which he did not fancy himself entirely familiar with!

Charles also thought that theology too often got in the way of understanding God. "God is not wont to philosophize about himself in the Bible. He does not chiefly use the third person. He does not say, 'Deity cannot do this,' and 'Deity cannot do that.' There is no such cold word in the Bible as Deity." Scholasticism in theology destroyed the living word, Charles said, making a dried specimen out of the flower of divine truth. What, then, was the ground of belief for a theologian, and how best could he communicate truth to the mass of believers?[10]

The Beechers were not alone among liberal evangelicals in questioning the validity of traditional methods of setting forth doctrines. Edwards Amasa Park addressed himself to the subject in 1839 in an essay called "Duties of a Theologian," which is worth considering here. In the first place, Park argued that the theologian should take precedence over the ordinary minister because the duties "of a pastor and preacher result and may be inferred from" those of the theologian. "To only three or four high-aiming intellects in as many ages has it been given of God to rise above the confiding assent of the vulgar, and to look with naked eye upon the mysteries of doctrine," said Park, discriminating between the leading minds—the Origens and Jeromes—and ordinary "system-makers and commentators." But such master intellects must not be blindly reverenced, for all had written as controversialists; and "when a man theorizes in view of an exigency, he is inclined to meet that exigency whether he meet the truth or not."

Of the same character were opinions which reflected personal idiosyncrasies and temperamental imbalances. Thus, those who defended Augustine's doctrine of Original Sin must recollect "the infelicities of his early life" which engendered "those ungracious conclusions," showing "how unsafe it is to seize at his results without examining his singular processes." And so with modern theologians:

> One divine has a phlegmatic temperament and loves to insist on human passivity; another has a sanguine temperament and loves to insist on human action and freedom; a third has a melancholic temperament and is fascinated with the inexplicable mysteries of God's moral system; a fourth has a bilious temperament and loves to combine the passive and the active, fore-knowledge and free-will.

The failure to recognize the origins and limitations of a "phlegmatic theology" or a "bilious" one had led, on the one hand, to terrible persecutions and, on the other, to the ascendancy of certain ideas to the exclusion of others. Hence Augustine's sway. Whatever his strengths in exposing the turpitude and concupiscence of human nature, "we can not but wish that in overpowering the intellect and taking the conscience by storm, he had also consulted the gentler and tenderer sensibilities, and given a more cheerful coloring to the messages of peace and love." Like Augustine, Calvin had put the stamp of his own stern personality on his doctrines, evincing none of "the mildness of Him, whose appropriate act it was to take little children into his arms and bless them."[11]

As for Jonathan Edwards, even those "ambitious to be called by his name" must acknowledge that "his failing was in too exclusive a regard to one portion of our sensibilities. He seemed to live apart from many of the innocent cravings and sympathies of his race." And if his grasp of human nature was defective, his depiction of the Creator was equally harsh and melancholy:

> He rehearsed the threatenings of his sovereign as if he had some

> peculiar right, and indeed he had, to tell on whom they would fall. He stood in the pulpit with a head unmoved and a still hand, and what he had written he had written. But his hearers looked up, and the tears stole down their cheeks, and they shook like aspen-leaves, and on some occasions screamed aloud.

It was not merely the congregations who shuddered and sobbed over Edwards's God. Park also recalled the fellow minister who was so scandalized that he yanked on Edwards's robe and cried, "Mr. Edwards! Mr. Edwards! is not God a merciful being,–is he not merciful?" Such a vision of the Creator was shocking to the feelings of Park and many of his generation. Charles Beecher pitied Edwards and suggested that he had been duped by Satan. "Not the worst of men deluded but the best . . . painfully misinformed concerning their best Friend!" So Beecher characterized the theology of Edwards's contemporaries and disciples. God could not be the monster of Edwards's depiction:

> Edwards had days which he devoted (with tears) to meditation on the sufferrings of the lost. But my sympathies are more moved toward that unhappy Being who holds the spider by a thread over the burning gulf, than toward the spider, for the latter is but an insect and his pains finite,--but the former? His misfortune (if I may say so) is infinite.

Park declared that Edwards's successors must not relinquish their claims to the spirituality and intellectual power that pervaded his writings, but they must supply his esthetic deficiencies and soften his "too great austerity." It was past time for theologians to consider all the worthy needs and capacities of humankind and to appeal to faculties other than the conscience:

> We need and crave a theology, as sacred and spiritual as his, and moreover one that we can take with us into the flower-garden, and to the top of some goodly hill, and in a sail over a tasteful lake, and into the saloons of music, and to the galleries of the painter and the sculptor, and to the repasts of social joy, and to all those humanizing scenes where virtue holds her sway not merely as that generic and abstract duty of a "love to being in general," but also the more familiar grace of a love to some beings in particular.

Edwards had ably fulfilled the duty of minute analysis and creative synthesis, but "another duty of a theologian is to associate his doctrines more intimately with what is delicate and refined in taste, comely, humane and magnanimous in sentiment."[12]

In this statement of Edwards A. Park, so similar in tone to Henry Ward Beecher's remarks on "sunshiny" clergymen, was a pronounced hostility to the aridity and austerity of doctrinal preaching. Park did not deny the value of theology for ordinary believers, but he did insist that it shed its Puritanic drabness and inculcate a greater sense of man's dignity. Here is seen the influence of William Ellery Channing who, more than any other critic of Calvinism, brought sweetness and light to the pulpit. Sacred and sublime topics, Channing maintained, were too often taught in such a way as to "narrow and degrade the hearers, disheartening and oppressing with gloom the timid and sensitive, and infecting coarser minds with the unhallowed spirit of intolerance." The mode of preaching favored by Calvinists produced depression and inertia in some, spiritual pride in others. He protested that "human nature requires for its elevation more generous treatment from the teachers of religion." His celebrated sermon of 1828, "Likeness to God," gave voice to the experience of many Christians outside his own small communion.[13]

The mellow, trustful religion of Harriet Porter's parents was obviously a projection of their own characters. They assumed that God would not treat them with severity because "God is good," an assumption which strict evangelicalism denounced as both presumption and a lowering of God to match human standards. But a sentiment similar to the Porters' had been uttered by Elder John Leland, a New England Baptist, a generation before:

> When we have the most of God in us, we most desire that *all*, without Exception; may be saved: and are our Wills better than the Will of God? at such Times, if it were in our Power, we would save all Men; and is Power wanting in God? These Things are often mentioned, but seldom canvassed fairly.

Such people were not Unitarians. Whether, like the Porters, they exhibited fine character and yet were accounted unconverted by the strenuous orthodox standard, or, like Leland, a minister who reported the kinds of speculative questions his parishioners posed, such people could be receptive to Channing's ideas.[14]

There was an inherent conflict between Channing and Edwards on the question of God's character, despite the striking similarity of their imagery. Edwards wrote that God's chief attribute was his glory, and that he made it known to his creatures:

> It is a thing infinitely good in itself, that God's glory should be *known* by a glorious society of created beings. And that there should be in them an *increasing* knowledge of God to all eternity, is worthy to be regarded by him, to whom it belongs to order what is fittest and best. If *existence* is more worthy than defect and nonentity, and if any *created* existence is in itself worthy to be, then *knowledge* is; and if any knowledge, then the most *excellent sort* of knowledge, *viz.*, that of God and his glory. This knowledge is one of the highest, most real, and substantial parts of all created existence, most remote from nonentity and defect.

There was a different emphasis in Channing's statement that "Likeness to God is the supreme gift. He can communicate nothing so precious, glorious, blessed as himself." Both perceived God as communicating himself to his creatures, and in this sense both believed that man partook of a continuous sacrament. But whereas Channing agreed with Edwards that this knowledge of God was analogical, he parted company with him in the latter's high conception of divine majesty and transcendence. For Channing, God was immanent, "the divine principle in us."[15]

The influence of both Channing and Edwards was clearest in the theology of Edward and Charles Beecher. They, of all the Beechers, produced the most fully developed, closely articulated theology, and through them we can extend this discussion to the rest of the family. Since Edward's was usually the leading mind of the pair, I shall begin with him. His private, not to say peculiar, theological vision came to him, it will be remembered, in a series of divine illuminations the nature of which remains rather vague. He did not consider himself a mystic and, in fact, believed that the intensity of his communion with God was only a heightened version of that promised to all believers. And yet he believed that he alone had received an authoritative revelation of God's truth, designed to overturn all previous systems and theories.

The doctrinal consequences of his experience were numerous. The chief of these was the affirmation of Channing's propositions about God. God's intelligence, goodness, and moral excellence were known through the correspondence of human consciousness with the divine. Furthermore, his power, even his omnipotence, was subjected to the principles of rectitude and goodness which were his chief glory. While the substance of Edward's doctrines was reinforced by what he learned from Channing, the scope of his system was Edwardsean. Like

Edwards, Beecher propounded a "system of the universe" and sought to prove that the end for which God designed, upheld, and perpetuated this system was the union of the eternal church with its creator. But, although Edwards had directed his efforts to demonstrating this, particularly in his *History of the Work of Redemption* and his *Dissertation Concerning God's Chief End in Creation*, he had not, in Beecher's opinion, answered the grave question: "Why is one part of God's creatures thus made the end of the creation? Why so valued, honored and exalted above the rest?" To answer this question Beecher proposed his theory of preexistence.[16]

Theodicy was the starting point of his inquiries, theodicy and the issue of just desert. The Pauline-Augustinian-Calvinist system had fastened a colossal error on Christianity, Beecher argued, because the system was "at war with the fundamental principles of honor and right, and hostile to the best interests of humanity." Not only did it impeach the goodness and justice of God, but by blinding men to the truth of his provisions for their salvation, it also prevented men from seeking saving faith. From the outset Beecher was concerned with presenting an alternative, a system that would vindicate human ethical standards. But he would not have said that merely human conceptions of right and wrong, decent and indecent, bind God. Rather, God "has, in his own mind, an eternal and immutable law of honor and right which he cannot disregard, and he is his own omniscient judge."

The intelligent creation looked to God for a transcendent ideal of benevolence. "The character of God is the sun of the moral world." Darken that character, and mankind and the angels would be plunged into confusion and gloom. The Augustinian doctrine of Original Sin had done precisely that to man, with incalculable damage to the cause of truth and piety and to the prosperity of the invisible church. Beecher reflected on this in 1827, when he entered his reservations about innate depravity in his commonplace book:

> There seems to be something in the nature of every human being morally odious as the certain cause of sin. This one would think is a calamity and not a crime, a ground of pity and not of condemnation. The idea of being by nature a child of wrath even in infancy when to all appearance the young being is ignorant of the cause of his being or his destiny, denotes not a crime but a calamity. And to call it voluntary [as New Haven Theology did] seems like removing a difficulty by language only. In short, original, native, entire depravity is a hard doctrine to be explained.

Under the Augustinian system, whether explained by Old or New School divines, "the question is, is not the present system a malevolent one?"[17]

If the system was malevolent, what must be the character of its author? Reasoning in this manner prostrated Beecher. The image of "a God selfish, dishonorable, unfeeling" blotted out every other conscious thought and feeling. Even at the depth of his despair, Beecher never called into doubt his own standards of honor and goodness, for these, he fervently believed, came from God himself. But this belief only worsened his dilemma. "Could he have trained me to hate himself?" Like John Leland, who had asked, "are our Wills better than the Will of God?" Edward Beecher could not surrender belief in the validity of his conceptions of morality, even when they appeared to conflict with God's.

Comparing his experience with that of other Christians, Beecher found reinforcement for this view. Many "free and powerful minds of New England" had recoiled from Calvinistic orthodoxy for the same reason. John Adams and William Ellery Channing were two such men. It was only popular prejudice against Unitarianism—prejudice the evangelicals had been quick to seize upon—that prevented others from following in the same track. The Old School had stigmatized such tendencies as "sceptical rationalism" and had charged them upon the New. And while the New School had dared to employ arguments of honor and right in teaching divine justice, it was only to preserve a system which Beecher believed incapable of being salvaged. Furthermore, the New School lowered its conception of human free agency by arguing that "the moral constitutions of men are [only] as good as the nature of free agency will allow." Bushnell, who occupied ground apart from both schools, declared a doctrine equally at variance with high conceptions of divine honor and rectitude. In Beecher's view, Bushnell approximated to the Hegelian tenet that moral evil is necessary as an educational provision. All these theories compromised the divine character by holding that God had so ordered things that his creatures were liable to punishment for possessing the very natures he had provided them.[18]

What was needed was a new theory to account for the entrance of moral evil. Such a theory must prove that God was entirely benevolent and fair, and that "no excuse or apology can be offered for those who began the revolt from God." This was an orthodox statement when Beecher offered it in 1827, but it contained a veiled allusion to the system he was laboring over in secret. He employed the language of New Haven to explain why moral evil had entered the divine economy, but with a twist:

> Moral power did not exist sufficient to prevent the entrance of some sin. This implies no imperfection in God. For free agency implies a natural power to sin, and moral omnipotence does not imply a power to present to free agents motives which do not exist.

The moral power of which Beecher spoke was to be found in disclosure of the character of God, which was the gravitational force of the moral universe. When that character was insufficiently known, "the entrance of moral evil will take place for want of motives powerful enough to prevent it." In other words, moral evil entered the universe because God could not show himself forth in a way to secure the unwavering love of all his creatures.

Beecher's hearers could not then know that the system which he taught had taken on extraordinary dimensions. The "conflict of ages" between the prevailing theological system and man's innate, God-given conception of just desert, between the character of God as presented by that system and man's innate ethical sense, could be quelled in only one way. That way was the system unfolded to Edward Beecher in his private communings with God:

> That, then, which I regard as having produced the great and fatal misadjustment of the system of Christianity, the effects of which I have endeavored to exhibit, is the simple and plausible assumption THAT MEN AS THEY COME INTO THIS WORLD ARE NEW-CREATED BEINGS. That they are NEW-BORN beings, is plain enough; that they are, therefore, NEW-CREATED beings, is certainly a mere assumption. True, it is a plausible assumption; and so was the old theory that the sun revolved around the earth.

By "new-created beings" Beecher meant the original souls of the men born into the present world. He pictured a previous state of existence for all souls during which they had rebelled against God, spurned his love, and thus come under his judgment. Beecher's system was essentially a political one, in which the personality of the leaders was the critical factor in the struggle. Hence his brother Charles's dictum that "theology is the politics of the universe." Faced with this celestial rebellion, God did not cut off the rebels without mercy. In his long-suffering love he made provision for amnesty. He even created another, material, world for the deserters and rebels to inhabit.

Their lives in the present world constituted a period of probation. These souls could be restored to grace by conformity to God's law and by relearning to love him. The world was a "moral hospital of the universe," and the entire material system was ordered to correspond to the spiritual. Men in this life received every help and encouragement to reform. There had never been a fall in Adam that had made men wretched and vicious and had corrupted the world they inhabited.[19]

The idea of preexistence was not new, but it had, on the whole, disreputable associations, Wordsworth notwithstanding. As a modern student put it, "It seems a fugitive word, escaped from a seance, wandering among us but not at home on the well-lighted streets of our empirical thoughts." Of Edward's family, only Charles and William accepted preexistence, and Charles was accused in later life of importing foul elements of "Indico-Persian mythology" into Christianity. The other Beechers admitted its congruence with the rest of Edward's system but complained that it was a hypothesis which settled nothing, for preexistence simply projected the problem of the Fall, and of hereditary wickedness, back in time. Furthermore, if men really were incarnations of their previous selves, of what use was their past experience if they recalled nothing of it?

Edward tried to explain to them that it was an all-sufficient theory because it vindicated God's goodness in ordaining a material system. The material world, its laws and operations, were wholly beneficial to man. His sin was not of material origin. "Sin originates in the spiritual world, from spiritual causes. Souls are sinful before they enter this material world. The soul is of Celestial origin. This is preexistence." Edward's emphasis upon the purity of the material world was intended as a deathblow to the Gnosticism he saw lingering in both Catholic and Protestant theology, with its suspicion of the body and the human passions. But he himself betrayed Gnostic influences in his conceptions of spiritual evil:

> The great idea is, evil entered in ages past, and introduced a kingdom hostile to that of God. The conflict of these kingdoms comes to its crisis here; and then cometh the end of this dispensation, and the eternal state of the universe begins.[20]

Edward might have expected Catharine, of all the family, to appreciate his system, since she had identified as defective the same aspects of their father's "liberal Calvinism." She, too, was seeking novel ways of eradicating those defects. To Edward's disappointment, Catharine received his theories with frank incredulity and cautioned him to reconsider his views. The thrust of her criticism was the utter improbability of Edward's scheme:

> I am however a little afraid that in the millenium your peculiar notion *not to be mentioned* about a *pre-existent state*, will not be found in the elementary works of mental philosophy or theology. One consideration I think ought to startle you in thinking of broaching such an opinion to man kind—and that is that no *probabilities* nothing short of demonstration could make mankind adopt a novelty as much contradicted by the obvious meaning of the Bible as it is by *consciousness* and by some of the *deductions* of reason as I believe.

Although, as she drily added, "you have data for judging of the correctness of your views which I have not," an ironical reference to his claims to divine illumination, Catharine would not concede that her brother's system overturned Calvinism. There were too many obvious objections to it. What had convinced Edward would not win over ordinary minds, which was what ordinary men were equipped with:

> *This* I can judge about and that is the amount of *testimony* and *evidence* which would be needful to make mankind throw away all their early notions and instilled principl[e] s. All their deference for past wisdom and investigation—all their prejudices against inovations and strange notions. You must find either *express testimony from God* or evidence that will amount to *demonstration* from other sources. Should you attempt to maintain the opinion you suggested without such a bulwark, it would only waken the idle wonder of those who know you not, and the regret of those who know and love you best.

Surely Edward must realize how visionary his theory was, how unnecessarily mystifying. And if he did not, he must at least admit the difficulties of getting around key points of Scripture. Catharine wanted to know, "What do you do with Adam on your scheme?" According to Genesis, "He once was holy and put in that state in this world." If all men came, as Edward held, from a previous state of existence which had left them depraved, did Adam "differ from all the rest of his race?" Or was Edward prepared to say that the Bible misrepresented Adam's condition?[21]

As her own views developed, Catharine became less concerned with accounting for man's innate depravity. With Edward, total depravity was not only a fact but the momentous fact of man's nature and destiny. He was trying to provide an alternative theory that would buttress the fact of man's entire sinfulness while exculpating God and vindicating his character. Catharine never denied that man was sinful, but she located that sinfulness elsewhere, accounting for it in terms of the malformation of mental and moral faculties and their operation in a limiting social environment. Her theology was fundamentally psychology, with a large element of moralistic reductionism. Her model of mental and emotional operations was relatively lacking in psychological depth, however, because she was unwilling or unable to deal with the darker strain in human nature, something which Edward and Charles—whatever their vagaries—acknowledged and insisted upon. She denied man's tragedy altogether. There was no possibility of deliverance or forgiveness because there was no "fallenness." Men differed widely in their capacities and endowments, but in the aggregate, man had as perfect a constitution as was possible under his circumstances. Whereas Edward spoke of this world as a "moral hospital," Catharine saw it as a nursery and a classroom.

In her *Elements of Mental and Moral Philosophy*, Catharine advanced the thesis that what theologians called depravity was actually "disordered mind." Infidels (whoever they might be) had seized upon the doctrine of total depravity to impugn God's honor. She admitted the force of this argument, given the current orthodox explanations of depravity. She impatiently brushed aside her father's explanation that the possession of free will involved liability to suffering and wrongdoing. Edward's argument for preexistence was even shallower and, worse than that, it contradicted the Bible, which gave a "full and clear account of the origin of our race—an account which forbids reliance on the dim light of tradition, or the vain speculations of poetry, or philosophy." Catharine proffered her own view, which she regarded as a fact and not a hypothesis.

Men cannot know the full extent of God's benevolent plan, but common sense and piety require men to believe that it is benevolent. What can be known of that plan shows that "what we can discern of ill, is the consequence of a wilful perversion of a noble nature, by *man himself*." Like the New Haven Theologians, she did not locate the source of this "wilful perversion" in the single transgression of Adam but represented it as an ongoing, natural process. Neither was it God's choice, for he looked on and sympathized with man's efforts to secure wholeness and sanity. When she spoke of "disordered mind," Catharine apparently meant a sort of moral insanity, which was, however, not incurable, since God provided countless aids and boundless encouragement, both in his Word and in his provision of social institutions.[22]

Her prognosis was optimistic. The cure lay ready to hand, if only religious teachers, especially mothers, would apply it. There were only two things needful: a "perfect and infallible standard of rectitude" by which man could measure his imperfection and toward which he could aspire, and motives powerful enough to uproot "already formed habits of self-indolence, in regard to our own best good, and of selfishness, in regard to the general happiness." Both these requisites could be found in God, who as a loving Friend would rejoice over man's recovery from selfishness and his advance toward a life of self-denying benevolence. Revelation showed that "the evil which man bewails, is not his solitary grief. His Creator shares in the sacrifice to redeem." Catharine placed a different construction on the traditional language of expiation. She viewed God not as a free sovereign bringing judgment against his criminal subjects but as a Father and protector:

> Mankind have been too apt to clothe the Father with all the terrific attribute[s] of indignation and punishment, while Jesus Christ retains all the lovely and endearing traits. Thus the character of the Deity is not preserved in its *true proportions*. But it is Jesus Christ who was the Judge and Governor of the people Israel, and the Father is never represented in Scripture, but in the most gentle and endearing characteristics.

God sometimes spoke wrathfully in the Old Testament, but that was the proper mode of address toward a superstitious, unfeeling, and ungrateful race.[23]

To illustrate her thesis that man's mind only required rectifying influences to achieve the holy healthfulness of benevolence, Catharine turned to recent history. Henry Martyn, the saintly missionary, showed the positive effects of religious nurture and self-culture. Lord Byron, "a noble mind in all the wild chaos of ruin and disorder," showed the converse. It was his vacillations between good and evil that fascinated Catharine. Byron possessed the potential for a high, selfless character, but it had been perverted by sensual excesses. He was "a singular combination of noble conceptions and fantastic caprices, of manly dignity and childish folly, of noble feeling and babyish weakness. . . . He sometimes seemed to gaze upon his own mind with wonder, to watch its disordered powers with curious enquiry, to touch its complaining strings, and start at the response; while often with maddening sweep he shook every chord, and sent forth its deep wailings to entrance a wondering world." Having painted this dark picture of a noble mind in ruins, Catharine nevertheless asserted that no one was too degraded and selfish to be saved from himself, not even a Byron.[24]

Yet her plan for universal restoration to moral sanity was balked by the plain fact that comparatively few of the world's creatures were saved from their constitutional weaknesses. She did not refer this fact, as Edward did, to God's decree of election. The "rectifying influence of that remedy for the disorders of the mind pointed out by Revelation" was available to all, without consideration of person or character. What was lacking was resolve on the part of godly men and women to exert themselves in behalf of their hapless brethren. Men could only be saved "by the instrumentality of their fellow beings," acting under God's encouragement, but those capable of acting to save their fellow men were unwilling to take up the task. "We thus learn the reason why the world is perishing."

The burden was not grievous. Men had to consecrate their lives to inculcating correct views of God, starting with receptive infant minds. Children were only too eager to believe what their parents told them. If parents were truthful, charitable, and self-sacrificing, children would learn to associate their character with that of their heavenly Parent. The life and precepts of Jesus could easily be made to govern a child's conduct so that obedience, generosity, and forbearance would become second nature. All branches of knowledge should be traced back to the "wisdom and goodness and skill of his Heavenly Parent," showing that God had designed the world to edify, shelter, and delight man. Thus gradually and imperceptibly would the child become, not only a believer in God and revelation, but actively benevolent and desirous of helping others to find the truth.[25]

Given Catharine's strictures on Edward's theory and her emphatic rejection of radical sinfulness, it is surprising that her brother's reaction to her *Elements* was so mild. While he criticized her for intruding too many technical controversies and thus cluttering her main outlines, he did not attack her leading ideas. For Catharine there was no "kingdom hostile to that of God," but rather a lifelong effort to subdue the elements of selfishness within oneself. Although Edward was pleased with his sister's uncommon independence of thought, there is no evidence that he took her seriously as a theologian. She directly challenged him in public and private, to refute her criticisms and prove the superiority of his own theories, but he steadfastly refused to be drawn into debate.

However he and Catharine may have differed as to God's purposes and operations, they agreed on his nature. There can be no doubt that it was Edward who influenced his brothers and sisters to believe in a God who felt and suffered for man. Nathaniel W. Taylor, Edward's teacher, would never have admitted such a possibility, for in his view:

> while I maintain that the happiness of God is affected by the moral conduct of creatures and painfully impaired by the existence of sin; while I might say that no language can too strongly describe his painful emotions toward it when compared with holiness, even that which represents him as *abhorring* iniquity and *shuddering* at the sight of it, still it will not follow that God is not perfectly blessed according to the true import of this language.

Lyman Beecher was inclined to be less dogmatic on this point but still took an orthodox stand. While he conceded that "there is no evidence that God is *constitutionally* incapable of pain" and that Scripture language depicted God as feeling rage, chagrin, and sorrow, "The scripture evidence is that the glorious tide of emotion that rolls through the mind of God is that of happiness—and no painful emotion suspends or neutralizes it." He himself had occasionally preached on the fatherhood of God but had not made it a major theme of the theology of moral government.[26]

When Edward seized upon and celebrated Channing's idea of the divine paternity, his father was receptive but expressed reservations about the suffering of God. Lyman told Isabella that she could have no abler spiritual counselor than her brother and urged her to contemplate his great theme, "the love of God," which Lyman understood in the Edwardsean sense:

> [It] will be the attraction of the intelligent universe and the theme of eternity—and the view which he gave you of God—as the subject of a personal interest in the friendship and sympathy and affectionate communion with every one of his creatures who love and approach and confide in him is most clearly revealed in the bible and needful to be understood and realised especially by us sinful creatures whom he has darkened and filled with fear and unbelief.

He could not, however, endorse the corollary to Edward's view of God, and cautioned Isabella not to take it too literally:

> That god should be susceptible of pain as well as pleasure on our account, might seem to our philosophy to follow and to be countenanced by the language of the bible—but in no such sense certainly as *Occasions* unmingled pain—or prevent[s] him from being every *moment* god over all, *blessed*, i.e., happy forever more. But you need not trouble yourself on this point. That he is happy in our happiness is certain from the nature of benevolence and the abundant testimony of his word. That he sympathises with us in all our sorrows and as a father pitieth his children, pitieth them that fear him cannot be denied and how he does it without to[o] much alloy to his blessedness we need no more attempt to comprehend than how he can uphold all things by the word of his power and not be tired, or administer the physical and moral government of the universe, and not be distracted by increasing and multitudinous attentions.[27]

Like Isabella, Thomas was drawn to Edward's God, even while repudiating the rest of his theology. Writing in 1840, Thomas declared that Edward's "belief as it regards the suffering of God is new—and I am exceedingly pleased with it--so much so that I believe it thoroughly and I think that no attribute of God is so lovely as this (viz.) his being affected either pleasantly or painfully by the good and bad actions of man." Instead of seeing the admission that God suffered as blasphemy, as an imputation of defect or imperfection to the deity, Thomas found that Edward's teaching "takes [away] that dark chilling cloud of *greatness in a particular way* that always bound me in my prayers and fettered my affections towards God." By making God more humanly intelligible and enabling Thomas to identify with him, Edward had done Thomas a great service. The younger brother went on to prove the validity of this doctrine by stressing the analogy between the human and the infinite mind:

> We know full well how much it adds to anyones character in our estimation to have the quality of humanity and tenderness in addition to the traits which are common to all minds. Then is it not manifestly unreasonable that we should deny an attribute as existing in the mind whose very essence is *love* which we are willing to adknowledge [*sic*] adds proportion harmony and loveliness to all other minds? And should we when we assume that God is a mild, great, good compassionate, and in short perfect being in all moral and intellectual points, deny in him that attribute which we see contributes particularly to the loveliness of human character?

And will not this idea be found consistent with the bible?[28]

Charles Beecher was also converted to the idea that God suffered and knew the pangs of sorrow and disappointment. When he was revising his book on the life of Christ, however, he acceded to Lyman's request to handle the subject cautiously. "The allusions to the sufferrings of the Messiah, I shall not introduce till after the Speech of Simeon," Charles wrote his father, "and then obscurely." He relied on the authority of Calvin Stowe for authentication of the belief, which the Stowes shared:

> I wish Prof. Stowe would have the kindness to translate for Harriet, and let her write down those passages he read to us one day from the German touching the knowledge had by the Jews in [the] time of Christ of a *sufferring* messiah. I can make some effective touches with them as I proceed.[29]

Edward rejoiced in Henry's acceptance of the same idea. Their frequent long conversations confirmed that Henry had also arrived at the belief that "This is the most fundamental doctrine in the whole range of theology. A denial of suffering love in God eclipses the sun of the Universe." When asked how he had arrived at this vision of God, Henry told Edward that "it came to him by a spiritual disclosure similar to my own." Henry preached this doctrine to millions, for his audience was as huge and varied as Edward's was small and select. These millions yearned, Henry said, for the "truth of Divine Fatherhood . . . addressed to *faith* and not to *philosophy*." In an 1884 sermon, "Our Father," he reiterated a theme he had stressed since the beginning of his ministry:

> Of all the names of God there is *none*, that brings Him home, to universal Consciousness, as Father—*Lord, King, Lion . . . Thunderer*, God of Battles—etc., limited and as human life grows better, die out. And at best, they are for *Adult*[s]. But, *Father*! The smallest child knows *that* name—and in general, it is a name showering upon us, the most *charming memories* and suggestions. In it are found all that *patience, love, service,* which infancy needs; it is in the Father (and Mother is wrapped up in it, and to the very, very *heart* that throbs in it) that feels the hidden reason for loving, which as yet, the child has not developed.

How like Jonathan Edwards, and yet how unlike him, Henry Ward Beecher sounded when he explained the reason of God's love:

> Parental love is not based upon *objective consideration.* The stream does not move because of the mill, but from its own *fulness*—from its own necessity and inward compulsion. The sun does not shine upon the persuasion of flowers, trees, and animals—but because it is so full of light and heat that it *must* distribute them.

The emanation of God's love which Henry preached was not, as in Edwards's thought, the fullness of divine glory lighting up the universe which reflected it back upon the source, so much as it was the warmth of a father caressing his fearful child. Furthermore, for Beecher, God's love for his children was unconditional and wholly spontaneous, having little or nothing to do with the obedience of the children.[30]

Henry also proclaimed another Beecher theme: "that the Family Relation, is made, in the Creative design of God, [and] becomes the interpreter of God, and the Commentary and theology, of his Nature and Government." He specifically rejected the language of moral government as a relic of "Scholastic Theology," with its monarchical assumptions. Edward, on the other hand, did not see any necessary conflict between divine government, in the theopolitical sense, and the family of God. "The family is a little model of the universal system under God and the church."

Edward's hostility to the Roman church stemmed in part from his belief that its doctrines of celibacy and its Gnostic hatred of the flesh were at war with the family. And in Harriet and Charles's view, it was precisely because God was an all-loving Father that he abhorred slavery. God was the author of sound social organization and the defender of the family in particular, as the institution most vulnerable to disintegration under slavery. He intended the family to serve not only the purposes of procreation and protection but also as a living symbol, as an emblem of his relation to man. This view was echoed by William Beecher, who taught that "God has so constituted the social system as to make us know what Love is," particularly in the human family, which was "Design'd to *show Love* and *its blessedness.*" Just as the husband and wife are one in a perfect union, just as parent and child are one, "such is God to his." God as the "Father of Spirits" "desires and seeks—the highest development, perfection and happiness of his children."[31]

Edward alone of all the Beechers employed the traditional metaphor of the marriage of Christ and the church, but even he feared that fellow evangelicals would be squeamish over the kind of sexual symbolism so freely used by their Puritan forebears. For the most part, the Beechers were content to agree with Henry's theology, as summarized by Charles:

> His theology consisted in this, that the character of the divine father, was *like* or fairly expressed by Jesus. And this (tho some call it Anthropomorphism) is after all the essence of all true theology.

And, whatever their critics might say, they maintained that evangelical preaching had always presented God as long-suffering, as much a man of sorrows as Christ, even while it had shrunk from the admission that such was the real nature of God.[32]

The anthropomorphism of which Charles spoke was not a simple conception. A theology which insisted so much on the fatherhood of God may seem to us banal or merely sentimental and not, as the Beechers thought, disturbing in its novelty. Catharine said to Andrew Dickson White that

> Tho' I am a full believer in the Supreme Divinity of Jesus Christ and a Trinity of Divine Reasons I regard Unitarianism as a protest of humanity against a *system of theology* at war equally with the Bible and common sense—and still more with the highest principles of our moral nature.

She, like Edward Beecher, "could not adore the character of God as it seemed to them to be represented in the conventional system," no matter how prayerfully they tried to reconcile the God of Augustine and Jonathan Edwards with the one they worshipped. When Edward, as a spokesman for orthodoxy, had been obliged to argue against Channing's views, he was won over to the Unitarian's position. "Appeals like these touched young Beecher's heart, a heart now thrilling with love to Christ. It was not the polemic but the love that felt such appeals." From the beginning of his ministry Edward had felt called to disseminate purer and more humane views of God, and found what he was seeking in Channing, amplified by his own theory of divine operation:

> This is my ideal of the glory of these United States and this as part of God's Universe. It will be a Universe of gentleness, condescenscion, patience, tenderness, unity, upheld and invigorated by infinite power.
>
> On this issue I desire to concentrate all truth, all history, all science, all languages, all analogies, all illustrations, all powers of style, all varieties of composition, all power of emotion. . . . Suffering is invaluable in the very idea of love in a system; sacrifice for others is the very basis of society forever.[33]

The representation of God's character in Timothy Dwight's *Theology* was very unlike the God preached by the children of Lyman Beecher; for in place of a glorified, unchanging, impassive deity, they worshipped a fond father. And whereas Dwight had considered Christ both in his roles as the tender, compassionate savior and as priest and judge, some of the Beechers emphasized the gentle Jesus who was at once elder brother and adoring shepherd, to the exclusion of the Christ of prophecy and priesthood. The transformation of Jesus Christ in the Beechers' imagination involved, and in fact required, the transfiguration of God to conform to their idea of his son's character. The qualities they attributed to Jesus were transferred to the Father. Yet it was more than a simple process of grafting specific Christ-like traits onto the Godhead, for many traditional divine attributes had to be suppressed, infused with new meaning, or denied outright. An example of this kind of assimilation was Edward Beecher's interpretation of divine omnipotence. Omnipotence was not, he said, "the exercise of mere naked power" but rather the operation of moral and spiritual power, specifically, the incalculable moral effect of God's self-disclosure through "the practical development of all his excellences."[34]

Another instance is one that recurred throughout the religious experience of the Beechers: the preoccupation with the honor and rectitude of God. Catharine, Edward, and Harriet, in particular, when confronted with painfully dissonant elements of their father's orthodoxy, decided the issue—or at least phrased their rejection of New Haven doctrine—in terms of orthodoxy's conflict with divine honor and equity. Their God, they seemed to be saying, must be more trustworthy than his. The same governing principle was implicit in the beliefs of the other Beecher children.

A third and final example of this tendency was the Beechers' use of the image of the family. They almost always spoke of the family in terms of domestic and private relations, completely excluding the economic, political, and tribal connotations of the family as represented in the Bible they always invoked. Even Edward, when he addressed the question of the political function of the family, referred to the higher politics of the celestial kingdom. The family of God was, then, characterized chiefly by emotional bonds and fulfilled emotional needs. The family was the channel of communion with its head, its divine Father. The Beechers insisted, of course, that the family was an important sphere of ethical activity; but even that element was lost in their rapturous transports over the boundless love and infinite tenderness of the family relation. Other theologians and preachers might go on talking about the rule of God and the obedience of his subjects, but the Beechers believed that their religion was far more spiritual, and they marveled aloud that Christians seemed so unwilling to dispense with the trappings of divine royalty and the goad of abject terror.

The Beechers insisted, then, upon a God who was not only loving but also honorable in his dealings with men. When, according to Edward, one sees that the acts and decisions imputed to God are at war with honor and right, "conviction of sin, confession and repentance, are impossible," for only when the sinner admits that "the conduct of God has been honorable and right, and that of the sinner dishonorable and wrong," can he bow down in humble contrition and ask God's forgiveness. Such a claim would have staggered Asahel Nettleton or Samuel Miller, for whom the probity of God was unquestionable. Furthermore, it was precisely such tendencies that had caused them to denounce the New Haven Theology and seek its destruction. Lyman Beecher and Nathaniel Taylor had argued vigorously and, as it seemed to their critics, intemperately, for moral government and the honor of God in language which suggested that New England orthodoxy denied both. Their insistence upon excising the doctrine of infant damnation from the body of orthodoxy was one result of reasoning in the New Haven fashion about God's purposes and character; their modifications of Original Sin was another. And yet, the arguments of Lyman's children went beyond mere logical extensions of New Haven Theology. They expressed a new concern for, as Thomas said, adding "humanity and tenderness" to God's character. As William told his congregations, "If God is love and we his children, then he is full of Pity—compassion, sorrow, *Long suffering*."[35]

It is a natural tendency of those who think about the existence and being of a god to picture him in human terms. For one thing, reasoning by analogy inevitably has that effect. For another, the language of Scripture is highly anthropomorphic. Some New England theologians, notably Jonathan Edwards, exalted God far above such human conceptions, comparing him most often to the sun rather than to human kings or wise men. In this view, the mind of God is totally inaccessible to his creatures. Edward Beecher rejected the Edwardsean concept and insisted that human ideas of time, space, and morality must agree with those of God, or at least be closely correlated. He went on to assert that men must judge revelation by the highest human ethical standard:

> Our ideas of the moral nature of God affect our belief or disbelief of all moral acts ascribed to him, and thus of the inspiration and interpretation of all professed revelations. This we cannot help, even if any deprecate it as rationalizing. But in fact, if we are made capable of *communion* with God, and the Bible affirms not only that we are, but that it is our chief end, then true human morality and divine morality must be coincident, and we are authorised and required to deal with all professed revelations on this principle.

Edward argued further that "God himself is truly correlated to the sanctified human mind, and his nature and attributes truly seen as adapted to harmonize, develop, vitalize, and fructify all its powers and emotions." A much more sweeping statement of the same idea was Catharine's conception of God as the great Happiness-maker, whose purpose was to elevate man through the gradual processes of nurture and education.[36]

The chief of God's attributes was paternity, but it was a paternity garlanded by the ineffable sweetness of a mother—so Mrs. Stowe told her juvenile readers in a parable published in 1858. And in *Woman in Sacred History* she described the God-given statutes of Moses as demonstrating a "peculiar and almost feminine tenderness and consideration for whatever is helpless and defenceless." Moses' "characteristic chivalry" was contrasted to the masculine selfishness of his sister, whom God punished with leprosy for her treachery against her brother, the all-forgiving and meek:

> Not the gentlest words of Jesus are more compassionate in their spirit than many of these laws of Moses. Some of them sound more like the pleadings of a mother than the voice of legal statutes. . . . He was like a mother in the midst of the great people whose sins, infirmities, and sorrows he bore upon his heart with scarcely a consciousness of self.

Moses, as the anointed of God, ruled and legislated in the manner of God himself, and God was both father and mother to his people. And if Moses distinguished himself by his maternal virtues, Christ was even more like a mother. The virgin birth guaranteed that he would be surpassingly womanly:

> We are led to see in our Lord a peculiarity as to the manner of his birth which made him more purely sympathetic with his mother than any other son of woman. He had no mortal father.

> All that was human in him was her nature; it was the union of the Divine nature with the nature of a pure woman. Hence there was in Jesus more of the pure feminine element than in any other man. It was the feminine element exalted and taken in union with divinity.

When Christ left his earthly home to undertake his Father's mission, he gathered a new family, his disciples, around him:

> We can see no image by which to represent the Master but one of those loving, saintly mothers, who, in leading along their little flock, follow nearest in the footsteps of Jesus. Jesus trusted more to personal love, in forming his church, than to any other force. . . . Jesus, that guest from brighter worlds, brought to this earth the nobler ideas of love, the tenderness, the truth, the magnanimity, that are infinite in the *All-loving.*

Catherine Sedgwick also attributed maternal impulses to God and was gratified to hear them expressed by Channing:

> His filial sentiment to the Deity always impresses me; it is not merely the confidence of a child to the father, but the tenderness that is most commonly felt to the mother; he is like the child who throws himself on the mother's bosom, sure there is repose there, and love enough for all his wants.

In his earnest but friendly debates with Mrs. Stowe over evangelical theology, Oliver Wendell Holmes found that they could agree on this point:

> Do you know that when I see the tenderness of you sweet kind women, I can understand Theodore Parker's insisting on the *maternal* element in the Divine being? I think the most encouraging hint with reference to the future of these helpless infants, whom we call men and women, is that He who made the heart of a mother would find it hard to quite give up a child. . . . You women are all Universalists.

And returning to a theme which obviously gave him peace, Holmes reiterated his belief that "I *must* love my Creator, for he is as kind as my father was, and as tender as my mother was. Otherwise he has made a creature better than himself, according to our human definition of better,—which is contrary to all reason, as it seems to me."[37]

Holmes hit upon the key when he spoke of a "creature better than himself," for these conceptions of God owed much to the prevalent

Victorian tendency to idealize and, in a sense, worship the father, mother, and home. When human parents were regarded with such awe and admiration, it must be a wonderful deity indeed who could surpass their kindness and watchfulness. By insisting as much as they did on the parental character of God and on the family ties of his children, the Beechers brought God down from heaven and installed him by the hearth. They had, in effect, made the ideal of parenthood the measure of God's goodness and greatness. A large element in their conception of divine goodness was hero-worship of their father. When Henry compared the Christian's love of God with the feelings of a small boy in pain nestling beside his father for comfort, the implication is clear. Catharine was even more explicit when she wrote, just before her death, of her yearnings for "the Heavenly Home." She told her sister Mary that mingled with her desire to see God was her longing for reunion with the man who had been both father and mother to her. Going home to God meant going "also to my earthly father that loved us so tenderly and thus enabled us to better understand 'Our Father in Heaven' and His love and care."[38]

For all their shared insistence on the loving-kindness and parental solicitude of God the Father, the Beechers were not unanimous in believing him to be the supreme deity. Christ still played a subordinate role in the theology of Catharine and Edward. They retained his atoning sacrifice in their systems. For Edward, the Atonement signified the miracle of the divine condescension, whereas Catharine thought only of its practical benefits to mankind. But in neither case did they fully develop or explain the Atonement itself. Charles did elaborate a theory of the Atonement congruent with Edward's scheme of preexistence. The elevation of Christ over the Father, Christomonism, was the keynote of the theology of Harriet, Henry, and Thomas.

Despite these differences, however, all the Beechers had departed so far from the orthodoxy of their father and his generation that by the 1850s, when they began publishing their most earnest statements in theology, none of them could have subscribed to the view of God presented in the following dialogue between the Reverend Edward Dorr Griffin and his unconverted daughter:

> "My child, where do you expect to spend your eternity?"
>
> "Why, papa, I think it most likely that I shall spend it in hell."
>
> "Well, my dear, that question God will decide, without asking counsel of you or me."

"I know that, papa, and I don't want any body else should decide it."

"Why, my dear?"

"Because he appears so good and so just."

"Do you think you deserve hell?"

"Oh, I know I do."

"What is the greatest desire of your heart?"

"To love and serve God all my days!"

Neither could the Beechers have greeted with anything but amazement and pity such a pious ejaculation as that of Thomas Robbins, who voiced a commonplace sentiment when he recorded in his diary, "This evening felt willing to be annihilated." They could not have accepted Robbins's standards of virtue or seen any necessity to celebrate God's majesty and justice by harping on his power to create and destroy arbitrarily.[39]

To pass from the Beechers' general view of God to their conceptions of the nature and mission of Christ in particular, it must be said at the outset that they seldom concerned themselves with formal Christology, even in writings devoted to the life and work of Jesus. Their ideas can best be understood by beginning with Lyman Beecher's view, as stated to his daughter Isabella:

> I acquiesce in Catherines advice that you cultivate an acquaintance with Christ—believing it well [constituted?] . . . . But if you love and obey and worship the father—You do approach [him] in the name of Christ. So long as you regard what he has *done* and the place he occupies as the ground of your acceptance. Praying in the name of Christ and having him as mediator does not mean that we pray to him—as Catholics do to Mary—to intercede for us—and that we may not pray to the father directly, but [rather] that we recognise his atonement and mediation as that which has opened the new and living way and authorised us to come boldly to the throne of grace. You may pray therefore as you find most easy and edifying tho—I would—if practicable pray to Christ as God.

Here we see Lyman guarding against any weakening of Trinitarianism while encouraging his child to find comfort and friendship in Christ.[40]

Catharine, in an apparent reversal of feeling, had moved away from her almost exclusive worship of Christ, relegating Christ to the role of exemplar of his Father's love. In her "Hymn for a Dying Bed," composed in anticipation of Louisa Wait's expiration, Catharine had called upon Christ for succor:

> And is there one who knows each grief,
> And counts the tears his children shed,
> Whose soothing hand can bring relief
> And smooth, and cheer their painful bed?
> Saviour, invisible, yet dear!
> Friend of the helpless, art thou near?

After recalling the pathetic scenes of Christ's lowly, despised, yet magnificent life on earth, Catharine went on to speak of his own struggles with Satan and his experience of death:

> And *Thou* hast tried the Tempter's power
> And felt his false and palsying breath,
> Has known the gloomy fears that wait
> Along the shadowy vale of Death—
> And what the dreadful pangs must be
> Of life's last parting agony.

It was not God who could support the perishing soul in its final confrontation with evil and its surrender to the fact of ultimate finiteness, but Christ:

> My only Hope! My Stay, My Shield!
> Thy fainting creature looks to Thee—
> Thy soothing peace, thy guidance yield
> In this, my last extremity;—
> With Thy dear, guardian hand to save
> I venture downward to the grave!

Catharine's hymn for her consumptive friend, written during her own mourning for Alexander Fisher, expressed both a desperate clinging to Christ and a shrinking from the God who had ordained men to be wretched and then punished them for enacting their misery and spiritual sickness on the only stage he had provided them.[41]

It was only after a prolonged exposure to Scottish realism, with its emphasis on the innate moral sense, and after searching the Scriptures with the express intent of disproving the orthodox explanation of God's dealings with man, that Catharine was able to be reconciled to the God whom she (in her imagination at least) had disavowed. Like the prodigal son returning to his father's house, Catharine discovered personal qualities in God which she had ignored or slighted during her period of rebellion against him. So complete was her reversion to God-worship that she almost, but not quite, approached the conservative Unitarian position which regarded Christ as quasi-divine and as the supreme ethical teacher.

Throughout her life Catharine Beecher made statements highly favorable to Unitarianism, describing that denomination as a body of sincere truth-seekers who had fled the confines of evangelicalism because of the bigotry and slavish scholasticism of its champions. Nevertheless, she could not bring herself to ally openly with the Unitarians. But her reservations about Unitarianism had nothing to do with the person or role of Christ:

> Now the great practical difficulty about Unitarianism is, that all moral men, though they think piety a very desirable thing, feel that they shall have a fair chance for eternity without it; and even those who are not strictly moral in every respect, feel but little more anxiety. Unitarianism destroys *the fear of evil consequences from neglect of duty*, so much more necessary in reference to duties relating to invisible things, which are realized only by faith.

If she could not join the Unitarians—"those who have too much conscience to live without any religion, and . . . too much reverence for the Bible to deny entirely its authority"—even less could she accept universalism.[42]

Why Catharine should have abandoned a Christocentric theology for one emphasizing the worship, or rather emulation, of the heavenly Father, is difficult to say. She herself never alluded to the sudden shift or offered any explanations of it. Possibly, her often expressed distaste for religious emotionalism caused her to shrink from fervid Christ-worship. Her rationalistic, decorous mind regarded displays of pietistic adoration with aversion and even contempt. Surrender to Christ, as experienced by Henry or Harriet, could not be pleasurable to their sister. Conjecture aside, it is clear that Catharine demoted Jesus from the object of worship and contemplation to the supreme educator: "In all the duties I urged, I always found authority and support in the Divine Word. I endeavored to present God as a loving Father, and to make it plain that his 'glory,' like that of earthly parents, consisted in the virtue and true happiness of all his children. I showed them that there are right ways and wrong ways of making ourselves and others happy; that Jesus Christ came to teach the only right way; and that those only can be truly and forever happy who make it their chief aim to follow his example and teachings." Elsewhere, in the same vein, she called Jesus "a messenger from the Creator" and a "noble benefactor." His work, she believed, was less to redeem man, in the sense of rescuing him from his fallen condition and reconciling him to God, than to instigate the individual's movement toward rectitude. There was no hint of justification by faith and no clear perception of what righteousness signified:

> Thus, if Christ is proved to be a messenger from God by miracles, whoever *practically believes* in Christ, believes in God also. And just so far as a man understands Christ's teachings *aright,* and *purposes* to obey him, and *carries out* this purpose, just so far he has faith, and love, and rep[e]ntance toward God and toward Christ. And as men are named by the name of those they obey, every man is a *true Christian* just so far as he understands Christ's teachings *aright* and *obeys* them.

The idea of Christian witness, so far as it occurred to Catharine, involved no prophetic duty and no sacrifice (other than the sacrifices required by moral self-regulation); for, as she gratefully observed, "the Christian profession has ceased to be a cross in any way, and has rather become honorable."[43]

Given this understanding of Christ, it is interesting that she felt compelled to set forth a theory of the Atonement when her system could have been complete without one. Her explanation of "Christ's atoning sacrifice" was consistent with her general position, which was both scriptural and moralizing but nondoctrinal. Thus she contented herself with paraphrasing the Gospel of John, while disclaiming any intent of providing a philosophical argument:

> God so loved the world that he gave his well-beloved and only-begotten Son to suffer and die for us. . . . And the history of the humiliation, sorrow, and painful death of God's only and well-beloved son is set forth as proof that God loves us even while we are sinners, and is *not willing* that we should perish. . . . That he has done this is proof also that there was some *impossibility* in saving us any other way. . . . There is no need of any explanation of the *causes* of this *impossibility*. . . .

She stubbornly refused to lose her readers in "the mists of metaphysical and theological technics." In her one extended discussion of the Atonement, Catharine again avowed that "the doctrine of the Atonement can be regarded simply as a fact without any reference to the philosophy of it, *i.e.*, the mode or *cause* of this fact." God had announced this fact in his revelation, and it was incumbent upon his children to believe him.[44]

Edward Beecher, of course, had no such disregard for "technics." Whereas Catharine's was a system of natural religion, his was eminently theocentric and eschatological. His view of the Atonement, that it served as the ultimate disclosure of God's self-sacrificing tenderness, was only fully developed by his brother Charles, who wrote *Redeemer and Redeemed* to elaborate the doctrines of Edward's *Concord of Ages.* In the *Concord*, Edward portrayed Calvary as both the literal and symbolic battleground between God and Satan, with Christ as the champion of God. "It was the cross which effected the final, irrevocable, and eternal defeat of the great antagonist of God, and a final and an eternal paralysis and destruction of his spirit and principles."

Satan had brought about the original celestial insurrection by convincing the human race that their Creator was unworthy of their obedience and love. As Edward imagined the scene, Satan had succeeded in universally subverting the souls of men in the millennia before the material creation. There was only one way to win them back:

> Charges had been made against [God] of undue assumption, unreasonable demands of suffering and obedience, undue self-exaltation, lawless despotism, and of unfeeling tyranny. How did he meet these charges? Not by words, but by acts. The creator, the upholder, the ruler of all worlds, laid aside his rights and glories; he came down in the place of a servant; he put himself under the law violated and dishonored, and fully honored and obeyed it. Nor was it an easy obedience. It required self-denial and suffering in the extreme; but he was obedient unto death, even the death of the cross.

With such a blazing example of God's self-sacrifice before them, the angels "rallied with new devotion around their great head," while mankind recoiled with horror from the Great Deceiver. Thus, the Atonement was not "a transient infliction of a penalty on Christ," but an act of infinite moral force, a force so great that it checked the kingdom of darkness, which had been bursting outward with centrifugal force, and reinstated the power of the kingdom of God, which operated through the centripetal forces of love and wisdom. From disorganization to reorganization, the universe was once again made whole.

The Atonement further contributed to the ultimate salvation of souls willing to love God by producing a "universal conviction that Christ deserved the highest honor" for vindicating the government of God. "And this reward was, power and authority to forgive all who should return to that law . . . for which he had created an enthusiasm unknown before his glorious example." Christ had upheld the law not by relieving men from fear of "the torments of Hell," but by instilling "admiration of the divine glory of suffering love, and a purpose to imitate it. This is the inspiration of Paul's ideal of sacrificial love, Phil. 3:8–10." This, in outline, was the theory of the Atonement which Charles Beecher decided to develop.[45]

Charles Beecher arrived at his Christology, as we have seen, with the help of Henry's liberal influence. "When I came up from New Orleans, I was a fatalist, and ready to dispute with any body," Charles somewhat inaccurately recalled. Placed under the guidance of Henry, who "ignored such points totally," Charles came to believe as his brother did:

> Do you ask what delivered me? What vanquished Skepticism, and *pride*, and ungovernable passions all at once? I answer, it was Jesus Christ—I cannot assign any other cause. When I remember all the past, when I recall all I have been, and thought and done, and then see what I am, I am utterly confounded, and *know* that no cause less than the power of a loving Savior is adequate to account for the change.

He addressed a plea to the readers of his first book, *The Incarnation*:

> But perhaps these pages may meet the eye of some unhappy wanderer on those sad confines between day and night, where doubt divides Christianity from Atheism. Perhaps such an one may be ready to turn from what is here written as a mere rhapsody. Beloved friend, listen to a simple closing confession. Once the writer of these pages wandered in those thankless realms where you now abide. . . . Years he wandered there. . . . After a series of internal changes, so gradual as to defy chronicling, he turned, benighted, to Jesus, whose character, considered purely as a work of art, he had, through all these wanderings, admired as perfect—against whom he had uttered no word of blasphemy. He prayed hypothetically, that Jesus, *if real*, would answer.

It was purely as an exercise, Charles added, that he had undertaken to study the life and character of Jesus in the Gospels. His hypothetical prayer was answered.[46]

The aim of *The Incarnation* was to illustrate the life of Christ through sketches of leading figures and major events of the Bible record. The book dealt briefly with Christological questions, such as the nature of Christ's temptation, his relationship with the other persons of the Trinity, and his human perfection. Beecher argued for a kenotic theory of the Incarnation, saying that Christ "emptied himself, suspended the full functions of deity," a theory his brother Henry also accepted. But neither of them developed this theory in its relation to their idea of the sufferings of the divine Christ. In this book, Charles stopped short of elucidating the meaning of the Atonement, leaving it to his sister Harriet, who contributed a poem, "Mary at the Cross," exalting the maternal sufferings and triumph of the Virgin, "his sole adorer, his best love." Beecher's next book, *David and His Throne*, described the Atonement in terms congruent with Edward's theory but stressing man's sinfulness rather than God's love:

> And what must be the eternal weight of meaning bound up in the death of such a Being? What does it signify, when such a One hangs expiring on a cross, under a sky of sackcloth, the rocks rending beneath? Sin—human sin—must be something far more dreadful than our darkened minds are willing to admit, when such facts as these pertain to the working out of atonement.[47]

Charles dedicated his major work, *Redeemer and Redeemed*, to his mother, "whom, next to my Redeemer, I most desire to meet in the Resurrection." The book was the fruit of twenty years of research and reflection, but Beecher offered his theory in an undogmatic spirit, saying, "a belief in the correct theory of atonement is not absolutely essential to salvation, but only a belief in the substance of the fact. . . . The sick man needs medicine, not a theory of medicine." For this reason, although he aimed at overturning the New England (or governmental) theory of the Atonement, he did not attack its proponents. Their error lay not in holding that the Atonement was intended primarily to declare God's righteousness, for that was a virtue of the New England theory, but in clinging to the notion that another divine purpose in the event was to show God's "disposition to punish."[48]

Charles's alternative was based upon an elaborate typology, which was rendered somewhat obscure by his overblown style. His theory fell into two major parts. In the first place, he held that Christ, though designated as ruler of the universe from the beginning of God's government, could not be invested with the actual title and power until he had proven himself worthy. By taking on human flesh, submitting to humiliation, and suffering unto death, he proved his obedience and loyalty to God, his solicitude for his fellow creatures. Rising again as the reborn Christ, Jesus attained his ordained authority and primacy over all the rest of the angelic race. Before his elevation to "headship of the universe," Christ was a human soul in a celestial body:

> The creature element in the person of the God-man, on the present supposition, is neither first-created in the order of time, nor of the angelic race, but created in heaven, and created human, like other glorified spirits.

The first-created, according to Beecher, was Lucifer rather than Christ, and it was between them that rulership of the universe was contested. The soul of Christ, elected to redeem the human race (which was, of course, a preexistent celestial race), was "Jesus Melchisedec, called to the high-priesthood before the world began." He alone of all the order of Melchisedec, the "royal family of the universe," as God's elect were known, resisted the blinding wiles of Lucifer. Lucifer hated and envied this royal order, the eternal invisible church of which all believers were members, and convinced them to usurp power from God, to seize their crown prematurely. After they had failed, they became subject to Lucifer, the "prime Secessionist of the skies." They had traded their celestial glory for the pottage of Lucifer's empty promises--all except Jesus Melchisedec, who was rewarded for his loyalty by being made second person of the Trinity.[49]

The second part of Beecher's theory developed the idea of Christ as the type of the scapegoat, driven out into the wilderness of Azazel. When Christ entered Hades after the Crucifixion, he entered the wilderness, coming under the power of death. He was the scapegoat, not because God required his degradation and death, but because there was no other way to supplant Satan. Satan had amassed tremendous power by various cunning strategies. As the firstborn of God, he had retained the "infinite affection" of his father, who either would not or could not cast him down from his eminence, even while repudiating his evil works. As leader of the celestial rebellion, Lucifer had won the loyalty of the human race and could exert moral blackmail against those who had repented of their betrayal of God but saw no way to reinstate themselves. He was also powerful because there was as yet no effective rebuttal to his charge that God was a self-regarding, pitiless despot. And finally, he was master of all the means of corrupting and seducing the unwary, blinding them to their duty to God. The death of Christ exposed Satan's lies and curbed his powers. "Thus the blood of Christ sufficed to purge heaven," as it "severed the last tie between Lucifer and a Father's love." It simultaneously demonstrated to the intelligent universe that God was fully capable of selfless love.[50]

Charles Beecher claimed that his theory of the Atonement accomplished a synthesis of all the valuable beliefs of the ages concerning the death of Christ. From primitive Christianity it took the belief that the Atonement was aimed at destroying Satan. It maintained unaltered the current Old School theory of the "full execution of justice," but made Satan, rather than Christ, the object of that justice. It also drew upon the New School doctrine that the Crucifixion and Resurrection were suasory in nature. Last, and most important, his theory did away with the shocking proposition that "God undertook to prove he would punish the guilty by undeserved suffering inflicted on the innocent," an idea so repugnant to man's moral sense that it made scoffers and skeptics out of high-minded men. Guilty man was redeemed by being enabled to love God unreservedly, seeing and worshipping him as he appeared in his true majesty and beauty. The sacrifice at Calvary called man home to the celestial existence he had known before this life, "when as a child he played about his father's knee in the heavenly home."[51]

This new theory of the Atonement was ingenious, labored, and totally uninfluential. Charles Beecher's critics professed to find it almost unintelligible, though fascinating in its way purely as cosmic drama. They tended to treat it as a mass of ancient errors and modern speculations. As one critic observed, after giving due credit to Beecher for his immense learning, "what is new is not true, and what is true is not new." Another complained of the dangerous tendency of "exalting to preternatural and almost Godlike energy the power of evil," an inheritance from Gnosticism. What distressed Noah Porter, and orthodox critics of Edward Beecher as well, was the brothers' fascination with Satanic power and demonology. The preexistence of Christ and Satan was not contested, but the Beechers' insistence on portraying Satan as the favorite son and near-successful rival of God was disturbing to minds that were content to explore the consequences and philosophy of the Atonement event. Not only did Edward and Charles believe that Satan had almost triumphed over Christ in the remote past, they also persisted in seeing him still at work everywhere, promoting discord and ignorance through "a delusive power in the higher regions of human thought." Thus rival theologies were laid at Satan's door, as part of his campaign to blind men to the true character of God.[52]

Redeemer and Redeemed was aimed at a scholarly audience. In his more ordinary discourses, Charles Beecher presented a view of the Atonement to which his brothers and sisters could subscribe. *The Divine Sorrow* was preached before his church at Georgetown, Massachusetts. In this sermon he held before his hearers the image of a suffering God, a conception that he and they knew was considered heretical. That God suffers for his people was, he insisted, not heresy but plain scriptural truth. "It will not avail to tell us of Anthropopathy," he declared. The subject of the Bible was God himself, and in it he aimed to "convince men that their sins do affect him painfully." What Christ felt, Jehovah felt also. The purpose of God in taking on human flesh was to "let sin act itself out in putting him to death." The Cross served to rivet the attention of mankind on a God who had striven with them in vain, to convince them once and for all of his compassion:

> God did not take flesh that he might be *able* to suffer, but that he might show forth his sufferings. He had suffered, as his plainest declarations show, ever since sin began, but could not say it plainly enough to be believed. The more he said it, the more Satan denied and men disbelieved it.

Let Beecher's detractors argue all they pleased about dogmas. They could not get away from the Bible itself, nor from the hymns offered up in every evangelical church, praising the self-sacrifice of God. "Would the power of these hymns be enhanced by the scientific reflection that God cannot possibly suffer?"[53]

Scientific reflection, as Charles called it, ultimately had little to do with the beliefs of Henry and Harriet and the millions who comprised their following. Henry's *Life of Jesus, the Christ* drew on the biblical scholarship of his day, but its acceptance has less to do with his research than with his hortatory and narrative skills. A blacksmith who wrote to him expressed the opinion that it was Beecher's own agony over the Tilton scandal which enabled him to write feelingly about Christ. Another admirer, a former preacher who had become "an Infidel," wrote that "you did what all others (and I have heard more than a hundred) have failed to do–given me a better idea of, and a warmer feeling towards, Jesus."

Beecher's sermon on Christ washing the disciples' feet was typical of the sermons his infidel correspondent had heard with genuine emotion. It was Beecher's ability to recreate the personality and experience of Christ and to make his congregations feel as if they were drawn irresistibly to that figure that made Henry's Christology so much more powerful than Edward's or Charles's. Their sister Harriet aimed at the same effect. She accepted Catharine and Charles's argument that the fact of an Atonement was crucial, while the specific theory was relatively unimportant. However, she insisted—as Catharine did not—that the believer must authentically experience the Atonement:

> And is there not a touchstone to try every theory of atonement? Whatever makes a man feel that he is only a spectator, an uninterested judge in this matter, is surely astray from the idea of the Bible. Whatever makes him feel that his sins have done this deed, that he is bound, soul and body, to this Deliverer, though it may be in many points philosophically erroneous, cannot go far astray.[54]

To round out this examination of the Beechers' transformation of the character of God, it must be emphasized that theirs was not a wholly sentimental image. They all professed, some more insistently than others, to draw their portrait from life, from God's self-revelation in Scripture. Thus, Charles found the most vivid picture in the Davidic Psalms, where the divine lineaments were purest and most forceful:

> Yet, strange to say, some of the people, in our day at least, will not say Amen, but think the character of Jehovah, as presented in these olden annals, repulsive, compared with the mild and merciful Saviour Jesus. Yet what can such persons do with David and this psalm, and his rapturous ascription to Jehovah of all the choicest, tenderest attributes of the Saviour's character. To our eyes and hearts it is most manifest that David's Lord, David's son, our Saviour, are one and the same lovely ideal.

Charles Beecher, like his sisters, reprobated the modern tendency to distinguish between the revelations of the Old and New Testaments as respectively lower and higher, cruder and finer. The Beechers rejected what they called scholasticism, on the one hand, and nonscripturalism, on the other. Partly under the influence of Calvin Stowe, they urged Christians to reaffirm the totality and continuity of the biblical revelation. Edward and Charles, especially, upheld the argument that the Gospels and the rest of the New Testament were incomprehensible without the living testimony of the Old. This was the message of Charles's *David and His Throne,* Harriet's *Woman in Sacred History*, and Edward's *History of Opinions on the Scriptural Doctrine of Retribution.* [55]

Though most of the Beechers shared a broadly scriptural outlook, there were remarkable divergences among them on the fundamentals of faith. Catharine, despite her special ties to Lyman, lamented his "soul-withering system" and claimed that "his disenthralled spirit" was "urging my hand as I write," inspiring her efforts to topple evangelical orthodoxy. She asserted that Lyman's *Autobiography*, far from presenting his triumphs as a theologian, was a record of failure as far as his children's conversion was concerned. "What anxiety, perplexity, disappointment, and agonizing fear are there recorded on the part of the father, and what sufferings and vain efforts on the part of the children!" Lyman's errors were those of a benighted generation. His allies and colleagues, "such as Dr. Taylor, Dr. Nettleton, Dr. [Nathaniel] Hewit, Dr. Tyler, Dr. Payson, Dr. Finney, and many others" had struggled valiantly to come to terms with their religious and dogmatic heritage:

> [They] made two great mistakes: the first was in representing the *emotive* part of love as the chief duty required, and the second was so representing God and Christ as to make it almost impossible to feel any other emotions than those of terror and aversion.

In this Lyman Beecher had been almost as culpable as his more conservative adversaries. Profoundly antagonized by what was, after all, Edwardsean piety, Catharine recoiled, taking refuge in a do-good theology from which emotionalism and intellectualism were equally absent. [56]

If Catharine wanted religion to be painless and sensible, her brother Charles retained the evangelical sense of struggle, of faith as the sole means of overcoming death and the Devil. The moral utilitarianism and practical good works of Catharine's scheme seemed inadequate and even dangerous to him. Writing to their father about certain modern tendencies in religion, Charles said:

> One thing is sufficiently evident to us both, and to all who attentively consider the signs of the times, viz., a tendency to idolise the human, and to leave out Christ crucified. And nothing can be more fatal than for a Christian minister to be led, beguiled, seduced,

by any pseudo-philanthropic scheme, away from the *cross*, and the atoning death of Christ.[57]

These were serious differences, but the true apostate among the Beechers was Henry, who almost dispensed with the scriptural basis so important to Catharine and the theology of reconciliation so central to Edward, Charles, and, in an undogmatic way, to Thomas. Thomas reminded his Elmira church that "every man of us is at this very moment a citizen of the kingdom of this world, presided over by Satan; or a citizen of the Kingdom of Heaven, presided over by Our Lord Jesus Christ." Every man, Thomas Beecher affirmed, could grow in grace so as to become a Christian through nurture, education, and prayerful self-examination. Nevertheless, all men failed sufficiently "to consider the things of their eternal life" and thus divided their loyalty between Satan and God. "Integrity or wholeness—holiness—is the definition of manhood. What we are, we must be with our whole being." No man need "reckon himself a cast-away" so long as he set his face heavenward with moral earnestness and complete dedication to the life in Christ. Wholehearted trust in God and a genuine desire to conform to his laws were the way of salvation. In this Henry and Thomas agreed, but Henry repudiated the evangelical belief in the power of evil, in what Bushnell (and Thomas Beecher with him) continued to fear as the Kingdom of Evil.[58]

As early as 1859, Henry was telling his audiences that the only necessity of Christian life was development of "a symmetrical Christian character, both contemplative and executive, both spiritual and philanthropic, both domestic and public." The previous year he had declared: "Piety before theology. Right living will produce right thinking." By piety he meant something both manly (practical, energetic, charitable, and chivalrous) and affective. He excoriated the "turbid sentimentalism" of mere theism and the "poverty-stricken" aridity of traditional theological activity. He interpreted Calvinism exclusively as the bulwark of "moral excellence and integrity of character," dismissing its doctrines as "the drippings of the old Roman hierarchy." Like Thomas and Harriet, he deplored the esthetic barrenness of Puritanic religion. Unlike them, however, he raised esthetics to the level of revelation, a revelation superior to virtually all others when it took the form of natural beauty. Henry regretted that his father's incapacity to grasp the revelatory power of Nature had cramped his theology, and reminded Yale seminarians how far theology had come since the older man's time:

> I recollect my dear old father talking about persons that worshipped God in clouds and saw the hand of God in beauty. He would say, "It is all moonshine, my son, with no doctrine nor edification nor sanctity in it at all, and I despise it."[59]

Henry Ward Beecher's nature writings, for which he became famous, strike a note much like the turbid sentimentalism that he complained of in others, and it would be easy to caricature his theological statements. His panegyrics on flowers captivated male and female readers alike, who followed his lead in worshipping God in Nature. John Calvin and Samuel Hopkins were all right in their day, but riper lessons could be found in violets in a mossy glade. Floral perfumes, Beecher wrote, were like "messengers from the spirit-world," while the trailing arbutus that braved spring snows was a sermon in itself. Beecher delighted his admirers by describing his elaborate tactics in stealing a dandelion through a fence or risking his clerical dignity to scramble down a riverbank in pursuit of wild primroses. If his father was incapable of considering the lilies of the field, his son went to the other extreme. Flowers were not merely aids to human spirituality. They delighted God himself, for "flowers may be said to live to God more than to men." More than any other creatures, flowers had a divine mission:

> Flowers are sent to do God's work in unrevealed paths, and to diffuse influence by channels that we hardly suspect. . . . Do we that look upon the kindled flowers, imagine what they have done, or are doing, to eyes that watch from afar. Because their life is not one fitted to commune with us, have they no life and communion the other way? Flowers may beckon toward us, but they speak toward heaven and God!

In short, flowers were sacramental.[60]

Although Harriet Stowe inclined toward Henry's view of natural beauty as an important means of communion with God, she retained a sense of realism in her view of Nature, deriving one of the chief supports of Calvinism from natural revelation:

> Now as Nature is, in many of her obvious aspects, notoriously uncompromising, harsh, and severe, the Calvinist who begins to talk to common-sense people has this advantage on his side,—that the things which he represents the Author of Nature as doing and being ready to do, are not very different from what the common-sense man sees that the Author of Nature is already in

> the habit of doing. The farmer who struggles with the hard soil, and with drouth and frost and caterpillars and fifty other insect plagues,—who finds his most persistent and well-calculated efforts constantly thwarted by laws whose workings he never can fully anticipate, and which never manifest either care for his good intentions or sympathy for his losses, is very apt to believe that the God who created nature may be a generally benevolent, but a severe and unsympathetic being, governing the world for some great, unknown purpose of his own, of which man's private improvement and happiness may not form a part.

Harriet was arguing that the calamities and hardships of man in the face of Nature—natural evil—predisposed him to Calvinistic views of moral evil and divine dispensation.[61]

Henry did not ignore natural and moral evil. There was more to the man than sentimental naturalism, for he was instrumental in advancing a doctrine of divine immanence. *Evolution and Religion* was the most forceful statement of this theme. There he acknowledged the presence of natural evil and the apparent wastefulness of the processes of growth, increase, and progressive development. "I am not ranked among the new theologists," he observed, "because I am not regarded as a theologian at any rate. . . . Nevertheless, I fight on my own hook." His fight, as he saw it, was to champion the idea that God is in Nature, that he reveals himself therein, and also that he dwells in history, shaping and directing it to a remote but glorious conclusion. That Beecher so understood his mission is clear from one of his letters, in which he praised Alexander V. G. Allen's essay on the spread of doctrines of divine immanence.[62]

Edward and Charles rejected this aspect of Henry's theology. God was transcendent. Even though history gave an ever purer disclosure of his character, it was a process he superintended as a sovereign directs the fate of his commonwealth. When Edward spoke of "evolution" and Charles of "historic fire," they meant that "history is, comprehensively speaking, the manifestation of God, in opposition to the manifestation of the evil one." In other words, they reasserted the Calvinist conception of the world as the theater of redemption, while adding the element of progressive revelation. They tried to disabuse Henry of his errors with respect to the "evolution of protoplasm and the primordial germ," and his heresy that mankind had only to outgrow its "basilar faculties" and develop eugenic knowledge to purge itself of brutish instincts and wolf-pack social behavior.

In 1884, Charles wrote Henry asking him to disavow the "dreadful things" reported—erroneously, he hoped—of a lecture defending evolution. With optimism bordering on self-deception, Charles regretfully conceded:

> I inferred from some remarks you made when I last saw you, that you had some slight differences of opinion in matters theologic from me and Edward. . . . We think man a fallen being, you think him a risen being,—but that need not prevent our writing letters to each other. Or is it a difference that must create a wide divergence—wider than might at first appear?

Sensing that Henry was in the vanguard of modern thought, while he and Edward appeared to be reactionaries, Charles made a stab at humor, saying, "It seems to me that a belief in the fall of man, may be tolerated in this era of liberty and liberality."[63]

Henry's reply must have mystified Charles, for it demonstrated a total lack of comprehension of Charles and Edward's system. "I am amazed or ought to be," Henry joked, "that you go back to Adam for an adequate supply of sin to furnish the needs of the world." The Augustinian doctrine of Original Sin was just so much "stale yeast" and he marveled at Charles's support of it. That his brothers had devoted their lives to destroying precisely that doctrine seems to have escaped Henry. Either he had not read their treatises or he wilfully misrepresented them. It was time, he told Charles, that men's "basilar powers" gave way to "the higher religious sentiments." By saying this, he was merely welding phrenological theory to evolutionary doctrine. He doubted whether further debate with his brothers would be profitable, and the discussion ended there. Henry simply could not take their concerns seriously. When he withdrew from the New York and Brooklyn Congregational Association in order to declare his independence of Congregational doctrine, Edward Beecher hastened to issue a public defense of Henry's orthodoxy, a fraternal gesture as unintelligible to Henry as it was crucial to Edward. Edward had spent the better part of his life trying to revolutionize society through theology, for only by knowing the truth about God and his ways could men be saved. The difference between the two men is summed up in a statement by one of Henry's young parishioners, who congratulated him on his intellectual honesty in withdrawing from the Association, and on the "practical effect" of his labors: "I find that, without any lack of zeal for knowing the truth, I am much more anxious to be right than to believe right." Although Henry himself might have considered such a testimony as an oversimplification of his teachings, another close friend asserted, "Belief with him was a matter of secondary importance; conduct was everything."[64]

Henry's watchword, as announced in *Life Thoughts*, was "Piety before theology." He defined piety as "right living" and told his readers that they must be good because wrongdoing and evildoing injured their heavenly Father. If Christians would only reflect upon their condition, they would realize that there was no need to be prideful, selfish, or mean-spirited. God expected nothing from them but what they could perform, given their education and constitutions. Men were only children, and God treated them accordingly:

> God Almighty is the mother, and the soul is the tired child. . . . The mother's arms encircle but one; but God clasps every yearning soul to his bosom, and gives it the peace which passeth understanding, beyond the reach of care or storm.
>
> I have been preaching that of all beings there is none so burdened, none so active, none that takes upon himself the garments of sorrow so universally and continually as God,—and what is there of patience, of labor, or suffering or watching that father and mother will not give rather than that the child should sicken and die, or rather than it should go wrong?[65]

The New Haven Theology aimed at vindicating the moral government of God from the charge that the divine ruler had arbitrarily entailed guilt upon a sinless race of his own creation. By the logic of the ultimate New Haven position, which fully developed the New England doctrine of actual sin, the guilt of sin belonged to the individual: "Sin is in the sinning." Lyman Beecher's children objected that Taylorism was not only inadequate to explain human depravity but also unfair to God by representing his actions and decisions in an absolutist light. It was hypocritical to talk of "moral government" when God still ruled by exercising arbitrary power and when he demanded instant submission to inequitable, unintelligible laws. Guilt or innocence, criminality or virtue, were meaningless terms when God required man to act according to a hopelessly flawed nature and yet exacted penalties for that very imperfection of nature.

True virtue in the regenerate man was supposed to mark his restoration to divine favor. Fired with love to God, the Christian would live according to the law of love to fellow creatures. This was more than right conduct, more than the Golden Rule. It was a love which overflowed ordinary human bounds, making the redeemed unconscious of their magnanimity, spontaneous in their altruism. If disinterested benevolence was the highest attainment of the Christian, as the Beechers were brought up to believe, then perhaps the same kind of love and self-sacrifice animated their Creator. The Beecher children saw nothing impious in arguing for an absolute moral identity between God and man. Disinterestedness lost its appeal when it was viewed as the attribute of a remote, dimly benignant sovereign. The character of God was immensely more attractive when seen as the disinterestedness of a devout mother or a selfless home missionary intensified and concentrated to equal God's omnipotence and omniscience.

The loftiest human ideal that the Beechers could conceive was a father, at once high-minded, spontaneously affectionate, actively benevolent, and powerful. Speaking of their father, Catharine asked:

> And was there ever a parent who, in the first period of family training, more perfectly exhibited the happy combination of strong and steady government with the tenderest love and sympathy, or whose children were better prepared to transfer the love and obedience of an earthly father to a Heavenly One?

Henry expressed the same feeling when he described how their father had comforted him as a child, and Charles, when he recalled that their father's love had provided not only consolation but security. Thus, when Edward Beecher presented to his brothers and sisters a Father even more perfect than the one they knew, they rushed to embrace him. They dethroned the constitutional monarch of Lyman's theology and instituted a new heavenly order, the family of God. If God was supremely paternal, as they held, then he could not be vindictive or hard-handed. Salvation in these terms was not amnesty or reconciliation, but homecoming. As William Beecher said, "*Pardon* is not salvation—*restoration to Love* is." Sin was due not to a depraved constitution but to ingratitude and lack of filial sympathy.[66]

In place of the sinner, there was the rebellious child. "Every sin you commit," Henry told his church, "is personal to God and not merely an infraction of his *law.*" How could men persist in disregarding their father's wishes and hopes, when their misbehavior pained him terribly? "It is casting javelins and arrows of base desire into his loving bosom." God's injunctions must be obeyed not out of mere superstitious regard for rules, but because disobedience threatened the father-child relationship. There was no hint in Henry's sermons that the Father would be angered and abandon the child, for divine love was unconditional. Knowing that God would bear with his every infirmity, the sinner could trust his Father to sympathize with his weaknesses and forgive his petty mistakes. God did not set up laws merely for the sake of exercising his authority, but rather to protect his children from their recklessness and ignorance. "Law without, is only an echo of God's heart-beat within."

The sinner's infractions of those laws, therefore, should not flood him with horror at the enormity of his guilt. What he should feel was sorrow and shame at the hurt he had inflicted upon the parent and remorse over his unworthiness. This was guilt, but of an untraditional kind. Guilt is central to the Augustinian formulation against which the Beechers were protesting, and there it is an existential fact as well as a motif of sacred history. Guilt in the Beechers' scheme was present, though unacknowledged as such, but it was purely private and personal. Moreover, it demonstrated the strength of the filial bond rather than opening a chasm between man and God which could be breached only by an act of divine condescension. It was only when the child was unable to feel and act upon his guilt that he was lost, for he was in danger of forgetting the great happiness of being forgiven.[67]

If a man's theology is truly a hereditary mansion, then the Beechers had abandoned the shelter of Puritanism well before 1859, when evangelicalism seemed to have begun its decline. In that year, as Catharine astutely noted, the great revival was instigated and led by laymen. And in 1860, sentiments like that of Oliver Wendell Holmes had lost their power to shock:

> I have in common with yourself, a desire to leave the world a little more human than if I had not lived; for a true humanity is, I believe, our nearest approach to Divinity, while we work out our atmospheric apprenticeship on the surface of this second-class planet.

Charles and Edward Beecher would have demurred from Holmes's remark, but not the other Beecher children. And in fact, even Edward and Charles Beecher's theology originated in similar impulses and needs. As much as they denounced self-deification and the denial of human tragedy, their principles and their deductions from those principles encouraged the more audacious, if less scientific, theological explorations of their brothers and sisters, who attached positive value to the humanization of the divine and the divinization of humanity.[68]

Faith and theology in the Beecher family was not a strictly private affair. Since they were ministers or, in the case of the women, virtually ministers, they aimed at communicating the results of their internal struggles to the masses of people who read their books and heard their lectures. This audience was predominantly middle-class and evangelical in background, and the view of God which the Beechers tried to establish was one that appealed to such people. The emphasis on domesticity, on the family of God as an enduring community, on the love of God as perfect and persevering—these ideas held undeniable attractions in an era when the nuclear family was made to bear such immense cultural and emotional weight. The sentimental subjectivism of views like the Beechers' was reflected, as they noted, in the hymns of the mid-nineteenth century. Henry Ward Beecher's favorite, "Jesus, Lover of My Soul, Let Me to Thy Bosom Fly," was simply one of hundreds of the same character, including his sister Harriet's most famous hymn, "Still, Still with Thee." The intensity of the Beechers' conception of God's parental bond to man reflected the inner experiences of people as diverse as Theodore Parker and Elizabeth Stuart Phelps Ward, Oliver Wendell Holmes and Andrew Jackson Davis. That intensity was not, of course, sustained, but the parental view of God became a permanent element of evangelical religion in America, notwithstanding neo-Calvinism, and the Beechers' contribution, for better or worse, was a large one.[69]

NOTES

CHAPTER 1

1. For a detailed, critical account of this earlier period, see Vincent Harding, "Lyman Beecher and the Transformation of American Protestantism, 1775-1863" (Ph.D. diss., University of Chicago, 1965).

2. Lyman Beecher, *Autobiography*, 2 vols., ed. Charles Beecher (New York, 1863), is one of the key sources for this study; quotations are from the modern edition by Barbara Cross (Cambridge, Mass., 1961), 1:159, chaps. 21 and 42. Rebecca Taylor Hatch, *Personal Reminiscences and Memorials* (New York, 1905), p. 35.

3. Timothy Dwight, *Travels in New England and New York*, 4 vols., ed. Barbara Miller Solomon (Cambridge, Mass., 1969), 2:256-57; Richard J. Purcell, *Connecticut in Transition, 1775-1818* (Washington, D.C., 1918); Alain C. White, comp., *History of the Town of Litchfield* (Litchfield, Conn., 1920); Emily Noyes Vanderpoel, comp., *Chronicles of a Pioneer School*, ed. Elizabeth C. B. Buel (Cambridge, Mass., 1903) and *More Chronicles of a Pioneer School* (New York, 1927); Samuel G. Goodrich, *Recollections of a Lifetime*, 2 vols. (New York, 1857); Harriet Porter Beecher to Nathaniel Coffin, Dec. 4, 1817 (SDML).

4. Lyman Beecher, preface to *Works*, 3 vols. (Boston, 1852).

5. Lyman Beecher, *Autobiography*, 2:399, 1:93; Hatch, *Personal Reminiscences*, p. 27; Calvin E. Stowe, "Sketches and Recollections of Lyman Beecher," *Congregational Quarterly* 6 (July 1864): 221; see Alpheus S. Packard on shift in New England speech, in Nehemiah Cleaveland, *History of Bowdoin College* (Boston, 1882), p. 89; Henry Ward Beecher, *Autobiographical Reminiscences*, ed. T. J. Ellinwood (New York, 1898), p. 86; John R. Dix, *Pulpit Portraits* (Boston, 1854), pp. 151-52; Henry P. Hedges, *History of the Town of East-Hampton* (Sag Harbor, N.Y., 1897), p. 163; James C. White, *Personal Reminiscences of Lyman Beecher* (New York, 1882).

6. Roxana Foote (1775-1816) was the daughter of Eli and Roxana Ward Foote of Guilford, Connecticut. Harriet Porter (1790-1835) was the daughter of Aaron and Paulina King Porter of Portland, Maine. The third wife, Lydia Beals Jackson of Boston, was a widow when Beecher married her in 1836 and took her children into his family.

7. Lyman Beecher, *Autobiography*, 1:35-38, 22; Hatch, *Personal Reminiscences*, p. 17; John P. Foote, *Memoirs of the Life of Samuel E. Foote* (Cincinnati, 1860), pp. 28-30.

8. Catharine E. Beecher, *Educational Reminiscences* (New York, 1874), p. 15; Roxana Foote Beecher to Harriet Foote, July 22, 1813 (Beecher-Scoville Family Papers, Yale); Lyman Beecher, *Autobiography*, 1:127, 130.

9. Catharine E. Beecher, *Educational Reminiscences*, pp. 9–12; Henry Ward Beecher, *Autobiographical Reminiscences*, pp. 34–35; John R. Howard, *Remembrance of Things Past* (New York, 1925), p. 246; Charles Beecher, "Life of Edward Beecher," MS (Illinois College Library), pp. 1–10.

10. Lyman Beecher, *Autobiography*, 1:217–18, 220–21; Vanderpoel, *Chronicles*, p. 149; Lyman Beecher to Nathaniel W. Taylor, Sept. 30, 1816 (Beecher-Scoville Family Papers, Yale).

11. Theodore and Elizabeth Tilton were parishioners and close friends of Henry Ward Beecher. Tilton, who was an active abolitionist and feminist, served under Beecher as managing editor of the *Independent*, a periodical owned by Henry C. Bowen, the founder of Plymouth Church in Brooklyn. Although the actual story of the transgression—if there was one—remains murky, it is plain that Beecher behaved in an indecorous and highly imprudent manner. It was rumored, long before Victoria Woodhull publicly accused Beecher of adultery, that he had seduced Bowen's wife, that she had fallen into a decline and died of a broken heart. Mrs. Woodhull charged that Elizabeth Tilton was the most recent of Beecher's paramours (local gossip attributing Mrs. Bowen's heartbreak to Beecher's inconstancy). Beecher's obstinate refusal to denounce the rumors and his signing of a "confession" forced on him by Tilton made the accusations highly plausible, when combined with Libby Tilton's equivocation and melodramatic gestures. The scandal was a piece of luck for Beecher's ecclesiastical foes, but his congregation backed him enthusiastically, through both church and civil trials, voting him a huge bonus to pay his legal fees. As religious scandals go, it was a stupendous one, but Beecher weathered it to remain the most popular clergyman of his time. For the effect of the scandal on his family, see chapters 4 and 10, below.

12. Henry Ward Beecher to Harriet Elizabeth Beecher, April 4, 1832, A. Perkins to Charles Perkins, Oct. 23, 1848, William H. Beecher to Henry Ward Beecher, Dec. 12, 1863, Charles Beecher to Harriet E. Beecher Scoville, Jan. 28, 1899 (Beecher-Scoville Family Papers, Yale); Lyman Beecher, *Autobiography*, 1:226; William C. Beecher and Samuel Scoville, *A Biography of Rev. Henry Ward Beecher* (New York, 1888), p. 128. The novels and poems of Harriet Beecher Stowe are full of saintly, ethereal women obviously modeled on her mother.

13. Lyman Beecher, *Autobiography*, 1:59, 2:26; Lyman Beecher to Harriet Porter, Sept. 16, 1817 (SDML): Isabella Beecher Hooker, *Womanhood: Its Sanctities and Fidelities* (Boston, 1873), pp. 24–25. Lyman stated that Roxana had attained the ideal of "disinterestedness" central to the theology of Samuel Hopkins. See Barbara M. Cross, *Horace Bushnell* (Chicago, 1958) for an illuminating analysis of middle-class popular piety in the mid-nineteenth century; her Radcliffe Ph.D. dissertation, 1956, contains a more extended discussion of the topic, centering on giftbooks and popular literary annuals.

14. Vanderpoel, *Chronicles*, p. 171.

15. Lyman Beecher to Harriet Porter, Sept. 9 [1817], Harriet Porter to Lyman Beecher, Sept. 11, 1817 (SDML).

16. Lyman Beecher to Harriet Porter, Sept. 9, 11, and Oct. 2, 1817 (SDML); Lyman Beecher, *Autobiography*, 1: 261–62.

17. Harriet Porter to Lyman Beecher, Sept. 22 and Oct. 13, 1817, Lyman Beecher to Harriet Porter, Sept. 16, 1817, Lyman Beecher to Nathaniel Coffin, Dec. 22, 1817 (SDML); *Autobiography*, 2:19. See Harriet Beecher Stowe, *Men of Our Times* (Hartford, 1868), pp. 506–07, on Harriet Porter, and Henry Ward Beecher, *Autobiographical Reminiscences*, pp. 70–71; Beecher and Scoville, *Henry Ward Beecher*, pp. 65–66; Lucy Jackson White, "Notes on the last days of Lyman Beecher," MS (SDML).

18. Henry Ward Beecher, Journal, Jan. 24, 1836 (Beecher-Scoville Family Papers, Yale); John Hooker to Isabella Homes Beecher, Nov. 11, 1839 (SDML); Lyman Beecher to Catharine E. Beecher, Dec. 3, 1823 (Beecher-Stowe Coll., SLR); James C. White, *Reminiscences of Lyman Beecher*, pp. 22, 33; Lyman Beecher, *Autobiography*, 1: 303–04.

19. Charles Beecher, preface to *Redeemer and Redeemed* (Boston, 1864); Charles Beecher to Harriet E. Beecher Scoville, Jan. 28, 1899 (Beecher-Scoville Family Papers, Yale).

20. Esther Beecher to Isabella Beecher Hooker, July 16, 1849, May 20 and July 7, 1844 (SDML); Harriet Beecher Stowe, *Household Papers and Stories* (Boston, 1896), pp. 421–22; Harriet Beecher Stowe to Henry Ellis Stowe [Dec. 16, 1855] (Beecher-Stowe Coll., SLR).

21. *Autobiography*, vol. 1, chaps. 2–11; D. Howe Allen, *The Life and Services of Rev. Lyman Beecher, D.D.* (Cincinnati, 1863), p. 3; Hedges, *History of East-Hampton*, p. 162.

22. Catharine E. Beecher, *Educational Reminiscences*, p. 15; Isabella Homes Beecher to John Hooker, Dec. 2, 1839 (SDML); Lyman Beecher, *Autobiography*, 1:11, 16, 26.

23. Horace Mann to Lydia B. Mann, April 11, 1822 (Horace Mann Papers, MHS); Vanderpoel, *Chronicles*, pp. 244, 250–51; Lyman Beecher, *Autobiography*, 1:226–27; Catharine E. Beecher, "The Slave's Prayer," in Julia Griffiths, ed., *Autographs for Freedom* (Boston, 1853), pp. 75–76; Catharine E. Beecher, *Religious Training of Children* (New York, 1864), p. 18; Lyman Beecher to Catharine E. Beecher, May 26, 1819 and Dec. 3, 1823 (Beecher-Stowe Coll., SLR); William H. Beecher to Edward Beecher, July 8, 1827 (Beecher Family Papers, MHCL); Henry Ward Beecher, *Norwood; or Village Life in New England* (New York, 1868), p. 181.

24. Charles Beecher, "Life of Edward Beecher," p. 84; Catharine E. Beecher, "Song of Remembrance," MS (Beecher-Stowe Coll., SLR); Lucy Jackson White, "Notes on the last days of Lyman Beecher," MS (SDML).

25. Catharine E. Beecher, *The Biographical Remains of George Beecher* (New York, 1844); Frederick Adolphus Porcher, "Memoirs," ed. Samuel G. Stoney, *South Carolina Historical and Genealogical Magazine* 47 (1947):210. Frederick Adolphus Porcher was a Southern aristocrat who found much to regret in Yankee character, particularly of the evangelical stripe. Porcher reported that George "used to talk with great complacency of the noble things he meant to do when he should have a church. He evidently intended to follow the footsteps of his father." George must have irritated Porcher greatly, for he noted acidly in his memoirs that this Beecher, after all, had amounted to very little.

26. Beecher and Scoville, *Henry Ward Beecher*, p. 32; Lyman Abbott, ed., *Henry Ward Beecher* (New York, 1883), p. vii; White, *History of Litchfield*, pp. 34–35.

27. Lyman Beecher, *Autobiography*, 1:248, 287, 302, 310, 342, 346–47.

28. I am indebted to Dr. David Musto for his assistance in interpreting the medical records of James C. Beecher.

29. Lyman Beecher, *Autobiography*, 1:387–91; Charles Beecher to William C. Beecher, April 17, 1887 (Beecher-Scoville Family Papers, Yale); Charles Beecher to Hattie and Eliza Stowe, July 23, 1896 (Beecher-Stowe Coll., SLR).

30. Catharine E. Beecher, *Religious Training*, pp. 18–19; Henry Ward Beecher, *Autobiographical Reminiscences*, p. 134; Abbott, ed., *Henry Ward Beecher*, pp. 25–26.

31. Vanderpoel, *Chronicles*, pp. 83, 97.

32. Mansfield, *Personal Memories*, p. 122.

33. Vanderpoel, *Chronicles*, p. 233; Catharine E. Beecher, *Educational Reminiscences*, p. 31; Lyman Beecher, *Autobiography*, 1:165, 397; Vanderpoel, *More Chronicles*, p. 116; Catharine E. Beecher to Louisa Wait, June 28, 1821 (Beecher-Stowe Coll., SLR).

34. Charles Beecher, "Life of Edward Beecher," pp. 3–4; Lyman Beecher to George A. Foote, Sept. 28, 1818, Jan. 9, 1819, and March 10, 1822 (Beecher-Scoville Family Papers, Yale); Lyman Beecher, *Autobiography*, 1:313, 316–17, 343.

35. Edward Beecher to Catharine E. Beecher, Dec. 11, 1822, Lyman Beecher to Catharine E. Beecher and Edward Beecher, Dec. 3, 1823 (Beecher-Stowe Coll., SLR); Catharine E. Beecher to Edward Beecher, April 25, 1826 (Beecher Family Papers, MHCL). See chap. 3, below, on the death of Catharine's fiancé. The property to which Lyman refers in his letter was probably the land and farmhouse he inherited from his uncle Lot Benton (*Autobiography*, 1:317).

36. Thomas K. Beecher, *Notable Sermons* (Elmira, N.Y., 1914), pp. 4–7; Lyman Beecher, *Autobiography*, 2:389, 427, 438.

37. Catharine E. Beecher, *Educational Reminiscences*, pp. 13–14; Henry Ward Beecher, *Autobiographical Reminiscences*, pp. 87–88; Isabella Beecher Hooker to John Hooker, Sept. 9, 1843 (SDML).

38. Charles Beecher, "Life of Edward Beecher," p. 2; Thomas K. Beecher, *Notable Sermons*, p. 7; Lyman Beecher, *Autobiography*, 1:391, 2:217–18; Henry Ward Beecher, *Norwood*, p. 547.

39. [Lyman Beecher], *Dialogue* (Sag Harbor, N.Y., 1806); Lyman Beecher to Richard S. Storrs, April 6, 1806 (Gratz Coll., HSP).

40. Thomas K. Beecher to Isabella Beecher Hooker, Jan. 9, 1843 (SDML); Henry Ward Beecher, "Bowdoin-Street Church," *Independent*, May 5, 1862.

41. Lyman Beecher, *Autobiography*, 1:29–30; Lyman Beecher, *Instructions for Young Christians* (Boston, 1834), pp. 21, 37, 48; Lyman Beecher, *A Guide to Piety; or, Directions to Persons Just Commencing a Religious Life* (Worcester, Mass., 1843), pp. 5, 16, 22, 27.

42. Lyman Beecher, *Autobiography*, 1:394–95; Charles Beecher to William C. Beecher, April 17, 1887 (Beecher-Scoville Family Papers, Yale); Edward Beecher to Catharine E. Beecher, April 1821 (Beecher-Stowe Coll., SLR); probably the book referred to is Michael Wigglesworth, *The Day of Doom: or a Poetical Description of the Great and Last Judgment* (1662), which enjoyed great popularity well into the nineteenth century.

43. Edward Beecher to Catharine E. Beecher, Nov. 13, 1822 (Beecher-Stowe Coll., SLR); Charles E. Stowe, *Life of Harriet Beecher Stowe* (Boston, 1889), p. 8.

44. Lyman Beecher, *Autobiography*, vol. 1, chaps. 34 and 46; Henry Ward Beecher, *Norwood*, p. 245; Harriet Beecher Stowe, *Sunny Memories of Foreign Lands*, 2 vols. (Boston, 1854), 1:41, 143, 178, 186; Catharine E. Beecher, "Song of Remembrance," MS (Beecher-Stowe Coll., SLR); Mansfield, *Personal Memories*, p. 140; undated clipping in Schoumaker scrapbook, James Chaplin Beecher papers in possession of Mrs. Alfred T. Abeles.

45. Goodrich, *Recollections*, 2:104; Lyman Beecher, *Autobiography*, 1:393–94.

46. Lyman Beecher, *Autobiography*, 1:33, 102, 165–66, 170–71; Vanderpoel, *Chronicles*, p. 150; Lyman Beecher to Nathaniel Wright, Jan. 1, 1840 and Nathaniel Wright to Lyman Beecher, Jan. 14, 1840 (Nathaniel Wright Papers, LC); Lyman Beecher, *Works*, 1:374; Charles R. Keller, *The Second Great Awakening in Connecticut* (New Haven, 1942), chap. 6; *History of Litchfield County, Connecticut* (Philadelphia, 1881), pp. 142–43.

47. Henry Ward Beecher, *Autobiographical Reminiscences*, p. 98; Horace

Bushnell, "The Age of Homespun," in *Work and Play* (New York, 1881), p. 396; Timothy Dwight, *Greenfield Hill* (New York, 1794), 5:223–24; Harriet Beecher Stowe, *Religious Studies* (Boston, 1896), p. 298.

48. Quoted in F. Ernest Stoeffler, *The Rise of Evangelical Pietism* (Leiden, 1965), p. 16.

49. Lyman Beecher, *Autobiography*, 1:208–09; Robbins, *Diary*, see various entries dated July 4; Goodrich, *Recollections*, 1:22, 355, 471.

50. Goodrich, *Recollections*, 2:78–81; Henry Ward Beecher, *Star Papers; or Experiences of Art and Nature* (New York, 1855), pp. 245–46. See also Richard L. Bushman, *From Puritan to Yankee: Character and Social Order in Connecticut, 1690–1795* (New York, 1967), on the transformation of the social ethos of Connecticut.

51. Goodrich, *Recollections*, 1:114; Lyman Beecher, *Autobiography*, 1:275; Harriet Porter Beecher to Nathaniel Coffin, Dec. 4, 1817, Harriet Porter to Lyman Beecher, Sept. 18, 1817 (SDML); Purcell, *Connecticut in Transition*, p. 331. "Toleration" was the term applied to the religious-political coalition of Jeffersonian Republicans (called Democrats) and dissenting denominations, which brought about the end of the Congregationalist establishment supported by the Federalists. The 1818 legislature secured a written state constitution and severed the church-state union.

52. Keller, *The Second Great Awakening in Connecticut*, p. 51. Lyman Beecher's dread of disestablishment was voiced in "The Toleration Dream," a heavy-handed satire reprinted as chapter 57 of his *Autobiography*, vol. 1.

CHAPTER 2

1. Lyman Beecher to Nathaniel W. Taylor, March 17, 1846, in *Autobiography*, 2:377–78. Useful background for this chapter is provided by Robert Baird, *Religion in America* (New York, 1856), which emphasizes the voluntaryistic and revivalistic character of American religion; Samuel J. Baird, *A History of the New School* (Philadelphia, 1868), a vitriolic but valuable tracing of the development of New School Presbyterian doctrine by an Old School partisan; Zebulon Crocker, *The Catastrophe of the Presbyterian Church in 1837* (New Haven, 1838), a temperate account of the events leading to the schism, by a New School man; George Marsden, *The Evangelical Mind and the New School Presbyterian Experience* (New Haven, 1970); and Sidney Mead, *Nathaniel William Taylor, 1786–1858: A Connecticut Liberal* (Chicago, 1942), an excellent treatment of the life and thought of Beecher's ally and closest friend.

2. Timothy Dwight, *Theology; Explained and Defended*, 5 vols. (Middletown, Conn., 1818), 5:565; Catherine M. Sedgwick, *Life and Letters*, ed. Mary E. Dewey (New York, 1871), p. 68.

3. Robert Baird, *Religion in America*, p. 412.

4. Mead, *Nathaniel W. Taylor*, pp. 100–01; William Chauncey Fowler, *Essays: Historical, Literary, Educational* (Hartford, 1876), pp. 53–57; Frank Hugh Foster, *A Genetic History of New England Theology* (Chicago, 1907), p. 365. Charles E. Cuningham, *Timothy Dwight* (New York, 1942), although an uninspired biography, contains useful material; Kenneth Silverman, *Timothy Dwight* (New York, 1969), focuses on his literary works.

5. Dwight, *Theology*, 5:219–20.

6. Ibid., 3:289–90.

7. Ibid., 1:115, 218, 224–28.

8. Ibid., pp. 182, 224–28, 251.

9. Ibid., pp. 248–49; "God To Be Believed Rather Than Man," "The Folly of

Trusting Our Own Hearts," and "The Preaching of Paul Before Felix," in *Sermons*, 2 vols. (New Haven, 1828), 1:40, 2:55–56, 483.

10. Dwight, *Theology*, 2:553.

11. "The Son of God" and "Tidings of a Saviour, Tidings of Great Joy," in *Sermons*, 1:116, 121, 190–91; *Theology*, 1:490, 2:3–15, 28, 503.

12. *Theology*, 1:525–27, 2:532.

13. Ibid., 4:458–68; "Secret Things Belong to God" and "Those Who Believe Not the Scriptures, Would Not Be Persuaded, Though One Rose From the Dead," in *Sermons*, 1:20, 2:111–12.

14. "Review of Dr. Dwight's Sermons," *Spirit of the Pilgrims* 2 (May-June 1829): 258; Lyman Beecher, *Autobiography*, 1:241–42.

15. Dwight, *Theology*, 1:309, 527, 2:15, 4:500–13, 5:25–33, 145. On preparationist theology, see Norman Pettit, *The Heart Prepared: Grace and Conversion in Puritan Spiritual Life* (New Haven, 1966).

16. Lyman Beecher, *Autobiography*, 1:29–30; Bennet Tyler, *Memoir of the Life and Character of Rev. Asahel Nettleton, D.D.* (Hartford, 1844), pp. 23–25, 64.

17. Tyler, *Memoir of Nettleton*, pp. 48, 145; Timothy Dwight, *Greenfield Hill*, pt. 1, pp. 479–80.

18. [Benjamin W. Dwight], "Biographical hints and facts respecting the late Revd Timothy Dwight," MS (Dwight Family Papers, Yale); [Timothy Dwight], "On the Manner in Which the Scriptures Are To Be Understood," *Panoplist and Missionary Magazine* 12 (May-June 1816): 193–203, 249–56; Timothy Dwight, "On Revivals of Religion," in *Sermons*, 1:228–38.

19. Geoffrey Nuttall, "The Influence of Arminianism in England," *The Puritan Spirit* (London, 1967), p. 77. See also C. C. Goen, "The 'Methodist Age' in American Church History," *Religion in Life* 34 (Autumn 1965): 562–72.

20. Jedidiah Morse to Dr. Kemp, Oct. 17, 1804, Morse to Joseph Lyman, Feb. 18, 1804, Leonard Woods to Morse, March 15 and Oct. 17, 1806, Asa McFarland to Morse, Sept. 8, 1806, and Elijah Parish to Morse [Dec. 11, 1806] (Morse Family Papers, Yale).

21. Morse to Leonard Woods, Oct. 21, 1806, Morse to Daniel Dana, Oct. 17, 1806, Morse to Dr. Lathrop, Nov. 18, 1807, Morse to Timothy Dwight, Feb. 22, 1808, Timothy Dwight to Morse, June 6, 1808, Abiel Holmes to Morse, Dec. 18, 1809 (Morse Family Papers, Yale). On Morse's life, see William B. Sprague, *Life of Jedidiah Morse, D.D.* (New York, 1874). See Geoffrey F. Nuttall, *Richard Baxter and Philip Doddridge: A Study in Tradition* (London, 1951).

22. Lyman Beecher to John Romeyn, Oct. 17, 1806, Lyman Beecher to Roxana Foote Beecher, Feb. 26, 1810, in *Autobiography*, 1:112, 133; Lyman Beecher, *Works*, 3 vols. (Boston, 1852), 2:13, 18, 156.

23. Nathaniel W. Taylor to Lyman Beecher, Jan. 14, 1819, in *Autobiography*, 1:284–87. On Emmons, see Foster, *Genetic History*, pp. 218, 345.

24. Mead, *Nathaniel W. Taylor*, chap. 6; Harriet Beecher Stowe, "Lyman Beecher," in Ferdinand Piper and Henry M. MacCracken, eds., *Lives of the Leaders of Our Church Universal* (Boston, 1879), 3:715.

25. Lyman Beecher, *Autobiography*, 2:53; Joseph F. Tuttle, *The Late Dr. Beecher* (New York, 1863), p. 9; Ebenezer Porter to Lyman Beecher, May 22, 1829, in *Autobiography*, 2:123.

26. Lyman Beecher to Benjamin Wisner, 1825, in *Autobiography*, 2:11; Samuel Baird, *History of the New School*, pp. 185–89.

27. Thomas Robbins, *Diary of Thomas Robbins, D.D., 1796–1854*, 2 vols., ed. Increase N. Tarbox (Boston, 1886), 1:230; Robert H. Nichols, *Presbyterianism in New York State*, ed. James H. Nichols (Philadelphia, 1963), pp. 110–11; Mars-

den, *Evangelical Mind*, pp. 40–42; Samuel Baird, *History of the New School*, p. 166.

28. Samuel Baird, *History of the New School*, pp. 180, 203; James Hadley, *Diary, 1843–1852*, ed. Laura Hadley Moseley (New Haven, 1951), p. 89; Lyman Beecher, *Autobiography*, 2:13.

29. Lyman Beecher to Asahel Hooker, March 13, 1825, Bennet Tyler to Lyman Beecher, Jan. 24, 1824, and Asahel Nettleton to Beecher, April 2, 1824, in *Autobiography*, 2:15, 1:408–10.

30. Calvin E. Stowe, "Lyman Beecher," p. 228; Nathaniel W. Taylor, *Concio ad Clerum: A Sermon Delivered in the Chapel of Yale College, Sept. 10, 1828* (New Haven, 1828).

31. Ebenezer Porter to Lyman Beecher, May 22, 1829, and Beecher to Porter, June 1829, in *Autobiography*, 2:119–20, 125–41. The most recent and best study of New Haven Theology is Earl A. Pope, "The Rise of New Haven Theology," *Journal of Presbyterian History* 44 (March, June 1966): 24–44, 106–21; the arguments of Taylor's critics are ably presented here. See also Claude Welch, *Protestant Thought in the Nineteenth Century* (New Haven, 1972), vol. 1, chap. 6; Foster, *Genetic History*; George Nye Boardman, *A History of New England Theology* (New York, 1899).

32. Charles G. Finney, *Memoirs* (New York, 1876), pp. 211, 314–17; Charles C. Cole, Jr., "The New Lebanon Convention," *New York History* 31 (Oct. 1950): 385–97. See H. Shelton Smith, *Changing Conceptions of Original Sin* (New York, 1955), chaps. 5 and 6 for the fullest discussion of New Haven doctrines of Original Sin. These did, in fact, resemble the views of Pelagius, the British monk whose commentary on Romans, written early in the fifth century, denied the argument that Original Sin was inherited from Adam, although sin had come into the world through him. Man, in the Pelagian view, is free not to sin. (See *Schaff-Herzog Encyclopedia of Religious Knowledge*.)

33. Lyman Beecher to Ebenezer Porter, June 1829, loc. cit.

34. Edward D. Mansfield, *Personal Memories* (Cincinnati, 1879), pp. 150–51; Timothy Flint, *Recollections of the Last Ten Years* (Boston, 1826), p. 46; Harding, "Lyman Beecher," pp. 434–35.

35. Samuel Baird, *History of the New School*, pp. 468–69.

36. [Nathaniel W. Taylor], *An Inquiry into the Nature of Sin as Exhibited in Dr. Dwight's Theology, with Remarks on an Examination of Dr. Taylor's and Mr. Harvey's Views on the Same Subject* (New Haven, 1829), p. 35; [Asa Rand], *Letter to Dr. Beecher* (Lowell, Mass., 1833), pp. 6–7.

37. Lyman Beecher, *Autobiography*, vol. 2, chap. 30.

38. Julian M. Sturtevant, *Autobiography* (New York, 1874), pp. 183, 194–200, 207; Beecher and Skinner, *Hints, Designed to Aid Christians* (Philadelphia, 1832), p. 18; A. T. Norton, *History of Presbyterianism in Illinois* (St. Louis, Mo., 1879), pp. 168, 184; Samuel Baird, *History of the New School*, pp. 472–73. See also John R. Willis, "The Yale Band in Illinois" (Ph.D. diss., Yale, 1946), pp. 177, 226–34, 248; Charles H. Rammelkamp, *Illinois College* (New Haven, 1928).

39. Lyman Beecher, *Autobiography*, vol. 2, chap. 31.

40. Tyler, *Memoir of Nettleton*, pp. 200–01, and chap. 13. Curtis M. Geer, *Hartford Theological Seminary, 1834–1934* (Hartford, 1934), is a pedestrian account of the East Windsor group and their seminary.

41. Chauncey A. Goodrich to Lyman Beecher, Aug. 3, 1834, Albert Barnes to Beecher, March 20, 1835, and Beecher to Nathaniel W. Taylor, April 25, 1835, in *Autobiography*, vol. 2, chap. 36, pp. 265–66; Richard Cary Morse to Louisa Morse, June 7 and 12, 1835 (Morse Family Papers, Yale).

42. "Dr. Beecher's Trial for Heresy," in Lyman Beecher, *Works*, 3:112–14,

117-33; Richard Cary Morse to Louisa Morse, June 13 and 19, 1835 (Morse Family Papers, Yale).

43. Ithamar Pillsbury to Samuel Miller, Sept. 17, 1835, and Asahel Nettleton to Samuel Miller [Sept. 17, 1835], Miller to Nettleton, Sept. 23, 1835, Feb. 9, 1836 (Samuel Miller Papers, Princeton); Lyman Beecher, *Autobiography*, 2:270-304; Lyman Beecher to William M. Engles [1836] (William M. Engles Coll., PHS); "Beecher's Views in Theology," *Biblical Repertory and Princeton Review* 4 (April, July 1837): 216-37, 364-407.

44. Calvin E. Stowe, MS sermon [ca. 1837] (Beecher-Stowe Coll., SLR); Edward Beecher to Lyman Beecher, Feb. 29, 1836 (Beecher Family Papers, MHCL); Edward Beecher to Lyman Beecher, Nov. 11, 1836 (Beecher-Stowe Coll., SLR).

45. Lyman Beecher to Thomas Brainerd, May 1837 (Gratz Coll., HSP); Henry B. Smith to George L. Prentiss, Nov. 2, 1840, in *Life and Letters of Henry Boynton Smith* (New York, 1881), p. 91; Lyman Beecher to Lydia Beals Jackson Beecher, July 24, 1839 (SDML); Henry P. Tappan, *Review of Edwards's "Inquiry into the Freedom of the Will"* (New York, 1839); Lyman Beecher, *Address, Delivered at the Tenth Anniversary Celebration of the Union Literary Society of Miami University* (Cincinnati, 1835), p. 3; review of Beecher's *Autobiography*, in *New Englander* 24 (April 1865): 405-06.

CHAPTER 3

1. Lyman Beecher, diary, Sept. 6, 1800, quoted by Harriet Beecher Stowe in "Catherine [*sic*] E. Beecher," *Our Famous Women* (Hartford, 1884), pp. 75-76; "Sketch of the life of Miss Catharine Beecher," May 20, 1878 (Beecher Family Papers, MHCL); Lyman Beecher, *Autobiography*, 1:149, 396.

2. Catharine E. Beecher, *Educational Reminiscences*; Catharine E. Beecher to Harriet Porter, quoted in *Autobiography*, 1:358.

3. Lyman Beecher, *Autobiography*, 1:363; Harriet Porter to Catharine E. Beecher, Sept. 18, 1817 (SDML); Catharine E. Beecher, *Educational Reminiscences*, p. 24; Lyman Beecher to Harriet Porter, Oct. 5, 1817 (SDML).

4. Catharine E. Beecher to Louisa Wait [June 1821], Catharine E. Beecher to Lyman Beecher, June 5, 1821 (Beecher-Stowe Coll., SLR).

5. John Hooker to Isabella Homes Beecher, March 4, 1840 (SDML); Catharine E. Beecher to Louisa Wait [Jan. 1822], March 25, 1822 (Beecher-Stowe Coll., SLR).

6. Lyman Beecher to Catharine E. Beecher, May 30, 1822, Edward Beecher to Catharine E. Beecher, May 30 and June 7, 1822 (Beecher-Stowe Coll., SLR).

7. Isabella Homes Beecher to John Hooker, July 2, 1841 (SDML).

8. Catharine E. Beecher to Edward Beecher, June 4 and July 1822 (Beecher-Stowe Coll., SLR); Lyman Beecher, *Autobiography*, 1:478n.

9. Lyman Beecher to Edward Beecher, Aug. 2, 1822 (Beecher-Stowe Coll., SLR).

10. Lyman Beecher, *Autobiography*, 1: 485-86.

11. Richard Cary Morse, MS [June 20, 1808?] (Morse Family Papers, Yale).

12. Edward Dorr Griffin to Ellen Maria Griffin, June 12, 1824, in William B. Sprague, *Memoir of the Rev. Edward D. Griffin, D.D.* (New York, 1839), pp. 146-47; [Theodore Bacon], *Delia Bacon* (Boston, 1888), p. 14.

13. Edward Beecher to Catharine E. Beecher, March 14, 21, and 26, 1822, Lyman Beecher to Catharine E. Beecher, Sept. 25, 1822 (Beecher-Stowe Coll., SLR).

14. Lyman Beecher to Catharine E. Beecher, Sept. 25, 1822, loc. cit.

15. Edward Beecher to Catharine E. Beecher, June 28, Aug. 19 and 23, 1822 (Beecher-Stowe Coll., SLR).

16. Catharine E. Beecher to Louisa Wait, Sept. 28, 1822 (Beecher-Stowe Coll., SLR).

17. Catharine E. Beecher to Edward Beecher, Oct. 9, 1822 (Beecher Family Papers, MHCL). Catherine M. Sedgwick, *A New England Tale* (New York, 1822), quotations from 1853 ed.

18. Catherine M. Sedgwick, *Life and Letters*, pp. 119, 150–51, 23n.

19. Ibid., p. 15; *A New England Tale*, pp. 225–26.

20. Catharine E. Beecher to Louisa Wait, Sept. 28, 1822, loc. cit.

21. Edward Beecher to Catharine E. Beecher, Oct. 27, 1822, Jan. 13, 1823 (Beecher-Stowe Coll., SLR); Edward Beecher to Caleb Fisher, Oct. 27, 1822 (Beecher-Scoville Family Papers, Yale); Alexander Metcalf Fisher, diaries, May 7, 1815 to Aug. 1, 1819 (Fisher Papers, Beinecke Library); Alexander M. Fisher, "Difficulties in the New Testament. Proposed for Solution," MS (Betts Coll. of Yale Autographs, Yale); Edwards A. Park, *Memoir of Nathanael Emmons* (Boston, 1861), pp. 234–36.

22. Fisher diaries, passim; D.[enison] Olmstead, "Anecdotes of Prof. Fisher" (Fisher Papers, Beinecke Library).

23. "Extract from Dr. Emmons Sermon Occasioned by the death of Prof. A. M. Fisher," June 9, 1822 (Fisher Papers, Beinecke Library); Park, *Memoir of Emmons*, pp. 433–37.

24. Lyman Beecher to Catharine E. Beecher, Oct. 27, 1822, Edward Beecher to Catharine E. Beecher, Nov. 13, 1822 (Beecher-Stowe Coll., SLR).

25. Catharine E. Beecher to Lyman Beecher, Jan. 1, 1823, Lyman Beecher to Catharine E. Beecher, Nov. 5, 1822 (Beecher-Stowe Coll., SLR); Lyman Beecher, *Autobiography*, 1:503–04.

26. Lyman Beecher to Catharine E. Beecher, Nov. 5, 1822, and Jan. 27, 1823, loc. cit.

27. Catharine E. Beecher to Lyman Beecher, Jan. 1 and Feb. 15, 1823, Lyman Beecher to Catharine E. Beecher, March 2, 21, and July 1823 (Beecher-Stowe Coll., SLR).

28. [Catharine E. Beecher], *Elements of Mental and Moral Philosophy* (Hartford, 1833); C. S. Watson to Mr. and Mrs. Charles Sedgwick, Dec. 4, 1829 (CSL).

29. Catharine E. Beecher to Edward Beecher, June 1 and 9, 1826, Lyman Beecher to Edward Beecher [July 28, 1826?] (Beecher Family Papers, MHCL); Catharine E. Beecher, "To those who profess or have the hope of piety in Miss Beecher's school," MS (SDML).

30. Catharine E. Beecher, *Educational Reminiscences*, p. 51.

31. Catharine E. Beecher to Edward Beecher, Aug. 23, 1828 (Beecher Family Papers, MHCL).

32. Catharine E. Beecher, *Letters on the Difficulties of Religion* (Hartford, 1836), and *The Moral Instructor; for Schools and Families: Containing Lessons on the Duties of Life, Arranged for Daily Study and Recitation* (Cincinnati, 1838). *Educational Reminiscences*, pp. 47, 52.

33. *Educational Reminiscences*, p. 52; Edward Beecher to Lyman Beecher, April 26, 1831 (Beecher Family Papers, MHCL).

34. Catharine E. Beecher, *Common Sense Applied to Religion; or, The Bible and the People* (New York, 1857) and *An Appeal to the People in Behalf of Their Rights as Authorized Interpreters of the Bible* (New York, 1860). Catharine E. Beecher to [Archibald Alexander], Oct. 18, 1831 (Gratz Coll., HSP); Hatch, *Personal Reminiscences*, p. 34; Catharine E. Beecher to Maria Park,

Aug. 23, 1856 (BPL); Catharine E. Beecher to Nathaniel Wright, Dec. 20, 1859 (Nathaniel Wright Papers, LC); Catharine E. Beecher to Henry Ward Beecher, Feb. 27, 1860 (Beecher-Scoville Family Papers, Yale); John Hooker to Isabella Homes Beecher, Jan. 31, 1840 (SDML).

35. [Catharine E. Beecher], "An Essay on Cause and Effect, in Connexion with the Doctrines of Fatalism and Free Agency," *American Biblical Repository*, 2d ser. 2 (Oct. 1839): 381–408; Leonard Woods, "Remarks on 'An Essay on Cause and Effect, in Connection [*sic*] with Fatalism and Free Agency,'" *American Biblical Repository*, 2d ser. 3 (Jan. 1840): 174–93. Charles Beecher to Lyman Beecher, Sept. 27, 1840 (Beecher-Stowe Coll., SLR); Lyman Beecher to George Beecher, Jan. 25, 1841 (Beecher-Trimble Coll., CHS).

36. Catharine E. Beecher, *Truth Stranger Than Fiction: A Narrative of Recent Transactions, Involving Inquiries in Regard to the Principles of Honor, Truth, and Justice, Which Obtain in a Distinguished American University* (New York, 1850). Leonard Bacon to Delia Bacon, May 26, 1847, "Protest of the Minority," Nov. 4, 1847 (Bacon Family Papers, Yale); Mary Beecher Perkins to Harriet Beecher Stowe, March 10 [1850] (SDML); Catharine E. Beecher to Caroline H. Dall, July 9, 1850 (Caroline H. Dall Papers, MHS). For a good secondary account of this episode, see Vivian C. Hopkins, *Prodigal Puritan: A Life of Delia Bacon* (Cambridge, Mass., 1959).

37. Harriet Beecher Stowe to Henry Ward Beecher and Lyman Beecher, Sept. 19 [1851] (Beecher-Scoville Family Papers, Yale); John Hooker to Isabella Beecher Hooker, July 4, 1852, Isabella Beecher Hooker to John Hooker, July 7, 1852, Mary Beecher Perkins to Lyman Beecher, Jan. 22, 1853, Isabella Jones Beecher to Isabella Beecher Hooker, April 4, 1860 (SDML); Charles Beecher to Henry Ward Beecher, April 12, 1857 (Beecher-Scoville Family Papers, Yale).

38. Catharine E. Beecher, *Biographical Remains of George Beecher* (New York, 1844); Catharine E. Beecher to [recipient unknown], Jan. 24, 1857 (BPL); Catharine E. Beecher to [Alonzo] Potter, April 1846 (Gratz Coll., HSP); Catharine E. Beecher to Andrew D. White, April 21, 1872 (White Papers, Cornell); Catharine E. Beecher, *Religious Training*, pp. 166–69.

39. Charles Beecher to Henry Ward Beecher, April 12, 1827 (Beecher-Scoville Family Papers, Yale); Charles Beecher to Isabella Beecher Hooker, May 15, 1857 (SDML); Harriet Beecher Stowe to Hatty Stowe [Jan. 1862] (Beecher-Stowe Coll., SLR); Harriet Beecher Stowe, "Catharine Beecher," p. 91; "Sketch of the life of Miss Catharine Beecher," MS (Beecher Family Papers, MHCL); Catharine E. Beecher, *Religious Training*, p. 380.

CHAPTER 4

1. This chapter is based primarily on letters in collections of the Stowe-Day Memorial Library, Hartford, and citations are to these, unless otherwise noted. "Memorandum made at Mrs. Beechers request, June 2, 1835," Isabella Homes Beecher to John Hooker, Nov. 9, 1839, Henry Ward Beecher to Isabella Homes Beecher, Jan. 11, 1839, Charles Beecher to Isabella Beecher Hooker, July 16, 1845. A note on Isabella's middle name: it is usually given as Holmes but she was, in fact, named after an aunt Homes.

2. Lyman Beecher to Isabella Homes Beecher, July 12, 1838, Mary Beecher Perkins to Isabella Homes Beecher [Jan. 1838?], Thomas K. Beecher to Isabella Homes Beecher, Jan. 24, 1838; James G. Pike, *Persuasives to Early Piety* (New York, 1837).

3. Lyman Beecher to Isabella Homes Beecher, March 3, 1838 and January 1839.

4. John Hooker, *Some Reminiscences of a Long Life, with a Few Articles on Moral and Social Subjects of Present Interest* (Hartford, 1899), pp. 27–31, 196–97. John Hooker to Isabella Homes Beecher, Sept. 18 and Oct. 6, 1839. Andrew Reed, *Martha; a Memorial of an Only and Beloved Sister* (New York, 1835); Isabella Homes Beecher to John Hooker, Sept. 25, 1839.

5. Isabella Homes Beecher to John Hooker, July 21, 1839, John Hooker to Isabella Homes Beecher, Sept. 18, 1839.

6. Lyman Beecher to John Hooker, Aug. 15 and Nov. 27, 1839, John Hooker to Isabella Homes Beecher, Dec. 11, 1839, Isabella Homes Beecher to John Hooker, Nov. 9 and Dec. 2, 1839, Mary Beecher Perkins to Isabella Homes Beecher, Nov. 29, 1839, Catharine Beecher to John Hooker, Nov. 17, 1839, Isabella Homes Beecher to Katharine Edes Beecher, Dec. 30, 1839.

7. John Hooker to Isabella Beecher Hooker, Oct. 4, 1849, Nov. 2, 1840, March 16 and July 20, 1841.

8. Isabella Homes Beecher to John Hooker, Aug. 30, 1839.

9. John Hooker to Isabella Homes Beecher, Jan. 7, 1841, and to Isabella Beecher Hooker, July 4, 1869.

10. John Pitkin Norton, Diaries, vol. 4, Jan. 15, 1842, vol. 5, Jan. 10, 1844, and vol. 7, July 25, 1844 (John Pitkin Norton Papers, Yale); Isabella Beecher Hooker to John Hooker, Jan. 4, 1843.

11. Isabella Beecher Hooker to John Hooker, March 19, 1847 and Feb. 14, 1862; Isabella Beecher Hooker to Harriet Beecher Stowe, July 31, 1849.

12. Isabella Beecher Hooker to John Hooker, Jan. 4, 1843; Esther Beecher to Isabella Beecher Hooker, July 7, 1844; Isabella Beecher Hooker to Esther Beecher [June 1847?]; John Hooker to Isabella Beecher Hooker, Feb. 24, 1854; Isabella Beecher Hooker to John Hooker, April 18, 1857, Aug. 7, 1859, Jan. 23, May 10, 15, 16, 19, and 23, 1860; Isabella Beecher Hooker to Alice Hooker, April 16, 1860.

13. Mary Beecher Perkins to Isabella Homes Beecher [1840], Nov. 5, 1844; Isabella Beecher Hooker to John Hooker, March 25, 1843; Catharine E. Beecher, *Essay on Slavery and Abolitionism, with Reference to the Duty of American Females* (Philadelphia, 1837), pp. 45–46; James G. Birney to Lewis Tappan, July 29, 1837, in *Letters of James Gillispie Birney*, ed. Dwight L. Dumond (New York, 1938), 1:400.

14. John Hooker, *Some Reminiscences*, pp. 23, 38–40; James W. C. Pennington, *The Fugitive Blacksmith; or, Events in the History of James W. C. Pennington*, 2d ed. (London, 1849), pp. 61–62; John Hooker to Isabella Homes Beecher, Sept. 5, 1839 and Oct. 4, 1840.

15. John Hooker to Isabella Beecher Hooker, Oct. 4, 1840 and Oct. 20, 1844; Isabella Beecher Hooker to John Hooker, Dec. 30, 1842 and Jan. 4, 1843; John Hooker, *Some Reminiscences*, pp. 342–43. "Abby Kellyism" is a reference to the behavior of female abolitionists who, like Abigail Kelley Foster (1810–87), addressed audiences of men and women. This breach of social decorum, like that of women praying before mixed assemblies in the previous generation, was supposed to show the terribly disrupting effect of Abolitionism on the social order. On Beecher's sermon on duelling, see *The Ballot Box a Remedy for National Crimes. A Sermon Entitled "The Remedy for Duelling," by Rev. Lyman Beecher, D.D.; Applied to the Crime of Slaveholding. By One of His Former Parishioners* (Boston, 1838), which simply and effectively substituted the words *slavery* and *slaveholder* for every occurrence of the words *duelling* and *duellist*.

16. John Hooker to Isabella Beecher Hooker, Jan. 3, 1843, July 23 and Dec. 22, 1844.

17. Isabella Beecher Hooker to John Hooker, June 30, 1852, Jan. 24, April 16,

and June 11, 1860; John Hooker to Isabella Beecher Hooker, May 13, 1860.

18. Isabella Beecher Hooker to John Hooker, April 16, April 28, and May 6, 1860; John Hooker to Isabella Beecher Hooker, May 13, 1860; Isabella Beecher Hooker to John Hooker, June 11, 1860.

19. Isabella Beecher Hooker to John Hooker, letters of May–July, 1860.

20. Isabella Beecher Hooker to John Hooker [July 18, 1852]; John Hooker to Isabella Beecher Hooker, April 26, 1861.

21. John Hooker to Isabella Beecher Hooker, March 15 and Oct. 16, 1864, and Dec. 25, 1869; Isabella Beecher Hooker to Alice Hooker Day, Oct. 13, 1870; Isabella Beecher Hooker to Samuel Bowles, March 26, 1877 (Samuel Bowles Papers, Yale); John Hooker, *Some Reminiscences*, p. 57; Isabella Beecher Hooker, "Argument of Mrs. Hooker," in *Memorial to the Congress of the United States* (Washington, D.C., 1872).

21. Isabella Beecher Hooker, "Report of the National Woman Suffrage and Education Committee," *Revolution*, vol. 8 (Aug. 10, 1871); Emanie Sachs, *"The Terrible Siren": Victoria Woodhull (1838–1927)* (New York, 1928).

23. Robert Shaplen, *Free Love and Heavenly Sinners*, is a popular account of the Beecher-Tilton scandal emphasizing its prurient aspects (New York, 1954); Harriet Beecher Stowe, *My Wife and I* (New York, 1871); Harriet Beecher Stowe to Mary B. Claflin, Dec. 24, 1872 (William Claflin Papers, RBH).

24. Isabella Beecher Hooker to John Hooker, June 15, 1860; Harriet Beecher Stowe to Eliza Stowe, May 11, 1873 (Beecher-Stowe Coll., SLR).

25. Kenneth R. Andrews, *Nook Farm: Mark Twain's Hartford Circle* (Seattle, 1969), chap. 2; Isabella Beecher Hooker to Alice Hooker Day, Jan. 4, 1894.

26. Isabella Beecher Hooker, Notebooks (SDML and CtHS); Isabella Beecher Hooker to Alice Hooker Day, April 17, 1877.

27. Harriet Beecher Stowe to Isabella Beecher Hooker, Feb. 11, 1883; William James to Isabella Beecher Hooker, Nov. 17, 1898; Isabella Beecher Hooker to Alice Hooker Day, Oct. 17, Nov. 14, Nov. 21, and Nov. 28, 1888, and Jan. 4, 1894.

CHAPTER 5

1. The chief source for this chapter is the MS "Life of Edward Beecher" by Charles Beecher. Edward kept diaries, quoted extensively by Charles, but these and the bulk of his other manuscripts are apparently lost (letter of John Beecher to the author, Aug. 9, 1968). Robert Merideth, *The Politics of the Universe* (Nashville, Tenn., 1968), takes not only its title but its analysis from Charles's MS.

2. "Life of Edward Beecher," pp. 89, 179.

3. Dix, *Pulpit Portraits*, p. 71; Ernest Calkins, *They Broke the Prairie* (New York, 1937), pp. 181–82.

4. Lyman Beecher to Catharine E. Beecher, May 26, 1819, Edward Beecher to Lyman Beecher, March 27, 1822, Edward Beecher to Catharine E. Beecher, Sept. 16, 1822 (Beecher-Stowe Coll., SLR); "Life of Edward Beecher," pp. 12, 16.

5. Edward Beecher to Catharine E. Beecher, Sept. 16, 30 and Dec. 11, 1822 (Beecher-Stowe Coll., SLR); Catharine E. Beecher to Edward Beecher, March 26, 1825, Mary Foote Beecher to Edward Beecher, April 4, 1826, Edward Beecher to Roxana Ward Foote, Jan. 25, 1826, Catharine E. Beecher to Edward Beecher, April 25 and June 19, 1826 (Beecher Family Papers, MHCL); Catharine E. Beecher, *Educational Reminiscences*, p. 31, and *Religious Training*, pp. 167–68.

6. Sturtevant, *Autobiography*, p. 93; Porcher, "Memoirs," p. 205; Catharine E. Beecher to Edward Beecher, April 25, 1826, Lyman Beecher to Edward Beecher [July 18, 1826?] (Beecher Family Papers, MHCL).

7. Lyman Beecher to Edward Beecher, Edward Beecher to Lyman Beecher, series of letters, Aug. 1826, Lyman Beecher to Edward Beecher, Sept. 5 and 12, 1826 (Beecher Family Papers, MHCL); "Life of Edward Beecher," p. 36; Park Street Church, Records, 1:214 (CL).

8. H. Crosby Englizian, *Brimstone Corner* (Chicago, 1968); Arcturus Z. Conrad, ed., *Commemorative Exercises at the One Hundredth Anniversary of the Organization of Park Street Church* (Boston, 1909); Park Street Church, Records, 1:22, and passim; Ebenezer Parker to Edward Beecher, March 22, 1830 (Archives of the Park Street Church).

9. Isabella Porter Jones, of Wiscasset, Maine.

10. "Life of Edward Beecher," p. 69.

11. Lyman Beecher to Edward Beecher, Nov. 21, 1826, Edward Beecher to Lyman Beecher, Dec. 4, 1826 (Beecher Family Papers, MHCL).

12. Edward Beecher, *President Beecher's Letters on the Subject of Baptism, Addressed to Rev. William Hague* (Boston, 1843), and *Baptism, with Reference to Its Import and Modes* (New York, 1849), the former being polemical in character, the latter disinterested and ecumenical.

13. Origenes, *Origen on First Principles,* trans. G. W. Butterworth (Gloucester, Mass., 1973); Charles Bigg, *The Christian Platonists of Alexandria* (New York, 1970); Henry Chadwick, *Early Christian Thought and the Classical Tradition: Studies in Justin, Clement, and Origen* (New York, 1966).

14. "Life of Edward Beecher," pp. 84, 409; Edward Beecher to Catharine E. Beecher, Aug. 19, 1822 (Beecher-Stowe Coll., SLR); Samuel J. Baird, *History of the New School*, p. 189; Edward Beecher to Lyman Beecher, Dec. 4, 1826 (Beecher Family Papers, MHCL).

15. Lyman Beecher, *Autobiography*, 1:82n, 2:224–25; Edward Beecher to Lyman Beecher, Oct. 15, 1828 (Beecher Family Papers, MHCL); "Life of Edward Beecher," pp. 46, 89.

16. Edward Beecher, request for dismission, Park Street Church, Records, 1:462 (CL); Lyman Beecher to William H. Beecher, Sept. 3, 1830, in *Autobiography*, 2:226; Colin B. Goodykoontz, *Home Missions on the American Frontier* (Caldwell, Idaho, 1939), pp. 195–97, 381–82; Willis, "The Yale Band in Illinois"; Rammelkamp, *Illinois College*.

17. Sturtevant, *Autobiography*, pp. 183–207; Willis, "The Yale Band," p. 226.

18. Sturtevant, *Autobiography*, chap. 15 and p. 225.

19. Ibid., p. 238; Willis, "The Yale Band," p. 197; Jonathan Baldwin Turner to Rhodolphia S. Kibbe, n.d., in Mary Turner Carriel, *Life of Jonathan Baldwin Turner* (Urbana, Ill., 1961), pp. 29, 34; "Life of Edward Beecher," pp. 101–04, 351–53; Thomas Kinnicut Beecher to Isabella Homes Beecher, Feb. 16, 1840 (SDML).

20. T. A. Post, *Truman Marcellus Post, D.D.* (Boston, 1891), p. 90; Edward Beecher, *Baptism*, p. 237; Sturtevant, *Autobiography*, pp. 249, 253; "Life of Edward Beecher," pp. 145–46.

21. "Life of Edward Beecher," pp. 152–264; Salem (Street) Congregational Church, Church Records, 1:355–416, 2:1–258, Samuel Tenney, "History of Salem Church (During Its First Nineteen Years)," MS (CL).

22. Amos Anson Phelps, *Letter to Professor Stowe and Dr. Bacon, on God's Real Method with Great Social Wrongs* (New York, 1848). Phelps's posthumous pamphlet was addressed equally to Edward Beecher, whom he considered his strongest opponent; Phelps did not live to revise and publish his letters to

Beecher. George W. Perkins to Amos A. Phelps, Aug. 30, 1845 (Antislavery MSS, BPL).

23. Edward Beecher, "Address," in *History of the Formation of the Ladies Society for the Promotion of Education at the West* (Boston, 1846), and *The Question at Issue. A Sermon Delivered at Brooklyn, New York, before the Society for the Promotion of Collegiate and Theological Education at the West* (Boston, 1850); Lyman Beecher, *A Plea for the West* (Cincinnati, 1835); Edward Beecher, *Papal Conspiracy Exposed* (Boston, 1855).

24. Isabella Beecher Hooker to John Hooker [July 18, 1852] (SDML); Salem (Street) Congregational Church, Church Records, 2:165, 228-30; Edward Beecher, *Address to the Citizens of Massachusetts. Read at the State Temperance Convention, Held Sept. 12 & 13, 1853* (n.p., 1853); George W. Bungay, *Off-Hand Takings; or, Crayon Sketches of Noticeable Men of Our Age* (New York, 1854), p. 342.

25. Edward Beecher to Henry Ward Beecher, Sept. 28, Oct. 5, and Oct. 11, 1848 (Beecher-Scoville Family Papers, Yale).

26. Edward Beecher, *The Conflict of Ages; or, the Great Debate on the Moral Relations of God and Man* (Boston, 1853); Moses Ballou, *The Divine Character Vindicated* (New York, 1854); Thomas Starr King, review, in the *Universalist Quarterly*, vol. 11 (Jan. 1854); Henry James, *The Nature of Evil* (New York, 1855).

27. James T. Powers to Henry Ward Beecher, June 4, 1855 (Beecher-Scoville Family Papers, Yale); Edward Beecher, letter of resignation, in the *Congregationalist*, Dec. 9, 1853.

28. Edward Beecher to Salem Church, Oct. 19, 1855, in Church Records, vol. 2 (CL); "Life of Edward Beecher," pp. 264-69, 291-96; *Historical Sketches. Central Congregational Church, Galesburg, Illinois, 1837-1962* (n.p., n.d.); Charles J. Sellon, *History of Galesburg* (Galesburg, Ill., 1857), pp. 21-23; Hermann R. Muelder, *Church History in a Puritan Colony of the Middle West* (Galesburg, Ill., 1937), pp. 49-57; Edward Beecher to Henry Ward Beecher, Oct. 4 and Nov. 13, 1855 (Beecher-Scoville Family Papers, Yale).

29. Calkins, *They Broke the Prairie*, pp. 171-79, 180-94; Alexander J. Schem, *The American Ecclesiastical Year-Book* (New York, 1860), 1:162; Edward Beecher and Charles Beecher, *The Result Tested. A Review of the Proceedings of a Council at Georgetown, Mass., Aug. 15, 16, and 22, 1863* (Boston, 1863).

30. *Galesburg* (Ill.) *Republican*, quoted in *New York Times*, Aug. 12, 1871; Noyes L. Thompson, *History of Plymouth Church* (New York, 1873), p. 269; "Life of Edward Beecher," chap. 42; Charles Beecher to Eunice Bullard Beecher, Feb. 25 and March 12, 1895 (Beecher-Scoville Family Papers, Yale).

31. *New York Times*, April 5 and 17, 1889, July 23, 1891, and Aug. 1, 1895; "Life of Edward Beecher," pp. 533-35; Isabella Porter Beecher to Frances Johnson Beecher [April 13, 1889] (James Beecher Family Papers, SLR); Isabella Beecher Hooker to Alice Hooker Day, April 12, 1889 and April 2, 1890 (SDML); Isabella Porter Beecher to Charles Beecher, July 20, 1894, in "Life of Edward Beecher," p. 536; Eunice Bullard Beecher to Harriet E. Beecher Scoville, June 21, 1892 (Beecher-Scoville Family Papers, Yale).

CHAPTER 6

1. Lyman Beecher, *Autobiography*, 2:461.

2. Nehemiah Cleaveland, *History of Bowdoin College*, pp. 452-53; Henry R. McCartney, *Address at the Funeral Service of the Rev. Charles Beecher* (Georgetown, Mass., 1900); Charles Beecher to Nathaniel Wright [Dec. 1838?] (Nathaniel

Wright Papers, LC); Charles Beecher to Lyman Beecher, Dec. 4, 1833 (Beecher-Stowe Coll., SLR).

3. Henry Ward Beecher to [William H. Beecher?], Dec. 14, 1832, Charles Beecher to William C. Beecher, April 17 and May 27, 1887, Charles Beecher to Harriet E. Beecher Scoville, Aug. 18, 1897 and Jan. 25, 1898 (Beecher-Scoville Family Papers, Yale); Harriet Beecher Stowe, "Henry Ward Beecher," pp. 530–33; Lyman Beecher to Isabella Homes Beecher, July 13, 1838 (SDML).

4. Charles Beecher to Lyman Beecher, Dec. 4, 1833 (Beecher-Stowe Coll., SLR).

5. Henry Ward Beecher, Journal, undated entry 1840 (Beecher-Scoville Family Papers, Yale); Katharine Edes Beecher to Mary Beecher Perkins and Thomas Clap Perkins, Nov. 3, 1834 (CHS).

6. Lyman Beecher, *Address [to] the Union Literary Society* (Cincinnati, 1835), known as *A Plea for Colleges*, p. 21; Henry Ward Beecher, Journal, Oct. 9, 1835 and March 23, 1837 (Beecher-Scoville Family Papers, Yale).

7. Catharine E. Beecher and Lyman Beecher to John Hooker, Nov. 17, 1839 (SDML).

8. Charles Beecher to Isabella Homes Beecher, Feb. 6, 1837 (SDML).

9. Charles Beecher to Isabella Homes Beecher, undated letter, 1837, and March 13, 1838 (SDML); Charles Beecher to Lyman Beecher, March 3, 1839 (Beecher-Stowe Coll., SLR); Charles Beecher to George H. Hastings, Aug. 30, 1938 (Beecher-Scoville Family Papers, Yale).

10. Charles Beecher to Nathaniel Wright, loc. cit.

11. Charles Beecher to Isabella Homes Beecher, Feb. 6, 1837 and March 13, 1838 (SDML); Henry Ward Beecher, Journal, March 21, 1837 (Beecher-Scoville Family Papers, Yale); George Beecher, diary, March 17, 1838, in Catharine E. Beecher, *Biographical Remains*, pp. 56–57.

12. Henry Ward Beecher, Journal, March 21, 1837; Lyman Beecher, *A Plea for Colleges*, p. 10.

13. Lyman Beecher to Isabella Homes Beecher, March 1838 (SDML).

14. Charles Beecher to Isabella Homes Beecher, July 6 and 18, 1838, and Jan. 11, 1840 (SDML).

15. Charles Beecher to Isabella Homes Beecher, Feb. 5, 1837 (SDML); Charles Beecher to Nathaniel Wright, loc. cit.

16. Charles Beecher to Nathaniel Wright, loc. cit. Although he presented this long missive as a reckless outpouring of spontaneous feeling, it was in fact a labored production. The chronological slips, or deliberate rewriting of history, enhanced the dramatic tension of the narrative.

17. Henry Ward Beecher to Isabella Homes Beecher, Jan. 11, 1839 (SDML); Lyman Beecher, *Autobiography*, 2:464. One of Charles's favorite recreations was floating down the Ohio River, which he called by its old French name.

18. Lyman Beecher to Isabella Homes Beecher, Sept. 12, 1838 and Jan. 1839, Lyman Beecher to Lydia Beals Jackson Beecher, May 1838, Charles Beecher to Isabella Homes Beecher, March 5, 1840 (SDML).

19. Charles Beecher to Lyman Beecher and Harriet Beecher Stowe, March 3, 1839 (Beecher-Stowe Coll., SLR).

20. Charles Beecher to Isabella Homes Beecher, April 12, May 29, and Nov. 18, 1839 (SDML); Charles Beecher to Catherine A. Foote, March 28 and May 20, 1839 (Beecher-Stowe Coll., SLR).

21. Charles Beecher to Isabella Homes Beecher, Sept. 12 and Nov. 18, 1839 (SDML); Charles Beecher to Lyman Beecher, quoted in Henry Ward Beecher, Journal, Sept. 1839 (Beecher-Scoville Family Papers, Yale).

22. Charles Beecher to Lyman Beecher, Nov. 10, 1839 (SDML).

23. Ibid.

24. Charles Beecher to Isabella Homes Beecher, Nov. 18, 1839 (SDML).

25. Ibid., and Charles Beecher to Isabella Homes Beecher, Jan. 1, 1840 (SDML).

26. Henry Ward Beecher, Journal, Oct. 25, 1838 (Beecher-Scoville Family Papers, Yale); Catharine E. Beecher to John Hooker, Nov. 27, 1839 (SDML); Lyman Beecher to Nathaniel Wright, Jan. 4, 1840, Nathaniel Wright to Lyman Beecher, Jan. 14, 1840 (Nathaniel Wright Papers, LC).

27. Charles Beecher to his family, in circular letter, March 18, 1840 (RBH); Charles Beecher to Lyman Beecher, Feb. 20 and April 2, 1840, Talbut Bullard to Lyman Beecher, enclosed in Charles Beecher to Lyman Beecher, Feb. 20, 1840 (SDML); Lyman Beecher, *Autobiography*, 2:465–66.

28. Charles Beecher to Lyman Beecher, Jan. 11 and March 4, 1840, Isabella Homes Beecher to Esther Beecher, Jan. 7, 1840, Charles Beecher to Isabella Homes Beecher, April 4, 1840 (SDML).

29. *Godey's Lady's Book* (Sept. 1840), pp. 116–24.

30. Charles Beecher to Isabella Homes Beecher, June 1, 1840 (Beecher-Stowe Coll., SLR); Charles Beecher to Lyman Beecher and Isabella Homes Beecher, June 20, 1840 (SDML).

31. [Isaac Taylor], *Natural History of Enthusiasm* (Boston, 1830), pp. 27, 46, 291, "Introductory Essay" to Jonathan Edwards, *An Inquiry into the Freedom of the Will* (London, 1831), p. lii.

32. *Autobiography*, vol. 2, chap. 49; Charles Beecher to Henry Wadsworth Longfellow, Oct. 5, 1840 (Houghton Library); Charles Beecher, *The Bible a Sufficient Creed: Being Two Discourses Delivered at the Dedication of the Second Presbyterian Church, Fort Wayne, Iowa* [sic] (Boston, 1846), and *The Incarnation; or Pen Pictures of the Virgin and Her Son* (New York, 1849).

33. Henry Ward Beecher to Lyman Beecher, March 18, 1843 and Sept. 13, 1844, Charles Beecher to Amelia Ogden, May 20, 1845 (Beecher-Stowe Coll., SLR).

34. Charles Beecher to Edward Beecher, June 16, 1846 (Beecher-Stowe Coll., SLR); Charles Beecher, preface to "Life of Edward Beecher," and *Redeemer and Redeemed: An Investigation of the Atonement and of Eternal Judgment* (Boston, 1864).

35. Joseph P. Moore, "History of the Churches in Fort Wayne (Indiana) Presbytery; To Which Is Added Biographical Sketches of Deceased Ministers, July 20, 1876," MS (PHS); James M. Whiton, *A Half Century of Church Life: A Discourse for the Semi-Centennial Anniversary of the First Free Presbyterian Church, Now and Since 1851, the First Congregational Church, of Newark, N.J.* (Newark, N.J., 1884), pp. 20–23; Charles Beecher to Lyman Beecher, Feb. 1, 1848, Harriet Beecher Stowe to Lydia Beals Jackson Beecher, Oct. 29 [1850] (Beecher-Stowe Coll., SLR); Esther Beecher to Isabella Beecher Hooker, March 30, 1850 and May 19 [1852], Isabella Beecher Hooker to John Hooker, June 25 and 30, 1852 (SDML); Charles Beecher and Sarah Coffin Beecher to Susan Maria Man McCulloch, Jan. 21, 1852, Hugh McCulloch to Charles Beecher, Feb. 9, 1852, Charles Beecher to "Brother Tyler," April 16, 1852 (McCulloch MSS, Indiana University).

36. Charles Beecher and Sarah Coffin Beecher to Susan Maria Man McCulloch, loc. cit.; Charles Beecher to Harriet Beecher Stowe, May 1, 1848 (Beecher-Stowe Coll., SLR).

37. Charles Beecher to Lyman Beecher, May 1848 (Beecher-Stowe Coll., SLR); Hugh McCulloch to Charles Beecher, Feb. 9, 1852, loc. cit.; Charles Beecher, diary, in Harriet Beecher Stowe, *Sunny Memories*, 2:180–81.

CHAPTER 7

1. *Life of Harriet Beecher Stowe*, comp. Charles E. Stowe (Boston, 1891), chaps. 1 and 2.

2. Ibid., pp. 33–39.

3. Ibid., pp. 39–43, 47–49, 512.

4. Ibid., chap. 3; Katharine Edes Beecher to Anna Edes, Feb. 26, 1835 (CHS); Frank R. Shivers, Jr., "A Western Chapter in the History of American Transcendentalism," *Bulletin of the Historical and Philosophical Society of Ohio* 15 (1957): 117–30; James M. Miller, *The Genesis of Western Culture: The Upper Ohio Valley, 1800–1825* (Columbus, Ohio, 1938).

5. *Life of Harriet Beecher Stowe*, chap. 4; Catharine E. Beecher to John A. Clarke, Nov. 22, 1837 and Calvin E. Stowe to A[bsalom] Peters, Feb. 1838 (Gratz Coll., HSP); *New York Times*, March 18, 1897.

6. Harriet Elizabeth Beecher to Elizabeth Lyman [ca. 1835] (CSL); Calvin E. Stowe to Harriet Beecher Stowe, Sept. 29 and 30, 1844, Harriet Beecher Stowe to Calvin E. Stowe, June 15, 1845 (Beecher-Stowe Coll., SLR); Lyman Beecher to Lydia Beals Jackson Beecher, July 28, 1845 (SDML).

7. Harriet Beecher Stowe to Calvin E. Stowe, Jan. 24, 1847 (Beecher-Stowe Coll., SLR); Mary R. Cabot, comp., *Annals of Brattleboro* (Brattleboro, Vt., 1922).

8. Harriet Beecher Stowe to Henry Ward Beecher and Eunice Bullard Beecher, Jan. 14, 1847 (Beecher-Scoville Family Papers, Yale).

9. Isabella Beecher Hooker to Harriet Beecher Stowe, July 31, 1849 (Beecher-Stowe Coll., SLR); Isabella Beecher Hooker to John Hooker [June 20, 1852] (SDML).

10. Harriet Beecher Stowe to Eliza Follen, Feb. 16, 1835, in *Life of Harriet Beecher Stowe*, p. 198; Harriet Beecher Stowe to Henry Ward Beecher, Feb. 1 [1851?] (Beecher-Scoville Family Papers, Yale); Harriet Beecher Stowe, preface, in Josiah Henson, *Father Henson's Story of His Own Life* (Boston, 1858).

11. Timothy Dwight, *Theology*, 1:483–84; Gordon Haight, *Mrs. Sigourney, The Sweet Singer of Hartford* (New Haven, 1930); Catharine E. Beecher, *Woman's Profession as Wife and Mother* (Philadelphia, 1872), p. 33.

12. Harriet Elizabeth Beecher to Georgiana May, May 1833, in *Life of Harriet Beecher Stowe*, p. 67; Charles Beecher to Isabella Homes Beecher, July 4, 1839 (SDML).

13. Harriet Beecher Stowe, *Sunny Memories*, 1:15–16, 186, 189, 315–16, 2:277. She also made the correlation (a tenet of Dwight's republicanism) between "popular freedom" and Protestant Sabbatarianism (2:411). Compare these views to Catherine Sedgwick's in her *Life and Letters*, pp. 192–93.

14. Harriet Beecher Stowe to Henry Ellis Stowe [Dec. 16, 1855] (Beecher-Stowe Coll., SLR); Catharine E. Beecher to her family, Feb. 3 [1856], Isabella Beecher Hooker to John Hooker, July 17, 1857 (SDML).

15. Susan Raymond Howard to Eunice Bullard Beecher, July 10, 1857 (Beecher-Scoville Family Papers, Yale); Isabella Beecher Hooker to John Hooker, July 17, 1857, Harriet Beecher Stowe to Lyman Beecher [July 9, 1857] (SDML).

16. Harriet Beecher Stowe to Catharine E. Beecher and Mary Beecher Perkins [1858] (Beecher-Stowe Coll., SLR); Harriet Beecher Stowe to Eliza and Hatty Stowe, Aug. 24, 1857, *Life of Harriet Beecher Stowe*, p. 323.

17. See, for example, Forrest Wilson, *Crusader in Crinoline* (Philadelphia, 1941), Charles Foster, *The Rungless Ladder* (Durham, N.C., 1954), and Alice C.

Crozier, *The Novels of Harriet Beecher Stowe* (New York, 1969). Annie Fields (*Life and Letters of Harriet Beecher Stowe* [Boston, 1898], p. 299) acknowledges only Harriet's dependence on Calvin's knowledge of the "literature of the past." Edmund Wilson, who calls Stowe "an odd Yankee character," notes that "Calvin's tendency, like that of his wife, was all to eliminate the rigors of the merciless and terrifying doctrines after whose founder he had been christened" (*Patriotic Gore* [New York, 1966], pp. 60–63). John S. Harker, "Life and Contribution of Calvin E. Stowe" (Ph.D. diss., University of Pittsburgh, 1951), is more concerned with Stowe's public services in the common school and religious education fields than in his scholarship or his ministry.

18. Harriet Beecher Stowe, "Henry Ward Beecher," p. 537.

19. Harriet Beecher Stowe to Calvin E. Stowe, June 8, 1836, in *Life of Harriet Beecher Stowe*, p. 81; William K. B. Stoever, "Henry Boynton Smith and the German Theology of History," *Union Seminary Quarterly Review* 24 (Fall 1968): 69–89. Stowe's attitudes toward the uses of biblical criticism are best seen in "The Right Interpretation of the Sacred Scriptures—The Helps and Hindrances," *Bibliotheca Sacra* 10 (Jan. 1853): 34–62, which was his inaugural address as professor of sacred literature at Andover, and "The Word of God," "The Religious Element in Education," and an untitled sermon on Eccles. 1:8–11, MSS sermons (Beecher-Stowe Coll., SLR).

20. Calvin E. Stowe, "Jonathan Edwards and his Theological School," MS (Beecher-Stowe Coll., SLR), and "Sketches and Recollections of Dr. Lyman Beecher," pp. 224–25.

21. Calvin E. Stowe, "Hebrew Belief in a Future Life," MS (Beecher-Stowe Coll., SLR), "The Eschatology of Christ, with Special Reference to the Discourses in Matt. XXIV. and XXV.," *Bibliotheca Sacra* 7 (July 1850): 452–78, and "The Prophet Jonah," *Bibliotheca Sacra* 10 (Oct. 1853): 739–64; Isabella Homes Beecher to John Hooker, Dec. 2, 1839 (SDML); Harriet Beecher Stowe to Charles E. Stowe, Sept. 27, 1879 (Beecher-Stowe Coll., SLR). She wrote from Florida to George Eliot, Feb. 8, 1872 (*Life of Harriet Beecher Stowe*, pp. 463–64): "I here set up our tent, he with German, and Greek, and Hebrew, devouring all sorts of black-letter books, and I spinning ideal webs out of bits that he lets fall here and there."

22. Harriet Beecher Stowe to Eliza and Hatty Stowe [ca. Aug. 1857], Sept. 1 and 5, 1857, in *Life*, pp. 320–26.

23. (Boston, 1859); quotations from 1896 edition.

24. Harriet Beecher Stowe to Catharine E. Beecher and Mary Beecher Perkins, loc. cit.

25. Review in *New York Times*, Nov. 19, 1859; James Russell Lowell to Harriet Beecher Stowe, Feb. 4, 1859, in *Life of Harriet Beecher Stowe*, pp. 333–36. John Ruskin's comment, on the other hand, betrays very little comprehension of this theological purpose (Ruskin to Harriet Beecher Stowe, n.d., in *Life*, pp. 336–38).

26. Harriet Beecher Stowe to Hatty Stowe [March 4, 1859] (Beecher-Stowe Coll., SLR).

27. Catharine E. Beecher to Henry Ward Beecher, Feb. 17, 1860 (Beecher-Scoville Family Papers, Yale).

28. Ibid.

29. Harriet Beecher Stowe to Hatty Stowe [Jan. 1862] and [Feb. 1862] (Beecher-Stowe Coll., SLR); Douglas C. Stange, "The Conversion of Frederic Dan Huntington (1859): A Failure of Liberalism?" in *Historical Magazine of the Protestant Episcopal Church* 37 (Sept. 1968): 287–98.

30. Harriet Beecher Stowe to Eliza, Hatty, and Georgiana Stowe, June

1, 1862 (Beecher-Stowe Coll., SLR); Henry Ward Beecher to Samuel and Harriet E. Beecher Scoville, June 17, 1862 (Beecher-Scoville Family Papers, Yale).

31. Harriet Beecher Stowe to Hatty and Eliza Stowe [Feb. 26, 1863?] (Beecher-Stowe Coll., SLR).

32. See Pension Office Records of Frederick William Stowe, Capt. 14th Mass. Infantry, Veterans Administration Records, National Archives. Fred had to abandon the study of medicine because of the injury to his skull, which, besides deafening his right ear, produced lasting symptoms such as "marked lethargy, pains in head, and symptoms of congestion of brain." Frederick Stowe to Harriet Beecher Stowe, Jan. 6, 1864, Harriet Beecher Stowe to Hatty and Eliza Stowe [April 5, 1864] (Beecher-Stowe Coll., SLR); Isabella Beecher Hooker to John Hooker, Oct. 16, 1864 (SDML).

33. Harriet Beecher Stowe to Hatty and Eliza Stowe, Nov. 13, 1864 [Nov. 1867?], and [1867?] (Beecher-Stowe Coll., SLR).

34. Frederick W. Stowe to Hatty and Eliza Stowe, Dec. 15, 1867, Frederick W. Stowe to Calvin E. Stowe [Dec. 1867], Harriet Beecher Stowe to Hatty and Eliza Stowe [Dec. 1867], Frederick W. Stowe to Harriet Beecher Stowe, Feb. 5, 1871 (Beecher-Stowe Coll., SLR); Harriet E. Beecher Scoville to Samuel Scoville, April 5, 1871, Henry Ward Beecher to Eunice Bullard Beecher, March 1, 1877 (Beecher-Scoville Family Papers, Yale).

35. Wilson, *Crusader in Crinoline*, p. 569; Harriet Beecher Stowe to Frederick W. Gunn, Jan. 12, 1864, and June 6 [1864] (Beecher-Scoville Family Papers, Yale); Harriet Beecher Stowe to Hatty Stowe, Nov. 2, 1863, Harriet Beecher Stowe to Charles E. Stowe, July 26, 1876 (Beecher-Stowe Coll., SLR); Susan Raymond Howard to Henry Ward Beecher, Sept. 1, 1878 (Beecher-Scoville Family Papers, Yale).

36. Eunice Bullard Beecher to Henry Ward Beecher, April 2, 1878, Harriet Beecher Stowe to Henry Ward Beecher, Jan. 27, 1882 (Beecher-Scoville Family Papers, Yale); Harriet Beecher Stowe to Charles E. Stowe [March 7, 1879] (Beecher-Stowe Coll., SLR).

37. Harriet Beecher Stowe to Charles E. Stowe [March 7, 1879], Calvin E. Stowe to Charles E. Stowe, March 7, 1879, Harriet Beecher Stowe to Charles E. Stowe, June 24, 1879 (Beecher-Stowe Coll., SLR).

38. Harriet Beecher Stowe to Charles E. Stowe, Feb. 4 [1881] (Beecher-Stowe Coll., SLR).

39. Ibid., Harriet Beecher Stowe to Charles E. Stowe, Sept. 27, 1879 and Feb. 16, 1881 (Beecher-Stowe Coll., SLR).

40. Harriet Beecher Stowe to Henry Ward Beecher, Jan. 27, 1882 (Beecher-Scoville Family Papers, Yale).

41. Herbert F. Beecher to Henry Ward Beecher, Sept. 15, 1872, Eunice Bullard Beecher to Henry Ward Beecher, April 1, 1877 (Beecher-Scoville Family Papers, Yale); *Life of Harriet Beecher Stowe*, p. 407.

42. Harriet Beecher Stowe to Charles E. Stowe, March 26, 1877 and April 9 [1877] (Beecher-Stowe Coll., SLR).

43. Harriet Beecher Stowe, *Agnes of Sorrento* (Boston, 1862), pp. 117–18, 247, 346, and *Sunny Memories*, 2:330–32.

44. Harriet Beecher Stowe to Charles E. Stowe, April 9 [1877], and Feb. 16, 1881 (Beecher-Stowe Coll., SLR).

45. Harriet Beecher Stowe to Charles E. Stowe, Sept. 27, 1879 (Beecher-Stowe Coll., SLR); Harriet Beecher Stowe, *My Wife and I* (New York, 1871), pp. 80–81.

46. Harriet Beecher Stowe, *Woman in Sacred History* (New York, 1873), pp. 211, 232–36, 303.

47. Harriet Beecher Stowe to Charles E. Stowe, Sept. 27, 1879 (Beecher-Stowe Coll., SLR); *Woman in Sacred History*, pp. 28, 361, 231.

48. Harriet Beecher Stowe, *Footsteps of the Master* (New York, 1877), pp. 64, 67, 70.

49. *The Minister's Wooing*, p. 207.

50. Harriet Beecher Stowe to Charles E. Stowe [Feb. 1881] and Feb. 16, 1881, Harriet Beecher Stowe to Mary Beecher Perkins, Dec. 3, 1879, and July 30 [1879] (Beecher-Stowe Coll., SLR); Harriet Beecher Stowe to Henry Ward Beecher, Sept. 8, 1881 (Beecher-Scoville Family Papers, Yale); Harriet Beecher Stowe to Susan Raymond Howard [ca. April 1887], in Fields, *Life and Letters of Harriet Beecher Stowe*, p. 391.

CHAPTER 8

1. James B. Pond to Emily Mervine Drury, Dec. 30, 1867 (Beecher-Scoville Family Papers, Yale); Edward W. Bok, comp., *Beecher Memorial* (Brooklyn, 1887), pp. 28–29; Henry Ward Beecher, *Norwood; or, Village Life in New England* (New York, 1868).

2. Henry Ward Beecher, *Autobiographical Reminiscences*, p. 31.

3. Ibid., pp. 134–35; Charles Beecher to William C. Beecher, April 17, 1887 (Beecher-Scoville Family Papers, Yale); Henry Ward Beecher, "The Rest of God," in *Evolution and Religion* (New York, 1885), p. 239.

4. Beecher and Scoville, *Biography of Henry Ward Beecher*, pp. 65–67, 128; *Autobiographical Reminiscences*, p. 70.

5. *Autobiographical Reminiscences*, pp. 105–06; Harriet Elizabeth Beecher to Elizabeth Lyman [n.d., ca. 1835] (CSL).

6. White, comp., *History of Litchfield*, pp. 34–35.

7. Abbott, ed., *Henry Ward Beecher*, pp. 29–35; George Montague to Sarah P. Ferry, Oct. 16, 1887, George Montague to Annie Scoville, Oct. 29, 1887, Henry Ward Beecher to Harriet Elizabeth Beecher, Dec. 5, 1831, March 8, April 5, and Dec. 14, 1832 (Beecher-Scoville Family Papers, Yale).

8. Richard Cary Morse to Louisa Morse, June 12, 1835 (Morse Family Papers, Yale); Henry Ward Beecher to [Iraneus] Prime, Feb. 18, 1863 (Gratz Coll., HSP); Henry Ward Beecher, Journal, Oct. 16, 1835 (Beecher-Scoville Family Papers, Yale).

9. Henry Ward Beecher, Journal, loc. cit.

10. Abbott, ed., *Henry Ward Beecher*, pp. 40, 490–91; Beecher and Scoville, *Biography of Henry Ward Beecher*, p. 164.

11. Abbott, pp. 35–37; Beecher and Scoville, p. 193.

12. Henry Ward Beecher, Journal, July 6, 1835, March 21 and Sept. 1836, Oct. 9 and Sept. 5, 1835.

13. Henry Ward Beecher to Margaret Groesbeck, in Journal, Oct. 29, 1835, Journal, May 4, 1837.

14. John H. Thomas, *An Historical Sketch of the Presbyterian Church of Lawrenceburgh, Indiana* (Lawrenceburgh, Ind., 1887), pp. 7–11; Jane Schaffer Elsmere, *Henry Ward Beecher: The Indiana Years, 1837–1847* (Indianapolis, 1973); Clifford Clark, Jr., "Henry Ward Beecher: Revivalist and Antislavery Leader: 1813–1867" (Ph. D. diss., Harvard University, 1967); James Barr Walker, *Experiences of Pioneer Life* (Chicago, 1881), pp. 185–86.

15. Henry Ward Beecher to George Beecher, Sept. 1838, in Beecher and Scoville, *Biography of Henry Ward Beecher*, pp. 161–62; Henry Ward Beecher, Journal, Sept. 27, 1838; Robert Hamilton Bishop to Henry Ward Beecher, in Lyman Beecher, *Autobiography*, 2:327–28; James H. Rodabaugh, *Robert Hamilton Bishop* (Columbus, Ohio, 1935), pp. 106–07, 116–17.

16. [Eunice Bullard Beecher], *From Dawn to Daylight; or, the Simple Story of a Western Home. By a Minister's Wife* (New York, 1859); Henry Ward Beecher, Journal, Aug. 3, 1835, and July 21, 1836, Eunice White Bullard to Olivia Polly Hill Bullard, July 4 and Nov. 8, 1834, Eunice Bullard Beecher to George Beecher, June 15, 1838, Eunice Bullard Beecher to Henry Ward Beecher, Sept. 20, 1843, Eunice Bullard Beecher to Harriet Beecher Stowe, Dec. 27, 1846 (Beecher-Scoville Family Papers, Yale); Thomas Kinnicut Beecher to Isabella Beecher Hooker, Dec. 15, 1843 (SDML); Katharine Edes Beecher to Mary Beecher Perkins and Thomas Clap Perkins, Feb. 26, 1835 (CHS).

17. Henry Ward Beecher, Journal, Sept. 27, 1838; Thomas, *Historical Sketch*, p. 11.

18. Henry Ward Beecher, Journal, Feb. 18, 1839.

19. Henry Ward Beecher, untitled sermon, Oct. 21, 1838 (Henry Ward Beecher Papers, LC); Henry Ward Beecher to [John?] Thomas, Oct. 1838, in Journal.

20. Ibid.

21. Ibid; L. C. Rudolph, *Hoosier Zion: The Presbyterians in Early Indiana* (New Haven, 1963), sustains Beecher's analysis of the causes of Presbyterian schism.

22. Julia Merrill Ketcham, "Reminiscences," MS (Indiana State Library) is valuable on this period of Beecher's life but contains some glaring inaccuracies and fanciful statements; Isabella Homes Beecher to John Hooker, Dec. 1, 1839 (SDML).

23. Henry Ward Beecher, Journal, Dec. 1839; Henry Ward Beecher to [Iraneus] Prime, Feb. 18, 1863, loc. cit.

24. Henry Ward Beecher to Isabella Homes Beecher, Jan. 30, 1840 (SDML); *From Dawn to Daylight*, p. 290.

25. Henry Ward Beecher, *Yale Lectures on Preaching* (New York, 1874), p. 47 (hereafter cited as vol. 1).

26. Henry Ward Beecher, Journal, undated entry 1840; Henry Ward Beecher, four MS sermons on baptism, Oct.–Nov. 1841 (Henry Ward Beecher Papers, LC); Elsmere, *Henry Ward Beecher*, p. 144.

27. Henry Ward Beecher, sermon on Mark 8:34, Jan. 21, 1838, MS outline (Henry Ward Beecher Papers, LC); Henry Ward Beecher, Journal, sermon outline [1840] and March 13, 1838; Henry Ward Beecher, *Eyes and Ears* (Boston, 1863), pp. 110–11; Henry Ward Beecher, "Sermon Preached at 2nd Chh Cincinnati," Aug. 20, 1843 (Henry Ward Beecher Papers, LC).

28. Henry Ward Beecher, *Eyes and Ears*, p. 111; Henry Ward Beecher, Journal, Oct. 25, 1837; Henry Ward Beecher, "Sermon Preached at 2nd Chh Cincinnati"; Henry Ward Beecher, *Autobiographical Reminiscences*, p. 91.

29. Abbott, *Henry Ward Beecher*, p. 37. See Lloyd J. Averill, *American Theology in the Liberal Tradition* (Philadelphia, 1967), and Kenneth Cauthen, *The Impact of American Religious Liberalism* (New York, 1962).

30. "Address of Rev. Henry Ward Beecher," in *Celebration of the Hundredth Anniversary of the Birthday of William Ellery Channing* (Boston, 1880), pp. 134–35.

31. Henry Ward Beecher, Journal, undated entry 1840.

32. George Beecher was found dead in the garden of his Chillicothe, Ohio, home on July 1, 1843, his double-barreled shotgun by his side. The coroner's inquest, held "at the suggestion of some of his friends," returned a verdict of accidental death, the theory being that he had discharged the first barrel at some birds and the second barrel had gone off accidentally. In Harriet Stowe's secondhand account of the incident, quoted in Lyman's *Autobiography*, the details of the death were edited out. The evening before his death, George had told his

congregation that he believed his death was imminent, and he had also patched up a bitter quarrel with the local Old School minister. Harriet Beecher Stowe to Henry Ward Beecher and Charles Beecher, July 4, 1843 (Beecher-Scoville Family Papers, Yale).

33. Harriet Beecher Stowe to Henry Ward Beecher and Charles Beecher, July 4, 1843 (Beecher-Scoville Family Papers, Yale); Henry Ward Beecher to Sarah Buckingham Beecher, Aug. 19, 1843 (Beecher-Trimble Coll., CHS); Henry Ward Beecher to George Beecher, n.d., in Lyman Beecher, *Autobiography*, 2:311–12.

34. Isabella Beecher Hooker to John Hooker, Jan. 16, 1841 (SDML); Henry Ward Beecher, sermon notes, Dec. 26, 1847, and Jan. 2, 1848, Henry Ward Beecher to Henry C. Bowen, Aug. 20, 1848, and Henry Ward Beecher, sermon notes, Feb. 5, 1848 (Beecher-Scoville Family Papers, Yale).

35. Walker, *Experiences*, pp. 190, 209; quotations from 1856 edition of *Philosophy*.

36. Elsmere, *Henry Ward Beecher*, chap. 4; Henry Ward Beecher, *Seven Lectures to Young Men* (Indianapolis, 1844); John R. Howard, *Henry Ward Beecher* (Boston, 1887), p. 49.

37. Henry Ward Beecher, sermon notes, Feb. 5, 1848 (Beecher-Scoville Family Papers, Yale).

38. Henry Ward Beecher to Harriet Beecher Stowe, July 25, 1848 (Beecher-Scoville Family Papers, Yale).

39. John H. Raymond to Henry Ward Beecher, Sept. 11, 1848 (Beecher-Scoville Family Papers, Yale).

40. Horace Bushnell, letters, May 30, 1849, Aug. 29, 1839, and May 11, 1858, in Mary Bushnell Cheney, *Life and Letters of Horace Bushnell* (New York, 1880), pp. 222, 225, 413–14.

41. Ibid., p. 281.

42. Ibid., p. 192.

43. A. Perkins to Charles Perkins, Oct. 23, 1848 (Beecher-Scoville Family Papers, Yale); Asa Fitch, diary, Oct. 29, 1865 (Fitch Family Papers, Yale); John Gough, *Autobiography and Personal Recollections* (Springfield, Mass., 1869), p. 83; Howard, *Henry Ward Beecher*, pp. 138–39.

44. Charles Jones to Henry Ward Beecher, Oct. 22, 1852 (Beecher-Scoville Family Papers, Yale).

45. Henry Ward Beecher to Charles Jones [Nov. 1852] (Beecher-Scoville Family Papers, Yale).

46. Harriet Beecher Stowe to Calvin E. Stowe [July 13–14, 1844] (Beecher-Stowe Coll., SLR); Edward Beecher to Henry Ward Beecher, July 12 and 14, 1875 (Beecher-Scoville Family Papers, Yale).

47. David O. Mears, *Autobiography* (Boston, 1920), p. 94; James L. Corning, *Personal Recollections of Henry Ward Beecher* (Brooklyn, ca. 1903), p. 8.

48. *Brooklyn Eagle* editorial, Oct. 4, 1872, quoted in Noyes L. Thompson, *History of Plymouth Church* (New York, 1873), pp. 16–17. Dr. Chapin, a Universalist, was pastor of the Church of the Divine Paternity and a close friend of Beecher's.

49. Henry Ward Beecher, "Working with Errorists," *Independent*, Jan. 13, 1859; Thomas Jefferson Sawyer, *Who Is Our God?* (New York, 1859); Henry Ward Beecher to "My dear friend," Oct. 24, 1882 (Lee Kohns Mem. Coll., NYPL); Edward Beecher to Henry Ward Beecher, Feb. 25, 1865, and Dec. 23, 1867 (Beecher-Scoville Family Papers, Yale).

50. *Celebration . . . of Channing*, pp. 135, 22; Sedgwick, *Life and Letters*, p. 60.

51. Henry Ward Beecher, "Speech of Mr. Beecher," in *Sixty-Second Anniversary Celebration of the New England Society in the City of New York* (New

York, 1868), p. 21; Thomas B. Macaulay, "Milton," in *Critical and Historical Essays* (London, 1890), 1:50–51; Henry Ward Beecher, *New Star Papers* (New York, 1873), pp. 403–05; *Celebration of Channing*, pp. 142–43.

52. Henry Ward Beecher, *New Star Papers*, p. 267; Mrs. C. A. Hulbert to Henry Ward Beecher, June 21, 1874 (Beecher-Scoville Family Papers, Yale).

53. Abbott, *Henry Ward Beecher*, pp. 480, 495.

54. Henry Ward Beecher, *New Star Papers*, pp. 304–05, 97–98; Henry Ward Beecher to Emily Mervine Drury, April 20, 1859 (Beecher-Stowe Coll., SLR); Henry Ward Beecher, *Norwood*, p. 77.

55. Lucy Jackson White, "Notes on the last days of Lyman Beecher," MS (SDML); Henry Ward Beecher, *Life Thoughts* (Boston, 1858), p. 182.

56. Henry Ward Beecher to Theodore Dwight Woolsey, March 27, 1862, Henry Ward Beecher to Moses S. Beach, April 7, 1868, Henry Ward Beecher to J. B. Ford and Co., Jan. 10, 1868 (Beecher-Scoville Family Papers, Yale).

57. Henry Ward Beecher to David O. Mears, July 14, 1876, Henry Ward Beecher to [?], Aug. 20, 1880 (Beecher-Scoville Family Papers, Yale); Henry Ward Beecher to Edwards A. Park, March [3, 1881] (Park Family Papers, Yale); Henry Ward Beecher, *Evolution and Religion* (New York, 1885), p. 255; Frank Hugh Foster, *The Modern Movement in American Theology* (New York, 1939), pp. 85–90; Henry Ward Beecher to —— Clark, Aug. 3 [1879?] (Beecher-Scoville Family Papers, Yale).

CHAPTER 9

1. Max Eastman, *Heroes I Have Known: Twelve Who Lived Great Lives* (New York, 1942), p. 113; this is one of several versions of the incident. Eastman's mother, Annis Ford Eastman, was associate pastor of Thomas Beecher's church in Elmira.

2. Thomas K. Beecher to Isabella Beecher Hooker, Aug. 3, 1846, Oct. 5, 1839 (SDML); Henry Ward Beecher to Eunice Bullard Beecher, March 12, 1863 (Beecher-Scoville Family Papers, Yale).

3. Thomas K. Beecher, "My Brother Henry," in *Notable Sermons* (Elmira, N.Y., 1914), p. 12; Thomas K. Beecher to Isabella Homes Beecher, Jan. 26, 1842 (SDML); Max Eastman, *Heroes I Have Known*, p. 113.

4. Thomas K. Beecher to Isabella Homes Beecher, Jan. 28 and Oct. 25, 1839, Feb. 16, 1840, and July 27, 1845, Thomas K. Beecher to Esther Beecher [Jan. 30, 1839] (SDML).

5. Thomas K. Beecher to Isabella Homes Beecher, Jan. 28, 1839 (SDML).

6. Thomas K. Beecher to Isabella Homes Beecher, March 22 [1840] (SDML).

7. Thomas K. Beecher to Lyman Beecher, Jan 4, 1842 (Beecher-Stowe Coll., SLR).

8. Charles Beecher to Lyman Beecher, Jan. 4, 1842 (Beecher-Stowe Coll., SLR); Lyman Beecher to James C. Beecher, Feb. [1845] and Oct. 30, 1845 (Thomas K. Beecher Coll., Cornell).

9. Charles Beecher to Isabella Homes Beecher, Jan. 26, 1842 (SDML).

10. Lyman Beecher to Chauncey A. Goodrich, Aug. 30, 1842 (Beecher-Scoville Family Papers, Yale); Thomas K. Beecher to Isabella Homes Beecher, Oct. 4 and Nov. 13, 1842, and Jan. 9, 1843 (SDML).

11. Thomas K. Beecher to Isabella Homes Beecher, Jan. 9 and Sept. 9, 1843 (SDML); faculty minutes of Illinois College, Nov. 3, 1841, and Feb. 2, 1843, quoted in Rammelkamp, *Illinois College*, pp. 78–80.

12. Thomas K. Beecher to Isabella Homes Beecher, Oct. 4, 1842, Jan. 9 and Sept. 9, 1843, and Nov. 13, 1842 (SDML).

13. Thomas K. Beecher to Isabella Homes Beecher, March [21], 1843 (SDML); W. M. L. DeWette, *Theodore; or, The Skeptic's Conversion: History of the Culture of a Protestant Clergyman*, trans. James Freeman Clarke, 2 vols. (Boston, 1841), 1:272.

14. DeWette, *Theodore*, 2:31-32, 79, 194-95.

15. Thomas K. Beecher to Isabella Homes Beecher, March [21] and Sept. 9, 1843 (SDML); Thomas K. Beecher, "My Brother Henry," p. 10.

16. Thomas K. Beecher, "My Brother Henry," pp. 8-10.

17. Harriet Beecher Stowe to Thomas K. Beecher, June 2, 1845, in Lyman Beecher, *Autobiography*, 2:367-74; "My Brother Henry," p. 10.

18. John H. Raymond, *Life and Letters*, p. 251; Thomas K. Beecher to Isabella Beecher Hooker, March 12 [1884] (SDML); Lyman Beecher, *Autobiography*, 2:507.

19. Lyman Beecher to Chauncey A. Goodrich, Aug. 30, 1842, Henry Ward Beecher to Eunice Bullard Beecher, Nov. 11, 1844 (Beecher-Scoville Family Papers, Yale); Hugh McCulloch, *Men and Measures*, pp. 148-49; Thomas K. Beecher to Isabella Beecher Hooker, Oct. 2, 1844 (SDML).

20. Thomas K. Beecher to Edward Beecher, Nov. 22, 1845 (Beecher Family Papers, MHCL); Thomas K. Beecher to Isabella Beecher Hooker, July 27, 1845 (SDML).

21. Thomas K. Beecher to Isabella Beecher Hooker, July 9, July 18, and Aug. 3, 1846 (SDML).

22. Thomas K. Beecher to Isabella Beecher Hooker, Aug. 22, Sept. 6, and Nov. 5, 1846 (SDML).

23. Thomas K. Beecher to [Isabella Beecher Hooker and Mary Beecher Perkins], July 25, 1846, James C. Beecher to Isabella Beecher Hooker, Nov. 29, 1847, Thomas K. Beecher to Lyman Beecher, Aug. 11, 1846, and Dec. 13, 1847 (SDML); James C. Beecher to Lyman Beecher, Nov. 22, 1847 (Beecher-Stowe Coll., SLR).

24. Thomas K. Beecher to Isabella Beecher Hooker, Feb. 10, 1847, Thomas K. Beecher to Lyman Beecher, May 18, 1847 (SDML).

25. Thomas K. Beecher to Lyman Beecher, Dec. 28, 1847 (Beecher-Stowe Coll., SLR); Lyman Beecher, *Autobiography*, 2:505.

26. Thomas K. Beecher to Lyman Beecher [July 1846] (SDML); Thomas K. Beecher to Harriet Beecher Stowe, July 30, 1846 (Beecher-Stowe Coll., SLR); Thomas Robbins, *Diary*, 2:905.

27. Thomas K. Beecher to Lyman Beecher [July 1846] (SDML); Thomas K. Beecher to Harriet Beecher Stowe, July 30, 1846, and Sept. 3, 1848 (Beecher-Stowe Coll., SLR).

28. Thomas K. Beecher to Harriet Beecher Stowe, Sept. 3, 1848, loc. cit.

29. Ibid.

30. Ibid.

31. Henry Ward Beecher to Thomas K. Beecher, Nov. 1848 (Thomas K. Beecher Papers, Cornell).

32. Ibid.; Henry Ward Beecher to John H. Raymond, Aug. 30, 1848 (Beecher-Scoville Family Papers, Yale).

33. Thomas K. Beecher to Olivia Langdon, June 1, 1889, Thomas K. Beecher to Isabella Beecher Hooker, Aug. 4, 1891 (SDML).

34. Olivia Day to Elizabeth W. Baldwin, April 14, 1849 (Baldwin Papers, Yale); James Hadley, *Diary, 1843-1852*, ed. Laura Hadley Moseley (New Haven, 1951), p. 227; John Hooker to Isabella Beecher Hooker, March 26, 1850 (SDML). See also Thomas K. Beecher to Isabella Beecher Hooker [1850], and Esther Beecher to Lydia Beals Jackson Beecher, May 20, 1850 (SDML).

35. Isabella Beecher Hooker to Henry Ward Beecher, May 1850 (SDML); *Elmira Advertiser*, March 15, 1900; John Pitkin Norton, diary, Sept. 28, 1851 (John Pitkin Norton Papers, Yale); Hadley, *Diary*, p. 237.

36. Hadley, *Diary*, passim.

37. Henry Ward Beecher to Thomas K. Beecher, Jan. 29, 1849 (Thomas K. Beecher Papers, Cornell); Harriet Beecher Stowe, *Oldtown Folks*, ed. Henry F. May (Cambridge, Mass., 1966), p. 403; Harriet Beecher Stowe to Isabella Beecher Hooker [Nov. 1850] (Beecher-Stowe Coll., SLR).

38. Thomas K. Beecher to Lyman Beecher, June 18, 1851 (SDML); Harriet Beecher Stowe to Isabella Beecher Hooker [Nov. 1850], loc. cit.; Thomas K. Beecher, *Our Seven Churches* (New York, 1870).

39. "Mr. [Henry Ward] Beecher's Part in the Organization of Churches in Brooklyn and Vicinity," typescript (Beecher-Scoville Family Papers, Yale); John Hooker to Isabella Beecher Hooker, May 11, 1853 (SDML); Lyman Beecher Stowe, *Saints, Sinners and Beechers* (Indianapolis, 1934), p. 358.

40. Olivia Day to Elizabeth W. Baldwin, June 18 [1853] (Baldwin Papers, Yale); Henry Ward Beecher to Thomas K. Beecher, Aug. 19, 1853 (BPL).

41. Mary Beecher Perkins to Isabella Beecher Hooker [May? 1854], Thomas K. Beecher to Isabella Beecher Hooker, Sept. 16, 1853 (SDML).

42. Thomas K. Beecher to Isabella Beecher Hooker [March 20, 1854] (SDML).

43. Thomas K. Beecher to Isabella Beecher Hooker, Aug. 26, 1856 (SDML); Thomas K. Beecher to Samuel Scoville, Feb. 7, 1870 (Beecher-Scoville Family Papers, Yale).

44. Thomas K. Beecher to Lyman Beecher and Lydia Beals Jackson Beecher, Jan. 9, 1857 (SDML); Harriet Beecher Stowe to Charles E. Stowe, June 24, 1879 (Beecher-Stowe Coll., SLR); David C. Robinson, *An Address in Memory of Thomas K. Beecher* (Elmira, N.Y. [1901?]).

45. W. S. B. Mathews, "A Remarkable Personality: Thomas K. Beecher," *Outlook* 82 (March 10, 1906): 557; Leonard Thurlow Beecher, *As It Was* (n.p., 1947), pp. 13–17; Annis Ford Eastman, *A Flower of Puritanism: Julia Jones Beecher, 1826–1905* (Elmira, N.Y., n.d.), pp. 40, 48.

46. Thomas K. Beecher to Isabella Beecher Hooker, Aug. 25, 1863, and Nov. 19, 1857; Thomas K. Beecher, "Saturday Miscellany," clipping in Ella L. Wolcott scrapbooks (SDML); Julia Jones Beecher to Olivia Langdon, Dec. 6, 1878 (SDML).

47. Julia Jones Beecher to Eliza Webster Jones, Jan. 13, 1867 (SDML); Henry Ward Beecher to Henry Allon, April 13, 1871 (Beecher-Scoville Family Papers, Yale); Thomas K. Beecher, "Saturday Miscellany," Aug. 8, 1879, and July 30, 1874, clippings in Ella L. Wolcott scrapbooks (SDML).

48. Thomas K. Beecher to [Frederick W. Beecher], May 20, 1865 (Beecher Family Papers, MHCL); Thomas K. Beecher, "Saturday Miscellany," Oct. 19, Sept. 15, Sept. 22, and Sept. 29, 1883, loc. cit. (SDML).

49. Thomas K. Beecher to James C. Beecher, 1855, quoted in Annis Ford Eastman, "Thomas K. Beecher and the Park Church," clipping in Ella L. Wolcott scrapbooks (SDML).

CHAPTER 10

1. Elizabeth Stuart Phelps Ward, *The Gates Ajar* (Boston, 1875), p. 74, Edmund H. Sears, *Foregleams and Foreshadows of Immortality*, 12th ed. (Philadelphia, 1874), p. 224; William Dean Howells, *The Undiscovered Country* (Boston, 1880), p. 72.

2. The term *Spiritualism* will be confined to the religious and social movement which arose after the Hydesville, New York, rappings of 1847; *spiritualism*

(without the capital) will be used when referring to spiritistic or psychic phenomena in general. *Spiritism*, a much-used alternative, was not employed by the Beechers. Except for Isabella, the Beechers were reluctant to associate themselves with Spiritualism.

3. Thomas H. Huxley to Alfred Russel Wallace [Nov. 1886?], in James Marchant, ed., *Alfred Russel Wallace: Letters and Reminiscences* (New York, 1916), p. 418; Gardner Murphy and Robert O. Ballou, eds., *William James on Psychical Research* (New York, 1960).

4. The novels referred to are *The Blithedale Romance* (Boston, 1852), *The Bostonians* (London, 1886), and *The Spirit-Rapper* (Detroit, 1854).

5. Lyman Beecher, *Autobiography*, 1:222–23, 2:351–53; D. Howe Allen, *Life and Services of Lyman Beecher*, p. 25.

6. Dwight, *Theology*, 5:407–550; Frank Podmore, *Modern Spiritualism* (London, 1902), 1:219, discusses the Universalist debate on immediate salvation versus future probation; Harriet Beecher Stowe, *The Minister's Wooing*, p. 62.

7. Lyman Beecher, *A Sermon Occasioned by the Lamented Death of Mrs. Frances M. Sands, of New Shoreham* (Sag Harbor, N.Y., 1806), pp. 11–12; "Theological Lectures," MS 1848 (McGraw Memorial Library, McCormick Theological Seminary).

8. Isabella Beecher Hooker to John Hooker, Aug. 5, 1860 (SDML); James C. Beecher to Frances Johnson Beecher, n.d. [before 1874] (Abeles Papers).

9. Horace Mann to Lydia B. Mann, April 11, 1822 (Horace Mann Papers, MHS).

10. Lyman Beecher, *Autobiography*, 2:414.

11. Andrew Reed, *Martha*, pp. 248, 257; Porcher, "Memoirs," p. 86.

12. "Memoir of the Life of President Dwight," in *Theology*, 1:lxxviii; Alexander M. Fisher, Diary III, Jan. 1, 1817 (Alexander Metcalf Fisher Coll., Beinecke Library, Yale); Mary Earhart, *Frances Willard* (Chicago, 1944), p. 58.

13. Earhart, pp. 87, 287; Porcher, p. 95.

14. Joseph Butler, *Analogy of Religion* (London, 1736); Samuel L. Clemens, *Captain Stormfield's Visit to Heaven*, in Ray B. Browne, ed., *Mark Twain's Quarrel with Heaven* (New Haven, 1970).

15. See sketches of Taylor in *Dictionary of National Biography* and in James Stephen, *Essays in Ecclesiastical History* (London, 1849), 2:384–459; Isaac Taylor to Ann Taylor Gilbert, n.d., in Doris Armitage, *The Taylors of Ongar* (Cambridge, 1939), p. 120.

16. Isaac Taylor, *Physical Theory of Another Life* (London, 1836), pp. 41, 74, 98, 108.

17. Ibid., pp. 129, 154–56, 192, 213, 224–25.

18. Ibid., pp. 122–26, 253–65.

19. [Catharine Beecher], *Elements*, pp. 356, 362, 365.

20. See sketch of Sears in *Dictionary of American Biography*; Richard Leopold, *Robert Dale Owen* (Cambridge, Mass., 1940); Robert Dale Owen, *Footfalls on the Boundary of Another World* (Philadelphia, 1860), p. 5.

21. Harriet Beecher Stowe to Robert Dale Owen, Dec. 8, 1860 (Dreer American Prose Writers Coll., HSP).

22. *Footfalls*, book 6, chap. 1; Harriet Beecher Stowe to Robert Dale Owen, Jan. 4, 1872 (Dreer American Prose Writers Coll., HSP); Harriet Beecher Stowe to Mary Lewes, Feb. 8, 1872, in *Life of Harriet Beecher Stowe*, pp. 464–66; Mary Lewes to Harriet Beecher Stowe, March 4, 1872 (Beecher-Stowe Coll., SLR).

23. Eunice Bullard Beecher to Henry Ward Beecher, April 1, 1877 (Beecher-Scoville Family Papers, Yale); *Foregleams*, pp. 44–45.

24. Ibid., pp. 44, 69.

25. Ibid., pp. 78–79, 225, 291.
26. Ibid., pp. 48–49.
27. *The Gates Ajar*, pp. 9, 52. Mark Twain's *Captain Stormfield* originated in his contempt for the grossly materialistic Heaven of Mrs. Ward.
28. Ibid., pp. 77, 94, 179–81, 217, 225, 230–44.
29. Isabella Beecher Hooker to Henry Ward Beecher, May 1850 (SDML).
30. Charles Beecher to Henry Ward Beecher, April 12, 1857 (Beecher-Scoville Family Papers, Yale).
31. *Life of Harriet Beecher Stowe*, pp. 422–38.
32. Ibid.
33. Florine Thayer McCray, *The Life-Work of the Author of Uncle Tom's Cabin* (New York, 1889), pp. 381–82.
34. MS in collections of the Congregational Library, Boston; a copy of Ross's narrative is also included in Stowe's MS sermon, "Three Contrasted Lives" (Beecher-Stowe Coll., SLR).
35. *Life of Harriet Beecher Stowe*, p. 437. Calvin also relished the witchcraft tales in Cotton Mather's *Magnalia Christi Americana*, one of his wife's favorite books.
36. See Stowe's "Three Contrasted Lives."
37. Harriet Beecher Stowe to Calvin E. Stowe, July [15?] 1844 (Beecher-Stowe Coll., SLR); Harriet Beecher Stowe to Henry Ward Beecher and Eunice Bullard Beecher [Winter?] 1844 (Beecher-Scoville Family Papers, Yale).
38. Harriet Beecher Stowe to Henry Ward Beecher and Eunice Bullard Beecher [Winter?] 1844 (Beecher-Scoville Family Papers, Yale).
39. Reprinted as a *Letter on Animal Magnetism by Rev. Dr. Beecher of the Presbyterian Church* (Philadelphia, 1844). Beecher was not, in fact, a D.D.
40. New York, 1846; Beecher's account is reprinted as an appendix.
41. Catharine Beecher, *Letters to the People on Health and Happiness* (New York, 1856), pp. 112–20.
42. Catharine E. Beecher to Z. P. Bannister [1849?] (Beecher Family Papers, MHCL). Dr. Ruggles and similar practitioners were satirized by James in the character of Dr. Selah Tarrant in *The Bostonians.*
43. Podmore, *Modern Spiritualism*, 1:175; Harriet Beecher Stowe, "Letter from Maine.—No. 1," reprinted in *Uncle Sam's Emancipation* (Phildelphia, 1853), p. 93; *Sunny Memories*, 2:187; Leopold, *Robert Dale Owen*, pp. 317–18.
44. Beecher and Scoville, *Biography of Rev. Henry Ward Beecher*, p. 363.
45. *Letters on Health and Happiness*, p. 161 and Note 4 (separately paginated), pp. 18, 27; "Sketch of the life of Miss Catharine Beecher by R.," MS (Beecher Family Papers, MHCL).
46. Samuel B. Brittan, *A Review of Rev. Charles Beecher's Report* (New York, 1853), pp. 20–21, 73; John S. Adams, *Review of the Conclusions of Rev. Charles Beecher* (New York, 1853).
47. Edward C. Rogers, *A Discussion on the Automatic Powers of the Brain* (Boston, 1853), pp. 22, 42–45, 51.
48. Brittan, pp. 46–47.
49. Podmore, *Modern Spiritualism*, 1:301; Andrew Jackson Davis, *The Penetralia; Being Harmonial Answers to Important Questions* (Boston, 1872), pp. 429, 502–16.
50. Brownson portrays his unnamed protagonist as a demon-possessed agent who triggers the revolutions of 1848 by allying with anti-Catholic, antimonarchical forces, and setting up a transatlantic "mesmeric battery" to transmit disruptive influences and augment the power of his coadjutors.
51. *Life of Harriet Beecher Stowe*, pp. 321–24, 349–52, 410–12; Harriet

Beecher Stowe to William Dean Howells, Nov. 25 [ca. 1870] (Houghton Library).

52. Harriet Beecher Stowe, "Henry Ward Beecher," pp. 539–40.

53. Harriet Beecher Stowe to [James C. Beecher], April [28, 1863] (Beecher-Stowe Coll., SLR).

54. Sarah L. Taylor, ed., *Fox-Taylor Automatic Writing, 1869–1892: Unabridged Record* (Boston, 1936), pp. 1–3.

55. *Christian Union*, Sept., Oct., 1870.

56. Ibid.

57. *Christian Union*, Nov. 7, 1870.

58. *Christian Union*, Nov. 26, 1870; Charles Beecher, *Spiritual Manifestations* (Boston, 1879), p. 41.

59. Beecher, *Spiritual Manifestations*, chap. 2; Podmore, *Modern Spiritualism*, 1:199–201.

60. Beecher, pp. 9, 12–13.

61. Ibid., chaps. 36 and 37.

62. Theodore Tilton, *Victoria C. Woodhull* (New York, 1871), pp. 5–8, 12–14; see Emanie Sachs, *"The Terrible Siren"* for the best biography of Mrs. Woodhull, based on interviews and extensive research.

63. Isabella Beecher Hooker to Alice Hooker Day, Nov. 4, 1870 (SDML).

64. It is difficult to say how many Notebooks survive. I have used two, spanning 1876–78. The first is in collections of the SDML, the second, in the Connecticut Historical Society. The latter may be consulted but nothing quoted from it. In deference to Mr. Joseph Hooker's wishes regarding that Notebook, I have made no direct quotations from either.

65. Alfred Russel Wallace, *My Life* (New York, 1905), 2:122. Graham Reed, *The Psychology of Anomalous Experience* (London, 1972) was helpful in placing these experiences in psychological perspective.

66. Martin Gardner, *Fads & Fallacies in the Name of Science.*

67. Isabella Beecher Hooker to John Stuart Mill, Aug. 9, 1869, in *Womanhood*, pp. 34–36.

68. James C. Beecher to [Frances Johnson Beecher], March 20 [ca. 1879] (Beecher-Stowe Coll., SLR). See also Pension Office records of the Veterans Administration (National Archives, RG 15).

69. Isabella Beecher Hooker to Alice Hooker Day, Nov. 4, 1870 (SDML).

70. Thomas K. Beecher, "Saturday Miscellany," *Elmira Daily Gazette*, March 12, 1872, May 17 and May 24, 1879, clippings in Ella L. Wolcott scrapbooks (SDML).

71. Harriet Beecher Stowe, "Mrs. A. D. T. Whitney," in *Our Famous Women*, p. 665; Mrs. Whitney was an author of children's books and a leading American Swedenborgian. Frances Johnson Beecher to James C. Beecher, March 30 and Oct. 10, 1885 (Abeles Papers).

72. "Anna Jones" to Isabella Jones Beecher, March 9, 1886 (Beecher Family Papers, MHCL); Isabella Beecher Hooker to Alice Hooker Day, April 1, 1890 (SDML); Sarah Coffin Beecher to Frederick W. Beecher, Nov. 20, 1894 (Beecher Family Papers, MHCL).

73. Julia Jones Beecher to Isabella Beecher Hooker, Jan. 1, 1901 (SDML); Annis Ford Eastman, *Flower of Puritanism*, p. 67.

74. Isabella Beecher Hooker to Alice Hooker Day, Oct. 30 and Nov. 21, 1888, March 5, July 1, Oct. 4, and Dec. 11, 1889, July 16 and Aug. 20, 1890, Nov. 28 and Dec. 15, 1893, Jan. 4 and April 15, 1894, Dec. 22, 1896 (SDML).

75. John Hooker, Notebook, "Spirit Friends" (SDML).

76. Hoxie Neale Fairchild, *Religious Trends in English Poetry* (New York,

1939–57), 1:535; Henry Ward Beecher, MS sermon fragment (Beecher-Scoville Family Papers, Yale).

CHAPTER 11

1. Charles Beecher to Oliver Wendell Holmes, March 21, 1881 (Houghton Library).

2. *The Modern Movement in American Theology*, p. 81; John E. Frazee, "Lyman Beecher: Theologian and Social Reformer" (Ph.D. diss., University of Edinburgh, 1936).

3. Dwight, *Theology*, 4:474, 1:79–84, 2:14, 1:447–67.

4. Lyman Beecher, "The Attributes and Character of God," in *Works*, 1:141–42; Lyman Beecher, *Autobiography*, 1:61; Nathaniel W. Taylor, *Lectures on the Moral Government of God* (New York, 1859), 1:265; Harriet Porter Beecher to Lyman Beecher, Sept. 22, 1817 (SDML); Harriet Beecher Stowe, "Lyman Beecher," in Piper and MacCracken, *Lives*, p. 720; Vanderpoel, *Chronicles*, p. 228.

5. Tyler, *Memoir of Nettleton*, p. 295; Frances M. Young, "Insight or Incoherence? The Greek Fathers on God and Evil," *Journal of Ecclesiastical History* 24 (April 1973): 118; Allen, *Life and Services of Lyman Beecher*, pp. 21, 27.

6. Nathaniel W. Taylor, *Concio ad Clerum*; Taylor, *Moral Government of God*, 2:345; Taylor, *Essays on Revealed Theology* (New York, 1859), pp. 186, 380–83.

7. Dwight, *Theology*, 1:223–58; Taylor, *Moral Government of God*, 2:302–11; Lyman Beecher, "The Decrees of God," in *Works*, 1:287–88.

8. Dwight, *Theology*, 2:35–69; Taylor, *Moral Government of God*, 1:344; Lyman Beecher, *Autobiography*, 1:31. See also Lewis Smith, "Changing Conceptions of God in Colonial New England" (Ph.D. diss., State University of Iowa, 1953).

9. See G. Ernest Wright, "Theology and Christomonism," in *The Old Testament and Theology* (New York, 1969), which develops the thesis of H. Richard Niebuhr.

10. Henry Ward Beecher, *Norwood*, p. 308; Charles Beecher, *The Divine Sorrow: A Sermon Preached in Georgetown, Mass., March 18, 1860* (Andover, Mass., 1860), p. 5.

11. "The Duties of a Theologian," *American Biblical Repository*, 2d ser. 2 (Oct. 1839): 348, 350–51.

12. Ibid., pp. 367, 370–74; Charles Beecher to Oliver Wendell Holmes, March 21, 1881, loc. cit.

13. William Ellery Channing, "Likeness to God," in *Works* (Boston, 1900), p. 301.

14. John Leland to Isaac Backus, April 17, 1789 (Isaac Backus Correspondence, Andover Newton Theological School).

15. Jonathan Edwards, *Dissertation Concerning God's Chief End in Creation*, in *Works*, ed. Sereno Edwards Dwight (New York, 1817), 3:19; Channing, "Likeness to God," pp. 291, 296.

16. "Life of Edward Beecher," p. 25; Edward Beecher, *Conflict of Ages*, pp. 493–97, 499.

17. *Conflict of Ages*, pp. 3, 27, 120; "Life of Edward Beecher," pp. 39–40.

18. *Conflict of Ages*, pp. 190, 117, 20, 128, 164, 181–82.

19. Edward Beecher, *An Address, Delivered at the Eighth Anniversary of the Auxiliary Education Society of the Young Men of Boston* (Boston, 1827), pp. 22–23; *Conflict of Ages*, pp. 211–12, 229–33.

20. Fred B. Craddock, *The Pre-Existence of Christ in the New Testament* (Nashville, 1968), p. 11. R. G. Hamerton-Kelly, *Pre-Existence, Wisdom, and the Son of Man* (Cambridge, 1973), treats the ontological problem of preexistence and offers a cogent definition of the concept itself. See Edward Beecher and Charles Beecher, *The Result Tested. A Review of the Proceedings of a Council at Georgetown, Mass., Aug. 14, 16, and 22, 1863* (Boston, 1863), p. 13.

21. Catharine E. Beecher to Edward Beecher, Aug. 23, 1828 (Beecher Family Papers, MHCL).

22. [Catharine E. Beecher], *Elements of Mental and Moral Philosophy*, pp. 257–71.

23. Ibid., pp. 275–77, 365, 329–32.

24. Ibid., pp. 346–49.

25. Edward Beecher to Lyman Beecher, April 26, 1831 (Beecher Family Papers, MHCL).

26. Taylor, *Moral Government of God*, 1:355; Lyman Beecher, "Theological Lectures," loc. cit.

27. Lyman Beecher to Isabella Homes Beecher, July 12, 1838 (SDML).

28. Thomas K. Beecher to Isabella Homes Beecher, March 22 [1840] (SDML).

29. Charles Beecher to Lyman Beecher, June 24, 1847 (Beecher-Stowe Coll., SLR). See F. F. Bruce, "The Servant Messiah," in *New Testament Development of Old Testament Themes* (Grand Rapids, Mich., 1968), pp. 83–99.

30. "Life of Edward Beecher," pp. 453–56; Henry Ward Beecher, "Our Father," MS sermon, Nov. 2, 1884 (Elsie and Philip D. Sang Coll., Knox College).

31. "Our Father"; Edward Beecher, *Papal Conspiracy*, pp. 150–52; Charles Beecher, *The God of the Bible Against Slavery* [New York, 1855]; Harriet Beecher Stowe, *Key to Uncle Tom's Cabin*; William H. Beecher, untitled MS sermon [Jan. 15, 1882] (Beecher Family Coll., Huntington Library).

32. "Life of Edward Beecher," pp. 85, 280; Charles Beecher to Hugh McCulloch, Jan. 7, 1889 (McCulloch MSS, Indiana University).

33. Catharine E. Beecher to Andrew Dickson White, April 21, 1872 (Andrew D. White Papers, Cornell); "Life of Edward Beecher," pp. 36–37, 284–85.

34. *Conflict of Ages*, p. 483.

35. Ibid., p. 114; William Beecher, MS sermon, loc. cit.

36. Edward Beecher, "Man the Image of God," *Bibliotheca Sacra* 7 (July 1850): 415–25; Edward Beecher, "The Great Religious Controversy in England, No. 4," *Independent*, Oct. 9, 1862.

37. Harriet Beecher Stowe, *Our Charley and What to Do With Him* (Boston, 1858), pp. 85–93, *Woman in Sacred History*, pp. 81–89, and *Footsteps of the Master*, pp. 70, 136–37; Catherine Sedgwick, *Life and Letters*, p. 247; Oliver Wendell Holmes to Harriet Beecher Stowe, Sept. 25, 1871, in *Life and Letters of Oliver Wendell Holmes*, 2:281.

38. Oliver Wendell Holmes to Harriet Beecher Stowe, n.d., *Life and Letters of Oliver Wendell Holmes*, p. 250; Catharine E. Beecher to Mary Beecher Perkins, April 29, 1878 (SDML).

39. Sprague, *Memoir of Griffin*, p. 155; Robbins, *Diary*, 1:25.

40. Lyman Beecher to Isabella Homes Beecher, Jan. 1839 (SDML).

41. Vanderpoel, *Chronicles*, pp. 250–51.

42. Catharine E. Beecher, *Letters on the Difficulties of Religion* (Hartford, 1836), pp. 296, 305.

43. Catharine E. Beecher, *Educational Reminiscences*, p. 47; Catharine E. Beecher, *An Appeal to the People*, pp. 166, 183, 258–59, 318.

44. Catharine E. Beecher, *Religious Training*, pp. 200–01, *Appeal to the People*, pp. 365, 373–74, *Elements of Mental and Moral Philosophy*, p. 317.

45. Edward Beecher, *Concord of Ages*, pp. 181–88; Edward Beecher to Charles Beecher, Jan. 1, 1886, in "Life of Edward Beecher," pp. 502–03.

46. Charles Beecher to Hugh McCulloch, Jan. 7, 1889, loc. cit.; Charles Beecher to Amelia Ogden, May 20, 1845 (Beecher-Stowe Coll., SLR); Charles Beecher, *The Incarnation*, pp. 20–21.

47. Ibid., pp. 200–08, 225–27; Charles Beecher, *David and His Throne* (New York, 1855), p. 225.

48. Charles Beecher, *Redeemer and Redeemed*, pp. 9, 52–58.

49. Ibid., pp. 21–24, 74.

50. Ibid., 72–73, 83, 144, 147–49.

51. Ibid., 160–62.

52. [Noah Porter], "Charles Beecher's New Theory of the Work of the Redeemer," *New Englander* 23 (April 1863): 369–71; Edward Beecher, "The Great Religious Controversy in England, No. 9" *Independent*, Nov. 13, 1862.

53. Charles Beecher, *The Divine Sorrow*, pp. 9, 13, 15.

54. Charles Smith to Henry Ward Beecher, Dec. 30, 1877, R. Dilks to Henry Ward Beecher, Sept. 3, 1866 (Beecher-Scoville Family Papers, Yale); Harriet Beecher Stowe, "A Scene in Jerusalem," in *Religious Studies* (Boston, 1896), p. 232.

55. Edward Beecher, *History of Opinions on the Scriptural Doctrine of Retribution* (New York, 1878).

56. Catharine E. Beecher, *Religious Training*, pp. 356, 342, 102, 117–18.

57. Charles Beecher to Lyman Beecher, May 1848 (Beecher-Stowe Coll., SLR).

58. Thomas K. Beecher, *Our Need and Our Plan* [Elmira, N.Y., ca. 1878], p. 16, and *Let Us Not Judge One Another Any More* [Elmira, N.Y., 1885], p. 4.

59. Henry Ward Beecher, *New Star Papers*, p. 328, *Life Thoughts*, pp. 2, 56, 210, *Yale Lectures on Preaching*, pp. 22, 55.

60. Henry Ward Beecher, *Eyes and Ears*, pp. 287, 294–98, 380–82.

61. Harriet Beecher Stowe, *Oldtown Folks*, pp. 402–03.

62. Henry Ward Beecher, *Evolution and Religion*, p. 290; Henry Ward Beecher to "My dear Friend," Oct. 24, 1882 (Lee Kohns Memorial Coll., NYPL); A. V. G. Allen, "The Theological Renaissance of the Nineteenth Century," *Princeton Review* 58 (1882): 263–82.

63. Edward Beecher, *Conflict of Ages*, p. 483; Charles Beecher, *Historic Fire* (Indianapolis, 1849), p. 22; "Life of Edward Beecher," pp. 447–48, 497–98, 468; Henry Ward Beecher, *Evolution and Religion*, pp. 215–16, 298; Charles Beecher to Henry Ward Beecher, Jan. 14, 1884 (Beecher-Scoville Family Papers, Yale).

64. Henry Ward Beecher to Charles Beecher, Jan. 19, 1884, Henry Ward Beecher Howard to Henry Ward Beecher, Oct. 11 [1883] (Beecher-Scoville Family Papers, Yale); Hugh McCulloch, *Men and Measures*, p. 143.

65. Henry Ward Beecher, *Life Thoughts*, p. 79; *Evolution and Religion*, pp. 290–91.

66. Catharine E. Beecher, *Religious Training*, p. 342; William H. Beecher, MS sermon fragment, n.d. (Beecher Family Coll., Huntington Library).

67. Henry Ward Beecher, *Life Thoughts*, pp. 103–04.

68. Catharine E. Beecher, *Appeal to the People*, p. 324; Oliver Wendell Holmes to Harriet Beecher Stowe, Sept. 13, 1860, in *Life and Letters of Oliver Wendell Holmes*, 1:265.

69. See David Singer, "God and Man in Baptist Hymnals, 1784–1884," *Midcontinent American Studies Journal* 9 (Fall 1968): 14–26; G. Ernest Wright, "Theology and Christomonism" (n. 9).

BIBLIOGRAPHY

The fullest references to my sources will be found in the endnotes. I list here only those sources which are essential to this study or which provide pertinent background material for scholars interested in the history of the Beecher family. Among the major primary sources, the so-called *Autobiography of Lyman Beecher*, a collection of his letters with brief essays by his children and fascinating but often inaccurate reminiscences by Beecher himself, is probably the most important single source. Others include Lyman Beecher's three-volume *Works*, Charles Beecher's manuscript "Life of Edward Beecher," Charles E. Stowe's *Life of Harriet Beecher Stowe*, and the collected sermons of Henry Ward Beecher, published as the *Plymouth Pulpit*.

Manuscript sources were equally important to this study, and I have been fortunate in receiving help and courtesies from dozens of research libraries, depositories of Beecher manuscripts. Of these collections the largest single groups belong to the Stowe-Day Memorial Library, Hartford. The Schlesinger Library in Cambridge, Massachusetts, has the valuable Beecher-Stowe Collection, along with the much smaller James C. Beecher Family Papers. Mrs. Margaret Abeles of Wilmette, Illinois, made available to me James Beecher papers not yet in the Schlesinger Library collection. The Beecher-Scoville Family Papers in Yale University's Sterling Memorial Library is another invaluable collection. The Mount Holyoke College Library owns another sizeable and extremely useful collection, the Beecher Family Papers. The Henry Ward Beecher Papers at the Library of Congress contain his earliest sermons, but comparatively few other documents such as letters or memoranda. The Mark Twain Papers at the University of California, Berkeley, were useful for the 1870s and 1880s.

Two denominational libraries, the Congregational Library in Boston and the Presbyterian Historical Society in Philadelphia, provided many books, pamphlets, local church histories, small numbers of manuscripts, and other items not available elsewhere. The Boston Public Library and the New York Public Library own many of the scarce or rare items among the Beechers' published works, as do the Beinecke Library at Yale, the Library of Congress, and the Historical Society of Pennsylvania. The libraries of Harvard and Yale Divinity Schools also own valuable collections, particularly in such areas as polemics, memoirs, theology, ecclesiastical proceedings, and church history.

Of secondary works, I am most indebted for information, background, and insight to the following: Kenneth Andrews, *Nook Farm*, Barbara Cross, *Horace*

Bushnell, Whitney R. Cross, *The Burned-Over District*, Douglas Elwood, *The Philosophical Theology of Jonathan Edwards*, Charles H. Foster, *The Rungless Ladder*, Charles I. Foster, *Errand of Mercy*, Vincent Harding, "Lyman Beecher," Joseph Haroutunian, *Piety versus Moralism*, Daniel W. Howe, *The Unitarian Conscience*, William A. Johnson, *Nature and the Supernatural in the Theology of Horace Bushnell*, Sidney E. Mead, *Nathaniel William Taylor*, Geoffrey F. Nuttall, *The Puritan Spirit*, Timothy L. Smith, *Revivalism and Social Reform*, Ernst F. Stoeffler, *The Rise of Evangelical Pietism*, and Claude Welch, *Protestant Thought in the Nineteenth Century.*

Two books in particular aided me in every aspect of my study: Sydney E. Ahlstrom, *A Religious History of the American People*, and Frank Hugh Foster, *A Genetic History of New England Theology.*

Following is a select list of sources, divided according to subject matter.

PRIMARY SOURCES

Major Published Works of the Beechers

Catharine Esther Beecher

An Appeal to the People in Behalf of Their Rights as Authorized Interpreters of the Bible. New York: Harper & Brothers, 1860.

Common Sense Applied to Religion; or, The Bible and the People. New York: Harper & Brothers, 1857.

Educational Reminiscences and Suggestions. New York: J. B. Ford and Co., 1874.

The Elements of Mental and Moral Philosophy, Founded Upon Experience, Reason, and the Bible. [Hartford: Peter B. Gleason & Co., 1831.]

An Essay on the Education of Female Teachers. Written at the Request of the American Lyceum, and Communicated at Their Annual Meeting. New York: Van Nostrand & Dwight, 1835.

An Essay on Slavery and Abolitionism, with Reference to the Duty of American Females. Philadelphia: Henry Perkins, 1837.

The Evils Suffered by American Women and American Children: the Causes and the Remedy . . . Also, An Address to the Protestant Clergy of the United States. New York: Harper & Brothers, 1846.

Letter, dated Round Hill, Northampton, Mass., May 26, 1850, concerning her book, *Truth Stranger Than Fiction.*

Letters on the Difficulties of Religion. Hartford: Belknap & Hamersley, 1836.

Letters to the People on Health and Happiness. New York: Harper & Bros., 1856.

The Moral Instructor; for Schools and Families: Containing Lessons on the Duties of Life, Arranged for Daily Study and Recitation. Cincinnati: Truman & Smith, 1838.

Religious Training of Children in the School, the Family, and the Church. New York: Harper & Brothers, 1864.

Truth Stranger Than Fiction. Boston: Phillips, Sampson & Co., 1850.

Catharine Esther Beecher and Harriet Beecher Stowe

The American Woman's Home. New York: J. B. Ford, 1869.

Principles of Domestic Science; as Applied to the Duties and Pleasures of Home. New York: J. B. Ford and Co., 1870.

Charles Beecher

The Bible a Sufficient Creed: Being Two Discourses Delivered at the Dedication of the Second Presbyterian Church, Fort Wayne, Iowa [sic], *February 22, 1846.* Boston: Christian World, 1846.

David and His Throne: Pen Pictures of the Bible. New York: J. C. Derby, 1855. Republished in 1861 under the title, *The Life of David, King of Israel, with an Introduction by Harriet Beecher Stowe.*

The Divine Sorrow: A Sermon Preached in Georgetown, Mass., March 18, 1860. Andover, Mass.: Warren F. Draper, 1860.

The Duty of Disobedience to Wicked Laws: A Sermon on the Fugitive Slave Law. New York: John A. Gray, 1851.

The Eden Tableau or Bible Object-Teaching: A Study. Boston: Lee and Shepard, 1880.

"Eoline; or the Wind-Spirit." *Godey's Lady's Book* 21 (Sept. 1840): 116–24.

The God of the Bible Against Slavery. [New York: American Anti-Slavery Society, 1885].

Historic Fire: An Address at the Anniversary of the Calliopean Society and Lyceum of Wabash College, July 18, 1849. Indianapolis: Douglass & Elder, 1849.

The Incarnation; or, Pictures of the Virgin and Her Son. New York: Harper & Bros., 1849.

Patmos, or the Unveiling. Boston: Lee and Shepard, 1896.

A Plea for the Maine Law: A Sermon Delivered in Surrey Chapel, Blackfriars, May 22nd, 1853. London: for the National Temperance Society by W. Tweedie [1853].

Redeemer and Redeemed; an Investigation of the Atonement and of Eternal Judgment. Boston: Lee and Shepard, 1864.

A Review of the "Spiritual Manifestations," Read Before the Congregational Association of New York and Brooklyn. New York: G. P. Putnam & Co., 1853.

A Sermon on the Nebraska Bill. New York: Oliver & Brothers, 1854.

Spiritual Manifestations. Boston: Lee and Shepard, 1879.

Edward Beecher

An Address, Delivered at the Eighth Anniversary of the Auxiliary Education Society of the Young Men of Boston, February 10, 1827. Boston: T. R. Marvin, 1827.

Address to the Citizens of Massachusetts. Read at the State Temp. Convention, held Sept. 12 & 13, 1853. N.p., n.d.

Baptism, with Reference to Its Import and Modes. New York: John Wiley, 1849.

The Concord of Ages; or, the Individual and Organic Harmony of God and Man. New York: Derby & Jackson, 1860.

The Conflict of Ages; or, the Great Debate on the Moral Relations of God and Man. Boston: Phillips, Sampson & Co., 1853.

"Dr. Beecher's Address." In *History of the Formation of the Ladies' Society at the West.* Boston, 1846.

Faith Essential to a Complete Education. An Address Delivered at the Anniversary of the Charlestown Female Seminary, July 31, 1845. Boston: Haskell & Moore, 1845.

History of Opinions on the Scriptural Doctrine of Retribution. New York: D. Appleton, 1878.

"Man the Image of God." *Bibliotheca Sacra* 7 (July 1850): 409–25.

Narrative of Riots at Alton: In Connection with the Death of Rev. Elijah P. Lovejoy. Alton, Ill.: G. Holton, 1838.

"The Nature, Importance, and Means of Eminent Holiness Throughout the Church." *American National Preacher* 10 (June and July 1835): 193–224.

The Papal Conspiracy Exposed, and Protestantism Defended, in the Light of Reason, History, and Scripture. Boston: Stearns & Co., 1855.

President Beecher's Letters on the Subject of Baptism, Addressed to Rev. William Hague. Boston: Washington Clapp, C. C. Dean, 1843.

"The Right Use of the Passions and Emotions in the Work of Intellectual Culture and Development." In *Lectures Delivered Before the American Institute of Instruction, at Providence, R.I., August, 1854.* Boston: Ticknor and Fields, 1855.

"The Works of Samuel Hopkins." *Bibliotheca Sacra* 10 (Jan. 1853): 63–82.

Edward Beecher and Theron Baldwin. *An Appeal in Behalf of Illinois College, Recently Founded at Jacksonville, Illinois.* New York: D. Fanshaw, 1831.

Edward Beecher and Thomas H. Skinner. *Hints, Designed to Aid Christians in Their Efforts to Convert Men to God.* Hartford: S. Andrus & Son, 1848.

Edward Beecher and Charles Beecher. *The Result Tested. A Review of the Proceedings of a Council at Georgetown, Mass., Aug. 15, 16, and 22, 1863.* Boston: Wright & Potter, 1863.

Eunice White Bullard Beecher

All Around the House; or, How to Make Homes Happy. New York: D. Appleton and Company, 1878.

From Dawn to Daylight; or, The Simple Story of a Western Home. By a Minister's Wife. New York: Derby & Jackson, 1859.

Henry Ward Beecher

Autobiographical Reminiscences of Henry Ward Beecher. Edited by T. J. Ellinwood. New York: F. A. Stokes Co., 1898.

Evolution and Religion. New York: Fords, Howard, & Hulbert, 1885.

Eyes and Ears. Boston: Ticknor and Fields, 1863.

Great Speech, Delivered in New York City on the Conflict of Northern and Southern Theories of Man and Society, January 14, 1855. Rochester, N.Y.: A. Strong & Co., 1855.

How to Become a Christian. New York: A. S. Barnes & Burr, 1862.

The Life of Jesus, the Christ. New York: J. B. Ford and Co., 1871.

Life Thoughts, Gathered from the Extemporaneous Discourses of Henry Ward Beecher. Boston: Phillips, Sampson and Company, 1858.

New Star Papers; or, Views and Experiences of Religious Subjects. New York: Derby & Jackson, 1859.

Norwood; or, Village Life in New England. New York: Charles Scribner, 1868.

Popular Amusements. The Races.—The Theatre. Edinburgh: Grant & Taylor, n.d.

Seven Lectures to Young Men, on Various Important Subjects. Indianapolis: W. H. Moore & Co., 1844.
Star Papers; or Experiences of Life and Art. New York: J. C. Derby, 1855.
A Summer Parish. New York: J. B. Ford and Co., 1875.
Woman's Duty to Vote. Speech by Henry Ward Beecher at the Eleventh Woman's Rights Convention. Held in New York, May 10, 1866. New York: American Equal Rights Association, 1867.
Yale Lectures on Preaching. New York: J. B. Ford and Co., 1872-74.

Lyman Beecher

An Address, Delivered at the Tenth Anniversary Celebration of the Union Literary Society of Miami University, September 29, 1835. Cincinnati: Cincinnati Journal, 1835.
The Autobiography of Lyman Beecher. Edited by Charles Beecher. 2 vols. New York: Harper & Bros., 1864.
The Autobiography of Lyman Beecher. Edited by Barbara Cross. Cambridge, Mass.: Harvard University Press, 1961. This John Harvard Library edition is more in the nature of an annotated reprint than a critical edition, numerous inaccuracies in the original going unnoticed and uncorrected, but I have taken my quotations from it, as it is the more accessible edition of the two.
A Dialogue, Exhibiting Some of the Principles and Practical Consequences of Modern Infidelity. Sag Harbor, N.Y., 1806.
God in the Storm . . . An Address by Lyman Beecher, D.D. on Board the Great Western, after the Storm Encountered on Her Voyage. New York: Robert Carter & Brothers, 1851.
A Guide to Piety; or, Directions to Persons Just Commencing a Religious Life. Worcester, Mass.: S. A. Howland, 1843.
Instructions for Young Christians. Cincinnati: Truman, Smith and Company, 1834.
A Plea for Colleges [see *An Address,* above, 1st entry].
A Plea for the West. Cincinnati: Truman and Smith, 1835.
A Sermon Occasioned by the Lamented Death of Mrs. Frances M. Sands of New Shoreham. Sag Harbor, N.Y.: Alden Spooner, 1806.
Sermons Delivered on Various Occasions. Boston: T. R. Marvin, 1828. This volume was collected in his *Works.*
To the Congregational Ministers and Churches of Connecticut. Reprinted from the *Christian Spectator,* n.d.
Views in Theology. Cincinnati: Truman and Smith, 1836. Collected in his *Works.*
Works, 3 vols. Boston: J. P. Jewett & Co., 1852-53.

Lyman Beecher and Asahel Nettleton

Letters of the Rev. Dr. Beecher and Rev. Mr. Nettleton, on the "New Measures" in Conducting Revivals of Religion. With a Review of a Sermon, by Novanglus. New York: G. & C. Carvill, 1828.

Thomas Kinnicut Beecher

A Candidate's Address to the Voters of the 19th District, N.Y. (Allegany, Steuben and Chemung Counties). Elmira, N.Y., 1880.
Christ Our Passover, April 25, 1886. Printed for the Park Church, Elmira, N.Y.

In Time with the Stars: Stories for Children. Elmira, N.Y.: Hosmer H. Billings, 1901.

Jervis Langdon, 1809–1870: Memorial Address. Privately printed.

Let Us Not Judge One Another Any More, Nov. 22, 1885. Printed for the Park Church, Elmira, N.Y.

Mr. Beecher's Prayers and Blessings for a Week, Taken by His Stenographer Without His Knowledge, the Summer Before His Death. [Elmira, N.Y., 1900].

Notable Sermons. Elmira, N. Y.: Osborne Press, 1914. This was intended to be a two-volume set, but the second was never published.

Of God's Temper and Man's Conditions, April 11, 1886. Printed for the Park Church, Elmira, N.Y.

Of Sabbaths or Rests, Dec. 19, 1885. Printed for the Park Church, Elmira, N.Y.

Olivia Lewis Langdon. [Elmira, N.Y., 1911].

Our Need and Our Plan, April 28, 1878, July 3, 1881, and Aug. 30, 1891. Printed for the Park Church, Elmira, N.Y.

Our Seven Churches. New York: J. B. Ford and Co., 1870.

A Sermon for the Citizens of Elmira. Elmira, N.Y.: Fairman & Caldwell, 1865.

Thanksgiving Sermon. Delivered November 26th, at a Union Service Held in the First Presbyterian Church at Elmira, New York, ed. and rev. Theron A. Wales. Elmira, N.Y.: Elmira Advertiser Association, 1907.

There Shall Arise False Christs, July 4, 1886. Printed for the Park Church, Elmira, N.Y.

The Wrath of Man Worketh Not the Righteousness of God, May 9, 1886. Printed for the Park Church, Elmira, N.Y.

William Henry Beecher

The Duty of the Church to Her Ministry. Batavia, N.Y.: Lucas Seaver, 1841.

A Letter on Animal Magnetism. Philadelphia: Brown, Bicking, & Guilbert, 1844.

Isabella Beecher Hooker

"Argument of Mrs. Hooker," in *Memorial of Elizabeth Cady Stanton, Isabella Beecher Hooker, Elizabeth L. Bladen, Olympia Brown, Susan B. Anthony, and Josephine L. Griffing, to the Congress of the United States, and the Arguments Thereon before the Judiciary Committee of the U.S. Senate, by Isabella Beecher Hooker, Elizabeth Cady Stanton, and Susan B. Anthony.* Washington, D.C.: Chronicle Publishing Co., 1872.

Confession of Faith, April 14, 1885. Privately printed.

Womanhood: Its Sanctities and Fidelities. Boston: Lee and Shepard, 1873.

John Hooker

A Discourse Delivered before the Willimantic Spiritualist Society. N.p.; Fowler & Miller, 1886.

"Experiences in the Investigation of Spiritualistic Phenomena and Reply to Objections." Reprinted from the *Psychical Review* (1894).

Some Reminiscences of a Long Life. With a Few Articles on Moral and Social Subjects of Present Interest. Hartford: Belknap & Warfield, 1899.

Harriet Beecher Stowe

Agnes of Sorrento. Boston: Houghton, Mifflin, 1896.

"Aunt Esther's Rules." *Our Young Folks* 1 (Sept. 1865): 591-94.

"Catharine E. Beecher" and "Mrs. A. D. T. Whitney." In *Our Famous Women.* Hartford: A. D. Worthington & Co., 1884.

Dred; a Tale of the Great Dismal Swamp. 2 vols. Boston: Phillips, Sampson and Co., 1856.

Footsteps of the Master. New York: J. B. Ford & Co., 1877.

Household Papers and Stories. Boston: Houghton, Mifflin, 1896.

Little Foxes. Boston: Fields, Osgood & Co., 1870.

"Lyman Beecher." In Piper and MacCracken, eds., *Lives of the Leaders of Our Church Universal*, 3:711-30. Boston: Congregational Publishing Society, 1879.

Men of Our Times; or Leading Patriots of the Day. Hartford: Hartford Publishing Co., 1868.

The Minister's Wooing. London: S. Low, Son & Co., 1859.

My Wife and I; or, Harry Henderson's History. New York: J. B. Ford and Co., 1871.

Oldtown Folks. Edited by Henry F. May. Cambridge, Mass.: Harvard University Press, 1966.

Our Charley, and What to Do with Him. Boston: Phillips, Sampson & Co., 1858.

Pink and White Tyranny: A Society Novel. Boston: Houghton, Mifflin, 1896.

Poganuc People: Their Loves and Lives. Boston: Houghton, Mifflin, 1896.

Queer Little People. Boston: Ticknor and Fields, 1868.

Religious Studies, Sketches and Poems. Boston: Houghton, Mifflin, 1896.

Sunny Memories of Foreign Lands. 2 vols. New York: J. C. Derby, 1854.

Uncle Sam's Emancipation; Earthly Care a Heavenly Discipline; and Other Sketches. Philadelphia: Willis R. Hazard, 1853.

Uncle Tom's Cabin; or, Life Among the Lowly. 2 vols. Boston: John P. Jewett, 1852.

We and Our Neighbors. New York: J. B. Ford, 1875.

Woman in Sacred History: A Series of Sketches Drawn from Scriptural, Historical, and Legendary Sources. New York: J. B. Ford and Co., 1873.

Calvin Ellis Stowe

"The Eschatology of Christ, with Special Reference to the Discourse in Matt. XXIV. and XXV." *Bibliotheca Sacra* 7 (July 1850): 452-78.

Introduction to the Criticism and Interpretation of the Bible, Designed for the Use of Theological Students, Bible Classes, and High Schools. Cincinnati: Corey, Fairbank & Webster, 1835.

A Letter to R. D. Mussey, M.D., on the Utter Groundlessness of All the Millennial Arithmetic. Cincinnati: J. B. Wilson, 1843.

Origin and History of the Books of the Bible, both the Canonical and the Apocryphal. Hartford: Hartford Publishing Co., 1867.

"The Prophet Jonah." *Bibliotheca Sacra* 10 (Oct. 1853): 739-64.

The Religious Element in Education. Boston: William D. Ticknor & Co., 1844.

Report on Elementary Public Instruction in Europe, Made to the Thirty-Sixth General Assembly of the State of Ohio, Dec. 13, 1837. Harrisburg, Pa.: Packer, Barrett and Parke, 1838.

"The Right Interpretation of the Sacred Scriptures– the Helps and the Hindrances." *Bibliotheca Sacra* 10 (Jan. 1853): 34-62.

"Sketches and Recollections of Dr. Lyman Beecher," *Congregational Quarterly*, 6 (July 1864): 221-35.

Memoirs, Biographies, Published Correspondence, etc.

Abbott, Lyman. "The Country Home of Rev. H. W. Beecher." *Brooklyn Advance* 2 (Sept. 1878): 1.

Abbott, Lyman, ed. *Henry Ward Beecher: A Sketch of His Career.* New York: Funk & Wagnalls, 1883.

Allen, Darcia Howe. *The Life and Services of Rev. Lyman Beecher, D.D. as President and Professor of Theology in Lane Seminary.* Cincinnati: Johnson, Stephens & Company. 1863.

Bacon, Leonard, et al. *Memorial of Nathaniel W. Taylor, D.D.* New Haven: Thomas H. Pease, 1858.

Badger, Joseph. *Memoir.* Hudson, Ohio: Sawyer, Ingersoll and Company, 1851.

Beecher, Leonard Thurlow. *As It Was.* N.p., Van der Veer Press, 1947.

Bok, Edward, comp. *Beecher Memorial: Contemporaneous Tributes to the Memory of Henry Ward Beecher.* Brooklyn, N.Y.: privately printed, 1887.

Bungay, George W. *Off-Hand Takings; or, Crayon Sketches of Noticeable Men of Our Age.* New York: DeWitt & Davenport, 1854.

Celebration of the One Hundredth Anniversary of the Birth-Day of William Ellery Channing at the Church of the Saviour, and at the Academy of Music, Brooklyn, N.Y., Tuesday and Wednesday, April 6 and 7, 1880. Boston, 1880.

Cheney, Mary Bushnell. *Life and Letters of Horace Bushnell.* New York: Harper & Brothers, 1880.

Cleaveland, Nehemiah. *History of Bowdoin College. With Biographical Sketches of Its Graduates.* Edited by Alpheus S. Packard. Boston: James Ripley Osgood & Co., 1882.

Corning, James L. *Personal Recollections of Henry Ward Beecher.* Brooklyn, N.Y.: Brooklyn Eagle Press, n.d.

Cornwell, Albert G. *The Lengthened Shadow of a Man: An Address Delivered on the Occasion of the Centennial of the Birth of Thomas K. Beecher.* Elmira, N.Y. [1924].

Day, Thomas and James Murdock. *Brief Memoirs of the Class of 1797.* New Haven, 1848.

"The Diary of Charles Peabody." Edited by William E. and Ophia D. Smith. *Bulletin of the Historical and Philosophical Society of Ohio* 11 (1953): 274–92.

Dix, John Ross. *Pulpit Portraits, or Pen-Pictures of Distinguished American Divines.* Boston: Tappan and Whittemore, 1854.

Eastman, Max. *Heroes I Have Known: Twelve Who Lived Great Lives.* New York: Simon & Schuster, 1942.

Eastman, S. E. *Address at the Unveiling of the Memorial Statue of Thomas K. Beecher.* Elmira, N.Y., 1901.

Edwards, B. B. "The Life and Character of Dr. DeWette." *Bibliotheca Sacra* 7 (Oct. 1850): 772–99.

——. *Memoir of the Rev. Elias Cornelius.* Boston: Perkins & Marvin, 1833.

Fairchild, Joy H. *Remarkable Incidents in the Life of Rev. J. H. Fairchild, Pastor of Payson Church, South Boston.* 4th ed. Boston: printed for the author, 1857.

Fields, Annie Adams. *Life and Letters of Harriet Beecher Stowe.* Boston: Houghton, Mifflin, 1897.

Flint, James. *Letters from America, Containing Observations on the Climate and Agriculture of the Western States.* Edinburgh: W. & C. Tait, 1822.

Flint, Timothy. *Recollections of the Last Ten Years, Passed in Occasional Residences and Journeyings in the Valley of the Mississippi.* Boston: Cummings, Hilliard, and Co., 1826.

Goodrich, Samuel G. *Recollections of a Lifetime.* 2 vols. New York: Miller, Orton and Mulligan, 1857.

Gough, John B. *Autobiography and Personal Recollections.* Springfield, Mass.: Bill, Nichols & Co., 1869.

Guernsey, A. H. "Lyman Beecher," *Harper's Monthly Magazine* 30 (May 1865): 697–710.

Hadley, James. *Diary, 1843–1852.* Edited by Laura Hadley Moseley. New Haven: Yale University Press, 1951.

Hatch, Rebecca Taylor. *Personal Reminiscences and Memorials.* New York: privately printed, 1905.

Howard, John Raymond. *Henry Ward Beecher: A Study of His Personality, Career, and Influence in Public Affairs.* Boston: Pilgrim Press, 1887.

——. *Remembrance of Things Past.* New York: Thomas Y. Crowell, 1925.

"Journal of Cyrus P. Bradley." Edited by George H. Twiss, *Ohio Archaeological and Historical Publications* 15 (Columbus, Ohio, 1906): 207–70.

"The Journal of Rev. and Mrs. Lemuel Foster," edited by Harry Thomas Stock. *Journal of the Presbyterian Historical Society* 11 (Sept. and Dec. 1921, and March 1922): 130–44, 156–70.

Letters of Theodore Dwight Weld, Angelina Grimké Weld, and Sarah Grimké. Edited by Gilbert H. Barnes and Dwight L. Dumond. 2 vols. New York, 1934.

McCartney, Henry R. *Address by Rev. Henry R. McCartney at the Funeral Services of the Rev. Charles Beecher.* Georgetown, Mass.: Advocate Printers, 1900.

McCulloch, Hugh. *Men and Measures of Half a Century: Sketches and Comments.* New York: Charles Scribner's Sons, 1889.

Mansfield, E. D. *Personal Memories, Social, Political, and Literary, with Sketches of Many Noted People, 1803–1843.* Cincinnati: Robert Clarke & Co., 1879.

Mathews, W. S. B. "A Remarkable Personality: Thomas K. Beecher." *Outlook* 82 (March 10, 1906): 555–61.

Mears, David Otis. *An Autobiography, 1842–1893.* Boston, 1920.

[Packard, Edward N.] *Memorial of Lieut. Frederick Henry Beecher, U.S.A.* Portland, Me.: Stephen Berry, 1870.

Pennington, James W. C. *The Fugitive Blacksmith; or, Events in the History of James W. C. Pennington.* 2d ed. London, 1849.

Perkins, Frances Johnson Beecher. "A Seven Years' Outing." *New England Magazine,* n.s. 22 (June 1900): 592–602.

Porcher, Frederick Adolphus. "The Memoirs of Frederick Adolphus Porcher," edited by Samuel Gaillard Stoney. *South Carolina Historical and Genealogical Magazine* 44 (1943): 65–80, 135–47, 212–19; 45 (1944): 30–40, 80–98, 146–56; 46 (1945): 25–39, 78–92, 140–58, 198–208; 47 (1946): 35–52, 83–108, 150–62, 214–27; 48 (1947), 20–25.

Post, T. A. *Truman Marcellus Post, D.D.: A Biography Personal and Literary.* Boston: Congregational Sunday-School and Publishing Society, 1891.

Raymond, John Howard. *Life and Letters.* New York: Fords, Howard & Hulbert, 1881.

Reed, Andrew. *Martha; a Memorial of an Only and Beloved Sister.* New York: Harper & Brothers, 1835.

Robbins, Sarah Stuart. *Old Andover Days: Memories of a Puritan Childhood.* Boston: Pilgrim Press, 1908.

Robinson, David C. "An Address in Memory of Thomas K. Beecher." N.p., 1901.

Sedgwick, Catherine M. *Life and Letters.* Edited by Mary E. Dewey. New York: Harper & Brothers, 1871.

Smith, Henry Boynton. *His Life and Work, Edited by His Wife.* New York: A. C. Armstrong & Son, 1881.

Sprague, William Buel. *Annals of the American Pulpit; or Commemorative Notices of Distinguished American Clergymen of Various Denominations.* Vol. 2. New York: Robert Carter & Brothers, 1859.

——. *The Life of Jedidiah Morse, D.D.* New York: Anson D. F. Randolph & Company, 1874.

——. *Memoir of the Rev. Edward D. Griffin, D.D.* New York: Taylor & Dodd, 1839.

Stanton, Henry B. *Random Recollections.* 2d. ed. New York: Macgowan & Slipper, 1886.

Stowe, Charles E. *Life of Harriet Beecher Stowe.* Boston: Houghton, Mifflin, 1889.

Sturtevant, Julian Monson. *An Autobiography.* Edited by J. M. Sturtevant, Jr. New York: Fleming H. Revell Co., 1896.

——. *The Memory of the Just, a Sermon Commemorative of the Life and Labors of the Rev. William Kirby.* New York: Baker, Godwin & Co., 1852.

Thomas K. Beecher, Teacher of the Park Church. Elmira, N.Y.: Park Church, 1900.

Tillson, Christiana Holmes. *A Woman's Story of Pioneer Illinois.* Edited by Milo M. Quaife. Chicago: Lakeside Press, 1919.

Tilton, Theodore. *Victoria C. Woodhull: A Biographical Sketch.* New York: The Golden Age, 1871.

Trollope, Frances. *Domestic Manners of the Americans,* ed. Donald Smalley. New York: Vintage Books, 1960.

Trumbull, Henry Clay. *My Four Religious Teachers.* Philadelphia: Sunday School Times Co., 1903.

Tuttle, Joseph F. *The Late Dr. Lyman Beecher.* New York: John A. Gray, 1863.

Tyler, Bennet. *Memoir of the Life and Character of Rev. Asahel Nettleton, D.D.* Hartford: Robins & Smith, 1844.

White, James C. *Personal Reminiscences of Lyman Beecher.* New York: Funk & Wagnalls, 1882.

Theological Writings, Tracts, etc.

Bacon, Leonard. "Concerning a Recent Chapter of Ecclesiastical History." *New Englander* 38 (Sept. 1879): 701–12.

——. *The Genesis of the New England Churches.* New York: Harper & Brothers, 1874.

Baird, Samuel J. *A History of the New School and of the Questions Involved in the Disruption of the Presbyterian Church in 1838.* Philadelphia: Claxton, Remsen & Haffelfinger, 1868.

"Beecher's Views in Theology." *Biblical Repertory and Princeton Review* 4 (April and July, 1837): 216-37, 364-407.
Bishop, Robert Hamilton. *Sketches of the Philosophy of the Bible.* Oxford, Ohio, 1833.
Bushnell, Horace. *Work and Play.* New York: Charles Scribner's Sons, 1881.
Debates and Proceedings of the National Council of Congregational Churches, Held at Boston, Mass., June 14-24, 1865. Boston: American Congregational Association, 1866.
"Declaration of Faith Set Forth by the National Council in 1865." *Congregational Quarterly* 10 (Oct. 1868): 377-78.
[Dwight, Timothy.] "A Brief Account of the Revival of Religion Now Prevailing in Yale-College, New-Haven," *Connecticut Evangelical Magazine* 3 (July 1802): 30-32.
Dwight, Timothy. *Sermons.* 2 vols. New Haven, 1828.
——. *Theology; Explained and Defended, in a Series of Sermons.* 5 vols. Middletown, Conn., 1818-19.
Fisher, George P. *Discussions in History and Theology.* New York: Charles Scribner's Sons, 1880.
Fisk, Wilbur. *Calvinistic Controversy: Embracing a Sermon on Predestination and Election.* New York, 1837.
Fowler, William Chauncey. *Essays: Historical, Literary, Educational.* Hartford, 1876.
Nettleton, Asahel. *Rev. Asahel Nettleton's Letter to Dr. Lyman Beecher, on Revivals.* N.p., ca. 1828.
"On the Atonement." *Connecticut Evangelical Magazine* 3 (March 1803): 332-38, 370-74.
[Rand, Asa.] *Letter to the Rev. Dr. Beecher on the Influence of His Ministry in Boston.* Lowell, Mass.: Rand and Southmayd, 1833.
Stuart, Moses. *A Sermon Preached at the Dedication of the Church in Hanover Street, Boston, March 1, 1826.* Andover: Flagg and Gould, 1826.
Taylor, Nathaniel W. *Essays, Lectures, Etc., Upon Select Topics in Revealed Theology.* New York: Austin & Smith, 1859.
[Taylor, Nathaniel W.] *An Inquiry into the Nature of Sin as Exhibited in Dr. Dwight's Theology, with Remarks on an Examination of Dr. Taylor's and Mr. Harvey's Views on the Same Subject.* New Haven, 1829.
Taylor, Nathaniel W. *Lectures on the Moral Government of God.* New York, 1859.

Denominational Publications, Histories of Churches, etc.

American Seamen's Friend Society. *Annual Reports.* New York: Stephen Hallet, 1856-61.
Andover Theological Seminary. *General Catalogue of the Theological Seminary, Andover, Massachusetts, 1808-1908.* Boston: Thomas Todd [1908].
The Articles of Faith, and the Covenant, of Park Street Church, Boston; with a List of the Members. Boston: T. R. Marvin, 1825.
The Articles of Faith and Covenant of the Hanover Church, Boston, with a List of the Members. Boston: T. R. Marvin, 1826.
Baird, Robert. *Religion in America; or, an Account of the Origin, Relation to the*

State, and Present Condition of the Evangelical Churches in the United States, with Notices of the Unevangelical Denominations. New York: Harper and Brothers, 1856.

Beecher, Willis J., comp. *Index of Presbyterian Ministers.* Philadelphia: Presbyterian Board of Publications, 1888.

Conrad, Arcturus Z., ed. *Commemorative Exercises at the One Hundredth Anniversary of the Organization of Park Street Church.* Boston: Park Street Church Centennial Committee, 1909.

Dexter, Henry M. *The Congregationalism of the Last Three Hundred Years, as Seen in Its Literature.* New York: Harper & Brothers, 1880.

Fiftieth Anniversary of the Organization of the Brick Church, Rochester, N.Y. Rochester, N.Y.: E. R. Andrews, 1876.

First Presbyterian Church, Batavia, N.Y. *Sesquicentennial History and Scrapbook, 1807–1959.* [Batavia, N.Y., 1959].

Griswold, Stephen M. *Sixty Years with Plymouth Church.* New York: Fleming H. Revell Company, 1907.

Hill, Charles J. *Historical Sketch of the South Congregational Church, Middletown, Conn.* Middletown, Conn.: Pelton & King, 1876.

Historical Papers Read at the Seventy-Fifth Anniversary of the Putnam Presbyterian Church, Zanesville, Ohio, December 18–21, 1910. Columbus, Ohio: The Champlin Press, ca. 1910.

Historical Sketches. Central Congregational Church, Galesburg, Illinois, 1837–1902. N.p., n.d.

Hoppin, James M. *The Office and Work of the Christian Ministry.* 2d ed. New York: Sheldon and Company, 1870.

Kingsbury, Addison. *Retrospection: an Historical Resumé of the Putnam Presbyterian Church, Zanesville, Ohio.* Zanesville, Ohio: Sullivan & Parsons, 1877.

A Layman [pseud.] *The Recent Attempt to Defeat the Constitutional Provisions in Favor of Religious Freedom Considered in Reference to the Trust Conveyances of Hanover Street Church.* 2d ed. Boston: Hilliard, Gray and Co., 1828.

Minutes of the General Assembly of the Presbyterian Church in the United States of America, 1831–37.

Minutes of the General Assembly of the Presbyterian Church [New School], 1838–58.

Moore, Joseph P. "History of the Churches in Fort Wayne (Indiana) Presbytery; To Which Is Added Biographical Sketches of Deceased Ministers. July 20, 1876." Typescript from MS in Presbyterian Historical Society.

New York Observer. Year Book and Almanac, 1871. New York: Sidney E. Morse, Jr. & Co., 1870.

Norton, A. T. *History of the Presbyterian Church in the State of Illinois.* Vol. 1. St. Louis, Mo.: W. S. Bryan, 1879.

One Hundredth Anniversary, First Congregational Church, Wellsville, New York. N.p., 1857.

The Sailor's Magazine, and Seamen's Friend, vols. 28–33 (Sept. 1855–Aug. 1861).

Schem, Alexander J. *The American Ecclesiastical Year-Book.* Vol. 1. New York: H. Dayton, 1860.

The Semi-Centennial Celebration of the Park Street Church and Society. Boston: Henry Hoyt, 1861.

Seventy-Fifth Anniversary of the Park Street Congregational Church. Boston: Brown & Clark, 1884.

Smyth, Egbert C. *Three Discourses upon the Religious History of Bowdoin College.* Brunswick, Me.: J. Griffin, 1858.
Thomas, John H. *An Historical Sketch of the Presbyterian Church of Lawrenceburgh, Indiana.* Lawrenceburgh, Ind., 1887(?).
Thompson, Noyes L. *The History of Plymouth Church.* New York: G. W. Carleton & Co., 1873.
" A Transcript of the Records of the Chillicothe [Ohio] Presbytery, vol. III, 1837–1846." Typescript in the Presbyterian Historical Society.
Whiton, James M. *A Half Century of Church Life: A Discourse for the Semi-Centennial Anniversary of the First Free Presbyterian Church, Now, and Since 1851, the First Congregational Church, of Newark, N.J.* Newark, N.J.: *Daily Advertiser*, 1884.
Year-Book of the American Congregational Union. New York and Boston, 1854–59, 1879–81.

SECONDARY SOURCES

Adams, John R. *Harriet Beecher Stowe.* New Haven, 1963.
Ahlstrom, Sydney E. "The Scottish Philosophy and American Theology," *Church History* 24 (Sept. 1955): 257–72.
Andrews, Kenneth R. *Nook Farm: Mark Twain's Hartford Circle.* N.p.: 1967.
Averill, Lloyd J. *American Theology in the Liberal Tradition.* Philadelphia, 1967.
Bainton, Roland H. *Yale and the Ministry.* New York, 1957.
Banner, James M., Jr. *To the Hartford Convention: The Federalists and the Origins of Party Politics in Massachusetts, 1789–1815.* New York, 1970.
Billington, Ray Allen. *The Protestant Crusade, 1800–1860: A Study of the Origins of American Nativism.* New York, 1938.
Birdsall, Richard D. *Berkshire County, a Cultural History.* New Haven, 1959.
——. "Ezra Stiles versus the New Divinity Men." *American Quarterly* 17 (Summer 1965): 248–58.
Boardman, George Nye. *A History of New England Theology.* New York, 1899.
Braden, Charles S. *Spirits in Rebellion: The Rise and Development of New Thought.* Dallas, Texas, 1963.
——. *These Also Believe: A Study of Modern American Cults and Minority Religious Movements.* New York, 1949.
Brauer, Jerald C., ed. *Reinterpretation in American Church History.* Chicago, 1968.
Brown, C. G. "Christocentric Liberalism in the Episcopal Church." *Historical Magazine of the Protestant Episcopal Church* 37 (March 1968): 5–38.
Brown, Herbert R. *The Sentimental Novel in America, 1789–1860.* Durham, N.C., 1940.
Brown, Jerry Wayne. *The Rise of Biblical Criticism in America, 1800–1870: The New England Scholars.* Middletown, Conn., 1969.
Bushman, Richard L. "Jonathan Edwards and Puritan Consciousness." *Journal for the Scientific Study of Religion* 5 (Fall 1966): 383–96.
——. *From Puritan to Yankee: Character and the Social Order in Connecticut, 1690–1765.* New York, 1967.
Calhoun, Daniel R. *Professional Lives in America: Structure and Aspiration, 1750–1850.* Cambridge, Mass., 1965.
Calkins, Earnest E. *They Broke the Prairie.* New York, 1937.

Carriel, Mary Turner. *The Life of Jonathan Baldwin Turner.* Urbana, Ill., 1961.

Carter, Paul A. *The Spiritual Crisis of the Gilded Age.* DeKalb, Ill., 1971.

Cauthen, Kenneth. *The Impact of American Religious Liberalism.* New York, 1962.

Chadwick, John W. *William Ellery Channing, Minister of Religion.* Boston, 1903.

Clark, Clifford E., Jr. "Henry Ward Beecher: Revivalist and Antislavery Leader, 1813-1867." Ph.D. dissertation, Harvard University, 1967.

Cole, Charles C., Jr. "The New Lebanon Convention." *New York History* 31 (Oct. 1950): 385-97.

——. *The Social Ideas of the Northern Evangelists, 1826-1860.* New York, 1954.

Cross, Barbara M. "Horace Bushnell." Ph.D. dissertation, Radcliffe College, 1956.

——. *Horace Bushnell: Minister to a Changing America.* Chicago, 1958.

Cross, Whitney R. *The Burned-Over District.* New York, 1965.

Crozier, Alice Cooper. *The Novels of Harriet Beecher Stowe.* New York, 1969.

Cuningham, Charles E. *Timothy Dwight, 1752-1817.* New York, 1942.

Dakin, Edwin F. *Mrs. Eddy: The Biography of a Virginal Mind.* New York, 1929.

DeMille, George E. *The Catholic Movement in the American Episcopal Church.* Philadelphia, 1950.

DesChamps, Margaret Burr. "Early Presbyterianism along the North Bank of the Ohio River." *Journal of the Presbyterian Historical Society* 28 (Dec. 1950): 207-20.

Detty, Victor C. *History of the Presbyterian Church of Wysox, Pennsylvania, 1791-1936.* Wysox, Pa., 1937.

Dorn, Jacob Henry. *Washington Gladden: Prophet of the Social Gospel.* Columbus, Ohio, 1967.

Doyle, Arthur Conan. *The History of Spiritualism.* 2 vols. New York, 1926.

Doyle, John H., comp. *The First Congregational Church of Toledo, a Narrative.* [Toledo, Ohio, 1914?].

Earhart, Mary. *Frances Willard: From Prayers to Politics.* Chicago, 1944.

Eastman, Annis Ford. *A Flower of Puritanism: Julia Jones Beecher, 1826-1905.* Elmira, N.Y., n.d.

Elsmere, Jane Shaffer. *Henry Ward Beecher: The Indiana Years, 1837-1847.* Indianapolis, 1973.

Elwood, Douglas. *The Philosophical Theology of Jonathan Edwards.* New York, 1960.

Englizian, H. Crosby. *Brimstone Corner: Park Street, Boston.* Chicago, 1968.

Everhart, J. F. *History of Muskingum County, Ohio.* Columbus, Ohio, 1882.

Fairchild, Hoxie Neale. *Religious Trends in English Poetry.* 4 vols. New York, 1939-57.

Faust, Clarence H. "The Decline of Puritanism." In Harry Hayden Clark, ed., *Transitions in American Literary History.* Durham, N.C., 1953.

Fitch, James Marston. "Our Domesticated Utopians." In *Architecture and the Esthetics of Plenty.* New York, 1961.

Fornell, Earl Wesley. *The Unhappy Medium: Spiritualism and the Life of Margaret Fox.* Austin, Texas, 1964. This is an example of a scholarly approach to Spiritualism which fails; it is largely a rehash of the primary sources, with no attempt at historical or biographical analysis.

Foster, Charles H. *The Rungless Ladder: Harriet Beecher Stowe and New England Puritanism.* Durham, N.C., 1954.

Foster, Charles I. *An Errand of Mercy: The Evangelical United Front, 1790–1837.* Chapel Hill, N.C., 1960.

Frazee, John Elmer. "Lyman Beecher, Theologian and Social Reformer." Ph.D. dissertation, University of Edinburgh, 1936.

Gabriel, Ralph Henry. *Religion and Learning at Yale.* New Haven, 1958.

Geer, Curtis Manning. *The Hartford Theological Seminary, 1834–1934.* Hartford, Conn., 1934.

Goen, C. C. "The 'Methodist Age' in American Church History." *Religion in Life* 34 (Autumn 1965): 562–72.

——. *Revivalism and Separatism in New England, 1740–1800.* New Haven, 1962.

Graff, Mary B. *Mandarin on the St. Johns.* Gainesville, Fla., 1953.

Grave, S. A. *The Scottish Philosophy of Common Sense.* Oxford, 1960.

Harding, Vincent. "Lyman Beecher and the Transformation of American Protestantism, 1775–1863." Ph.D. dissertation, University of Chicago, 1965.

Harker, John S. "The Life and Contributions of Calvin Ellis Stowe." Ph.D. dissertation, University of Pittsburgh, 1951.

Haroutunian, Joseph. *Piety versus Moralism: The Passing of the New England Theology.* New York, 1932.

Hedges, Henry P. *A History of the Town of East-Hampton, N.Y.* Sag Harbor, N.Y., 1897.

Henry, Stuart C. *Unvanquished Puritan: A Portrait of Lyman Beecher.* Grand Rapids, Mich., 1973.

Hibben, Paxton. *Henry Ward Beecher: An American Portrait.* New York, 1927. Typical of the muckraking biographies of the 1920s and 1930s, it is inaccurate and untrustworthy in many of its details.

Hopkins, Vivian C. *Prodigal Puritan: A Life of Delia Bacon.* Cambridge, Mass., 1959.

Howard, Leon. *The Connecticut Wits.* Chicago, 1943.

Howe, Daniel W. *The Unitarian Conscience: Harvard Moral Philosophy, 1805–1861.* Cambridge, Mass., 1970.

Hutchinson, William R. *The Transcendentalist Ministers: Church Reform in the New England Renaissance.* Boston, 1965.

"Jacksonville Centennial Number." *Journal of the Illinois State Historical Society* 18 (April 1925).

Johnson, William A. *Nature and the Supernatural in the Theology of Horace Bushnell.* Lund, Sweden, 1963.

Jones, Howard Mumford. "The Unity of New England Culture." In *Proceedings of the Massachusetts Historical Society* 79 (1967): 74–88.

Keller, Charles R. *The Second Great Awakening in Connecticut.* New Haven, 1942.

Kerber, Linda K. *Federalists in Dissent: Imagery and Ideology in Jeffersonian America.* Ithaca, N.Y., 1970.

Kerr, Howard. *Mediums, and Spirit-Rappers, and Roaring Radicals: Spiritualism in American Literature, 1850–1900.* Urbana, Ill., 1972.

Kirkham, E. Kay. *A Survey of American Church Records for the Period before the Civil War East of the Mississippi.* Salt Lake City, Utah, 1959.

Leopold, Richard W. *Robert Dale Owen, a Biography.* Cambridge, Mass., 1940.

Lewis, Thomas H. *Zanesville and Muskingum County, Ohio.* Vols. 1 and 2. Chicago, 1927.

Ludwig, Allan L. *Graven Images: New England Stonecarving and Its Symbols.* Middletown, Conn., 1966.

McGiffert, Michael. "American Puritan Studies in the 1960's." *William and Mary Quarterly* 27 (Jan. 1970): 36–67.

McLoughlin, William G. *The Meaning of Henry Ward Beecher.* New York, 1970.

——. *Modern Revivalism: Charles Grandison Finney to Billy Graham.* New York, 1959.

Magoun, George F. *Asa Turner: A Home Missionary Patriarch and His Times.* Boston, 1889.

Marsden, George M. *The Evangelical Mind and the New School Presbyterian Experience.* New Haven, 1970.

Mead, Sidney E. *Nathaniel William Taylor, 1786–1858: A Connecticut Liberal.* New Haven, 1967.

Melder, Keith. "Ladies Bountiful: Organized Women's Benevolence in Early 19th-Century America." *New York History* 48 (July 1967): 231–54.

Michaelson, Robert S. "The Protestant Ministry in America: 1850 to the Present." In *The Ministry in Historical Perspectives,* edited by H. Richard Niebuhr and Daniel D. Williams. New York, 1956.

Miller, James M. *The Genesis of Western Culture: The Upper Ohio Valley, 1800–1825.* Columbus, Ohio, 1938.

Monk, Robert C. *John Wesley, His Puritan Heritage: A Study of the Christian Life.* Nashville, 1966.

Morse, Jarvis Means. *A Neglected Period of Connecticut's History, 1818–1850.* New Haven, 1933.

Muelder, Hermann R. *Church History in a Puritan Colony of the Middle West.* Galesburg, Ill., 1937.

Munger, Theodore T. *Horace Bushnell, Preacher and Theologian.* Boston, 1899.

Nichols, James H. *Romanticism in American Theology: Nevin and Schaff at Mercersburg.* Chicago, 1961.

Nichols, Robert H. *Presbyterianism in New York State.* Edited by James H. Nichols. Philadelphia, 1963.

Niebuhr, H. Richard. *Radical Monotheism and Western Culture.* New York, 1943.

Nuttall, Geoffrey F. *The Puritan Spirit: Essays and Addresses.* London, 1967.

——. *Richard Baxter and Philip Doddridge: A Study in Tradition.* London, 1951.

Patterson, Robert L. *The Philosophy of William Ellery Channing.* New York, 1952.

Pearson, Samuel C., Jr. "From Church to Denomination: American Congregationalism in the Nineteenth Century." *Church History* 38 (March 1969): 67–87.

Pettit, Norman. *The Heart Prepared: Grace and Conversion in Puritan Spiritual Life.* New Haven, 1966.

Pope, Earl A. "The Rise of the New Haven Theology." *Journal of Presbyterian History* 44 (March, June 1966): 24–44, 106–21.

Power, Richard L. *Planting Corn Belt Culture: The Impress of the Upland Southerner and Yankee in the Old Northwest.* Indianapolis, 1953.

Purcell, Richard J. *Connecticut in Transition, 1775–1818.* Washington, D.C., 1918.

Putnam, Ellen Day, comp. *Some Chronicles of the Day Family.* Cambridge, Mass., 1893.

Rammelkamp, Charles H. *Illinois College: A Centennial History, 1829–1929.* New Haven, 1928.

Rourke, Constance M. *Trumpets of Jubilee: Henry Ward Beecher, Harriet Beecher Stowe, Lyman Beecher, Horace Greeley, P. T. Barnum.* New York, 1927.

Rudolph, L. C. *Hoosier Zion: The Presbyterians in Early Indiana.* New Haven, 1963.

Sachs, Emanie. *"The Terrible Siren": Victoria Woodhull (1838–1927).* New York, 1928.

Schneider, Norris F. *Y Bridge City: The Story of Zanesville and Muskingum County, Ohio.* Cleveland, 1950.

Scott, Donald Moore. "Watchmen on the Walls of Zion: Evangelicals and American Society, 1800–1860." Ph.D. dissertation, University of Wisconsin, 1968.

Shivers, Frank R., Jr. "A Western Chapter in the History of American Transcendentalism." *Bulletin of the Historical and Philosophical Society of Ohio* 15 (1957): 117–30.

Silverman, Kenneth. *Timothy Dwight.* New York, 1969.

Singer, David. "God and Man in Baptist Hymnals, 1784–1844." *Midcontinent American Studies Journal* 9 (Fall 1968): 14–26.

Sklar, Kathryn Kish. *Catharine Beecher: A Study in American Domesticity.* New Haven, 1973.

Smith, Lewis. "Changing Conceptions of God in Colonial New England." Ph.D. dissertation, State University of Iowa, 1953.

Smith, Timothy L. *Revivalism and Social Reform.* New York, 1965.

Stange, Douglas C. "The Conversion of Frederic Dan Huntington (1859): A Failure of Liberalism?" *Historical Magazine of the Protestant Episcopal Church* 37 (Sept. 1968): 287–98.

Stoeffler, F. Ernst. *The Rise of Evangelical Pietism.* Leiden, 1965.

Stoever, William K. G. "Henry Boynton Smith and the German Theology of History." *Union Seminary Quarterly Review* 24 (Fall 1968): 69–89.

Stowe, Lyman Beecher. *Saints, Sinners and Beechers.* Indianapolis, 1934.

Strong, Leah A. *Joseph Hopkins Twichell, Mark Twain's Friend and Pastor.* Athens, Ga., 1966.

Swift, David Everett. "Conservative versus Progressive Orthodoxy in Latter 19th Century Congregationalism." *Church History* 16 (March 1947): 22–31.

Thomas, Benjamin P. *Theodore Weld: Crusader for Freedom.* New Brunswick, N.J., 1950.

Thompson, Ernest T. *Changing Emphases in American Preaching.* Philadelphia, 1943.

Thompson, J. Earl, Jr. "Lyman Beecher's Long Road to Conservative Abolitionism." *Church History* 42 (March 1973): 89–109.

Wagenknecht, Edward. *Harriet Beecher Stowe: The Known and the Unknown.* New York, 1965.

Wakefield, Gordon S. *Puritan Devotion: Its Place in the Development of Christian Piety.* London, 1957.

Walker, George Leon. *Some Aspects of the Religious Life of New England with Special Reference to Congregationalists.* New York, 1897.

Welch, Claude. *Protestant Thought in the Nineteenth Century, I: 1799–1870.* New Haven, 1972.

White, Alain C., comp. *The History of the Town of Litchfield, Connecticut, 1720–1920.* Litchfield, Conn., 1920.

Willis, John R. "The Yale Band in Illinois." Ph.D. dissertation, Yale University, 1946.

Wilson, Edmund. *Patriotic Gore: Studies in the Literature of the American Civil War*, pp. 3–72. New York, 1966.

Wilson, Forrest. *Crusader in Crinoline: The Life of Harriet Beecher Stowe.* Philadelphia, 1941.

Wishy, Bernard. *The Child and the Republic: The Dawn of Modern American Child Nurture.* Philadelphia, 1968.

Wood, Raymond L. "Lyman Beecher, 1775–1863: A Biographical Study." Ph.D. dissertation, Yale University, 1961.

Wright, G. Ernest. *The Old Testament and Theology*. New York, 1969.

Wright, Louis B. *Culture on the Moving Frontier*. Bloomington, Ind., 1955.

Wyatt-Brown, Bertram. *Lewis Tappan and the Evangelical War Against Slavery.* Cleveland, 1969.

INDEX